Vegans Know How to Party

Over 465 Recipes including Desserts, Appetizers, Main Dishes, and More

Also by Nancy Berkoff, EdD,RD

Vegan Seafood — Beyond the Fish Shtick for Vegetarians

Vegan Menu for People with Diabetes

Vegan Microwave Cookbook

Vegan Meals for One or Two — Your Own Personal Recipes

Vegan in Volume — Vegan Quantity Recipes for Every Occasion

Vegan Passover Recipes — Eggless & Dairy-free Dishes

Dedication

This book is dedicated to Dr. Williard F. Zahn, who demonstrates every day that lemons are best used in lemonade, that a picture is worth a thousand words (especially when seen with friends), and that there is unbelieveable enjoyment in the preparation and sharing of a nosh!

Acknowledgments

Special thanks to the following people who contributed their time and talents towards production and editing of this book: Ed Coffin; Keryl Cryer; Julia Diggs, RD; David Herring, MS; Reed Mangels, PhD, RD; Charles Stahler, and Debra Wasserman. Thanks to Linda Long for providing the incredible photos appearing in this book and David Kliger for assisting Linda with some of the photography. Finally, thank you to Debra Wasserman for the book cover design and being the managing editor for this book project. You are all greatly appreciated!

Vegans Know How to Party

Over 465 Recipes including Desserts, Appetizers, Main Dishes, and More

By Chef Nancy Berkoff, EdD,RD

 From The Vegetarian Resource Group
Baltimore, Maryland

A Note to the Reader

The contents of *Vegans Know How to Party* and our other publications, including web information, are not intended to provide personal medical advice. Medical advice should be obtained from a qualified health professional. We often depend on product and ingredient information from company statements. It is impossible to be 100% sure about a statement, information can change, people have different views, and mistakes can be made. Please use your own best judgement about whether a product is suitable for you. To be sure, do further research or confirmation on your own.

© Copyright 2011, The Vegetarian Resource Group
P.O. Box 1463, Baltimore, MD 21203.

Library of Congress Cataloging-in-Publication Data

Berkoff, Nancy.
  Vegans know how to party : over 465 vegan recipes including desserts, appetizers, main dishes, and more / by Nancy Berkoff.
      p. cm.
  Includes index.
    ISBN 978-0-931411-33-5 (pbk.)
  1. Vegan cooking. 2. Entertaining. 3. Cookbooks. I. Vegetarian Resource Group. II. Title.
  TX837.B777 2011
  641.5'636--dc22

                                                    2010037281

Printed in the United States of America

10 9 8 7 6 5 4 3 2 1

Table of Contents

SECTION I ❧ DESSERTS

SECTION II ❧ APPETIZERS / PARTY FOOD

SECTION III ❧ ENTERTAINING A CROWD

Introduction

Party Fare the Vegan Way

This book will give you details on preparing scrumptious vegan party foods from ingredients you probably keep in your refrigerator and pantry or that can be purchased in your local market. Pasta, rice, barley, couscous, beans and legumes, and potatoes can all form the base of vegan appetizers and entrées. Firm tofu and soy or rice milk are refrigerated ingredients that can also be the beginning of a great appetizer, entrée, soup, or dessert.

You can decide on the amount of time and money you have for your party-prep effort. An easy, but probably the most costly, way to prepare party food is to use convenience products. For example, veggie burgers are available in a variety of flavors and are simple to prepare. You can use veggie burgers for patty melts or hamburger platters. Pile high raw vegetables (sliced tomato, lettuce, onion, bell pepper, shredded carrot, etc.) and you have a quick entrée. A veggie burger can be the basis for a slice of meat-loaf, Salisbury steak, Swiss steak, or country-fried steak. Taking it a step further, veggie burgers can be cooked and crumbled into tomato sauces (to make a vegetarian "meat" sauce), used as a filling for tacos and burritos, served as a pizza topping, or used in casseroles, such as tamale pie, chili, or shepherd's pie.

Veggie hot dogs can be can be grilled indoors, barbecued outdoors, or steamed on the stove. Slice veggie hot dogs into casseroles or soups to add an extra element of flavor. Make bagel-veggie hot dogs by toasting the bagel, slicing the hot dog length-wise, cooking it (barbecued, grilled, or microwaved), and then cutting the soy hot dog to fit the bagel. Wrap the bagel in foil and keep hot in a low oven. Serve this with relish, ketchup, and mustard, and baked chips or veggie sticks for a fast party meal.

There are numerous frozen, ready-to-use vegan entrées available today, which may include pasta or bean combinations. These can be heated and served as is, or add a sauce or garnish to personalize them.

Pasta is another easy way to go. Prepare a marinara sauce (tomato sauce with vegetables), add sautéed or steamed mushrooms, minced garlic, and extra tomatoes and serve over cooked pasta for a fast entrée. Or toss pasta with sauce, place it in a baking pan, amd top with chopped tomatoes, bell peppers, and onions. Cover and bake until hot for a quick vegetarian casserole. Additions to the tomato sauce can include chopped seasonal vegetables (such as summer squash, carrots, and different varieties of mushrooms), cooked lentils or white beans, and roasted garlic and fresh chopped herbs (try basil or oregano). For a color and flavor difference, use vegan pesto sauce (basil or spinach puréed with pine nuts, olive oil, and garlic).

Beans and legumes are simple to prepare (use canned or dried) and versatile. Make a hearty four-bean soup (try kidney, navy, garbanzos, and black-eye peas); pair it with a baked potato (topped with chopped veggies), steamed rice, or pasta salad and you have a terrific entrée. Or season red or black beans with onion, cumin, and pepper and serve the beans on a steaming bed of white or brown rice. Cooked beans can be puréed and seasoned and used as a sauce to top pasta, rice, or other cooked grains. You can toss cooked beans into a rice pilaf for another fast entrée.

Baked potatoes can be topped with chopped fresh and cooked vegetables, cooked beans, salsa, or vegan margarine. If you have space at your party, create a baked potato bar on a side table and let your guests create their own hot potato specialties. The same can be done with a pasta bar. Have several types of cooked pasta, several sauces (all without meat and dairy), and chopped fresh and cooked vegetables. Guests can then make their own entrées.

If you have the time to create vegan dishes from scratch, you may want to make your own veggie burgers with combinations of beans and grains. See Chapter 9 for some ideas. The same recipes can be used to form cutlets and loaves. Prepare these ahead of time; cook and freeze to be used as needed.

Tofu can be scrambled, just like eggs and used as an ingredient in stir-fries, casseroles, and as a filling for hot sandwiches. Just remember that tofu should be seasoned or it will come across as unexciting. Tofu can be marinated and used as a substitute for eggs or meat. A school we visited made a "turkeyless" tetrazini, using cubed tofu (which they had marinated in poultry seasoning) to replace the meat.

Speaking of tofu, it can be used in many vegan dessert creations. We have included recipes for tofu cheesecake, tofu chocolate chip coookies, and chocolate tofu mousse. This cookbook includes frozen dessert recipes as well. Also, there are ready-to-use soy dessert items, such as soy ice cream and pies, available in stores today.

Most commercial sorbets and fruit ices are vegan (read the labels) and can be used in place of ice cream for sundaes or other ice cream creations. If you have extra fruit, such as strawberries or melon, you can purée and freeze it to create your own sorbet. For vegan desserts, you can use apple juice or orange juice concentrate, rice syrup, or maple syrup as sweeteners.

Fresh sliced fruit, sprinkled with cinnamon makes a refreshing dessert. For a warm treat, try baked apples or pears with cinnamon, ginger, and maple syrup. Cobblers can be made by thickening canned apples or peaches with cornstarch and then topping the fruit with granola mixed with dried fruit.

You'll find many recipes and suggestions for party preparations throughout this book. Select what suits your time and budget, invite some friends over, and let the good (vegan) times rolls!

Using This Book

This book is divided into three sections. The first two are food preparation sections and the last section is devoted to party planning and resources.

The DESSERTS section includes "how to's" and recipes for preparing a wide assortment of cakes, cookies, muffins, pies, parfaits, baked desserts, fruit desserts, frozen creations, and hot and cold beverages. The APPETIZER / PARTY FOOD section includes savory suggestions for crispy and crunchy appetizers, dips and spreads, salads, hot and cold sandwiches, ethnic specialties, hearty soups and sauces, vegetable and grain creations, and some fast entrées. The ENTERTAINING A CROWD section will help you when you go shopping for vegan ingredients and products, are planning party meals, working with caterers, or preparing for special audiences.

You will find balance in the dishes and menu suggestions. The majority of recipes are healthy, with an attempt to hold down the amount of fat and calories. There are occasional flights of fancy, with cheesecake and creamy cake frosting recipes. Also, we've included suggestions for planning party menus for people with diabetes as well as lowfat ideas.

The recipes and suggestions in this book are generally designed to serve about six people. Chapter 19 shows how to plan for larger parties up to 25 people. If you are interested in increasing recipe yields found throughout Sections I and II, refer to Chapter 19 for an easy recipe-increased formula.

As you browse through the recipes, you will see this book was constructed to enable you to offer a variety of dishes to your guests. Think buffets and receptions with hot and cold food, rather than heavy sit-down meals. Over the years, we have found offering several dishes, rather than a set meal, is a successful formula. Your guests can create the meal they desire. This is especially helpful if you have guests who avoid certain ingredients, such as wheat or nuts, or if you have guests with varying palates. For example, in a medium-sized group, you may have someone who is allergic to nuts, someone who is avoiding wheat, someone who likes their food to be "firehouse" hot, and someone who prefers their food to be on the mild side. Offering a selection of menu items solves these issues without having to prepare 10 versions of the same dish.

You will find that most of the recipes are mildly spiced or seasoned. It's easy to add spices or seasoning, but you can't take them out! We suggest you prepare a selected recipe for the first time as written, and make notes about modifying it for the next time.

A Note About the Recipes

- Unless noted, for fruit and vegetable recipes, any form, such as canned, frozen (always thawed), or fresh is acceptable. If a particular type is needed, it will be noted in the recipe.

- If a recipe calls for precooked rice or grains, such as "use one cup cooked rice," we will put the raw amount with which to start in parentheses, such as use one cup cooked long-grain rice (start with $1/2$ cup uncooked).

- If using canned beans or vegetables, rinse them with cold water before adding them to the recipe.

- Unless noted, lowfat or low-sodium products may be used, such as soy sauce (available as low-sodium), coconut milk (available lowfat), tofu and soymilk (available lowfat), etc.

- It is not a good idea to substitute different types of flour in baking recipes, unless you are very familiar with how they work. If you would prefer to use specific types of flour, prepare half a recipe, using your preferred flour, to see if other ingredients need adjustment. Never replace more than one ingredient in a recipe at a time. If you substitute more than one ingredient, and the results are not satisfactory, you won't know which ingredient caused the problem.

- Roasted soy nuts and soy butter may be used instead of peanuts and peanut butter if preferred.

The Party's No Fun If Someone Gets Sick

Not only does party food need to taste good, it must be safely prepared and served. Just because there are no animal products, doesn't mean there aren't any food-borne illness-causing bacteria lurking around. Bacteria like protein, whether it's from meat or from beans, rice, pasta, soy products, etc. Bacteria don't grow well below 40 degrees or above 140 degrees; so keep food either hot or cold, but not in-between.

Have lots of towels, soap, bleach or bleach alternatives around. If you use sponges and towels, sanitize them frequently with diluted bleach or in the dishwasher. Bacteria are rendered harmless by water that is over 180 degrees or by chlorine, so make your choice (you don't need both).

Avoid cross contamination (spreading bacteria from one utensil or food to another utensil or food) by sanitizing your hands and your utensils every time you switch dishes. You don't have to peel fruit and veggies, if you don't want to, but you do have to wash and scrub them well.

Label and date prepared food and ingredients. Do a refrigerator-sweep at least every 5 days and discard what does not resemble what it says it is on the label. If you think you won't have time to eat something you have freshly cooked in a day or two, freeze it.

Don't forget to thaw foods in the refrigerator, not on the counter. Invest in a thermometer to check the refrigerator, the freezer, and the oven. This will not only keep foods safe, but also keep them fresher, and in the case of the oven, foods will be cooked properly. If you have a dishwasher, you might want to put the thermometer in it to be sure it's getting up to a sanitizing temperature.

Remember that everything can be cleaned and sanitized. This includes oven racks, the counter tops, the inside of the freezer, the interior of the dishwasher, and the pantry shelves.

Store foods safely. In the pantry, everything should be off the floor in airtight containers and there should be enough room between boxes, cans, and containers so that air can circulate. The same goes for the refrigerator and the freezer. If air can't get around, then the cool air can't get around either. If anything might drip in the refrigerator, place it on the bottom shelf, so it can't drip on foods beneath it.

Don't get too attached to pots, pans, and utensils. If they rust, scratch, chip, corrode, crack, or discolor, it's time to say "bye bye."

Always wash your hands and use separate handwashing facilities for food and hands. That means no washing your hands in the same sink in which the lettuce is sitting. In order to get rid of bacteria on the skin, you have to soap and lather for at least 20 seconds and then thoroughly rinse.

Useful Equipment

Culinary apprentices are told that a good cook can prepare any dish with just a knife, a cutting board, and some assorted pots, pans, and bowls. This is true, but there are some pieces of equipment that can improve efficiency and generally make life easier. Vegan foods require the same amount of chopping, slicing, and combining as any type of menu.

Depending on the size of your kitchen, you may already have many of these items. They are not required, just handy to cut down on the time you spend in the kitchen, so you can enjoy your guests:

1. Blender or food processor: useful for puréeing soups and sauces, and finishing salad dressings. You could use a manual food mill (or your mixer may come with a mill or ricer attachment), but the blender or food processor allows you to choose from many different textures.

2. Mixer: mixing quantity foods by hand can develop muscles (and frustration). Choose the size of mixer best suited to your production sizes. Standard attachments should include a dough hook, a paddle, and a whisk. Other attachments may include a grinder (for vegetables, potatoes) or a ricer.

3. Slicer: if you will be slicing a lot of veggies (eggplant, potatoes, tomatoes, onions, and zucchini), you may want to think about investing in a slicer. Do some online shopping to locate small, home-size electric slicers.

4. Rice cooker: can also be used to steam other grains. Depending on the amount of rice you will be preparing every day and for parties, this could come in handy.

5. Knives and cutting boards: sharp sturdy knives are essential. Chef's knives should fit your hand, meaning the handle is comfortable to grasp and the knife blade feels like the right length to you. Think of selecting a knife as if you were selecting a piece of sporting equipment. Have enough cutting boards so you can clean and sanitize one while using another.

6. Serving platters and bowls: select platters and bowls that fit in your cabinets, are easy to clean, can stand hot and/or cold, and won't chip or discolor. Select serving spoons, tongs and forks that match your serving platters and bowls.

7. Storage containers: should be washable, nonreactive (won't interact with acid foods), stand up to hot and/or cold, and be easy to label.

We'll speak about more party equipment, such as silverware, linen, and beverage containers later in this book. Now it's time to start planning your next party!

Section 1 ❧ Desserts

INTRODUCTION TO DESSERTS

Who doesn't love dessert? Along with making them attractive and tasty, it is possible to sneak some healthy stuff into desserts. Luscious and decadent treats can also have extra vitamins and minerals in them. Dried fruit (such as dates, golden raisins, figs, peaches, nectarines, apples, cherries, and blueberries) are sweet and moist and add color, flavor, texture, and some fiber and nutrients to desserts. The same goes for chopped nuts, nut and apple butter, fresh, canned, and frozen fruit, and fruit juices or concentrates (used for sweetening).

Some of us have lots of time to create end-of-the-meal wonders. For those of us short on preparation time there are still lots of ways to create signature desserts. Cookies are a good example of this.

If you purchase ready-to-eat vegan cookies, build a cookie ice cream sandwich with a scoop of frozen soy yogurt, sorbet, or soy ice cream. This can be made ahead of time, wrapped, and then used as needed. For calorie-controlled or lower sugar modifications and lower fat desserts, use graham crackers and frozen soy yogurt (if you can't find frozen soy yogurt, purchase refrigerated soy yogurt and freeze it in individual serving dishes). If the weather is too cold for frozen desserts, use a small amount of peanut butter or other nut butters or apple butter and fruit preserves for a filling.

Crumbled cookies can be used to garnish pudding, custard, cream pies, and even hot cereals. Crumbled cookies can be used just like graham cracker crumbs to create whole or individual pie crusts or tart shells.

The key to sumptuous quick desserts is having the right ingredients on hand. Here is a guide for you. The list looks extensive, but you won't be necessarily stocking everything. Plan the types of desserts you'd like to create and shop accordingly:

Freezer: unbaked pie shells, frozen uniced vegan sheet cakes (make them from scratch and freeze them or purchase already baked), frozen uncut brownies, cookie dough, muffin batter, fruit juice concentrates, vegan whipped topping, and assorted frozen vegan ice creams and sorbets. If you can't find frozen or refrigerated cookie dough or muffin batter, you can make your own. Frozen dough or batter should last about one month in a properly working freezer or one week in a refrigerator. We have found refrigerated vegan and gluten-free cookie dough at Whole Foods and other natural foods stores.

Refrigerator: prepared vegan cheesecakes, fresh garnishing fruit (such as fresh berries, kiwi fruit, bananas, pineapple, etc.), flavored soy and/or rice milk, solid vegan chocolate (for shaving and melting), and vegan sour cream, yogurt, and cream cheese. Consider edible flowers, which can be found in the produce section of many grocery stores and at farmers' markets.

Pantry: canned fruit toppings and pie fillings, unfilled tart shells (individual size, pastry and graham cracker crust), chopped nuts, vegan pudding mixes, shredded coconut, chocolate and/or carob chips, fruit preserves (such as apricot, raspberry, and orange marmalade), maple syrup, and vegan fruit-flavored syrups.

The concept behind quick-and-easy desserts is to create a wonderful menu without a lot of kitchen time. You can cut out small rounds of cake, purchase unfilled tart shells, or even hollow out day-old cupcakes and fill or top these with the following:

- apricot preserves with chocolate pudding, amaretto-flavored vegan whipped cream (just add an ounce of liqueur or extract to the whipped cream while you're whipping it), and garnished with shaved chocolate
- raspberry preserves, chocolate pudding, orange-flavored (use Triple-Sec or orange extract) vegan whipped cream, and garnished with candied orange peel and chocolate shavings
- orange marmalade, orange pudding (vanilla pudding flavored with fresh orange zest or orange extract), chocolate-flavored vegan whipped cream (use cocoa powder), and garnished with carob or chocolate chips
- raspberry preserves, vanilla pudding or soy ice cream, rum-flavored vegan whipped cream, and garnished with fresh berries
- raspberry preserves, mocha pudding (add espresso powder to chocolate pudding) or chocolate soy ice cream, vegan whipped cream, and garnished with crushed espresso beans

At a recent Sunday brunch, we saw a kid's version of this dessert: a chocolate shell filled with grape jelly, chocolate pudding, vegan whipped cream, and garnished with peanut butter chips.

Pre-baked tart shells offer lots of room for creativity. Be sure to spread a thin layer of preserves or glaze (bakers like to use apricot glaze) on the bottom of the shell to prevent sog, then layer on the vegan ice cream or pudding, vegan whipped cream, and garnishes.

You can create attractive desserts that are as pleasing to the eye as to the taste buds by using pre-baked items. For example, defrost frozen white or yellow vegan cake, purée some strawberries to create a coulis (flavor with liqueurs, maple syrup, or extracts), and serve the cake on a pool of deep red strawberry coulis garnished simply with some fresh mint. Create your own chocolate decadence by layering vegan brownies (thawed from the freezer) with vegan ice cream, cookie crumbs, whipped cream, and shredded coconut or chopped nuts.

If you have a little more time, create your own version of English trifle with frozen or leftover sheet cake (cut into strips), fruit preserves, pudding, and whipped cream. Or bake a quick pie by adding canned pie fruit to a frozen pie shell and top with streusel (made with flour, vegan margarine, and sugar); roll out a second pie shell to create a top, or bake as a one-crust pie and top later with cookie crumbs, sliced fresh fruit, or vegan whipped cream.

No one will know if you made that tofu cheesecake or not, if you individualize it. See a basic cheesecake recipe in Chapter 2. Top with pie filling, sliced, stewed fruit or preserves, flavored vegan whipped cream, and cookie crumbs or serve on a bed of sliced fresh fruit and fruit coulis, garnished with a liqueur (think cassis, honeydew, crème de menthe, etc.). You can whip up individual cheesecakes (use individual graham-cracker crust shells) and do the same.

Quick breads, such as carrot cake, banana bread, and zucchini bread are fast to mix up and fit at every meal. Add extra shredded veggies, mashed bananas, dried fruit, or nuts. Bake in cake pans, muffin tins, or loaf pans; bake off extra and freeze to be used as needed. Serve quick breads warmed with an accompaniment of soy yogurt and fruit. Slice and toast quick breads and serve with sliced fruit, vegan ice cream, frozen yogurt or sorbet, or fruit preserves. Instead of bread, also use quick breads as a base for bread pudding.

Tofu can be your friend when thinking about fast desserts. Combine silken tofu with vegan pudding mixes and you'll get a creamy pie filling or pudding that can be used for lower fat desserts. Use tofu pudding to create "cream" pies or individual tarts. Simply fill baked, cooled pie shells (here's where you can use your cookie crumbs) or individual tart shells with your tofu-based pudding. You can also blend tofu with pie filling (such as blueberry, cherry, or peach) and refrigerate or freeze pies or tarts. Tofu pumpkin custard can be made by blending tofu with canned pumpkin, seasoned with lemon zest and pumpkin pie spices, such as cinnamon, nutmeg, mace, cloves, and ginger, and allowed to cool in the refrigerator until firm.

Up for more fast dessert ideas? Thaw frozen vegan biscuits (prepare and bake extra biscuits, allow to cool, wrap, and freeze until needed), split and top with thawed, frozen strawberries, chopped canned peaches, pie filling, or seasonal berries mixed with apricot jam (apricot jam is fairly neutral, and is used in desserts for glazing and moistening), and garnish with vegan whipped cream or ice cream for a fast short cake. Or you can spread softened vegan ice cream or sorbet on one sheet cake, top with a second, and freeze. Cut into portions while still frozen (it's easier), top with fruit sauce or fruit preserves for a fast ice cream cake. Frozen waffles can be toasted and topped with ice cream or sorbet and fruit or create mini banana splits (these can be pre-made and stored in the freezer until ready to use). Slice pound cake or quick breads in thin slices; toast (or not) and serve with fruit.

Here's a simple idea. Peel a fresh juice orange (not a navel orange), slice it crosswise, arrange the slices in a bowl, drizzle with rice syrup, and a hint of vanilla extract; garnish with minced walnuts or fresh mint and serve.

You can go retro and offer banana splits, sundaes, and even dessert beverages. Think malteds (use malt powder or nutritional yeast) and ice cream sodas. Try this simple, yet elegant idea: serve a scoop of soy ice cream with several gourmet cookies, a twist of candied fruit peel, and some fresh mint or chocolate pieces. For the more sophisticated palate, offer a sampler plate of several sorbets (think passion fruit, mango, citrus, pear, melon). This is great for the calorie- or fat-conscious guest. Top brownies or cookies with vegan ice cream and garnishes and you have a quick dessert with lots of curb appeal.

Speaking of retro, parfaits can be pretty and easy to assemble. Get some glass parfait dishes and layer with sliced fresh fruit, vegan pudding, chopped nuts, cookie crumbs, and a garnish.

Fruit sauces are easy to make (and a great way to use those extra strawberries that are looking a bit peaked). To prepare a pint (2 cups) of fruit sauce, purée 3 cups of fruit (fresh or frozen); and warm 2 Tablespoons of rice syrup. Add the syrup to the fruit purée, blend, then add a bit of lemon juice for some tang. Refrigerate until ready to use. An alternative to fruit sauces are compotes. Simply stew fruit combinations (fresh or dried) until tender, spice and flavor, and serve hot or cold.

Some fruit has its own natural container. Take advantage of this. Serve a scoop of frozen soy yogurt in a quarter cantaloupe, Persian melon, or honeydew melon. Garnish it with fresh berries and you've got a simple (and healthy) dessert. Oranges or grapefruit can be scooped out and the pulp replaced with sorbet or sherbet or even stuffed with whole grapes dipped in sugar and then frozen.

When is the last time you had a banana split? It was probably too long ago. We bet your guests are thinking the same thing. Offer mini-splits, with sliced bananas and a dab of chocolate, strawberry, and pineapple sauce, topped with vegan whipped cream and chopped nuts, then serve in a small sundae glass or a brandy snifter. Or go for the whole banana, served in a classic split bowl or on a soup plate. For an adult spin, offer mint or chocolate liqueurs as one of the toppings.

A spectacular presentation is an apple or lemon sorbet served in a red Delicious apple shell. Apples are hollowed, and the shells and tops are retained. To create the sorbet, the apple pulp is puréed with Calvados (apple brandy) and apple juice concentrate. Or instead use apple pulp, fresh lemon juice, and apple juice concentrate. The sorbet is spooned into the apple shells, the tops are placed back on, and the whole fruit is frozen for at least an hour. Served in a brandy snifter or cut glass bowl, the apples glisten and the flavor is breath taking.

Vegan ice cream and sorbet are all good candidates for "a la mode," served on top or on the side of freshly baked vegan pies, layer cakes, cookie assortments, or sliced seasonal fruit. Wolfgang Puck serves maple ice cream with freshly baked apple pie at several of his restaurants. It is one of the most popular dessert items on the menu. You can create maple vegan ice cream by allowing vegan vanilla ice cream to soften, mixing well with maple syrup, and allowing to refreeze until hard enough to serve.

Remember enjoying a popsicle on a hot day? Offer your guests adult versions of that childhood favorite with Grand Marnier and rice syrup, lime and raspberry juice, espresso and almond milk, or a blueberry and Champagne popsicle. Fruit ice can also serve as an intermezzo or even as a sauce for a hot entrée. A quick cranberry ice can be made by blending jellied cranberry sauce with lemon-lime or grapefruit soda and then freezing it.

Create your own vegan ice cream soda. You may want to scour thrift stores for old-fashioned ice cream glasses and long-handled spoons. Imagine these combinations: coffee ice cream with espresso syrup, coconut ice cream with carob syrup, cherry vanilla ice cream with maple syrup, peach ice cream with peach syrup, or coffee ice cream with almond syrup; the list goes on and on.

If you'd like to "cook" with ice cream, than think of traditional ice cream creations. Baked Alaska, ice cream bombes, and ice cream pies have stood the test of time. Baked Alaska is a mound of hard-frozen ice cream covered with a thin layer of white or yellow cake and coated with an outside layer of whipped cream. The whole creation is quickly browned, most easily nowadays with a chef's portable torch, and then frozen. If you're game for playing with a little bit of dessert fire, you can find small butane torches at most gourmet food shops or restaurant supply houses. Traditionally, baked Alaska is flamed and paraded around the dining room, for effect, before being served. If this sounds like too much pageantry, you can create individual baked Alaskas, using orange shells as a mold.

Bombes are created by filling half-moon shaped molds with ice cream, leaving a hollowed out section in the center of the mold. The hollowed-out section is filled with two complimentary flavors of ice cream and/or sorbet and the whole mold is frozen until firm. The bombe is unmolded, resembling half a globe, and sliced to reveal the different layers. Try vegan vanilla ice cream with orange sorbet, chocolate and coffee ice cream, or strawberry ice cream with lemon sorbet combinations.

Ice cream pies are easy. Prepare and cool vegan pie shells including graham cracker or chocolate cookie pie shells. Fill with softened vegan ice cream and freeze until firm. Top with cake or cookie crumbs, shaved dark chocolate or carob chips, fresh or frozen berries, or chopped nuts. Remember, ice cream pies will melt more quickly than packaged ice cream, so keep them stored in the back of the freezer, away from the door. Ice cream pies should be portioned while still hard (frozen) for ease of service.

A very retro ice cream dessert is the snowball. Right up there with "Leave it to Beaver," snowballs are very popular and very easy to create. The idea is to roll a scoop of ice cream in crumbs of some sort and then to top it with a hot sauce, such as chocolate or maple. The "crumb" portion could be shredded coconut, chopped pistachios, peanuts, pecans, hazelnuts, or walnuts, cake or cookie crumbs, chopped candy bars or peppermint candy, or even cold cereal. A restaurateur we know creates snowballs for every season, dyeing coconut red and blue for the Fourth of July, red and green for Christmas, and all the colors of the rainbow for Easter. We're waiting for the Valentine snowball, a scoop of vegan chocolate chip ice cream rolled in chopped maraschino cherries and chopped almonds, served with a chocolate-cherry sauce. Fortunately, there is a large variety of soy- and rice-based frozen vegan ice cream flavors with which to create.

Be sure to accessorize your vegan ice cream or sorbet. Serve ice cream on petite blueberry or strawberry waffles, á la Scandinavia or wrapped into thin, cooled pancakes. Ice cream should never stand alone on the plate. So give it some cookie company. Cones come in several varieties. Fresh berries, slices of apple or pears, or chocolate-dipped apricots or biscotti can be the cherry on top for your ice cream offerings.

As noted above, cookies can be fun or swanky. Scoop some frozen dough and bake off fresh cookies as they are needed for your party or event. You don't have to prepare cookies from scratch to have "home-baked" cookies. You can prepare cookies from mixes and refrigerate for several hours until you are ready to bake off your cookies. Add chopped nuts, chips, orange or lemon zest, or chopped dried fruit to the mix to create new flavors. For a different texture, add cold cereal, like crumbled corn flakes, Grapenuts, or crisped rice for crispy textures; add chopped pineapple, raisins and other dried fruit, and applesauce to cookie mix to make soft cookie bars. These can be served topped with apple butter or peanut butter or dessert sauces.

To make a signature cookie, bake half way and press vegan chocolate chips, chopped nuts, chopped fruit, chopped granola, or minced cinnamon candy onto the top of the cookies and allow to finish baking. You can impress your guests with a new sauce such as a quick sauce made by puréeing thawed frozen strawberries and mixing it with a little orange juice concentrate or spiced applesauce.

For really quick desserts, you need to hone your shopping skills. For example, many Asian markets sell sweet tofu, a silken tofu poached in a sweet syrup. Although many of the syrups used with the tofu are refined-sugar based, you can find some rice syrup products. Vegan pudding mixes, frozen vegan desserts, and even ripe seasonal fresh fruit can be quickly plated and served to guests. If you find a really good vegan bakery nearby, you may want to purchase a whole cake, rather than just several slices. Wrap the cake whole or in slices in several layers of waxed paper and then in airtight containers. You'd be surprised how handy having frozen chocolate cake or carrot cake can be!

The following chapters will give you many more ideas for offering desserts as part of a special meal or as a stand-alone treat. You will find information on various ingredients and advice on how to use vegan ingredients to replace non-vegan ingredients, such as dairy milk, eggs, and refined sugar.

Chapter 1: PIES AND TARTS

Pastry flour is the best choice for pie dough and pastry crust. You can find whole wheat, unbleached, and white pastry flour in many markets. Pastry flour produces a flaky crust that has some "chew" to it. Although less healthy than vegetable oil, solid vegetable fat, such as vegan margarine or shortening, makes the best pie crust. Do not use "diet" margarines for pie crust, as they will produce an undesirable texture. At the time of this writing, we had baking success with Earth Balance vegan margarine. If you would like to use vegetable oil, you may want to increase the strength of your flour, using bread flour instead of pastry flour. Water or vegan milks can be used to create good pie dough and pastry crusts. Always add cold liquid to pastry dough. Hand mixing is the best way to create pastry dough. Pastry dough can be used for pie crusts, tart shells, fruit turnovers, and filled, savory turnovers, such as empanadas (a Central American potato and vegetable snack).

Pie dough and crust are fairly easy products to create. Remember to measure accurately, mix correctly, and have the oven at the proper temperature. Too much liquid will create a mushy crust that browns too quickly. You may get the same result from an oven that is too hot.

If you get impatient using recipes, we'll let you in on an old pastry chef's secret. Pie crust and pastry dough can be made with the 3-2-1 method: three parts flour to two parts fat to one part liquid. So, if you use three cups of flour, you'd use two cups of fat and one cup of liquid.

If you make pie dough infrequently, you don't need to invest in a rolling pin. You can roll dough out with a clean wooden dowel, which is very inexpensive and found in most hardware stores. Or you can use a sturdy, round drinking glass or a wine bottle.

For most pastry chefs, the difference between a pie and a tart is size and number of crusts. Pies are bigger, and can have two crusts. Tarts are smaller and usually have only a bottom crust. Baked pies, turnovers, and tarts hold up well to freezing. Take advantage of seasonal fruit and make apple, peach, apricot, pear, plum, or berry pies in season. Bake them, cool, wrap well, and freeze them for future use.

Bake off and freeze some unfilled pie crusts when you are creating a batch of pies, or purchase frozen vegan pie crusts. You can create refrigerator or frozen pies by filling thawed crusts with tofu pudding or custard, fresh berry fillings or sorbet.

You can use pastry dough to create turnovers. Cut small circles of pastry dough. Fill dough with a small amount of pie filling, fold over, crimp edges (press down to create a closure) with a fork, then bake. You can create savory turnovers by filling them with small amounts of curried potatoes, seasoned mashed potatoes mixed with cooked, diced vegetables, mashed beans and vegetables, or thick chili.

Once the fruit is peeled, fruit fillings are easy to prepare. The cooked juice fruit filling method works for fruit that requires little cooking, such as fresh cherries, berries, peaches or apricots, or canned or frozen fruit. Juice is drained from the fruit (if you don't get any juice when peeling and cutting fruit, you can use a small amount of crushed fruit, or canned or frozen fruit juice). Juice is placed in a pot and brought to a boil. Cornstarch is combined with a small amount of water or juice to create a smooth paste. The boiling juice is brought to a simmer and the cornstarch is whisked in. This is stirred until it becomes clear and slightly thickened. Sweetener is added, if desired, at this time. The cooked juice is poured over the fruit, tossed, and allowed to cool. When cool, it can be use to create baked or refrigerator pies.

To prevent a soggy pie bottom, you may want to reduce the liquid you use by one quarter. Bake unfilled pie crusts on the bottom oven rack at high heat for several minutes to remove some of the moisture. If your unfilled pie crust tends to bubble, you can "blind bake," that is, place a second, empty pie tin over the unfilled baking crust, or cover the unfilled pie crust with clean (washed and dried) uncooked beans. The beans will not interfere with the baking crust. They are removed before the pie crust is filled, and can be used in bean recipes. Don't put hot pie filling in unbaked pie shells, as this creates a lot of trapped moisture.

Pie Crust Guidelines

A terrific pie filling needs a great pie crust. To make your crust from scratch, follow these guidelines:

- There are four ingredients in a crust: flour, fat, liquid, and salt. Flour is necessary to form the structure and bulk of the crust; fat to add moisture and help keep the crust flaky; liquid to keep the dough somewhat pliable; and salt to enhance the flavor and brown the crust.

- Before making crusts, chill the fat (vegan shortening or margarine) and the liquid (soy or rice milk or water). Chilling will prevent the fat pieces from dissolving into the flour. Stir the flour and salt together in a large bowl. Cut the chilled margarine or shortening into the dry mixture using a pastry cutter or by pinching the fat into the mixture with your hands. The resulting mixture should have fat lumps no larger than peas.

- Pour in the chilled liquid, a small amount at a time, mixing gently with a fork until the dough is wet enough to be packed into a ball. The dough should be handled as little as possible to prevent the blending of all of the fat lumps. A crust with no fat lumps will become dense and hard.

- Split dough into two equal amounts; roll into balls; and wrap in plastic before placing them in the refrigerator. Chilling for at least 30 minutes will prevent the flour from absorbing the fat and give the crust a lighter texture when baked. Well-wrapped chilled crust can last 3 days in the refrigerator.

- Generously dust a clean, dry surface with flour and remove one of the packages of dough from the refrigerator. Flatten the dough slightly and dust the top of the dough with flour before rolling it out with a rolling pin or wooden dowel.

- Start rolling at the center of the dough and work outwards. Some people prefer doing this between sheets of parchment paper or plastic wrap because it makes cleaning up easier.

- Quickly roll the dough into a circle, either $1/4$- or $1/8$-inch thick. The size of the circle should be approximately 4 inches wider in diameter than the pie pan. You don't want to overwork the dough, as you'll lose some of the flakiness. Roll the dough only as much as is needed.

- Position the dough in the pan correctly by folding the dough in half and then in half again to make quarters. Gently pick the dough up and place it into the pan so that the center point is in the center of the pan. Unfold the dough in the pan and it should be perfectly centered. If the dough cracks a little during this process, press it back together with your fingers or patch the cracks with a bit of dough from the outer edges.

- Press the crust firmly into the pan and trim any excess dough from the edge. Leave a $1/4$-inch flap of dough around the edge for fluting or later sealing on the top crust.

Once the pie is filled, you'll want to top it with a second crust. To make a standard top crust, roll the dough out and lay it carefully over the pie. Seal its edges to the lower crust by using a small amount of water as an adhesive. Use your fingers to pinch the edges together.

If you'd like a latticework pie, follow the following steps:

1. On a lightly floured surface, roll refrigerated dough out to $1/4$-inch in thickness.
2. Cut the dough into strips approximately 1 inch wide, keeping all the dough strips the same width.
3. Moisten the edge of the pie with a small amount of water, and begin laying the strips across the pie one at a time. Press the ends of the strips firmly to the edge of the pie and remove any excess length.
4. Once the pie has been covered with strips, the top can be brushed with a cinnamon/sugar combination. Your pie is ready to bake.

Vegan Sugars
Domino's Organic Sugar
Florida Crystals Organic Sugar
Great Eastern Sun Organic Raw Cane Sugar
Hain Organic Brown Sugar and Organic Powdered Sugar
Rapadura Whole Organic Sugar and Organic Powdered Sugar
Shady Maple Farms Granulated Maple Sugar
Wholesome Sweeteners Organic Light and Dark Brown Sugar, Organic Powdered Sugar,
    Organic Sucanat, and Organic Turbinado Sugar

Vegan Liquid Sweeteners
Aunt Patty's offers raw organic agave syrup both bottled for consumers and in bulk for food service.
Visit <www.AuntPattys.com> or call (800) 456-7923.

Florida Crystals offers Organic Brown Rice Syrup. See <www.floridacrystals.com> or
call (877) 835-2828.

Great Eastern Sun offers Sweet Cloud Organic Sweeteners including Organic Brown Rice Malt Syrup,
Organic Barley Malt Syrup, Organic Corn Malt Syrup, and Organic Wheat Syrup.
Visit <www.great-eastern-sun.com> or call (800) 334-5809.

Great Northern Maple Farms offers Organic Maple Syrup. Visit <www.greatnorthernmaple.com>
or call (418) 485-7777.

Lundberg offers Organic Sweet Dreams Brown Rice Syrup. Visit <www.lundberg.com>
or call (530) 882-4551.

Maple Grove Farms produces maple syrup in Vermont. Some of their syrups are fruit flavored. Visit
<www.maplegrove.com> or call (802) 748-5141.

Maple Valley Syrup has a line of organic maple syrup. For information, visit
<www.maplevalleysyrup.com> or call (800) 760-1449.

Shady Maple Farms manufactures maple syrup in Canada. Visit <www.shadymaple.ca>
or call (905) 206-1455.

Spring Tree Maple Syrup manufactured in Canada is available in various sizes. Visit
<www.springree.com> or call (802) 254-8784.

Suzanne's Specialties produces several different varieties of liquid sweeteners including organic barley
malt, organic blackstrap molasses, organic agave syrup, and Just-Like-Honey (made with rice nectar).
For information visit <www.suzannes-specialties.com> or call (800) 762-2135.

Wax Orchards manufactures Fruit Sweet and Pear Sweet. For information visit
<www.waxorchards.com> or call (800) 634-6132.

Wholesome Sweeteners offers Organic Blackstrap Molasses, Organic Light Corn Syrup, and Organic
Blue Agave Nectar. For information visit <www.whoesomesweeteners.com> or call (800) 680-1896.

Powdered Vegan Egg-Replacers

Bob's Red Mill, 5209 SE International Way, Milwaukie, OR 97222 offers Vegetarian Egg Replacer made with whole soy flour, wheat gluten, corn syrup, and kelp. Visit <www.bobsredmill.com> or call (800) 349-2173.

Ener-G Foods, Inc., PO Box 84487, Seattle, WA 98124 manufactures Ener-G Egg Replacer (a combination of various starches) that simply necessitates adding water. For information visit <www.ener-g.com> or call (800) 331-5222.

Canbrands Specialty Foods, PO Box 117, Gormley, Ontario L0H 1G0 Canada also manufactaures Egg Replacer in a powdered form. For further information visit <www.canbrands.ca> or call (905) 761-5008.

Vegan Pre-made Pie Crusts

Natural Feast Pie Shells are available from Natural ME, Inc., 150 Main Street, Suite 11, Richmond, ME 04357. The pie shells can be ordered online at <www.naturalfeast.com> or by calling (866) 628-6346.

Wholly-Wholesome Frozen Pie Shells available as traditional, whole wheat, or spelt as well as graham and chocolate pie crusts sold in the grocery section are distributed by The Run-A-Ton Group, Inc., PO Box 2205 Morristown, NJ 07962. Visit <www.whollywholesome.com> or call (800) 247-6580.

VEGAN PIE CRUSTS

Cookie Crumb Pie Crust

Makes one 9-inch crust or 8 servings

1¹/₂ cups vegan cookie crumbs
3 Tablespoons sugar
6 Tablespoons vegan margarine, cut into small pieces

Preheat oven to 400 degrees. Place all ingredients in a food processor or blender and process until combined. Press evenly into a 9-inch pie pan. Bake crust for 5 minutes or until crust is set. Allow crust to cool before filling.

Variations: Use leftover vegan vanilla, chocolate, lemon, or ginger cookies, graham crackers, or vanilla wafers. You can also use crumbled cold cereal instead of the cookie crumbs.

Creative Suggestion: To assemble a "mud" pie, fill cookie crumb crust with one layer of coffee vegan soy ice cream and one layer of chocolate frozen dessert. Sprinkle with slivered almonds and chocolate or carob chips. Place in your freezer and allow pie to chill for 30 minutes before serving.

Total Calories Per Serving: 275   Total Fat as % of Daily Value: 24%   Protein: 3 gm   Fat: 16 gm
Carbohydrates: 27 gm   Calcium: 15 mg   Iron: 0 mg   Sodium: 257 mg   Dietary Fiber: 2 gm

Chocolate Cups

Makes approximately 2 dozen cups

4 ounces (¹/₂ cup) vegan chocolate or carob chips
24 small cupcake papers

Place chips in a microwave-safe bowl and microwave on HIGH for 2 minutes, or until melted. Stir. Or place chips in a small pot, stirring, and cook for 3-4 minutes, or until melted.

Place cupcake papers on a large microwave-safe plate. Brush a thin layer of chocolate into the papers, using a pastry brush or the back of a spoon. Chill in the refrigerator for 5 minutes. Repeat brushing the chocolate onto the cups to make the cups thicker and thicker. If you need to remelt the chocolate, microwave on HIGH for 20 seconds or until melted. Repeat until all chocolate is used.

Refrigerate cups for at least 30 minutes. Peel away paper to reveal chocolate cups.

Total Calories Per Chocolate Cup: 22   Total Fat as % of Daily Value: <1%   Protein: <1gm   Fat: 1 gm
Carbohydrates: 3 gm   Calcium: 1 mg   Iron: <1 mg   Sodium: 0 mg   Dietary Fiber: <1 gm

Basic Pie Crust

Makes two 9-inch pie crusts

1 cup frozen vegan margarine
2 cups all-purpose flour (or 1 cup whole wheat and 1 cup all-purpose flour)
¹/₂ teaspoon salt
¹/₂ cup ice water
Flour for dusting surfaces
Two 9-inch pie plates

Preheat oven to 425 degrees. Cut margarine into small pieces. Place margarine in a food processor canister or blender. Add flour and salt. Pulse (turn on and off) mixture until it looks like coarse crumbs (similar to oatmeal). Slowly add the water just enough for dough to hold together; you don't want thin dough. Divide the dough in half, wrap, and freeze for 10 minutes.

Flour a clean surface and place one piece of dough on it. Roll out, using a rolling pin, a tall round glass, or clean wooden dowel. Roll to approximately ¹/₂-inch thickness. Place your pie tin in the center of the dough and ensure the dough is 1-2 inches larger than the pie plate. Fold dough in quarters. Place in pie tin and unfold carefully. Crimp edges or fold dough edge under. Repeat with second piece of dough or reserve second piece of dough for a top crust.

Use a "blind baking" technique so that the bottom of the crust does not bubble up. Weigh down bottom of crust with uncooked beans (these can be used again for baking or can be cooked). Or, weigh down the bottom of the crust with several smaller (in diameter) pie tins.

If filling a pie, bake crust for only 3-4 minutes, so that the bottom crust will not be soggy. If completely baking crust, allow crust to bake for 10-12 minutes, or until golden brown.

Total Calories Per Serving: 314   Total Fat as % of Daily Value: 34%   Protein: 3 gm   Fat: 22 gm
Carbohydrates: 24 gm   Calcium: 5 mg   Iron: <1 mg   Sodium: 328 mg   Dietary Fiber: 1 gm

PIES

Apple Pies

So, what type of apples do you like? Green, golden, pink, or red? Sugary sweet or puckery sour? And how do you like to eat your apples? Piping hot, baked with raisins and walnuts? Cold and crunchy, right from the refrigerator? Or do you prefer one of America's favorite desserts, apple pie?

The flavor of your pie will be decided by the apple variety you select. Red Delicious are the good ol' standbys of eating apples, but they can be cooked for a firm, rather than soft, pie filling. Mix the Red with the Golden Delicious for a change of pace. If you like the sweetness of Red Delicious, you'll like Cameo (very sweet with a nice crunch), Fuji (sweet and crunchy), and Gala (a cross between a Golden Delicious and the New Zealand Orange Red). For a more rounded flavor, sweet with some overtones of tang, choose Braeburn, Pink Lady, or Jonagold. Look in farmers markets or specialty produce stores for heirloom or antique varieties, such as Maiden Blush, Winesap, or MacIntosh or for fairly new varieties, such as Honeygold and its brand new cousin, Honeycrisp. If you'd like to stay with cooking apples, look for Rome, Granny Smith, or Pippins. Cooking varieties handle heat better, as they have more fiber and less juice. This allows them to hold their shape when being baked, sautéed, broiled, or microwaved.

Nothing beats the smell of a freshly baked apple pie. Depending on your time and your equipment you may elect to bake apple pies strictly from scratch or indulge in a little speed scratch.

The ultimate in speed scratch pie baking is the purchase of frozen, vegan, ready-to-bake pies such those sold by Natural Feast <www.naturalfeast.com>. Bake off pies as you need them, making them a signature dish by garnishing pies just removed from the oven with shredded, vegan sharp cheddar cheese or with a drizzle of melted vegan cinnamon candies or melted caramels. If you'd like to do a bit of hands-on baking, but don't feel like rolling out the pie crust or peeling apples, purchase frozen vegan pie crusts and canned apple pie filling. Toss canned filling with your favorite aromatic spice blend and chopped walnuts, pecans, raisins, dried cranberries, or diced dried figs. Top with a second crust, with a crust cut into lattice strips, or with a streusel topping. Prepare ahead of time and refrigerate until you are ready to bake them.

Baking Your Pie

Baking apple pie from scratch is one of the easier dessert tasks. Here are some tips to ensure that your apple or other fruit pies are top of the line:

- Preheat the oven to the temperature recommended in the recipe. If a recipe calls for the pie to go in at a high temperature first, and to finish baking at a lower temperature; do it! The two-temperature method helps high-fat crusts to become flaky and tender. Remember that convection ovens bake approximately 25 degrees hotter than traditional or conduction ovens (ovens without fans to circulate the heat). Adjust temperatures accordingly.

- Baking a pie with a raw fruit filling will take at least 30 minutes total cooking time. Apple and pear pies usually cook for approximately 45 minutes. When using a canned filling, the pie will normally bake at a higher temperature for a shorter period of time to thoroughly bake the crust and heat the filling up. To check if the filling is done, insert a knife into the center of the pie. If there's no resistance, the pie is done. To check if the crust is done, insert a knife into the crust. If you feel the knife puncture the crust, it's done. If the pie is not quite done but the top or edges are becoming too dark, loosely cover the top of the pie with aluminum foil to shield it from the heat.

- When you remove the pie from the oven, place it on a rack. This allows even cooling so your pie won't sag to one side. As the pie cools, the filling will settle, and the top will even out.

- Don't attempt to cut hot pies. Plan ahead so your pies are at room temperature before serving them.

- Never reheat pies in a microwave. Microwave ovens will make the crust soggy. You'll need to plan to have some room in a moderate (about 300 degree) oven to re-warm pies.

Making Apples into Pie Filling

Apple pies can range from simple and traditional to modern and fusion. You can use one type of apple, a mixture of sweet and tart apples, or pear and apple combinations. Filling add-ins can include dried cherries, golden raisins, currants, dried cranberries, and finely chopped nuts.

A rule of thumb for filling a 9-inch pie crust is usually eight to nine medium apples tossed with 6 ounces (about $3/4$ cup) sugar and 2 ounces (about $1/4$ cup) of all-purpose or whole-wheat flour. Spices, totaling 1 Tablespoon all together, can include ground cinnamon, nutmeg, mace, clove, cardamom, lavender, ginger, and/or dried orange zest.

Slice peeled and cored apples into even slices that are no thicker than $1/2$ inch. Thin slices help to ensure even baking. If fresh apples aren't available, you can use frozen, thawed apple slices, or fresh, ripe pears. Place about half of the apples into an unbaked bottom crust and dust with half of the sugar, flour, and spice mixture. Top with the remaining apples and sprinkle them with the rest of the sugar.

Tarte Tatin

Tarte Tatin is apple pie, all grown up and back from a Continental tour. It's really an upside down apple tart, topped with a caramel sauce. As with many culinary discoveries, the tatin is thought to have been a delightful accident. The story goes that Stephanie Tatin, half of a sister team running the Hotel Tatin in Beuvron, France, was having a bad kitchen day in 1889. She started to make a traditional apple pie but left the apples cooking in butter and sugar for too long. Smelling the burning, she tried to rescue the dish by putting the pastry base on top of the pan of apples and quickly finishing the cooking by putting the whole pan in the oven. After turning out the upside down tart, she was surprised to find how much the hotel guests enjoyed the dessert.

To create your own vegan tatin, peel some tart apples, such as Granny Smiths, rub them with lemon juice, halve them, and core them. Place slices of vegan margarine on the bottom of a pan that can handle the stove and the oven, and sprinkle with sugar. Place the apples on top with their stem ends up, going round the pan. Bring to a simmer on top of the stove. Keep cooking until a fragrant, light mahogany caramel bubbles up in between the apples. Then, place the pan into the oven until the apples are tender. Remove the pan, and let the apples cool. Top with either your own pie dough or puff pastry and return to the oven for 15 more minutes. Let the tart cool, and flip out onto a serving platter. You should have tender, caramel soaked apple halves and a crispy bottom crust. Top with a dollop of vegan Devon cream (see page 60) or a scoop of vegan vanilla frozen dessert. Call it "apple pie with an attitude," and start dishing.

Accesorize the Pie

Apple pie can stand well on its own, but a little bit of company will enhance it even more.

- A La Mode: top hot or warm pie with a generous serving of traditional vanilla vegan frozen dessert or lemon or ginger sorbet.

- With a Dollop: top warm or cold pie with vegan Devon cream (see page 60) flavored with vanilla extract, rum extract, almond extract, orange zest, minced fresh ginger, or crushed dried lavender.

- Cheese, Please: serve pie in a pool of vegan cheese sauce, topped with melted shredded vegan cheese or accompanied by a petite wedge.

PIE RECIPES

Maple Apple Pie
Fills one 9-inch pie shell serving 8

Two frozen 9-inch pie crusts, thawed
8 large green apples, peeled, cored, and sliced or diced
$1/2$ cup maple syrup
1 Tablespoon molasses
1 Tablespoon brown sugar
1 teaspoon ground cinnamon
$1/2$ teaspoon ground nutmeg
$1/2$ teaspoon ground ginger
$1/2$ teaspoon lemon zest
$1/4$ cup all-purpose or whole wheat flour
1 Tablespoon water or apple juice

Preheat oven to 400 degrees. Place one piece of pie shell in a 9-inch pie pan and crimp or fold edges. Bake for 3 minutes. Allow shell to cool.

Place apples in large bowl. Mix in remaining ingredients and toss to combine. Fill pie shell and cover with top crust. Place on a baking sheet and center in the middle of an oven rack. Allow to bake for approximately 40 minutes or until filling is bubbly and crust is just golden.

Total Calories Per Serving: 463   Total Fat as % of Daily Value: 34%   Protein: 4 gm   Fat: 22 gm
Carbohydrates: 62 gm   Calcium: 33 mg   Iron: 1 mg   Sodium: 331 mg   Dietary Fiber: 3 gm

Apple Cream Pie
Fill one 9-inch pie shell serving 8

2 pounds peeled, cored, and thinly sliced, green apples
$3/4$ cup sugar
2 Tablespoons whole wheat or all-purpose flour
2 teaspoons ground cinnamon
$1/2$ teaspoon allspice
$1/2$ teaspoon nutmeg
3 Tablespoons vegan margarine
$1 1/2$ cups vegan Devon cream (see page 60)
Two 9-inch pie crusts, unbaked

Preheat oven to 400 degrees. Toss apples with sugar, flour, and spices and arrange in the bottom of one pie shell. Combine margarine and cream in a small pan. Simmer, stirring, until margarine is melted and well incorporated with the cream. Pour over apples. Cover with top crust. Bake for approximately 40 minutes or until filling is bubbly and crust is just golden.

Total Calories Per Serving: 515   Total Fat as % of Daily Value: 43%   Protein: 4 gm   Fat: 28 gm
Carbohydrates: 62 gm   Calcium: 11 mg   Iron: <1 mg   Sodium: 388 mg   Dietary Fiber: 2 gm

Red Cinnamon Apple Pie

Fills one 9-inch pie crust serving 8

1¹/₂ cups apple juice
6 ounces vegan hard cinnamon candy
¹/₂ teaspoon vanilla extract
2 pounds peeled, cored, and sliced baking apples
2 Tablespoons cornstarch
1 pre-baked 9-inch pie crust

Preheat oven to 400 degrees. Combine juice, candy, and vanilla in a small pot and simmer until candy is dissolved. Stir to combine. Add apples. Allow mixture to cook, stirring, until apples are tender, about 10 minutes. Combine cornstarch with two Tablespoons of cooking liquid to create a slurry. Whisk cornstarch slurry into filling and combine well. Allow apples to cool. Place in pie shell. Allow pie to chill in refrigerator for at least 2 hours before serving.

Total Calories Per Serving: 323   Total Fat as % of Daily Value: 17%   Protein: 2 gm   Fat: 11 gm
Carbohydrates: 55 gm   Calcium: 11 mg   Iron: <1 mg   Sodium: 165 mg   Dietary Fiber: 2 gm

Apple Pie without Added Sweetener

Fills one 9-inch pie shell serving 8

3 Tablespoons cornstarch
1 Tablespoon ground cinnamon
¹/₂ teaspoon nutmeg
¹/₂ teaspoon mace
1 cup unsweetened apple juice concentrate
2 pounds peeled, cored, and thinly sliced baking apples
Two 9-inch pie crusts, unbaked

Preheat oven to 350 degrees. Whisk together the cornstarch, cinnamon, nutmeg, mace, and ¹/₄ cup of the apple juice concentrate. Place apples in a small pot and simmer in the remaining apple juice until tender, about 10 minutes. Add the cornstarch mixture, stirring, and allow apples to simmer until thickened. Pour apples into one crust and cover with a top crust. Bake 30 minutes or until crust is brown.

Total Calories Per Serving: 426   Total Fat as % of Daily Value: 34%   Protein: 4 gm   Fat: 22 gm
Carbohydrates: 53 gm   Calcium: 27 mg   Iron: 1 mg   Sodium: 331 mg   Dietary Fiber: 3 gm

Pie-Eyed Apple Pie (Apple Pie with Whiskey)

Fills one 9-inch pie shell serving 8

Two unbaked 9-inch pie crusts
³/₄ cup sugar
2 Tablespoons whole wheat or all-purpose flour
¹/₈ teaspoon salt
1 teaspoon ground cinnamon

¹/₄ teaspoon ground ginger
¹/₄ teaspoon ground nutmeg
1¹/₂ pounds peeled, cored, and sliced green apples
2 Tablespoons vegan margarine
2 Tablespoons whiskey (optional)

Preheat oven to 450 degrees. Place bottom crust into a 9-inch pie plate.

In a small bowl, mix together sugar, flour, salt, cinnamon, ginger, and nutmeg. Place apples in a large bowl and sprinkle with sugar mixture. Toss until apples are thoroughly coated.

Place apples in pie crust. Dot apples with margarine, then sprinkle with whiskey, if desired. Cover with top crust. Seal edges and cut steam vents in top. Bake for 10 minutes. Lower oven temperature to 350 degrees and bake pie an additional 30 minutes. Serve warm.

Total Calories Per Serving: 459   Total Fat as % of Daily Value: 38%   Protein: 4 gm   Fat: 25 gm
Carbohydrates: 55 gm   Calcium: 10 mg   Iron: <1 mg   Sodium: 388 mg   Dietary Fiber: 2 gm

Spicy Apple Pie Filling

Fills one 9-inch pie shell serving 8

One prepared 9-inch pie crust recipe (or two frozen pie crusts, thawed)
8 large green apples, peeled, cored, and sliced or diced
¹/₄ cup maple syrup
1 Tablespoon molasses
1 teaspoon ground cinnamon
¹/₂ teaspoon each ground nutmeg and ground ginger
¹/₂ teaspoon lemon zest
¹/₄ cup all-purpose or whole wheat flour
1 Tablespoon water or apple juice

Preheat oven to 400 degrees. Place one piece of pie dough in a 9-inch pie pan and crimp or fold edges. Bake for 3 minutes. Allow pie crust to cool.

Place apples in a large bowl. Mix in remaining ingredients and toss to combine. Place in the pie crust. Cover with remaining piece of dough. Fold top dough over the bottom. Cut several slits in top crust to allow steam to escape. Place pie on a baking sheet and put in oven. Allow to bake for 15 minutes, or until top crust is golden and filling is bubbly.

Notes: 1. If one crust pie is preferred, top apples with cake crumbs or chopped nuts.
2. If a lattice crust is preferred, roll out top crust and cut into strips. Place dough strips in a lattice pattern on top of apples.
3. If desired, ¹/₄ cup raisins may be added to apple filling.

Variations: 1. For blueberry pie, use 4 cups blueberries instead of apples.
2. For blueberry-apple pie, use 2 cups of blueberries and 2 large apples.
3. For peach pie, use 8-10 peeled fresh peaches, pitted and sliced (about 4 cups).
4. For apricot pie, used 14-16 peeled fresh apricots, pitted and sliced (about 4 cups).

Total Calories Per Serving (not variations): 444   Total Fat as % of Daily Value: 34%   Protein: 4 gm   Fat: 22 gm
Carbohydrates: 57 gm   Calcium: 26 mg   Iron: <1 mg   Sodium: 330 mg   Dietary Fiber: 3 gm

OTHER TYPES OF PIE

Raw Peach Pie Filling

Makes one 9-inch pie serving 8

This recipe requires some pre-preparation and a food processor. If you use the Almond Pecan crust recipe below, this will be a raw vegan dessert.

$^1/_2$ cup whole, shelled pecans
4 cups whole fresh peaches (about 5 pounds)
$^1/_2$ cup chopped dried pineapple
$^3/_4$ cup chopped fresh pineapple
$^1/_2$ teaspoon apple pie spice (available in the spice section of the market, usually a
    combination of cinnamon, nutmeg, cloves, mace, and ginger)
$^1/_2$ teaspoon cinnamon
$^2/_3$ cup pitted soft dates
$1^1/_2$ cups fresh berries or frozen, thawed berries for garnish
One pre-baked pie crust or Almond Pecan Crust (recipe below)

In a small bowl, cover pecans with water and soak for 8-12 hours. Drain and rinse pecans. Set aside.
    Peel and halve peaches, reserving skin. Remove pit and thinly slice flesh. Set aside.
    In a food processor or blender, blend peach skin with pecans, dried and fresh pineapple, spices, and dates.
    In pie shell, layer half of peach slices in an overlapping circle. Evenly spread half of pineapple mixture over peach slices. Repeat with remaining peach slices and pineapple mixture.
    Garnish with fresh berries. This pie can be served immediately or refrigerate and serve chilled.

Total Calories Per Serving: 355   Total Fat as % of Daily Value: 33%   Protein: 4 gm   Fat: 21 gm
Carbohydrates: 39 gm   Calcium: 28 mg   Iron: 1 mg   Sodium: 165 mg   Dietary Fiber: 5 gm

Raw Almond-Pecan Pie Crust

Makes one 9-inch pie crust serving 8

This crust is flavorful and moist, but not crisp. Expect it to crumble as the pie is dished out onto individual dessert plates.

1 cup shelled whole unsalted almonds
$^1/_2$ cup shelled whole unsalted pecans
$^1/_3$ cup chopped pitted soft dates
3 Tablespoons water
Vegetable oil spray

In separate bowls, cover almonds and pecans with water and let soak for 8 hours. Drain and rinse.
    In a food processor, grind almonds to a consistency of chunky peanut butter. Place in a medum-size bowl and set aside.

In a food processor, grind pecans to a consistency of chunky peanut butter and stir into almond meal. Set aside.

In a food processor, blend dates, and water until smooth. Stir into nut mixture until thoroughly mixed and dough-like in consistency. Shape nut mixture into a ball and place on 12-inch length of waxed paper. Top with another 12-inch length of waxed paper. Flatten ball with palm of hand. Using rolling pin, roll out dough into a circle 10 inches in diameter.

Carefully remove top sheet of paper. Spray 9-inch pie pan with oil. Invert pie crust into pie pan, pressing gently. Trim excess crust and press gently to even edges of dough.

Place crust in a food dehydrator set at 125 degrees for 2 hours. (Or preheat conventional oven to 250 degrees and immediately turn off heat. Let crust sit in oven with door closed until it is dry and set, about 30 minutes.)

Total Calories Per Serving: 220   Total Fat as % of Daily Value: 29%   Protein: 5 gm   Fat: 19 gm
Carbohydrates: 10 gm   Calcium: 58 mg   Iron: 1 mg   Sodium: 0 mg   Dietary Fiber: 4 gm

Peach Cheesecake Pie

Makes one 9-inch pie serving 8

2 cups vegan cream cheese
¼ cup sugar
1 Tablespoon soy, almond, or rice milk
¼ teaspoon vanilla extract
1 prebaked and cooled 9-inch graham cracker crust
2 cups peeled, thinly sliced very ripe peaches or canned, drained peaches
¼ cup apricot jam

Place cream cheese and sugar in a bowl and beat together until smooth. Beat in milk and vanilla. Pour into pie shell. Place peaches in single layer on top of cream filling. Place apricot jam in a 1-cup microwave bowl and heat on HIGH for 30 seconds or until liquid. This can also be done on top of the stove in a small pot over high heat.

Allow mixture to cool slightly. Pour over peaches. Allow pie to chill in the refrigerator for at least 2 hours before serving.

Note: Very ripe, peeled apricots, nectarines, plums, or strawberries (sliced) or blueberries (slightly mashed) may be used in place of the peaches.

Total Calories Per Serving: 367   Total Fat as % of Daily Value: 33%   Protein: 4 gm   Fat: 22 gm
Carbohydrates: 40 gm   Calcium: 7 mg   Iron: <1 mg   Sodium: 485 mg   Dietary Fiber: 1 gm

Fresh Peach Pie

Makes one 9-inch pie serving 8

One unbaked 9-inch pie crust
4 cups peeled, pitted, and sliced ripe fresh peaches
2 teaspoons unbleached flour
¼ cup peach preserves
1 teaspoon fresh lemon juice
½ teaspoon ground cinnamon
¼ teaspoon ground nutmeg

Preheat oven to 400 degrees. In the unbaked crust of your choice, arrange the peach slices, in overlapping circles. Sprinkle peaches lightly with flour. Combine peach preserves, lemon juice, cinnamon, and nutmeg in a saucepan and heat until just bubbling. Pour glaze over the peaches, then place in oven and bake for 10 minutes. Turn down heat to 375 degrees and continue baking for an additional 30-35 minutes, or until crust is golden. Serve at room temperature or cold.

Total Calories Per Serving: 200   Total Fat as % of Daily Value: 17%   Protein: 2 gm   Fat: 11 gm
Carbohydrates: 23 gm   Calcium: 7 mg   Iron: <1 mg   Sodium: 164 mg   Dietary Fiber: 2 gm

Easy Blueberry Pie

Makes one 9-inch pie serving 8

3½ cups fresh or frozen, thawed blueberries, divided
1½ cups water
1½ cups sugar
½ cup orange juice
2 Tablespoons cornstarch
¼ cup water
One pre-baked 9-inch pie shell

Place 2 cups of blueberries in a pot with 1½ cups of water over medium heat for 5 minutes. Stir in sugar and orange juice, and cook, stirring for another 5 minutes. In a small bowl, combine cornstarch and ¼ cup cold water, and add to cooked blueberries. Stir until thickened. Cool. Pour into pie shell and cover with remaining blueberries. Refrigerate for at least 2 hours before serving.

Total Calories Per Serving: 353   Total Fat as % of Daily Value: 17%   Protein: 2 gm   Fat: 11 gm
Carbohydrates: 62 gm   Calcium: 8 mg   Iron: <1 mg   Sodium: 165 mg   Dietary Fiber: 2 gm

Blueberry Apple Pie

Makes one 9-inch pie serving 8

³/₄ cup sugar
1 Tablespoon cornstarch
¹/₂ teaspoon salt
5 cups peeled and thinly sliced apples of your choice
1 cup fresh or frozen thawed blueberries
1 teaspoon lemon juice
2 unbaked 9-inch pie crusts
2 teaspoons vegan margarine

Preheat oven to 400 degrees. In a large bowl, stir together sugar, cornstarch, and salt. Add apples, blueberries and lemon juice; toss to coat the fruit. Cover a pie pan with one of the crusts to form the bottom crust. Add fruit filling. Dot with margarine. Add top crust; seal and crimp edges. Bake for 30-40 minutes or until crust is golden and apples are tender.

Total Calories Per Serving: 442   Total Fat as % of Daily Value: 36%   Protein: 4 gm   Fat: 23 gm
Carbohydrates: 55 gm   Calcium: 9 mg   Iron: <1 mg   Sodium: 481 mg   Dietary Fiber: 2 gm

Strawberry Rhubarb Pie

Makes one 9-inch pie serving 8

Two 9-inch pie crusts
4 cups washed and diced fresh rhubarb (be certain to remove all leaves and discard)
    or frozen, thawed, unsweetened rhubarb
1 cup rice syrup or maple syrup
6 Tablespoons arrowroot
2 cups sliced fresh or frozen, thawed, unsweetened strawberries
1 teaspoon grated fresh orange zest
2 Tablespoons unbleached white flour

Fit bottom crust into a 9-inch pie plate. Refrigerate for 30 minutes. Put sliced rhubarb into a colander with a bowl underneath. Pour syrup over rhubarb and allow syrup to drain for 1 hour. In a large pot, mix arrowroot with half of the drained syrup (about ¹/₂ cup). Heat until thickened, stirring over low heat, then add the remaining syrup.

Preheat oven to 350 degrees. Mix rhubarb and strawberries together in a glass or plastic bowl. Mix zest and flour into syrup mixture. Add syrup mixture to the fruit mixture. Pour fruit mixture into prepared pie shell. Roll out top crust and place on top. Join crusts, crimping edges with a fork. Put several slashes through top crust so steam can escape.

Bake 1 hour. Allow pie to cool, then refrigerate for at least 2 hours to set.

Total Calories Per Serving: 461   Total Fat as % of Daily Value: 35%   Protein: 5 gm   Fat: 22 gm
Carbohydrates: 60 gm   Calcium: 94 mg Iron: 1 mg   Sodium: 336 mg   Dietary Fiber: 3 gm

Silky Lemon Pie

Makes one 9-inch pie serving 8

3 cups unsweetened pineapple juice
¹/₂ cup orange juice concentrate
¹/₂ cup evaporated cane juice or rice syrup
6 Tablespoons cornstarch
¹/₂ teaspoon pure lemon extract
2 Tablespoon vegetable oil
¹/₂ teaspoon salt
1 Tablespoon freshly grated lemon rind
6 Tablespoons fresh lemon juice
1 pre-baked 9-inch pie crust

Whisk all filling ingredients in a pot, away from heat, until smooth. Place pot on medium-high heat and stir constantly until the filling is thick and clear yellow. Pour into a baked pie shell and chill until firm. If you like, top with vegan Devon cream (see page 60), whipped vegan cream cheese, or sliced strawberries.

Total Calories Per Serving: 338   Total Fat as % of Daily Value: 22%   Protein: 2 gm   Fat: 14 gm
Carbohydrates: 50 gm   Calcium: 21 mg   Iron: 1 mg   Sodium: 312 mg   Dietary Fiber: 1 gm

Holiday Pumpkin Pie

Makes one 9-inch pie serving 8

1¹/₄ pounds soft or silken tofu (about 4 cups)
16-ounce can unsweetened pumpkin purée (about 2½ cups)
³/₄ cup maple syrup
³/₄ cup sugar
¹/₃ cup unbleached all-purpose flour
1 Tablespoon ground cinnamon
1 teaspoon ground ginger
1 teaspoon ground nutmeg
One unbaked 9-inch pie crust

Preheat oven to 400 degrees. Place all the ingredients except the pie crust into a blender or food processor canister and process until smooth. Pour mixture into the unbaked pie crust. Bake for 30 minutes, then turn the oven down to 350 degrees and bake for another 30-45 minutes or until the filling is set. Serve warm or chilled.

Total Calories Per Serving: 372   Total Fat as % of Daily Value: 18%   Protein: 7 gm   Fat: 12 gm
Carbohydrates: 60 gm   Calcium: 63 mg   Iron: 2 mg   Sodium: 229 mg   Dietary Fiber: 2 gm

TARTS AND MORE

Red Cherry Tart
Serves 8-10

1½ pounds fresh red cherries

Pie Crust:
1¼ cups whole wheat pastry flour
¼ teaspoon salt
1 teaspoon sugar
3-5 Tablespoons ice water
½ cup vegan shortening

Almond Flour:
⅓ cup whole wheat pastry flour
⅓ cup sugar
2 teaspoons vanilla extract
2 teaspoons almond extract

Pie Filling:
2 Tablespoons sugar

Stem and pit the cherries. Set aside.

Sift together the dry ingredients for the pie crust. Cut in shortening with a pastry cutter or fork. Once it resembles small pebbles, add water, starting with 3 Tablespoons and adding more if needed. Turn the dough out onto plastic wrap or wax paper. Roll dough into a ball and refrigerate for 1 hour.

Remove dough from refrigerator and roll dough out into a 10-inch tart pan. If the dough does not roll out easily, spray your hands with vegetable oil and spread the dough out evenly. Cover with plastic or wax paper and refrigerate for about 30 minutes.

Preheat oven to 400 degrees. Sift together flour and sugar for almond flour into a large bowl. Stir in vanilla and almond extract. Remove dough from refrigerator. Spread almond flour evenly over the bottom of the tart crust.

Toss cherries with 2 Tablespoons sugar, then place in tart pan, in a single layer. Use all the cherries, forcing them to fit, if necessary. The tighter the fit, the juicier your tart will be.

Place the tart pan on the lowest rack of the oven and cook there for 10 minutes at 400 degrees. After 10 minutes lower the temperature to 375 degrees and bake for another 10 minutes; then place tart pan in the middle of the oven and lower temperature to 350 for another 30 minutes. Let cool on a rack then serve warm at room temperature or chilled.

Note: A tart pan is lower and wider than a pie pan. If you don't have a tart pan, use 2 pie pans, placing the crust dough only half way up the pan sides.

Total Calories Per Serving: 286   Total Fat as % of Daily Value: 20%   Protein: 4 gm   Fat: 13 gm
Carbohydrates: 40 gm   Calcium: 21 mg   Iron: 1 mg   Sodium: 76 mg   Dietary Fiber: 4 gm

Chocolate Tofu Pie

Makes one 9-inch pie serving 8

¼ cup melted vegan margarine
1 cup vegan graham cracker crumbs
1¼ pounds firm tofu, cut into small cubes (about 4 cups)
1 cup rice syrup or maple syrup
½ cup vegan margarine
1 Tablespoon vanilla extract
⅔ cup unsweetened cocoa powder

Preheat oven to 350 degrees. Combine the melted margarine and crumbs and pat into a pie pan. Bake for 20 minutes or until golden. Remove crust from oven and allow crust to cool.

Place tofu in a food processor canister and process until very smooth. Add the other filling ingredients and process until well combined. Fill the baked, chilled crust with the tofu mixture and refrigerate for at least 1 hour before serving.

Total Calories Per Serving: 342   Total Fat as % of Daily Value: 29%   Protein: 7 gm   Fat: 19 gm
Carbohydrates: 40 gm   Calcium: 64 mg   Iron: 2 mg   Sodium: 265 mg   Dietary Fiber: 3 gm

Fruit Tart with Apricot Glaze

Makes 8-10 tarts

6 Tablespoons cold margarine
2 cups all-purpose flour or 1 cup whole wheat flour plus 1 cup all-purpose flour
2 teaspoons sugar
4-5 Tablespoons water
3 green apples (about 1 pound)
2 Tablespoons sugar
1 teaspoon orange zest
1 teaspoon ground ginger
½ cup apricot jam

Preheat oven to 350 degrees. Cut margarine into small pieces and place in the canister of a food processor or blender. If no machine is available, this can be done by hand. Add flour, 2 teaspoons sugar, and one Tablespoon of water and combine until crumbs start to form. Add water slowly, only until a nonsticky dough is formed. Wrap in plastic or waxed paper and freeze for 15 minutes.

Roll tart dough out on a clean surface to a 1-inch thickness. Line a 9-inch pie pan or individual tart pans with dough. Pinch ends of dough around the edge of the pan.

Peel apples and slice very thin. Layer apples into pan with a little overlap between pieces. In a small cup, combine 2 Tablespoons sweetener, zest, and ginger and sprinkle over apples. Bake uncovered for 20 minutes, or until apples are soft. Cover and bake 20 more minutes.

Heat jam in the microwave or in a small pot on the stove. Remove tarts from oven and brush with jam. Allow tart to cool for 10 minute before serving.

Note: Fresh ripe pears, peaches, apricots, or plums can be used instead of apples in this recipe.

Total Calories Per Serving: 288   Total Fat as % of Daily Value: 13%   Protein: 3 gm   Fat: 9 gm
Carbohydrates: 49 gm   Calcium: 14 mg   Iron: <1 mg   Sodium: 106 mg   Dietary Fiber: 2 gm

Individual Strawberry Tarts
Makes 8-10 tarts

Crust:
1/4 cup vegan margarine
1/4 cup vegan shortening
Vegetable oil spray
1/2 cup whole-wheat pastry flour
1 1/2 cups all-purpose flour
1 Tablespoon sugar
1 teaspoon salt
1 Tablespoon canola oil
1/4 cup ice-cold water

Filling:
6 cups washed and stemmed strawberries
1/2 cup sugar
2 Tablespoons frozen apple juice concentrate
1/4 teaspoon salt
1/2 teaspoon vanilla extract
3 Tablespoons cornstarch, dissolved in 1/2 cup water

To prepare pie crust, chill the margarine and shortening in the freezer for 10 minutes.

Preheat oven to 350 degrees and lightly spray muffin tin(s) with oil (prepare sufficient muffin tins to make 8-10 tarts). In a food processor, combine the flours, sugar, and salt. Add the margarine, shortening, and canola oil. Process until moistened and well combined. Gradually add the cold water and process until a nonsticky dough forms. Shape into a ball, wrap in plastic or wax paper, and chill for at least 30 minutes.

Remove from refrigerator and roll out to a 1/4-inch thickness. Cut into circles that are slightly larger than the size of the cups of the muffin tin. Place each circle in a muffin cup and pierce bottom with a fork, to allow steam to escape. Bake crust for 25 minutes, or until the edges are lightly browned. If desired, you can use the "blind baking" method described at the beginning of this chapter (see page 18). Remove from oven and allow crust to cool.

To prepare pie filling, purée 2 cups of the strawberries in a food processor until very smooth. In a medium pot, combine the strawberry purée, sugar, apple juice concentrate, salt, vanilla extract, and cornstarch mixture. Bring to a fast boil over medium heat. Let boil for 3 minutes, or until thick. Remove from stove and allow mixture to cool. Cut the remaining strawberries into quarters and stir into the cooled strawberry mixture.

To assemble tarts, remove the baked crusts from the muffin tins. Arrange on a serving platter or on individual dishes. Spoon the filling into the crusts and chill for at least 1 hour before serving.

Total Calories Per Serving: 337   Total Fat as % of Daily Value: 21%   Protein: 4 gm   Fat: 14 gm
Carbohydrates: 49 gm   Calcium: 24 mg   Iron: 1 mg   Sodium: 411 mg   Dietary Fiber: 4 gm

Apple Dumplings

Makes approximately 5 servings (depending upon the size of the apples)

Dough:
2 cups all-purpose flour
2 teaspoons baking powder
¹/₂ teaspoon salt
3 Tablespoons plus ¹/₂ Tablespoon sugar
3 Tablespoons cold vegan margarine, cut into pieces
2 Tablespoons cold vegetable shortening
¹/₂ cup plus ¹/₂ Tablespoon soy coffee creamer (*Silk* brand works well)

To prepare dough, sift together the flour, baking powder, salt, and 3 Tablespoons of sugar (the rest will be used in the assembly) in a bowl. Blend in margarine and shortening with a pastry blender or your fingertips until crumbly. Add ¹/₂ cup nondairy creamer (the rest will be used in the assembly) and stir with a fork just until the mixture is moistened. Do not overmix.

On a lightly floured surface, gently knead the dough 7 to 8 times or until a soft dough forms (be careful not to overwork the dough). Wrap in plastic or wax paper and set aside.

Filling:
¹/₃ cup sugar
1¹/₂ teaspoons light molasses
¹/₂ pound apples, such as Granny Smith, peeled, cored, and cut into ¹/₂-inch pieces (about 3 cups total)
¹/₃ cup dried cranberries
¹/₃ cup coarse, fresh bread crumbs
1¹/₂ Tablespoons vegan margarine
¹/₄ teaspoon ground nutmeg
¹/₄ teaspoon ground cinnamon

Mix the sugar and molasses until thoroughly combined.

In a medium bowl, combine all remaining filling ingredients until the apples are coated. Set aside.

Syrup:
1 cup sugar
2 Tablespoons blackstrap molasses
1¹/₂ cups unfiltered apple cider

In a small bowl, stir sugar with the molasses until combined.

In a small pot, bring molasses mixture to a boil. Reduce heat and add cider; stir and allow mixture to simmer for 5 minutes or until thickened. Set aside. Keep hot until ready to assemble.

Preheat the oven to 425 degrees.

Using a rolling pin, roll out the dough into an approximately 16- x 11-inch rectangle, with ³/₄-inch thickness. Halve dough lengthwise, then cut crosswise in thirds to form 6 squares.

Divide the filling evenly into the centers of the squares. Bring all 4 corners together over the filling and pinch together to seal, forming a little bundle.

Spray a large glass or ceramic baking dish liberally with oil. Transfer the dumplings to the baking dish and arrange about 1 inch apart. Brush tops with remaining ¹/₂ Tablespoon creamer and sprinkle with remaining ¹/₂ Tablespoon sugar.

Pour the hot syrup over the dumplings. Bake dumplings for 20-25 minutes or until they are golden brown. Serve immediately.

Total Calories Per Serving: 527   Total Fat as % of Daily Value: 26%   Protein: 6 gm   Fat: 17 gm
Carbohydrates: 86 gm   Calcium: 136 mg   Iron: 1 mg   Sodium: 579 mg   Dietary Fiber: 3 gm

Fast Fruit Crisp

Makes 8-10 servings

Topping:
1 cup all-purpose flour (or ¹/₂ cup all-purpose plus ¹/₂ cup whole wheat flour)
¹/₂ cup cold vegan margarine, cut into small pieces
¹/₂ cup sugar or brown sugar
1 teaspoon cinnamon
1 teaspoon nutmeg
¹/₂ teaspoon orange zest

Filling:
8 green apples, cored, peeled, and sliced, or 4 cups sliced, canned or fresh, peeled
    peaches or apricots, or 4 cups fresh, ripe pears, cored, peeled, and sliced, or
    3 cups frozen blueberries (not thawed) plus 1 cup sliced apples or pears
3 Tablespoons all-purpose or whole wheat flour
¹/₄ cup maple syrup
1 teaspoon cinnamon
1 teaspoon orange zest

Preheat oven to 400 degrees.

To prepare topping, place all topping ingredients in a food processor canister or blender or combine by hand until well mixed. Set aside.

To prepare fruit filling, combine fruit with remaining ingredients in a large bowl. Spread fruit mixture in a deep casserole dish. Sprinkle topping over fruit, resembling crumbs.

Bake for 20 minutes or until topping is golden and fruit is tender.

Notes: If you would like to microwave this recipe, place fruit filling in a 2-quart microwave-proof casserole dish. Place dish on an inverted plate in the microwave (if you have a microwave rack, use that). Microwave on HIGH for 6-7 minutes, rotating twice or until a knife inserted in the center comes out dry. This recipe freezes well.

Total Calories Per Serving: 323   Total Fat as % of Daily Value: 17%   Protein: 2 gm   Fat: 11 gm
Carbohydrates: 55 gm   Calcium: 18 mg   Iron: <1 mg   Sodium: 92 mg   Dietary Fiber: 3 gm

Apple-Maple Topping

Makes 1½ cups, enough to top one 9-inch pie or 8 servings

Use this as a hot topping for vegan frozen desserts, pancakes, or waffles, or to top a baked pie.

¼ cup apple juice
2 teaspoons apple juice concentrate
2 baking apples, cored, peeled, and diced (about ½ cup)
¾ cup maple syrup
1 Tablespoon vegan margarine

Place apple juice, concentrate, and apples in a medium-size pot. Bring to a fast boil, reduce heat to simmer while stirring. Cook mixture for 6-8 minutes or until apples are tender. Add syrup and margarine and stir. Allow topping to cook for 2 more minutes. Serve warm or refrigerate until ready to use.

Total Calories Per Serving: 113   Total Fat as % of Daily Value: 2%   Protein: <1 gm   Fat: 1 gm
Carbohydrates: 26 gm   Calcium: 22 mg   Iron: <1 mg   Sodium: 14 mg   Dietary Fiber: <1 gm

MICROWAVE BAKING TECHNIQUES

Remember that baking is closer to chemistry than any other type of cooking. This is especially true with microwave baking. When measuring dry ingredients (such as flour, sugar, baking powder, or baking soda), do so in a measuring cup or with measuring spoons. Be certain to level your measures, so that you are getting accurate amounts. The same goes for vegan margarine or shortening, you have to level your measures to get consistent, accurate amounts. If a recipe calls for sugar, do not substitute liquid sweeteners, such as maple syrup or molasses. It just won't work due to the interplay of dry and moist ingredients. There are some recipes that call just for sugar. After experimenting with various sweeteners, we found that only sugar worked in these few recipes.

Margarine and oil are not interchangeable in baking recipes. We've tried to keep most recipes as lowfat as possible. When a recipe calls for oil, melted margarine won't do and when you see melted margarine, oil won't do. This goes back to the chemistry of baking.

When measuring liquids, such as water, applesauce, milk or oil, get down to eye level with the measure. Looking down at a measuring cup does not give you an accurate view of the amount. You've either got to get down to its level or bring it up to yours.

Baking powder is a chemical leavening agent and loses its intensity over time, or if exposed to too much heat during storage. To get the best results, make sure your baking powder is fresh. Store it away from heat and moisture.

You'll note that most of the recipes in the other chapters of this book do not include salt. Baking recipes require salt to ensure adequate leavening (rising). Baking powder and baking soda interact with salt. If you need to eliminate salt from baking recipes, you'll have to experiment so you get the right amount of "rise." Salt substitutes cannot take the place of salt in baking recipes.

We have used silken tofu to replace eggs in many baking recipes. Two Tablespoons of silken tofu corresponds roughly to 1 large egg. If you are comfortable using powdered egg replacer, you can use the equivalent of one egg's worth of egg replacer for every 2 Tablespoons of silken tofu listed in the recipe. For more information on using egg replacer, see Chapter 16, on using vegan ingredients.

Pie fillings can be made in a microwave and some pie crust can be "baked" in a microwave. Remember, if you want a browned crust, you will not be getting it in a microwave, unless the microwave has a browning element. Graham cracker and nut crusts work well in a microwave, as the deep color is already in the ingredients. You may want to prepare several piecrusts at a time and refrigerate or freeze them until needed. This makes it easy to prepare a fast dessert, especially during fresh fruit season.

To make a fresh fruit pie, you can peel and slice very ripe fruit, such as peaches or apricots. Prepare a cornstarch slurry (follow the cornstarch package directions) and mix with a small amount of sugar. Toss the fruit and cornstarch together to coat the fruit, add to a pie shell, and you've got instant pie. This works well with ripe strawberries, blueberries, a berry and banana combo, raspberries, gooseberries, boysenberries, figs, and plums.

If your microwave is too small to accommodate an entire pie shell, or if you don't need a whole pie, you can cut recipes in half and make individual tarts. If you don't want to bother with the pie crust, simply prepare the filling and serve it in individual bowls.

Microwave Gingersnap Crust
Makes one 9-inch crust or 8 servings

Use extra cookies to make a spicy pie crust.

1½ cups vegan ginger snap cookies
5 Tablespoons vegan margarine, softened

Smash gingersnaps to form small crumbs. Mix crumbs and margarine well in a 9-inch microwaveable pie pan. Press mixture firmly and evenly into the pan. Microwave on HIGH for 2 minutes. Cool before filling.

Note: Vegan graham crackers can be substituted for the gingersnaps.

Total Calories Per Serving: 239   Total Fat as % of Daily Value: 17%   Protein: 2 gm   Fat: 11 gm
Carbohydrates: 33 gm   Calcium: 32 mg   Iron: 3 mg   Sodium: 335 mg   Dietary Fiber: 1 gm

Microwave Fruit Pie Fillings

Apple Pie
Makes enough to fill one 9-inch pie crust

4 cups baking apples, peeled, cored, and sliced
⅔ cup sugar
½ teaspoon cinnamon
2 Tablespoons flour

Combine all ingredients and mix well. Pour into a baked gingersnap or graham cracker crust. Set the pie on a piece of waxed paper and microwave on HIGH for 12-14 minutes, or until fruit is tender. Allow pie to cool for 10 minutes before slicing.

Variations: Use sliced peeled fresh pears, peaches, or apricots instead of apples. Fresh or frozen berries can be used in place of apples; however, if berries are very juicy, use 3 cups rather than 4 cups.

Total Calories Per Serving (Filling only): 124   Total Fat as % of Daily Value: <1%   Protein: <1 gm   Fat: <1 gm
Carbohydrates: 32 gm   Calcium: 6 mg   Iron: <1 mg   Sodium: <1 mg   Dietary Fiber: 2 gm

Raisin Pie

Makes enough to fill one 9-inch pie crust or 8 servings

$^2/_3$ cup sugar
2 Tablespoons cornstarch
1 cup water
2 cups raisins
$^1/_4$ cup orange juice
1 Tablespoon orange zest
2 Tablespoons lemon juice
$^1/_4$ teaspoon ground ginger

In a 2-quart bowl or casserole, mix sugar, cornstarch, water, and raisins. Microwave on HIGH for 6 minutes or until thickened, stirring every 2 minutes. Stir in juices, zest, and ginger. Pour into baked shell. Set pie on waxed paper in the microwave and microwave on MEDIUM for 6 minutes, or until bubbly.

Total Calories Per Serving (Filling only): 245	Total Fat as % of Daily Value: <1%	Protein: 2 gm	Fat: <1 gm
Carbohydrates: 64 gm	Calcium: 29 mg	Iron: 1 mg	Sodium: 6 mg	Dietary Fiber: 2 gm

Chapter 2: CAKES, QUICK BREADS, MUFFINS, AND DESSERT SAUCES

Cakes and their cousins, quick breads and muffins, are favorite desserts. They can be a big hit, served warm from the oven or at room temperature with a scoop of sorbet.

Cake baking is both science and art. Quick breads, such as carrot cake or zucchini bread, and muffins are a little more forgiving than layer or sponge cakes. Cupcakes can be made from most cake or quick bread batters and are very durable, as they can be baked ahead, frozen, then thawed as needed. Cake baking takes patience, an accurate oven, attention to recipe instructions, and the use of properly measured ingredients.

Professional chefs will tell you to make a trial run with a baking recipe, rather than trying it out for the first time on the day of a big event. Baking ingredients interact with each other to create an acceptable product. If you would like to try to substitute or add ingredients, do it one ingredient at a time, so you know what worked and what didn't. For example, if you would like to exchange orange juice concentrate for maple syrup, and shredded coconut for chopped walnuts in the same cake recipe, select one ingredient change and prepare the recipe. If it is a success, you can try the one-ingredient changed recipe with a second ingredient change. Make sure to add notes to the recipe, so you'll remember it for the next time.

Cake Success

Here are some tips for cake and muffin success:

- Ingredients should be used as listed in recipes, in the amounts listed. Invest in a set of measuring cups and measuring spoons.

- Use the sweetener specified in the recipe. When you see sugar listed as an ingredient in the recipes, we are referring to products such as Sucanat, beet sugar, turbinado sugar, or other vegan sweeteners available in your area. They should have the texture of granulated white sugar. You can make your own vegan powdered sugar by processing sugar in a spice grinder or food processor until it is powdery. Do not substitute a liquid vegan sweetener for sugar in recipes, unless you are willing to experiment with the balance of all the ingredients. Rice syrup, maple syrup, applesauce, or orange juice concentrate are all fine sweeteners. However, 2 Tablespoons of rice syrup are not equivalent to 2 Tablespoons of sugar in a baking recipe. You will be skewing the ratios, and may not get the desired end result. It is possible to use different sweeteners than specified in the recipes, understanding that you'll need to do your own "tweaking."

- Use the fat specified in the recipe because different fats and oils work in vastly different ways. For example, sesame and peanut oil have distinctive tastes and colors. Oil has a different melting point than margarine. Margarine contains more air than oil, and so will yield a different product, etc. Baking is chemistry and one of the ways to get the "experiment" to come out right is to use the right "chemicals."

- Soymilk (not lowfat or no-fat soymilk) is the safest milk to use with these baking recipes. The flavor and fat content is the right balance for a good end result. If a recipe simply says "vegan milk," you may use soymilk, rice milk, or almond milk. Again, you may use a different vegan milk than specified in the recipe, but give yourself some time for "tweaking."

- Use the cake pan or muffin tin size specified in the recipe. An oversized pan will cause baked goods to bake too fast, resulting in a burnt outside and a raw middle. An undersized pan can result in the cake spilling over the sides of the pan, a sunken center, and a raw middle. If you are not certain about a pan size, measure the pan across the top from one inside edge to the opposite inside edge.

- Prepare pans according to recipe directions. Don't assume that every cake pan is greased and floured. If you do grease a pan, be certain it is done evenly.

- Combine ingredients in the order listed.

- Mix cake for the amount of time listed in the recipe. Over- or underbeating baked goods can result in cake or muffins that are too dense and don't rise properly. Spread batter evenly in the prepared pans.

- Bake at the temperature specified in the recipe. An overhot oven will result in a flat, cracked-on-top, burnt-on-the-outside, raw-in-the-middle cake. A too-cool oven can result in a sticky-on-the-outside, crumbly-in-the-center cake. This may take some planning if you are baking several different items at the same time. Use the doneness method specified in the recipe.

- Allow cake or muffins to cool slightly before removing from pans or tins, so they don't crack, stick, or break.

Cake Tidbits

Most cake batters can be used to make cupcakes. Line muffin tins with baking paper or parchment and fill ⅔ full. A recipe for a one-layer cake should yield about 12-15 cupcakes. A recipe for one loaf of quick bread, such as zucchini bread, also should yield about 12-15 muffins.

Moist cakes, such as chocolate cake and carrot cake, can be baked ahead of time and frozen until needed. If you need the oven space, you can bake most cakes at least 2 days ahead of time. Store single-layer cakes in the baking pan, if possible, and seal tightly with foil or plastic wrap. If you plan on doing a lot of baking, you may want to invest in a domed, glass or plastic, cake saver. Cakes with frosting or fillings should be stored in the refrigerator.

Icing on the Cake

For presentation, you can prepare and decorate two of the same cakes. Place one cake at the edge of a serving platter. Slice the second cake and arrange those slices around the uncut cake. This looks good, and saves you from cutting too much cake. If time or space doesn't allow you to slice cake in front of guests, slice cake in the kitchen and place on plates, decorating with a sprinkle of fresh berries or a strawberry half. Arrange plates around the beverage area or on a dessert table.

If you would like to frost a cake, make certain it is cool. Place the first layer, top-side down, on a plate or serving platter. Place a small amount of frosting in the middle of the layer and spread gently in a circular movement, with a spatula or the back of a spoon. For smooth frosting, a pastry chef's secret is to very thinly frost a cake (it won't look pretty at this point, and some crumbs may even be visible through the frosting). Then refrigerate the cake for at least 30 minutes. This is called the "crumb" layer. When the first layer of frosting has had time to set, you can add a second layer of frosting. You don't use any more frosting than if you apply the frosting all at one time and you'll find it much easier to create an even, elegant frosting with this method. Think of it as first applying a coat of primer and then adding the final paint coat. Refrigerate all frosted cakes and cupcakes.

Frosted or not, you'll probably want to decorate your cake or cupcakes. Frost your cake, or spread a thin layer of jam or fruit preserves, nut butter (such as cashew or almond butter), or apple butter on your cake or cupcakes. Decorate with any of the following:

- Thin banana slices dipped in orange juice (to prevent browning)

- Chopped nuts

- Shredded coconut

- Carob or chocolate chips

- Flaked or grated carob or chocolate
- Fresh mint leaves and raspberries
- Petals from edible flowers, or small whole flowers
- Sliced grapes (sliced side up, so as not to make the cake soggy)
- Dried fruit or grated, peeled, fresh ginger

Dessert sauces can be used instead of cake frosting. You can pour a small pool of sauce on a dessert plate and place a small piece of unfrosted cake on top of the sauce. This looks very elegant and is a classical method for cake service. You can also place cake on a plate, and have the sauce in a serving bowl with a small ladle, allowing guests to choose the amount of sauce they would like. In addition to being colorful and flavorful, many dessert sauces contain less sugar or fat than frostings.

Get it on the Plate

Whether you bake a cake or purchase it from a bakery, you'll need to cut it into slices to serve it. To give you an idea of serving amounts, a 9 x 13-inch sheet cake can be cut into 30-35 small servings (about 2 x 2 inches). A single layer cake, usually 9 or 10 inches in diameter (the size of a big dinner plate) can be cut into about 30 small servings if you use the following method: about 3 inches from the outside of the cake, cut a circle all around the interior of the cake (you can gently place an inverted paper salad plate over the middle of the cake to use as a guide). Cut slices around the outside circle of the cake and plate. Then cut slices from the inner circle as needed. This works well for large layer cakes or wedding cakes. Everyone gets a small, even, square-ish serving of cake.

CAKE AND CUPCAKE RECIPES

Vanilla (White) Cake

Makes one 9 x 13-inch cake (8 large servings) or 24 cupcakes

Vegetable oil spray
1¹/₃ cups sugar
¹/₂ cup vegan margarine
3 cups unbleached flour
1 Tablespoon baking powder
³/₄ Tablespoon salt
2 cups soymilk, rice milk, or other vegan milk
1 Tablespoon each vanilla extract and almond extract

Preheat oven to 325 degrees. Spray a 9 x 13-inch pan or 24 cupcake tins with oil and set aside. Using an electric mixer or in a large bowl with a hand held mixer, mix the sugar and margarine together until light and fluffy. In another bowl, sift together the flour, baking powder, and salt. Add dry ingredients into the margarine mixture, alternating with the milk, and continuing to beat the mixture well between each addition. Add the vanilla and almond extract and beat the mixture an additional 2 minutes at medium speed. Pour the batter into the pan. Bake for 30 minutes or until an inserted toothpick comes out clean. Allow to completely cool before frosting.

Total Calories Per Serving Cake: 427   Total Fat as % of Daily Value: 19%   Protein: 7 gm   Fat: 12 gm
Carbohydrates: 72 gm   Calcium: 194 mg   Iron: 1 mg   Sodium: 959 mg   Dietary Fiber: 2 gm

Vanilla (White) Cake II

Makes two 8-inch layers or 8 servings

Vegetable oil spray
2³/₄ cups all-purpose white flour
2¹/₂ teaspoons baking powder
¹/₂ teaspoon salt
2 teaspoons powdered egg replacer (see page 21)
¹/₄ cup water
³/₄ cup soymilk
¹/₂ cup water
¹/₂ cup softened vegan margarine
1³/₄ cups sugar
1¹/₂ teaspoons vanilla extract

Preheat oven to 375 degrees. Spray two 8-inch pans with oil.

Combine flour, baking powder, and salt and set aside. Mix egg replacer and ¹/₄ cup water and set aside. Mix soymilk and ¹/₂ cup water, and set aside.

In the large bowl of an electric mixer, beat margarine until it is creamy, about a minute. Gradually add sugar until well creamed. Beat in vanilla. Add mixed dry ingredients and mixed soymilk/water alternately to creamed margarine, sugar, and vanilla, beating after each addition. Begin and end with flour mixture. Add mixed egg replacer along with the third addition of liquid. Turn evenly into pans.

Bake for 30-35 minutes, or until done (toothpick inserted into cake comes out clean). Remove from oven and let cool on a cake rack for 10 minutes. Remove from pans and let cool on rack until cold. Frost cake as desired.

Total Calories Per Serving: 437   Total Fat as % of Daily Value: 18%   Protein: 5 gm   Fat: 12 gm
Carbohydrates: 78 gm   Calcium: 123 mg   Iron: 1 mg   Sodium: 401 mg   Dietary Fiber: 1 gm

Lemon-Vanilla Cake

Makes one 9 x 13-inch pan or 8 large servings

Vegetable oil spray
3 cups unbleached flour
1¹/₂ cups sugar
1 Tablespoon baking soda
1¹/₂ teaspoons salt
1 cup water
¹/₂ cup lemon juice
¹/₄ cup safflower oil
3 Tablespoons vanilla
¹/₂ Tablespoon lemon oil (optional)
2 Tablespoon cider or white vinegar

Preheat oven to 350 degrees. Lightly spray a 9 x 13-inch pan and set aside.

In a large bowl, sift together the flour, sugar, baking soda, and salt. In another bowl, place the water, lemon juice, oil, vanilla, and lemon oil (if using), and whisk well to combine. Add the wet ingredients to the dry ingredients and whisk well to combine. Drizzle the vinegar over the top of the batter and whisk quickly to thoroughly incorporate. Pour batter into the prepared pan. Bake for 20-25 minutes or until an inserted toothpick comes out clean. You can serve this cake plain or frosted.

Total Calories Per Serving: 393   Total Fat as % of Daily Value: <1%   Protein: 5 gm   Fat: 4 gm
Carbohydrates: 75 gm   Calcium: 9 mg   Iron: <1 mg   Sodium: 909 mg   Dietary Fiber: 1 gm

Moist Chocolate Cake
Makes one 9 x 13-inch pan (8 large servings) or 24 cupcakes

3 cups all-purpose flour
2 cups sugar
2 Tablespoons baking soda
1 Tablespoon salt
½ cup unsweetened cocoa powder
¾ cup vegetable oil
1 Tablespoon vanilla extract
2 Tablespoons white vinegar
2 cups water
Vegetable oil spray

Preheat oven to 350 degrees. Mix the dry ingredients in one bowl and then add the wet ones, and mix until smooth and well combined. Spray pans and pour into a 9 x 13-inch pan or 24 cupcake tins. Bake at 350 degrees for approximately 20-25 minutes (cupcakes) or 50 minutes (9 x 13-inch pan). Test with a toothpick to make sure center is baked. Cool cake and ice with your favorite frosting.

Total Calories Per Serving Cake: 557   Total Fat as % of Daily Value: 31%   Protein: 6 gm   Fat: 20 gm
Carbohydrates: 89 gm   Calcium: 14 mg   Iron: 1 mg   Sodium: 1817 mg   Dietary Fiber: 3 gm

Moist Chocolate Cake II

Makes one 8-inch layer or 8 servings

1½ cups unbleached white flour
½ cup unsweetened cocoa powder
1 teaspoon baking soda
½ teaspoon salt
1 cup sugar
½ cup vegetable oil
1 cup cold brewed coffee or brewed grain coffee substitute
2 teaspoons vanilla extract
2 teaspoons cider vinegar

Preheat the oven to 375 degrees. Sift together flour, cocoa, baking soda, salt, and sugar into an ungreased 8-inch square pan.

In a 2-cup measuring cup, measure and mix the oil, water, coffee, and vanilla. Slowly pour the oil mixture into the baking pan and mix the batter with a fork or a small whisk. When the batter is smooth, add the vinegar and stir quickly. There will be some bubbling in the batter while the baking soda and vinegar are reacting. Stir only until the vinegar is evenly distributed throughout the batter; you will be able to tell because the batter color becomes consistent.

Bake cake for 25-30 minutes or until a toothpick comes out clean. Allow cake to cool on a rack. Be certain the cake is completely cooled before frosting.

Total Calories Per Serving: 314   Total Fat as % of Daily Value: 21%   Protein: 3 gm   Fat: 14 gm
Carbohydrates: 46 gm   Calcium: 10 mg   Iron: 1 mg   Sodium: 304 mg   Dietary Fiber: 2 gm

Devil's Food Cake

Makes one 9 x 13-inch pan or 12 servings

2 cups sugar
4 cups all-purpose flour
8 Tablespoons unsweetened cocoa powder
1 teaspoon salt
4 teaspoons baking soda
2 cups water
2 cups vegan mayonnaise
1 teaspoon peppermint extract
Vegetable oil spray

Preheat oven to 350 degrees. In a large bowl, sift together the sugar, flour, cocoa, and salt. Stir the baking soda in the water until dissolved. Add to the flour mixture. Add the mayonnaise and peppermint extract. Stir until smooth.

Spray a 9 x 13-inch pan with oil. Pour batter into pan. Bake for 30 minutes, or until a toothpick inserted into the center comes out clean.

Total Calories Per Serving: 528   Total Fat as % of Daily Value: 38%   Protein: 5 gm   Fat: 25 gm
Carbohydrates: 67 gm   Calcium: 11 mg   Iron: 1 mg   Sodium: 841 mg   Dietary Fiber: 2 gm

Sponge-Style Birthday Layer Cake
Makes two 8-inch layers or 8 servings

Cake:
2 cups white flour
$\frac{1}{2}$ cup soy flour
2 teaspoons baking soda
2 teaspoons cream of tartar
$\frac{1}{2}$ cup brown sugar
Vegetable oil
$\frac{1}{2}$ cup orange juice
$\frac{1}{2}$ cup cold water
2 teaspoons vanilla extract
$1\frac{1}{2}$ cups sliced bananas

Filling:
$\frac{1}{4}$ cup vegan margarine
4 Tablespoons powdered sugar
1 Tablespoon lemon juice
$\frac{1}{4}$ teaspoon vanilla extract
1 cup raspberry jam

Preheat oven to 325 degrees. To prepare cake, sift together all the dry ingredients except the sugar. Whisk together sugar, oil, orange juice, water, and vanilla. Gently add in bananas and mix only to combine. Pour this mixture into the dry ingredients and beat well until smooth. Grease (don't spray) two 8-inch cake pans and split the mixture between them. Bake cake in oven for 35-40 minutes or until golden.

Let the two layers cool. To make the filling, first beat the margarine in a bowl until soft. Sift and beat in the powdered sugar gradually. Add the lemon juice and vanilla. Add a little warm water, soymilk, or rice milk if required to give a fluffy consistency.

Spread raspberry jam over one layer and spread some of the lemon icing over the other layer. Invert one covered layered so the raspberry and the lemon icing meet. Cover the top of the cake with more lemon icing. Allow cake to stand for at least 1 hour before cutting.

Total Calories Per Serving: 396   Total Fat as % of Daily Value: 10%   Protein: 7 gm   Fat: 6 gm
Carbohydrates: 78 gm   Calcium: 42 mg   Iron: 1 mg   Sodium: 377 mg   Dietary Fiber: 3 gm

Applesauce Cake

Makes one 9 x 13-inch pan or 8 large servings

1 cup all-purpose flour
1 cup whole wheat flour
1 cup sugar
1 Tablespoon cornstarch
2 teaspoons baking soda
$\frac{1}{2}$ teaspoon salt
$\frac{1}{2}$ teaspoon cinnamon
$\frac{1}{4}$ teaspoon ginger
$\frac{1}{8}$ teaspoon cloves
$\frac{1}{4}$ teaspoon mace
$2\frac{1}{3}$ cups unsweetened applesauce
$\frac{1}{2}$ cup raisins
Vegetable oil spray

Preheat oven to 325 degrees. Mix the dry ingredients together; then add the applesauce and raisins and stir until well combined.

Spray a 9 x 13-inch pan with oil. Add batter to pan. Bake for 45-60 minutes. Test by inserting a toothpick into the center; it's done when the toothpick comes out clean.

Total Calories Per Serving: 291   Total Fat as % of Daily Value: <1%   Protein: 4 gm   Fat: <1 gm
Carbohydrates: 71 gm   Calcium: 14 mg   Iron: 1 mg   Sodium: 463 mg   Dietary Fiber: 3 gm

Autumn Pear Cake

Makes one 9 x 13-inch or two 8 x 8-inch pans or 8 large servings

Vegetable oil spray
2 pounds very ripe pears (about 6 cups)
6 Tablespoons lemon juice
$2\frac{1}{2}$ cups all-purpose flour
1 Tablespoon baking powder
$\frac{1}{4}$ teaspoon salt
$\frac{1}{8}$ teaspoon ground cloves
$\frac{1}{4}$ teaspoon ground ginger
1 cup sugar
$\frac{1}{2}$ cup puréed silken tofu
$\frac{3}{4}$ cup vegetable oil
$\frac{1}{4}$ cup maple syrup
2 Tablespoons hot water

Place a rack in the middle of the oven and preheat oven to 400 degrees. Spray a 9 x 13-inch pan (or two 8-inch square pans) with vegetable oil and then line pan(s) with parchment paper. Peel and core pears, and cut into $\frac{1}{4}$-inch chunks. Place lemon juice in a medium bowl and add pears, turning to coat well. Set aside.

Maple Apple Pie
Page 25

Moist Chocolate Cake
Page 45
with Vegan Buttercream Frosting
Page 58

In a large bowl, combine the dry ingredients and mix well. Add the tofu and vegetable oil and beat into a very stiff batter. Gently fold the pears into the batter. Turn the batter into the prepared cake pan(s), smooth the top with a wet spatula, and sprinkle with a little sugar.

Bake 10 minutes; reduce heat to 350 degrees and bake another 40-50 minutes or until the top is golden brown and a skewer inserted into the middle of the cake comes out clean. Remove pan from the oven. Use the edges of the parchment paper to lift the cake from the pan and transfer it to a plate.

To prepare the glaze, place the maple syrup in a bowl and add hot water. Stir well. Brush over the top of the cake. Let the cake cool for 15 minutes before serving. Serve warm or cool.

Total Calories Per Serving: 520   Total Fat as % of Daily Value: 31%   Protein: 5 gm   Fat: 20 gm
Carbohydrates: 81 gm   Calcium: 129 mg   Iron: 1 mg   Sodium: 270 mg   Dietary Fiber: 5 gm

Tomato Soup Cake
Makes three 9-inch layers or 8 large servings

This recipe is adapted from Los Angeles Unified School District recipe files, circa 1930's.

Vegetable oil spray
4 cups all-purpose flour
2 cups sugar
1½ Tablespoons baking powder
2 teaspoons baking soda
2 teaspoons ground allspice
2 teaspoons ground cinnamon
1 teaspoon ground cloves
2¼ cups condensed canned vegan tomato soup
1 cup vegan margarine or shortening
½ cup firm tofu
½ cup water

Preheat oven to 350 degrees. Spray pans with vegetable oil and lightly flour pans. In large bowl, combine and mix all dry ingredients. Place dry ingredients in a bowl of a mixer. Using the paddle or whisk attachment, beat in soup, margarine or shortening, and water. Beat for 3 minutes or until well combined.

Divide batter and pour into pans. Bake for 30-40 minutes or until toothpick inserted in center of cake comes out clean. Allow cake to stand for 10 minutes before removing from pan.

Total Calories Per Serving: 705   Total Fat as % of Daily Value: 35%   Protein: 9 gm   Fat: 23 gm
Carbohydrates: 113 gm   Calcium: 150 mg   Iron: 1 mg   Sodium: 1,147 mg   Dietary Fiber: 3 gm

Peach Cobbler Cake

Makes one 8-inch layer or 8 servings

¾ **cup whole wheat flour**
¼ **cup soy flour**
2 **teaspoons baking powder**
½ **teaspoon each cinnamon and nutmeg**
½ **cup sugar**
⅔ **cup soymilk**
¼ **teaspoon almond extract**
16-ounce **can sliced peaches, drained and cut into small pieces (about 2¼ cups)**
Vegetable oil spray

Preheat oven to 350 degrees. In a medium bowl combine the flour, soy flour, baking powder, cinnamon, nutmeg, and sugar. Stir until well combined. Add soymilk and almond extract and stir just until blended. Gently stir in the peaches.

Spray pan with oil. Pour the batter into the pan. Bake 35-40 minutes, until a toothpick inserted in the center comes out clean. Allow cake to cool before cutting.

Total Calories Per Serving: 130   Total Fat as % of Daily Value: 1%   Protein: 4 gm   Fat: 1 gm
Carbohydrates: 28 gm   Calcium: 112 mg   Iron: 1 mg   Sodium: 132 mg   Dietary Fiber: 3 gm

Cinnamon-Spicy Bean Cake

Makes one 9 x 13-inch pan or 8 large servings

¼ **cup vegan margarine**
4 **Tablespoons silken tofu**
2 **cups cooked, mashed pinto beans**
1 **cup all-purpose flour**
1 **cup sugar**
1 **teaspoon baking soda**
2 **teaspoons ground cinnamon**
½ **teaspoon each ground cloves and nutmeg**
¼ **teaspoon salt**
2 **cups peeled, cored, diced green apples**
¾ **cup raisins or dried cranberries**
¼ **cup chopped walnuts (optional)**
1 **Tablespoon vanilla extract**
Vegetable oil spray

Preheat oven to 375 degrees. Place margarine in a large bowl and mash with fork to soften. Add tofu slowly, beating to incorporate. Blend in beans. Sift together dry ingredients and spices. Mix mixture into beans, blending well to combine. Mix in apples, raisins, nuts, and vanilla.

Spray a 9 x 13-inch baking pan with oil. Pour batter into pan. Bake for 40 minutes or until a toothpick inserted in the center comes out dry.

Total Calories Per Serving: 473   Total Fat as % of Daily Value: 13%   Protein: 14 gm   Fat: 8 gm
Carbohydrates: 88 gm   Calcium: 73 mg   Iron: 4 mg   Sodium: 286 mg   Dietary Fiber: 9 gm

Carrot Cake

Makes one 9-inch layer or 8 servings

Vegetable oil (for pan)
2 cups whole wheat flour
1 Tablespoon each baking powder and baking soda
½ teaspoon salt
1¼ cups water
1¼ cups chopped dates
1 cup raisins
1 Tablespoon each cinnamon and ground ginger
½ Tablespoon each ground cloves and ground nutmeg
½ cup shredded carrots
½ cup chopped walnuts
⅓ cup frozen orange juice concentrate

Preheat oven to 375 degrees. Lightly oil a 9-inch springform pan and set aside.

In a small bowl, sift together the flour, baking powder, baking soda, and salt and set aside. In a small saucepan, combine the water, dates, raisins, cinnamon, ginger, cloves, and nutmeg. Bring to a boil, reduce heat, and simmer for 5 minutes. In a large bowl, place the shredded carrots, pour the hot liquid mixture over the top, and allow mixture to cool completely. Add the walnuts and orange juice concentrate to the carrot mixture and blend well. Add the dry ingredients to the wet ingredients and stir well to combine. Pour the batter into the prepared springform pan. Bake for 45 minutes or until an inserted toothpick comes out clean.

Total Calories Per Serving: 324   Total Fat as % of Daily Value: 7%   Protein: 8 gm   Fat: 5 gm
Carbohydrates: 69 gm   Calcium: 147 mg   Iron: 2 mg   Sodium: 814 mg   Dietary Fiber: 8 gm

Frozen Raw Birthday Cake

Makes one bundt cake or 8-inch round deep casserole-size cake (8 servings)

2 cups dried organic figs, soaked overnight in water
2 cups of dried pitted organic dates, soaked overnight in water
1½ cups shelled organic almonds
8 ripe bananas

Soak fruit in separate bowls. The water level should be about half full. Don't completely cover the fruit.

Remove stems from soaked figs. Purée figs and set aside. Purée dates and put in a separate bowl. Chop almonds in food processor or blender and set aside. Peel and purée the bananas in a blender or food processor.

To assemble the cake, place almonds in the bottom of a bundt cake pan or 8-inch round, deep casserole. The second layer is the puréed figs, then almonds; then puréed bananas, almonds, dates, almond, figs, etc., ending with almonds. Cover and freeze for at least 4 hours.

To serve, remove from the freezer, place upside down on a plate, and allow cake to sit a few minutes until thawed enough to release from the pan. Serve immediately.

Total Calories Per Serving: 400   Total Fat as % of Daily Value: 20%   Protein: 8 gm   Fat: 13 gm
Carbohydrates: 69 gm   Calcium: 108 mg   Iron: 2 mg   Sodium: 2 mg   Dietary Fiber: 11 gm

Tofu Cheese Pie
Makes one 9-inch pan or 8 servings

Cheese pie has a more silky texture than traditional cheesecake. The textures reflect regional preferences.

2¼ cups softened vegan cream cheese
1 cup sugar
1½ Tablespoons lemon juice
1 teaspoon vanilla extract
One 9-inch prepared graham cracker crust
1 cup vegan cherry pie filling or ¾ cup orange marmalade mixed with ¼ cup
** drained, canned pineapple tidbits or fresh, minced pineapple**

Preheat oven to 350 degrees. Combine cream cheese, sugar, lemon juice, and vanilla until smooth and pour into the graham cracker crust. Bake for 40-50 minutes, or until golden on top.

Chill for at least 2 hours. Top with pie filling. Chill for at least 1 hour before serving.

Variations: Bake in various sized pans and create a series of small pies, tiered, and decorated with edible flowers. Create individual cheese pies by baking in muffin tins. Vary the toppings, including using a melted chocolate glaze or fresh raspberry purée.

Total Calories Per Serving: 518   Total Fat as % of Daily Value: 36%   Protein: 3 gm   Fat: 23 gm
Carbohydrates: 74 gm   Calcium: 11 mg   Iron: <1 mg   Sodium: 528 mg   Dietary Fiber: <1 gm

Tofu Cheesecake
Makes two 9-inch pans or 16 servings

This recipe is fast to make and has a very creamy texture. Serve with a topping of thawed, frozen berries or fresh, sliced fruits.

Crust:
1½ pounds vegan graham cracker or cookie crumbs
½ cup maple syrup
¼ cup melted margarine
1 Tablespoon orange zest

Filling:
2 pounds silken tofu, drained
½ pound pressed tofu (see note below)
⅓ cup orange juice concentrate
4 Tablespoons apple butter
2 teaspoons orange zest
2 Tablespoons cornstarch dissolved in 6 Tablespoons of soy or rice milk

Preheat oven to 350 degrees. Prepare crust in a large mixing bowl by combining all pie ingredients until crumbs are moistened. Press crumbs into pie tins, muffin, or tart tins (for individual cheesecakes). Bake at 350 degrees for about 5 minutes (or until firm). Allow crust to cool.

Preheat oven to 350 degrees. Place all filling ingredients in a blender or food processor and blend until mixture is smooth. Pour into cooled crusts. Bake for 30 minutes or until top of cheesecake is slightly browned. Cool and refrigerate until set, about 2 hours.

After cheesecake sets, serve it with fresh or frozen, thawed blueberries, strawberries, or canned chopped pineapples. If appropriate, add a small amount of liqueur as a topping.

Note: To make pressed tofu, simple place firm tofu in a strainer or colander, cover with paper towels, and weigh down with several dinner plates. Allow tofu to drain for at least 4 hours.

Total Calories Per Serving: 274   Total Fat as % of Daily Value: 11%   Protein: 8 gm   Fat: 7 gm
Carbohydrates: 44 gm   Calcium: 52 mg   Iron: 2 mg   Sodium: 344 mg   Dietary Fiber: 1 gm

Chocolate Tofu Cheesecake
Makes one 9-inch pan or 8 servings

Filling:
1¼ cups vegan chocolate chips
3½ cups extra-firm silken tofu
¼ cup maple syrup
1 Tablespoon vanilla extract
⅛ teaspoon salt

Crust:
1½ cups vegan graham cracker crumbs
3 Tablespoons unsweetened cocoa powder
1 Tablespoon sugar
½ cup vegetable oil

Melt the chocolate chips in the microwave or over a double boiler until smooth. Press the tofu to remove any excess moisture. (You can do this by placing the tofu between two plates and putting a heavy weight on top. Leave weight on for at least one hour, then pour off liquid before using the pressed tofu.) In a food processor canister or blender, combine the pressed tofu, melted chocolate chips, and remaining filling ingredients and purée until smooth. Set aside.

Preheat oven to 325 degrees. In a small bowl, combine graham cracker crumbs, cocoa, and sugar, stirring until well combined. Drizzle in oil, mixing mixture with your hands until thoroughly combined. Firmly press into the bottom of a greased 9-inch springform pan and set aside. Pour filling over top of crust and bake at 325 degrees for 45 minutes. Allow cheesecake to cool for at least 4 hours before attempting to cut.

Total Calories Per Serving: 499   Total Fat as % of Daily Value: 39%   Protein: 11 gm   Fat: 26 gm
Carbohydrates: 60 gm   Calcium: 63 mg   Iron: 4 mg   Sodium: 345 mg   Dietary Fiber: 3 gm

Quick Bread and Muffin Recipes

Chocolate Raspberry Muffins
Makes 12 muffins

Vegetable oil spray
1¹/₂ cups unbleached all-purpose flour
¹/₄ cup unsweetened cocoa powder
¹/₂ cup brown sugar
1¹/₂ teaspoons baking powder
1 teaspoon ground cinnamon
¹/₂ teaspoon baking soda
¹/₂ teaspoon salt
1 cup vegan buttermilk (1 cup soymilk mixed with 2 teaspoons white vinegar)
¹/₄ cup vegetable oil
2 Tablespoons applesauce
1 cup fresh, washed or frozen, thawed raspberries
1 teaspoon vanilla extract

Preheat the oven to 400 degrees. Spray a 12-cup muffin pan with vegetable oil.

In a medium-size bowl, combine all the dry ingredients (flour, cocoa powder, sugar, baking powder, cinnamon, baking soda, and salt).

In a large bowl, stir together the wet ingredients (vegan buttermilk, oil, vanilla, and applesauce) until well combined. Stir in the dry mixture until just combined. Do not over mix. Gently fold in the raspberries.

Divide the batter evenly among the prepared muffin cups, filling them about two-thirds full. Bake for 12-15 minutes or until a wooden toothpick inserted in the center of a muffin comes out clean. Cool on a rack for 5 minutes.

Total Calories Per Serving: 141   Total Fat as % of Daily Value: 8%   Protein: 3 gm   Fat: 5 gm
Carbohydrates: 21 gm   Calcium: 74 mg   Iron: <1 mg   Sodium: 222 mg   Dietary Fiber: 2 gm

Banana Blueberry Muffins

Makes 12 muffins

Muffin papers
2 very ripe mashed bananas (about 2$\frac{1}{2}$ cups)
$\frac{1}{2}$ cup sugar
$\frac{1}{2}$ teaspoon baking powder
$\frac{1}{2}$ teaspoon salt
$\frac{3}{4}$ cup all-purpose flour
$\frac{1}{2}$ cup whole wheat pastry flour
1$\frac{1}{2}$ teaspoons powdered egg replacer
2 Tablespoons water
$\frac{1}{2}$ cup washed, fresh or frozen, thawed blueberries

Preheat oven to 350 degrees. Line muffin cups with paper muffin liners.

In a large bowl combine mashed bananas, sugar, baking powder, salt, and flours; mix until smooth. In a small bowl or cup combine egg replacer and water; stir into banana mixture. Fold in blueberries.

Spoon batter evenly, about $\frac{1}{4}$ cup each, into muffin cups. Bake in oven for 20-25 minutes, or until golden brown. Cool on a rack.

Total Calories Per Serving: 122　　Total Fat as % of Daily Value: <1%　　Protein: 2 gm　　Fat: <1 gm
Carbohydrates: 30 gm　　Calcium: 16 mg　　Iron: <1 mg　　Sodium: 117 mg　　Dietary Fiber: 2 gm

Whole Wheat Apple Muffins

Makes 12 muffins

2 cups whole wheat flour
2 Tablespoon sugar (may use $\frac{1}{4}$ cup sugar for sweeter muffins)
1 Tablespoon baking powder
$\frac{1}{4}$ teaspoon salt
1 teaspoon cinnamon
1$\frac{1}{4}$ cups water
$\frac{1}{2}$ cup applesauce
1$\frac{1}{2}$ cups peeled, cored, and chopped green apples

Preheat oven to 425 degrees. Combine flour, sugar, baking powder, salt, and cinnamon in large mixing bowl. Combine water and applesauce in another bowl. Add chopped apple to dry ingredients and mix to coat apple. Add water mixture to dry ingredients. Mixture will be thick.

Spoon mixture into non-stick muffin tins sprayed with vegetable oil spray. Bake at for about 20 minutes or until lightly browned. Allow muffins to cool on rack.

Total Calories Per Serving: 90　　Total Fat as % of Daily Value: <1%　　Protein: 3 gm　　Fat: <1 gm
Carbohydrates: 21 gm　　Calcium: 75 mg　　Iron: 1 mg　　Sodium: 171 mg　　Dietary Fiber: 3 gm

Dessert Sauces

Melba Sauce
Makes 4 servings

1 cup thawed frozen raspberries
¹⁄₂ cup currant or apricot jelly
2 teaspoons cornstarch
1 Tablespoon cold water

In a small sauce pot, mash berries. Add jelly and quickly bring to a boil. Reduce heat. In a small cup, create a slurry with cornstarch and water. Stir cornstarch into berries. Cook, stirring, until clear and slightly thickened, about 5 minutes.

Total Calories Per Serving: 131   Total Fat as % of Daily Value: <1%   Protein: <1 gm   Fat: <1 gm
Carbohydrates: 32 gm   Calcium: 15 mg   Iron: <1 mg   Sodium: 13 mg   Dietary Fiber: 2 gm

Vegan Caramel Sauce
Makes 1½ cups

¹⁄₄ cup soy or rice milk
³⁄₄ cup sugar
¹⁄₃ cup maple syrup or brown rice syrup
1 Tablespoon water
1 Tablespoon arrowroot
2 Tablespoons vegan margarine
1 Tablespoon vanilla

Place the milk, sugar, and maple syrup in a small saucepan and whisk well to combine. Cook over medium heat for 3 minutes, while whisking occasionally. In a small bowl, whisk together the water and arrowroot, and then whisk the mixture into the saucepan. Cook the mixture, while whisking constantly, an additional 2-3 minutes or until it thickens. Remove the saucepan from the heat and whisk in the remaining ingredients.

Serve warm as a topping for cakes, desserts, non-dairy frozen desserts, or as a dipping sauce for fruit. Store in an airtight container in the refrigerator, and reheat as needed.

Total Calories Per Serving: 136   Total Fat as % of Daily Value: 4%   Protein: <1 gm   Fat: 3 gm
Carbohydrates: 28 gm   Calcium: 19 mg   Iron: <1 mg   Sodium: 27 mg   Dietary Fiber: <1 gm

Summer Dessert Sauce

Serves 5

Vegetable oil spray
$1/2$ cup pitted, peeled, and diced fresh, ripe apricots
1 cup pitted, peeled, and diced fresh, ripe peaches
$1/4$ cup chopped fresh strawberries
1 cup pitted, peeled, and diced fresh, ripe plums
1 Tablespoon orange juice concentrate
Water or orange juice, as needed

Heat a large skillet and spray with oil. Add all fruit and sauté quickly, stirring, just until fruit begins to wilt, about 2 minutes. Pour sautéed fruit into a blender. Add orange juice concentrate and process until just smooth, not totally puréed. If sauce is thicker than desired, add a small amount of water or juice and process briefly to combine.

Total Calories Per Serving: 34   Total Fat as % of Daily Value: <1%   Protein: <1 gm   Fat: <1 gm
Carbohydrates: 9 gm   Calcium: 5 mg   Iron: <1 mg   Sodium: <1 mg   Dietary Fiber: 1 gm

Spiced Apple Syrup

Serves 5

1 cup water
6 ounces apple juice concentrate, thawed
2 Tablespoons sugar
1 Tablespoon cornstarch
1 teaspoon cinnamon
$1/2$ teaspoon nutmeg
$1/2$ teaspoon ground ginger
$1/2$ teaspoon vanilla extract

In a small sauce pot, combine water, concentrate, sugar, cornstarch, and cinnamon. Heat, stirring until mixture becomes clear, about 10 minutes. It will be thin. Add remaining ingredients and cook for an additional 3 minutes. Serve warm.

Total Calories Per Serving: 41   Total Fat as % of Daily Value: <1%   Protein: <1 gm   Fat: <1 gm
Carbohydrates: 10 gm   Calcium: 2 mg   Iron: <1 mg   Sodium: 2 mg   Dietary Fiber: <1 gm

Frostings

Cream Cheese Spread with Fruit

Serves 8-10

Use as a cake frosting or filling and as a dip for plain cookies, wafers, or for sliced fruit.

1 cup vegan cream cheese
1 teaspoon fresh orange zest
$\frac{1}{2}$ cup fruit preserves, such as apricot, raspberry, or orange marmalade
$\frac{1}{4}$ cup chopped fresh or frozen, thawed, and well-drained strawberries

Place cream cheese in a medium-size bowl. If necessary, whisk with a fork to soften. Add remaining ingredients and mix well to combine.

Spread with a spatula on a cooled cake, muffins, or cupcakes, or place in a bowl and serve as a fruit dip. Refrigerate extra spread.

Note: For a smoother spread, place all ingredients in a blender or food processor canister and purée.

Total Calories Per Serving: 140   Total Fat as % of Daily Value: 8%   Protein: 1 gm   Fat: 5 gm
Carbohydrates: 23 gm   Calcium: 4 mg   Iron: <1 mg   Sodium: 166 mg   Dietary Fiber: <1 gm

Vegan Buttercream Frosting

Makes 2 cups or 8 servings

$\frac{1}{2}$ cup softened vegan margarine
$\frac{1}{4}$ cup soy, rice, or almond milk
3 cups powdered sugar
$1\frac{1}{2}$ Tablespoons vanilla extract

Using an electric mixer or in a large bowl with a hand held mixer, place the margarine and milk, and cream them together. Add half of the powdered sugar, and beat well to combine. Add the remaining ingredients and continue to beat the mixture until light and fluffy.

Variations: For a Berry Frosting, add $\frac{1}{4}$ cup mashed fresh or frozen berries, such as raspberries, strawberries, or blueberries.
For a Chocolate Frosting, add $\frac{1}{2}$ cup cocoa powder or $\frac{1}{3}$ cup melted vegan chocolate chips.
For a Coffee Frosting, substitute cold coffee or espresso for the milk in the recipe.
You can also stir in chopped nuts, chopped vegan chocolate, shredded coconut, or chopped fruit into the basic Vanilla Buttercream Frosting recipe to create additional variations.

Total Calories Per Serving (not variations): 278   Total Fat as % of Daily Value: 17%   Protein: <1 gm   Fat: 11 gm
Carbohydrates: 45 gm   Calcium: 11 mg   Iron: <1 mg   Sodium: 95 mg   Dietary Fiber: <1 gm

Pineapple-Coconut Tofu Frosting

Makes frosting for one 9 x 13-inch cake or 8 large servings

12 ounces silken extra-firm tofu (about 1¹⁄₂ cups)
¹⁄₂ cup frozen pineapple-orange juice concentrate, thawed
2 Tablespoons maple syrup
1¹⁄₂ teaspoons cider or white vinegar
1 Tablespoon cornstarch
1 Tablespoon water
2 teaspoons rum extract
¹⁄₂ teaspoon coconut extract

Press the silken tofu by placing a colander over a bowl and then put a paper coffee filter in the colander. Place the block of tofu in the coffee filter, cover the tofu with another coffee filter, place a plate on top of the filter, and place a large can or other heavy object on top of the plate. Place the colander in the refrigerator for 1 hour to drain.

Meanwhile, in a small saucepan, place the pineapple-orange juice concentrate, maple syrup, and cider vinegar. Bring to a boil, reduce the heat to low, and simmer for 5 minutes.

In a small bowl, whisk together the cornstarch and water. Pour the cornstarch mixture into the simmering juice mixture and continue to cook, while whisking constantly, until the mixture thickens. In a food processor canister or blender, place the pressed silken tofu, thickened juice mixture, and rum and coconut extracts, and purée for 1-2 minutes or until very smooth and creamy. Spread the tofu frosting over the top only of a cooled cake.

Total Calories Per Serving: 60   Total Fat as % of Daily Value: <1%   Protein: 3 gm   Fat: <1 gm
Carbohydrates: 12 gm   Calcium: 24 mg   Iron: <1 mg   Sodium: 37 mg   Dietary Fiber: <1 gm

Lemon Frosting

Makes enough to frost one 8-inch cake or 8 servings

¹⁄₂ cup softened vegan margarine
¹⁄₂ cup vegan cream cheese
2 Tablespoons soy or rice milk
4 cups powdered sugar
1 Tablespoon lemon juice
2 Tablespoons lemon zest
1 Tablespoon vanilla

Using an electric mixer or in a large bowl with a hand held mixer, place the margarine, cream cheese, and milk and cream them together. Add half of the powdered sugar and beat well to combine. Add the remaining ingredients and continue to beat the mixture until light and fluffy.

Total Calories Per Serving: 378   Total Fat as % of Daily Value: 21%   Protein: <1 gm   Fat: 14 gm
Carbohydrates: 65 gm   Calcium: 6 mg   Iron: <1 mg   Sodium: 173 mg   Dietary Fiber: <1 gm

Vegan Chocolate Ganache

Makes 2 cups or 8 servings

¾ cup soy, rice, or almond milk
¼ cup vegan margarine
1½ cups vegan chocolate chips

In the top part of a double boiler, place the milk and margarine, and heat together until the margarine melts. Add the chocolate chips, continue to cook while stirring constantly until the chocolate chips have melted completely and the mixture is very smooth.

Use the ganache, warm, as a glaze for cakes or use as a dip or coating for fruit or nuts, or when cool, use as a filling for cakes and desserts. Store any excess in an airtight container in the refrigerator.

Total Calories Per Serving: 211   Total Fat as % of Daily Value: 23%   Protein: 2 gm   Fat: 15 gm
Carbohydrates: 21 gm   Calcium: 42 mg   Iron: 1 mg   Sodium: 60 mg   Dietary Fiber: 2 gm

Tofu Cream Frosting

Makes 1¼ cups, enough for one 8-inch layer cake (8 servings)

1 cup firm tofu (half pound)
2 Tablespoons each vegetable oil and lemon juice
3 Tablespoons maple syrup
¼ teaspoon salt
½ teaspoon vanilla extract

Combine all the ingredients in a blender and blend until very smooth. Scrape the sides of the blender often with a rubber spatula to get the frosting completely smooth.

Total Calories Per Serving: 60   Total Fat as % of Daily Value: 5%   Protein: 2 gm   Fat: 3 gm
Carbohydrates: 6 gm   Calcium: 15 mg   Iron: <1 mg   Sodium: 97 mg   Dietary Fiber: <1 gm

Vegan Devon Cream

Makes about 3 cups or 8 servings

Devon cream is thick, luxurious, and not as fluffy as whipped cream. Will hold for several hours in the refrigerator and it can be rewhipped, if necessary.

1 cup chilled soy non-dairy coffee creamer (such as Silk™ brand)
3 Tablespoons vegan cream cheese (such as Tofutti™ brand)
2 Tablespoons sugar
¼ teaspoon fresh lemon zest

Put creamer and cream cheese in a large, chilled bowl. Use an electric mixer and beat at high speed until it gets fluffy. Sprinkle sugar a little at a time, beat and taste until desired sweetness is reached. Mix in lemon zest and use to frost cake or as a base for creamy desserts.

Total Calories Per Serving: 58   Total Fat as % of Daily Value: <1%   Protein: <1 gm   Fat: 3 gm
Carbohydrates: 7 gm   Calcium: <1 mg   Iron: <1 mg   Sodium: 50 mg   Dietary Fiber: <1 gm

Soy Whipped Cream

Makes ½ cup

2 Tablespoon soymilk powder
½ cup ice water
½ teaspoon vanilla extract

Place all ingredients in a chilled bowl. Using an electric hand mixer or a wire whisk, whip until stiff peaks are formed. Keep cold until ready to use.

Total Calories Per 2 TB Serving: 12   Total Fat as % of Daily Value: <1%   Protein: 1 gm   Fat: <1 gm
Carbohydrates: 1 gm   Calcium: 5 mg   Iron: <1 mg   Sodium: 56 mg   Dietary Fiber: <1 gm

Vegan Pastry Cream

Makes 3 cups

½ cup unbleached flour
2 cups soymilk, rice milk, or other vegan milk divided into ½ cups
⅓ cup sugar
¼ cup lemon juice
2 Tablespoons grated lemon zest
½ Tablespoon vanilla extract

In a small bowl, place the flour and whisk in ½ cup milk, and set aside. In a small saucepan, place the remaining milk and sugar and whisk to combine. Add the flour mixture to the liquid ingredients and whisk well to combine. Cook the mixture over medium heat, while whisking constantly, for 5-6 minutes or until thickened. Add the remaining ingredients, whisk well to combine, and cook the mixture an additional 1 minute.

Remove the saucepan from the heat and transfer the mixture to a glass bowl. Place a piece of waxed paper or plastic wrap directly on top of the pastry cream to prevent a skin from forming on the top. Place the pastry cream in the refrigerator for several hours to cool completely. Use as a filling for pies, tarts, pastries, or phyllo dough, or as a topping for desserts.

Total Calories Per 2 TB Serving: 30   Total Fat as % of Daily Value: <1%   Protein: 1 gm   Fat:<1 gm
Carbohydrates: 6 gm   Calcium: 30 mg   Iron: <1 mg   Sodium: 11 mg   Dietary Fiber: <1 gm

Vegan Powdered Sugar

Makes 2 cups

2 cups sugar
½ cup cornstarch

In a blender or food processor, blend sugar and cornstarch for 1 minute. Scrape the sides down and blend an additional 30 seconds. Store in an airtight container.

Total Calories Per 2 TB Serving: 112   Total Fat as % of Daily Value: 0%   Protein:<1 gm   Fat: 0 gm
Carbohydrates: 29 gm   Calcium: <1 mg   Iron: <1 mg   Sodium: <1 mg   Dietary Fiber: <1 gm

Chapter 3: COOKIES

Everybody likes to munch on a cookie. If you purchase ready-to-eat cookies for your party, build a cookie ice cream sandwich with a scoop of vegan sorbet or vegan ice cream. This may be made ahead of time, wrapped, and used as needed. For calorie-controlled or low sugar modifications use vegan graham crackers; for lower fat restrictions use sorbet or fruit ices. Too cold for ice cream? Use peanut butter or apple butter and fruit preserves for a filling.

Create individual dessert pizzas with cookies or prepare large dessert pizzas for special activities, rather than cake. Crumbled cookies can be used to garnish pudding, cream pies, and even hot cereals. Garnish the morning oatmeal with crumbled gingersnaps or oatmeal raisin cookies and see the great response. Crumbled cookies can be used just like graham cracker crumbs to create whole or individual pie crusts or tart shells.

Review the cake baking suggestions in Chapter Two. They are the same for cookies. In order to get successful batches of cookies, you should use the specified ingredients, add them in the specified order, and mix and bake according to directions. If you would like to change ingredients, prepare a batch with only one ingredient changed at a time.

You don't have to prepare cookies from scratch to have "home-baked" cookies. There are some easy-to-use vegan cookies mixes available, many of which only need the addition of water. You can prepare the mixes and refrigerate the dough for several hours until you are ready to bake your cookies.

Add chopped nuts, chips, orange or lemon zest, or chopped dried fruit to the mix to create new flavors. For a different texture, add cold cereal (such as crumbled corn flakes, Rice Krispies™, or Grapenuts™), chopped pineapple, raisins, dried fruit, and applesauce to the cookie mix to make soft cookie bars. These can be served topped with powdered sugar, apple butter or peanut butter, or frosting. If you would like "from scratch" cookies, but don't think you'll have the time to prepare them when party time comes around, do some pre-preparation. Make up the dry components of the cookie mixes and store labeled in airtight containers in a dry, cool place. When you are ready to bake, most of the work will already be done. You'll just need to add some vegetable oil, margarine, juice, or vegan milk, depending on the recipe.

Pinwheel cookies can be prepared from two different cookie doughs. Select two different colors, such as a brown carob and a golden vanilla. Chill dough slightly to make it easier with which to work. Roll out cookie dough into thin, about $1/2$-inch sheets. Stack the sheets and lightly roll, so they adhere to each other. Roll up the combined doughs into a tight, long oval, resembling a roll of coins. Slice the dough into 1-inch thick coins, arrange on a nonstick cookie sheet, and bake.

You can find organic, vegan brown sugar or dried, crystallized date or palm sugar. Brown vegan sugar has a different texture that is sometimes required in baking recipes to obtain the desired results. You can use carob powder instead of cocoa powder, carob chips instead of chocolate chips, or soy butter instead of nut butters if you like. If you can't find vegan powdered sugar you can grind vegan sugar in a food processor or grinder until it has a powdery texture. Some people add a bit of cornstarch to increase the powdery texture. See Chapter 2 for a recipe for vegan powdered sugar.

The good news about most cookies is they can be baked, properly cooled, and stored in airtight containers for several days. That makes many cookies the perfect bake-ahead party food. If you are giving guests favors to take home, think about a small tin of carefully baked home-baked cookie assortments.

Cookies to the Max!

Here are some ideas for add-ins when you're whipping up a batch of cookies (these ingredients can be added to cookie mixes or pressed into frozen cookie dough as a garnish):

- chocolate chip cookies: add chopped walnuts, macadamias, pistachios, peanuts, almonds or pecans, or chopped or shredded coconut
- oatmeal cookies: add raisins or chopped dates, apricots, prunes, figs, or dried peaches, chopped crystallized ginger, or carob chips
- vanilla cookies: add dried or fresh lemon or orange zest, fruit preserves (such as raspberry or cherry), orange marmalade, apricot jam, or flavored extracts (such as almond, rum, or orange)

Or create a "dessert pizza." Bake oversized cookies and top as follows:

- sauce: fruit preserves or jam, peanut, apple, hazelnut, soy, cashew or almond butter, creamy cake frosting, flavored vegan cream cheese (whip pineapple tidbits, fresh or frozen berries or peach pieces into cream cheese)
- toppings: shredded coconut, melted vegan chocolate, peanut butter chips, raisins or chopped dried fruit (remember dried cherries, blueberries, apples, peaches, and nectarines), chopped nuts, fresh berries, canned or fresh pineapple, peaches, apricots

RECIPES

Banana Orange Oatmeal Cookies

Makes about 32 small (2-inch) cookies

¹/₂ cup softened vegan margarine
2 Tablespoons silken tofu or powdered egg replacer to equal one egg
¹/₄ cup very ripe mashed banana
1 teaspoon vanilla extract
¹/₂ cup vegan brown sugar or palm or date sugar (with moist texture of brown sugar)
1 Tablespoon fresh orange zest
2 cups whole wheat flour
1 teaspoon baking powder
1¹/₂ cups rolled oats (not instant)
1 cup raisins
Vegetable oil spray

Preheat oven to 350 degrees. Place margarine and tofu or egg replacer in a bowl and mash together. Add banana and vanilla and mix until as smooth as possible. Add sweetener and zest and combine. Set aside.

In a large bowl, combine flour, baking powder, oats, and raisins. Add banana mixture to dry mixture and mix until well combined.

Spray baking sheet with oil. Drop cookie dough by teaspoonfuls, leaving 1-2 inches between each cookie. Bake for 10-15 minutes or until golden brown. Cool cookies on a rack.

Total Calories Per Serving (2 cookies): 207	Total Fat as % of Daily Value: 11%	Protein: 6 gm	Fat: 7 gm
Carbohydrates: 33 gm	Calcium: 42 mg	Iron: 2 mg	Sodium: 88 mg	Dietary Fiber: 4 gm

Glazed Ginger-Almond Cookies

Makes about 30 small (2-inch) cookies

$^2/_3$ cup molasses
$^1/_3$ cup softened vegan margarine
$^1/_4$ cup apple juice concentrate
1 teaspoon vanilla extract
4 Tablespoons silken tofu
2 cups all-purpose flour
2 cups whole wheat flour
$^1/_2$ cup sugar
4 teaspoons dry ground ginger
$^1/_2$ teaspoon ground cloves
1 teaspoon orange zest
1 teaspoon baking soda
$^1/_2$ teaspoon baking powder
Vegetable oil spray
$^1/_4$ cup apple juice concentrate (for glaze)

Preheat oven to 350 degrees. In a large bowl, combine molasses, margarine, concentrate, and vanilla. In a small bowl, whisk tofu until fluffy. Add to molasses mixture and stir to combine. In a medium bowl, combine flours, sugar, ginger, cloves, zest, baking soda, and baking powder and mix. Mix dry mixture slowly into molasses mixture. Mix and knead until smooth.

Place dough on a clean surface and divide into two balls. Roll each ball into a long tube, about 2 inches in diameter. Wrap in plastic or waxed paper and refrigerate for 30 minutes.

Spray a baking sheet with oil. Unwrap dough and cut into thin slices, about 1-inch thick. Place on sheet. Brush each cookie with a little apple juice concentrate. Baking 10 minutes or until a light brown.

Total Calories Per Serving (2 cookies): 223   Total Fat as % of Daily Value: 6%   Protein: 4 gm   Fat: 4 gm
Carbohydrates: 43 gm   Calcium: 48 mg   Iron: 2 mg   Sodium: 140 mg   Dietary Fiber: 2 gm

Apple Snacking Cookies

Serves 6

This is a cross between moist cake and cookie.

1 cup whole wheat flour
1 teaspoon nutmeg
1 teaspoon cinnamon
$^1/_2$ teaspoon ginger
1 teaspoon baking soda
3 Tablespoons sugar
3 Tablespoons vegetable oil
4 Tablespoons silken tofu, whisked until fluffy
1 Tablespoon maple syrup
2 cups peeled, cored, shredded green apples

¹/₄ cup chopped dates
¹/₄ cup chopped pecans or walnuts (optional)
Vegetable oil spray

Preheat oven to 350 degrees. In a medium bowl, combine flour, nutmeg, cinnamon, ginger, baking soda, and sugar. In a large bowl, combine oil, tofu, and maple syrup. Mix in apples, dates, and nuts (if desired). Slowly mix in dry ingredients and stir only until combined (don't over mix).

Spray an 8 x 8-inch baking pan with oil. Add batter. Bake for 30-40 minutes or until knife inserted in center comes out clean. Cut into squares and serve warm or cool.

Total Calories Per Serving: 259   Total Fat as % of Daily Value: 14%   Protein: 8 gm   Fat: 9 gm
Carbohydrates: 40 gm   Calcium: 39 mg   Iron: 2 mg   Sodium: 310 mg   Dietary Fiber: 4 gm

Fruit Pizza
Serves 8

Make as one big cookie, instead of a special event cake, or make as individual cookies. Please note that this recipe is high in fat.

2 recipes unbaked cookie crumb crust using vegan ginger snaps (see page 21)
1 cup vegan cream cheese
1 teaspoon vanilla extract
¹/₄ cup sugar
1 cup sliced bananas (dip in orange juice to prevent browning, if desired)
1 cup peeled sliced kiwi fruit
¹/₂ cup drained, crushed pineapple
¹/₄ cup dried berries, such as blueberries or cranberries
¹/₂ cup shredded coconut (optional)
¹/₂ cup water
¹/₄ cup sugar
³/₄ cup orange juice
2 Tablespoons lemon juice
2 Tablespoons cornstarch

Preheat oven to 350 degrees. Press ginger snap crust into two 9-inch pizza pans or a thin baking sheet. Bake 5 minutes and allow crust to cool.

In a medium-size bowl, mix cream cheese, vanilla, and ¹/₄ cup sugar. Spread over cooked crust. Arrange bananas, kiwi fruit, pineapple, berries, and coconut (optional) over cream cheese. Put in refrigerator.

In a small pot, combine water with ¹/₄ cup sugar, orange and lemon juice, and cornstarch, whisking constantly. Bring to a fast boil, reduce heat and allow mixture to simmer, whisking constantly about 3 minutes, until thickened. Allow mixture to cool. Pour evenly over pizza and allow fruit pizza to cool in refrigerator at least 1¹/₂ hours before serving.

Total Calories Per Serving: 720   Total Fat as % of Daily Value: 46%   Protein: 7 gm   Fat: 30 gm
Carbohydrates: 107 gm   Calcium: 80 mg   Iron: 6 mg   Sodium: 834 mg   Dietary Fiber: 4 gm

Gingerbread Cookies
Makes about 3 dozen cookies

$1/2$ cup brown sugar
$1/4$ cup maple syrup
$1/4$ cup molasses
$1/2$ cup mashed banana
$2^{1}/_{2}$ Tablespoons grated fresh ginger
$1/8$ cup vegetable oil
$1/4$ teaspoon vanilla extract
1 cup all-purpose flour
1 cup whole wheat flour
1 teaspoon baking soda
1 teaspoon baking powder
$1/2$ teaspoon salt
$1/4$ Tablespoon cloves
$1/4$ Tablespoon nutmeg
$1/4$ Tablespoon cinnamon

Preheat oven to 350 degrees. In large mixing bowl, combine brown sugar, syrup, molasses, banana, ginger, oil, and vanilla. Beat until all ingredients are well combined and banana is smooth.

In a separate bowl, combine flour, baking soda, baking powder, salt, cloves, nutmeg, and cinnamon. Stir until well combined. Mix dry and moist ingredients gingerly until thoroughly combined.

Roll dough into small balls (about 2 Tablespoons each). Place balls of dough on cookie sheets and bake for approximately 10 minutes or until golden. Allow cookies to cool on a rack.

Serve warm or cool, or place in an air-tight container and store in a cool, dry place for up to 1 week.

Total Calories Per Serving (2 cookies): 134   Total Fat as % of Daily Value: 11%   Protein: 2 gm   Fat: 7 gm
Carbohydrates: 18 gm   Calcium: 31 mg   Iron: 1 mg   Sodium: 172 mg   Dietary Fiber: 1 gm

Apricot and Raisin Bars
Makes approximately 16 bars

Vegetable oil spray
1 cup quick-cooking oats (not old-fashioned or steel cut)
1 cup whole wheat flour
$1/3$ cup sugar, brown sugar, or date sugar
$1/4$ teaspoon ground cinnamon
1 teaspoon ground ginger
$1/4$ teaspoon salt
$1/4$ teaspoon baking soda
3 Tablespoons apple juice
$1/3$ cup vegetable oil
$1/4$ cup apricot jam or preserves (or other flavor jam)
2 Tablespoons apple juice
1 cup diced dried apricots (or other type of dried fruit)

Preheat oven to 350 degrees. Spray cookie sheet with oil and set aside.

Mix together oats, flour, sweetener, cinnamon, ginger, salt, and baking soda in a bowl until well combine. In a cup, whisk together 3 Tablespoons of juice with the oil. Combine with oat mixture until blended. Set aside 1 cup of the oat mixture. Press the remaining mixture evenly into the cookie sheet.

In a small bowl, combine the jam and 2 Tablespoons of apple juice. When well mixed, stir in the dried apricots and combine. Evenly spread apricot mixture over oat mixture in cookie sheet. Top with reserved oat mixture. Press down lightly to remove air and to even the cookies. Bake for 30 minutes, or until golden. Remove from oven and allow bars to cool before cutting.

Total Calories Per Serving: 134   Total Fat as % of Daily Value: 8%   Protein: 3 gm   Fat: 5 gm
Carbohydrates: 20 gm   Calcium: 9 mg   Iron: 1 mg   Sodium: 58 mg   Dietary Fiber: 2 gm

Fudge without the Oven Cookies
Makes about 2 dozen cookies

2 cups sugar
¹/₂ cup soymilk
¹/₃ cup unsweetened cocoa powder
¹/₄ cup vegan margarine
¹/₂ cup smooth peanut butter
1 cup shredded coconut
1¹/₂ teaspoons vanilla extract
2¹/₂ cups quick oats

Place sugar, soymilk, and cocoa in a medium pot and bring to a fast boil, stirring constantly. Reduce heat and allow mixture to simmer, stirring for 2 minutes. Remove from heat and quickly stir in remaining ingredients. Mix well to combine. Drop tablespoonfuls onto waxed paper. This mixture hardens fast, so be prepared to work quickly.

Total Calories Per Serving (2 cookies): 475   Total Fat as % of Daily Value: 31%   Protein: 10 gm   Fat: 20 gm
Carbohydrates: 67 gm   Calcium: 43 mg   Iron: 3 mg   Sodium: 92 mg   Dietary Fiber: 5 gm

Banana and Oat Cookies with Dates
Makes approximately 3 dozen cookies

2¹/₂ cups sliced bananas
2 cups rolled oats
1 cup chopped dates
¹/₃ cup vegetable oil
1 teaspoon vanilla extract

Preheat oven to 350 degrees. In a large bowl, mash the bananas. Stir in remaining ingredients. Mix well and let set for 15 minutes.

Drop by teaspoonful onto ungreased cookie sheets. Bake for 20 minutes or until light brown.

Total Calories Per Serving (2 cookies): 144   Total Fat as % of Daily Value: 8%   Protein: 3 gm   Fat: 5 gm
Carbohydrates: 22 gm   Calcium: 13 mg   Iron: 1 mg   Sodium: <1 mg   Dietary Fiber: 3 gm

No Bake Chocolate, Peanut, and Oatmeal Cookies

Makes about 2 dozen cookies

Please note that these cookies should only be served on special ocassions due to their high fat content.

¹/₃ cup vegan chocolate chips
¹/₄ cup vegan margarine
¹/₂ cup brown sugar
¹/₂ cup soy or rice milk
1 teaspoon vanilla extract
2 cups peanut butter
3 cups instant oats
2 cups shredded coconut

In a large sauce pan, melt chocolate chips, margarine, and sugar; stir and cook until smooth. Add milk and bring to a fast boil. Allow mixture to boil, stirring for 2 minutes. Reduce heat and add vanilla and peanut butter. Cook and stir until peanut butter is completely blended into the mixture.

Meanwhile, in a separate bowl, mix oats and coconut together. Add oatmeal-coconut mixture to the mixture containing peanut butter and stir until dry ingredients are coated. Drop by heaping spoonfuls onto waxed paper and let cool.

Total Calories Per Serving (2 cookies): 697   Total Fat as % of Daily Value: 68%   Protein: 20 gm   Fat: 44 gm
Carbohydrates: 58 gm   Calcium: 67 mg   Iron: 4 mg   Sodium: 249 mg   Dietary Fiber: 7 gm

Pumpkin Pie Cookies

Makes approximately 2 dozen cookies

1 cup vegan shortening
1 cup sugar
1¹/₂ cups unsweetened canned or cooked, puréed pumpkin
Powdered egg replacer plus water for 1 egg equivalent
2 cups all-purpose flour
1 teaspoon baking soda
1 teaspoon cinnamon
¹/₂ teaspoon nutmeg
¹/₂ teaspoon salt
¹/₂ cup vegan carob or chocolate chips
Vegetable oil spray

Preheat oven to 375 degrees. Cream shortening, sugar, and pumpkin together. Add egg replacer and mix well. Sift in dry ingredients and mix thoroughly. Add in chips and mix thoroughly.

Spray baking sheets with oil. Drop heaping spoonfuls onto baking sheets. Bake approximately 20-30 minutes. When done, let cookies cool and then spread on paper towels to dry.

Total Calories Per Serving (2 cookies): 292   Total Fat as % of Daily Value: 23%   Protein: 3 gm   Fat: 15 gm
Carbohydrates: 36 gm   Calcium: 12 mg   Iron: 1 mg   Sodium: 325 mg   Dietary Fiber: 2 gm

Crispy Cocoa Cookies

Makes approximately 2 dozen cookies

6 Tablespoons vegan margarine
4 Tablespoons sugar
$^1/_2$ teaspoon vanilla extract
1 Tablespoon cocoa powder
$1^1/_2$ cups whole wheat flour
4 Tablespoons crushed cornflakes

Preheat oven to 350 degrees. In a large bowl, cream margarine and sugar. Add vanilla and cocoa, mix well to combine. Add flour and mix well to combine. Mix in crushed cornflakes. Roll into teaspoon-sized balls and flatten slightly with a fork. Bake on a tray for 20-25 minutes. Cool for 5 minutes on tray then cool completely on a wire rack.

Total Calories Per Serving (2 cookies): 120	Total Fat as % of Daily Value: 9%	Protein: 2 gm	Fat: 6 gm
Carbohydrates: 16 gm	Calcium: 5 mg	Iron: <1 mg	Sodium: 46 mg	Dietary Fiber: 2 gm

Cranberry Cookies

Makes approximately 2 dozen cookies

2 cups whole wheat flour
1 teaspoon baking soda
$^1/_2$ teaspoon ground ginger
$^1/_2$ teaspoon ground nutmeg
$^1/_2$ teaspoon salt
3 cups quick cooking oats
1 cup vegan shortening
$1^1/_2$ cups chopped dried cranberries
$1^1/_2$ cups firmly packed brown sugar
Vegetable oil spray

Preheat oven to 375 degrees. In a large bowl, combine flour, baking soda, ginger, nutmeg, salt, and oats. Cut in shortening until particles are very fine. Add cranberries and brown sugar. Mix until well blended. Chill in the refrigerator for at least 1 hour.

Roll out dough to $^1/_4$-inch thickness and cut into 3-inch rounds. Spray cookie sheets with oil. Bake on greased cookie sheets for 12-15 minutes or until lightly browned. Cool on rack.

Total Calories Per Serving (2 cookies): 462	Total Fat as % of Daily Value: 26%	Protein: 10 gm	Fat: 17 gm
Carbohydrates: 69 gm	Calcium: 51 mg	Iron: 3 mg	Sodium: 333 mg	Dietary Fiber: 7 gm

Oatmeal Cookies without the Oven

Makes about 3 dozen cookies

2 cups sugar
1/2 cup soymilk
1/4 cup vegan margarine
2 Tablespoons unsweetened cocoa powder
3 cups quick oats
3/4 cup chopped walnuts
1 teaspoon vanilla extract

Combine sugar, soymilk, margarine, and cocoa in a medium pot. Bring to a fast boil and boil, stirring, for 2 minutes. Remove from heat and add oats, nuts, and vanilla. Stir well until combined.

Drop by spoonfuls onto waxed paper. Mixture will be slightly loose, and will firm up as it dries. Allow cookies to set for at least 2 hours before serving.

Total Calories Per Serving (2 cookies): 245   Total Fat as % of Daily Value: 11%   Protein: 6 gm   Fat: 7 gm
Carbohydrates: 41 gm   Calcium: 26 mg   Iron: 2 mg   Sodium: 24 mg   Dietary Fiber: 3 gm

Gooey Carob No-Bake Cookies

Makes approximately 3 dozen cookies

3/4 cup maple syrup
1/2 cup soymilk (vanilla flavor is okay to use)
1/4 cup vegan margarine
1 Tablespoon carob powder
3 cups quick oats
3/4 cup of raisins or chopped nuts
2 Tablespoons carob powder

Combine maple syrup, soymilk, margarine, and 1 Tablespoon carob powder in a medium-size pot over medium heat. Bring to a boil and boil for 2 minutes, stirring. Remove from heat and briskly stir in oats and raisins or nuts. Stir thoroughly. Spread onto a cookie sheet lined with wax paper. Sprinkle 2 Tablespoons carob powder over cookies.

Allow cookies to chill in refrigerator for at least 1 hour. Cut into squares to serve.

Total Calories Per Serving (2 cookies): 182   Total Fat as % of Daily Value: 6%   Protein: 5 gm   Fat: 4 gm
Carbohydrates: 33 gm   Calcium: 38 mg   Iron: 2 mg   Sodium: 26 mg   Dietary Fiber: 4 gm

Peanut and Carob Cookies

Makes approximately 2 dozen cookies

$\frac{1}{2}$ **cup vegan margarine**
1 cup brown sugar
$\frac{1}{4}$ **cup soft tofu**
1$\frac{1}{2}$ cups whole wheat flour
$\frac{3}{4}$ **teaspoon baking soda**
$\frac{1}{8}$ **teaspoon salt**
$\frac{1}{2}$ **cup peanut butter**
$\frac{3}{4}$ **cup carob chips**

Preheat oven to 375 degrees. Cream margarine and sugar together. Add tofu and combine well. In a separate bowl, combine flour, soda, and salt. Combine with margarine mixture. Add peanut butter and mix well. Melt carob chips in the microwave or in a small pot on top of the stove. Blend 1 cup of cookie dough with the melted carob. Fold the carob dough into the peanut butter dough until it looks marbled. Roll into 1$\frac{1}{2}$-inch balls, press with a fork, and bake on an ungreased cookie sheet for about 5 minutes or until slightly browned.

Total Calories Per Serving (2 cookies): 263   Total Fat as % of Daily Value: 20%   Protein: 5 gm   Fat: 13 gm
Carbohydrates: 32 gm   Calcium: 26 mg   Iron: 1 mg   Sodium: 225 mg   Dietary Fiber: 3 gm

Molasses Cookie Bars

Makes approximately 2 dozen cookies

1 cup packed brown sugar
$\frac{3}{4}$ **cup vegetable oil**
$\frac{1}{4}$ **cup molasses**
Powdered egg replacer plus water equivalent for 2 eggs
2$\frac{1}{4}$ cups unbleached all purpose flour
2 teaspoons baking soda
1 teaspoon ground cinnamon
1 teaspoon ground ginger
$\frac{1}{2}$ **teaspoon ground cloves**
$\frac{1}{4}$ **teaspoon salt**
3 Tablespoons unbleached flour
2 Tablespoons sugar

Preheat oven to 325 degrees. Mix brown sugar, oil, molasses, and egg substitute in a large bowl with an electric mixer on medium. You can mix by hand, but it needs to be very fluffy. Stir in the remaining ingredients, except the sugar.

Roll into tablespoon-sized balls of dough. Roll each ball in sugar. Shake off excess. Then place 1-2 inches apart on ungreased sheet. Bake for 13-16 minutes or until set (they will appear dry). Allow bars to cool on wire rack.

Total Calories Per Serving (2 cookies): 310   Total Fat as % of Daily Value: 20%   Protein: 3 gm   Fat: 13 gm
Carbohydrates: 45 gm   Calcium: 33 mg   Iron: 1 mg   Sodium: 266 mg   Dietary Fiber: 1 gm

Peanut Butter and Jelly Cookies

Makes approximately 3 dozen cookies

1 cup peanut butter
2 cups whole wheat flour
1 teaspoon powdered egg replacer mixed with 2 Tablespoons warm water
1 teaspoon vanilla extract
2 Tablespoons your favorite preserves, jam, or jelly

Preheat oven to 350 degrees. Place peanut butter, flour, egg replacer, and vanilla in a bowl and stir until well-blended. Form into small balls (about 1 teaspoon's worth) and place on a cookie sheet. The dough might be crumbly, but the heat of your hands should help to hold it together. Using a fork, flatten the cookies, making a cross-stitch pattern by pressing the fork down in one direction, and then another. Poke a tiny hold in the center of each cookie and fill with small amount of the preserves, jam, or jelly.

Bake for 5-6 minutes. Watch carefully, as these cookies burn easily. Remove cookies from the oven, let cool for 1 minute, than transfer to a plate to cool.

Total Calories Per Serving (2 cookies): 135   Total Fat as % of Daily Value: 11%   Protein: 5 gm   Fat: 7 gm
Carbohydrates: 14 gm   Calcium: 11 mg   Iron: 1 mg   Sodium: 67 mg   Dietary Fiber: 3 gm

Rugelach

Makes approximately 30 rugelach

This is a vegan version of the traditional Eastern European treat (a miniature, chewy Danish).

Dough:
1/2 cup vegan cream cheese
1 cup vegan margarine
1 cup flour
1/4 teaspoon salt
Flour for rolling dough

Filling:
1/2 cup carob or chocolate chips or apricot preserves (you can alternate fillings)
1/2 cup finely chopped walnuts or pistachios
1/4 cup sugar mixed with 2 teaspoons ground cinnamon
1 Tablespoon vegetable oil

Vegetable oil spray

Blend together dough ingredients. This works best if you use your hands. Roll into a ball and wrap in plastic or waxed paper. Freeze for at least 2 hours.

Preheat oven to 375 degrees. Remove dough from freezer and place on a well-floured surface. Roll very thin into a rectangular shape. Spread chips or preserves in a thin layer, covering all the dough. Sprinkle with nuts, and then sugar. Slice the dough into small triangles. Roll from the broad end to the tip, so rugelach resembles a small crescent. Brush with oil.

Spray cookie sheets with oil. Bake on cookie sheet 12-15 minutes or until golden. Allow rugelach to cool before serving.

Total Calories Per Serving (2 rugelach): 213   Total Fat as % of Daily Value: 25%   Protein: 2 gm   Fat: 16 gm
Carbohydrates: 13 gm   Calcium: 4 mg   Iron: <1 mg   Sodium: 179 mg   Dietary Fiber: 1 gm

Crispy Rice Cookies
Makes about 4 dozen

2 cups vegan margarine
2 cups sugar
2 teaspoons vanilla
3 cups all-purpose flour
2 teaspoons baking soda
2 teaspoons cream of tartar
1½ cups Rice Krispies™-style cold cereal

Preheat oven to 350 degrees. Cream margarine and sugar together. Add vanilla and mix well. Add flour, baking soda, and cream of tartar and mix well. Fold in the Rice Krispies™-style cereal. Place a heaping teaspoon at a time on ungreased cookie sheet and bake 10-12 minutes. Allow to cool before serving.

Total Calories Per Serving (2 cookies): 259   Total Fat as % of Daily Value: 23%   Protein: 2 gm   Fat: 15 gm
Carbohydrates: 30 gm   Calcium: 3 mg   Iron: 1 mg   Sodium: 227 mg   Dietary Fiber: <1gm

Sugar Cookies
Makes about 20 cookies

1½ cups all-purpose flour
½ cup sugar
½ teaspoon baking soda
½ teaspoon salt
½ cup oil
1 Tablespoon vanilla extract
1 Tablespoon maple syrup
1 teaspoon powdered egg replacer mixed with 1 Tablespoon water
Ground cinnamon to sprinkle on top (optional)

Mix dry ingredients in a bowl, except for cinnamon. Mix moist ingredients in a separate bowl. Stir moist ingredients into dry ingredients. Form dough into a big ball. (If it sticks together well, then it's the right consistency. If not, then add a bit of water and mix it well.) Wrap dough in plastic or waxed paper and chill for 1 hour.

   Preheat oven to 375 degrees. Form dough into teaspoon-sized balls and roll into cinnamon, if desired. Place on ungreased cookie sheet. Flatten each ball a little bit. Bake cookies for about 7 minutes, watching carefully as they burn easily. Allow cookies to cool on a rack.

Total Calories Per Serving (2 cookies): 285   Total Fat as % of Daily Value: 17%   Protein: 2 gm   Fat: 11gm
Carbohydrates: 46 gm   Calcium: 4 mg   Iron: <1 mg   Sodium: 179 mg   Dietary Fiber: 1 gm

Cherry Almond and Chocolate Chip Cookies

Makes approximately 2¹/₂ dozen or 30 cookies

½ cup soymilk, water, or apple juice
½ cup maple syrup
½ cup vegetable oil
1 teaspoon vanilla extract
¼ teaspoon almond extract
1 cup unbleached flour
1 cup whole wheat pastry flour
1 teaspoon baking powder
½ teaspoon baking soda
¼ teaspoon salt
³/₄ cup vegan chocolate chips
¹/₃ cup dried cherries
¹/₃ cup sliced almonds
Vegetable oil spray

Preheat oven to 350 degrees. In a medium-size bowl, whisk together the soymilk, maple syrup, oil, vanilla, and almond extract and set aside. In a large bowl, place flours, baking powder, baking soda, and salt and stir well to combine. Add the wet ingredients to the dry ingredients and stir well to combine. Fold the remaining ingredients into the cookie dough.

Lightly spray cookie sheets. Drop the dough by teaspoonfuls, spacing them 2 inches apart, onto the prepared sheets. Bake at 350 degrees for 10-15 minutes or until cookies are set and lightly browned on the bottom and around the edges. Allow the cookies to cool on the cookie sheets for a few minutes before transferring to a rack to cool completely. Repeat the baking procedure for the remaining cookie dough. Store the cookies in an air-tight container.

Total Calories Per Serving (2 cookies): 213   Total Fat as % of Daily Value: 17%   Protein: 3 gm   Fat: 11 gm
Carbohydrates: 26 gm   Calcium: 50 mg   Iron: 1 mg   Sodium: 119 mg   Dietary Fiber: 2 gm

Pinwheel Cookies

Makes about 4¹/₂ dozen or 54 cookies

2½ cups all-purpose flour
¼ teaspoon salt
1 cup vegan margarine
1 cup sifted powdered sugar
2 Tablespoons silken tofu
1 teaspoon vanilla extract
1 teaspoon almond extract
2 teaspoons beet juice (drained canned beets works) or 2 teaspoons cherry juice

Beat margarine in a mixer bowl with an electric mixer for 30 seconds. Beat in powdered sugar until fluffy. Add tofu and extracts; beat well. Add the dry ingredients. Beat until just combined. Divide dough in half. Mix beet or cherry juice into one portion of dough to give it a red color. Chill dough for 1 hour or until easy to handle.

Divide each portion of dough in half. On lightly floured surface, roll out each of the four balls of dough to form an 8-inch square. Place a white square of cookie dough on top of a red square of cookie dough. Roll up, jelly roll style. Repeat with remaining dough. Wrap the rolls in waxed paper and chill for at least 2 hours.

Preheat oven to 375 degrees. Cut chilled dough into $1/4$-inch thick slices. Place on ungreased cookie sheets. Bake for 8-10 minutes or until edges are firm and bottoms are light brown. Remove cookies and cool on wire racks.

Total Calories Per Serving (2 cookies): 109	Total Fat as % of Daily Value: 9%	Protein: 1 gm	Fat: 6 gm
Carbohydrates: 12 gm	Calcium: 3 mg	Iron: <1 mg	Sodium: 73 mg	Dietary Fiber: <1 gm

Vegan Lemon Square Cookies
Makes approximately 15-18 cookies

Shortbread:
1½ cups all-purpose flour
2 Tablespoons sugar
¾ cup cold vegan margarine

Lemon curd:
12 ounces soft silken tofu (about 1½ cups)
1 cup fresh lemon juice
2 Tablespoons grated lemon zest
¾ cup sugar
1 teaspoon vegan lemon gel powder or ⅛ teaspoon saffron threads dissolved in
  1 Tablespoon cold water (optional to get yellow color)
3-4 cups all-purpose flour

Place oven rack in the middle position and preheat oven to 325 degrees.

Prepare shortbread layer by first sifting together flour and sugar into a large bowl. Cut margarine into small chunks and scatter over flour/sugar mixture. Cut together margarine, flour, and sugar using a pastry blender or fork until the resulting mixture is the size of small peas. Press mixture into the bottom and $1/2$ inch up the sides of an ungreased 9 x 13-inch baking pan using your fingers or the back of a wooden spoon. Bake shortbread layer approximately 30 minutes or until golden brown.

While shortbread cools, prepare lemon curd by first, puréeing tofu in a food processor canister. Add lemon juice, zest, sugar, and lemon gel powder or saffron threads and process until thoroughly mixed. Continue processing while adding flour gradually until well blended. Allow lemon curd to chill for at least 2 hours in the refrigerator.

Pour lemon curd batter over cooled shortbread crust. Bake until lemon curd is bubbly and starts to turn golden around the edges. Remove pan from oven and let rest on a rack until cool to touch. Chill at least 1 hour in the refrigerator before cutting into bars and serving.

Total Calories Per Serving (1 cookie): 274	Total Fat as % of Daily Value: 14%	Protein: 5 gm	Fat: 9 gm
Carbohydrates: 42 gm	Calcium: 15 mg	Iron: 1 mg	Sodium: 93 mg	Dietary Fiber: 1 gm

Fudge Brownies

Makes 10

Vegetable oil spray
³/₄ cup crumbled light silken tofu
¹/₂ cup each water and maple syrup
¹/₂ cup unsweetened carob powder (roasted variety works well) or cocoa powder
2 Tablespoons vegetable oil
1 Tablespoon vanilla extract
1¹/₄ cups whole wheat pastry flour
1 cup sugar
¹/₄ teaspoon baking powder
¹/₄ teaspoon cinnamon
¹/₄ teaspoon salt
¹/₂ cup walnuts

Preheat oven to 350 degrees. Spray an 8 x 8 x 2-inch baking pan with oil and set aside.

Place the tofu, water, maple syrup, carob or cocoa powder, oil, and vanilla extract in a blender and process until completely smooth. Place the remaining ingredients except the walnuts in a medium mixing bowl and stir until well combined. Pour the blended mixture into the dry ingredients and stir. Fold in the walnuts.

Pour the batter evenly into the prepared baking pan. Bake for 40 minutes. Cool brownies, then cut into squares and serve.

Total Calories Per Serving: 250   Total Fat as % of Daily Value: 9%   Protein: 4 gm   Fat: 6 gm
Carbohydrates: 47 gm   Calcium: 46 mg   Iron: 1 mg   Sodium: 79 mg   Dietary Fiber: 4 gm

Date Crumb Squares

Makes about 12 squares

¹/₂ cup whole pitted dates
4 cups oat flour
4 cups rolled oats
³/₄ cup chopped walnuts or pecans
1 cup vegetable oil
1 cup maple syrup
1 teaspoon almond extract
¹/₂ teaspoon salt

The day before, soak the dates in 1 cup of water to soften. Drain, put the dates in a food processor canister and process until smooth.

Preheat the oven to 350 degrees. In a large bowl, combine the flour, rolled oats, and walnuts or pecans and mix together well. In another bowl, blend together the oil, maple syrup, almond extract, and salt. Add the wet ingredients to the flour mixture and mix well.

Press half of the mixture into a greased 12 x 6-inch baking pan. Spread the puréed dates over the mixture, top with the remaining half of the flour mixture, and press down lightly. Bake for 30 minutes or until lightly browned. Let cool and cut into squares.

Total Calories Per Serving: 666   Total Fat as % of Daily Value:43 %   Protein: 17 gm   Fat: 28 gm
Carbohydrates: 85 gm   Calcium: 75 mg   Iron: 5 mg   Sodium: 108 mg   Dietary Fiber: 10 gm

Chocolate Chip Cookies
Makes about 3 dozen cookies

1³/₄ cups flour
1 teaspoon salt
1 teaspoon baking powder
1 cup vegan margarine
³/₄ cup brown sugar
³/₄ cup sugar
1 teaspoon vanilla extract
2 teaspoons powdered egg replacer plus 2 Tablespoons water
1¹/₂ cups vegan chocolate chips
Vegetable oil spray

Preheat oven to 350 degrees. In a large bowl, combine flour, salt, and baking powder. Cut in margarine with a fork. Work mixture until it resembles moist bread crumbs. Mix in sweeteners, vanilla, and egg replacer/water mixture and mix until well combined. Mix in just enough water to barely moisten mixture. Stir in chocolate chips. Mixture should be very stiff.

Spray baking sheets with oil. Drop dough by rounded spoonfuls, about 1 inch apart. Bake for 10-12 minutes, or until golden. Cool cookies on rack.

Total Calories Per Serving (2 cookies): 321   Total Fat as % of Daily Value: 26%   Protein: 2 gm   Fat: 17 gm
Carbohydrates: 42 gm   Calcium: 35 mg   Iron: 1 mg   Sodium: 290 mg   Dietary Fiber: 1 gm

Peanut 'Spiders'
Makes about 24 'spiders'

Vegetable oil spray
1¹/₂ cups vegan chocolate or carob chips
1¹/₂ cups chow mein noodles
1 cup salted peanuts

Spray a serving platter with oil. In a 3-cup microwave-safe container, melt chips in microwave on HIGH for 2 minutes or melt slowly in a small pot on top of the stove, stirring constantly. Remove chips from microwave or stove and stir until smooth. Allow melted chips to cool for 15 minutes. Stir in chow mein noodles and peanuts until well combined. Drop by teaspoonfuls onto the serving platter. Allow 'spiders' to dry for 30 minutes, during which time they will harden, allowing them to be picked up by hand. Serve as dessert 'cookies' or use to decorate cupcakes or cakes.

Total Calories Per Serving (2 "spiders"): 197   Total Fat as % of Daily Value: 20%   Protein: 3 gm   Fat: 13 gm
Carbohydrates: 19 gm   Calcium: 15 mg   Iron: 1 mg   Sodium: 103 mg   Dietary Fiber: 3 gm

Chapter 4: PARFAITS AND PUDDINGS

Parfaits

Parfaits are quick to prepare, can be made ahead of time or at the last moment, or be prepared during the event by the host or the guests. They can be made to look elegant or fun and don't require exact shapes and cuts. Parfaits can be assembled from extra ingredients (leftovers), such as canned or frozen fruit, pudding, silken tofu, cold cereal, cookies, cake, vegan frozen dessert, as well as seasonal ingredients, including fresh fruit.

If you bake cookies, cakes, or muffins, bake extra or store "crumbles" of packaged items in the freezer for use in assembling multi-layered parfaits. You'll need glass or plastic ware to layer in, as seeing layers is half the fun. Since glassware varies, it's difficult to give exact measurements in every recipe.

When planning parfaits, think variety in textures and temperatures. In the summer you may want a cold layer, in the winter a warm layer. Crumbly textures can be cake, muffins, sweet rolls, sweet bagels (such as cinnamon raisin); crunchy layers can be crumbled cookies, chopped nuts, granola, cold cereal, sweet bagels, unsalted tortilla chips, chocolate or carob chips, or shredded coconut; creamy layers can be pudding, vegan Devon cream (see recipe on page 60), sweet tofu, mashed banana or cooked, puréed pumpkin; cool layers can be sorbet, frozen rice, soy, or nut ice cream, frozen pudding, chilled apple sauce, chilled fruit preserves or chilled fruit; and warm layers can be heated maple syrup, heated pie filling, heated applesauce or canned fruit, or heated fruit preserves.

To jazz up layers, add little 'zinger' touches, such as minced fresh ginger, fresh lemon, orange, or lime zest, a dash of apple or orange juice concentrate, or some toasted coconut.

You can make vegan puddings, custards, or mousses from scratch or from mixes. You'll select the method according to your level of kitchen expertise and available time. If you prepare desserts from scratch you can control the amount of sweetness and the flavor intensity, but it takes time and patience. Mixes save time and generally guarantee a consistent outcome.

PARFAIT AND PUDDING RECIPES

Chocolate Pudding in a Snap!
Serves 4

One package of tofu (any firmness, about 8- to 10-ounce package or 1½ cups)
2-3 teaspoons of soy or rice milk
½ cup unsweetened cocoa or carob powder
Maple syrup to taste

Place all ingredients in a blender canister and process until smooth and uniform. Pour into a serving bowl or separate dishes. Cover, put in refrigerator, and allow pudding to chill for at least 1 hour.

Variations:
- Freeze instead of refrigerating for a frozen chocolate pudding.
- Pour into a baked, cooled pie shell or individual tart shells and garnish with chocolate or carob chips and/or coconut or chopped berries and serve as a chocolate cream pie/tart.
- Instead of cocoa or carob powder, add ½ cup very ripe, mashed bananas for a banana pudding (all other ingredients remain the same).

- In addition to cocoa, add 2-3 teaspoons of instant coffee for a mocha pudding.
- Instead of cocoa, add $^1/_2$ cup puréed canned or very ripe, fresh, peeled peaches or apricots.
- Instead of cocoa, add $^1/_2$ cup puréed, drained pineapple tidbits.
- Instead of cocoa, add $^1/_2$ cup puréed fresh, very ripe strawberries or blueberries.
- Instead of cocoa, add 2 teaspoons vanilla extract and a bit more maple syrup for a vanilla pudding.

Total Calories Per Serving (not variations): 69   Total Fat as % of Daily Value: 3%   Protein: 10 gm   Fat: 2 gm
Carbohydrates: 7 gm   Calcium: 63 mg   Iron: 2 mg   Sodium: 102 mg   Dietary Fiber: 4 gm

There are several national brands of vegan pudding mixes, including Oetker's Simple Organics™ and Mori-nu Mates™. Check your local market, read labels carefully, and make some sample batches. If you purchase vegan vanilla pudding mix, you can usually create your own flavors with different extracts, such as rum, orange, or almond, or with a small amount of puréed fruit, such as strawberries or blueberries. Prepare pudding mixes with regular or lowfat soymilk, rice milk, almond milk, or other veggie milks. For extra flavor, you may want to try vanilla-flavored vegan milk.

From-scratch puddings can be made from silken tofu or veggie milk and cornstarch mixtures. We've included several recipes in this chapter for you. From-scratch puddings take a bit of time, stirring and measuring, and may require more setting time (time it takes to get firm enough to serve) than mixes.

Puddings can serve two purposes. Made according to directions, they are smooth, firm desserts. With the addition of a little extra liquid, and with a little bit more whisking, they can serve as silky, creamy dessert sauces. Think about using pudding-sauces to dress fruit salad or to accompany frozen desserts or baked desserts.

Seasonal Strawberry Parfait
Serves 4

1 cup strawberry sorbet
1 cup strawberry soy or rice ice cream
1 cup crumbled cake or muffins
1 cup diced fresh or frozen, thawed strawberries
1 cup vegan Devon cream (optional; see recipe on page 60)

Have four parfait glasses ready. Layer $^1/_4$ cup sorbet, $^1/_4$ cup vegan ice cream, $^1/_4$ cup cake crumbles, and ¼ cup strawberries into each glass. Top parfait with Devon cream or extra strawberries. Serve immediately or place in freezer until ready to serve.

Note: Cover parfaits if they are going in the freezer, so they don't absorb any freezer flavors.

Variations:
1. Use vanilla ice cream and fresh or frozen blueberries instead of strawberry ice cream and strawberries.
2. Use orange sorbet, chocolate ice cream, crumbled chocolate cake or muffins, and chopped navel oranges.
3. Use raspberry sorbet, vanilla ice cream, and fresh or frozen, thawed raspberries instead of strawberry sorbet, strawberry ice cream, and strawberries.
4. Use pineapple sorbet, vanilla ice cream, and crushed fresh or canned pineapple instead of strawberry sorbet, strawberry ice cream, and strawberries.

5. Use peach sorbet, peach, or vanilla ice cream, and fresh or canned peaches or apricots instead of strawberry sorbet, strawberry ice cream, and strawberries.

6. Use lemon sorbet, vanilla ice cream, and diced fresh seedless grapes.

7. Use orange sorbet, chocolate ice cream, chocolate cake crumbles, and diced fresh or canned plums.

8. Use peanut butter vegan ice cream, vanilla ice cream, sliced bananas, crumbled vegan graham crackers, and fruit preserves for a 'peanut butter and jelly' parfait.

Total Calories Per Serving (not variations): 110   Total Fat as % of Daily Value: 5%   Protein: 1 gm   Fat: 3 gm
Carbohydrates: 21 gm   Calcium: 30 mg   Iron: 1 mg   Sodium: 67 mg   Dietary Fiber: 2 gm

Trifle Parfait
Serves 4

Can be easily doubled, tripled, or quadrupled.

2 cups prepared vegan pudding (flavor of your choice)
8 Tablespoons fruit preserves
2 cups each raspberries and blueberries
1 Tablespoon sugar (if desired)
2 teaspoons fresh orange zest
2 cups yellow or white cake crumbles

Select four tall parfait glasses, iced tea glasses, or clear tumblers. Layer one-quarter of each ingredient, in order listed, into glasses. Cover and refrigerate for at least 1 hour before serving.

Total Calories Per Serving: 439   Total Fat as % of Daily Value: 11%   Protein: 8 gm   Fat: 7 gm
Carbohydrates: 88 gm   Calcium: 230 mg   Iron: 3 mg   Sodium: 180 mg   Dietary Fiber: 7 gm

Banana Pudding Parfait
Serves 4

Can be easily doubled, tripled, or quadrupled.

1 cup vanilla wafers, vegan graham crackers, or plain, vanilla-flavored cookies
2 cups prepared vegan vanilla pudding
2 cups mashed banana
1 cup vegan Devon cream (see page 60) or puréed sweet tofu
4 teaspoons toasted almonds

Line 4 parfait glasses with crumbled cookies. Layer pudding, then banana. Top with cream or tofu. Garnish with almonds.

Note: If you are going to serve this parfait as soon as it is assembled, or if you have a lot of freezer space, you can use vanilla ice cream instead of pudding (but will have to serve these fast). If you are going to pre-make the parfaits and refrigerate them first, toss mashed bananas with several Tablespoons of orange juice to prevent browning.

Total Calories Per Serving: 464   Total Fat as % of Daily Value: 26%   Protein: 9 gm   Fat: 17 gm
Carbohydrates: 71 gm   Calcium: 175 mg   Iron: 2 mg   Sodium: 428 mg   Dietary Fiber: 3 gm

Raspberry Brownie Parfait

Serves 4

1 cup raspberry sorbet
1 cup raspberry fruit preserves
1 cup crumbled vegan brownies

Layer each parfait cup with thin layers of each ingredient. Plan to serve immediately or freeze until ready to serve.

Variations: To make this a "black and white" parfait, use a layer of brownies and a layer of white cake or crumbled vanilla cookies. You can also, add chopped pecans or walnuts as a garnish, if desired.

Total Calories Per Serving: 265   Total Fat as % of Daily Value: 3%   Protein: 1 gm   Fat: 2 gm
Carbohydrates: 62 gm   Calcium: 19 mg   Iron: 1 mg   Sodium: 46 mg   Dietary Fiber: 1 gm

Strawberry-Yogurt Parfaits

Makes 8 servings

Two 8-ounce containers strawberry or vanilla soy yogurt
2 cups sliced fresh, or frozen, thawed strawberries
Granola for topping (about 1 cup)

Select eight parfait glasses. For each serving, layer ¼ cup each of yogurt and fruit in the parfait dish; repeat each layer, then do the same for the other glasses. Top with granola. Chill at least 1 hour before serving.

Total Calories Per Serving: 141   Total Fat as % of Daily Value: 8%   Protein: 5 gm   Fat: 5 gm
Carbohydrates: 20 gm   Calcium: 85 mg   Iron: 1 mg   Sodium: 23 mg   Dietary Fiber: 3 gm

Colorful Fruit Parfaits

Serves 6

2 cups vanilla soy yogurt
¼ teaspoon almond extract
½ cup chopped cantaloupe or Crenshaw melon
½ cup chopped fresh or frozen, thawed strawberries
½ cup peeled, chopped kiwi fruit
2 Tablespoons sliced almonds

Mix yogurt and almond extract together in a small bowl. Alternate layers of fruit and yogurt mixture in parfait glasses, beginning and ending with fruit. Top with almonds. Chill for at least 1 hour before serving.

Note: Feel free to add even more chopped fruit on top for a pretty presentation.

Total Calories Per Serving: 114   Total Fat as % of Daily Value: 5%   Protein: 4 gm   Fat: 3 gm
Carbohydrates: 18 gm   Calcium: 118 mg   Iron: 1 mg   Sodium: 31 mg   Dietary Fiber: 1 gm

Crunchy Lime Parfait

Serves 8

2 cups granola
1 cup vegan cream cheese
1½ cups firm silken tofu
½ cup soymilk
½ cup sugar
¼ cup fresh lime juice
1 Tablepoon fresh lime zest

Process granola in a blender or food processor canister until it has the consistency of coarse flour. Remove from canister. Set aside.

Place cream cheese, tofu, soymilk, sugar, lime juice, and lime zest in the canister. Purée until smooth and well blended.

To assemble, put about 2 Tablespoons of ground granola in the bottom of eight parfait glasses or wine glasses. Pour the cream cheese-tofu mixture over the granola. Top with approximately 1 more Tablespoon of granola. Refrigerate at least 2 hours before serving.

Total Calories Per Serving: 296   Total Fat as % of Daily Value: 18%   Protein: 7 gm   Fat: 12 gm
Carbohydrates: 39 gm   Calcium: 49 mg   Iron: 2 mg   Sodium: 188 mg   Dietary Fiber: 3 gm

Kids-Can-Cook Strawberry Parfaits

Serves 4

1 package (4 serving size, about 5 ounces) vegan instant vanilla pudding mix
Soy or rice milk as indicated on pudding package (usually 2 cups)
2 cups chopped fresh or frozen, thawed strawberries
2 Tablespoons strawberry jam

Prepare vanilla pudding according to package directions, except do not chill immediately. In a small bowl, stir together strawberries and jam. In each of four parfait glasses, layer ¹/₈ of the pudding and ¹/₈ of the strawberry sauce. Repeat layers. Chill at least 1 hour before serving.

Total Calories Per Serving: 109   Total Fat as % of Daily Value: 3%   Protein: 4 gm   Fat: 2 gm
Carbohydrates: 20 gm   Calcium: 164 mg   Iron: 1 mg   Sodium: 60 mg   Dietary Fiber: 2 gm

Kids Can Cook No-Bake Layered Parfait

Serves 8

14 whole vegan graham crackers
One package (4 servings, about 5 ounces) vegan instant vanilla pudding mix
2 cups cold soy or rice milk
2 cups soy fruit-flavored yogurt
1½ cups fruit preserves

Line a 9 x 9-inch square pan with graham crackers, breaking crackers if necessary. Prepare pudding with milk as directions indicate; let stand 5 minutes. Then blend pudding with yogurt. Spread half of the pudding mixture over graham crackers. Place another layer of graham crackers on top. Spread remaining pudding mixture over crackers. Add another layer of crackers. Spread preserves over the top. Cover, and refrigerate for at least 2 hours before serving.

Total Calories Per Serving: 344   Total Fat as % of Daily Value: 6%   Protein: 6 gm   Fat: 4 gm
Carbohydrates: 71 gm   Calcium: 168 mg   Iron: 2 mg   Sodium: 197 mg   Dietary Fiber:2 gm

Frozen Berry Crunch Bars
Makes 8 bars

1 cup silken tofu
**1 cup frozen, thawed or fresh mashed berries (strawberries, raspberries, blue-
    berries, or a mixture)**
1 Tablespoon apple juice concentrate
$\frac{1}{3}$ cup crushed cold cereal
8 small (2-3 ounce) paper cups
8 popsicle™ sticks or rigid straws

In a large bowl, mix tofu with berries and concentrate very well. Put one teaspoon of cold cereal in the bottom of each paper cup. Spoon tofu mixture over cereal. Try to pack mixture down firmly into cups; don't leave any air bubbles. Freeze for 1 hour and then insert 1 stick or straw into the center of the freezing mixture. Allow bars to freeze for 2 more hours, or until frozen solid. To serve, peel away paper cups or let the guests do it!

Total Calories Per Serving: 25   Total Fat as % of Daily Value: <1%   Protein: 2 gm   Fat: <1 gm
Carbohydrates: 4 gm   Calcium: 14 mg   Iron: 1 mg   Sodium: 28 mg   Dietary Fiber: 1 gm

Traditional Trifle
Serves 10

10 slices (4 x 5-inch) vegan vanilla cake
$\frac{3}{4}$ cup jam or fruit preserves
$\frac{1}{2}$ cup sherry or apple juice concentrate
5 cups chilled prepared vegan pudding (flavor of your choice)
3 Tablespoons sugar

Spread the cake with jam, and then cut into small squares. Select a large glass bowl or deep serving dish. Arrange cake in bowl. Pour on sherry or concentrate and allow cake to soak for 10 minutes in the refrigerator.

Beat the pudding with a fork and pour evenly over cake. Sprinkle sugar on top of pudding. Chill for at least 1 hour before serving. If desired, garnish with slivered almonds, shredded coconut, carob or chocolate chips, canned, drained mandarin oranges, or additional jam or fruit preserves.

Total Calories Per Serving: 474   Total Fat as % of Daily Value: 17%   Protein: 9 gm   Fat: 11 gm
Carbohydrates: 85 gm   Calcium: 256 mg   Iron: 3 mg   Sodium: 296 mg   Dietary Fiber: 1 gm

Fast Trifle-Misu

Serves 12

Trifle and tiramisu are traditional layered holiday desserts, made a day ahead to allow the flavors to combine. This is a large "community" parfait. Please note this is a high-fat dish.

2 cups diced, drained canned peaches
2 Tablespoons peach liqueur (traditional, but optional) or peach nectar
2 cups frozen, thawed blueberries
2 Tablespoons Midori or melon liqueur (traditional, but optional) or grape juice
3 cups vegan Devon cream (see page 60 for recipe)
1 teaspoon vanilla extract
1 teaspoon rum extract
1 teaspoon lemon extract
3 Tablespoons sugar
4 cups prepared vegan vanilla pudding
2 cups frozen, thawed raspberries
24 thin cake slices (2 x 6-inch pieces)

In a small bowl, combine peaches with peach liqueur. In a small bowl, mix blueberries with Midori. Divide Devon cream into three bowls containing one cup of cream in each. Mix vanilla extract into one bowl, rum extract into one bowl, and lemon extract and sugar into another bowl. In a small bowl, mix vanilla pudding and raspberries.

   Assemble trifle as follows: Line the bottom of a deep, round bowl with vegan cake. Alternate layers of pudding, vanilla cream, peaches, rum cream, blueberries, and lemon cream, and cake slices until bowl is filled. Chill for at least 3 hours before serving.

Total Calories Per Serving: 562   Total Fat as % of Daily Value: 31%   Protein: 10 gm   Fat: 20 gm
Carbohydrates: 86 gm   Calcium: 207 mg   Iron: 2 mg   Sodium: 592 mg   Dietary Fiber: 3 gm

Creamy Chocolate Pudding

Serves 4

¹/₂ cup sugar
¹/₄ cup unsweetened cocoa powder
4 Tablespoons cornstarch
2¹/₂ cups regular or lowfat soy or rice milk
1 teaspoon vanilla extract

Place sweetener, cocoa, and cornstarch in a microwave-safe bowl and stir. Whisk in milk and vanilla extract. Microwave pudding, uncovered, for 6-8 minutes on HIGH, stopping every 2 minutes to stir, or until mixture is boiling and getting thick. Remove from microwave and pour into individual serving dishes or leave in bowl. Chill for at least 2 hours before serving.

Variations:
1. For vanilla pudding, leave out cocoa, decrease sugar to ¹/₃ cup, increase vanilla to 2 teaspoons.
2. During Passover, use potato starch instead of cornstarch, and almond milk instead of soy or rice milk.

Total Calories Per Serving (not variations): 204   Total Fat as % of Daily Value: 5%   Protein: 5 gm   Fat: 3 gm
Carbohydrates: 43 gm   Calcium: 193 mg Iron: 2 mg   Sodium: 72 mg   Dietary Fiber: 2 gm

Quick Pudding
Serves 4

⅓ cup sugar
3 Tablespoons cornstarch
2¼ cups vegan milk
1 teaspoon vanilla extract
1 cup vegan chocolate or carob chips

Mix sugar and cornstarch together in a microwave-safe bowl. Whisk in milk and extract. Microwave on HIGH for 5 minutes, stirring once. Remove from microwave and quickly stir in chocolate or carob chips until melted. Microwave for 1 more minute, if needed to melt chips.

Pour into individual bowls or large serving bowl. Refrigerate for at least 2 hours before serving.

Total Calories Per Serving: 346   Total Fat as % of Daily Value: 22%   Protein: 5 gm   Fat: 14 gm
Carbohydrates: 55 gm   Calcium: 181 mg   Iron: 2 mg   Sodium: 69 mg   Dietary Fiber: 3 gm

Rice Pudding with Peaches
Serves 4

1 cup cooked white rice (start with about ⅓ cup uncooked rice), cooled
½ cup soy or rice milk (reduced fat is okay)
½ cup chopped and peeled fresh peaches or drained and chopped canned peaches
2 Tablespoons silken tofu
2 Tablespoons sugar
1 Tablespoon cornstarch
1 Tablespoon vegan margarine
¼ teaspoon cinnamon
¼ teaspoon vanilla extract
¼ teaspoon ginger
⅛ teaspoon nutmeg

In a microwave-safe bowl, combine all ingredients and mix well. Microwave on HIGH for 5 minutes, or until mixture is thickened and starting to set. Serve warm, or allow pudding to cool.

Note: This can be done on the stove by combining all ingredients in a medium-sized pot and cooking over medium heat, stirring, until mixture begins to thicken.

Total Calories Per Serving: 143   Total Fat as % of Daily Value: 6%   Protein: 5 gm   Fat: 4 gm
Carbohydrates: 23 gm   Calcium: 57 mg   Iron: 1 mg   Sodium: 72 mg   Dietary Fiber: 1 gm

Chocolate Pudding in a Mug
Serves 5

5 Tablespoons cornstarch
10 Tablespoons each cocoa powder and sugar
5 cups soy or rice milk
1 Tablespoon vanilla extract

Select five large microwave-safe coffee mugs. In each mug combine $1/5$ of the cornstarch, cocoa, and sugar in milk (1 Tablespoon cornstarch, 2 Tablespoons cocoa, etc.). Stir in milk and mix until well combined. Microwave each mug on HIGH for 1 minute or until mixture boils. Remove from microwave and stir in vanilla. Allow pudding to chill in refrigerator for at least $1^{1}/_{2}$ hours before serving right in the mug! If you would like to prepare this in a glass measuring cup, you can see when the mixture boils.

Total Calories Per Serving: 159   Total Fat as % of Daily Value: 8%   Protein: 9 gm   Fat: 5 gm
Carbohydrates: 25 gm   Calcium: 312 mg   Iron: 3 mg   Sodium: 117 mg   Dietary Fiber: 4 gm

Chocolate Tofu Mousse
Serves 6

2 cups puréed silken tofu
1¼ cups vegan chocolate chips
3 Tablespoons maple syrup
Sliced fruit for garnish (optional)
Prebaked and cooled pie or graham cracker crust (optional)

Place tofu in a blender. Melt chips in the microwave or on top of the stove. Add maple syrup to melted chocolate and mix to combine. Pour chocolate into tofu and process until creamy. Pour into a serving bowl or individual dishes or you can create a pie by pouring the mousse into a prepared pie shell. Allow mousse to chill for at least 2 hours before serving.

Total Calories Per Serving: 221   Total Fat as % of Daily Value: 17%   Protein: 6 gm   Fat: 11 gm
Carbohydrates: 30 gm   Calcium: 45 mg   Iron:2 mg   Sodium: 68 mg   Dietary Fiber: 2 gm

Banana Tofu Pudding
Serves 4

2 cups silken tofu
2 ripe, peeled bananas (about 1¼ cups)
1 teaspoon vanilla extract
2 Tablespoons orange juice extract

Place all ingredients in a food processor canister or blender and process until smooth. Pour into serving bowl or individual dishes or into a prepared pie crust. Allow pudding to chill for 2 hours before serving.

Total Calories Per Serving: 83   Total Fat as % of Daily Value: 2%   Protein: 8 gm   Fat: 1 gm
Carbohydrates: 12 gm   Calcium: 43 mg   Iron: 1 mg   Sodium: 96 mg   Dietary Fiber: 1 gm

Baked Lemon-Coconut Pudding

Serves 6

½ cup sugar
1 cup self-raising flour
1 teaspoon powdered egg replacer (not mixed with water)
⅓ cup shredded coconut
2 Tablespoons fresh lemon zest
½ cup soymilk
2 Tablespoons melted vegan margarine
1 teaspoon vanilla extract
½ cup sugar
½ cup fresh lemon juice
Hot water (about 1 cup)
1 teaspoon vanilla extract

Preheat oven to 350 degrees. In a 2-quart baking dish, combine ½ cup sugar, flour, egg replacer, coconut, and lemon zest. Stir in soymilk, margarine, and vanilla. The mixture will be smooth, but sticky.

In a small bowl, combine ½ cup sugar and lemon juice. Add enough hot water to bring the fluid up to 1½ half cups. Add 1 teaspoon vanilla extract. Pour liquid gently over the pudding mixture. Bake uncovered for 30 minutes or until set (toothpick inserted in center comes out moist, but clean). Serve warm or cold.

Total Calories Per Serving: 326   Total Fat as % of Daily Value: 15%   Protein: 3 gm   Fat: 10 gm
Carbohydrates: 58 gm   Calcium: 32 mg   Iron: 1 mg   Sodium: 45 mg   Dietary Fiber: 1 gm

Baked Farfel Pudding

Serves 10

2½ cups matzo farfel
½ cup boiling water
¾ cup melted vegan margarine
1 cup peeled, cored, and very thinly sliced green apple
4 teaspoons powdered egg replacer mixed with 4 Tablespoons water
Vegetable oil spray
4 teaspoons ground cinnamon
1 teaspoon lemon zest

Preheat oven to 350 degrees. Place farfel in a medium-size bowl. Pour boiling water over farfel and let soften for 3 minutes, then drain. Discard water. Mix margarine, apple, and egg replacer in a large bowl until well combined.

Spray a 9 x 13-inch baking dish with oil. Place farfel mixture in a dish. Sprinkle cinnamon and zest on top. Bake for 20 minutes or until firm.

Total Calories Per Serving: 153   Total Fat as % of Daily Value: 20%   Protein: 1 gm   Fat: 13 gm
Carbohydrates: 7 gm   Calcium: 1 mg   Iron: <1 mg   Sodium: 109 mg   Dietary Fiber: <1 gm

Coconut Milk Rice Pudding

Serves 8

2¹/₂ cups coconut milk
2 cups cooked, then cooled brown or white long grain rice
2 Tablespoons sugar
1 teaspoon of vanilla extract

Place coconut milk in a heavy, medium-sized pot and simmer until warm. Add cooked rice and heat, stirring for 5 minutes or until hot. Stir in sugar and vanilla, and simmer until pudding thickens slightly and is still soupy. Remove from heat and chill 1 hour before serving. Pudding will tighten up as it chills.

Total Calories Per Serving: 202   Total Fat as % of Daily Value: 22%   Protein: 3 gm   Fat: 14 gm
Carbohydrates: 16 gm   Calcium: 16 mg   Iron: 3 mg   Sodium: 9 mg   Dietary Fiber: <1 gm

Coconut Pudding

Serves 4

1 pound soft tofu (about 2¹/₂ cups)
¹/₂ cup sugar
1¹/₂ teaspoons vanilla extract
¹/₂ cup shredded coconut

Whip the tofu, sugar, and vanilla extract in a blender or food processor canister until stiff and creamy. Transfer to a bowl. In the bowl, fold the coconut into the tofu mixture. Pour the pudding into four parfait glasses or individual dessert bowls and chill for at least 30 minutes before serving.

Total Calories Per Serving: 206   Total Fat as % of Daily Value: 9%   Protein: 8 gm   Fat: 6 gm
Carbohydrates: 31 gm   Calcium: 44 mg   Iron: 1 mg   Sodium: 100 mg   Dietary Fiber: <1 gm

Sweet Carrot Pudding

Serves 6

1 pound carrots, sliced thinly (about 3¹/₂ cups)
Water or soymilk to moisten (about 1-1¹/₂ cups)
1-2 teaspoons nutmeg, to taste
1-2 teaspoons ground cinnamon, to taste
¹/₂-1 teaspoon cloves, to taste
¹/₂-1 teaspoon ground ginger, to taste
¹/₃ cup maple syrup
3 Tablespoons cornstarch
6 Tablespoons cold water

Steam, boil, or microwave carrots until tender. Place carrots and any cooking liquid in a food processor canister or blender. Purée carrots and cooking liquid until as smooth as possible. This is where you would add water or soymilk, if necessary, to create a thick liquid (think: creamed corn). Pour the purée into a medium pot, add spices as desired, and maple syrup and allow to heat, stirring, for 10 minutes.

In the meantime, mix cornstarch with the cold water until completely dissolved and smooth. Whisk the starch into the carrots, stirring constantly. Bring to a fast boil and boil, stirring, for 1 minute. Remove immediately from the stove and cool by separating into several bowls and placing on ice. When pudding has cooled to at least warm, place in the refrigerator and allow to set for at least 2 hours before serving.

Total Calories Per Serving: 109   Total Fat as % of Daily Value: 2%   Protein: 2 gm   Fat: 1 gm
Carbohydrates: 25 gm   Calcium: 86 mg   Iron: 1 mg   Sodium: 72 mg   Dietary Fiber: 2 gm

Cooked Custard
Serves 8

1 quart soymilk, rice milk, or almond milk (flavored is okay)
$^2/_3$ cup arrowroot or cornstarch
$^1/_2$ cup maple syrup
1 teaspoon vanilla extract
$^1/_4$ teaspoon almond extract
$^1/_4$ teaspoon salt

In a medium-size pot, mix the milk, arrowroot or cornstarch, maple syrup, vanilla and almond extract, and salt and whisk well to combine. Cook over medium heat, whisking constantly, until the mixture has thickened. Pour into a serving bowl or individual dishes. Allow custard to chill for at least 2 hours before serving.

Total Calories Per Serving: 144   Total Fat as % of Daily Value: 5%   Protein: 3 gm   Fat: 2 gm
Carbohydrates: 29 gm   Calcium: 162 mg   Iron: 1 mg   Sodium: 132 mg   Dietary Fiber: <1 gm

Apricot Whip
Serves 6

Use as a dessert on its own, a parfait layer, a dressing for fresh fruit salad, a pie filling, or a cake topping.

1 cup dried apricots (or other dried fruit)
Water or orange juice to cover apricots
$4^1/_2$ cups silken tofu
$^1/_2$ cup sugar

Place apricots in enough water or juice just to cover. Allow apricots to soak until soft, about 1 hour, depending on the toughness of the apricots. Use only enough liquid to cover, so you don't create a soggy product.

When apricots are soft, drain and save liquid. Blend the tofu, apricots, and sugar in a blender or food processor canister. Add enough reserved liquid to make a thick liquid (think: thin cake batter). Process till smooth and fluffy.

Ladle into a serving bowl or individual dishes. Refrigerate for at least 1 hour before serving.

Total Calories Per Serving: 155   Total Fat as % of Daily Value: 2%   Protein: 10 gm   Fat: 1 gm
Carbohydrates: 28 gm   Calcium: 62 mg   Iron: 2 mg   Sodium: 130 mg   Dietary Fiber: 1 gm

Chapter 5: BAKED DESSERTS

There are many desserts that are very popular and delicious, but defy being categorized as cakes, pies, or cookies. In this chapter you will find cobblers, bettys, crisps, short cakes, kugels (baked puddings), bread puddings, dumplings, and other baked dessert combinations. There are others with less familiar names that are equally tasty, such as pandowdies, clafloutis, and buckles.

These desserts make wonderful party offerings, as most are moist and don't mind sitting on a dessert table for extended periods of time. Many of these treats can be made by approximation, rather than requiring the exacting measurement and temperatures of some cakes and cookies. They can be served on their own or paired with frozen vegan desserts.

Cobblers and crisps are combinations of fruit and biscuit- or crumb-style toppings that are baked together. Most can be made with fresh seasonal fruit or frozen fruit. They have their origins in Europe, especially the United Kingdom and France, and in early American cooking. These treats are generally quick to assemble and relatively foolproof. They can be served for brunch or at an afternoon reception, picnic, classroom party, or festive dinner.

Serving these desserts is very easy. Scoop them with a large serving spoon or an ice cream scoop into a small bowl or a dessert plate. You can serve them without adornment, or top them with a small amount of sorbet, fresh or frozen (thawed) berries, a mixture of dried fruit and nuts, a combination of black and gold raisins, or thin slices of fresh, seasonal fruit.

For a very fast, very elegant dessert, Athens Foods <www.athensfoods.com> and other companies offer frozen mini phyllo dough shells. These are individual vegan dessert shells that come fully baked in plain- or graham-flavored. They can be thawed and filled, or baked again with a filling. Fill plain phyllo shells with pie filling, soy yogurt and fruit, sorbet and chopped nuts, soy pudding, or tofu cheesecake for sweet menu items. You can also plan to use the plain-flavored shells for savory dishes, such as five-bean chili, vegan "ground" beef, chopped Tofurky™ and gravy, or avocado and salsa for savory dishes.

COBBLER RECIPES

Apple Cobbler
Serves 6

1¹/₂ cups all-purpose flour
2 teaspoons baking soda
¹/₂ teaspoon cinnamon
¹/₄ teaspoon salt
¹/₄ cup applesauce
¹/₂ cup lowfat soymilk
¹/₂ cup apple juice
Vegetable oil spray
4 cups peeled, cored, and thinly sliced apples
1 teaspoon cinnamon
1 teaspoon orange zest

Preheat oven to 350 degrees. Mix flour, baking soda, cinnamon, salt, applesauce, soymilk, and apple juice in a large bowl until well combined.

Spray a 9 x 13-inch baking dish with oil. Spread mixture in pan. Add apples on top of crust. Sprinkle with cinnamon and zest. Bake for 30 minutes or until crust is golden and fruit is tender.

Total Calories Per Serving: 175   Total Fat as % of Daily Value: 2%   Protein: 4 gm   Fat: 1 gm
Carbohydrates: 39 gm   Calcium: 34 mg   Iron: 1 mg   Sodium: 527 mg   Dietary Fiber: 2 gm

Quince and Mince Cobbler
Serves 8

Filling:
Vegetable oil spray
1 cup diced dried pitted prunes
1 cup golden raisins
1 cup black raisins
²/₃ cup diced pitted dates
1 cup diced dried apricots
¼ cup diced crystallized or dried ginger
½ teaspoon nutmeg
½ teaspoon cinnamon
½ teaspoon cardamom
⅛ teaspoon cloves
1 cup evaporated cane juice or rice syrup
1 cup apple juice or apple cider
¼ cup orange juice
¼ cup brandy (optional)
4½ cups peeled, cubed fresh quince

Cobbler:
¾ cup whole wheat flour
¾ cup all-purpose flour
1 cup evaporated cane juice or rice syrup
1 Tablespoon baking powder
½ cup vegetable oil
1½ cups soymilk

Preheat oven to 350 degrees. Spray bottom and sides of a 9 x 13-inch baking dish with oil. Combine all the filling ingredients in a large bowl. Set aside.

In a separate medium-size bowl, combine all cobbler ingredients and mix well. Pour cobbler mixture into prepared baking pan. Stir filling ingredients and carefully layer over cobbler ingredients. Bake cobbler in oven for 1 hour or until fruit is tender. Remove and allow cobbler to cool for at least 30 minutes before serving.

Total Calories Per Serving: 664   Total Fat as % of Daily Value: 22%   Protein: 6 gm   Fat: 14 gm
Carbohydrates: 136 gm   Calcium: 203 mg   Iron: 2 mg   Sodium: 211 mg   Dietary Fiber: 7 gm

Tropical Cobbler

Serves 8

2¹/₂ cups dried fruit combination, such as pineapple and papaya
Water to cover fruit
Vegetable oil spray
1 cup grated carrot
¹/₂ cup peeled and cored grated green apple
¹/₄ cup peeled, thinly sliced fresh lemon or lime
1 cup drained, canned pineapple tidbits
³/₄ cup rice or almond milk
3³/₄ cups unbleached white flour
2 teaspoons baking powder
1 cup peeled, sliced bananas (wait to slice bananas until needed, to avoid browning)

Preheat oven to 375 degrees. Place dried fruit in a bowl and just cover with water. Soak dried fruit in water for 1 hour or until tender. Drain and reserve liquid.

Spray a 9 x 13-inch baking dish with oil. Combine soaked fruit, carrots, apples, and lemon slices in a large pot. Add ³/₄ cup of reserved liquid and simmer for 30 minutes or until dried fruit is very soft. Cool and spread in prepared dish.

Squeeze canned pineapple as dry as possible. Discard liquid. Mix pineapple and milk together in a large bowl. Add flour and baking powder and mix until well combined. This is your crust.

To assemble cobbler, arrange banana slices on top of dried fruit. Drop Tablespoonfuls of crust dough onto fruit and bananas. Bake for 20 minutes or until biscuit topping is golden. Allow cobbler to cool for 20 minutes before serving.

Total Calories Per Serving: 286   Total Fat as % of Daily Value: 2%   Protein: 7 gm   Fat: 1 gm
Carbohydrates: 63 gm   Calcium: 117 mg   Iron: 1 mg   Sodium: 146 mg   Dietary Fiber: 4 gm

Blackberry Cobbler

Serves 6

3 cups fresh blackberries (or other berries)
³/₄ cup water
2 teaspoons cinnamon
1 cup sugar
1 cup self-rising flour
2 Tablespoons silken tofu
¹/₃ cup vegan margarine

Preheat oven to 350 degrees. Wash blackberries and spread on the bottom of a greased 8 x 8-inch baking dish. Add water and sprinkle with cinnamon. Combine sugar and flour. Whisk tofu, then cut tofu into sugar and flour until crumbly. Layer mixture over top of fruit. Melt margarine and drizzle over topping. Bake 35 minutes or until bubbly.

Total Calories Per Serving: 334   Total Fat as % of Daily Value: 14%   Protein: 5 gm   Fat: 10 gm
Carbohydrates: 57 gm   Calcium: 34 mg   Iron: 1 mg   Sodium: 105 mg   Dietary Fiber: 4 gm

Strawberry Rhubarb Cobbler

Makes 12

2 pounds fresh rhubarb washed, leaves removed, and chopped
4 cups sliced frozen, thawed or fresh strawberries
2 Tablespoons lemon juice
$2^3/_4$ cups sugar
$^1/_3$ cup cornstarch
Vegetable oil spray
$3^3/_4$ cups all-purpose flour
1 teaspoon baking powder
1 teaspoon baking soda
$^1/_2$ teaspoon salt
$1^1/_4$ cups vegan margarine
$1^1/_2$ cups soymilk mixed with 1 Tablespoon vinegar (soy buttermilk)
4 Tablespoons puréed silken tofu
1 teaspoon vanilla extract

In a 3-quart pot, combine the rhubarb, strawberries, and lemon juice. Cover and cook over medium heat for 5 minutes. In a small bowl, whisk together 1 cup sugar and cornstarch. Gradually stir the cornstarch mixture into the rhubarb mixture; heat to boiling. Lower heat, cook, stirring constantly for 4 minutes, then set aside to cool slightly.

Preheat the oven to 350 degrees. Spray a 9 x 13-inch baking dish with oil; set aside. In a large bowl, combine 3 cups flour, 1 cup sugar, baking powder, soda, and salt. Cut 1 cup margarine into chunks; add to the flour mixture. With a pastry blender or 2 knives, cut in the margarine until the mixture resembles coarse crumbs.

In a small bowl, beat together the soy buttermilk, tofu, and vanilla. Stir the buttermilk mixture into the flour mixture just until combined. Spread half the batter evenly in the greased pan; spread the rhubarb filling over the batter. Drop the remaining batter by heaping Tablespoonsful over the rhubarb filling.

In a 1-quart pot over low heat, melt remaining $^1/_4$ cup margarine. Stir in the remaining $^3/_4$ cup flour and $^3/_4$ cup sugar until the mixture resembles coarse crumbs. Sprinkle crumbs over the top of the batter. Bake the cobbler for 40-45 minutes, or until it is golden brown and bubbly. Cool cobbler for 10 minutes. Spoon into individual serving dishes; serve warm or cold.

Total Calories Per Serving: 555   Total Fat as % of Daily Value: 29%   Protein: 8 gm   Fat: 19 gm
Carbohydrates: 89 gm   Calcium: 144 mg   Iron: 1 mg   Sodium: 434 mg   Dietary Fiber: 4 gm

Red, White, and Blue Cobbler

Serves 6

½ cup vegan margarine
½ cup sugar
1 teaspoon vanilla extract
1 cup all-purpose flour
1 teaspoon baking powder
¼ teaspoon salt
½ cup soy or rice milk
1 cup fresh or frozen, thawed blueberries
2 cups diced fresh rhubarb
⅔ cup sugar

Heat oven to 375 degrees. Cream margarine, sugar, and vanilla together. Mix together flour, baking powder, and salt. Combine dry mixture and milk with the margarine and sugar mixture. Gently fold in blueberries. Pour into 2-quart casserole or an 8 x 8-inch casserole dish. Top with rhubarb. Sprinkle sugar over the rhubarb. Bake for 40 minutes or until bubbly.

Total Calories Per Serving: 390   Total Fat as % of Daily Value: 23%   Protein: 3 gm   Fat: 15 gm
Carbohydrates: 61 gm   Calcium: 109 mg   Iron: 1 mg   Sodium: 311 mg   Dietary Fiber: 2 gm

Blueberry Cobbler

Serves 6

⅔ cup whole wheat flour
½ cup sugar
1½ teaspoons baking powder
¼ teaspoon salt
⅔ cup soy or rice milk
2 cups fresh or frozen, thawed blueberries
Vegetable oil spray

Preheat oven to 350 degrees. Combine dry ingredients, then add milk and whisk until smooth. Spray an 8 x 8-inch baking dish with oil. Pour flour mixture into pan and sprinkle blueberries on top. Bake for 40 minutes or until bubbly.

Total Calories Per Serving: 149   Total Fat as % of Daily Value: 2%   Protein: 3 gm   Fat: 1 gm
Carbohydrates: 35 gm   Calcium: 107 mg   Iron: 1 mg   Sodium: 232 mg   Dietary Fiber: 3 gm

CRUMBLE RECIPES

Fresh Fruit Crumble

Serves 8

Topping:
Vegetable oil spray
2¹/₂ cups unbleached flour
1 cup apple butter
¹/₄ cup applesauce

Preheat oven to 375 degrees. In a large bowl, combine flour, apple butter, and sauce until crumbly.

Spray a 9 x 13-inch baking dish with oil. Put aside ¹/₂ cup of mixture and press remainder into dish.

Filling:
3 cups peeled and diced fresh fruit (berries, apricots, peaches, ripe persimmons, nectarines, and plums work well)
¹/₄ cup peeled, diced fresh orange (seeds removed)
¹/₈ cup raisins (or dried berries)
1 teaspoon fresh orange zest
1 Tablespoon fresh lemon juice

Combine filling ingredients in large pot; heat over medium heat, stirring constantly, until fruit is soft and mixture is slightly thickened. If more sweetness is desired, add 2 teaspoons of orange juice.

Spread fruit over topping. Crumble remaining topping over fruit. Bake 30 minutes or until bubbly.

Total Calories Per Serving: 253   Total Fat as % of Daily Value: 2%   Protein: 5 gm   Fat: 1 gm
Carbohydrates: 58 gm   Calcium: 24 mg   Iron: 1 mg   Sodium: 4 mg   Dietary Fiber: 4 gm

Peach-Cherry Crumble

Serves 8

2¹/₂ cups unbleached flour
1 cup apple butter
¹/₄ cup applesauce
Vegetable oil spray
4 cups cooked sour cherries, drained (can use canned or frozen, thawed cherries)
¹/₂ cup diced cooked peaches (can use canned, frozen or freshly cooked)

Preheat oven to 375 degrees. In a large bowl, combine flour, apple butter, and applesauce until crumbly. Put aside ¹/₂ cup of mixture and press remainder into a vegetable oil sprayed 9 x 13-inch dish.

Mix cherries and peaches together and spread over crust. Sprinkle remaining flour mixture over fruit. Bake for 30 minutes until bubbly and golden brown. Serve warm or cold.

Total Calories Per Serving: 214   Total Fat as % of Daily Value: 2%   Protein: 5 gm   Fat: 1 gm
Carbohydrates: 48 gm   Calcium: 20 mg   Iron: 1 mg   Sodium: 4 mg   Dietary Fiber: 3 gm

Apple Crumble

Serves 6

Vegetable oil spray
1¹/₂ cups diced dried apples
¹/₄ cup apple juice
1¹/₈ cups applesauce
1 cup peeled, cored, and diced fresh apples
1 teaspoon cinnamon
¹/₈ teaspoon nutmeg
¹/₂ cup apple butter
¹/₈ cup applesauce
³/₄ cup rolled oats
¹/₈ cup wheat germ
¹/₂ teaspoon cinnamon
¹/₈ teaspoon ginger

Preheat oven to 375 degrees. Spray a 9 x 13-inch dish with oil.

In a large pot, combine dried apples, juice, 1¹/₈ cups applesauce, fresh apples, cinnamon, and nutmeg and simmer until dried and fresh apples are tender, about 12-15 minutes. When mixture is tender, spread evenly in the pan.

In a small pot, heat apple butter and ¹/₈ cup applesauce over low heat until well combined. Add rolled oats, wheat germ, cinnamon, and ginger. Remove from heat and cool. Spread over apples.

Bake for 35 minutes or until bubbly and golden.

Total Calories Per Serving: 174   Total Fat as % of Daily Value: 5%   Protein: 4 gm   Fat: 2 gm
Carbohydrates:38 gm   Calcium: 17 mg   Iron: 1 mg   Sodium: 3 mg   Dietary Fiber: 4 gm

Apple Crumble II

Serves 6

1 cup all-purpose flour
³/₄ cup packed brown sugar
¹/₂ cup oats (not quick-cooking)
¹/₄ cup softened vegan margarine
2 cups apple pie filling (or 1¹/₂ cups peeled, cored, and thinly sliced apples tossed
**   with ¹/₂ cup peach preserves)**
2 teaspoons ground cinnamon

Preheat oven to 350 degrees. Create a crumble mixture by combining flour, sugar, and oatmeal with margarine until very crumbly. Place half of mixture in an 8 x 8-inch baking dish. Pour pie filling on top of crumble. Top pie filling with remaining mixture. Sprinkle with cinnamon. Bake for 35 minutes. Serve warm or cold.

Total Calories Per Serving: 496   Total Fat as % of Daily Value: 12%   Protein: 5 gm   Fat: 8 gm
Carbohydrates: 103 gm   Calcium: 40 mg   Iron: 2 mg   Sodium: 162 mg   Dietary Fiber: 4 gm

CRISP RECIPES

Cherry Crisp
Serves 8

**1 pound stemmed and pitted fresh red or white cherries, or frozen, thawed
unsweetened cherries**
1 cup vegan margarine
1¼ cups sugar
¼ cup unbleached white flour
¼ cup whole wheat flour
1 teaspoon almond extract

Preheat oven to 350 degrees. Combine cherries, ½ cup margarine, and ¾ cup sugar in a large pot. Cook over medium heat until the cherries are soft and tender. Using a slotted spoon, transfer the cherries to a 9 x 13-inch baking dish.

Sift together flours, remaining ½ cup sugar, and almond extract. Using your fingers or a pastry cutter, work the remaining margarine into the dry ingredients until the mixture resembles coarse crumbs. Spread the flour mixture over the cherries and bake for 12 minutes or until bubbly.

Total Calories Per Serving: 376   Total Fat as % of Daily Value: 34%   Protein: 2 gm   Fat: 22 gm
Carbohydrates: 44 gm   Calcium: 11 mg   Iron: <1 mg   Sodium: 184 mg   Dietary Fiber: 2 gm

Pear Cranberry Crisp
Serves 8

Vegetable oil spray
4½ cups peeled, cored, and thinly sliced pears
¾ cup fresh cranberries
1 Tablespoon lemon juice
1 Tablespoon all-purpose flour
½ cup maple or rice syrup
½ cup all-purpose flour
½ cup old-fashioned oats
½ cup walnut pieces
⅓ cup vegan margarine
½ cup brown sugar

Preheat oven to 375 degrees. Lightly spray an 8 x 8-inch baking dish.

In a large bowl mix the pears and cranberries with the lemon juice, 1 Tablespoon of flour, and sweetener. Mix just enough to coat evenly. In another bowl mix ½ cup flour, oats, walnuts, brown sugar, and vegan margarine until it resembles crumbs. Place the fruit in an even layer in the pan and sprinkle the topping over it. Bake 25-30 minutes or until browned and crisp on top and bubbly.

Total Calories Per Serving: 346   Total Fat as % of Daily Value: 18%   Protein: 5 gm   Fat: 12 gm
Carbohydrates: 56 gm   Calcium: 45 mg   Iron: 1 mg   Sodium: 67 mg   Dietary Fiber: 5 gm

Baked Apples with Ginger

Serves 8

Vegetable oil spray
2 pounds peeled, cored, and thinly sliced fresh apples and/or ripe pears
⅛ cup apple cider
⅛ cup apple butter
3 Tablespoons preserved ginger
½ cup rolled oats
¼ cup applesauce
¼ cup crumbled vegan ginger cookies
⅛ teaspoon ginger
Pinch cinnamon
Pinch nutmeg

Preheat oven to 375 degrees. Spray a 9 x 13-inch baking dish with oil. Place sliced apples in dish. Add cider, apple butter, and preserved ginger and toss gently until ingredients are well combined.

In a small bowl, mix oats, applesauce, cookies, ginger, cinnamon, and nutmeg until well combined. Spread oat mixture over apples and press down. Bake for 35 minutes, until apples are soft and topping is crisp.

Total Calories Per Serving: 132   Total Fat as % of Daily Value: 2%   Protein: 2 gm   Fat: 1 gm
Carbohydrates: 29 gm   Calcium: 17 mg   Iron: 1 mg   Sodium: 47 mg   Dietary Fiber: 3 gm

Berry Crunch

Serves 6

½ cup berry juice (strawberry or blueberry) or apple juice
1½ Tablespoons quick-cooking tapioca
⅓ cup apple butter
⅛ cup fruit jam
1 cup each unbleached flour and quick-cooking oatmeal
¼ cup toasted wheat germ
¼ teaspoon double-acting baking powder
¼ teaspoon baking soda
Vegetable oil spray
3 cups fresh or frozen, thawed berries (your choice)

Preheat oven to 325 degrees. Mix berry juice and tapioca in a non-reactive bowl (glass or plastic) and let stand for 15 minutes.

In a medium-size pot, heat apple butter and jam over low heat, stirring, until well combined. Remove from heat. Mix flour, oats, wheat germ, powder, and soda into juice and stir until well combined.

Spray a 9 x 13-inch baking dish with oil. Place half the oat mixture into the dish, scatter berries over the oats, spread tapioca mixture over the berries, and complete with remaining oats mixture. Bake crunch for 30 minutes or until topping is brown.

Total Calories Per Serving: 274   Total Fat as % of Daily Value: 5%   Protein: 8 gm   Fat: 2 gm
Carbohydrates: 56 gm   Calcium: 37 mg   Iron: 2 mg   Sodium: 77 mg   Dietary Fiber: 6 gm

BAKED PUDDING RECIPES

Bread and Butter Pudding
Serves 6

1 cup firm tofu
4 Tablespoons vanilla soy yogurt
1 cup soymilk
1 teaspoon orange zest
1 Tablespoon maple syrup
4 Tablespoons brown sugar
½ teaspoon each cinnamon and allspice
½ teaspoon nutmeg
Vegetable oil spray
9 slices bread (or however many fit the dish)
¼ cup raisins

Preheat oven to 375 degrees. Place tofu, yogurt, soymilk, zest, maple syrup, brown sugar, and spices in a blender canister and process until smooth.

Spray an 8 x 8-inch baking dish with oil. Tightly line bottom of pan with bread. Pour on some of the tofu mixture. Add another layer of bread and pour on some more mixture. Repeat until bread and tofu mixture are used up. Sprinkle top with raisins. Cover and bake for 30 minutes. Remove cover, spray top of pudding with oil, and allow pudding to bake for 5 more minutes, or until golden.

Total Calories Per Serving: 282   Total Fat as % of Daily Value: 5%   Protein: 9 gm   Fat: 3 gm
Carbohydrates: 54 gm   Calcium: 190 mg   Iron: 3 mg   Sodium: 517 mg   Dietary Fiber: 2 gm

Mexican Bread Pudding (Capirotada)
Serves 8

Vegetable oil spray
9 slices toasted white bread
4 cups black tea brewed with 1 cinnamon stick and 4 teaspoons brown sugar
5 slices vegan soy cheese
1 cup thinly sliced, peeled apples
1 cup thinly sliced, peeled bananas
½ cup raisins

Preheat oven to 375 degrees. Spray an 8 x 8-inch baking dish with oil.

Tightly layer bread into a single layer in bottom of pan. Pour a small amount of tea over bread to moisten. Top bread with a thin layer of cheese, apples, bananas, and a sprinkle of raisins. Create a second layer of bread, pressing down. Repeat with tea, cheese, etc. Continue until all ingredients are used up. Cover and bake for 30 minutes. Uncover and spray with oil. Bake for 5 more minutes or until golden on top.

Total Calories Per Serving: 233   Total Fat as % of Daily Value: 6%   Protein: 5 gm   Fat: 4 gm
Carbohydrates: 45 gm   Calcium: 83 mg   Iron: 2 mg   Sodium: 426 mg   Dietary Fiber: 2 gm

Vegan Noodle Kugel
Serves 5

Vegetable oil spray
One 12-ounce package wide vegan noodles (lasagna noodles work well)
1½ cups silken tofu
¾ cup sugar
1 teaspoon cinnamon
1 teaspoon vanilla extract
2 teaspoons orange zest
½ cup raisins
½ cup drained, chopped canned peaches
1½ cups peeled, cored, and cubed green apples
¼ cup applesauce

Preheat oven to 400 degrees. Spray a loaf pan (about 4 inches deep and 8 inches long) with oil. Cook noodles according to package directions, drain, and cool. Using a blender or mixer, purée tofu with sugar, cinnamon, vanilla, and zest.

In a large bowl, combine raisins, peaches, apples, and applesauce. Whip in tofu mixture. Add in noodles and mix until well combined. Pour into loaf pan and bake for 30 minutes, or until golden.

Variations: For different flavors, use pineapple or apricots instead of peaches and dried cranberries and cherries or apricots instead of raisins. Whole wheat noodles can be used in this recipe.

Total Calories Per Serving: 458	Total Fat as % of Daily Value: 5%	Protein: 10 gm	Fat: 2 gm
Carbohydrates: 104 gm	Calcium: 37 mg Iron: 2 mg Sodium: 61 mg	Dietary Fiber: 9 gm	

Chocolate Cherry Bread Pudding
Serves 6

Pudding will be flat, but moist. Also, note this dish is high fat!

¾ cup vegan chocolate chips
¾ cup vegan margarine
⅔ cup sugar
½ cup puréed silken tofu
1 cup ground almonds
⅓ cup dry bread crumbs
1 pound canned or frozen, drained sour cherries
Vegetable oil spray

Set a rack in the middle of the oven. Preheat oven to 350 degrees.

Melt the chocolate chips in a microwave or in a small pot on the stove. In a separate bowl beat the margarine with half the sweetener until soft and light. Place melted chocolate in a large bowl. Whisk in margarine, then whisk in tofu. Combine the almonds and crumbs together and stir into chocolate mixture. Fold in cherries.

Spray a loaf pan (about 4 inches deep and 8 inches long) with oil. Pour in batter. Bake for 30 minutes, or until solid.

Total Calories Per Serving: 586   Total Fat as % of Daily Value: 62%   Protein: 8 gm   Fat: 40 gm
Carbohydrates: 53 gm   Calcium: 94 mg   Iron: 2 mg   Sodium: 236 mg   Dietary Fiber: 5 gm

Chocolate Bread Pudding
Serves 8-10

2¹/₂ cups chocolate soymilk
3 Tablespoons unsweetened cocoa
1 pound loaf of bread torn into pieces (about 18 slices of bread)
2 Tablespoons brandy (optional)
¹/₂ cup dried cherries
1 cup sliced bananas (wait to peel until needed, to avoid browning)
¹/₂ cup sugar
1 teaspoon cinnamon
1 teaspoon vanilla
¹/₈ teaspoon salt
Vegetable oil spray

Preheat oven to 350 degrees. In a medium-size pot, heat ¹/₂ cup of soymilk to nearly boiling. Remove from heat and add cocoa, whisking until lumps disappear. Add remaining soymilk, whisking to combine. Place bread pieces in a large bowl and pour cocoa/soymilk mixture over them and mix until all the bread is coated. Allow bread to soak for 20 minutes.

In a small bowl, pour brandy over cherries and set aside until cherries have plumped, about 30 minutes. If not using brandy, use warm water.

Lightly spray an 8 x 8-inch square baking dish. In a blender or food processor canister, purée bananas with sugar, cinnamon, vanilla, and salt. Pour banana mixture over bread mixture, add soaked cherries, and stir to combine evenly.

Spread pudding into prepared pan, in an even layer. Bake pudding on center rack of oven for 25-30 minutes or until pudding is set and firm to touch. Cool slightly before serving.

Total Calories Per Serving: 257   Total Fat as % of Daily Value: 5%   Protein: 7 gm   Fat: 3 gm
Carbohydrates: 51 gm   Calcium: 183 mg   Iron: 3 mg   Sodium: 458 mg   Dietary Fiber: 3 gm

Sweet Vegetable Kugel

Serves 12

Vegetable oil spray
2 cups peeled, shredded raw sweet potatoes
2 cups shredded raw carrots
2 cups peeled, shredded raw apples
2 cups matzo meal
2 teaspoons cinnamon
2 teaspoons nutmeg
1/2 cup sugar
1/2 teaspoon salt
1 cup melted vegan margarine

Preheat oven to 325 degrees. Spray a 9 x 13-inch pan with oil. Combine sweet potatoes, carrots, and apple in a large mixing bowl. Add the matzo meal, spices, sugar, and salt, and mix well. Stir in the margarine until well combined. Scrape the mixture into the baking pan, spreading evenly and smoothing the top. Cover and bake for 45 minutes, then remove cover and bake for another 10 minutes. Allow kugel to cool for at least 10 minutes before serving.

Total Calories Per Serving: 231   Total Fat as % of Daily Value: 23%   Protein: 1 gm   Fat: 15 gm
Carbohydrates: 24 gm   Calcium: 13 mg   Iron: <1 mg   Sodium: 235 mg   Dietary Fiber: 2 gm

Matzo Kugel with Fruit

Serves 6

Vegetable oil spray
3 boards of matzo
Boiling water to cover matzo
1/4 cup sugar
1/4 teaspoon each cinnamon and ground ginger
1/4 teaspoon salt
2 cups cored, peeled, and grated green apples
1/4 cup each dried apricots, pitted prunes, and black raisins
2 Tablespoons vegetable oil
2/3 cup mashed firm tofu

Preheat oven to 350 degrees. Spray a 9-inch springform pan or an 8 x 8-inch baking dish with oil. Break matzo into small pieces and put them into a large bowl. Pour boiling water over matzo to soften and drain off all water immediately (you don't want to end up with mush). Mix in remaining ingredients and mix well. Pour into pan and press evenly.

   Bake for 1 hour or until lightly browned around the edges. Cool at least 10 minutes before removing from pan.

Variations: For a different flavor, use pineapple tidbits in place of apples. A quarter cup chopped walnuts or pecans can be added as well.

Total Calories Per Serving: 209   Total Fat as % of Daily Value: 8%   Protein: 4 gm   Fat: 5 gm
Carbohydrates: 39 gm   Calcium: 22 mg   Iron: 1 mg   Sodium: 122 mg   Dietary Fiber: 2 gm

Cinnamon Matzo Balls
Makes about 14 dessert balls

Matzo balls don't just belong in soup!

1 cup vegan margarine
¹⁄₂ cup sugar
¹⁄₂ teaspoon vanilla extract
1³⁄₄ cups matzo meal or matzo cake flour
1 teaspoon cinnamon
¹⁄₂ teaspoon ground ginger

Preheat oven to 350 degrees. Allow margarine to soften at room temperature.
   Place margarine in a medium-size bowl. Cream together margarine and sugar. Mix in vanilla.
   Sift together matzo meal, cinnamon, and ginger. Mix into margarine/sugar mixture. Cover and place in the refrigerator for at least 1 hour.
   Shape into 1-inch round balls and place on ungreased baking sheet. Bake matzo balls for 15 minutes or until lightly golden. Allow dessert balls to cool before serving. Can be dusted with cinnamon or rolled in finely chopped almonds prior to serving.

Total Calories Per Serving (2 balls): 312   Total Fat as % of Daily Value: 38%   Protein: 1 gm   Fat: 25 gm
Carbohydrates: 20 gm   Calcium: 1 mg   Iron: <1 mg   Sodium: 209 mg   Dietary Fiber: <1 gm

Apple Brown Betty
Serves 6

1¹⁄₂ pounds green apples
4 slices whole wheat bread
¹⁄₂ cup vegan margarine
³⁄₄ cup brown sugar
2 Tablespoons water

Preheat oven to 375 degrees. Peel, core, and slice apples. Place the bread slices in a food processor and blend to make fresh crumbs. Rub a 1-quart baking dish thickly with margarine and then sprinkle liberally with brown sugar. Add alternating layers of sliced apples, sugar, and bread crumbs, then repeat, ending with bread crumbs. Thickly sprinkle with sugar and dot with leftover margarine. Sprinkle water on top. Bake for 40 minutes or until browned.

Total Calories Per Serving: 372   Total Fat as % of Daily Value: 25%   Protein: 3 gm   Fat: 16 gm
Carbohydrates: 57 gm   Calcium: 74 mg   Iron: 1 mg   Sodium: 333 mg   Dietary Fiber: 2 gm

MICROWAVE BAKED DESSERT RECIPES

The recipes in this section are prepared in a microwave. If a microwave is not available, you can bake these recipes in the same size pan in a 375-degree preheated oven.

Gingerbread

Makes an 8 x 8 x 2-inch pan or 9 servings

¹/₂ cup vegan margarine
¹/₂ cup brewed espresso or strong coffee
4 Tablespoons silken tofu
¹/₂ cup sugar
¹/₂ cup molasses
1¹/₂ cups all-purpose flour
2 teaspoons baking powder
2 teaspoons ground ginger

Place margarine and coffee in a small bowl and microwave on HIGH for 30 seconds or until margarine is melted.

In a large bowl, beat tofu and sugar together. Add molasses. Mix in coffee. Sift together flour, baking powder, and ginger. Mix into liquid and stir well to combine.

Add to an 8 x 8 x 2-inch microwaveable baking dish or square casserole. Microwave on HIGH for 8 minutes, or until a toothpick inserted in the center comes out clean.

Total Calories Per Serving: 276   Total Fat as % of Daily Value: 15%   Protein: 5 gm   Fat: 10 gm
Carbohydrates: 42 gm   Calcium: 115 mg   Iron: 2 mg   Sodium: 228 mg   Dietary Fiber: 1 gm

Fruit and Nut Bread

Makes an 8 x 8 x 2-inch pan or 9 servings

Vegetable oil spray
1 cup chopped dates
¹/₄ cup chopped raisins
³/₄ cup chopped pecans or walnuts
1¹/₂ teaspoons baking soda
³/₄ cup hot tap water
3 Tablespoons margarine, softened
4 Tablespoons silken tofu
1 teaspoon lemon zest
¹/₂ teaspoon vanilla extract
1 cup sugar
1¹/₂ cups all-purpose flour, sifted

Spray an 8 x 8 x 2-inch microwaveable baking pan or square casserole with oil. Set aside.

In a large bowl, combine dates, raisins, nuts, and baking soda. Mix in water and margarine. Cover and let stand for 30 minutes. Stir in remaining ingredients until well blended. Pour into baking pan.

Microwave on HIGH for 8 minutes, or until toothpick inserted in center comes out clean. Let stand for at least 10 minutes before serving.

Total Calories Per Serving: 331   Total Fat as % of Daily Value: 15%   Protein: 8 gm   Fat: 10 gm
Carbohydrates: 55 gm   Calcium: 31 mg   Iron: 1 mg   Sodium: 272 mg   Dietary Fiber: 3 gm

Pumpkin Bread

Makes a 9 x 5-inch or 8 x 4-inch loaf pan with 10 slices

Don't wait for the holidays to quick-bake this wonderful cake-bread.

1 cup all-purpose flour
³/₄ cup sugar
1 teaspoon baking powder
1 teaspoon baking soda
1 teaspoon cinnamon
1 teaspoon ginger
¹/₂ teaspoon nutmeg
¹/₄ teaspoon cloves
¹/₂ cup oil
4 Tablespoons silken tofu
¹/₂ cup chopped walnuts, almonds or mixed nuts (optional)
1 cup canned pumpkin (unsweetened)
Vegetable oil spray

In a medium-size mixing bowl, mix all ingredients until well combined.

Spray a loaf pan with vegetable oil or line it with waxed paper. Spread batter evenly in the pan.

Place an inverted shallow bowl or saucer in the center of the microwave or use a microwave baking rack. Place the loaf pan on the bowl or rack. Microwave on MEDIUM for 9 minutes. Rotate and microwave on HIGH for 2-5 minutes. Check for doneness with a toothpick inserted in the center.

Note: If possible, use a loaf pan with straight, rather than sloped sides for microwave baking.

Variations:
Applesauce Bread: use 1 cup of sweetened applesauce to replace the pumpkin.
Carrot Bread: use 2 cups finely grated fresh carrots instead of the pumpkin.
Zucchini Bread: use 1¹/₂ cups finely grated fresh, unpeeled zucchini to replace the pumpkin.

Total Calories Per Serving: 259   Total Fat as % of Daily Value: 22%   Protein: 5 gm   Fat: 14 gm
Carbohydrates: 28 gm   Calcium: 51 mg   Iron: 1 mg   Sodium: 204 mg   Dietary Fiber: 2 gm

Banana Bread with Whole Wheat

Makes a 8 x 4-inch or 9 x 5-inch loaf with 10 slices

Use this as a dessert, the foundation of a warm breakfast, or as sandwich bread.

1 cup whole wheat flour
1/2 cup all-purpose flour
1/2 cup sugar
1/4 cup oil
1/4 cup soy, almond, or rice milk (you can use vanilla-flavored)
4 Tablespoons silken tofu
1 cup very ripe bananas, mashed
1 Tablespoon lemon juice
1 teaspoon baking soda
1/2 teaspoon salt
1/2 cup chopped walnuts, almonds, pecans, or mixed nuts (optional)

Place all ingredients in a large mixing bowl and combine until smooth.

Line the bottom of a loaf pan with waxed paper. Place an inverted saucer or microwave rack in the center of the microwave. Pour batter into loaf pan. Place pan on saucer or rack and microwave on MEDIUM for 8 minutes. Rotate pan. Microwave on HIGH for another 4-8 minutes, until no uncooked batter can be seen and cake springs back to touch. Let stand for 5 minutes before slicing.

Total Calories Per Serving: 217   Total Fat as % of Daily Value:14 %   Protein: 6 gm   Fat: 9 gm
Carbohydrates: 28 gm   Calcium:29 mg   Iron: 1 mg   Sodium: 274 mg   Dietary Fiber: 3 gm

Creamy Ginger and Date Bread

Makes one 12 x 8-inch dish or two 8 x 4-inch loaves with 12-14   servings

You should microwave each loaf separately. This recipe freezes well and can be used as a cake or bread.

1 cup all-purpose flour
1/4 cup softened vegan margarine
1/2 cup brown sugar or sugar
4 Tablespoons silken tofu
1/2 cup vegan sour cream or plain soy yogurt
1 teaspoon ginger
1/2 teaspoon nutmeg
1/2 teaspoon cinnamon
1/2 teaspoon vanilla extract
1/2 teaspoon baking soda
1/4 teaspoon salt
1/2 cup finely chopped dates
1 Tablespoon molasses

Put all ingredients in a large mixing bowl and blend to combine. Invert a saucer in the middle of the microwave or insert a microwave rack. Pour the batter into a 12 x 8-inch microwaveable baking dish or shallow casserole. Microwave on HIGH for 5-8 minutes or until a toothpick inserted in the center comes out clean.

Total Calories Per Serving: 146   Total Fat as % of Daily Value: 6%   Protein: 3 gm   Fat: 4 gm
Carbohydrates: 24 gm   Calcium: 30 mg   Iron: 1 mg   Sodium: 159 mg   Dietary Fiber: 1 gm

Raisin and Orange Cake

Makes an 8 x 4-inch or 9 x 5-inch loaf pan with 10 slices

1 cup raisins
1 cup water
2 Tablespoons fresh orange zest
$1/2$ cup sugar
$1/3$ cup softened vegan margarine
4 Tablespoons silken tofu
2 teaspoons orange juice concentrate
2 teaspoons baking powder
$1/2$ teaspoon baking soda
$1/2$ teaspoon salt
$1/4$ teaspoon nutmeg
$1/2$ teaspoon ground ginger
$1^{1}/_{3}$ cups all-purpose flour

In a large bowl, combine raisins and water. Microwave on HIGH for 2 minutes. Stir in zest. Allow mixture to cool.

In a separate large bowl, combine all ingredients except flour. Mix until well blended. Add in flour and mix well. Add raisin mixture and blend well.

Place an inverted saucer or microwave rack in the center of the microwave. Line the bottom of a loaf pan with waxed paper. Pour batter into loaf pan. Microwave on MEDIUM for 9 minutes. Rotate pan. Microwave on HIGH for 3-6 minutes or until no uncooked batter can be seen and cake springs back when touched. Allow cake to cool for 5 minutes before slicing.

Total Calories Per Serving: 198   Total Fat as % of Daily Value: 9%   Protein: 2 gm   Fat: 6 gm
Carbohydrates: 35 gm   Calcium: 64 mg   Iron: 1 mg   Sodium: 328 mg   Dietary Fiber: 1 gm

Graham Cracker Molasses Bread

Makes an 8 x 4-inch or 9 x 5-inch loaf with 10 slices

Use this as sandwich bread or the base for a super sorbet sundae.

¾ cup vegan graham cracker crumbs
¾ cup all-purpose flour
1 teaspoon baking soda
½ teaspoon salt
½ cup chopped raisins or dates
¾ cup soymilk
1 Tablespoon lemon juice
¼ cup molasses
¼ cup oil

In a large bowl, combine all ingredients and mix until well blended. Line the bottom of a loaf pan with waxed paper. Pour in the batter. Cover with vented plastic wrap. Microwave on MEDIUM for 5-9 minutes or until bread springs back when touched. Cool at least 5 minutes before slicing.

Total Calories Per Serving: 162   Total Fat as % of Daily Value: 9%   Protein: 2 gm   Fat: 6 gm
Carbohydrates: 25 gm   Calcium: 46 mg   Iron: 1 mg   Sodium: 292 mg   Dietary Fiber: 1 gm

Chapter 6: BEVERAGES

Planning

Beverages are a necessary part of any party meal. Beverages can serve as appetizers, a meal, dessert accompaniments, and even as dessert itself. Appetizer beverages should be flavorful without being filling. Icy orange-pineapple juice or a tomato juice cocktail would be good examples. In selecting dessert beverages, the rule of thumb is: the richer or sweeter the dessert, the less rich or sweet the beverage. For example, if you're serving a chocolate cheesecake for dessert, simply brewed coffee or ice tea would be a good choice in beverages. If dessert is sliced oranges with fresh mint, vanilla smoothies or flavored iced tea would make a good accompaniment.

When attempting to figure out beverage quantity needs, you need to consider the weather. On a hot day, cold or iced beverages will be in great demand; the same goes for hot beverages on cold days.

Serving containers: how large are the cups or glasses you plan to use; you need to figure that people will fill their cups or glasses to the top at least twice.

Menu: if you will be putting out beverages in advance of the meal, you can plan that people will drink a glass or cup or two before the meal, and then another one or two with the meal; if your food is spicy, plan on people drinking more than if the food is mild.

Variety: will you be serving only one or two beverages throughout the entire meal or party, or offering a large variety; if only one or two, assume people will drink three or four cups or glasses; if you are serving different beverages for the meal and dessert, for example, sparkling water with dinner, and hot coffee with dessert, plan on people having one or two glasses or cups of each.

Service: will people be serving themselves or will they be served; people tend to drink less when served.

Depending on the time of year and your guests' preferences, you will probably want to serve at least one hot and one cold beverage. Some people seem to drink iced tea no matter how cold the weather, and others cannot live without their hot coffee, even during a heat wave.

When planning beverage service, remember the ice and containers to keep drinks cold, or the warmers, especially if you will be serving beverages over several hours. You don't want to spend your party time running to the store for ice, or brewing endless pots of tea or coffee. If you or your friends don't have a large coffee warmer, check with your local school or community center to see if they can loan you one. If necessary, you can rent large coffee warmers from a local party rental center.

Tea: Brew It and Ice It!

Hot and cold tea have been a popular beverages in many countries for many centuries. Green and black tea comes from the same plant, a bush that is a member of the camellia family. Green tea is dried for a shorter time than black tea and is not allowed to go through the short fermenting process that black tea does. Green tea and black tea have about the same amount of caffeine.

Many people are trying to cut back on their caffeine. Black tea and green tea are available in a decaffeinated form. Many herbal teas are made from dried flowers, bark, and herbs and may not contain caffeine. Read the label of any tea product before purchasing to be sure that no caffeine-containing or stimulating ingredients, such as guarana or cola, have been added.

The Perfect Brew

Chilling tea certainly makes it refreshing during the warm weather months. Leaf or herb teas are easy to brew and chill and do not contain the extra flavorings or sweeteners that instant teas may have.

To brew the perfect pitcher of tea for chilling, bring the amount of water you need to a rolling boil. While the water is boiling, measure the amount of tea you're going to use into a clean glass or china container. (Plastic and metal tend to pick up extra flavors.) Pour a small amount of boiling water over your tea and let it steep for a minute. Add the remainder of the boiling water and allow tea to steep to the desired strength. Don't leave the tea in for too long, as it will give an acid taste. Put your tea in the refrigerator and allow it to cool for several hours. Brewed tea will keep its flavor for at least 2 days in the refrigerator, so you don't have to brew it every day.

Cubed Iced Tea

Iced tea on its own has a wonderful flavor, but sometimes you get the urge to dress it up. Rather than using sugar or flavored syrups, create fruity ice cubes that can be added to ice tea. In addition to great flavor, you'll be sneaking in some extra nutrition. Try freezing orange, apple, or cranberry juice or apricot, pear, peach, mango, or strawberry nectar in ice cube trays. Add several flavors at a time to create your own taste sensation.

Cold tea can be a fast thirst quencher or you can pile a tall glass full of orange, fresh pineapple, grapefruit, or fresh ripe peach slices and some fresh berries for a beverage and a dessert all rolled into one. Along with chopped fresh mint, add a splash of iced tea to fruit salads for a "secret" ingredient. Brewed teas can be mixed with fruit juice or puréed fruit and frozen and served as a refreshing, low-calorie summer treat.

Ethnic Ice Tea

Leaf tea makes a nice iced tea, but sometimes it's nice to branch out! Browse the shelves of ethnic markets (or food websites) for the following brew-ables. In addition to exciting new flavors, most of these products are caffeine-free!

Central America: Jamaica (say "ha-mie-cah") is a dried hibiscus flower that brews up a brilliant crimson color. Brew jamaica as you would leaf tea.

Korea: Roasted corn and roasted barley are sold in the coffee and tea section of Korean markets. The roasted corn has a naturally sweet flavor and a delicate yellow color. The barley has a nutty, full roasted flavor and a golden brown color. Add several teaspoons to 2 cups of boiling water and allow the mixture to boil for 2-3 minutes. Some people like to brew the corn and barley together. An extra added dividend: don't strain out the corn and barley and munch on it as a high fiber snack.

China and South East Asia: Chrysanthemums make a beautiful flower arrangement on the table and a give a beautiful bouquet in your cup. Purchase dried chrysanthemums in the tea section of the market and brew the dried flowers as you would leaf tea.

Japan: Peel and slice ginger, letting several small slices steep in boiling water for several minutes. The ginger tea will take on a delicate, pale green color and have a mild but stimulating flavor.

South Africa: When brewed, roobia looks like a cup of orange pekoe (traditional black leaf tea) and has a mild, pleasant taste. Taken from the bark of a tree that grows only in South Africa, roobia has no caffeine. Look for it in health and natural food stores.

Coffee

You have many choices when selecting coffees. It may be easier for you to use instant coffee for a large number of guests rather than brewing it. If you are serving iced coffee, you can brew the coffee several days ahead of time. There are flavored coffees available in both instant and brewing forms.

No matter what type of coffee you select, keep the following in mind:

- Coffee pots and containers should be very, very clean, so the coffee does not pick up any off tastes.

- Do not boil coffee; boiling causes bitter and acid flavors to develop.

- Use cold water to make instant or brewed coffee.

- The longer coffee beans or coffee powder is exposed to air, the more flavor it loses. Store coffee in airtight containers, in dry, cool places. If you will be storing opened coffee for more than one week, store it in the freezer.

- For ground coffee beans, estimate about 1-2 level Tablespoons of coffee for each cup (8 ounces) water. For instant coffee, follow label instructions, as coffee powders differ in strength.

Beverages can also be a meal item or a dessert. Smoothies, made with combinations of fruit and veggie milks, or milkshakes can be warm weather breakfast entrées or one of the dessert offerings at a party. Before serving them at a party, have a tasting "session" to try out your blender and to see how various ingredients taste when blended together.

RECIPES

Note: All the beverage recipes can easily be doubled, tripled or expanded further if needed. The amounts currently listed can be easily prepared on most usual kitchen equipment. If you need to make large amounts, you will probably have to do it in batches.

Tropical Smoothie

Serves 6

3 cups peeled, seeded, and diced ripe papaya
2 cups vanilla soy yogurt
2 cups crushed ice

Place papaya and yogurt in a blender and process until smooth. Slowly add ice and process until smooth. Serve immediately.

Variations: If papaya is not available, use frozen, thawed mango chunks, fresh ripe mango, or fresh ripe pineapple.

Total Calories Per Serving: 94   Total Fat as % of Daily Value: 2%   Protein: 3 gm   Fat: 1 gm
Carbohydrates: 18 gm   Calcium: 150 mg   Iron: 1 mg   Sodium: 11 mg   Dietary Fiber: 2 gm

Banana Vanilla Shake
Serves 5

1¹/₂ cups mashed, banana (approximately 2 bananas)
1 Tablespoon vanilla extract
2 cups ice
2 cups vegan milk (plain or vanilla soy, rice, or almond milk)
1 Tablespoon apple juice concentrate

Place all ingredients in the canister of a blender and process until smooth. Serve immediately.

Total Calories Per Serving: 124   Total Fat as % of Daily Value: 3%   Protein: 5 gm   Fat: 2 gm
Carbohydrates: 22 gm   Calcium: 42 mg   Iron: 1 mg   Sodium: 56 mg   Dietary Fiber: 3 gm

Frozen Smoothie
Serves 4

1¹/₂ cups very ripe peeled bananas frozen for at least 1 hour
1¹/₂ cups fresh or frozen, thawed sliced or diced strawberries
1 Tablespoon frozen orange juice concentrate
1¹/₂ cups apple juice or cider

Place all ingredients in a blender. Process mixture until smooth. Serve immediately.

Variations: Take advantage of the seasons and the sales at the market and use raspberries, blueberries, peaches, peach, apricot, or pear nectar, and apple juice concentrate in this recipe.

Total Calories Per Serving: 121   Total Fat as % of Daily Value: 0%   Protein: 1 gm   Fat: 0 gm
Carbohydrates: 30 gm   Calcium: 21 mg   Iron: 1 mg   Sodium: 4 mg   Dietary Fiber: 3 gm

Pumpkin Smoothie
Serves 4

1 cup unsweetened canned pumpkin
1 cup vanilla soy yogurt
¹/₂ teaspoon cinnamon
¹/₄ teaspoon nutmeg
1 Tablespoon brown sugar
2 cups ice cubes

Place all of the ingredients in a blender and process until smooth. Serve in small glasses, as this is very rich.

Total Calories Per Serving: 80   Total Fat as % of Daily Value: 2%   Protein: 2 gm   Fat: 1 gm
Carbohydrates: 16 gm   Calcium: 117 mg   Iron: 1 mg   Sodium: 155 mg   Dietary Fiber: 2 gm

Frozen Orange Mango Smoothie

Serves 5

4 cups frozen mango pieces (purchase frozen or cut and freeze fresh mango)
1 cup orange juice
¹/₄ cup lime juice
¹/₄ cup frozen, thawed diced strawberries
¹/₂ cup crushed ice

Place mango, juices, and berries in the canister of a blender. Process mixture until smooth. Add ice and process for desired texture. Serve immediately.

Total Calories Per Serving: 116   Total Fat as % of Daily Value: 1%   Protein: 1 gm   Fat: 1 gm
Carbohydrates: 30 gm   Calcium: 22 mg   Iron: 0 mg   Sodium: 4 mg   Dietary Fiber: 3 gm

Strawberry-Banana-Apple Smoothie

Serves 4

1 cup soy or rice milk
¹/₂ cup apple juice
1 cup cored and chopped apple
¹/₂ cup chopped frozen banana
¹/₂ chopped fresh banana
3 cups frozen strawberries

Add all ingredients into a blender and blend until smooth. Serve immediately or refrigerate until ready to serve.

Total Calories Per Serving: 16   Total Fat as % of Daily Value: 3%   Protein: 4 gm   Fat: 2 gm
Carbohydrates: 24 gm   Calcium: 47 mg   Iron: 1 mg   Sodium: 36 mg   Dietary Fiber: 4 gm

Chocolate-Banana-Peanut Butter Smoothie

Serves 4

2 cups peeled, mashed frozen banana
1 cup vanilla soymilk
2 Tablespoons wheat germ
2 Tablespoons cocoa powder
2 Tablespoons peanut butter
1 cup ice

Place all ingredients in a blender canister and blend until very smooth and thick. Serve immediately.

Total Calories Per Serving: 198   Total Fat as % of Daily Value: 7%   Protein: 7 gm   Fat: 6 gm
Carbohydrates: 34 gm   Calcium: 37 mg   Iron: 2 mg   Sodium: 73 mg   Dietary Fiber: 6 gm

Watermelon-Apple Smoothie
Serves 4

2 cups peeled, cored, and diced apples
1 cup fresh watermelon cubes
1 cup crushed ice

Place all ingredients in a blender and blend until very smooth and thick. Serve immediately.

Total Calories Per Serving: 44   Total Fat as % of Daily Value: 0%   Protein: 0 gm   Fat: 0 gm
Carbohydrates: 12 gm   Calcium: 6 mg   Iron: 0 mg   Sodium: 1 mg   Dietary Fiber: 2 gm

Sangria (Red Wine with Fruit)

Basic Sangria Proportions:
2 parts wine
1 part orange juice
$1/4$ part brandy
$1/4$ part orange-flavored liqueur
$1/2$ part lemon-lime soda

Sangria is a fruity wine punch that is served cold. Using the proportions above, if you use one measuring cup as a "part," you would get a yield of about 5 cups or 40 ounces (ten 4-ounce [$1/2$ cup] servings).

Total Calories Per Serving: 83   Total Fat as % of Daily Value: 0%   Protein: 0 gm   Fat: 0 gm
Carbohydrates: 5 gm   Calcium: 7 mg   Iron: 0 mg   Sodium: 3 mg   Dietary Fiber: 0 gm

Wine and Citrus Aperitif
Makes 2½ quarts or 10 cups

Called "Vin de Pamplemousse," this interesting adult beverage can be refrigerated for up to 4 weeks.

1 white grapefruit
2 red grapefruits
$1^1/2$ Meyer lemons
One 2-inch piece vanilla bean, split lengthwise
Three 8-ounce (750-ml) bottles crisp white wine
$1^1/2$ cups vodka
$3/4$ cup plus 2 Tablespoons sugar

Select grapefruit that smell fragrant and floral when skin is lightly scratched. Wash all fruit and slice into ½-inch-thick rounds. Combine ingredients in a nonreactive container and stir to dissolve sugar.

    Cover container and store in a cool, dark place or in a refrigerator for 1 week. Check once a day, stirring. Taste and adjust to suit your taste, adding more sugar if it is not too sweet, or adding more fruit and wine if it seems too sweet. After 3 days, strain out and discard solids and let aperitif sit covered and undisturbed for 2 days so that the cloudy bits settle.

    Carefully strain liquid through several layers of cheesecloth, but stop pouring when you get to the cloudy part at bottom. The process can be repeated until crystal clear or not, depending on how you like the appearance.

Place in clean wine bottles and cork tightly. Refrigerate. Serve chilled in fluted, stemmed glasses.

Total Calories Per Serving: 215   Total Fat as % of Daily Value: 0%   Protein: 0 gm   Fat: 0 gm
Carbohydrates: 22 gm   Calcium: 11 mg   Iron: 0 mg   Sodium: 4 mg   Dietary Fiber: 0 gm

Virgin Bloody Mary

Serves 8

4 cups tomato juice
¼ teaspoon prepared horseradish
⅛ teaspoon onion powder
2 bay leaves
¼ teaspoon fresh ground black pepper
¼ teaspoon paprika
⅛ teaspoon garlic powder
¼ teaspoon hot sauce
¼ teaspoon lemon juice
1 teaspoon lime juice
¾ teaspoon celery salt
⅓ teaspoon hot sauce
1 teaspoon chili powder

Combine all ingredients into a glass or plastic pitcher and mix well. Cover and refrigerate for at least 1 hour before serving. You can make this a day ahead of time.

Before serving remove the bay leaves. Serve in chilled glasses.

Total Calories Per Serving: 21   Total Fat as % of Daily Value: 0%   Protein: 1 gm   Fat: 0 gm
Carbohydrates: 5 gm   Calcium: 12 mg   Iron: 1 mg   Sodium: 331 mg   Dietary Fiber: 0 gm

Sparkling Fruit Punch

Serves 14

7 cups chilled pineapple juice
4 cups sparkling water or seltzer
¾ cup frozen orange juice concentrate
½ cup thinly sliced, peeled lemons or limes
2 cups fresh or frozen, thawed berries
One 8-ounce bottle (750 ml) chilled champagne or lemon-lime soda (optional)

Combine all ingredients in a chilled punch bowl. If not serving immediately, wait to add seltzer and/or champagne. Keep cold with ice.

Total Calories Per Serving: 124   Total Fat as % of Daily Value: 0%   Protein: 1 gm   Fat: 0 gm
Carbohydrates: 28 gm   Calcium: 33 mg   Iron: 1 mg   Sodium: 4 mg   Dietary Fiber: 2 gm

Banana-Orange Punch

Serves 6

2 cups peeled, puréed banana
2 cups orange juice
1 cup pineapple juice
3 cups seltzer or sparkling water
2 cups lemon or orange sorbet

Place banana purée in a blender. Add orange and pineapple juice and process until smooth. Just before serving, add the seltzer and mix well. Put a spoonful of sorbet in each glass and fill with punch.

Total Calories Per Serving: 197   Total Fat as % of Daily Value: 0%   Protein: 2 gm   Fat: 0 gm
Carbohydrates: 48 gm   Calcium: 18 mg   Iron: 0 mg   Sodium: 2 mg   Dietary Fiber: 2 gm

Sparkling Peach Punch

Serves 10-12

5 cups puréed canned or fresh, ripe peaches
1 cup orange juice
1 cup peach nectar
1 Tablespoon fresh, peeled, and minced ginger
1 quart chilled sparkling water (about 4 cups)

Combine all ingredients in a large punch bowl. Chill with ice or refrigerate for 2 hours before serving.

Total Calories Per Serving: 58   Total Fat as % of Daily Value: 0%   Protein: 1 gm   Fat: 0 gm
Carbohydrates: 14 gm   Calcium: 9 mg   Iron: 0 mg   Sodium: 42 mg   Dietary Fiber: 1 gm

Autumn Apple Punch

Serves 12

1½ quarts apple juice or cider (about 6 cups)
2 cinnamon sticks
8 whole cloves
3 Tablespoons fresh sliced, peeled ginger
1½ cups pineapple juice
½ cup lemon juice
1 quart orange juice
4 cups sparkling water

Place all ingredients except sparkling water in a large pot. Bring to a fast boil, reduce heat, and allow punch to simmer for 5 minutes. Remove from heat, remove cinnamon, cloves, and ginger and cool. When punch is cool, stir in sparkling water and serve immediately.

Total Calories Per Serving: 18   Total Fat as % of Daily Value: 0%   Protein: 1 gm   Fat: 1 gm
Carbohydrates: 28 gm   Calcium: 23 mg   Iron: 1 mg   Sodium: 9 mg   Dietary Fiber: 1 gm

Sunshine Punch

Serves 20

1¹⁄₂ cups frozen, thawed lemonade concentrate
1¹⁄₂ cups frozen, thawed orange juice concentrate
2 teaspoons vanilla extract
2 teaspoons almond extract
5 quarts cold water (20 cups)
3 cups orange sorbet

Combine all ingredients in a large bowl or several pitchers. Mix well. Serve immediately, with ice or allow punch to chill for 2 hours before serving.

Total Calories Per Serving: 108	Total Fat as % of Daily Value: 0%	Protein: 1 gm	Fat: 0 gm
Carbohydrates: 26 gm	Calcium: 8 mg	Iron: 0 mg	Sodium: 2 mg	Dietary Fiber: 0 gm

Four Fruit Punch

Serves 6

This recipe contains no carbonation and no ice cream. This is our family's punch recipe. We serve it for all special occasions.

2 cups orange juice
2 cups lemonade
1 cup pineapple juice
1 cup grapefruit juice

Mix ingredients together. Chill and serve in a punch bowl.

Total Calories Per Serving: 113	Total Fat as % of Daily Value: 0%	Protein: 1 gm	Fat: 0 gm
Carbohydrates: 28 gm	Calcium: 42 mg	Iron: 1 mg	Sodium: 6 mg	Dietary Fiber: 0 gm

Sweet Lassi (Sweet Yogurt Drink)

Serves 3

2 cups vanilla soy yogurt
¹⁄₈ teaspoon black pepper
1 Tablespoon sugar
1 cup crushed ice

Place all ingredients in a blender and process until smooth. Serve immediately.

Total Calories Per Serving: 149	Total Fat as % of Daily Value: 4%	Protein: 4 gm	Fat: 3 gm
Carbohydrates: 26 gm	Calcium: 267 mg	Iron: 1 mg	Sodium: 18 mg	Dietary Fiber: 1 gm

Vegan Eggnog

Serves 8

One 10-ounce packages of silken regular or lowfat tofu (about 2¹/₂ cups)
2 cups vanilla soy or rice milk
1 Tablespoon vanilla extract
¹/₄ cup sugar
2 Tablespoons maple syrup
¹/₄ teaspoon turmeric (for yellow color)
¹/₂ to 1 cup rum or brandy (optional)
1 teaspoon nutmeg

In a blender or food processor canister, combine all ingredients except nutmeg; blend thoroughly. Pour into pitcher or individual glasses. Allow eggnog to chill for at least 1¹/₂ hours before serving. Garnish each serving with nutmeg.

Total Calories Per Serving: 128   Total Fat as % of Daily Value: 3%   Protein: 4 gm   Fat: 2 gm
Carbohydrates: 14 gm   Calcium: 38 mg Iron: 1 mg   Sodium: 36 mg   Dietary Fiber: 1 gm

Ice Cream Soda

Serve 1

This beverage needs to be made right before they are to be consumed, as they rapidly lose their fizz.

1 Tablespoon orange juice concentrate
¹/₄ cup sorbet or vegan ice cream (flavor of your choice)
³/₄ cup (6 ounces) sparkling water or seltzer

You'll need a chilled, 8-ounce (1 cup) glass and an ice cream scoop. Place the orange juice concentrate in the bottom of the glass and top with sorbet. Quickly add sparkling water (watch out for the froth) and serve immediately.

Notes: If you have the freezer space, you can add the concentrate and sorbet to glasses and keep them cold until ready to add the "bubbles." If you'd like to have a soda bar, set up the ingredients in the order listed, and have the guests assemble their own.

Total Calories Per Serving: 81   Total Fat as % of Daily Value: 0%   Protein: 0 gm   Fat: 0 gm
Carbohydrates: 20 gm   Calcium: 6 mg   Iron: 0 mg   Sodium: 1 mg   Dietary Fiber: 0 gm

Italian Soda

Serves 1

¹/₄ cup crushed ice
¹/₂ cup rice milk
¹/₄ cup juice or nectar (your choice of flavor)
¹/₂ cup sparkling water

Put ice in a chilled 10-ounce (1¼ cups) glass. Fill halfway with rice milk. Fill remainder of glass with juice and sparkling water. Serve immediately.

Note: Assemble these as you would an ice cream soda, right in front of your guests.

Total Calories Per Serving: 89   Total Fat as % of Daily Value: 2%   Protein: 0 gm   Fat: 1 gm
Carbohydrates: 9 gm   Calcium: 104 mg   Iron: 0 mg   Sodium: 45 mg   Dietary Fiber: 0 gm

Strawberry Lemonade
Serves 6

2 cups fresh lemon juice
4 cups of cold water
2 cups fresh or frozen strawberries
4 Tablespoons sugar (or more, is desired)

Place all ingredients in a blender and process until smooth. Serve immediately.

Variation: This works well with fresh or frozen raspberries.

Total Calories Per Serving: 66   Total Fat as % of Daily Value: 0%   Protein: 1 gm   Fat: 0 gm
Carbohydrates: 17 gm   Calcium: 17 mg   Iron: 0 mg   Sodium: 18 mg   Dietary Fiber: 1 gm

Hot Drinks

Hot Cranberry Punch
Serves 6

2 cups cranberry juice
2 cups orange juice
½ cup sugar
1 cup water
1 Tablespoon lemon juice
1 cinnamon stick

Combine all of the ingredients in a large microwave-safe bowl. Microwave on HIGH for 8 minutes or until mixture boils. Alternately, you can boil all the ingredients on the stove for 3 minutes. Remove from heat, remove cinnamon stick, and serve hot.

Total Calories Per Serving: 148   Total Fat as % of Daily Value: 0%   Protein: 1 gm   Fat: 0 gm
Carbohydrates: 37 gm   Calcium: 12 mg   Iron: 0 mg   Sodium: 3 mg   Dietary Fiber: 0 gm

Spiced Cider

Serves 8

1 gallon apple juice
4 cinnamon sticks
4 whole cloves
4 Tablespoons sliced, peeled fresh ginger

Warm apple juice by placing in a large pot on the stove and bringing to a simmer, or place in a large, clean coffee urn. When juice is warm, add cinnamon, cloves, and ginger and allow cider to simmer for 10 minutes. Serve warm, being careful not to serve the whole spices.

Total Calories Per Serving: 250   Total Fat as % of Daily Value: 2%   Protein: 1 gm   Fat: 1 gm
Carbohydrates: 62 gm   Calcium: 89 mg   Iron: 3 mg   Sodium: 20 mg   Dietary Fiber: 3 gm

Party Hot Cocoa

Serves 4

4 cups plain or vanilla soy or rice milk
2 cups water
4 Tablespoons unsweetened cocoa powder
3 Tablespoons sugar
½ teaspoon vanilla extract
Dash of cinnamon

Heat milk and water in a small saucepan (if using soymilk, whisk briskly to avoid curdling). Add cocoa, sugar, and vanilla; stir until smooth. Sprinkle with cinnamon and serve hot.

Variation: For a mocha cocoa, use 2 cups of brewed coffee in place of the water.

Total Calories Per Serving: 185   Total Fat as % of Daily Value: 8%   Protein: 12 gm   Fat: 5 gm
Carbohydrates: 25 gm   Calcium: 93 mg   Iron: 5 mg   Sodium: 135 mg   Dietary Fiber: 4 gm

Chai Masala

Serves 4

1 Tablespoon fresh grated ginger (or more, if you like it "hot")
4 cups water
4 black tea bags
1 teaspoon ground cinnamon
1 teaspoon cloves
1 teaspoon whole cardamon pods
½ teaspoon nutmeg
½ teaspoon ground black pepper
½ cup soymilk
4 Tablespoons sugar

Fill saucepan or pot with water and add ginger and bring to boil. Add tea and spices and simmer for 5 minutes or longer, depending on how flavorful you like your tea (you can simmer for as long as 20 minutes without hurting the brew, although 10 minutes will give you a pretty strong flavor). Then remove cardamom and simmer again until very dark, about 8 minutes. Remove from heat, and whisk in soymilk and sugar. Return to heat and bring to boil to bring out flavor. Turn off heat. Strain, if desired, and serve hot or chilled.

Total Calories Per Serving: 74   Total Fat as % of Daily Value: 1%   Protein: 2 gm   Fat: 1 gm
Carbohydrates: 16 gm   Calcium: 17 mg   Iron: 1 mg   Sodium: 24 mg   Dietary Fiber: 1 gm

Cinnamon Hot Chocolate

Serves 5

8 Tablespoons unsweetened cocoa powder
4 Tablespoons brown sugar
1 Tablespoon cinnamon
5 cups chocolate soy or rice milk

In a medium-size pot, mix together cocoa, brown sugar, and cinnamon until well combined. Add 1-2 Tablespoons of milk and stir thoroughly to make a paste. Add the rest of the milk and stir until smooth. Warm over very low heat for 10-20 minutes, stirring; the longer you stir, the thicker and smoother it gets. Serve hot.

Note: If you use soymilk, you'll need to stir briskly so it does not curdle.

Total Calories Per Serving: 185   Total Fat as % of Daily Value: 8%   Protein: 8 gm   Fat: 6 gm
Carbohydrates: 28 gm   Calcium: 33 mg   Iron: 5 mg   Sodium: 33 mg   Dietary Fiber: 6 gm

Orange Berry Herbed Tea

Serves 5

3 cups water
4 herbal tea bags
1/4 cup fresh orange slices
1 cup cranberry juice
1/2 cup sliced or frozen, thawed strawberries or raspberries

Pour water into a medium-size pot and bring to a boil. Add tea bags and oranges and steep for 2 minutes. Add juice and remove from heat. Allow tea to steep for 5 minutes. Remove tea bags. Add berries and allow tea to steep for 1 minute.

To serve, place a slice or orange and some berries in heated cups, pour hot tea over garnish, and serve immediately.

Total Calories Per Serving: 37   Total Fat as % of Daily Value: 0%   Protein: 0 gm   Fat: 0 gm
Carbohydrates: 9 gm   Calcium: 9 mg   Iron: 0 mg   Sodium: 3 mg   Dietary Fiber: 0 gm

Chapter 7: FRUIT DESSERTS AND FROZEN DESSERTS

Everyone is always after us to eat more fruit. How better to include more servings of fruit and fruit juice on the menu than in fruit desserts. With lots of fresh, frozen, and dried products available, fruit desserts are quick and convenient to prepare and look beautiful on the plate. Fruit desserts can take the place of high-fat desserts, offering flavor and texture in place of sugar and fat.

Remember that fruit desserts can only be as good as the ingredients you select. Use fresh fruit in season, such as strawberries, pineapple, oranges, grapefruit, kiwi fruit, berries, and pears. Switch to frozen or canned versions out-of-season. Frozen mango and papaya chunks can be added in small amounts to give an everyday fruit salad a bit of a kick.

Handle fresh or frozen thawed fruit with care to ensure the maximum in flavor, color and nutrition. Here are some fresh fruit handling tips:

- Always wash the exterior of fruit before cutting, even if you are going to peel it.
- Prepare the fruit as close to serving as possible. Try to capture all the juice from cutting and add the juice to the fruit salad. To prevent browning, squeeze lemon or lime juice on the fruit.
- If you need to work ahead, cover the fruit tightly with plastic wrap or put it in an airtight container. Store it in the coolest part of the refrigerator.
- When buying ready-cut fruit salad, check dates.
- Store cut fruit in plastic or glass. There may be some interaction between the natural acid in fruit and metals.

Fruit Salads

Fruit salad is about simplicity. Handle fruit as little as possible and prepare as close to serving time as you can. If you are preparing a fruit salad with dressing, add the dressing just before serving to avoid a soggy salad. Fruit salad should always be kept cold to prevent colorless or tasteless salads. If you are using canned fruit, chill it before adding to fresh fruit salads.

Citrus salads are refreshing. Use fresh oranges and pink or red grapefruit in season to create salads "with zest." First, zest several oranges and grapefruit and put the zest in a bowl. Segment the oranges and grapefruit, catching the juice to add to the salad. Try to remove as much of the membrane between the segments as possible, as this may be bitter. If the citrus is not sweet enough, add orange juice concentrate or a sweetener.

Think about using fruit salad as a base for a cold entrée. Chilled fruit salad with soy yogurt dressing makes a cool summer breakfast entrée. Pear and apple salad with crumbled soy cheddar cheese and walnuts makes a refreshing luncheon entrée. Try a sweet fruit and pasta salad, using canned peaches or frozen mango cubes, citrus segments, and bowtie pasta as the base, tossed with cinnamon and maple syrup.

Dress up a fruit salad with a blend of purple or white grape juice, rice syrup, and lemon juice; a purée of bananas, maple syrup, and lemon juice; or a more elaborate combination of whipped silken tofu topping, orange juice concentrate, and orange marmalade.

If fresh fruit is not in season, create a cooked fruit salad. Stew dried fruit combinations, such as dried plums (formerly known as prunes!), raisins, and apricots with peeled and diced fresh apples. Flavor the stewed fruit with apple or orange juice, cinnamon, and orange zest. Serve hot or cold on its own or as a topping for sliced cake or sorbet.

Do you have to make fruit salad for a large crowd? Try the following idea to minimize labor while impacting flavor. Combine diced canned or frozen peaches and mandarin orange segments with their juice along with raisins, fresh or canned pineapple chunks, frozen mango or papaya chunks, and dried apricots, dried plums, dried cranberries, or dried apple pieces. Refrigerate for at least 2 hours to allow the dried fruit to plump up. Right before serving, add in fresh or frozen, thawed sliced strawberries or blueberries or kiwi fruit segments. This can be served on its own or topped with sorbet or another vegan frozen dessert.

Fresh berries served chilled on their own or with sorbets are easy and fast to assemble. Pair strawberries with orange sorbet. Or pair blueberries or raspberries with lemon or strawberry sorbet. If you have extra berries, purée them with a small amount of orange juice or apple juice concentrate and use as a dessert sauce.

Melon can be sliced, wedged, or balled, served chilled on its own, soaked in white wine, or sprinkled with fresh orange or lemon zest. Serve a trio of melon slices studded with a chiffonade (finely shredded or cut as thin as possible) of fresh mint or sprinkled with berries. Create your own honeydew or watermelon sorbet by puréeing melon with a small amount of fruit juice concentrate or fruit liqueur and freezing it in individual serving dishes.

Frost grapes, strawberries, or melon balls by moistening grapes with water or apple juice before freezing; berries and melons have sufficient natural moisture. Simply place fruit in a single layer on a baking sheet (use parchment paper) and allow to cool in the freezer until frosty but not frozen. Serve as soon as removed from the freezer.

Fresh peaches, plums, and apricots can be cut and sprinkled with orange zest and orange juice concentrate and allowed to marinate overnight in the refrigerator. Serve garnished with raisins and nuts or use as part of a sorbet sundae. If there's room on the grill, wrap peach or apricot halves seasoned with cinnamon and ginger in foil, and allow the fruit to cook until just tender. Use as a "fire and ice" dessert with sorbet or soy ice cream.

Frozen Desserts

What could be more luscious, more decadent, more comforting, more refreshing, and more indulgent than frozen dessert? If you will be offering a simple scoop, you'll want some sauce to pretty up the plate. This can be a simple fruit coulis. Purée fruit, such as fresh or frozen strawberries, raspberries, or blueberries. If needed, sweeten with a small amount of orange juice concentrate. Chocolate sauce is a popular ice cream treat, made simply by melting vegan chocolate chips in the microwave or on top of the stove. If you'd like a thick chocolate sauce, simply melt the chips; for a thinner sauce, stir in a small amount of water. If you would like a dignified sauce for your ice cream, go with the classics. A melba sauce is traditionally made with raspberries, currant jelly, and kirsch (a liqueur resembling schnapps). For an updated version, you can use apricot glaze or preserves to replace the currant and jelly and omit the kirsch.

When is the last time you had a banana split? It was probably too long ago! We bet your guests are thinking the same thing. Offer mini-splits, with sliced bananas and a dab of chocolate, strawberry, and pineapple sauce, topped with chopped nuts, served in a small sundae glass or a brandy snifter. Or go for the whole banana, served in a classic split bowl or a soup plate. For an adult spin, offer mint or chocolate liqueurs as one of the toppings. Or go for broke and flambe (douse the dessert in a small amount of brandy or liqueur and to set it on fire). A grown-up version of the banana split, bananas foster, is a New Orleans tradition. Bananas are flamed at the table with brown sugar and orange liqueur and served over French vanilla ice cream. You can make a vegan version with orange juice concentrate, brown sugar, and just enough vodka to "flame" the dessert.

Offer sorbets for a light texture and flavor. A spectacular presentation is an apple or lemon sorbet served in a red Delicious apple shell. Apples are hollowed, and the shells and tops are retained. To create the sorbet, the apple pulp is puréed with Calvados (apple brandy) or apple juice concentrate. The sorbet is then spooned into apple shells, the tops are placed back on, and the whole fruit is frozen for at least an hour. Served in a brandy snifter or cut glass bowl, the apples glisten and the flavor is breathtaking.

Sorbets can be part of a frozen fruit salad entrée, served with chilled seasonal fruit and frosted grapes or berries. To frost grapes, wash and dry them well, dip in powdered vegan sugar (see Chapter 2 for recipe) and freeze for several minutes.

Vegan frozen desserts are all good candidates for "a la mode," served on top or on the side of freshly baked pies, layer cakes, cookie assortments, sliced seasonal fruit, hot-from-the-kitchen doughnuts, or cream puffs and éclairs.

Even lighter than sorbet are fruit ices. Remember enjoying a popsicle™ on a hot day? Why not offer your guests healthy versions of that childhood favorite with lime and raspberry, espresso and soy cream, or blueberry and Champagne popsicles™?

Frozen Dessert Toppings

A scoop of sorbet, fruit ice, or vegan ice cream starts a wonderful dessert with the addition of one or two toppings. Choose from the following:

fresh/frozen berries	flavored syrups	sliced bananas
shredded coconut	canned fruit	flavored vegan whipped cream
malt powder	crumbled cookies	chocolate, carob, or peanut butter chips
crystallized ginger	crunchy peanut butter	crumbled plain or chocolate-covered pretzels
pie filling	chopped nuts	

FRUIT DESSERT RECIPES

Cranberry Waldorf Salad

Serves 8

1¹⁄₂ cups fresh or frozen, thawed cranberries
2 cups sugar
2 cups cored, not peeled, diced red apples
¹⁄₂ cup chopped celery
¹⁄₂ cup seedless red grapes, halved
¹⁄₂ cup chopped walnuts
¹⁄₄ cup vegan mayonnaise

In food processor canister, coarsely chop cranberries, and then stir in sugar. Cover and chill 4 hours. Drain cranberries for about 2 hours, reserving liquid for another use. In a large bowl, stir together remaining ingredients and gently stir in drained cranberries.

Note: This salad is not too sweet. It would be a good addition to a dessert table with a lot of cookies, cakes, and other sweet desserts. This salad can also be used as an accompaniment to cooked entrées.

Total Calories Per Serving: 269   Total Fat as % of Daily Value: 7%   Protein: 0 gm   Fat: 5 gm
Carbohydrates: 58 gm   Calcium: 7 mg   Iron: 0 mg   Sodium: 48 mg   Dietary Fiber: 2 gm

Fruit Salad with Yogurt Dressing
Serves 10

2 cups cored, chopped apples (not peeled)
2 cups peeled and chopped oranges
1¹⁄₂ cups sliced bananas
1 cup cored, peeled, and chopped pears
¹⁄₂ cup frozen, thawed blueberries
¹⁄₂ cup chopped peaches or apricots
1 cup drained pineapple chunks
¹⁄₂ cup shredded coconut
¹⁄₂ cup finely chopped walnuts
¹⁄₄ cup maple syrup
2 cups strawberry soy yogurt

Combine all fruit in a large bowl. In a small bowl, combine coconut, walnuts, syrup, and yogurt, and mix well. Toss fruit and dressing. Refrigerate for at least 2 hours before serving.

Total Calories Per Serving: 195   Total Fat as % of Daily Value: 9%   Protein: 3 gm   Fat: 6 gm
Carbohydrates: 35 gm   Calcium: 113 mg   Iron: 1 mg   Sodium: 8 mg   Dietary Fiber: 4 gm

Pear and Date Salad with Mint
Serves 8

3 Tablespoons olive oil
1 Tablespoon balsamic vinegar
1 Tablespoon fresh lemon juice
2 Tablespoon maple syrup
3 cups torn Romaine lettuce
¹⁄₂ cup minced fresh mint
3 seeded, cored, and diced ripe pears
2 cups peeled, chopped fresh oranges or peaches
¹⁄₂ cup chopped dates

In a small bowl, combine oil, vinegar, juice, and syrup until well blended.

To assemble salad, arrange Romaine on a serving platter or on individual plates. Top Romaine with a thin layer of mint, then pears, then oranges or peaches, and finish with dates. Just before serving, drizzle on dressing, or serve dressing on the side.

Total Calories Per Serving: 172   Total Fat as % of Daily Value: 9%   Protein: 2 gm   Fat: 6 gm
Carbohydrates: 33 gm   Calcium: 65 mg   Iron: 1 mg   Sodium: 10 mg   Dietary Fiber: 6 gm

Fruit Salad with Citrus-Cilantro Dressing
Serves 10

3 cups canned, drained pineapple chunks
3 cups peeled and chopped red grapefruit
2 cups sliced fresh or frozen, thawed strawberries
1½ cups mango pieces (frozen, thawed or fresh)
½ cup orange juice
⅓ cup lime juice
3 Tablespoons chopped fresh cilantro
2 Tablespoons orange juice concentrate

Combine pineapple, grapefruit, strawberries, and mango in a large serving bowl; set aside.

In a small pot, combine orange juice, lime juice, and cilantro. Bring to a boil, reduce heat, and simmer for 5 minutes. Strain and discard cilantro. Stir in concentrate.

Allow dressing to cool. Pour over fruit mixture and toss until evenly coated.

Total Calories Per Serving: 85   Total Fat as % of Daily Value: 0%   Protein: 1 gm   Fat: 0 gm
Carbohydrates: 22 gm   Calcium: 32 mg   Iron: 1 mg   Sodium: 3 mg   Dietary Fiber: 3 gm

Main Dish Fruit Salad
Serves 8

½ cup vegan mayonnaise
1 Tablespoon lemon juice
2 teaspoons sugar
2 cups sliced bananas
1½ cups cantaloupe or honey dew chunks
½ cup diced peaches or apricots
1 cup pineapple chunks
1 cup seedless grapes
1 cup sliced fresh or frozen, thawed strawberries
1½ cups cubed watermelon
3 cups flavored soy yogurt (your choice)
Mandarin orange segments to garnish

In a bowl combine mayonnaise, lemon juice, and sugar; stir well and set aside. In another bowl combine all fruit.

To serve, toss fruit salad with dressing, portion onto individual serving dishes, top with yogurt, and garnish with mandarin oranges.

Total Calories Per Serving: 258   Total Fat as % of Daily Value: 17%   Protein: 4 gm   Fat: 11 gm
Carbohydrates: 36 gm   Calcium: 166 mg   Iron: 1 mg   Sodium: 101 mg   Dietary Fiber: 3 gm

Blueberry and Pasta Fruit Salad

Serves 10

1 pound frozen vegan tortellini or mini vegan ravioli
1 cup frozen, thawed blueberries
1 cup sliced fresh or frozen, thawed strawberries
1½ cups mandarin orange segments, drained
1 cup sliced green grapes
¼ cup sliced almonds
½ cup prepared creamy-style salad dressing

Cook pasta, drain, and allow to cool. In a large bowl, add pasta and salad ingredients. Pour dressing over salad and toss lightly. Refrigerate for at least 2 hours before serving.

Total Calories Per Serving: 205   Total Fat as % of Daily Value: 9%   Protein: 1 gm   Fat: 6 gm
Carbohydrates: 34 gm   Calcium: 25 mg   Iron: 2 mg   Sodium: 419 mg   Dietary Fiber: 3 gm

Pineapple Boat

Serves 6-8

1 fresh pineapple (about 1½ pounds)
2 fresh oranges
4-5 bananas, peeled and sliced (about 3 cups)
1 cup fresh or frozen, thawed blueberries

Begin by thoroughly washing the outside of the pineapple. Lay the pineapple down on a large plate or cutting board with the top facing you. With a large sharp knife, cut the pineapple in half from the bottom to the top so that each half has half of the green leafy top.

Using a curved grapefruit knife, cut around the inside of one of the pineapple halves about ³/₄ inch from the outside, being careful not to cut through the skin of the pineapple. Then cut the inside into 4 or 5 lengthwise wedges, being careful not to cut through the skin. Begin removing the wedges from both sides of the pineapple, using the knife to release any pineapple that was not cut through. Then slide the knife under the center wedges to loosen them. Cut the wedges into bite-sized pieces and place them in a large mixing bowl along with any juice. Repeat with the other half.

Wash and peel the oranges, separate into sections, cut the sections into bite-sized pieces, and add to the mixing bowl. Peel and slice the bananas and add to the mixing bowl. Add the blueberries and mix all the fruit together. Spoon the fruit back into the hollowed out pineapple halves, so that it is mounded above the pineapple. Serve and enjoy!

Note: If the pineapple boat fruit salad is being prepared for the main course, plan on one pineapple half for each person. For a side dish or dessert, one pineapple half can serve up to 4 people.

Total Calories Per Serving: 141   Total Fat as % of Daily Value: 0%   Protein: 2 gm   Fat: 0 gm
Carbohydrates: 36 gm   Calcium: 37 mg   Iron: 1 mg   Sodium: 2 mg   Dietary Fiber: 5 gm

Avocado Fruit Salad

Serves 8

4 ripe avocados
4 ripe bananas
4 navel oranges
4 ripe pears
¹/₂ cup (or less) vegan mayonnaise

Peel and slice avocados and fruit and place in a mixing bowl. Add several spoons of mayonnaise, just to moisten and stir mixture together. Chill for at least 1 hour before serving.

Total Calories Per Serving: 366   Total Fat as % of Daily Value: 35%   Protein: 3 gm   Fat: 23 gm
Carbohydrates: 41 gm   Calcium: 48 mg   Iron: 1 mg   Sodium: 93 mg   Dietary Fiber: 12 gm

Minted Fruit Salad

Serves 6

¹/₂ cup unsweetened apple juice
¹/₂ cup each cored and sliced red apple and green apple
1¹/₂ cups cored and sliced ripe pears
1 cup peeled and sliced oranges
1 cup peeled and sliced bananas
2 Tablespoons chopped fresh mint

Place the apple juice in a large bowl and add the remaining ingredients. Toss gently so all the ingredients are coated with the juice. Cover and chill for at least 1 hour before serving.

Total Calories Per Serving: 79   Total Fat as % of Daily Value: 0%   Protein: 1 gm   Fat: 0 gm
Carbohydrates: 20 gm   Calcium: 21 mg   Iron: 0 mg   Sodium: 1 mg   Dietary Fiber: 3 gm

Summer Fruit Salad

Serves 6

2 cups of any of the following: seedless watermelon, honeydew, cantaloupe, cut into ³/₄-inch chunks
2 cups of any of the following: peaches, nectarines, plums, pears, cut into bite-size chunks
2 cups of any of the following: cherries (pitted), blueberries, raspberries, blackberries, strawberries, gooseberries
3 Tablespoons fresh lime juice
2 Tablespoons sugar or to taste

Place fruit in a glass or plastic serving bowl and toss gently to combine. Chill for at least 1 hour. Whisk lime juice and sugar together in a small bowl and pour over fruit before serving. Toss to combine.

Total Calories Per Serving: 85   Total Fat as % of Daily Value: 0%   Protein: 1 gm   Fat: 0 gm
Carbohydrates: 22 gm   Calcium: 14 mg   Iron: 1 mg   Sodium: 1 mg   Dietary Fiber: 2 gm

Grilled Fresh Fruit Kebobs with Ginger and Mint

Serves 10

Marinade:
½ cup rum or orange juice mixed with 1 teaspoon rum extract
2 Tablespoons maple syrup
2 Tablespoons fresh lemon juice
1 teaspoon minced fresh ginger

Kebobs:
8 green apples, cored, peeled, cut into 10 pieces each
8 ripe pears, cored, peeled, cut into 10 pieces each
8 small bananas, peeled and sliced into 10 pieces each
1 medium cantaloupe or small honeydew, seeded, peeled, and cut into chunks (or use a melon baller to create balls)
1 medium fresh pineapple, peeled, cored, top off, and cut into 1-inch chunks (about 2½ cups)
10 red seedless grapes or small fresh strawberries, washed

Dip:
2 cups plain or lemon-flavored soy yogurt
2 Tablespoons maple syrup
1 Tablespoon minced fresh ginger
1 Tablespoon minced fresh mint

Prepare marinade by mixing all marinade ingredients in a plastic or glass bowl together until well combined. Place apples, pears, bananas, melon, and pineapple in the marinade. Allow kebobs to marinate in the refrigerator for at least 1 hour.

While fruit marinates, prepare dip by mixing all dip ingredients together until well combined. Place dip in a serving bowl and refrigerate until needed.

Remove fruit from marinade and retain marinade. Preheat broiler or heat barbecue grill. Assemble kebobs by threading one type of each fruit on 10 skewers.

Place the kebobs in a shallow pan, and top with marinade. Broil or grill quickly, about 3-4 four minutes, just until the fruit gets the slightest bit soft. Remove from heat.

Thread grapes or strawberries onto each skewer. Serve by arranging kebobs on a platter, with the dipping sauce in the middle.

Total Calories Per Serving: 332   Total Fat as % of Daily Value: 2%   Protein: 4 gm   Fat: 2 gm
Carbohydrates: 75 gm   Calcium: 121 mg   Iron: 1 mg   Sodium: 19 mg   Dietary Fiber: 9 gm

Puff Pastry Apple Flower
Makes 8 apples

3 boxes (1 pound or 16 ounces) vegan frozen puff pastry or phyllo dough
6 small red apples
¹/₄ cup sugar
4 Tablespoons ground cinnamon
6 Tablespoons melted vegan margarine
3 cups lemon sorbet (if desired, for garnish)

Preheat oven to 400 degrees. Measure each apple (with a tape measure, or with your eye). You will need to cut eight sheets of dough for each apple. Each sheet should be 3-4 inches wider than the apple, to form petals. Cuts sheets and set aside.

Core each apple, but do not cut all the way through. If you like, you can cut small patterns into the top of the apple, as the top will show through the pastry. Some people like to cut tiny triangles, resembling flower petals.

Combine sugar, cinnamon, and margarine in a small bowl. Place a baking rack on a solid baking sheet. Place each apple upside down on the rack, leaving space for the pastry dough. Brush each pastry sheet with margarine mixture. One at a time, wrap eight pastry sheets, with side containing margarine placed towards the apple, around the apple, alternating placement, so the corners do not meet. Place in oven and bake until pastry sheets are just golden brown, about 20 minutes.

Remove from oven, and turn over gently, placing on serving platter or on individual dessert plates. If desired, serve with a small scoop of sorbet. Serve immediately.

Total Calories Per Serving: 319   Total Fat as % of Daily Value: 18%   Protein: 4 gm   Fat: 12 gm
Carbohydrates: 50 gm   Calcium: 53 mg   Iron: 3 mg   Sodium: 366 mg   Dietary Fiber: 5 gm

Maple-Baked Pears with Raspberries
Serves 6-8

3 Tablespoons apple juice
1 Tablespoon fresh lemon juice
2 Tablespoons maple syrup
1 Tablespoon apple juice concentrate
1 teaspoon fresh lemon zest
¹/₂ teaspoon powdered ginger
3-4 ripe pears
1¹/₂ cups fresh or frozen (thawed) raspberries
2 Tablespoons shaved vegan dark chocolate (optional)

Preheat oven to 375 degrees. Combine apple and lemon juice, maple syrup, concentrate, zest, and ginger in a small bowl and mix well. Pour mixture in a shallow baking pan that is long enough to accommodate 6-8 pear halves. Cut pears in half and remove seeds and stems. Place pear halves, cut side down, onto juice mixture. Bake for 12-15 minutes, until pears just begin to soften. Turn pear halves over and bake another 5-7 minutes, or until fork-tender.

Remove from oven. Place pear halves on a serving platter or on individual plates. Drizzle with juice mixture from bottom of baking pan. Just before serving, top with raspberries and chocolate (if desired).

Total Calories Per Serving: 91   Total Fat as % of Daily Value: 0%   Protein: 1 gm   Fat: 0 gm
Carbohydrates: 23 gm   Calcium: 21 mg   Iron: 1 mg   Sodium: 3 mg   Dietary Fiber: 5 gm

Baked Apples with Vegan Oatmeal Cookie Topping
Serves 4

Vegetable oil spray
2 pounds granny smith apples or other baking apples (4 medium apples)
¼ cup raisins
2 Tablespoons maple syrup
1 Tablespoon lemon juice
10 vegan oatmeal cookies (see recipe on page 63 or packaged oatmeal cookies)
½ cup apple or pineapple juice

Preheat the oven to 350 degrees. Spray an 8 x 8-inch dish with oil.

In a large bowl, mix together the raisins, maple syrup, and lemon juice. Peel and very thinly slice the apples. After each apple is sliced, add it to the bowl and stir with the wet ingredients. Once all the apples are added to the bowl, mix well and pour into the oiled baking dish. Crumble the vegan oatmeal cookies over the apples and distribute evenly. Slowly pour the juice over the cookie topping. Bake for 40 minutes.

Total Calories Per Serving: 336   Total Fat as % of Daily Value: 10%   Protein: 5 gm   Fat: 7 gm
Carbohydrates: 68 gm   Calcium: 40 mg   Iron: 1 mg   Sodium: 143 mg   Dietary Fiber: 7 gm

Frozen Fruit Salad
Serves 8

6 ounces vegan cream cheese
3 Tablespoons vegan mayonnaise
1 cup drained, crushed pineapple
2 cups drained fruit cocktail
1 cup small-cubed, drained extra-firm tofu
2 cups sliced bananas
1 cup vegan Devon cream (see page 60 for recipe)

Cream cream cheese and mayonnaise together in a large bowl. Mix in pineapple, fruit cocktail, tofu, and bananas. Fold in Devon cream.

Pour into 8 x 8-inch freezer-safe pan or several small pans (do not use metal). Cover with plastic and freeze for at least 3 hours. Serve frozen, cut into squares.

Total Calories Per Serving: 181   Total Fat as % of Daily Value: 13%   Protein: 3 gm   Fat: 9 gm
Carbohydrates: 22 gm   Calcium: 18 mg   Iron: 1 mg   Sodium: 154 mg   Dietary Fiber: 2 gm

FROZEN DESSERT RECIPES

Basic Vegan Soy Ice Cream
Makes approximately 3 cups

You'll need the following equipment for this recipe: blender or food processor and a home ice cream machine (manual, freezer-type or electric).

1 cup soy yogurt (flavor of your choice)
1³/₄ cups soymilk
¹/₃ cup maple syrup
2 teaspoons vanilla extract

Combine all ingredients in a blender or food processor canister and blend until smooth. Blend in any desired flavoring ingredients (see below). Pour into an ice cream machine, and freeze following the manufacturer's instructions.

Variations: For various flavors, add to the food processor:
For Peach or Apricot Soy Ice Cream, blend in 1 cup well-drained, chopped canned peaches or apricots
For Banana Soy Ice Cream, blend in 2 cups mashed bananas
For Strawberry Soy Ice Cream, blend in 1 cup frozen, partially thawed strawberries (not fresh). This works well with frozen, partially thawed blueberries as well.
For Pineapple Soy Ice Cream, blend in 1 cup of well-drained pineapple tidbits.
You can also use vanilla or chocolate soymilk, or add vanilla, almond, or orange extract to plain soymilk with this recipe.

Total Calories Per Serving: 243	Total Fat as % of Daily Value: 6%		Protein: 9 gm	Fat: 4 gm
Carbohydrates: 43 gm	Calcium: 212 mg	Iron: 3 mg	Sodium: 91 mg	Dietary Fiber: 2 gm

Vegan Ice Cream Cake
Serves 8-10

Two 10-ounce containers of soy ice cream (flavors of your choice)
1 package vegan chocolate snaps cookies (about 10-12 ounces)

Let the soy ice cream soften at room temperature; only let it soften so it is workable. You don't want it to melt. Crumble the cookies by hand or in a food processor.

Line a large mixing bowl with plastic wrap. Empty one ice cream container into the bowl and spread out the ice cream so it forms a two-inch layer on the bottom and up the sides of the bowl. Sprinkle half the cookie crumbs on this layer. Empty the second ice cream container on top of the crumbs and press down to form a thick, flat layer. Sprinkle the remaining crumbs. Cover and allow cake to freeze for at least an hour.

When you are ready to serve, invert your container onto a serving plate, and you have a two-layer ice cream cake with chocolate crumbs in the center and on the bottom. If you would like, make extra crumbs and sprinkle on top.

Variations: This can be made with a variety of cookie crumbs and vegan ice cream or sorbet flavors. We enjoyed:

Ginger snaps with orange sorbet
Ginger snaps with strawberry vegan ice cream
Ginger snaps with raspberry sorbet
Chocolate snaps with chocolate vegan ice cream
Chocolate snaps with raspberry sorbet
Chocolate snaps with peanut butter vegan ice cream

Total Calories Per Serving: 246   Total Fat as % of Daily Value: 11%   Protein: 0 gm   Fat: 7 gm
Carbohydrates: 41 gm   Calcium: 0 mg   Iron: 1 mg   Sodium: 112 mg   Dietary Fiber: 2 gm

Strawberry Ice Cream with Cashews
Makes 4 cups

You will need a juicer, blender, and ice cream maker to prepare this recipe.

1¼ pounds fresh, organic strawberries, hulled
1 cup young coconut water (drained right from a fresh coconut)
½ cup cashews or cashew pieces
¾ cup packed pitted dates

Run the strawberries through a juicer to make about 2 cups juice. If you don't get 2 cups, add water, more strawberries, or orange juice to make up the difference.

Combine the coconut water and cashews in a blender. Blend on high until smooth. With the motor running, gradually add the strawberry juice and dates and blend until smooth. Place the mixture in the freezer for 40 minutes or in the refrigerator for 4 hours.

Pour the mixture into an ice cream maker and freeze according to the manufacturer's instructions. Serve immediately or transfer to airtight containers and store in the freezer until ready to serve.

Total Calories Per Serving: 308   Total Fat as % of Daily Value: 20%   Protein: 7 gm   Fat: 13 gm
Carbohydrates: 47 gm   Calcium: 61 mg   Iron: 3 mg   Sodium: 68 mg   Dietary Fiber: 7 gm

Strawbery-Citrus Granita with Mint
Serves 6

1½ cups frozen strawberries
2 cups crushed ice
⅓ cup sugar
4 fresh mint leaves, minced
½ cup fresh lemon juice (see note)

Place all ingredients in a blender or food processor canister and process until combined. Serve immediately or place in individual serving dishes and freeze until ready to serve.

Note: When squeezing fresh lemon juice, carefully cut the lemons in half. After juicing, scoop out remaining pulp. Using lemon halves as serving dishes, spoon granita into lemon halves and freeze.

Variation: This can also be done with orange juice and orange halves.

Total Calories Per Serving: 59   Total Fat as % of Daily Value: 0%   Protein: 0 gm   Fat: 0 gm
Carbohydrates: 15 gm   Calcium: 8 mg   Iron: 0 mg   Sodium: 5 mg   Dietary Fiber: 1 gm

Chocolate Tofu Ice Cream
Makes 6 cups

³/₄ cup sugar
¹/₂ cup water
2 cups vegan chocolate chips
1¹/₂ pounds silken tofu (about 3¹/₂ cups)
1¹/₂ cups soy or rice milk
2 Tablespoons vanilla extract

Place the sugar and water in a small pot and simmer for 5 minutes to thoroughly dissolve and form a syrupy consistency. Remove the pot from the heat and set aside.

Place the chocolate chips in the top of a double boiler (over simmering water) and allow the chocolate chips to melt (or you can melt the chips in a microwave). Set aside.

In a food processor canister, process the tofu to a smooth purée. Add the syrup mixture, melted chocolate chips, milk, and vanilla, and process for 1-2 minutes or until very smooth and creamy. Taste and add additional sugar or vanilla, if desired.

If you have an ice cream maker, transfer the mixture to the ice cream maker and freeze according to the manufacturer's instructions. Or pour the mixture into a large shallow pan and place it in the freezer. Stir the mixture every hour or so to give it a smooth texture. When completely frozen, remove it from the freezer and allow it to sit at room temperature for 15 minutes. Transfer the mixture to a food processor, process until smooth, and transfer the mixture to an airtight container. Return it to the freezer and freeze until solid.

Total Calories Per Serving: 391   Total Fat as % of Daily Value: 23%   Protein: 10 gm   Fat: 15 gm
Carbohydrates: 54 gm   Calcium: 129 mg   Iron: 3 mg   Sodium: 68 mg   Dietary Fiber: 3 gm

Cranberry Sorbet
Makes about 6 cups

1¹/₂ pounds fresh or frozen, thawed cranberries (about 4 cups)
3 cups apple juice
2 cups water
1¹/₄ cups sugar
3 Tablespoons lemon juice

In a medium-size pot, place the cranberries, apple juice, and water, and cook the mixture over low heat for 3-4 minutes or until cranberries begin to "pop." Remove the pot from the heat. Pass the mixture through a sieve that is placed over a bowl, pressing on the mixture with the back of a spoon to separate the pulp from the skins. Discard the skins, add the remaining ingredients to the cranberry purée, and stir well to combine.

Pour the mixture into an ice cream maker and freeze according to the manufacturer's instructions.

If an ice cream maker is not available, place sorbet mixture in a plastic container, cover, and chill for 3-4 hours or until partially frozen. Process sorbet mixture in a blender or food processor canister. Return the mixture to the plastic container, cover, and freeze 3 additional hours. Repeat the processing procedure, transfer back to the plastic container, cover, and freeze until solid.

Total Calories Per Serving: 232   Total Fat as % of Daily Value: 0%   Protein: 0 gm   Fat: 0 gm
Carbohydrates: 60 gm   Calcium: 12 mg   Iron: 1 mg   Sodium: 10 mg   Dietary Fiber: 1 gm

Pineapple-Orange Sorbet
Serves 6

2 cups canned, crushed pineapple
1¹/₂ cups mashed bananas
2 cups orange juice
1 teaspoon vanilla extract

Drain the crushed pineapple and reserve the juice. Line a large casserole with plastic, and spread the drained pineapple evenly over the plastic. Top the pineapple with the bananas. Cover and place the casserole in the freezer for several hours or until fruit is thoroughly frozen.

In a blender or food processor canister, combine the frozen fruit, reserved pineapple juice, and the remaining ingredients, and blend until smooth. Serve immediately in chilled glasses.

Total Calories Per Serving: 113   Total Fat as % of Daily Value: 0%   Protein: 1 gm   Fat: 0 gm
Carbohydrates: 28 gm   Calcium: 19 mg   Iron: 0 mg   Sodium: 2 mg   Dietary Fiber: 2 gm

Coconut-Cinnamon Frozen Dessert
Serves 6

3 cups soy or rice milk
1³/₄ cups lowfat coconut milk
³/₄ cup sugar
¹/₃ cup apple juice
1 teaspoon vanilla extract
1 Tablespoon cinnamon
¹/₄ teaspoon nutmeg

In a large bowl, whisk together all ingredients. If you have an ice cream maker, transfer the mixture to the ice cream maker, and freeze according to the manufacturer's instructions. Or pour the mixture into a large shallow pan and place it in the freezer. Stir the mixture every hour or so to give it a smooth texture. When completely frozen, remove it from the freezer, and allow it to sit at room temperature for 15 minutes. Transfer the mixture to a food processor, process until smooth, and transfer the mixture to an airtight container. Return it to the freeze and freeze until solid.

Total Calories Per Serving: 204   Total Fat as % of Daily Value: 10%   Protein: 4 gm   Fat: 7 gm
Carbohydrates: 43 gm   Calcium: 230 mg   Iron: 2 mg   Sodium: 64 mg   Dietary Fiber: 1 gm

Peppermint and Chocolate Frozen Dessert

Makes 7 cups

1 quart soy or rice milk
2 cups cold, brewed peppermint tea
1 cup maple syrup
3 Tablespoons agar-agar flakes
1 teaspoon vanilla extract
1¹/₂ cups vegan chocolate chips

Place all of the ingredients, except the chocolate, in a large pot and simmer over low heat for 5-7 minutes, stirring to thoroughly dissolve the agar-agar flakes. Remove from heat and set aside to cool.

Freeze the mixture in an ice-cream maker per machine instructions. When partially frozen, add in chocolate chips. Transfer to an airtight container and keep frozen until ready to serve.

If an ice cream maker is not available, pour the mixture into a large shallow pan, and place in the freezer. Stir the mixture every hour or so to give it a smooth texture. When completely frozen, remove it from the freezer, and allow it to sit at room temperature for 15 minutes. Transfer the mixture to a food processor and process until smooth. Transfer the mixture to an airtight container and fold in the chocolate. Return the mixture to the freezer and freeze until solid.

Note: Agar-agar comes from seaweed and can be found in most Asian markets, especially Chinese, Thai, and Japanese, at Seventh-day Adventist stores (some churches with large Adventist populations have stores), in Whole Foods, and some gourmet stores, such as Bristol Farms. Some baking supplies shops may stock it as well.

Total Calories Per Serving: 300   Total Fat as % of Daily Value: 14%   Protein: 4 gm   Fat: 9 gm
Carbohydrates: 52 gm   Calcium: 245 mg   Iron: 2 mg   Sodium: 61 mg   Dietary Fiber: 2 gm

Section 2 ❦ Appetizers / Party Food

Introduction to Appetizers and Party Food

Appetizers are versatile menu items. A party meal can consist of a large variety of hot and cold appetizers. This allows your serving area to fill with a wonderful variety of colors and aromas. Guests can create the meal of their dreams, and serving is a snap. A few assorted types of appetizers paired with beverages covers the refreshments for short receptions or get-togethers.

Appetizers are meant to perk up the taste buds. They are small in size but big in flavor. Not originally meant to be a meal, many people are electing to have appetizer and desert receptions during holidays and celebrations. Appetizers allow guests to select the types and amounts of food they care to eat, as well as offering an opportunity to move about and speak to a large number of the other guests.

Remember to keep service as simple as possible. Plan the menu so the guests don't have foods that have to be cut or are awkward to eat while standing. Offer foods that will hold up well for several hours while people graze. The chapters in this section will give you ideas for a wide range of appetizers and wonderful party food. Here is some background information to get your education started.

Canapés: Canapés, bite-sized open-faced sandwiches, are the perfect palette for international vegetarian flavors. Use different breads and spreads to represent various parts of the world. Pita, tortillas, or phyllo dough cut into small "puffs," polenta squares grilled or roasted, Lebanese cracker bread, blinis (small buckwheat pancakes, traditionally served with sour cream), and Norwegian flat bread are just some of the breads you can use to carry a variety of savory vegan spreads. Think about focaccia with rosemary, oregano, and garlic oil; polenta (baked corn meal) squares with sun-dried tomatoes; tortillas with shredded vegan cheese; or mini bagels with cucumber and dill vegan cream cheese and thinly sliced smoked tofu. To top canapés, use flavored vegan cream cheese, unflavored yogurt or sour cream with cilantro, chilies, capers, sweet onions, soy sausage or smoked tofu, smoked mushrooms, pimientos, cornichons (spicy, small pickles from France), and olives.

Middle Eastern Dips: Hummus is a Middle Eastern and Mediterranean cold sauce/dip made with mashed garbanzo beans, tahini (sesame seed paste), garlic, lemon juice, olive oil, and cayenne. You can prepare your own or purchase premade hummus. Several companies are offering flavored hummus, adding roasted peppers, roasted garlic, olives, and other savory flavors. Babaganoujh is prepared like hummus, using roasted eggplant purée instead of garbanzos. Both can be made lower fat than traditional dips made with vegan sour cream or mayonnaise and are still creamy and spicy. Eggplant caviar is made by first roasting eggplant until they are almost puréed. Then mix the roasted eggplant with sautéed onions, peppers, and garlic. Serve these dips as toppings for canapés, as dips for vegetables and breads, or as ingredients for layered dips (recipes in future chapters).

Turnovers: Every country seems to have a version of the savory turnover. Boreks are spinach and cheese pies made with phyllo. Calzone are miniature stuffed pizzas. Empanadas and samosas are small savory fried potato and vegetable pies. Whatever you call them, they are easy and economical to make, requiring a savory filling and rolled out dough that is quickly filled and baked or fried. They can be made ahead of time and cooked off as needed.

<u>Asian Finger Food</u>: Vegetable tempura, vegan egg rolls, and spring rolls are fast to make and do well on reception tables. You can make your own tempura batter and not use eggs. Think about using green beans, carrots, sweet potatoes, mushrooms, zucchini, and peppers for tempura. Egg rolls are fried and spring rolls are usually steamed, but they can share the same fillings. Make sure you purchase vegan wrappers. Offer a variety of dipping sauces, including miso, soy sauce, hot sauces flavored with chilies and ginger, and mustards.

<u>Central American Fare</u>: Central American flavors are always popular and can be used to enliven mild appetizers. Different types of salsa, such as salsa verde made with tomatillos and green chilies or roasted mango chili, can be offered on crudite (crunchy vegetable) platters for color and flavor. Mini enchiladas, quesadillas, or chiles rellenos also add color and crunch to holiday receptions.

<u>Cheese Platters</u>: To segue away from savory appetizers to sweet, offer sliced vegan cheese platters with accompanying fresh fruit, dried fruit, and nuts. Cheese platters can serve as both appetizers and desserts. There are several types of soy cheeses that slice nicely for buffets.

<u>Vegan Meatballs</u>: Every country seems to have a meatball recipe and everyone seems to like meatballs. They are an easy and economical item that can be made ahead of time and frozen until ready to use. Meatballs stand up well to extended periods of heat on the serving line. To make a basic meatball "international," serve with Indonesian or Indian curry sauce, Swedish "cream" sauce, Thai style with sweet and sour sauce, or Mexican with roasted chili and cilantro sauce. We have included several "neatball" recipes in Chapter 13.

<u>Rumaki</u>: Rumaki, traditionally made with chicken livers, water chestnuts, and bacon, is a popular holiday appetizer. Nobody seems to know the origin of this appetizer that combines disparate ingredients, but it has stood the test of time. Prepare vegan rumaki with tempeh, water chestnuts, and vegan bacon strips. In recent years, there have been rumaki variations, including the addition of a sliver of pineapple, vegan shrimp or scallops in place of the liver, and macadamia nuts instead of water chestnuts.

<u>Sushi</u>: Sushi has become very popular and seems to be on every buffet table. Check with a local natural foods store, such as Whole Foods, rather than preparing vegan sushi yourself. Of course, if you have the time, you might want to attend one of the many sushi academies that have sprung up all over the country. Be sure to have wasabi (a powered, spicy plant that resembles watercress and grows in riverbeds) and pickled ginger on hand. Depending on available ingredients or time, sushi combinations of nori (dried seaweed wrapper), sushi rice, and a filling of chopped smoked tofu and vegan cream cheese or romaine, sushi rice, and slivered cucumbers hold up well.

<u>Salads</u>: For salads, keep it simple and savory. For example, toss roasted beets with greens and orange segments and a drizzle of olive oil. Layer a Caprese salad, with fresh basil leaves, thinly sliced tomatoes, thinly sliced vegan mozzarella, and a splash of balsamic vinegar.

A great big bowl of salad can be a centerpiece for your appetizer party or serve salads in individual edible bowls of taco shells, hollowed bread, or tomato shells. Here are some more appetizer salad ideas:

- baby lettuces with soy cheese strips, black olives, almonds, tomatoes, and chopped Tofurky™
- mixed greens with grapes, pears, pistachios, nutritional yeast, and dried cranberries
- romaine and raddichio topped with broiled or grilled tofu or seitan, red onions, peppers, and tomatoes
- salad greens with black beans, corn, tomatoes, onions, and vegan soy cheese
- salad greens with soy bacon bits, shredded carrots, hearts of palm, and beets
- fresh spinach with balsamic-marinated strawberries, pecans, and oranges

Sandwiches: In a sandwich, vegetables should be included as part of the team. The idea is to create a pleasing combination, using vegetables as flicks of flavor, added texture, and spectrums of color. Add a mild sandwich filling and fantastic bread, and you've got a great sandwich.

For example, take a thick piece of crusty whole wheat bread, add a slice or two of vegan deli slices, and top with grated raw red and yellow beets and carrot, shredded cucumbers, and sweet Vidalia onion. Top with a small amount of mashed garlic, several dashes of a mild vinegar, and chopped walnuts. You can replace the bread with a tortilla. Roll up with filling and toppings, and finely shredded salad greens. How about finely diced avocado and fresh tomato on a baguette, flavored with a squeeze of fresh lime juice, chopped green onions, and sunflower seeds? This can also be rolled into a tortilla. Focaccia bread has structure, flavor, and a hearty texture. Pile it high with grated, shredded, and chopped vegetables and your favorite salad dressing for an open-faced delight. If you'd like your focaccia to go really Mediterranean, add tapenade (an olive and garlic spread). For cool focaccia, use shredded cucumbers, tomatoes, shredded spinach, and fresh mint, along with a spread of lemony, garlicky hummus.

Burgers: If the weather is prime for firing up the grill, add vegan burgers to the appetizer menu. You can prepare regular-size burgers and cut them in quarters to serve as appetizers. Think about appetizer burgers topped with:

- garlic-sautéed mushrooms
- wild mushrooms sautéed in wine with sesame seeds
- vegan bacon bits, onion rings, and mango salsa
- pineapple and jerk seasoning
- teriyaki sauce, pineapple, and tomatoes
- sautéed onions and peppers

Better Than Sliced Bread

Sandwiches are all about the bread and the condiments; here are some ideas to get you started.

Bread: pita, ciabatta, focaccia, baguette, oat-wheat, onion-herb, sour dough, tomato-basil, poblano chili, garlic-sesame

Condiments: sun-dried tomato spread, Dijon mustard (combine with favorite salad dressings), wasabi horseradish, cranberry sauce or relish, chutneys, cilantro-lime vegan mayonnaise, creamy horseradish (grated horseradish combined with vegan sour cream or mayonnaise), or sweet onion relish

To Add to Sandwich Fillings:
- roast or grilled sliced seitan with roasted red onions and pickles
- roasted onions with vegan bacon bits
- sautéed mushrooms and corn
- raw shredded beets, summer squash
- roasted eggplant slices
- fresh spinach tossed with orange juice and vinegar
- chopped artichoke hearts
- mashed avocado
- chopped fresh chilies
- sliced roasted vegetables
- sun-dried tomatoes
- sprouts of all kinds

Some Combo Ideas:
- portabello mushrooms with onions, peppers, romaine, and tomato
- teriyaki tofu with lettuce, tomatoes, red onions, and olives
- spicy seitan with chili-mayonnaise, tomatoes, and shredded carrots
- Tofurky™ with chilies, olives, cucumbers, onions, and greens

Chapter 8: CRISPY AND CRUNCHY APPETIZERS

Fresh fruit and vegetables are probably about the most luscious foods around; however, humans do not live by juicy tomatoes slices or succulent peaches alone! Sometimes we crave a little crunch or just want something that's not in season. That's when fruit and vegetable chips come in. Contrary to popular opinion, potatoes are not the only veggie around that can be "chipped." If it can be sliced and dried, a fruit or vegetable can be made into a crunchy, tasty chip. Why risk burns and extra calories from deep-frying when you can bake/dry crispy party snacks?

We have had great success "chipping" the following:
Vegetables: sweet potatoes, yams, beets, carrots, turnips, winter squash, onions, and of course, potatoes (besides the white variety, we have tried Yukon golds and Peruvian purples)
Fruit: apples (all varieties), pears, peaches, plums, apricots, and (with a little patience) strawberries
More Exotic: salsify (a root veggie which resembles a white carrot), celery root (the bulbous root of the celery plant), Jerusalem artichoke, portobello mushrooms, lotus root, daikon radish, taro root, fennel (also called sweet anise), ginger root, and horseradish (for flavoring only; eating horseradish chips on their own could be dangerous!).

You can chip your fruit several different ways, depending on the equipment you have on hand and the amount of time you have. Our favorite (because it takes the least amount of time and equipment and gives a crisp chip) is using a hot (475 degrees or higher) oven. You can also use a dessicator (a drying oven), an outdoor barbecue, or natural sunlight.

For the oven method, simply preheat your oven to 475 degrees (500 is even better if you can do that without switching over to "broil"). Have baking sheets available that are either lined with parchment or sprayed lightly with oil. Wash and thoroughly dry the fruit or vegetable. You can leave the peel on or off, as you prefer. Just note, if the peel is on, it will toughen a bit, giving two textures to the chip (the interior flesh will be crisp and the exterior peel will be chewy). Slice the fruit or vegetable as thinly as possible, then place single-file on the sheet (no overlaps). Bake until the chips are crisp. This can take from 8-15 minutes depending on what fruit or vegetable you are using and how hot and consistent your oven is. If you have a convection oven (forced air), the "chipping" should go more quickly.

Using the dessicator or the sun method will give more of a chewy treat rather than a true chip. With the dessicator, slice the fruit or vegetable as thinly as possible, place on desiccating trays, and allow drying. If you have the time and the space to do the natural sun method, you would place thin slices of fruit or vegetables on clean screens and allow drying in the sun (the same method used commercially to produce raisins and sun-dried tomatoes). The dessicator method can take from several hours up to a day, depending on your equipment. The sun method can take several days. Remember that you will need to be able to keep your drying produce away from "natural" invaders, like animals and insects. And be sure to check the weather forecast before you set out to "chip" the natural way. Rain showers can wipe out the whole crop. Both the dessicator and the natural method will probably require that you turn your chips at least once to guarantee uniform drying.

For those of you that like to play with fire, thinly slice your produce of choice, place it on a tray of fine screening (or make a tray with several layers of foil) and place it on the barbecue grill (or in a smoker). You'll have to turn the chips to allow for the unevenness of the heat, but you get a really unique flavor.

No matter which method you choose, remember that thinness is the key. The thinner the slice, the crisper or dryer your chip will be. Thick slices will result in a soggy product.

If making chips and crispy snacks for a party, be sure to plan ahead. Some require at least overnight cooking. Which ever way you make your chips, you will need to store them in a dry place in an airtight container. If stored properly, they should retain their crispness for about a week. We usually layer them between paper towels or cheesecloth in airtight tins or plastic bags to maintain maximum crispness.

Vegetable chips can be flavored with dried herbs or spices. Fill a paper bag with carrot or beet chips; add some garlic powder, onion powder, and white pepper and shake until the chips are all coated. Use the same technique with potato or onion chips, using chili powder. Fruit chips can be flavored with ground cinnamon, ginger, nutmeg, mace, cocoa powder, and dried orange or lemon zests. Don't flavor the chips until right before you are ready to serve them.

If you can get past the snacking phase, use fruit chips to top cobblers or crisps, in granola or cold cereal, or to garnish rice puddings or sorbet. Vegetable chips can be crumbled on top of casseroles and cooked vegetables or grains, used as a garnish for soups, or used instead of croutons in salads.

As hard as we tried, we could not come up with a successful banana "chip" unless we used a lot of oil. However, if you have any need for banana "flakes," simply bake thin banana slices as per directions for apple chips.

If you have extra bagels, you can make bagel chips. Very carefully slice any variety of bagel into $1/4$-inch slices. Lay the slices on an ungreased baking sheet. Lightly spray each bagel slice with vegetable oil spray and sprinkle with your choice of herbs or seasoning salts on top. Suggested toppers include garlic powder, dried parsley, onion powder, dried oregano, cayenne, or cinnamon. Toast in a 350-degree oven for 9-12 minutes or until crisp and light brown.

Chips That Don't Add to Your Hips

- Bake-frying can be used to cook any type of chip, not just tortilla chips. For extra flavor, spray the chips lightly with oil before baking. The resulting fat grams are negligible.

- Boost chip flavor by sprinkling chips with spices, such as ground cumin or coriander, or dried herbs, such as oregano or basil.

- For a colorful presentation, use both yellow and blue corn tortillas. Blue corn tortillas are available at most supermarkets; you may even be able to find red (tomato) and green (spinach) tortillas.

- Wedges of pita bread make good chips. Lightly spray them with olive oil and sprinkle with salt, pepper, and dried herbs or cumin.

Chips and More

Need to assemble party appetizers in a hurry? Learn how to use the "open and pile" method, as follows: open a bag of baked tortilla chips and pile on a microwaveable dinner plate. Open a can of vegetarian refried beans and pile on top of the chips (spread them around so they're evenly distributed.). If you've got some sliced olives, pile them on top of the beans. Open a bag of vegan sliced cheese, crumble, and pile on top of the olives. Place your creation in the microwave and microwave on HIGH for 2 minutes or until the cheese is melted and the beans are hot.

This works with any kind of chip, so think pita chips or veggie chips. You can find red, green, and blue tortilla chips, as well as flavored bagel chips. If you have a little more time and some leftover beans, you can mash them instead of using the canned refried beans. If you'd like more crunchiness, purchase a bag of chopped onions or fresh salsa in the produce section of your market.

Another variation on this theme would be using canned, drained artichokes (packed in brine or water, not marinated), and croutons instead of chips for the base. Top with a small amount of vegan mayonnaise, then shredded vegan cheese, olives or garbanzo beans, and canned drained tomatoes. Microwave as above. If a microwave is not available, preheat the oven to 400 degrees, place your goodies in an ovenproof pie pan or a shallow casserole, and bake for 5-10 minutes or until the dish is heated through.

Quick Dips

You'll probably want to have some dip ingredients for last minute party appetizers.

To create sweet dips, have on hand:
>   peanut butter, soy butter, or other nut butters
>   apple butter
>   ripe bananas
>   raisins or dried cranberries
>   orange juice concentrate
>   (optional) fresh or frozen, thawed strawberries

To make savory dips, you'll want:
>   soy sour cream, unflavored soy yogurt, or silken tofu
>   canned or cooked garbanzo beans or white beans
>   prepared salsa or canned chopped tomatoes
>   fresh bell pepper (any color)
>   fresh parsley

You'll need ingredients with which to dip. Here are some suggestions.

Sweet:
>   pretzels
>   fresh apples or pears
>   fresh pineapple
>   fresh grapes
>   fresh strawberries
>   frozen whole strawberries
>   dried apple, mango, pineapple, and papaya slices

Savory:
>   fresh or dried breadsticks
>   tortillas
>   baked tortilla chips or veggie chips
>   pita bread
>   bagels
>   fresh veggies, such as carrots, radishes, cherry tomatoes, celery, jicama, cucumbers, zucchini, and even fresh corn in season (doesn't have to be cooked, just washed)
>   wedges of hot or cold baked potatoes make good dip-ees

To make a quick sweet vegetarian dip:
Place a small amount of nut butter or apple butter in a mixing bowl. Stir to soften. In a separate bowl, mash a banana with berries and/or orange juice concentrate. Combine banana with nut butter and mix until well combined. You can add in chopped nuts, chopped dates, crumbled cold cereal, or fresh berries, depending on customer preference.

To make a quick savory dip:

Place soy yogurt, vegan sour cream, or tofu in a blender or food processor canister. Add a small amount of salsa or drained canned tomatoes, canned beans, some chopped bell peppers (or fresh chili, for heat), and parsley. Blend until smooth. Chill for 10 minutes prior to serving.

Fast and Crunchy Popcorn

Popcorn is festive, filling, and easy to make. Whether air-popped, microwaved, or popped in your fireplace, you can season popcorn for a tasty crowd pleaser. You'll want to premix you flavorings and place them in a bowl big enough for you to toss the popcorn in. Toss the popcorn while it's hot, even if you are serving it later, so the flavor can permeate all the popcorn. Here are some ideas, working with about 6 cups of popped popcorn (about $1^1/_2$ cups unpopped popcorn):

1. Red Hot Chili Popcorn: Combine 2 Tablespoons chili powder, 1 teaspoon red pepper flakes, and $^1/_2$ teaspoon garlic powder in a large bowl
2. Holiday Sweet Spice Popcorn: Combine 2 Tablespoons ground cinnamon, 1 teaspoon ground ginger, 2 teaspoons sugar, and $^1/_2$ teaspoon ground nutmeg
3. Curry Popcorn: Combine 2 Tablespoons curry powder, 1 teaspoon ground cumin, and $^1/_4$ teaspoon dry mustard
4. Pizza Popcorn: Combine 2 Tablespoons garlic powder, 1 teaspoon red pepper flakes, 1 teaspoon dried basil, and 1 teaspoon dried oregano
5. Power Punch Popcorn: Combine 2 Tablespoons nutritional yeast, 2 teaspoons dried parsley, and 1 teaspoon onion powder

APPETIZER RECIPES

Herb Mix for Vegetable Chips

Makes $^1/_2$ cup

Store this mix in an airtight container.

2 Tablespoons dill weed
2 Tablespoons dried oregano
2 Tablespoons dried sage
2 teaspoons dried thyme
2 teaspoons garlic powder

Combine all ingredients until well mixed. Store in an airtight container. Shake to mix before using.

Total Calories Per 1/2 Cup Mix: 88   Total Fat as % of Daily Value: 3%   Protein: 4 gm   Fat: 2 gm
Carbohydrates: 19 gm   Calcium: 404 mg   Iron: 13 mg   Sodium: 18 mg   Dietary Fiber: 9 gm

Herb Mix for Fruit Chips

Makes $^1/_2$ cup

This mix enhances the natural sweetness of the fruit.

2 Tablespoons cinnamon

Colorful Fruit Parfaits
Page 81

Hot Veggie Pizza Squares
Page 166

2 Tablespoons ground nutmeg
2 teaspoons ginger powder
1 teaspoon clove powder
1 teaspoon mace
1 teaspoon sugar

Combine all ingredients until well mixed. Store in an airtight container. Shake to mix before using.

Total Calories Per 1/2 Cup Mix: 153   Total Fat as % of Daily Value: 10%   Protein: 2 gm   Fat: 7 gm
Carbohydrates: 27 gm   Calcium: 215 mg   Iron: 7 mg   Sodium: 13 mg   Dietary Fiber: 12 gm

Apple or Pear chips
Serves 8

Use fruit at the height of ripeness for wonderful flavor.

3 large apples or pears, peeled and thinly sliced
2 teaspoons cinnamon
2 teaspoons ginger powder

Preheat oven to 450 degrees. Place fruit slices on baking sheets that have been lined with parchment or non-stick pans. Be sure that fruit does not touch (single-file placement). Bake until fruit is crispy, about 8 minutes in a convection oven or up to 15 minutes in a conventional oven.

Remove fruit from oven, sprinkle lightly with cinnamon and ginger. Allow to cool, then store between sheets of paper towels in an airtight container.

Note: The same method can be used for ginger chips, omitting the seasonings, using $3/4$ cup sliced, peeled ginger root. Use ginger chips as a (very) spicy snack or as a garnish for baked goods or to "heat" up granola or trail mix.

Total Calories Per Serving: 30   Total Fat as % of Daily Value: 0%   Protein: 0 gm   Fat: 0 gm
Carbohydrates: 8 gm   Calcium: 10 mg   Iron: 0 mg   Sodium: 0 mg   Dietary Fiber: 1 gm

Carrot or Beet Chips
Serves 8

These veggies can be baked with or without seasoning.

2 cups thinly sliced, peeled carrots or beets (raw)
1 Tablespoon onion powder
1 teaspoon white pepper

Preheat oven to 450 degrees. Place veggie slices on baking sheets that have been lined with parchment or non-stick pans, being sure that veggies do not touch. Bake until veggies are crisp, about 5 minutes in a convection oven or up to 10 minutes in a conventional oven. Remove from oven; sprinkle lightly with onion powder and pepper. Allow chips to cool, then store between sheets of paper towels in an airtight container.

Total Calories Per Serving: 17   Total Fat as % of Daily Value: 0%   Protein: 0 gm   Fat: 0 gm
Carbohydrates: 4 gm   Calcium: 15 mg   Iron: 0 mg   Sodium: 23 mg   Dietary Fiber: 1 gm

Strawberry or Apricot Chips
Serves 6

These are moist fruits, so they require a bit more attention and will give a chewier product. They won't be as pretty as apple chips, but the concentrated flavor more than makes up for it.

1¹/₂ cups thinly sliced fresh strawberries or pitted fresh apricots
2 teaspoons ginger powder

Preheat oven to 450 degrees. Carefully arrange fruit slices (you may have to prod them into uniform shapes, as the slicing may have smooshed some of the slices) on baking sheets, which are covered with parchment or are non-stick. Bake for 3 minutes, turn slices over, and allow chips to bake until dry (from 5-8 minutes depending on the amount of moisture in the fruit). Remove from oven, sprinkle with ginger, and allow cooling.

Total Calories Per Serving: 15   Total Fat as % of Daily Value: 0%   Protein: 0 gm   Fat: 0 gm
Carbohydrates: 4 gm   Calcium: 7 mg   Iron: 0 mg   Sodium: 1 mg   Dietary Fiber: 1 gm

Baked Sweet Potato Chips
Makes approximately 3¹/₂ cups

Here's a colorful alternative to white potato chips. Make a batch of each and combine.

3 large sweet potatoes or yams (about 1¹/₂ pounds)
Vegetable cooking spray
1 Tablespoon garlic powder

Preheat oven to 350 degrees. Peel sweet potatoes or yams and slice thin, as if for a thick potato chip. Cover a cookie sheet or baking pan with foil and spray lightly with vegetable spray. Lay sweet potato chips on the foil, rubbing each one slightly in the veggie spray. Then lightly spray the tops with veggie spray. Sprinkle evenly with garlic powder. Bake for 20 minutes, turn, sprinkle other side with garlic powder and bake for another 10 minutes. Remove from oven, allow chips to cool, and store in an air-tight container.

Total Calories Per Serving: 121   Total Fat as % of Daily Value: 0%   Protein: 3 gm   Fat: 0 gm
Carbohydrates: 28 gm   Calcium: 41 mg   Iron: 1 mg   Sodium: 72 mg   Dietary Fiber: 4 gm

Lowfat Potato Chips
Serves 6

1¹/₂ pounds scrubbed Idaho or russet potatoes
2 teaspoons malt or balsamic vinegar
¹/₂ teaspoon salt
¹/₂ teaspoon black pepper

Place oven rack in the center of oven. Preheat oven to 350 degrees. Slice potatoes very thinly and arrange directly onto oven rack in a single layer; bake until golden brown and crispy, about 8-10 minutes. Place in serving bowl and sprinkle lightly with vinegar, salt, and pepper.

Total Calories Per Serving: 89   Total Fat as % of Daily Value: 0%   Protein: 2 gm   Fat: 0 gm
Carbohydrates: 20 gm   Calcium:15 mg   Iron: 1 mg   Sodium: 394 mg   Dietary Fiber: 3 gm

Lower Fat Pasta Chips

Serves 24

1 pound uncooked lasagna noodles (whole wheat or spinach are fine)
2 teaspoons vegetable oil
¼ cup water
Vegetable oil spray
⅓ cup vegan grated Parmesan cheese
2 teaspoons each dried basil and dried oregano
2 teaspoons parsley flakes
1 teaspoon garlic powder

Cook noodles according to package directions, omitting salt. This is usually in 4 quarts of boiling water for 7-10 minutes or until soft. Drain well. Separate noodles carefully, laying them on a flat surface.

Preheat oven to 400 degrees. Combine oil and water in a small bowl; stir well and brush both sides of lasagna noodles. Spray a baking sheet with oil. Cut each noodle crosswise into 2-inch pieces and arrange in a single layer on baking sheet. Set aside.

In a small bowl combine Parmesan cheese, basil, oregano, parsley, and garlic powder; stir well. Sprinkle a small amount of the mixture on each chip. Bake for 10 minutes or until crisp and golden. Cool and store in an airtight container until ready to serve.

Total Calories Per Serving: 62   Total Fat as % of Daily Value: 0%   Protein: 2 gm   Fat: 0 gm
Carbohydrates: 15 gm   Calcium: 23 mg   Iron: 1 mg   Sodium: 22 mg   Dietary Fiber: 2 gm

Toasted Pita Chips

Serves approximately 6

Turn extra pita chips into party food; add your favorite savory spices to vary the flavor.

3 pita pockets
1 teaspoon garlic powder (optional)

Preheat oven to 325 degrees. Split each pita pocket in half. Cut each half into 6 triangles. Arrange in single layers on baking sheets. Sprinkle lightly with garlic powder, if desired. Bake chips for 8 minutes or until they are lightly browned and crisp. Store in airtight container until ready to serve.

Total Calories Per Serving: 83   Total Fat as % of Daily Value: 0%   Protein: 3 gm   Fat: 0 gm
Carbohydrates: 17 gm   Calcium: 26 mg   Iron: 0 mg   Sodium: 161 mg   Dietary Fiber: 1 gm

Baked Tortilla Chips

Serves 18-20

4 each yellow and blue 6-inch diameter corn tortillas
Vegetable oil spray
Salt and black pepper to taste

Preheat oven to 375 degrees. Cut each tortilla into 6 wedges. Arrange the wedges in a single layer on non-stick baking sheets. Lightly spray the chips with oil and sprinkle with salt and pepper. Bake the chips until lightly browned and crisp, about 10 minutes turning once. Be careful not to let them burn. Transfer the chips to a rack to cool.

Variation: To make cinnamon chips, toss sugar with ground cinnamon and sprinkle on chips instead of salt and pepper.

Total Calories Per Serving: 26   Total Fat as % of Daily Value: 0%   Protein: 1 gm   Fat: 0 gm
Carbohydrates: 5 gm   Calcium: 9 mg   Iron: 0 mg   Sodium: 5 mg   Dietary Fiber: 1 gm

Flavored Bagel Chips

Makes approximately 20 chips or 1 serving

Savory, crisp or crisp and mild, your choice!

2 plain, whole wheat, sesame, or poppy seed bagels
Vegetable oil spray
$\frac{1}{8}$ teaspoon each garlic powder and onion powder
$\frac{1}{8}$ teaspoon cumin
$\frac{1}{8}$ teaspoon oregano
$\frac{1}{8}$ teaspoon nutritional yeast

Preheat oven to 400 degrees. With a very sharp knife, carefully slice bagel into extremely thin slices. Place slices on an ungreased baking sheet. Lightly spray with cooking spray. Sprinkle with seasonings. Bake for 3-4 minutes until lightly browned. Be careful; they burn easily. Store in an airtight container for up to 3 days.

Total Calories Per Serving: 462   Total Fat as % of Daily Value: 5%   Protein: 18 gm   Fat: 3 gm
Carbohydrates: 91 gm   Calcium: 165 mg   Iron: 11 mg   Sodium: 798 mg   Dietary Fiber: 4 gm

Soynuts

Makes $1\frac{1}{2}$ cups or two $\frac{3}{4}$ cup servings

1 cup dry soybeans
Water to cover soybeans
Vegetable oil spray
Salt to taste (if desired)

Place soybeans in water and soak for 3 hours. Drain and pat dry.

Preheat oven to 350 degrees. Spray baking sheet with oil. Spread soybeans on the sheet in a single layer. Let soybeans cook for 30-40 minutes, stirring every 10 minutes. Nuts are done when they are golden and crispy. Remove from oven and, if desired, sprinkle with salt. Serve warm or cold.

Total Calories Per Serving: 387   Total Fat as % of Daily Value: 29%   Protein: 34 gm   Fat: 19 gm
Carbohydrates: 28 gm   Calcium: 258 mg   Iron: 15 mg   Sodium: 2 mg   Dietary Fiber: 9 gm

Chock Full Trail Mix

Makes about 5 cups or ten $1/2$ cup servings

1 cup cashew pieces
1 cup shelled peanuts
1 cup broken banana chips
1 cup vegan chocolate or carob chips
1 cup dried pineapple chunks
$1/2$ cup coconut flakes

Combine ingredients in a large mixing bowl. Store trail mix in an airtight container until ready to serve.
    Eat in moderation since this mix is high in fat.

Total Calories Per Serving: 347   Total Fat as % of Daily Value: 38%   Protein: 6 gm   Fat: 25 gm
Carbohydrates: 37 gm   Calcium: 24 mg   Iron: 2 mg   Sodium: 11 mg   Dietary Fiber: 5 gm

Spicy Sunflower Seed Mix

Makes 2 cups or four $1/2$ cup servings

Enjoy this unique snack mix.

1 cup hulled sunflower or pumpkin seeds
$1/4$ cup sesame seeds
3 Tablespoons Braggs Liquid Aminos, tamari, or soy sauce
1 Tablespoon water
$1 1/4$ teaspoons cumin
1 teaspoon cayenne

Soak sunflower/pumpkin and sesame seeds in Braggs and water mixed together for at least 2 hours. The seeds will start to plump.

    Stir in spices and spread evenly on a parchment lined or nonstick baking sheet. Bake in preheated 150-degree oven overnight.

    Cool completely on baking sheet and store in an airtight container. Eat in moderation since this mix is high in fat.

Total Calories Per Serving: 276   Total Fat as % of Daily Value: 37%   Protein: 12 gm   Fat: 24 gm
Carbohydrates: 9 gm   Calcium: 57 mg   Iron: 4 mg   Sodium: 761 mg   Dietary Fiber: 5 gm

Crunchy Roasted Beans

Makes 4 cups or eight $^1/_2$ cup servings

Turn extra beans into party food. These take at least 5 hours of preparation and cooking time.

6 cups uncooked soybeans or garbanzo beans
$^1/_2$ cup chunked celery
3 Tablespoons olive oil
2 Tablespoons curry powder

Soak beans in cold water for at least 2 hours. Drain and discard water. Place soaked beans in a large pot, add celery, and cook until soft, about 40-50 minutes. Drain and discard celery. Preheat oven to 200 degrees (a low oven). Spread olive oil evenly on a baking sheet. Roll the beans in the olive oil until well coated. Slowly roast the beans in the oven for 4-8 hours. Remove from the oven when crunchy. Toss in curry powder. Store roasted beans in an airtight container in the refrigerator for up to 14 days.

Total Calories Per Serving Using Soybeans: 226   Total Fat as % of Daily Value: 20%   Protein: 17 gm
Fat: 13 gm   Carbohydrates: 14 gm   Calcium: 133 mg   Iron: 8 mg   Sodium: 1 mg
Dietary Fiber: 5 gm

Total Calories Per Serving Using Garbanzo Beans: 192   Total Fat as % of Daily Value: 9%   Protein: 9 gm
Fat: 6 gm   Carbohydrates: 27 gm   Calcium: 44 mg   Iron: 3 mg   Sodium: 10 mg
Dietary Fiber: 8 gm

Crunchy Party Mix

Makes approximately 10 cups

Purchase cold cereal when it is on sale to use as party mix later.

1 cup Cheerios™ or oat cereal
4 cups your favorite vegan dry cereal
1$^1/_2$ cups pretzel sticks
2 cups unsweetened apple juice
1 Tablespoon soy sauce
$^1/_2$ teaspoon garlic powder
1 teaspoon onion powder
1 teaspoon dry parsley

In a large microwave-safe bowl, combine dry cereals, add pretzel sticks, and mix. In a separate bowl, combine apple juice, soy sauce, and seasonings. Brush $^1/_2$ of the liquid on the cereals and toss. Microwave 3 minutes on high. Stir and brush on $^1/_2$ of the liquid. Remove and let cool. Serve warm or cold.

Alternately, oven bake at 300 degrees for 30 minutes. At 15 minutes, stir and apply the remaining liquid. Cook the remaining 15 minutes or until the mix is a golden brown. Remove and let cool. Serve warm or cold.

Total Calories Per Serving (will vary): 143   Total Fat as % of Daily Value: 2%   Protein: 4 gm   Fat: 1 gm
Carbohydrates: 30 gm   Calcium: 18 mg   Iron: 4 mg   Sodium: 499 mg   Dietary Fiber: 2 gm

Spicy Garbanzo Snack

Makes approximately 2 cups or 2 servings

These are great as a party snack or as a garnish for salads, soups, and entrées.

2 cups canned, drained garbanzo beans
Vegetable oil spray
1 Tablespoon chili powder
1 Tablespoon cracked black pepper

Preheat oven to 400 degrees. Rinse garbanzos and pat dry. Spray baking sheet with oil. Place garbanzos on sheet and sprinkle with chili powder and pepper. Roll garbanzos around on sheet to coat. Place in oven for 15-20 minutes or until crunchy. Stir once half way through cooking. Serve hot or cold.

Total Calories Per Serving: 306   Total Fat as % of Daily Value: 5%   Protein: 13 gm   Fat: 3 gm
Carbohydrates: 58 gm   Calcium: 101 mg   Iron: 5 mg   Sodium: 757 mg   Dietary Fiber: 13 gm

Garlic and Herb Pretzels

Makes about 12 pretzels or 12 servings

Your guests will appreciate that you baked these pretzels.

2 packages of yeast
1¹/₂ cups warm water
1 teaspoon salt
1 teaspoon sugar
4-5 cups all-purpose flour
2 cloves garlic, crushed
1 Tablespoon dried basil
1 Tablespoon dried parsley
2 teaspoons salt

Preheat oven to 425 degrees. Dissolve yeast in water. Add salt, sugar, and 2 cups of the flour. Mix in crushed garlic and herbs. Add 2 cups more of the flour and keep adding until dough is no longer sticky. Roll into snakes and shape into pretzels. Bake for 10 minutes or until brown. Pretzels will be the consistency of bread when removed from the oven, and will harden over two or three days. Sprinkle with salt while still warm.

Total Calories Per Serving: 158   Total Fat as % of Daily Value: 0%   Protein: 5 gm   Fat: 0 gm
Carbohydrates: 33 gm   Calcium: 18 mg   Iron: 2 mg   Sodium: 583 mg   Dietary Fiber: 2 gm

Caraway and Rye Crackers

Makes about 10 very large crackers or 30 small crackers

2 cups rye flour
2 cups wheat flour
1 Tablespoon caraway seeds
1/2 cup olive oil
1/4 teaspoon baking soda
1 cup water
Flour (to coat preparation surface)

Preheat oven to 300 degrees. Combine all ingredients in a large bowl and mix well. Roll the mixture into a 1-inch thick sheet on a cold, lightly floured surface to prevent sticking. Cut into shapes using cookie cutters or use a knife to cut desired shape. Bake on ungreased baking sheets for 30 minutes or until golden.

Total Calories Per Large Cracker: 264	Total Fat as % of Daily Value: 18%	Protein: 5 gm	Fat: 12 gm
Carbohydrates: 36 gm	Calcium: 14 mg	Iron: 1 mg	Sodium: 1 mg	Dietary Fiber: 4 gm

Roasted Red Pepper Crostini

Serves approximately 24

1 French baguette (about 24 inches long)
1 Tablespoon olive oil
30 pitted black olives
1 cup roasted and seed red bell peppers cut into thin strips (or you can purchase canned whole pimientos)
1/3 cup chopped fresh tomatoes
3 cloves garlic, chopped
2 teaspoons olive oil
1/4 teaspoon kosher or coarse salt
1/4 teaspoon black pepper
1/8 teaspoon sugar
1/4 cup minced fresh parsley

Preheat oven to 450 degrees. Cut baguette into 24 slices and brush with olive oil; place on ungreased baking sheet. Bake for 5-6 minutes or until lightly browned. Remove from oven and set aside. In a food processor, combine olives, peppers, tomatoes, garlic, olive oil, salt, pepper, and sugar. Process briefly; you want the mixture to be chunky. Spread mixture onto baguette slices. Arrange on serving platter. Garnish with fresh parsley.

Note: You can make this recipe a day in advance and assemble the day of the party.

Total Calories Per Serving: 107	Total Fat as % of Daily Value: 4%	Protein: 3 gm	Fat: 3 gm
Carbohydrates: 18 gm	Calcium: 35 mg	Iron: 1 mg	Sodium: 313 mg	Dietary Fiber: 1 gm

Eggplant Frisbees

Serves 6-8

The young at heart will enjoy this fun finger food dish. For a spicier (and smaller) version, use Asian eggplant.

4 cups (one medium) eggplant, peeled, sliced ¼ inch thick
Vegetable oil spray
½ cup grated vegan cheese
¼ cup wheat germ
¼ cup sunflower seeds
⅛ cup minced onion

Preheat oven to 350 degrees. Spray baking sheet with vegetable oil spray. Place in oven and allow baking sheets to heat for 1 minute. Place eggplant on sheets and lightly brown eggplant slices on both sides (you'll probably need to turn the slices one time for even browning). Sprinkle cheese, wheat germ, sunflower seeds, and onion on top of each eggplant slice. Bake eggplant for 3 minutes or until cheese is melted. Serve eggplant immediately on its own, or with salsa or hummus.

Total Calories Per Serving: 96   Total Fat as % of Daily Value: 5%   Protein: 3 gm   Fat: 4 gm
Carbohydrates: 9 gm   Calcium:94 mg   Iron: mg   Sodium: 132 mg   Dietary Fiber: 3 gm

Sweet Treats

Kettle Corn

Serves approximately 8-10

Kettle corn is a combination of sweet and salty. It's a little tricky to prepare, but it's worth the effort.

½ cup vegetable oil
2 cups unpopped popcorn kernels
½ cup sugar
Salt to taste

Heat oil in a large pot with a lid. When oil is hot, add kernels. When the first kernel pops, carefully add sugar and stir. Put the top on the pot and turn down the heat. Shake constantly. Pay attention to the heat, as you want to pop the corn without burning the sugar or your fingers.

When all the corn is popped, quickly shake on salt and serve. Serve this hot or warm. When it cools, it gets sticky and soggy.

Total Calories Per Serving: 417   Total Fat as % of Daily Value: 25%   Protein: 8 gm   Fat: 17 gm
Carbohydrates: 62 gm   Calcium: 5 mg   Iron: 3 mg   Sodium: 5 mg   Dietary Fiber: 9 gm

Granola

Makes about 5 cups or 5 servings

Add your favorite dried fruit to create your own "signature" granola.

Vegetable oil spray
3 cups old-fashioned oats (not quick oats)
1 cup unsweetened corn flakes
$1/2$ cup toasted wheat germ
$1/4$ cup chopped almonds
1 teaspoon cinnamon
$1/2$ teaspoon nutmeg
$1/2$ teaspoon salt
$1/2$ cup apple juice concentrate
$1/2$ cup molasses
1 teaspoon vanilla extract
$1^1/2$ cups dried fruit (apple slices, peaches, apricots, figs, etc.)

Preheat oven to 300 degrees. Coat 2 baking sheets with oil spray. Place oats in a large bowl and sprinkle with enough water to dampen. Add corn flakes, wheat germ, almonds, cinnamon, nutmeg, and salt.

In small bowl combine apple concentrate, molasses, and vanilla. Pour over oat mixture and mix until evenly coated. Spread granola mix onto baking sheets. Bake until golden brown, about 30-35 minutes, turning every 10 minutes for even browning. Remove from oven, stir in fruit, return to oven, and bake 5 additional minutes. Let cool and store in an airtight container.

Total Calories Per Serving: 473   Total Fat as % of Daily Value: 12%   Protein: 11 gm   Fat: 8 gm
Carbohydrates: 97 gm   Calcium: 133 mg   Iron: 7 mg   Sodium: 307 mg   Dietary Fiber: 9 gm

Chewy Granola Bars

Makes about 24 small bars

Who needs packaged bars when you can make your own? These are great for gift baskets, too.

2 cups vegan crisped rice cold cereal
2 cups old-fashioned oats (not quick oats)
1 cup dried cranberries, raisins, or any other chopped dried fruit
$1/2$ cup hulled unsalted sunflower seeds
$1/2$ cup chopped almonds
Vegetable oil spray
1 cup corn syrup
$3/4$ cup sugar
1 Tablespoon vegan margarine

In a large bowl, combine rice cereal, oats, dried fruit, sunflower seeds, and almonds. Mix together; pull the pieces of fruit apart if they stick together. Spray a baking pan (9 x 13-inch works well) with vegetable oil spray.

In a medium-size pot, heat corn syrup until it starts to boil; add sugar and turn down heat to simmer. Add margarine and stir until sugar is thoroughly dissolved. Remove pot from stove and stir in dry ingredients. Mix until well combined.

Place mixture in pan, spreading it out evenly. Place a sheet of wax paper over mixture and press down so mixture is even and flat. You can use the side of a can to roll the top of the mixture, if necessary. Remove wax paper, cover lightly, and let set for at least one 1 hour before cutting into 24 bars.

Total Calories Per Serving: 127   Total Fat as % of Daily Value: 5%   Protein: 2 gm   Fat: 3 gm
Carbohydrates: 25 gm   Calcium: 13 mg   Iron: 1 mg   Sodium: 38 mg   Dietary Fiber: 1 gm

Applesauce Leather
Serves 4-6

Kids of all ages will enjoy the instant fruit flavor and the chewy texture of fruit leather.

2 cups peeled, cored, and chopped green apples
¼ cup lemon juice
¼ cup sugar
1 teaspoon cinnamon

Preheat oven to 150 degrees. Place apples in a pot and add 1 inch of water or apple juice. Simmer apples over medium heat, about 20 minutes or until very soft. Place in blender and add remaining ingredients. Blend well.

To dry in an oven, spread mixture on a parchment-lined sheet pan or a non-stick baking pan. Dry until fruit feels "tough", but still a little soft. Time will vary depending on oven. Remove the leather while it is still warm and roll it up.

Total Calories Per Serving: 78   Total Fat as % of Daily Value: 0%   Protein: 0 gm   Fat: 0 gm
Carbohydrates: 21 gm   Calcium: 5 mg   Iron: 0 mg   Sodium: 3 mg   Dietary Fiber: 1 gm

Berry Leather
Serves 4-6

4 cups puréed fresh or frozen, thawed berries
¼ cup sugar

Preheat oven to 150 degrees. Combine berries and sugar in a medium pot. Add 1 inch of water or fruit juice. Cook on low just until heated. If desired, strain through cheesecloth to remove seeds.

To dry in an oven, spread mixture on parchment-lined baking sheet or nonstick pan. Dry until fruit feels tough; but still a little soft. Time will vary depending on oven. Remove the leather while it is still warm and roll it up.

Total Calories Per Serving: 118   Total Fat as % of Daily Value: 1%   Protein: 2 gm   Fat: 1 gm
Carbohydrates: 28 gm   Calcium: 47 mg   Iron: 1 mg   Sodium: 2 mg   Dietary Fiber: 9 gm

Chapter 9: PARTY SANDWICHES

Since that compulsive gambler the Earl of Sandwich popularized eating on the run, we have been toasting, open-facing, baking, dipping, grilling, wrapping, and stacking sandwiches. Sandwiches fit into every course of any meal. From eye-opening breakfast biscuit sandwiches to delicate canapés to Dagwoods, sandwiches are so beloved that there are restaurants dedicated exclusively to them.

Hot and cold vegan sandwiches can be just as easy to offer. Go beyond "salad on a roll" or grilled veggie sandwiches; think veggie wraps with lots of mixed greens, hummus, chopped walnuts, and smoked tofu or a veggie "french dip" with grilled and marinated portobellos and mushroom broth stepping in for the beef and the au jus.

For cold weather, create a baked, stacked sandwich with a vegan cheese strata. Stratas are created by stacking layers of bread and cheese in a baking pan, covering them with a "custard" of soymilk and herbs, and then baking the dish in the oven. The resulting hot "sandwich" is a pleasure to serve.

Sandwiches are hot weather fare as well. While the barbecue or grill is hot, toss thinly sliced, marinated eggplant, carrots, and summer squash (sliced lengthwise), sliced bell peppers, wedged red and white onions, and mushrooms and cook until tender. Chill until ready to use. Marinate tomatoes, cucumbers, green and wax beans, and mushrooms in vinegar, dried herbs, and chopped onions. Chop lettuce, radishes, green and black olives, and pickles, rinsed alfalfa and soybean sprouts, drained and rinsed canned black, kidney, red, and garbanzo beans; open some salsa and mix up some hummus and you're ready to assemble veggie sandwiches.

Stuff whole wheat and plain pita bread with grilled veggies, radishes, hummus, olives, and sprouts. Wrap flour, tomato, and blue corn tortillas with marinated veggies, beans, lettuce, and salsa. Try wrapping with cracker bread, spring roll wrappers, and soft pizza crust.

Instead of a veggie burger, top a burger bun with grilled veggies, pickles, and salsa. Create a summer sub with grilled and marinated vegetables, dried herbs, and salad greens on a crusty baguette or in a demi-loaf of walnut-green onion or black olive-sun dried tomato.

Have a Slice

Bread adds interest to the sandwich; here are some of the possibilities:

French or Italian bread	Sour dough
Whole wheat	Whole wheat with wheat berries
Seedless rye	Dark rye
Rye with seeds	Pumpernickel
Raisin or cinnamon raisin bread	Fruit and nut breads
Flavored breads, usually crusty breads flavored with minced black olives, green onions, walnuts, or dijon mustard	

If you like to make party sandwiches with different breads, but are afraid leftover bread will go to waste, wrap it very well and freeze it. Thaw frozen bread without unwrapping it, to keep in moisture. Crusty breads should not be wrapped, if possible, as the crust will become soggy. For protection, loose brown paper or paper towels can be used to protect the bread while keeping the crust.

If possible, store bread you are going to use within a day or two at room temperature. Refrigerating bread speeds up staling, and bread may absorb flavors from the refrigerator. Don't forget, stale bread can be used for toasting, for bread pudding, or for croutons.

Sandwich Making 101

Sandwiches consist of an edible casing, such as bread, rolls, tortillas, pita, or lettuce leaves; spreads, such as vegan mayonnaise, salad dressing, vegan margarine, avocado, nut butters, or hummus; and a filling, which is usually the "heart" of the sandwich.

Good-quality breads provide excellent texture and flavor, fiber, nutrients, and eye appeal. If you're cooking cornbread, bake off an extra pan spread extra thin. Slice and use the corn bread for the base of appetizer sandwiches. Spreads keep the bread from absorbing too much moisture. This helps to maintain the appropriate texture. Spreads also add flavor, and can add nutrients, such as in the case of nut butters, hummus, or vegetable spreads. You can prepare a fast, savory spread by combining vegan mayonnaise with Dijon or spicy prepared mustard, white pepper, and a splash of lemon juice. Create simple, elegant hot or cold sandwiches with two slices of bread or two halves of a roll, such as a grilled vegetable submarine sandwich or a marinated portobello sandwich with a rosemary baguette.

Open-faced sandwiches are made with one slice of bread or one half of a roll. These sandwiches can be part of a hearty meal, such as a grilled veggie burger served on a half of a toasted sesame roll, or be a large appetizer, such as a slice of crusty baguette, topped with a slice of ripe tomato and shredded fresh basil. Try an open-faced sliced Tofurky™ sandwich, served on a slice of crusty bread, and tossed with vegan bacon-flavored mayonnaise or a cornbread open-faced sandwich, topped with thinly sliced pears, vegan pepperoni, and shredded vegan cheese.

Wraps are sandwiches in which the fillings are wrapped in bread, such as a tortilla or pita, or in a lettuce or cabbage leaf. Multidecker sandwiches are made with more than two slices of bread. For example, a vegan club sandwich might be constructed by toasting three slices of wheat bread. On the first piece of bread, vegan mayonnaise and several slices of tomatoes are arranged; a second piece of toast is placed on top of the tomatoes. The second slice of bread would have thin slices of avocado and shredded lettuce. The third slice of bread tops the avocado slices. To cut into quarters, draw an imaginary "x" across the bread, dividing the bread into four triangles. Place a toothpick in the center of each triangle, for a total of four toothpicks. Cut across the imaginary "x" to cut the sandwich into quarters. Arrange so the crust side is facing the plate and the cut side, showing all the ingredients, is facing up.

If you have the time for fancy presentation, you can create checkerboard sandwiches. This takes a bit of coordination. You need to bake or purchase unsliced square (traditionally-shaped) bread loaves. You'll want two colors, such as a light whole wheat and a sour dough or a sour dough and a pumpernickel.

To prepare a checkerboard, you'll want two loaves of unsliced day-old bread for each checkerboard you want to create. (Not stale bread, but bread that's a little more dry than fresh, so it can be sliced without tearing.) Cut the ends off each loaf and save for bread crumbs or croutons. Slice each loaf lengthwise, not up and down as you usually slice bread. Select the same number of slices from each loaf. Spread each slice with a thin layer of fillings, such as soy cream cheese, jam, nut butters, guacamole, or hummus; make sure the flavors go with each other. Reassemble a "loaf," alternating the different types of bread. Press down on the "loaf" and let it stand refrigerated for at least several hours. Slice the checkerboard as you would a regular loaf of bread. You'll see a checkerboard of bread and a rainbow of colors. Serve as individual slices as is, or top with a small garnish, such as a dab of salsa, a tomato rose, a thin slice of cucumber, or half a strawberry.

If you don't have the time for such a "spiffy" presentation, use cookie cutters to shape bread, top with sandwich filling, and serve as a mini-sandwich or a large appetizer. If the bread tends to tear when you are cutting it, freeze it for about an hour and cut it while frozen.

You'll need unsliced bread to make pinwheel sandwiches. Cut the unsliced loaves in $1/2$-inch slices, and then cut each slice in half crosswise. Slightly flatten slices with a rolling pin or wooden dowel.

Spread with a very thin layer of margarine or vegan mayonnaise and then a fairly smooth sandwich filling, such as hummus, vegan cream cheese with or without finely chopped vegetables, chopped oilves or dried fruit, or vegan deli slices. Roll up tightly. You can fasten the sandwich with a frilled toothpick, or seal with a small amount of vegan margarine or cream cheese. Serve whole or slice. Plan ahead so you can chill checkerboard or pinwheel sandwiches for several hours before slicing and serving.

Use Convenience as the Key

Convenience vegan sandwich items are available and easy to use. Check out the plethora of veggie burgers; you can find them made of grains, vegetables, corn, mushrooms, soy, and gluten in a variety of flavors (we've seen Southwestern, barbecued, smoked, and Cajun). Treat these burgers as people use traditional burgers and offer them on their own or in combos. Pile on the toppings: tomato, lettuce, raw or grilled onions (have several types), sliced garlic, avocado wedges, shredded veggie mixes, salsa, fresh and pickled chilies, veggie chili beans, and chopped olives are some that come to mind. Offer a vegan "chili size" with a veggie burger topped with vegan five bean chili, complimented with a corn and pepper salad and some green and red cabbage tossed with oil, vinegar, and chopped onions. Treat vegan hot dogs the same way, offering them on their own or paired with a salad or topping.

Alternative meats are easy to use. Made from soy or wheat they are available in turkey, chicken, beef, and ham look-alikes, with assorted seasonings. Vegan soy cheese is on the market in assorted flavors as well. Offer these as hot or cold deli sandwiches, subs or hoagies, melts, dips (with mushroom gravy), or grilled or barbecued.

Go Ethnic

In Spain or Cuba, panini, or pressed sandwiches, are all the rage. Get out your trusty sandwich press (or use a grill or a large skillet and weigh down the sandwiches with several dinner plates) and do a vegan panini with crusty French bread filled with thinly sliced tomatoes, peppers, onions, garlic, and mashed beans or with salsa and marinated tofu, or with hummus, shredded carrots, and chopped onions.

In South America, tapas are bite-sized sandwiches originally served with the mid-day glass of wine. Today, a tapas assortment is a popular light lunch. Offer vegan toppings on flat bread, pita, and baguette, all cut to bite-size pieces.

The original wrap, the burrito, is a perfect vegan offering. Fill burritos with different varieties of seasoned beans, crunchy veggies, potatoes, rice, corn, salsa, or steamed veggies, paired with veggie chili, potato salad, or fresh fruit and you have a fast and colorful vegan meal. Do you have extra Caesar salad? Supplement the traditional Romaine salad with thin slices of red onion, orange or grapefruit segments, chopped peanuts, and chopped dates. Create a dressing with vegan mayonnaise, lime juice, a little vinegar and peanut butter, whipped until creamy. Mix the salad with the dressing and either stuff the mixture into a pita, roll a wrap, or serve on a crusty roll for a Thai-Caesar sandwich.

Falafel (garbanzo beans mashed, formed into patties and fried) in pita with shredded veggies, burritos, hummus on lavash (flatbread), and bean and vegetable curries on injera (Ethiopian flat bread) are some vegan-friendly sandwiches. Experiment with naan, roti, or dosa (Indian breads) and vegetable curries or fill spring roll wrappers with crunchy vegetables, Asian basil and fresh spinach for cold spring rolls, and pizza dough or calzones as stuffed pizza.

Finally, who says peanut butter is just for the small fry? It was good enough for Elvis! Offer peanut butter combined with fruit preserves (remember, many vegans do not use white sugar, so watch the jelly and jam labels), fresh sliced apples, strawberries, pears, peaches, pineapple, and bananas, canned sliced peaches or pineapple, wheat germ, mashed frozen or fresh berries, and even sweet onion. Serve on a variety of breads, such as seven-grain, pumpkin, pumpernickel, rye, or even white. Grill the peanut butter sandwiches and pair with a fruit skewer or coleslaw with chopped dates and pineapple.

Vegan Sandwich Ingredient Ideas

Fillings: peanut, almond, and soy butter, tofu chunks, alternative meats, cooked and seasoned beans, such as vegan refried beans, black beans with garlic, and navy beans with onions and chilies, vegan soy cheese, plain and flavored hummus

Condiments: vegan mayonnaise (available commercially or make your own), mustard, ketchup, horse-radish, salsas (tomato, mango, citrus, etc.), chutneys (mint, mango, etc.), hot sauce, soy sauce, minced garlic, oil and vinegar, mashed avocado. *Note*: Worcestershire sauce is not vegetarian, as traditional Worcestershire contains anchovies. There are vegan varieties.

Crunchy stuff: pickled cucumbers, carrots and cauliflower, pepperocini and chili peppers, sliced fresh radishes, cucumbers, chopped celery, shredded carrots, sliced tomatoes and bell peppers, broccoli florets, chopped onions, shredded fresh beets and red cabbage

Green stuff: head lettuce and leaf lettuce leaves (romaine, iceberg, Boston, etc.), spinach leaves, shred-ded green cabbage, baby lettuce mix, Caesar salad mix (without the eggs and anchovies)

More stuff: olive assortment, canned or cooked garbanzo beans, sliced mushrooms, fresh parsley and cilantro, fresh basil, bean sprouts, chopped peanuts, soy nuts, wheat germ, nutritional yeast, flavored croutons, soy yogurt (available commercially)

Vegan Mayonnaise

Makes 1 pint

Use this as a base for vegan salad dressings, dips, or sauces. Add chopped onions, capers, minced garlic, chopped pickles, or tomato purée for different flavoring.

12 ounces (drained) silken tofu
2 Tablespoons fresh lemon juice
1 Tablespoon vinegar
2 teaspoons apple juice concentrate
2 teaspoons prepared mustard
Salt and pepper to taste

Place tofu in blender or food processor and blend until creamy (about 30 seconds). Add remaining ingredients and blend until well combined. Store, covered, in the refrigerator until ready to use.

Total Calories Per 1 Pint: 270   Total Fat as % of Daily Value: 17%   Protein: 25 gm   Fat: 11 gm
Carbohydrates: 17 gm   Calcium: 150 mg   Iron: 4 mg   Sodium: 132 mg   Dietary Fiber: 1 gm

Walnut Paté

Makes 2 cups or sixteen 2 Tablespoon servings

Use this paté as a sandwich spread with fresh, sautéed, or grilled vegetables or as a replacement for mayonnaise or salad dressing. This recipe freezes well and will keep in the refrigerator for up to 3 days.

4 Tablespoons vegetable oil
³/₄ cup chopped onions
1¹/₄ cups chopped fresh button mushrooms
4 cloves garlic, minced
1¹/₄ cups chopped walnuts
4 Tablespoons chopped fresh parsley
1 Tablespoon soy sauce
2 teaspoons white pepper

Sauté onions, mushrooms, and garlic in olive oil until very soft. Place in blender or food processor and purée. Add remaining ingredients. Process paté until smooth (if the mixture is too thick, it can be thinned with vegetable stock or lemon juice). Chill for at least 1 hour before serving.

Total Calories Per Serving: 97   Total Fat as % of Daily Value: 14%   Protein: 2 gm   Fat: 9 gm
Carbohydrates: 3 gm   Calcium: 13 mg   Iron: 0 mg   Sodium: 65 mg   Dietary Fiber: 1 gm

Croque Monsieur

Makes 2 servings

4 slices white or sour dough bread
4 slices vegan mozzarella cheese
2 slices vegan "ham" slices
2 teaspoons Dijon mustard
2 Tablespoons melted vegan margarine

Preheat oven to 325 degrees. Assemble sandwiches as follows: one slice bread, one slice mozzarella, one slice "ham", a second slice of mozzarella. Spread one teaspoon of mustard on a second slice of bread and top sandwich with this slice. Put margarine on the side of the sandwich facing up.

Place sandwich in an ovenproof frying pan with the side not containing margarine facing down. Brown this side and then turn and brown the side containing margarine.

Place the sauté pan in the oven and heat until the cheese is totally melted. Serve immediately.

Note: Croque Madame: another bistro classic, uses sliced "chicken" instead of ham.

Total Calories Per Serving: 677   Total Fat as % of Daily Value: 56%   Protein: 9 gm   Fat: 36 gm
Carbohydrates: 67 gm   Calcium: 793 mg   Iron: 5 mg   Sodium: 1641 mg   Dietary Fiber: 5 gm

More Sandwich Ideas

Bread: white, wheat, rye pumpernickel, sour dough, whole wheat, olive, sun dried tomato, herbed, raisin, date nut, Boston brown bread

Rolls: seeded, herbed, baguette, foccacia

Crackers: wheat, rye, Melba toast, rye, Scandinavian cracker bread

Flat breads for rolling: pizza shells, tortillas, flavored wraps, cracker bread, vegetables (such as zucchini, cut in thin, lengthwise strips)

Vegetables

Roasted eggplant	Grilled tomatoes	Roasted onions	Spinach
Shredded carrots	Baby lettuce mixes	Cucumbers	Sliced mushrooms
Radicchio	Endive	Sprouts (bean, alfalfa, radish, sunflower, etc.)	
Sliced bell peppers/chilies			

Spreads and Condiments

Vegan mayonnaise	Mustards	Salsa	Nut butters (peanut, almond, soy, etc.)
Soy yogurt	Hummus	Paté	Mashed, seasoned tofu
Tofu	Bean spreads	Guacamole	Tapenade (olive spread)
Apple butter	Salad dressings	Chutney	Flavored vegan cream cheese

Garnishes

Pickled vegetables (cucumbers, carrots, onions, celery)

Raisins, dried fruit (apples, apricots, nectarines, cranberries)

Vegetable brochettes (skewers of cherry tomatoes, radishes, summer squash, mushrooms, carrots, sweet onions)

Black and green olives

Broccoli and cauliflower florets and asparagus spears

Side Dishes

Pasta, macaroni, hot potato salad, sweet potato salad, five bean salad

Baked fries: spicy with peel-on, sweet potato, eggplant, tempura style

Sliced seasonal fresh vegetables

Sliced seasonal fresh fruit

Freshly made vegetable chips: white and sweet potato, carrot, beet, taro, rutabaga

Top that Burger or Veggie Hot Dog

Separate your burgers from the other burgers on the block. Offer a wide assortment of toppings (build your own or preassembled) to add that extra accent. No one will notice the fat is missing!

Veggies: cucumbers (sliced lengthwise), shredded carrots, broccoli, radish, alfalfa and soy bean sprouts, bell pepper slices, shredded and leaf iceberg, chilies (of various "heat") red leaf, romaine, Bibb lettuces, fresh spinach, endive, yellow and red tomatoes, red, yellow, white, sweet onion slices, minced fresh garlic, raw and sautéed button mushrooms, thinly sliced jicama

Fruit: fresh, thinly sliced pineapple and peaches

Pickled stuff: cucumbers (sweet and savory chips, slices, spears), carrot slices, green tomatoes, green and black olives, cabbage (kimchi), daikon radish, baby corn, celery slices, gardenia (a mixture of pickled vegetables), pepperocini (sweet Italian peppers), artichoke hearts, heart of palm, capers, watermelon rind

Condiments: ketchup, flavored ketchup, vegan mayonnaise, flavored vegan mayonnaise, red and green Tabasco sauce, various hot sauces, selection of salsa, chutneys, mustard, flavored mustards, grated horseradish, salad dressings, pickle relish, pepper relish, vegan steak sauce, soy sauce, flavored vinegars, barbecue sauce, chopped fresh herbs (basil, oregano, rosemary, etc.), fresh cilantro.

The Five Commandments of Moist Lowfat Burgers

Moistness rules when it comes to burgers; follow these six rules and you should have perfect results every time.

1. To add moistness to veggie "ground round" or TVP, add some mashed fresh avocado or thawed frozen avocado pulp. Avocado has a neutral flavor and a rich, creamy texture, which will make lean ingredients moist. Yes, avocado contains fat, but it is the unsaturated, "good" kind of fat.
2. A touch of tomato purée, ketchup, or chopped, deseeded fresh tomatoes helps ensure moistness.
3. When preparing lowfat burger mixtures, add small amounts of cold water, vegetable stock, or tomato juice.
4. Experiment with a moist stuffing, such as chopped and steamed mushrooms or onions, or barbecued or baked beans or black beans.
5. Include moist toppings, such as thick slices of beefsteak tomatoes, salsa, or chutney.

Burger Ideas

Hit a creative wall when it comes to new veggie burger ideas? Here are just a few ideas that can be made with a basic veggie burger mix (see recipes):

Baked or Grilled Mushroom Burgers	White and Black Bean Burgers
Chili Bean Burgers	Grilled Eggplant Burgers
Jalapeño Red Bean Burgers	Lentil Burgers
Lentil Carrot Burgers	Oat Burgers
Portobello Burgers	Roasted Veggie Burgers
Spicy Black Bean Burgers	White Bean and Rice Burgers
Yam and Brown Rice Burgers	Grated Beet Burgers

VEGGIE BURGERS AND SANDWICH RECIPES

Multi-Veggie Burger
Makes 10 burgers

If you don't have the tofu called for in this recipe, you can substitute prepared and cooled mashed potatoes.

14 small baking potatoes (about 3 pounds), cooked and peeled
1 pound onions, diced
8 ounces mushrooms, diced
2 pounds carrots, diced and cooked
2 pounds cooked green peas
1½ pounds cooked corn
8 ounces firm tofu
1½ cups (14 ounces) dry bread crumbs

Mash cooked potatoes. Set aside.

Heat and grease a griddle. Sauté onions and mushrooms until tender. Combine mushrooms with mashed potatoes in a large mixing bowl. Add remaining ingredients, except crumbs. Mix thoroughly. Add just enough crumbs to have mixture form patties. Form into 10 (about 3-ounce) patties. Cook on a hot griddle or bake at 350 degrees in the oven until browned on both sides.

Total Calories Per Burger: 444   Total Fat as % of Daily Value: 5%   Protein: 17 gm   Fat: 4 gm
Carbohydrates: 90 gm   Calcium: 161 mg   Iron: 5 mg   Sodium: 215 mg   Dietary Fiber: 17 gm

Basic Veggie Burgers
Makes 8-10 burgers

This is a great "pantry" recipe, as many of the ingredients should be on your shelf. This is also a terrific way to use leftover veggies. If you don't have the tofu used in this recipe, you can substitute prepared and cooled mashed potatoes.

1¹/₂ cups canned sliced carrots, drained (reserve liquid)
1¹/₂ cups canned cut green beans, drained
1¹/₂ cups cooked pinto or red beans
2¹/₂ cups dry bread crumbs
2 Tablespoons vegetable oil or melted vegan margarine
1 Tablespoon dried parsley
¹/₂ cup ketchup or chili sauce
2 Tablespoons silken tofu
¹/₂ teaspoon white pepper
¹/₂ teaspoon celery salt
1 teaspoon onion powder

Preheat oven to 325 degrees. Place carrots, green beans, and pinto or red beans in a blender or food processor and purée until almost smooth.

Place mixture in a large bowl. Stir in remaining ingredients until well combined. If mixture is too thick, add some of the reserved carrot liquid; if it is too thin, add additional bread crumbs.

Form mixture into burgers and place on a non-stick baking sheet (or spray with vegetable oil spray). Bake for 30-40 minutes or until thoroughly heated and lightly browned.

Note: This mixture can be pressed into a standard-size loaf pan and baked as a loaf at the same temperature and same amount of time as the burgers.

Total Calories Per Burger: 235   Total Fat as % of Daily Value: 9%   Protein: 8 gm   Fat: 6 gm
Carbohydrates: 39 gm   Calcium: 103 mg   Iron: 3 mg   Sodium: 717 mg   Dietary Fiber: 5 gm

Tofu Burgers

Makes 6-7 burgers

These burgers can be baked or pan-fried. Also use them as "meatballs" and microwave them in sauce.

2 cups firm tofu, drained and crumbled
1 clove garlic, minced
$\frac{1}{8}$ cup onions, minced
$\frac{1}{2}$ cup wheat germ
$\frac{1}{2}$ cup dry bread crumbs
1 Tablespoon soy sauce
$\frac{1}{4}$ cup fresh parsley, chopped
$\frac{1}{2}$ cup celery, minced
$\frac{1}{4}$ cup bell peppers, chopped
$\frac{1}{2}$ cup water or carrot juice
Oil for frying

In a large bowl, mash tofu until almost smooth. Add all ingredients except water or juice and combine until well mixed. Slowly add water or juice until mixture is thick enough to form burgers.

Form into small burgers and refrigerate for 30 minutes. Fry in oil until browned or bake at 350 degrees for 20 minutes, until heated and browned.

Total Calories Per Burger: 142   Total Fat as % of Daily Value: 8%   Protein: 11 gm   Fat: 5 gm
Carbohydrates: 16 gm   Calcium: 199 mg   Iron: 3 mg   Sodium: 261 mg   Dietary Fiber: 3 gm

Portobello and Spinach Sandwich

Makes 4 sandwiches

1 cup roasted red bell pepper strips or canned pimento strips
4 portobello mushroom caps
Vegetable oil spray
4 slices sweet onion
2 teaspoons minced fresh garlic
40 fresh spinach leaves (about 2 cups)
4 crusty bread rolls
8 slices tomato

If using canned pimento, drain, wash, and pat dry. Set aside.

Spray grill or frying pan with vegetable oil. Place portobello caps on a grill or in a pan and grill until tender. Set aside. Keep grill or pan hot.

Put onion and garlic in pan and sauté until onion is tender, about 2 minutes. Add spinach and peppers, toss and heat only until spinach just begins to wilt, about 1 minute.

To assemble, first split rolls. Place 2 slices of tomato on one half of each roll. Place 1 portobello cap on top of tomato. Garnish with spinach combination.

Note: If desired, top with shredded vegan mozzarella soy cheese and broil for 30 seconds or until the cheese is bubbly.

Total Calories Per Sandwich: 250   Total Fat as % of Daily Value: 14%   Protein: 10 gm   Fat: 9 gm
Carbohydrates: 35 gm   Calcium: 177 mg   Iron: 5 mg   Sodium: 303 mg   Dietary Fiber: 6 gm

Fast Garden Wraps

Makes 4 entrées or 8 appetizers

Four 12-inch spinach tortillas
Vegetable oil spray
1¹⁄₂ cups crumbled firm tofu (flavored, if desired)
¹⁄₄ cup crumbled vegan cheese
4 cups fresh, cleaned spinach

Preheat skillet. Lightly toast tortillas, for about 30 seconds on each side, one at a time, depending on the size of your skillet. Cover with a clean kitchen towel and set aside.

Spray heated skillet with oil and add in tofu and cheese, cook and stir for 2 minutes. Add spinach, and cook and stir until greens are wilted, about 2-3 minutes.

Divide spinach mixture into four equal parts. Place one part at one edge of each tortilla and roll tightly. Serve hot, or place in low oven (about 200 degrees) for up to 10 minutes to keep warm.

Total Calories Per Serving: 376   Total Fat as % of Daily Value: 19%   Protein: 17 gm   Fat: 13 gm
Carbohydrates: 47 gm   Calcium: 192 mg   Iron: 2 mg   Sodium: 129 mg   Dietary Fiber: 1 gm

Hot Spinach Toasts

Serves 12

2 cups thawed, drained and squeezed chopped spinach
12 slices whole wheat bread (thinly sliced, if you can find it)
¹⁄₄ cup chopped onion
2 cloves garlic, minced
Vegetable oil spray
²⁄₃ cup plain soy yogurt or drained silken tofu mixed with 1 Tablespoon lemon juice
¹⁄₄ teaspoon ground nutmeg

Preheat broiler (or oven to 400 degrees). Ensure all the water that can be is squeezed from the spinach.

Trim crusts from the bread. Cut bread into triangles or squares and place on a baking sheet. Broil or bake until toasted.

Heat a frying pan and spray with vegetable oil. Sauté onion and garlic until soft, about 2 minutes. Set aside. Place spinach in a large bowl. Mix in onion/garlic mixture, yogurt, and nutmeg and toss to combine. Microwave on HIGH for 2 minutes to heat (or place in a baking dish and heat in 400-degree oven for 5-6 minutes or until hot). Top bread with spinach mixture and serve.

Total Calories Per Serving: 77   Total Fat as % of Daily Value: 2%   Protein: 4 gm   Fat: 1 gm
Carbohydrates: 14 gm   Calcium: 31 mg   Iron: 1 mg   Sodium: 171 mg   Dietary Fiber: 2 gm

Hot Veggie Pizza Squares

Serves 6

One 10-inch frozen vegan pizza shell or 6 individual frozen pizza shells
¼ cup shredded vegan mozzarella
⅓ cup shredded or chopped vegan sausage or deli slices
¾ cup canned, drained sliced mushrooms
½ cup diced onions
¼ cup diced green bell peppers
½ cup fresh shredded zucchini or summer squash
1 cup chopped fresh tomatoes or canned, diced, drained tomatoes
2 Tablespoons fresh shredded basil

Preheat oven to 450 degrees. Place pizza dough on non-stick baking sheet or spray a regular pan with vegetable oil and then place dough. Sprinkle pizza dough evenly with each ingredient. Bake for 8-10 minutes or until crust is golden and vegetables have lost their crispness.

Variations: If you like, prepare your favorite pizza dough and freeze it for use in this recipe. If you can't find or prepare vegan pizza dough, prepare biscuits and use as the crust. In a pinch, you can use vegan English muffin halves. If desired, top pizza with more shredded vegan mozzarella cheese or a sprinkle of nutritional yeast. Finally, if vegan mozzarella isn't available, you can grate an equal amount of seitan.

Total Calories Per Serving: 308   Total Fat as % of Daily Value: 7%   Protein: 1 gm   Fat: 5 gm
Carbohydrates: 55 gm   Calcium: 151 mg   Iron: 5 mg   Sodium: 627 mg   Dietary Fiber: 4 gm

Hot Sauerkraut-Potato Bread

Makes 2 loaves (about 12 servings)

Vegetable oil spray
2 packets (½ ounce or 2 Tablespoons) dry yeast
1½ cups warm water
1 cup mashed potatoes
5 Tablespoons sugar
2 teaspoons salt
1 teaspoon caraway seeds
4 Tablespoons oil
3 cups drained and chopped sauerkraut
8 cups all purpose flour or 2 cups whole wheat flour and 6 cups all purpose flour

Preheat oven to 350 degrees. Spray two loaf pans or 9 x 5-inch baking pans with oil.
   Place yeast in a large glass or plastic bowl. Pour water over yeast and stir until dissolved.
   Stir in potatoes, sugar, salt, caraway seed, oil, sauerkraut, and flour. Place on clean surface and knead for 2 minutes. Cover with a clean towel and place in a warm spot, such as a gas oven with a pilot light, warm corner of the kitchen, etc. Allow dough to rise until it doubles in size, about 50-60 minutes.
   Punch dough to remove bubbles. Shape into two smooth loaves. You can moisten your hands with cold water to smooth the surface of the loaves, if desired. Place dough in baking pans. Cover and let rise for a second time, about 40-50 minutes. Bake, uncovered, for 45-50 minutes or until golden brown.

Note: Serve bread hot from oven or reheat in oven or microwave. Serve with mustard dipping sauce, sliced vegan hot dogs or deli slices, or pair with chili.

Total Calories Per Serving: 393   Total Fat as % of Daily Value: 9%   Protein: 10 gm   Fat: 6 gm
Carbohydrates: 74 gm   Calcium: 29 mg   Iron: 2 mg   Sodium: 670 mg   Dietary Fiber: 4 gm

Italian Melts

Serves 6

This versatile sandwich method is very popular. Try it with different filling combinations, one "melty" and one firm. Suggestions: vegan cheddar cheese and sliced tomato or nut butters and sliced fresh pineapple, or vegan mozzarella cheese and sautéed mushrooms or sweet onions.

2 loaves crusty Italian or French bread
6 teaspoons softened vegan margarine
1 clove garlic, minced
6 slices vegan mozzarella cheese
12 slices vegan pepperoni

Preheat oven to 400 degrees. Cut bread into 12 thin slices. In a small bowl or cup, combine margarine and garlic until blended.

Place 6 slices of bread on a baking sheet. Spread each slice with one teaspoon of garlic spread. Place one slice of cheese and two slices of pepperoni on top of garlic spread. Cover with a slice of bread. Place sandwiches in oven and bake for 3-5 minutes, or until cheese is bubbly.

Note: If desired, spray the top of the sandwiches with vegetable oil for a crispier sandwich. For a pressed sandwich, or panini, spray the top of the sandwiches with vegetable oil and weigh down sandwiches with several oven-proof plates prior to placing in the oven. If you like this effect, you may want to check out electric sandwich presses, sold in most appliance department and on the web.

Total Calories Per Serving: 216   Total Fat as % of Daily Value: 22%   Protein: 2 gm   Fat: 14 gm
Carbohydrates: 14 gm   Calcium: 179 mg   Iron: 2 mg   Sodium: 517 mg   Dietary Fiber: 1 gm

Spicy Sandwiches

Serves 4

8 slices whole wheat bread
1/2 cup vegan cream cheese
1/4 cup prepared horseradish
1/2 cup each peeled, thinly sliced cucumbers and thinly sliced tomatoes

Spread all 8 slices of bread with equal amounts of the cream cheese/horseradish mixture. Top four of the bread slices with cucumber slices and thinly sliced tomato slices. Cover with remaining four slices of bread. Chill for 20 minutes before serving.

Total Calories Per Serving: 211   Total Fat as % of Daily Value: 12%   Protein: 6 gm   Fat: 8 gm
Carbohydrates: 31 gm   Calcium: 53 mg   Iron: 2 mg   Sodium: 464 mg   Dietary Fiber: 5 gm

Tofu Caprice Sandwiches

Serves 6

3 loaves Italian or crusty French bread, cut into halves lengthwise
12 slices ripe tomato
1 pound smoked tofu, cut into twelve slices
12 leaves fresh basil
3 teaspoons vinegar
2 teaspoons olive oil
Cracked black pepper to taste

If desired, lightly toast or broil bread in a hot oven. Cut each half loaf of bread into three pieces. Place on individual appetizer plates or on a serving platter.

To assemble the sandwiches, place a slice of tomato on each bread piece. Top with a slice of tofu, then a basil leaf. Repeat. Drizzle top with vinegar and olive oil. Very lightly sprinkle with black pepper. Serve immediately.

Total Calories Per Serving: 157   Total Fat as % of Daily Value: 13%   Protein: 8 gm   Fat: 8 gm
Carbohydrates: 13 gm   Calcium: 173 mg   Iron: 2 mg   Sodium: 131 mg   Dietary Fiber: 2 gm

Mediterranean Mushroom Sandwiches

Serves 6-8

6-8 large portobello mushroom caps
¼ cup olive oil
2 teaspoons dried oregano
2 cloves garlic, minced
2 teaspoons dried parsley
1 teaspoon cracked black pepper
Vegetable oil spray
¼ cup fresh lemon juice
6-8 pieces pita bread
1 cup chopped red bell pepper
1 cup sliced black olives

Wash and destem mushrooms. In a large bowl, combine olive oil, oregano, garlic, parsley, and black pepper. Add mushrooms, being certain each cap is coated. Cover and allow mushrooms to marinate for 10 minutes.

Spray a large skillet with oil and allow to heat. Remove portobellos from marinade and sauté until just tender. If desired, use remaining marinade as a cooking liquid for the mushrooms. Sprinkle mushrooms with lemon juice while they are sautéeing. Remove mushrooms.

Cut or split open the pita bread to form a pocket. Place one portabollo cap in each pita. Garnish with red pepper and olives. Serve warm.

Total Calories Per Serving: 297   Total Fat as % of Daily Value: 19%   Protein: 8 gm   Fat: 12 gm
Carbohydrates: 40 gm   Calcium: 81 mg   Iron: 2 mg   Sodium: 525 mg   Dietary Fiber: 4 gm

Curried "Egg" Salad Sandwiches with Apples

Serves 10

2 cups drained, crumbled extra-firm tofu
2 Tablespoons prepared chutney
1/2 cup minced celery
2 teaspoons curry powder
1/8 teaspoon cinnamon
1/8 teaspoon ground cardamom
1/8 teaspoon black pepper
1/2 cup vegan mayonnaise
2 Tablespoons Dijon mustard
10 slices vegan bread of choice
1 cup peeled, thinly sliced green apples
10 leaves Romaine lettuce, washed and dried

Combine tofu, chutney, celery, curry powder, cinnamon, cardamom, black pepper, mayonnaise, and mustard in a large bowl and mix well. Place bread on a serving platter or on individual plates. Top each piece of bread with several slices of apples and one slice of Romaine. Top with curried salad. Refrigerate until ready to use.

Total Calories Per Serving: 208   Total Fat as % of Daily Value: 18%   Protein: 7 gm   Fat: 11 gm
Carbohydrates: 17 gm   Calcium: 161 mg   Iron: 2 mg   Sodium: 290 mg   Dietary Fiber: 2 gm

Avocado Pitas

Makes 4 entrées or 8 appetizers

1 cup avocado slices
1/2 cup chopped plum (Roma) tomato
2 Tablespoons chopped onion
1 clove garlic, minced
1 teaspoon black pepper
1/4 cup drained, canned or cooked black beans
4 vegan pita bread

Combine avocado, tomato, onion, garlic and pepper in a medium bowl. Gently mix in black beans. Split pitas and stuff with filling. Chill for 20 minutes before serving.

Total Calories Per Serving: 276   Total Fat as % of Daily Value: 14%   Protein: 8 gm   Fat: 9 gm
Carbohydrates: 42 gm   Calcium: 64 mg   Iron: 2 mg   Sodium: 352 mg   Dietary Fiber: 6 gm

Spinach and Portobello Sandwiches

Serves 6-8

2 Tablespoons olive oil
1 cup roasted red peppers or canned, drained pimentos, sliced in long, thin strips
  (about 1/2 pound)
6-8 large portobello mushroom caps
6-8 thin slices onion
2 cloves garlic, minced
1 Tablespoon ground oregano
2 cups loosely-packed fresh spinach leaves
6-8 crusty rolls, split in half
6-8 slices ripe tomato
6-8 slices vegan mozzarella cheese

Pour 1 Tablespoon of oil into a large skillet and heat. Add peppers and quickly sauté to coat with oil. Remove and set aside. Add portobellos to the skillet and sauté until tender, 5-10 minutes, depending on the mushrooms. Remove from skillet and set aside.

Add remaining oil to skillet and warm. Add onions, garlic, and oregano and cook, tossing, until onions are soft. Add spinach, cooking quickly and tossing until spinach is just wilted. Add red peppers and stir and cook until well combined.

To assemble, first place split rolls on serving platter or individual plates. Place a portobello cap on each roll and top with spinach mixture, one slice of tomato, and one slice of cheese. Close rolls to allow cheese to slightly melt.

Note: If desired, portobellos can be grilled on a barbecue, rather than in a skillet. Drizzle oil on portobellos as they are grilling so they do not dry out. If you want, assembled sandwiches can be wrapped in foil and placed in a 400-degree oven for 2-3 minutes to melt cheese. Do not heat for a prolonged time, as the spinach will be overcooked.

Total Calories Per Serving: 240   Total Fat as % of Daily Value: 15%   Protein: 6 gm   Fat: 10 gm
Carbohydrates: 32 gm   Calcium: 227 mg   Iron: 2 mg   Sodium: 704 mg   Dietary Fiber: 3 gm

Major Wraps

Serves 8-10

Filling:
1 cup minced, peeled, broccoli stalks (not florets)
1 cup minced, peeled carrots
1/4 cup minced green onions
3/4 cup minced fresh fennel
4 Tablespoons chopped fresh parsley
1/2 cup chopped fresh tomatoes
2 Tablespoons drained capers
2 cups minced or ground pistachios
1/2 cup minced or ground cashews
1/4 cup minced red peppers

¼ cup minced celery
1 cup minced fresh mushrooms

Sauce:
1 Tablespoon lime juice
1 Tablespoon cilantro
¼ cup sesame oil
¼ cup rice wine vinegar
1½ Tablespoons sugar
2 teaspoons soy sauce
2 Tablespoons crumbled nori (dried seaweed), optional
2½ Tablespoons minced fresh garlic
2 teaspoons cracked black pepper
2 teaspoons onion powder
2 teaspoons hot sauce, optional

8-10 large, cleaned lettuce leaves

Prepare sauce by combining all sauce ingredients together in a medium bowl. Refrigerate 30 minutes.

Prepare filling by tossing all filling ingredients in a large bowl until well combined. Toss with sauce until well coated. Allow filling to chill for 20 minutes.

To assemble, place approximately ¼ cup of filling at the end of each lettuce leaf. Gently and firmly roll up, as tightly as you can. Serve whole, or cut into 2-inch lengths.

Total Calories Per Serving: 329   Total Fat as % of Daily Value: 38%   Protein: 10 gm   Fat: 25 gm
Carbohydrates: 22 gm   Calcium: 84 mg   Iron: 3 mg   Sodium: 229 mg   Dietary Fiber: 6 gm

Baked Avocado Sandwiches
Makes 4 entrées or 8 appetizers

1-2 large avocados (about 1 pound)
4 crusty rolls
1 cup shredded Romaine lettuce
½ cup shredded red cabbage
½ cup peeled, thinly sliced cucumbers
½ cup grated carrots
2 Tablespoons chopped green onions

Preheat oven to 400 degrees. Slice avocados as thinly as possible. Split rolls in half and place on a non-stick baking sheet. Cover split rolls with overlapping avocado slices. Bake sandwiches for 5 minutes or until rolls are crispy. Remove from oven, quickly top with remaining ingredients and serve immediately.

Total Calories Per Serving: 289   Total Fat as % of Daily Value: 25%   Protein: 6 gm   Fat: 17 gm
Carbohydrates: 33 gm   Calcium: 79 mg   Iron: 2 mg   Sodium: 245 mg   Dietary Fiber: 8 gm

Tofu "Fillet" Sandwich with Tartar Sauce

Serves 4

12 ounces extra-firm tofu, drained and pressed (about 1½ cups), sliced 1-inch thick
⅓ cup cornmeal
¼ cup flour
¼ cup dry bread crumbs
1 Tablespoon lemon pepper or Italian seasoning blend
Vegetable oil spray
4 vegan whole wheat sandwich buns
½ cup vegan mayonnaise
2 teaspoons minced pickles
2 teaspoons minced onion
2 teaspoons lemon juice
¼ teaspoon black pepper
½ cup shredded lettuce
4-6 tomato slices

Mix cornmeal, flour, bread crumbs, and lemon pepper in a large bowl. Place slices of tofu in breading and cover thoroughly on both sides. Spray a large skillet with oil and heat. Place "fillets" in pan, and sauté until golden on both sides. Alternately, you may preheat oven to 425 degrees, spray a baking sheet with oil, and bake "fillets" for 5 minutes or until golden on each side.

Line a large plate with paper towels. Set fillets to drain on towels. To make vegan tartar sauce, mix vegan mayonnaise, pickle, and onion in a small bowl. Add lemon juice and pepper to taste.

Place 4 bun halves on a serving platter. Top each half with a fillet, vegan tartar sauce, lettuce, and tomatoes and top with remaining bun halves.

Total Calories Per Serving: 501   Total Fat as % of Daily Value: 40%   Protein: 17 gm   Fat: 26 gm
Carbohydrates: 49 gm   Calcium: 210 mg   Iron: 4 mg   Sodium: 543 mg   Dietary Fiber: 6 gm

Vegan Eggplant and Pepper Sandwich with Pesto

Serves 8-10

Pesto Sauce:
4 cloves garlic, minced
1 cup fresh, finely shredded basil leaves
1 cup fresh, finely shredded spinach
2 teaspoons nutritional yeast

Filling:
1 large round eggplant, peeled and sliced ¼-inch thick (about 1½ pounds or 3½ cups)
2 teaspoons olive oil or olive oil spray
2 teaspoons balsamic vinegar
1 red bell pepper, deseeded and sliced ¼-inch thick (about 6 ounces or 1 cup)
1 cup thinly sliced onions
¾ cup thinly sliced tomatoes

3 cups washed and dried fresh spinach
8 pieces vegan focaccia squares or pieces of crusty bread, cut 6 x 6-inches

To prepare pesto, place all sauce ingredients in a blender or food processor canister and process until smooth. Set aside.

Preheat grill or large skillet. Brush eggplant lightly with a drop of olive oil and 1 teaspoon balsamic vinegar and grill. In a large skillet, add remaining olive oil and heat. Add peppers and onions and cook, stirring until very soft. Spread ¼ cup pesto on top and bottom of each focaccia square. Layer eggplant, red peppers, onions, tomato, and fresh spinach. Grill sandwiches in dry pan or griddle over medium heat for 4 minutes. Or, preheat oven to 425 degrees, place sandwiches on a non-stick baking sheet and bake for 3 minutes or just until hot.

Total Calories Per Serving: 321   Total Fat as % of Daily Value: 7%   Protein: 11 gm   Fat: 4 gm
Carbohydrates: 61 gm   Calcium: 191 mg   Iron: 5 mg   Sodium: 601 mg   Dietary Fiber: 8 gm

Apple "Cheese" Melt
Serves 4

8 slices whole grain or oat bread
1 cup peeled, thinly sliced apples (your choice)
4 slices vegan cheese
Vegetable oil spray

Toast bread lightly. Place bread on a clean surface. Cover 4 slices with apples and cheese. Cover with remaining bread slices. Coat a large skillet with oil. Allow to heat. Place one or two sandwiches (depending on the size of your skillet) in the pan and allow to brown on one side. Flip sandwich and allow to brown on other side. Cut in halves or quarters and serve immediately.

Note: This can be done open-faced on a broiler, or baked closed-faced in a 400-degree oven, if desired.

Total Calories Per Serving: 189   Total Fat as % of Daily Value: 7%   Protein: 6 gm   Fat: 4 gm
Carbohydrates: 33 gm   Calcium: 192 mg   Iron: 2 mg   Sodium: 445 mg   Dietary Fiber: 5 gm

Kids Can Cook Peanut Butter, Banana, and Applesauce Sandwich
Serves 4-6

8 slices wheat bread
1 cup applesauce
8 Tablespoons peanut butter (or soy, hazelnut, or cashew butter)
1 cup peeled and sliced bananas
2 teaspoons cinnamon

Toast bread and set aside. Place applesauce in a microwave-safe bowl and heat on high for 40 seconds or until warm (or heat on top of the stove in a small pot). Allow nut butter to come to room temperature. Spread nut butter on toast and top with sliced bananas. Top bananas with applesauce and a sprinkle of cinnamon. Top with second piece of toast. This is a gushy, mushy sandwich best served in a bowl!

Total Calories Per Serving: 411   Total Fat as % of Daily Value: 29%   Protein: 14 gm   Fat: 19 gm
Carbohydrates: 55 gm   Calcium: 73 mg   Iron: 3 mg   Sodium: 469 mg   Dietary Fiber: 9 gm

Mediterranean Kale Sandwich

Serves 4

2 Tablespoons olive oil
3 cloves garlic, minced
4 cups washed and cut kale (about 1-2 bunches), torn into 2-inch length pieces
1 teaspoon crushed red pepper flakes
2 Tablespoons drained capers
¼ cup pitted, diced black olives
8 slices sour dough, rosemary, or olive bread
1 Tablespoon nutritional yeast

Heat olive oil in a large skillet. Add garlic and cook until soft, but not brown, about 1 minute. Add kale, red pepper flakes, capers, and olives, stirring briskly to coat mixture. Turn kale mixture to coat with oil. Cover and simmer, stirring occasionally, for 5 minutes or just until kale becomes soft (there will be some residual cooking, and you don't want soggy kale). Remove from heat. Place 4 bread slices on a serving platter. Top with kale, sprinkle with yeast, and cover with remaining bread. Cut in halves or quarters and serve immediately.

Total Calories Per Serving: 172   Total Fat as % of Daily Value: 14%   Protein: 6 gm   Fat: 9 gm
Carbohydrates: 20 gm   Calcium: 124 mg   Iron: 2 mg   Sodium: 349 mg   Dietary Fiber: 4 gm

Tempeh Salad Sandwich

Serves 4

1½ cups tempeh (about 12-ounces)
½ cup grated carrots
¼ cup minced sweet onions
2 teaspoons fresh lemon juice
1 Tablespoon minced fresh parsley
2 teaspoons curry powder
½ teaspoon hot sauce
¼ cup vegan mayonnaise
4 pitas

Cube tempeh and steam for 10 minutes or until soft. Allow tempeh to cool.

In a large bowl mash cooled tempeh with a fork. Mix in the carrots, celery, and onions, and stir until well combined. In a small bowl, mix lemon juice, parsley, curry powder, and hot sauce. Mix tempeh and mayonnaise together.

Cut pitas into halves or quarters and stuff with tempeh salad. Serve warm or cold.

Total Calories Per Serving: 389   Total Fat as % of Daily Value: 26%   Protein: 17 gm   Fat: 17 gm
Carbohydrates: 42 gm   Calcium: 133 mg   Iron: 3 mg   Sodium: 427 mg   Dietary Fiber: 2 gm

Club Sandwich

Serves 4

8 strips cooked vegan "bacon"
3 Tablespoons vegan mayonnaise
12 slices of toasted bread
24 thin slices of tomatoes (about 3 tomatoes)
24 lettuce leaves
8 slices vegan "turkey"

To assemble, break bacon slices in half. Set aside. Place 4 slices of bread on a serving platter. Spread lightly with mayonnaise. Top with 4 bacon halves and 2 slices of tomato. Add a second slice of bread. Spread lightly with mayonnaise. Top with lettuce and 2 slices of turkey. Cover with third bread slice. Cut into quarters and arrange on serving platter. If necessary, used frilled toothpicks (frilled, so the guests can see them and not bite into them) to keep sandwiches together.

Total Calories Per Serving: 376   Total Fat as % of Daily Value: 20%   Protein: 14 gm   Fat: 13 gm
Carbohydrates: 46 gm   Calcium: 160 mg   Iron: 5 mg   Sodium: 1042 mg   Dietary Fiber: 5 gm

Hummus with Red Bell Pepper Sandwich

Serves 4

2 cups canned, drained or cooked garbanzo beans
1/2 cup chopped and seeded roasted red bell pepper (or canned, drained pimentos)
1/2 teaspoon ground cumin
2 Tablespoons lemon juice
3 Tablespoons tahini (sesame seed paste)
1 clove garlic, minced
8 slices whole wheat bread
2 cups thoroughly washed alfalfa or radish sprouts
8 tomato slices
8 avocado slices

Place garbanzos in a blender or food processor canister. Add bell pepper, cumin, lemon juice, tahini, and garlic and process to a smooth consistency. If a thinner consistency is desired, add some more lemon juice, tahini, or water. Makes about $1^3/_4$ cups or enough for 4 or more sandwiches. If tahini is not available, purchase prepared hummus and blend with roasted red bell pepper.

Spread hummus generously on both top and bottom slices of bread. Top 4 slices of bread with sprouts, tomatoes, and avocados. Cover with remaining bread, cut, and serve.

Total Calories Per Serving: 419   Total Fat as % of Daily Value: 24%   Protein: 17 gm   Fat: 16 gm
Carbohydrates: 59 gm   Calcium: 148 mg   Iron: 5 mg   Sodium: 318 mg   Dietary Fiber: 318 gm

Chapter 10: ETHNIC SPECIALTIES

Ethnic cuisines are a perfect fit for vegetarian parties. Many ethnic cuisines are vegetable- and grain-based, rather than having meat as the centerpiece. The exciting flavors of ethnic cuisines eliminate palate boredom and make for great theme meals.

A perfect example is ratatouille, that internationally famous vegetable stew from Southern France. Eggplant is the main character, supported by summer squash, garlic, onions, tomatoes, peppers, olives, and fresh parsley. Some chefs cook all the vegetables separately, combining them just before service. Others allow the flavors to marry. As with any regional dish, proportions and consistency vary; your ratatouille may be smooth or choppy, full of tomatoes, or garlicky. Even the service temperature is open for debate, as ratatouille is served hot, cold, and at room temperature. Ratatouille can be served as an appetizer, main course, side dish, or used as a bed for grilled vegetables, potatoes, or alternative meats such as smoked seitan or roasted tofu. Ratatouille is economical and wonderful to consume. Take advantage of seasonal bounty to make several batches of ratatouille and freeze for later use.

Eggplant is the star in several other ethnic stews. Romanian cooks create "ghivetch," in which eggplant is mixed with bell peppers, onions, garlic, carrots, okra, mushrooms, green and wax beans, peas, summer squash, potatoes, and parsley. In Turkey you'll find your eggplant in "imam bayildi," a stew of braised eggplant, onions, tomatoes, and garlic. In the Middle East you'll encounter veggie "Mousakka," made with eggplant, chickpeas, tomatoes, and onions.

You won't find ratatouille in Spain, but you will find "menestra de legumbres," a vegetable ragout of wax beans, peas, cauliflower, artichokes (use canned if fresh aren't available), potatoes, carrots, asparagus, and mushrooms, which are simmered on the stove first and then baked with a chili-spiked stock.

Potatoes crisscross the international dateline for veggie delights. Colcannon, Ireland's savory staple is a combination of mashed potatoes (try this with Yukon golds for a buttery yellow dish), sautéed onions, sautéed shredded kale or cabbage, and butter and milk (you can use vegan margarine and soymilk). Colcannon is a meal in itself or can be paired with bean soup or lentil stew for a hearty meal. Himmel und Erde (heaven and earth), a German favorite, can be made veggie by omitting the bacon from stewed potatoes, apples, salt, pepper, and vinegar garnished with crisp onion rings. In South Africa, sliced potatoes are cooked in stock (you can use veggie stock or broth) along with green beans and onions. An Indian potato-based stew has onions, tomatoes, and peas seasoned with ginger, garlic, cumin, turmeric, chili pepper, cilantro, and garam masala (a lovely spice bouquet). "Yataklete kilkil" is an Ethiopian potato stew, seasoned with garlic and ginger, and filled out with carrots, green beans, onions, bell peppers, green onions, and chili peppers.

In Java, "gado-gado" is a complex festival dish with potatoes seared in a peanut and coconut milk sauce; this is added to tofu cakes, yard beans (you can use whole green beans), bean sprouts, and spinach (all cooked) and served over tomatoes and lettuce (uncooked). This would be a fun buffet presentation, offering potatoes, sauce, tofu, and cooked veggies in separate chafing dishes with the salad items iced down at the end of the buffet line.

Corn may be confined to the Americas, but this did not limit the number of ways it is used by regional cooks. New England cooks adapted succotash from Native Americans, combining fresh corn kernels with green beans in the summer and limas in the winter. The southern colonies put their own twist on succotash, using butter beans and wax beans. "Maquechou" is a Creole corn dish, combining fresh corn, onions, garlic, bell peppers, tomatoes, and red pepper flakes. In Mexico, you'll find corn mixed with summer squash, green beans, tomatoes, onions, and hot peppers to create "colache."

Whether you spell it "pasta e fagioli" or "pasta fazole," the famous pasta, bean and vegetable soup, resembling a thin stew, makes a wonderful vegan entrée. Dried pasta is cooked and drained and the water from the pasta is then used to cook the beans. This was a traditional way to preserve as many nutrients as possible (and to save on water). "Fagioli al'uccelletto" is a warm dish using cooked dried beans that have been tossed with garlic, sage, and tomatoes and seasoned with wine vinegar right before serving.

Dried pigeon peas can be found in Indian stores, or you could substitute black-eyed peas if you have a hankering to create "sambar." Dried beans are stewed with eggplant, onions, green beans, carrots, and tomatoes and seasoned with tamarind pulp, chopped fresh coconut, turmeric, cilantro, cumin, and mustard seeds. Served with crisp papadum or moist naan (Indian breads) or accompanied with basmati or long-grained rice, sambar makes a spicy entrée.

Learn to work with phyllo dough (you can purchase it frozen) and offer your guests Middle Eastern "cigars." Phyllo becomes the wrap for mashed potatoes, chopped pistachios, caramelized onions, minced garlic, and chives. Or invent your own fillings, using Middle Eastern flavorings.

Fava beans (you can purchase them dried or canned) with garlic, lemon, and olive oil are a popular Lebanese appetizer, as is eggplant and chickpeas baked with tomatoes, onion, and garlic. Or try baby okra (available fresh or frozen) simmered in tomato sauce with garlic.

Many of the ingredients in your kitchen, such as cabbage, onions, tomatoes, carrots, green beans, vegetable and mushroom stock, chopped peanuts, fresh ginger and garlic, and fresh and dried chilies are prime ingredients in Asian cuisine. To capture authentic flavors, you may want to investigate stocking some of the herbs, spices, and condiments found in ethnic markets.

Asian cuisine has a range of finger foods, served with fragrant teas and cool beers. Spring rolls are large won ton, filled with an assortment of chopped and wok-fried or steamed vegetables, salad greens, and a variety of sprouts. For a Thai flavor, add fresh ginger, garlic, cilantro, fresh chili, and brown sugar. For Chinese, use bean sprouts, soy sauce, garlic, and black pepper. Spring rolls can be fried or steamed and should be accompanied with dipping sauces. Remember to purchase eggless wrappers (such as rice paper) in Asian markets.

Won tons have traditional names that are meant to be as much fun as the savory bites, including "money bags" and "son-in-law pouch." Fill eggless wrappers with the same ingredients as spring rolls and steam or fry, offering several different types on one plate.

Looking to add some Japanese flair to your menu? Tempura can be purchased frozen, ready-to-fry, or can be made from scratch. Purchase tempura flour (which is more finely ground and seasoned than most Asian flours). Coat sweet potato strips, zucchini, and carrots with tempura flour, dip into a beaten silken tofu, and deep fry in hot oil until golden brown. Serve with preserved ginger and soy sauce. Offer tempura as an appetizer, as a light entrée, or as a garnish.

Dipping Sauces

A small bowl of dipping sauce can heighten the enjoyment of Asian finger foods and of fresh vegetables. Ranging from a small dish of soy sauce to complex sauces, dipping sauces should be served with won tons, spring rolls, noodles, tempura, and satays (skewered, thin slices of tofu, tempeh, or seitan, and carrots, mushrooms, or water chestnuts).

To whip up some fast sauces, try the following:

Sesame Seed Sauce: Toast sesame seeds in a dry pan until seeds are golden brown. Grind the seeds in a food processor and add oil until a paste is formed. Flavor with soy sauce, sugar, miso, and white pepper.

Soy and Ginger Sauce: Combine minced fresh ginger, soy sauce, and sugar. Mix well and serve immediately (this sauce does not hold up well when stored).

Lemon and Garlic Sauce: Combine fresh lemon juice, soy sauce, chopped red chilies, chopped fresh garlic, and a small amount of sugar. Serve immediately.

Cilantro and Chili Sauce: Combine vegan hoison sauce, chopped fresh cilantro, chopped red chilies, and a small amount of brown sugar. Serve immediately.

Thai Peanut Sauce: Sauté chopped onions until soft and slowly stir in peanut butter, chopped garlic, minced fresh ginger, chili powder, and coconut milk. Stir until thickened. Add ground cumin and lemon juice, then garnish with chopped peanuts and serve hot.

A Bowl of Yum

Every country in the world has its answer to a bowl of chicken soup. Here's a vegan Asian tour. Think about offering a soup and salad bar with Asian-accented soups.

YUM is a flavor unique to Thailand, combining sour, salty, spicy, and aromatic all in one bowl. This taste bud heaven is made with lime or tamarind, fresh chili, lemon grass, and fresh ginger cooked into a vegetable or mushroom stock with a little coconut milk and some shredded cabbage. TOM YUM is the vegetarian-Thai answer to that comforting bowl of chicken soup. Not only will it comfort, but is will also surprise, delight, and cheer.

Chinese vegetarian sweet corn soup is almost an entrée in a bowl. A creamy appearance is made with creamed corn and corn flour, with no dairy present. Tofu pieces are cut and added to boiling vegetable or mushroom stock, then stirred and thickened with creamed corn and corn flour. Flavor comes from adding soy sauce and fresh green onions. Just as a note, creamed corn is made by puréeing cooked corn and mixing it with a slurry of cornstarch and water.

Vegetarian Japanese udon noodle soup can be made from prepared miso broth to which is added soy sauce, minced green onions or leeks, and udon noodles (thick, wheat noodles). This soup can be garnished with scrambled tofu and fresh peas.

From Burma we get Twelve Varieties Soup. Vegetable broth is loaded up with tofu pieces, mushrooms, garlic, onions, ginger, green beans, cauliflower, cabbage, spinach, bean sprouts, and green onions, and flavored with cilantro, soy sauce, and lime!

Korean dumpling soup uses rice paper wrappers to enrobe minced garlic, cabbage, bean sprouts, mushrooms, and onions, which are simmered in a broth flavored with soy sauce, onions, and fresh ginger. Sometimes served with sautéed spinach, this soup is sure to chase away the blues.

A Fast Asian Culinary Vocabulary Lesson

Chinese Five Spice: a powdered blend of star anise, fennel, black pepper, cloves, and cinnamon. Used to flavor sauces and noodle dishes.

Hoison Sauce: used in Chinese cuisine, this sweet and sour sauce has soy sauce, tamarind, and chili as some of its ingredients. Read the label to ensure that it is vegan.

Lemon Grass: is a long-stemmed herb that has a citrus flavor. Fresh lemon grass has the most flavor and is used in Thai, Vietnamese, and Chinese dishes, such as Thai coconut or hot and sour soup. If fresh lemon grass is not available, use lemon zest instead.

Miso: this fermented soybean paste is a staple of Japanese seasoning. Available in different strengths and colors (white, brown, red, and black), miso can be used to flavor soups, marinades, and dips.

Rice Flour: makes a delicate breading that gives a light crunch to fried dishes.

Rice Vermicelli: these dried, thin, glass-like noodles can be soaked and used in stir-fries or soups or can be quickly deep fried for a crunchy garnish or to form an edible basket.

Rice Vinegar: is clear, mild, and sweet-tasting vinegar, suited to Japanese and Singapore cuisine. If not available, diluted white wine vinegar can be used.

Sesame Oil: is dark brown oil with a nutty, rich flavor. Do not refrigerate, as it will cloud. Use it for Chinese, Korean, and Japanese dishes.

Soy Sauce: there are many varieties of soy sauce; do a tasting and decide which type suits your menu.

Tamarind: sold as a paste, tamarind can be used as a "sour" wherever lemon might be used.

Wasabi: also called Japanese horseradish, wasabi is a river vegetable with a root resembling dark green ginger. Sold as a paste or a powder, wasabi is very hot and can be used sparingly in soups and as a condiment.

Wrappers: finger food and dumplings are popular in Asian cuisines. Won ton wrappers are small squares traditionally made of wheat flour and egg dough; vegans can use rice-based wrappers instead. Spring roll wrappers are a larger version of won ton, or can be made from rice flour. Rice paper wrappers are very thin, made from rice flour and water and must be brushed with water before using so they become flexible.

Ready to Go Middle Eastern?

Stock Your Spice Rack: caraway seeds, cumin, fenugreek, mint, oregano, paprika, and parsley
And Your Pantry: almonds, bulgur, chickpeas, eggplant, raisins, grape leaves, sesame paste, pine nuts, and lentils

So You Can Make:
Dolmas: grape leaves stuffed with rice, onions, raisins, and pine nuts

Pide: Middle Eastern pizza made with flatbread

Tahini: roasted ground sesame paste, used for flavoring and for the base of hummus

Mezze: the Middle Eastern version of anitpasto

Falafel: ground chickpeas, formed into patties and fried or baked, served with tahini.

Stuffed pita sandwiches: use your imagination with chickpeas, cooked bulgur, grilled fresh veggies

Tabbouleh: bulgur and parsley salad

Pizza Anyone?

Pizza is inherently vegetarian. If striving to create a classic pizza (a la Naples), it must be baked on a hot brick or stone surface, not a pan. The crust is thin and crisp, and except for the raised edges, should not exceed $^3/_8$ inch. Chopped tomatoes are used, not a sauce. Plum tomatoes are the tomato of choice.

Pizza Margherita one of the most popular traditionally topped pizza, consisting of tomatoes (just chopped tomatoes, not sauce), (vegan) mozzarella, olive oil, and (vegan) shredded Parmesan cheese. The aforenamed Margherita was an Italian queen, well known for her love of pizza.

Siciliana-style pizza is generally shaped into a rectangle, has a thicker crust, and is traditionally topped with tomatoes and tomato sauce, (vegan) parmesan cheese, black olives, smoked tofu or nutritional yeast instead of anchovies, and seasoned with oregano.

Schiacciata is pizza-like dough that has been popular in Florence since the 1500's. Served more as an accompaniment rather than an entrée this "pizzette alla fiorentina" is flavored with rosemary or sage and olive oil. It's prepared without tomatoes.

Pizza can be designed to serve from one to many people. This makes it ideal as a vegetarian offering. Ready-to-use frozen pizza shells makes offering different vegetarian pizza easy. Some frozen pizza shells require proofing, which can be done as a "cold-proof" in the refrigerator (keep several of all sizes at the ready in the refrigerator). Check the ingredients. Pizza dough should be vegetarian and many are vegan (no dairy or animal products).

Fresh or frozen pizza shells can be made into a quick meal. Top shells with tomato sauce (straight from the can or seasoned with tomato purée, fresh or dried basil and oregano, chopped tomatoes, onions, and peppers, etc.) and offer ingredients such as sliced mushrooms, peppers, onions, and garlic, spicy sprouts (try radish or broccoli sprouts), broccoli or cauliflower florets, shredded carrots, capers (the pickled plant, not the fish), artichoke hearts, chopped tomatoes, seasoned tofu, veggie crumbles, and for the more adventurous, diced pineapple. For variety, make individual calzone with the same ingredients; an advantage of a calzone is that it can be premade, frozen (uncooked or cooked), and then heated as needed.

United Nations of Pizza

Fusion is in the pizza world. Think about ingredients from all over the world: teriyaki tofu, pickled ginger, Moroccan harissa (fiery pepper and chili sauce), Indian chutneys or dal (spicy, thin lentil stew), tandoori potatoes, soyrizo (vegan, spicy sausage), and seasoned beans can all find a home on top of a pizza crust.

Supplement tomato sauce with fruit or vegetable salsas, using fresh red or yellow tomatoes, green, yellow, red, or orange bell peppers, tomatillos, mango, papaya, pineapple, or oranges to flavor the salsas. Leave red entirely behind and use a pesto (fresh basil and pine nut sauce) topped with vegan sour cream and vegetarian caviar or smoked tofu (how decadent! how Russian!).

You can also wrap traditional pizza toppings in lavash (flat bread) or stuff a pita with them. We've seen pizza "scones" offered in several cafes in Southern California (scones dotted with shredded basil, chopped tomatoes, diced soy pepperoni, and topped with smoked vegan mozzarella). Prepare a "Very Veggie Pita Pizza" by coating the inside of a pita with marinara sauce, stuff with sliced mushrooms, chopped tomatoes, onions, and bell peppers, minced garlic, and diced olives, heat in oven or microwave, then serve hot.

Pizza Toppings

1. <u>Veggies</u> (raw, grilled, sautéed, or steamed)
   sliced or diced onions, bell peppers, artichoke hearts, mushrooms (button, portobellos, shiitake, enoki, etc.), arugula (bitter greens), tomatoes, green and black olives, capers, eggplant, zucchini

2. <u>Herbs</u> (fresh and dried)
   basil, oregano, rosemary, whole or diced garlic, thyme, red pepper flakes, chopped parsley, cilantro

3. <u>Vegan Cheese and Meat Alternatives</u>
   soy cheddar, jack, and mozzarella; soy sour cream
   crumbled soy bacon bits, crumbled "ground round" (soy ground beef), diced veggie meats, sliced veggie pepperoni

4. <u>Beyond the Usual</u>
   pineapple, vegetarian caviar, sprouts (broccoli, radish, sunflower), roasted fruit (pears, apples), habanero chilies, chocolate chips, chopped peanuts, smoked or grilled seitan, sesame seeds, chopped pistachios

Here's Some Pizza Vocabulary in Italian

<u>alla napoletana</u>: neapolitan style, with tomatoes, mozzarella, and basil

<u>con cipolle</u>: with onions

<u>con ramerino</u>: with rosemary

<u>con aglio</u>: with garlic

<u>al pesto</u>: with basil sauce

<u>pommodori e carciofi</u>: with tomatoes and artichokes

<u>aubergine e mozzarella</u>: with eggplant and mozzarella

RECIPES
Note: all recipes can be easily doubled, tripled, or quadrupled

Hearty and Healthy Pizza
Makes one 12-inch pizza or 8 slices

One 12-inch vegan pizza crust, unbaked, ready to use

Sauce:
2 cups prepared tomato sauce
1/2 cup tomato purée
1/3 cup shredded carrots
3 cloves garlic, minced
1/4 cup shredded fresh basil
1/2 ounce dried oregano
1/2 ounce black pepper

Topping:
1/2 cup thinly sliced green bell pepper
1/2 cup diced Roma tomatoes
1/3 cup minced broccoli florets
1 pound finely shredded fresh spinach (about 4½ cups)
1/3 cup thinly sliced white or red onions
3/4 cup shredded vegan mozzarella

Heat tomato sauce, tomato purée, carrots, and garlic in a saucepan until carrots are soft. Add basil, oregano, and pepper and allow sauce to simmer for 30 minutes.

To assemble, first preheat oven to 400 degrees. Spread sauce over pizza crust evenly. Arrange topping ingredients over sauce, finishing with cheese. Bake until crust is browned and cheese is melted, about 15 minutes, depending on your oven. Serve hot.

Total Calories Per Slice: 192	Total Fat as % of Daily Value: 5%	Protein: 5 gm	Fat: 3 gm
Carbohydrates: 35 gm	Calcium: 183 mg Iron: 3 mg	Sodium: 791 mg	Dietary Fiber: 4 gm

Thai Vegetable Wrap
Serves 8

1 pound extra-firm tofu, drained (about 2 cups drained)
1 cup each thinly sliced green bell pepper and red bell pepper
1 cup thinly sliced onions
1 cup shredded carrots
Vegetable oil spray

Sauce:
2 cups coconut milk
4 Tablespoons red curry paste (make sure there is no fish flavor!)
2 teaspoons maple syrup

2 Tablespoons vinegar
2 teaspoons minced fresh ginger
1 teaspoon red pepper flakes
2 cloves garlic, minced
3 Tablespoons cornstarch
8 spring roll wrappers or whole wheat tortillas

Slice tofu into thin strips and set aside.

To prepare sauce, place coconut milk in a medium pot and bring to a fast boil. Reduce to simmer and add curry paste, syrup, vinegar, ginger, red pepper, and garlic. Mix and allow sauce to simmer. In a small cup, combine cornstarch with just enough water to make a slurry, about 1-2 Tablespoons. Add cornstarch slurry to sauce. Stir and allow sauce to cook until thickened, about 5 minutes.

Heat a wok or pot with deep sides. Spray with vegetable oil. Add tofu and stir-fry 1 minute. Add peppers, onions, and carrots and stir-fry. Stir in sauce and allow mixture to cook for 1 minute.

Lay wraps on platter. Place about ¹/₂ cup filling on each wrap. Roll up and serve.

Notes: Curry paste can be found in the gourmet or ethnic section of many markets. Check out Southeast Asian and Indian markets as well and make sure there is no fish sauce in the curry paste you purchase. If you like, use reduced-fat canned coconut milk for the sauce. For a fancy presentation, cut each wrap in half and place in a circle around the rim of a serving plate. Stack the center of plate with fresh bean sprouts, sliced fresh chilies, lime wedges, and fresh basil leaves.

Total Calories Per Serving: 397   Total Fat as % of Daily Value: 29%   Protein: 12 gm   Fat: 19 gm
Carbohydrates: 47 gm   Calcium: 131 mg   Iron: 5 mg   Sodium: 535 mg   Dietary Fiber: 3 gm

Stuffed Mushrooms with Couscous
Serves 5-6

¹/₂ cup vegetable broth
¹/₄ cup instant couscous
1 teaspoon ground black pepper
2 Tablespoons minced fresh basil
2 teaspoons nutritional yeast
Vegetable oil spray
2 cloves garlic, minced
¹/₄ cup chopped onions
1 Tablespoon soy sauce (low-sodium soy sauce is fine)
1 cup white wine or water
12-14 fresh small button mushrooms, stems removed, washed

In a small pot, bring vegetable broth to a boil. Stir in couscous, then remove from heat. Cover and allow to sit for 5 minutes or until all liquid is absorbed. Mix in pepper, basil, and yeast. Set aside.

Preheat oven to 350 degrees. Spray a frying pan with oil and allow to heat. Sauté garlic and onions until soft, about 2 minutes. Stir in soy sauce and wine or water and allow mixture to simmer for 4 minutes. Add mushrooms. Cook until mushrooms are tender, about 10 minutes. Save cooking liquid.

Place mushrooms in a baking dish. Fill with couscous. Sprinkle a small amount of cooking liquid over each mushroom. Cover and bake for 10 minutes or until hot.

Total Calories Per Serving: 68   Total Fat as % of Daily Value: <1%   Protein: 2 gm   Fat: <1 gm
Carbohydrates: 7 gm   Calcium: 46 mg   Iron: 1 mg   Sodium: 288 mg   Dietary Fiber: 1 gm

Stuffed Grape Leaves I

Serves 10-12

2 cups vegetable broth
1 cup uncooked brown rice
1/2 cup chopped green onions
1/4 cup finely chopped celery
1/4 cup finely chopped fresh mint
1 Tablespoon olive oil
2 Tablespoons vinegar
1 Tablespoon lemon juice
1/2 cup raisins (white raisins are traditional)
1/4 cup pine nuts
1 teaspoon ground black pepper
1/2 teaspoon dried ground oregano
35 grape leaves, drained and rinsed
2 teaspoons olive oil
1 teaspoon vinegar
2 teaspoon lemon juice

Pour broth into a medium-size pot and bring to a fast boil. Stir in rice, reduce heat, cover and allow to simmer for 40 minutes or until all water is absorbed. Fluff rice and allow rice to cool.

Preheat oven to 350 degrees. In a medium-size bowl, mix rice with onions, celery, mint, 1 Tablespoon of oil, vinegar, lemon juice, raisins, pine nuts, pepper, and oregano. Place grape leaves on a clean surface. Place about 2 Tablespoons of filling on leaf (depending on size of leaf) and roll up, first folding the sides in. Place stuffed grape leaves in a baking dish and drizzle with 2 teaspoons oil, vinegar, and lemon juice. Cover and bake for 10-15 minutes or until warmed through. If you like, you can microwave the grape leaves for 4-5 minutes on HIGH or until warmed. Serve warm or cold.

Note: Grape leaves are available canned or jarred in Mediterranean, Greek, and Middle Eastern markets, as well as some natural food stores. If you're really careful, you could use steamed, cooled romaine or kale leaves instead of grape leaves.

Total Calories Per Serving: 151   Total Fat as % of Daily Value: 8%   Protein: 3 gm   Fat: 5 gm
Carbohydrates: 24 gm   Calcium: 50 mg   Iron: 1 mg   Sodium: 162 mg   Dietary Fiber: 2 gm

Stuffed Grape Leaves II
Makes about 30 stuffed grape leaves

1 cup olive oil
3 cups chopped onion
1 cup short-grain rice
3 Tablespoons tomato paste
$^1/_2$ cup water
Lemon pepper or ground black pepper, to taste
1 teaspoon dry mint, crumbled
1 teaspoon dried dill
1-2 Tablespoons minced fresh parsley
3 Tablespoons fresh lemon juice
Salt to taste
About 30 brined grape leaves, rinsed in cold water and patted dry

For steaming:
2 large onions, peeled, sliced (about 2 cups)
1 head leaf lettuce, such as romaine

Heat olive oil in large saucepan on medium-high heat. Add onion and cook until transparent, about 4-5 minutes. Add rice and tomato paste; stir to combine until rice is evenly coated with tomato paste. Add water and bring to boil. Reduce heat to medium and simmer until liquid evaporates and rice is tender. Add pepper, mint, dill, parsley, lemon juice, and salt. Stir and taste; adjust seasoning as needed. Set aside to cool completely.

To stuff grape leaves, arrange 1 grape leaf, smooth side down, on a kitchen towel. Trim stem flush with leaf. Spoon about 1 Tablespoon filling onto leaf near stem end and roll up filling tightly in leaf, folding in sides and squeezing roll to pack filling. (Roll should be about $3^1/_2$ inches long.) Make more rolls in same manner. Line bottom of 8-quart heavy pot with onion slices and top with lettuce leaves. Arrange stuffed grape leaves, seam sides down, close together in layers over leaves. Add enough water to come $^1/_2$-inch below top of stuffed grape leaves. Cover with lettuce leaves. Bring to boil on high heat. Cover, reduce heat to low, and simmer 45 minutes. Remove from heat. Cool and refrigerate. Store chilled up to one week. Serve cold.

When serving, first prepare tazaziki sauce. To make tazaziki, a yogurt-based sauce that accompanies these stuffed grape leaves, combine 3 cups plain soy yogurt, 1 large hothouse (seedless or Persian) cucumber (about 1 cup, finely diced), and 2 teaspoons dried mint (crumbled). Add salt and garlic powder to taste.

Note: If desired, add either $^1/_2$ cup pine nuts or 3 Tablespoons currants to the rice filling when you add the mint.

Total Calories Per Stuffed Grape Leaf: 90	Total Fat as % of Daily Value: 11%	Protein: 1 gm	Fat: 7 gm
Carbohydrates: 6 gm Calcium: 24 mg	Iron: 1 mg Sodium: 16 mg	Dietary Fiber: 1 gm	

Stuffed Arepas
Makes 12 arepas

Arepas are Latin American corn cakes. They can be made unstuffed or stuffed with savory fillings.

2 cups instant masa flour (found in Central American markets or online)
1 teaspoon salt
3 cups boiling water
Vegetable oil spray
Wax paper

For stuffing:
1¹/₂ cups bean chili or ³/₄ cup shredded vegan cheese or 1 cup salsa

Combine flour and salt in a large bowl. Slowly stir in water until it becomes a soft, not sticky, dough. Cover and let stand 5 minutes. Remove and place on floured surface and knead for 3 minutes.

Preheat nonstick pan or grill. Spray hands with vegetable oil. Shape dough into small balls (about 3 inches in diameter). Place dough balls between two pieces of wax paper and flatten to ³/₄ inch thickness. Spray pan or grill with vegetable oil. Cook arepas over medium heat, turning and cooking until both sides are golden brown.

Remove from heat, place a Tablespoon of stuffing on one end of the arepa, fold over and serve immediately. If the arepas are too stiff to fold, simply top them with chili, cheese, or salsa.

Note: Instant masa flour may also be called "tamale mix," and generally contains corn flour, salt, and baking powder. Check the ingredients to ensure that it is vegan.

Total Calories Per Arepa: 105   Total Fat as % of Daily Value: 4%   Protein: 4 gm   Fat: 2 gm
Carbohydrates: 18 gm   Calcium: 42 mg   Iron: 2 mg   Sodium: 346 mg   Dietary Fiber: 3 gm

Vegetable Gratins
Gratins are comfort foods in every French home. Unfortunately, in the States, gratins have been relegated to gloppy, boxed mixes with cardboard textures and blah flavors. A vegetable gratin can be a wonderful dinner, when prepared with a little love and a little care.

A gratin is a cooked vegetable tossed with a flavorful sauce, topped with bread crumbs, and browned in the oven. Here are some tips for a successful gratin:

1. After cooking vegetables, drain them well. Any excess water will dilute sauce and make the vegetables soggy. Gratins can go beyond potatoes (choose starchy or baking potatoes for gratins, as they will absorb the sauce). Think spinach (squeeze excess water from spinach after cooking; if using frozen spinach, there's no need to cook it, just thaw and squeeze), broccoli or cauliflower (cut into florets and steam briefly; frozen broccoli or cauliflower does not need to be cooked, just thawed and drained), Swiss chard (cut leaves into ¹/₂-inch strips), winter squash (cut into peeled, 2-inch pieces), zucchini (cut into thin slices), mushrooms (use fresh, sliced mushrooms), and chopped onion.

2. All sauces can be jazzed up with herbs. For each cup of sauce, add two teaspoons of dried or 1 Tablespoon of fresh, chopped herbs. Since gratin sauces are generally mild, think about using tarragon, basil, oregano, thyme, and marjoram for some extra flavor.

3. If you decide to use vegan soy cheese in your gratin, be sure to melt a small amount in a small dish before using it in the gratin. Different brands of soy cheese melt differently. You'll want to be sure you have the right product.

4. Use as heavy a baking dish as you have for a gratin. This helps with even heating.

5. When broiling to brown the top, keep the oven door open a crack to allow excess steam to escape. This will give you a crisp top.

Okay, so now you're ready to make your gratin. Prepare about one cup of a vegan cream or bechamel sauce (see page 321 for recipe) or make a cup of cream sauce, by puréeing $3/4$ cup of silken tofu with $1/4$ cup soymilk. Cook, stirring, over medium heat, add a small amount of cayenne and nutmeg, and cook until mixture is hot. Have your cooked veggies (about $1 1/2$ cups) drained; this is a great place to use leftover veggies.

Heavily grease a baking dish. Toss the veggies and the sauce together in the dish and bake for 10 minutes at 425 degrees. Sprinkle with bread crumbs and broil for 1 minute or until golden. If you like, you can toss the veggies and sauce together in the baking dish and refrigerate it, uncooked, until you're ready to prepare it. You can wait up to 3 days to cook it.

Korean "Soon" Tofu Stew
Serves 4

2 teaspoons sesame oil
$1/2$ cup diced onions
1 Tablespoon crushed red pepper
2 cloves garlic, finely chopped
One 12-ounce package silken tofu (about $1 1/2$ cups)
$1 1/2$ cups sliced fresh mushrooms (any variety)
2 teaspoons toasted sesame seeds
8 cups of water
$1/2$ cup chopped green onions
1 cup washed, fresh spinach leaves

Heat oil in large pot. Sauté onions and red pepper until onions are soft. Add garlic and cook for 1 minute longer. Add tofu, mushrooms, sesame seeds, and water. Bring to a fast boil. Reduce heat and simmer for 5 minutes. Be sure to break up the soft tofu in the pot; this will help to create a gravy-like consistency in the soup. Allow stew to simmer until mushrooms are soft. Just before serving, sprinkle chopped green onions and spinach leaves on top of stew. Serve with sticky or short-grained white rice.

Total Calories Per Serving: 110   Total Fat as % of Daily Value: 8%   Protein: 8 gm   Fat: 6 gm
Carbohydrates: 9 gm   Calcium: 50 mg   Iron: 1 mg   Sodium: 41 mg   Dietary Fiber: 1 gm

Indian Cuisine

Garam Masala
Makes about $^1/_4$ cup or 6 Tablespoons

This is a savory, versatile spice blend that can be used to make anything from chai masala (spiced tea) to flavored potatoes, rice, and curries.

5 teaspoons coriander seeds
1 Tablespoon cumin seeds
1 Tablespoon black pepper
1 teaspoon each whole cloves, cinnamon, and green cardamom pods

Heat a medium-size skillet until very hot. Toast coriander and cumin seeds for about 3 minutes. Remove from skillet, cool, and combine with other ingredients. (You'll need to grind the spices, either by hand with a mortar and pestle or with a spice grinder or food processor.) Store in a glass (not metal) container, in a cool, dark place. The mixture will keep its pungency for up to 4 months.

Total Calories Per Serving: 83   Total Fat as % of Daily Value: 6%   Protein: 3 gm   Fat: 4 gm
Carbohydrates: 16 gm   Calcium: 192 mg   Iron: 9 mg   Sodium: 22 mg   Dietary Fiber: 8 gm

Indian Lentil Stew
Serves 8-10

1 cup masoor dal (red lentils; if not available, use standard gray lentils)
2 cups peeled and cubed boiling potatoes
1 cup peeled and sliced carrots
4 cups vegetable stock
2 Tablespoons vegetable oil
$^1/_2$ cup chopped onion
2 cloves garlic, minced
1 Tablespoon each minced fresh green chili and minced fresh ginger
2 teaspoons ground cumin
2 teaspoons ground coriander
1 teaspoon cayenne powder
$^1/_2$ teaspoon garam masala (see recipe above)
$^1/_8$ teaspoon turmeric

Rinse lentils to remove dust. Combine lentils, potatoes, and carrots in a large bowl. Pour stock over mixture, cover, and set aside.

In a large pot, heat oil and sauté onion until soft. Add garlic, green chili, and ginger, and sauté 1 more minute. Add lentil mixture to onions. Bring to a fast boil. Mix in remaining spices. Reduce heat, cover, and simmer for at least 1 hour, or until lentils are tender. Serve stew over steamed rice.

Total Calories Per Serving: 82   Total Fat as % of Daily Value: 1%   Protein: 3 gm   Fat: <1 gm
Carbohydrates: 17 gm   Calcium: 27 mg   Iron: 2 mg   Sodium: 468 mg   Dietary Fiber: 4 gm

Vegetable Curry with Fruit
Serves 5

1¹/₂ cups chunked extra-firm tofu
³/₄ cup canned pineapple tidbits, not drained
1 teaspoon paprika
2 teaspoons ground cumin
1 teaspoon ground coriander
2 teaspoons ground turmeric
1 teaspoon chopped fresh cilantro
Vegetable oil spray
³/₄ cup sliced onion
1¹/₂ cups boiled, peeled, and cubed potatoes (or drained, canned potatoes)
¹/₂ cup soymilk
2 Tablespoons fruit chutney

Place the tofu in a large bowl. In a small bowl, mix the pineapple with juice and all the ground spices and cilantro. Pour over the tofu and allow tofu to marinate for at least 2 hours (it can marinate for up to 10 hours, if you'd like to do some pre-preparation).

Spray a large skillet with oil and heat. Add onion and cook until softened, about 3 minutes. Add the potatoes, tofu, pineapple, and marinade to the onions and simmer for 10 minutes. Slowly stir in soymilk; you may not want to add the entire amount, depending on the desired thickness. Stir in the fruit chutney. Cover and simmer for 5 minutes, or until heated through. Serve over steamed rice.

Total Calories Per Serving: 189   Total Fat as % of Daily Value: 12%   Protein: 14 gm   Fat: 7 gm
Carbohydrates: 19 gm   Calcium: 577 mg   Iron: 4 mg   Sodium: 26 mg   Dietary Fiber: 4 gm

Gobi Aloo (Southeast Asian Cauliflower and Potatoes)
Serves 5

1 large head cauliflower (about 1¹/₂ pounds or 6 cups)
3 medium boiling potatoes (about 1 pound or 4 cups)
Vegetable oil spray
1 teaspoon whole mustard seeds
1 bayleaf
3 whole cloves
2 pods green cardamom
1 cup sliced onions
1 teaspoon ground coriander
1 teaspoon cumin seeds
¹/₂ teaspoon ground turmeric

Cut the cauliflower into small bite-sized pieces (roughly 1-inch cubes). Set aside. Place potatoes in a pot, cover with water, and allow potatoes to boil until soft. While the potatoes are cooking, heat a large skillet with oil until it is very hot. Add the mustard seeds and wait until they start popping. Add bay leaves, cardamom, and cloves. Cook, stirring for 2 minutes and add onions. Cook onions until soft, and stir in coriander and cumin.

Add the cauliflower and cook for 2 minutes. Lower heat and cover. While the cauliflower is simmering, peel and cut potatoes into bite-sized pieces. Add to skillet. Add turmeric and stir. If dry, add up to $^1/_2$ cup of water. Continue to stir and simmer until cauliflower and potatoes are tender. Serve hot.

Total Calories Per Serving: 139   Total Fat as % of Daily Value: 1%   Protein: 4 gm   Fat: 1 gm
Carbohydrates: 31 gm   Calcium: 60 mg   Iron: 2 mg   Sodium: 15 mg   Dietary Fiber: 6 gm

South Indian Pilau (Pilafed Rice)
Serves 5

1 cup basmati rice
Vegetable oil spray
$^1/_2$ cup thinly sliced onion
2 whole green cardamom pods
2 Tablespoons minced fresh green chili
1 whole clove
$^1/_8$ teaspoon ground cinnamon
1 bay leaf
1 cup mixed peas and cubed carrots
$^1/_2$ teaspoon dried coriander
1 clove garlic, minced
$^1/_4$ teaspoon ground ginger
$^1/_4$ teaspoon chili powder
$^1/_3$ cup tomato purée
1 cup water

Rinse rice in cold water and set aside. Spray a large pot with oil and cook onions and cardamom, stirring, for about 2 minutes. Add chili and stir to combine. Add clove, cinnamon, and bay leaf and cook until onions turn golden brown, about 4-5 minutes. Add peas and carrots, coriander, garlic, ginger, and chili powder and stir to combine. Add the tomato pureé and water and bring to a boil. Stir in rice.

Reduce the flame and cover. Stir mixture after it has been simmering for 5 minutes. Allow pilau to simmer until all the moisture has evaporated and the rice is tender, about 10 minutes.

Total Calories Per Serving: 76   Total Fat as % of Daily Value: <1%   Protein: 3 gm   Fat: <1 gm
Carbohydrates: 17 gm   Calcium: 21 mg   Iron: 1 mg   Sodium: 92 mg   Dietary Fiber: 1 gm

Hungarian Cuisine

Hideg Almaleves (Cold Apple Soup)
Serves 5

This is a lovely summer soup. Serve it as a dessert, garnished with lemon sorbet or vanilla soy ice cream.

3 cups red and green apples, cored, peeled, and diced
$^1/_2$ cup sugar
2 teaspoons lemon zest

3 cups hot water
½ cup white wine or ¼ cup unsweetened apple juice
2 Tablespoons flour
2 Tablespoons cold water
½ cup vegan sour cream

Combine apples, sugar, zest, and hot water in a medium pot; cover and cook on medium heat until apples are tender, about 30 minutes. Add the wine or juice and continue to cook. In a small cup, combine flour and cold water to make a smooth paste. Add several spoonfuls of hot soup to paste to temper it (make it easier to combine into soup). Add paste to soup, stirring vigorously to incorporate. Simmer for 5 minutes. Remove from heat, cover, and place in refrigerator to cool for at least 2 hours before serving. Stir in sour cream before serving.

Total Calories Per Serving: 208   Total Fat as % of Daily Value: 6%   Protein: 1 gm   Fat: 4 gm
Carbohydrates: 39 gm   Calcium: 6 mg   Iron: 0 mg   Sodium: 130 mg   Dietary Fiber: 1 gm

Komenymagos Leves (Caraway Seed Soup)
Serves 6

This is a real peasant soup, requiring few ingredients and not much money to make. It can be a light soup, good for serving before a heavy meal.

2 Tablespoons caraway seeds
6 cups boiling water
2 Tablespoons vegan margarine
4 Tablespoons flour
½ cup vegan sour cream
½ cup croutons

In a medium pot, combine caraway seeds and water. Simmer, covered for 15 minutes. In a small cup, combine margarine and flour to form a paste. Add several spoonfuls of hot soup to the paste to temper. Add paste to hot soup and stir vigorously to combine. Cover and allow soup to simmer until thickened, about 20 minutes. Place 1-2 Tablespoons of sour cream in each soup bowl. Pour soup over cream and garnish with croutons. Serve hot.

Total Calories Per Serving: 127   Total Fat as % of Daily Value: 12%   Protein: 2 gm   Fat: 8 gm
Carbohydrates: 13 gm   Calcium: 18 mg   Iron: 1 mg   Sodium: 165 mg   Dietary Fiber: 1 gm

Szarittott Babfozelek (White Beans with Sour Cream)

Serves 5

A light entrée or a hearty side dish, this is the perfect recipe for leftover cooked beans or green beans. It actually gets better the second day, so make extra to enjoy again.

3 cups cooked or canned white beans (approximately 1¹/₂ cups uncooked beans)
1 Tablespoon vegan margarine
³/₄ cup chopped onions
2 Tablespoons flour
1 Tablespoon vinegar
³/₄ cup cold water
¹/₂ cup vegan sour cream

Rinse and drain cooked or canned beans. Set aside. In a medium-size frying pan, heat margarine. Add onions and allow to brown, about 3 minutes. Stir in flour to blend. Add vinegar and cold water to make a thick sauce. Stir in beans. Allow dish to heat for 5 minutes on medium heat. Right before serving, stir in sour cream.

Variation: This dish works well with cooked green or wax beans instead of white beans.

Total Calories Per Serving: 196   Total Fat as % of Daily Value: 4%   Protein: 11 gm   Fat: 3 gm
Carbohydrates: 32 gm   Calcium: 103 mg   Iron: 4 mg   Sodium: 293 mg   Dietary Fiber: 7 gm

Tofu Paprikash

Serves 5

A spin on the traditional and omnipresent paprikash stews. This can be made a day ahead of time and reheated when ready to serve.

2 teaspoons vegan margarine
¹/₂ cup onions, sliced thin
1 pound smoked firm tofu, drained and cut into cubes
1 Tablespoon ground paprika
1 cup vegan sour cream

Heat margarine in a medium frying pan. Add onions and cook until browned, about 3 minutes. Add tofu and paprika and continue to cook, stirring, for 8 minutes, or until tofu is heated. Stir in sour cream, cook for 3 additional minutes, and serve immediately over cooked noodles.

Total Calories Per Serving: 222   Total Fat as % of Daily Value: 21%   Protein: 9 gm   Fat: 13 gm
Carbohydrates: 18 gm   Calcium: 187 mg   Iron: 2 mg   Sodium: 284 mg   Dietary Fiber: 1 gm

Dill and Mushroom Sauce

Makes about 2 cups or 4 servings

Serve this savory sauce over baked or mashed potatoes, barley or rice pilaf, baked or grilled tofu or seitan, or even use as a base for a soup!

2 Tablespoons vegan margarine
¹/₂ cup finely chopped onions
¹/₄ cup finely chopped fresh mushrooms
2 Tablespoons flour
¹/₂ cup vegetable stock
1 Tablespoon chopped fresh dill
1 teaspoon lemon juice
¹/₂ cup vegan sour cream

Melt margarine in a medium-size frying pan. Add onions and mushrooms and cook for 2 minutes. Stir in flour until well incorporated. Add stock, reduce heat and cover. Allow sauce to cook until thickened, about 20 minutes. Stir in dill, juice, and sour cream and allow sauce to cook, stirring, for 3 minutes.

Total Calories Per 1/2 Cup: 118   Total Fat as % of Daily Value: 8%   Protein: 2 gm   Fat: 5 gm
Carbohydrates: 16 gm   Calcium: 44 mg   Iron: 1 mg   Sodium: 261 mg   Dietary Fiber: 1 gm

Krampampuli (New Year's Eve Punch)

Serve 10

This hot and spicy beverage is served hot on Sylvester night (New Year's Eve). It is usually made with brandy, but you can use apple cider instead.

¹/₂ cup chopped dried figs
¹/₂ cup chopped dates
¹/₂ cup candied ginger or fruit peel
³/₄ cup sugar
2 Tablespoons orange zest
1 cup brandy or apple cider
4 cups red wine or 3 cups wine and ¹/₄ cup vinegar
2 cinnamon sticks
2 cups hot brewed tea
³/₄ cup orange juice
¹/₂ cup lemon juice

Place figs, dates, and ginger in a large, non-reactive bowl. Sprinkle sugar and zest over fruit and toss to combine. Cover and allow fruit to stand for at least 1 hour. Pour brandy and wine (or cider, wine, and vinegar) over fruit. Cover and allow punch to stand for ¹/₂ hour. Place cinnamon, tea, and juices in a medium-size pot and bring to a boil. Pour over the fruit and serve hot with a little fruit in each glass.

Total Calories Per Serving: 270   Total Fat as % of Daily Value: 1%   Protein: 1 gm   Fat: 1 gm
Carbohydrates: 36 gm   Calcium: 49 mg   Iron: 2 mg   Sodium: 10 mg   Dietary Fiber: 3 gm

Balinese Cuisine

Nasi Goreng (Fried Rice)
Serves 6

Found widely in Bali, nasi goreng is traditionally flavored with shrimp; we've used seitan. If you would like to be really authentic, hunt down kecap manis (Indonesian sweet soy sauce). If you can't locate it, use ketchup (originally a Chinese-Indian condiment) instead.

Vegetable oil spray
2 cloves garlic, minced
1 cup chopped red bell pepper
³/₄ cup diced smoked seitan or tempeh
1¹/₂ cups shredded green cabbage
¹/₂ cup fresh green beans, cut into small pieces
2¹/₂ cups cooked white rice
¹/₂ cup chopped fresh tomato
2 Tablespoons tomato sauce
2 Tablespoons kecap manis or ketchup
1 Tablespoon soy sauce

Heat a wok or deep frying pan and spray with vegetable oil. Add garlic and bell pepper and sauté over high heat for 1 minute. Add seitan or tempeh and sauté, stirring briskly for 1 minute. Add cabbage and green beans and sauté until cabbage and beans are tender, about 4 minutes.

Lower heat and mix in rice, tomatoes, tomato sauce, kecap manis or ketchup, and soy sauce. Stir to mix well and allow to heat, about 4 minutes. Serve hot.

Total Calories Per Serving: 147   Total Fat as % of Daily Value: 4%   Protein: 6 gm   Fat: 3 gm
Carbohydrates: 25 gm   Calcium: 49 mg   Iron: 2 mg   Sodium: 264 mg   Dietary Fiber: 2 gm

Jukut Urap (Balinese Vegetable Salad)
Serves 5

Balinese vegetarian cooking utilizes lots of seasonal vegetables. You can mix and match crunchy and leafy vegetables in this recipe.

¹/₂ cup cabbage, cut into small chunks
¹/₂ cup packed fresh spinach leaves
¹/₂ cup fresh green beans, cut into 1-inch pieces
¹/₂ cup fresh soy bean sprouts
Vegetable oil spray
2 Tablespoons chopped onions
2 cloves garlic, minced
¹/₄ cup chopped fresh tomato
3 Tablespoons seeded and chopped fresh hot chili peppers
2 Kaffir lime leaves (optional)

1 teaspoon sugar
2 teaspoons cracked black pepper
2 Tablespoons fresh lime juice

Lightly blanch (par-cook) cabbage, spinach, beans, and sprouts separately. Do this by bringing a pot of water to boil. Lower vegetables into the water for only 1-2 minutes until the cabbage, spinach, and sprouts wilt slightly and the beans show a slight tenderness. Remove vegetables with a slotted spoon and place in a colander. Spray for several seconds with cold water to stop cooking. Set aside.

Spray a small frying pan with oil. Add onion, garlic, tomatoes, and chilies and sauté until tender, about 2 minutes. In a large bowl, mix par-cooked vegetables with garlic mixture, Kaffir leaves, sugar, pepper, and lime juice. Serve at room temperature.

Total Calories Per Serving: 29   Total Fat as % of Daily Value: 1%   Protein: 2 gm   Fat: 1 gm
Carbohydrates: 6 gm   Calcium: 26 mg   Iron: 1 mg   Sodium: 9 mg   Dietary Fiber: 1 gm

Gado Gado (Vegetable Salad with Potatoes)
Serves 6

Traditionally served with peanut sauce, you can offer a variety of condiments, including mango and tomato salsas, chutneys, and chopped fresh fruit.

1½ cups Russet-style potatoes, cooked, peeled, and thinly sliced
½ cup fresh green beans, par-cooked (see note) and cut into 1-inch pieces
¼ cup shredded carrots
1 cup cauliflower florets, par-cooked
1 cup green cabbage, shredded and par-cooked
1 cup bean sprouts, par-cooked
½ cup extra-firm tofu, drained and cut into 1-inch pieces
½ cup peeled cucumber, thinly sliced

Attractively arrange vegetables, except cucumber, on a serving platter. Top with tofu and cucumber. Serve with peanut sauce or other sweet and sour dipping sauce.

Note: Parcooked means just briefly placed in boiling water and immediately removed. For sprouts and greens (like cabbage), you may want to dunk them in ice water after removing from boiling water to stop the cooking. Think about vegetables that are only about 40 percent cooked.

Total Calories Per Serving: 69   Total Fat as % of Daily Value: 3%   Protein: 5 gm   Fat: 2 gm
Carbohydrates: 10 gm   Calcium: 71 mg   Iron: 1 mg   Sodium: 16 mg   Dietary Fiber: 2 gm

Sambal Kacang (Peanut Sauce)
Serves 6

Serve with vegetable salads, over rice, or as a dipping sauce for vegetables. Make it as fiery as you dare!

¼ cup smooth peanut butter
1 clove garlic, minced
½ teaspoon cayenne
1 teaspoon chopped and seeded fresh chilies
1 Tablespoon sugar
2 Tablespoons fresh lime juice
1 Tablespoon coconut milk
1 teaspoon soy sauce
1 teaspoon kecap manis or ketchup
¼ cup water

Place all ingredients in a small pot. Bring to a boil, stirring constantly. Lower heat to simmer, stir occasionally and cook until thickened, about 15 minutes. Can be served hot or cold.

Total Calories Per Serving: 80   Total Fat as % of Daily Value: 9%   Protein: 3 gm   Fat: 6 gm
Carbohydrates: 5 gm   Calcium: 7 mg   Iron: 0 mg   Sodium: 116 mg   Dietary Fiber: 1 gm

Gulai Daun Bayem (Spinach in Coconut Milk)
Serves 5

You won't have any trouble getting everyone to eat their spinach with this creamy, spicy dish.

1 cup coconut milk
1 Tablespoon seeded and chopped fresh green chilies
1 clove garlic, minced
½ cup chopped onions
1½ pounds fresh spinach (about 8 cups), cleaned

In a deep frying pan or Dutch oven, combine coconut milk, chilies, garlic, and onions. Bring to a boil and boil for 2 minutes. Add spinach and cook quickly, stirring. The spinach will cook rapidly in the hot liquid. When spinach is tender, about 2 minutes, serve immediately.

Total Calories Per Serving: 129   Total Fat as % of Daily Value: 16%   Protein: 5 gm   Fat: 10 gm
Carbohydrates: 8 gm   Calcium: 148 mg   Iron: 5 mg   Sodium: 115 mg   Dietary Fiber: 3 gm

Sicilian and Italian Cuisine

Pasta Pugliesi
Serves 4

This is an example of a dish that creates its own sauce.

¹/₄ cup olive oil
4 cloves garlic, minced
2 teaspoons red pepper flakes
1 pound uncooked pasta, such as small shells, rotini, or fusilli
1¹/₂ cups fresh broccoli florets
1 teaspoon chopped fresh parsley

Place olive oil in a frying pan and heat. Quickly sauté garlic and red pepper flakes for 2 minutes. Set aside.

Cook pasta according to package directions until just tender (al dente). Drain, but save pasta water and cook broccoli in same water. Drain and set aside.

Place olive oil in large pot and heat for 1 minute. Add parsley and stir to combine. Toss in pasta and broccoli, remove from heat, then serve.

Variation: Alternate broccoli with finely chopped kale or broccoli rabe (a type of green, found in Italian and specialty produce stores).

Total Calories Per Serving: 553   Total Fat as % of Daily Value: 24%   Protein: 16 gm   Fat: 15 gm
Carbohydrates: 87 gm   Calcium: 41 mg   Iron: 4 mg   Sodium: 64 mg   Dietary Fiber: 4 gm

Basic Tomato Sauce (Salsa di Pomodoro)
Makes about 3¹/₂ cups or 7 servings

From Naples comes pommarola, the famous tomato sauce of Italy. There are many Neapolitan tomato sauces. We have included several for you to play with. Add fresh or dried herbs, pickled capers, chopped olives, fresh tomatoes, or onions to create new sauces. The basic tomato sauce freezes well.

4 cups peeled and chopped fresh tomatoes or drained, chopped canned tomatoes
¹/₂ teaspoon black pepper
¹/₄ cup olive oil

In a large pot, combine tomatoes and pepper. Cook over medium heat, stirring, for 30 minutes or until tomatoes are very soft and mushy. Remove from heat, stir in olive oil, cover, and refrigerate until ready to use.

Total Calories Per 1/2 Cup Serving: 84   Total Fat as % of Daily Value: 12%   Protein: 1 gm   Fat: 8 gm
Carbohydrates: 3 gm   Calcium: 9 mg   Iron: 0 mg   Sodium: 4 mg   Dietary Fiber: 1 gm

Tomato Sauce II (Salsa Napoletana)

Makes about 2 cups or 4 servings

Use this Neapolitan sauce to top veggie pizzas, to toss with pasta, couscous, brown rice, or quinoa, or to top a grilled veggie sandwich.

1³/₄ cups canned, diced, drained tomatoes
¹/₄ cup chopped onions
5 whole peppercorns
1 bay leaf
¹/₄ cup chopped carrots
2 cloves garlic, peeled
1 teaspoon dried thyme
2 Tablespoons olive oil
3 Tablespoons red wine, if desired

Place tomatoes in a large sauce pan. Add onions, peppercorns, bay leaf, carrots, and garlic. Cook for 15 minutes, covered, over medium heat. Remove from heat and strain. Return to heat, add thyme, olive oil, and red wine and allow sauce to simmer for at least 30 more minutes or until sauce is very flavorful and slightly thickened.

Total Calories Per 1/2 Cup Serving: 88   Total Fat as % of Daily Value: 11%   Protein: 1 gm   Fat: 7 gm
Carbohydrates: 6 gm   Calcium: 19 mg   Iron: 1 mg   Sodium: 266 mg   Dietary Fiber: 1 gm

Tomato Sauce III (Sugo di Pomodoro Fresco)

Makes enough for 1 pound (uncooked) pasta or 4 servings

This is an uncooked tomato sauce, great for fresh tomatoes that are ripe or overly ripe. This sauce is not meant to sit, as it is at its flavor peak freshly prepared and served. The sauce will not freeze well, so make just enough and top al dente pastas, rice, and steamed greens with it.

1¹/₂ pounds (about 4 cups) peeled and seeded chopped fresh tomatoes
3 chopped green onions
2 cloves garlic, minced
3 Tablespoons chopped fresh basil
2 Tablespoons olive oil

Combine all ingredients in a glass or plastic bowl (no metal). Spoon over hot pasta and serve.

Total Calories Per Serving: 115   Total Fat as % of Daily Value: 7%   Protein: 2 gm   Fat: 11 gm
Carbohydrates: 12 gm   Calcium: 31 mg   Iron: 1 mg   Sodium: 10 mg   Dietary Fiber: 3 gm

Garlic and Oil Sauce (Aglio e Olio)

Makes enough sauce for $1^1/_2$ pounds (uncooked) pasta or about 6 servings

Although fairly high in fat, this backbone of Southern Italian cuisine is meant to be used sparingly to merely coat pasta or vegetables. Be sure to allow the garlic to become only golden brown, never to scorch. Burnt garlic gives bitterness to cooked dishes. Add finely minced vegetables or onions to create new flavors.

$^3/_4$ cup olive oil
5 cloves garlic, minced
$^1/_3$ cup fresh, chopped parsley
$^1/_2$ teaspoon oregano
$^1/_2$ teaspoon white pepper

Heat olive in a frying pan for 2 minutes. Add garlic, cooking over low heat, stirring, until garlic is golden (not brown, which will taste terrible), about 3 minutes. Stir in parsley, oregano, and pepper. Cook and stir for 1 minute.

Total Calories Per Serving: 244   Total Fat as % of Daily Value: 27%   Protein: <1 gm   Fat: 30 gm
Carbohydrates: 1 gm   Calcium: 7 mg   Iron: 0 mg   Sodium: 1 mg   Dietary Fiber: 0 gm

Green Sauce I (Pesto Sauce)

Makes enough for 1 pound (uncooked) pasta or 4 servings

Genoa is the main city of Liguria, on the northwest coast of Italy. Genoa's traditional sauce is pesto, made with a mortar and pestle to crush pine nuts and herbs, to extract flavor. We've modernized the technique, using less elbow grease and more electricity. Serve pesto over hot or cold pasta, cold or heated vegetables, or use as a dip for fresh breadsticks.

$^1/_2$ cup olive oil
1 cup fresh basil leaves, washed
4 cloves garlic, peeled
2 Tablespoons pine nuts
1 Tablespoon chopped fresh parsley

Combine all ingredients in a blender and process until smooth.

Variations: Pesto is usually made with basil and pine nuts. Some chefs like to use fresh spinach (frozen does not work well) to replace some or all of the basil. Walnuts can be used to replace some or all of the pine nuts to create a new flavor.

Total Calories Per Serving: 276   Total Fat as % of Daily Value: 46%   Protein: 1 gm   Fat: 30 gm
Carbohydrates: 2 gm   Calcium: 28 mg   Iron: 1 mg   Sodium: 3 mg   Dietary Fiber: 1 gm

Green Sauce II (Salsa Verde)
Makes enough for 1 pound (uncooked) pasta or 4 servings

Bread is an essential part of every Italian regional cuisine. This uncooked sauce utilizes extra pieces of bread, with the flavor of Sicily. Use as a salad dressing for chilled pasta, rice, or tofu or for grilled vegetables.

3 slices white bread
½ cup wine vinegar
3 Tablespoons chopped fresh parsley
3 Tablespoons capers
4 cloves garlic, minced
2 Tablespoons olive oil

Tear bread and soak in vinegar for 10 minutes. Squeeze bread dry and place in blender or food processor. Blend with parsley, capers, and garlic until just smooth. Add olive oil and blend only until combined.

Total Calories Per Serving: 125   Total Fat as % of Daily Value: 8%   Protein: 2 gm   Fat: 12 gm
Carbohydrates: 12 gm   Calcium: 55 mg   Iron: 1 mg   Sodium: 323 mg   Dietary Fiber: 1 gm

Roasted Vegetable Sauce Abruzzi
Makes enough sauce for 2 pounds of pasta (uncooked) or about 8 servings

The wonderful farmlands of Abruzzi inspired this colorful sauce. Make several batches at once, serving one as a vegetable entrée and puréeing the others to be used as a sauce, or even a soup with pasta, cooked beans, or steamed or baked polenta (corn meal prepared as a thick cereal).

4 sprigs parsley
½ cup chopped carrots
1 stalk chopped celery
1 clove garlic, peeled
¼ teaspoon dried oregano
2 Tablespoons olive oil
1 cup chopped onions
½ cup chopped bell peppers
1½ cups peeled and diced boiling potatoes
¾ cup diced zucchini

Place parsley, carrots, celery, garlic, and oregano in a food processor or blender and process until finely chopped. Preheat oven to 375 degrees. Grease baking dish with olive oil. Layer remaining ingredients in the dish, sprinkling each layer with the parsley blend. Bake covered for 45 minutes or until vegetables are tender. Serve as a casserole or purée and serve as a sauce. After puréeing, the sauce can be frozen for up to 2 months.

Total Calories Per Serving: 64   Total Fat as % of Daily Value: 5%   Protein: 1 gm   Fat: 3 gm
Carbohydrates: 8 gm   Calcium: 15 mg   Iron: 0 mg   Sodium: 10 mg   Dietary Fiber: 1 gm

Kenyan Cuisine

Ugali
Serves 5-6

Ugali is traditionally served in Kenya to accompany meat as a starchy side dish. We like to serve it with sukuma wiki (steamed or boiled greens) and grilled vegetables. It is typically made with maize or semolina flour, but you can use cornmeal.

2 cups yellow cornmeal
4 cups water
1 teaspoon ground white pepper

Sift cornmeal. Place water in a large pot and bring to a boil. Slowly sprinkle cornmeal over boiling water, stirring constantly until all the cornmeal is incorporated into the water. Be sure to stir briskly to avoid lumps. Lower heat and simmer covered for 20 minutes or until the mixture is very thick. Add pepper, stir well, cover and cook for an additional 5 minutes. Serve hot.

Total Calories Per Serving: 203   Total Fat as % of Daily Value: 1%   Protein: 5 gm   Fat: 1 gm
Carbohydrates: 43 gm   Calcium: 4 mg   Iron: 1 mg   Sodium: 2 mg   Dietary Fiber: 4 gm

Saladi
Serves 4

This is a salad "relish" or a chopped vegetable dish served as a "cool" condiment with a meal that may have a lot of spice from chili or other hot peppers. It is a combination of seasonal vegetables served without dressing. There should be chopped chilies or hot sauce on the tables, as well as a vinegar-and-oil style dressing to add as desired.

2 cups green cabbage, washed and chopped
1 cup red cabbage, washed and chopped
1/2 cup carrots, grated
1/2 cup sweet onions, diced
1/2 cup sweet red pepper, diced

In a medium-size, non-reactive bowl combine all ingredients, tossing well. Cover and allow relish to chill for at least 1 hour before serving.

Total Calories Per Serving: 35   Total Fat as % of Daily Value: 0%   Protein: 1 gm   Fat: 0 gm
Carbohydrates: 8 gm   Calcium: 41 mg   Iron: 1 mg   Sodium: 22 mg   Dietary Fiber: 3 gm

Tomato, Corn, and Kale Stew

Serves 5

This can be made with kale, collards, or mustard greens. If you can't find fresh greens, look for frozen. Allow the frozen greens to thaw and squeeze all the water from it before adding to the stew.

¼ cup vegetable broth
2 cloves garlic, mashed
½ cup onions, chopped
1 cup chopped canned tomatoes with juice
2 pounds fresh kale, washed and chopped
2 cups frozen corn, thawed
1 cup canned tomato sauce

In a large pot, heat broth on high heat for 1 minute. Add garlic and onions and quickly cook until just soft, about 1 minute. Add tomatoes and juice and allow mixture to cook for 3 minutes. Add kale, lower heat, and allow dish to cook until kale is soft, about 10-15 minutes. Add corn and sauce and cook, stirring, for 10 minutes. Serve hot with chapati, ugali, or over steamed white rice.

Total Calories Per Serving: 186   Total Fat as % of Daily Value: 4%   Protein: 10 gm   Fat: 2 gm
Carbohydrates: 40 gm   Calcium: 267 mg   Iron: 4 mg   Sodium: 427 mg   Dietary Fiber: 7 gm

Groundnut Stew

Serves 5

The nuts mellow out the flavor and add smoothness to the sauce. If you like, you can add some grilled or baked diced tofu as an extra ingredient.

Vegetable oil spray
2 cups onions, chopped
1 cup green bell peppers, chopped
2 cloves garlic, peeled and mashed
2 cups canned tomato sauce
2 cups frozen corn, thawed
1 cup canned white or red beans, drained
½ teaspoon ground black pepper
½ teaspoon red pepper flakes
½ cup smooth peanut butter

Spray a large pot with oil and allow to heat. Add onions, peppers, and garlic and cook until soft, about 3 minutes. Add remaining ingredients, except peanut butter, cover, and allow stew to simmer over low heat for 30 minutes. Stir in peanut butter. Continue to stir and cook until well blended and sauce of stew has thickened to desired texture. Serve over steamed white rice.

Total Calories Per Serving: 322   Total Fat as % of Daily Value: 22%   Protein: 14 gm   Fat: 14 gm
Carbohydrates: 41 gm   Calcium: 70 mg   Iron: 3 mg   Sodium: 729 mg   Dietary Fiber: 10 gm

Polish Cuisine

Strawberry or Blueberry Soup (Zupa Jagodowa)
Serves 4

Sweet figures very highly in Polish cuisine. Until only a few years ago, many kitchens had very few appliances or conveniences. Sweet soups made with fresh fruit were an easy way to create dessert items in basic kitchens. If you must, you can use frozen, thawed berries instead of fresh.

1 pound fresh strawberries or blueberries, cleaned
1¼ cups water
3 Tablespoons sugar
1 Tablespoon fresh lemon juice
½ cup soy coffee creamer or vanilla soy or rice ice cream
2 cup cooked, cooled noodles (optional)

Place fruit in a medium-size pot, add water and bring to a quick boil. Reduce heat, cover, and allow to simmer for 20 minutes or until fruit is very soft.

Place in blender and purée. Return purée to pot, add sugar, lemon juice, and vegan creamer or ice cream. Stir and allow soup to simmer for 5 minutes. Chill soup for at least 2 hours before serving.

Note: It is traditional to eat this soup on its own or served over cold noodles.

Total Calories Per Serving: 86   Total Fat as % of Daily Value: 1%   Protein: 2 gm   Fat: 1 gm
Carbohydrates: 19 gm   Calcium: 65 mg   Iron: 1 mg   Sodium: 14 mg   Dietary Fiber: 2 gm

Sour Pickle Soup (Zupa Ogorkowa)
Serves 6

Sour is a popular flavor for appetizers, entrées, and side dishes in Polish cuisine. Usually, sour pickle soup is made with beef broth; we've used vegetable broth instead. Serve this soup as is or add chopped, cooked pasta, or additional diced, cooked potatoes for more body.

6 cups vegetable broth
½ cup shredded carrots
½ cup diced celery
1 cup peeled fresh potatoes, diced
1 cup garlic or dill pickles, shredded
Flour, as needed (about ¼ cup)

Place broth in pot, bring to quick boil, reduce heat, and allow broth to simmer. Add carrots, celery, and potatoes and simmer for 15 minutes. Add pickles and simmer for 30 minutes or until potatoes are tender. If a thicker soup is desired, mix together equal parts flour and water to make a paste. Add slowly, stirring and allow soup to simmer until it is lightly thickened.

Total Calories Per Serving: 66   Total Fat as % of Daily Value: <1%   Protein: 1 gm   Fat: <1 gm
Carbohydrates: 15 gm   Calcium: 12 mg   Iron: 1 mg   Sodium: 1,127 mg   Dietary Fiber: 1 gm

Quick Borscht
Serves 6

1 pound can shredded beets, not drained
2 cups water
3 Tablespoons frozen lemonade, thawed (or 2 Tablespoons frozen lemon juice and
** 1 Tablespoon sugar)**

In a large bowl, combine beets, water, and lemonade slowly together until all ingredients are well mixed. Blend until puréed. Chill for at least 2 hours before serving. Enhance with vegan sour cream.

Total Calories Per Serving: 39   Total Fat as % of Daily Value: 0%   Protein: 1 gm   Fat: 0 gm
Carbohydrates: 10 gm   Calcium: 14 mg   Iron: 1 mg   Sodium: 108 mg   Dietary Fiber: 1 gm

Borscht
Serves 6

Borscht has many variations among the Eastern and Central European countries. Serve this hot or cold.

2 bunches beets with greens (about 8-9 medium beets)
½ cup chopped onion
1 pound can stewed tomatoes
3 Tablespoons fresh lemon juice
⅓ cup sugar

Scrub and clean beets, but don't peel them. Save the greens. Place beets in large pot, add onion and cover with 3 quarts of water. Simmer for 1 hour or until beets are very tender. Remove beets from water, but save the water. Discard onions. Finely chop beets and return to water. Wash and chop greens and add to water. Add tomatoes, lemon juice, and sweetener. Cook borscht over medium heat for 30 minutes or until greens are tender. Chill for at least 2 hours before serving.

Total Calories Per Serving: 139   Total Fat as % of Daily Value: 3%   Protein: 3 gm   Fat: 2 gm
Carbohydrates: 29 gm   Calcium: 34 mg   Iron: 1 mg   Sodium: 397 mg   Dietary Fiber: 3 gm

Cabbage Soup (Kapusniak)
Serves 6

A staple soup of Polish cuisine, made with staple ingredients. Make an extra batch and freeze it.

2 Tablespoons vegan margarine
2 cups shredded green cabbage
½ teaspoon black pepper
3 cups water
2 cups peeled and diced potatoes
½ cup chopped fresh tomato

Place margarine in a soup pot and melt. Add cabbage and pepper and sauté until cabbage is browned, about 7 minutes. Add water, potatoes, and tomato and cook covered for 20 minutes or until potatoes are tender.

Total Calories Per Serving: 78   Total Fat as % of Daily Value: 6%   Protein: 1 gm   Fat: 4 gm
Carbohydrates: 10 gm   Calcium: 20 mg   Iron: 0 mg   Sodium: 49 mg   Dietary Fiber: 2 gm

Pierogi (Boiled Dumplings)
Serves 5 (6 pierogis per serving)

Pierogis are Polish cuisine's ode to ravioli, won ton, and other filled dumplings. Traditional fillings usually start with either potatoes or sauerkraut. You can experiment with sweet potatoes, polenta (corn meal mush), shredded green or red cabbage, or chopped nuts. Make several batches of pierogi and freeze them for future use.

1½ cups sifted all-purpose flour
½ teaspoon salt
¼ teaspoon baking powder
½ cup vegan margarine
Approximately ¼ cup water

Preheat oven to 400 degrees. Sift together dry ingredients. Cut in margarine, adding enough water to just hold the mixture together. On a floured board, roll out, like a piecrust. Cut into 3-inch squares. Place about 1 teaspoonful filling (recipe follows) in the center of each square. Fold squares so filling is completely covered. Press edges together with a fork. Place on a non-stick cookie sheet and bake for 20 minutes, or until golden brown.

Total Calories Per Serving: 297   Total Fat as % of Daily Value: 28%   Protein: 4 gm   Fat: 18 gm
Carbohydrates: 29 gm   Calcium: 19 mg   Iron: 2 mg   Sodium: 450 mg   Dietary Fiber: 1 gm

Pierogi Filling
Serves 5

¾ cup minced onion
2 Tablespoons vegan margarine
2 cups cooked kasha (approximately ¾ cup uncooked; prepared according to package directions)

Place onions and margarine in frying pan and sauté until onions are just soft. Add kasha and continue to cook, tossing, until kasha is combined with onions.

Note: Another traditional filling is mashed potatoes mixed with sautéed onions.

Total Calories Per Serving: 112   Total Fat as % of Daily Value: 7%   Protein: 2 gm   Fat: 5 gm
Carbohydrates: 16 gm   Calcium: 10 mg   Iron: 1 mg   Sodium: 51 mg   Dietary Fiber: 2 gm

Dill Sauce
Makes about 1 cup or 4 servings

This sauce is perfect to serve over boiled or baked potatoes or pierogi. Serve it cold, as a salad dressing.

2 Tablespoons vegan margarine
2 Tablespoons flour
$^1/_2$ cup vegetable stock
1 Tablespoon chopped fresh dill
$^1/_2$ cup vegan sour cream (or $^1/_2$ cup silken tofu with 2 Tablespoons lemon juice)

Place margarine and flour in the top of a double boiler. Stir to blend. Add stock and cook, stirring until thickened and smooth. Remove from stove, then quickly stir in dill and sour cream.

Total Calories Per Serving: 74   Total Fat as % of Daily Value: 9%   Protein: 1 gm   Fat: 6 gm
Carbohydrates: 5 gm   Calcium: 14 mg   Iron: 1 mg   Sodium: 169 mg   Dietary Fiber: <1 gm

Sweet and Sour Red Cabbage
Serves 5

This recipe reflects the Polish taste for sweet and sour items, in this case combined into one dish. Serve this dish as an accompaniment to braised potatoes or to pierogi. Also use as an underliner for entrées.

3 cups shredded red cabbage
$^1/_2$ cup green or tart apple, peeled and chopped
2 cups boiling water
1 Tablespoon apple juice concentrate
$^1/_2$ teaspoon ground allspice
4 Tablespoons vinegar

Combine all ingredients in a large pot. Bring quickly to a boil, reduce heat, and allow cabbage to simmer until cabbage is tender, about 20 minutes.

Total Calories Per Serving: 23   Total Fat as % of Daily Value: 0%   Protein: 1 gm   Fat: 0 gm
Carbohydrates: 5 gm   Calcium: 22 mg   Iron: 0 mg   Sodium: 9 mg   Dietary Fiber: 1 gm

Baked Apples with Fruit Preserves and Nuts
Serves 6

This simple dessert can also be made with pears. You can serve it with soy or rice ice cream.

6 baking apples, washed and cored
6 Tablespoons each sugar and strawberry or apricot fruit preserves
$^1/_2$ cup chopped walnuts

Preheat oven to 350 degrees. Place apples in baking dish, being sure they are touching each other, fitting tightly in the dish. Place 1 Tablespoon of sugar in the core of each apple, followed by 1

Tablespoon preserves. Sprinkle with nuts. Fill baking dish with 1 inch of water. Bake apples for 30 minutes or until tender. Serve warm or allow apples to chill.

Total Calories Per Serving: 278   Total Fat as % of Daily Value: 10%   Protein: 2 gm   Fat: 7 gm
Carbohydrates: 57 gm   Calcium: 26 mg   Iron: 1 mg   Sodium: 9 mg   Dietary Fiber: 6 gm

Indonesian Desserts

Fragrant fresh fruit and fruit juices are plentiful in Indonesia and make lovely desserts.

Coconut Rice

Serves 4

Two 14-ounce cans unsweetened coconut milk
1½ cups Jasmine rice
1 teaspoon each ground ginger and ground cardamom
2 teaspoons sugar

In a medium-size saucepan, combine milk and rice. Bring to a boil, stirring occasionally. Reduce heat to low, cover, and cook for 10 minutes, stirring occasionally so rice does not stick.

Uncover, continue to cook over low heat, stirring, and adding ginger, cardamom, and sugar. Stir and cook until rice is creamy and tender, about 15 minutes. If more liquid is required, water can be added (no more than ½ cup at a time). This dish should be eaten in moderation due to its high fat content.

Total Calories Per Serving: 482   Total Fat as % of Daily Value: 66%   Protein: 6 gm   Fat: 43 gm
Carbohydrates: 25 gm   Calcium: 45 mg   Iron: 7 mg   Sodium: 30 mg   Dietary Fiber: 1 gm

Kolak Pisang (Sweet Banana Compote)

Serves 5

From West Java, this compote is an indulgence. Traditionally, it is flavored with daun pandan, a fragrant, flat leaf whose closest relative is the pine.

5 ripe, medium-size bananas, peeled and cut into thick 2-inch slices
1 Tablespoon lemon juice
1 cup water
1 cup palm or turbinado sugar
4-inch piece of daun pandan or 1 teaspoon ground cardamom and 1 teaspoon
**   ground clove**
½ cup coconut milk
1 Tablespoon cornstarch mixed into 2 Tablespoons cold water

Toss bananas with lemon juice, cover, and set aside. In a medium-size pot, boil water, sugar and seasonings (daun pandan or cardamom and clove) until they are thick and syrupy, about 10 minutes. Lower heat and add coconut milk, slowly stirring. Add cornstarch and mix well to combine. Add bananas, lower heat, and allow dish to simmer until thickened (like a thin custard), about 15 minutes, stirring occasionally. Serve hot alone or over lemon sorbet.

Total Calories Per Serving: 351   Total Fat as % of Daily Value: 8%   Protein: 2 gm   Fat: 5 gm
Carbohydrates: 81 gm   Calcium: 15 mg   Iron: 2 mg   Sodium: 134 mg   Dietary Fiber: 3 gm

Chapter 11: SOUPS

Soups can be meals in themselves. They can be the item around which the entire party meal is planned or can be a flavorful meal starter or side dish.

Soups can be thin or thick, chewy or smooth, and hot or cold. If soup is to be the main event, plan on serving each guest about 1 to $1^1/_2$ cups; if the soup is a starter or side dish, plan on about $^1/_2$ a cup. Serve hot soup in warmed cups or bowls. If your dishware is oven-proof, leave soup bowls or cups in a 200-degree oven for about 10 minutes. This should be long enough to warm them, but not so long that they will be difficult to handle. Or, if you have extra help, run soup bowls or cups under hot water and dry them quickly before filling with soup.

Garnishing Soups

Most soups can be made ahead and frozen or refrigerated until needed. Soups rely on the quality of the ingredients, so take advantage of seasonal vegetables. Select the freshest vegetables or the highest quality frozen or canned ingredients. Garnishes add more interest to soup. They can even do some positive "false" advertising. For example, you can make a fat-free soup look really, really creamy by garnishing it with a small scoop (about the size of two teaspoons) of vegan cream cheese or sour cream.

Here are some other soup garnishing ideas:

- popcorn
- seasoned croutons
- crumbled vegan breakfast strips
- crumbled vegan ground round or vegan sausage
- thin strips of vegan alternative meats
- shredded vegan cheese
- thinly sliced fresh radish or Daikon radish
- baked carrot, sweet potato, beet, or tortilla chips
- toasted pita or bagel chips
- chopped green, yellow, or red bell pepper
- thinly sliced green or black olives
- corn kernels
- chopped sweet, yellow, or green onions
- salsa

Start From the Beginning

If you have the desire to make soup from scratch, start with the stock. If you have the time and the room on the stove, you can make your own stock. In place of chicken or beef bones, use sliced fresh mushrooms. Cook mushrooms with carrots, onions, celery, and a sachet of whole peppercorns, parsley stems, and dried thyme. Cook the stock at least 1 hour until it is flavorful. Strain, cook properly, and store in the refrigerator or the freezer. To make a heartier vegetable stock, before you add the mushrooms to the stock sear them in the oven topped with a small amount of tomato purée and vegetable oil until very brown. Cook seared mushrooms with carrots, onions, celery, chopped tomatoes or tomato purée, and a sachet. Allow stock to cook at least 1 hour until very flavorful. Cool and refrigerate or freeze. Vegetable stocks are getting more popular and can be used instead of chicken or beef stock.

If you are purchasing vegetarian stock bases, become a label reader. Be sure the main ingredients are vegetables and spices, not fat and salt. You may have to pay a bit more for the higher quality base, but it's worth it for the flavor and the reduced salt and fat content. If you purchase reduced fat and/or sodium stock bases, be sure to add herbs and spices to replace the flavor lost by the reduction. Reduced fat and salt bases are very helpful. Just remember that fat and salt add flavor to soups, so their absence must be accounted for.

Thick without the Fat

Soups can be thickened. Traditionally, soups were thickened with whole milk, cream, sour cream, or pastes made with equal parts flour and fat. Switching to nonfat milk doesn't cut it, as it won't yield a desirable texture. There are lots of thickening options that offer flavor and texture while remaining vegetarian. Mashed potato mix is actually easier to work with than flour or cornstarch and may have the extra added attraction of being fortified with vitamin C. Just be careful. If you add too much, you'll have soup the texture of mashed potatoes, so have a steady hand. Low-fat soy yogurt or silken tofu can be used as thickeners. They give a silky, full texture and the yogurt adds a pleasant tang. Puréed carrots, turnips, parsnips, parsley root, celery root, and winter squash and cooked, mashed sweet potatoes are also natural thickeners, perfect for winter holiday soups. Cooked beans can be puréed and added to soup. They add extra protein, texture, and flavor. Puréed beans can be thickened alone and used as dips and sauces. Puréed beans can be added to soups with strong or diverse flavors, such as split pea, lentil, vegetable, chowders, and three-bean soups. Silken tofu can be added to purée- or "cream of" soups, such as asparagus, broccoli, cauliflower, potato, mushroom, celery, carrot, and New England-style chowders.

Vegetarian soups may benefit from lots of extras, but not from extra salt or fat. We've heard the complaint that food tastes "flat" without salt and has no texture without fat. That only happens if nothing is done to replace what is taken out. Salt won't be missed in a vegetable soup that is flavored with browned garlic and onion, minced oregano and thyme, and a reduction of puréed carrots, peppers, and tomatoes. (To "reduce" is to allow liquids to boil or simmer [depending on how delicate they are] until they are at least one half of their original volume.) Fat won't be missed in a minestrone soup that is packed with white and red beans, fresh basil, spinach and tomato pasta, and white and black pepper. Do take out the fat and salt by selecting lower fat stock bases, choosing reduced fat, using fresh or frozen ingredients, rather than canned, when possible, and by sautéing soup ingredients with vegetable oil spray or stock rather than large amounts of oil. But don't take out the fat and salt without adding something just as tasty. Nobody will thank you for trying to make them healthy with soup that tastes like dishwater.

We don't always have time to start from scratch. Canned or frozen soups can form a base for muscular soups. Tomato soup and cream soups can be reconstituted with soymilk, yogurt, and soft or silken tofu. Add vegan frozen mini-ravioli, tortellini, or chunks of smoked or flavored tofu as an extra ingredient and top with shredded vegan cheese, vegan bacon crumbles, and shredded fresh spinach. Add extra beans and pasta to minestrone and vegetable soups. Purée extra portions of vegetables, such as carrots, celery, and mushrooms and add to vegetable, split pea, and bean soups. Add cooked, diced potatoes and carrots to vegetable soups. For extra fiber, add cut corn, beans, and tomatoes to vegetable soups and chowders. Make a fast vegetable chowder by combining canned tomato soup with canned, chopped tomatoes, canned or frozen cut corn, cooked, diced potatoes, sliced mushrooms, and diced frozen or canned carrots. Thicken with tofu or soy yogurt or mashed potato mix.

Have a "stone soup" party. Stone soup is an old tale about building soup with magic stones and water. Of course, after the magic stones had simmered for a while, they needed the enhancement of some carrots, celery, onions, peppers, mushrooms… You get the picture. You provide the "cream" in the form of tofu or mashed potato mix. Ask everyone to bring one nutritious item to add to the stone soup; record the creation and give all participants the recipe.

Show your guests that vegetable stock can be made to look and taste creamy with the addition of cream of rice cereal; the same effect can be achieved by cooking rice right in the stock (rather than cooking rice separately and then adding). A good example of this is Greek "Chicken" and Lemon soup (avgolomono), which looks creamy but contains no dairy products. Rice is cooked right in chicken broth (you can find vegan "chicken" style stock bases in most markets); lemon juice adds a flavorful tang and helps to "cloud" the broth. Garnished with shredded Chik'n™ or Tofurky™, this can be a lowfat soup that looks and tastes as if it was cooked with lots of cream.

Root Vegetables 101

All root vegetables share the common bond of long storage capability and the ability to hold up under heat, including in soup. After that, each has a distinct personality. Test your root vegetable vocabulary with the following; how many can you identify, or better yet, how many uses can you devise for each:

> Traditional: beets, carrots, garlic, horseradish, onions (yellow, white, red, green, pearl), parsnips, potatoes, radish, rutabaga, sweet potatoes, turnips
>
> Out of the Mainstream: celery root, chervil, chicory, sunchokes, Jerusalem artichoke, jicama, lotus root, salsify, shallot, taro, water chestnut, kohlrabi
>
> New and Improved: icicle, golden and white beets, white and purple carrots, planet and finger carrots, purple- and red-topped baby turnips, purple potatoes

Bake, Steam, Grill, Roast

Root vegetables are willing partners in your kitchen, allowing you to use every cooking method imaginable. They can be boiled, steamed, baked, grilled, fried, braised, roasted and stir-fried in their entirety or minced, sliced, diced, julienned, or tourneed (cut into seven-sided foot-ball shaped portions). Roots can be mashed (think rosemary and garlic mashed potatoes), puréed (think purée of carrot soup), baked (think gratin of winter root vegetables), used in breads (think potato-garlic focaccia), and desserts (think carrot cake, sweet potato custard), done up in a wok (think ginger and garlic water chestnut and lotus root), tossed into salads (think crispy radishes, marinated onions), and used to create the soup du jour (think beet-based borscht, cream of onion, and sunchoke).

Beet-ing a Path

Beets have enjoyed a great deal of popularity through the past two centuries as a plant that is totally utilizable. The leaves can be steamed or braised and served as a side dish (beet greens are spicy and slightly acidic, so they should be mixed with mellow greens, such as spinach, rather than being served on their own) or raw in salads and the root can be used as an ingredient for entrées, side dishes, soups, and even desserts (grated fine and used in quick breads and muffins).

Beets may look unapproachable and tough, but remember that they have been grown for their sugar throughout history. Fresh beets are easily prepared. Buy them with the tops off (unless you'd like to add beet greens to your menu) and store them refrigerated until ready to use. To minimize a beet-red kitchen staff, scrub beets well and cook (they can be boiled, steamed, or roasted) unpeeled. Once cooked, the peels are easily removed by hand. Boiled or steamed beets can be finished on the grill to caramelize their sugar content. Season fresh or canned beets with dill, parsley, fennel, lemon, or tarragon. Raw beets can be finely shredded and used as a salad garnish. Combine sliced fresh or canned beets with sliced potatoes to create a rosy, creamy gratin (toss vegetables with a Béchamel sauce, top with grated cheese and brown). For a unique side dish, serve a warm salad of sliced, roasted beets (simply clean beets, place on a sheet pan, and roast in a hot oven until easily pierced with a fork; allow to cool and peel) tossed with walnuts or pecans, mandarin orange segments, olive oil, cracked black pepper, and a dash of dried tarragon.

Borscht is a traditional beet soup. Russian-style borscht is a clear, deep purple-red beet broth garnished with shredded beets, boiled potatoes, and sour cream and it can be served hot or chilled. Ukrainian-style borscht is a hearty beef and vegetable (heavy on shredded cabbage, diced onions, turnips, and potatoes) hot soup that used beets to add sweetness and color. Try seitan instead of beef in this type of borscht.

Turn Up the Heat

Root vegetables are the ultimate ingredient for soups and stews. Root vegetables, more so then most other vegetables, improve with cooking, adding flavor, color, and texture. Turnips and rutabagas have authoritative flavors, so use them as the star ingredient in soups. Beets will turn everything rosy, so consider what you would like your presentation to be. Daikon radish and lotus root (available canned if you can't find them fresh or frozen) take on the flavor of their pot-mates. Carrots, parsnips, and sweet potatoes add sweetness. Potatoes, parsley root, and taro are very high in starch and when mashed or puréed will add thickness to soups; Jerusalem artichoke, carrots, and celery root are higher in water content, adding moisture but not much thickening. The natural thickening ability of some root vegetables translates into creamy, full soup textures. This enables you to create luxurious soups without dairy products, perfect for heart-healthy and vegetarian menu selections.

Leek and potato soup (when served cold, it becomes "vichyssoise," created by a French chef working in New York City, named after Vichy, his native region in France) can be made quickly by sautéing cubed peeled potatoes and diced leeks in olive oil or vegan margarine, covering with broth, and allowing to simmer until the potatoes are soft (see recipe on page 214). Potage Crecy is a classic purée of carrot soup, prepared with puréed carrots (cook carrots with a small amount of rice or potato until soft enough to be processed through a food mill or food processor), stock, shallots, and thickened with heavy cream and butter. An updated version can be made vegan by increasing the amount of rice or potato, using vegetable stock or carrot juice instead of chicken stock, and omitting the cream and butter. The color is vibrant and the natural sugar and fiber in the carrots makes for a sweet, full-bodied soup. Potage Crecy can be made a day or two ahead of time and stored in the refrigerator until ready to heat (see recipe on page 216).

Here are some more ideas for soups including root vegetables: white minestrone (include several types of potatoes, onions, and turnips), red pepper, celery root, and corn chowder, Jerusalem artichoke and tomato chowder, turnip, leek, and brown rice soup, Ukrainian borscht with beet greens and seitan, four onion soup, lentil carrot soup, ginger and carrot soup, purple potato chowder, and garlic potato soup with rosemary.

Who Needs Cream?

The following ingredients added to soup give the taste, appearance, and mouthfeel of cream without the fat calories; they can be blended in by mixing or puréed in a food processor:

Lowfat tofu

Mashed sweet potatoes

Soymilk powder

Rice (cooked right in the soup)

Prepared mashed potatoes or mashed potato mix

Puréed root vegetables (such as carrots, turnips, or parsnips)

Cream of rice or cream of wheat cereal

Puréed or cream corn

Build a Meal with Soup

Base a cold-weather meal around a bowl of steaming hot, aromatic soup. Here are some building blocks:

COLD	HOT	BREADS
Carrot Raisin Salad	Vegan Mac & Cheese	Breadsticks
Herbed Potato Salad	German Potato Salad	Corn Bread (add cut corn, chopped bell peppers, or shredded vegan cheese)
Red or Green Cabbage Slaw	Hot Spiced Beans	Corn or Flour Tortillas
Corn Salad	Vegetarian Chili	Biscuits
Baby Green Salad	Rice Pilaf	Herbed Rolls
Pasta Salad	Baked Potato (white or sweet)	English Muffin Pizzas
Marinated Mushrooms	Vegetable and Pasta Stir-Fries	Garlic Bread
Beet Salad	Vegan Spring Rolls	Steamed Dumplings

Mix and Match Soups

No time to make soups from scratch? Here are some ideas for mix-and-match soups made with ingredients from your cold and dry storage.

1. Split pea and lentil: add cooked lentils (you can purchase them canned) to canned split pea soup and dilute according to package directions. Add chopped onions and shredded smoked tofu or chopped veggie hot dogs during cooking for more flavor.
2. Purée Mongole: a classic soup of tomatoes and split peas. Combine canned tomato soup and canned split pea soup and prepare according to package directions. Drained, chopped canned tomatoes can be added for more texture.
3. Five-bean soup: add five types of cooked beans of your choice to canned or frozen vegetable or minestrone soup and cook until flavors are blended.
4. "Neatball" soup: add frozen vegan meatballs to frozen or canned vegetable soup until meatballs are thoroughly cooked. Add cooked pasta or rice for extra body.

5. Black bean soup: combine canned black beans with canned or frozen vegetable soup. Cook thoroughly. Purée some or all of the soup for a smooth texture.

6. Hot Gazpacho: combine canned tomato soup with prepared salsa. Dilute with tomato juice or vegetable cocktail juice. As heating, add lemon or lime juice, a small amount of vinegar and onion and garlic powder for flavor.

7. Cream of Spinach: Combine canned or frozen vegan potato soup with frozen vegan creamed spinach. If not available, could mix frozen, thawed, well-drained chopped spinach with a small amount of soy sour cream. Allow soup to cook until thoroughly heated.

8. Tomato-Corn Chowder: Combine canned tomato soup with canned or frozen corn chowder; dilute with soymilk or a combination of plain soy yogurt and water. Add drained, chopped tomatoes and frozen or canned, drained cut corn for extra texture.

9. Cabbage-Vegetable Soup: purchase ready-cut cole slaw mixes (a mixture of raw shredded cabbage and carrots). Steam or sauté with a small amount of vegetable stock until tender. Add to canned or frozen vegetable soup and allow soup to cook until thoroughly heated.

RECIPES

Note: All the soup recipes can be easily doubled, tripled, or quadrupled.

Savory Sweet Potato Soup

Serves 10

This soup is pretty and flavorful and tastes even better the next day.

³/₄ cup chopped onions
¹/₄ cup chopped celery
¹/₂ cup chopped carrots
2 cloves garlic, minced
1 gallon vegetable stock
3 pounds peeled and diced fresh sweet potatoes (about 7 cups)
1 Tablespoon ground cinnamon
1 teaspoon ground nutmeg
1 teaspoon ground ginger
2 Tablespoons maple syrup
1 cup puréeed silken tofu

Place onions, celery, carrots, and garlic in a dutch oven or heavy pot with a small amount of stock. Sauté until vegetables are soft, about 2 minutes.

Add rest of stock, sweet potatoes, and spices. Simmer covered until potatoes are very soft, about 45 minutes. Place soup in a blender or food processor and purée until smooth. Return to stove, add syrup and tofu, stir, and remove from heat.

Total Calories Per Serving: 187   Total Fat as % of Daily Value: 2%   Protein: 4 gm   Fat: 1 gm
Carbohydrates: 41 gm   Calcium: 87 mg   Iron: 1 mg   Sodium: 1,332 mg   Dietary Fiber: 5 gm

Vegetable Stock

Makes 2 gallons

1 Tablespoon vegetable oil
2 cloves garlic, chopped
2 Tablespoons chopped onions
2 gallons water
¾ cup dry white wine (optional)
1½ cups minced carrots
2 cups sliced fresh mushrooms
¾ cup minced celery
½ cup sliced leeks (yellow onions can be used, as well)

Sachet (use a coffee filter for your sachet if you don't have cheesecloth):
2 bay leaves
10 parsley stems
2 teaspoon whole black peppercorns
1 whole clove
1 teaspoon dried thyme

Add oil to a 2-gallon pot (or two 1-gallon pots) and heat. Add garlic and onions and sauté until they are translucent, about 3 minutes. Add all remaining ingredients. Bring to a fast boil, lower heat, cover, and allow stock to simmer for 1 hour. Strain, cool, and refrigerate or freeze.

Total Calories Per Stock: 300   Total Fat as % of Daily Value: 24%   Protein: 8 gm   Fat: 15 gm
Carbohydrates: 38 gm   Calcium: 185 mg   Iron: 5 mg   Sodium: 217 mg   Dietary Fiber: 10 gm

Vegan Vichyssoise

Serves 6

This is the perfect cool start for a spicy meal or the hot start for a hearty winter's meal.

3 large Russet or baking potatoes, peeled and diced (about 4 cups)
3 cups mushroom stock
1 bunch leeks (about 4 leeks)
2 Tablespoons vegan margarine
2 cups puréed silken tofu
Salt and white pepper to taste
¼ cup vermouth (authentic, but optional)

Place potatoes in large pot and cook in stock until they are soft enough to mash. Wash leeks and slice thinly, using only the white sections. Melt margarine in large frying pan and sauté leeks over medium-low heat until tender. Drain potatoes and return liquid to pot. Mash potatoes. Return potatoes to stock and add leeks and tofu. Season soup with salt and freshly ground black pepper. Stir in vermouth. Serve very hot (don't boil) or extremely cold. Garnish with chives.

Total Calories Per Serving: 308   Total Fat as % of Daily Value: 14%   Protein: 12 gm   Fat: 9 gm
Carbohydrates: 48 gm   Calcium: 156 mg   Iron: 4 mg   Sodium: 552 mg   Dietary Fiber: 4 gm

Pasta e Fagioli (say it "pasta fa-zool")

Serves 5

This Italian soup/stew is a winter staple. Save broken pasta (such as lasagna) and leftover beans to use in this thrifty, flavorful, and versatile dish. This dish can be served with lots of crusty hot bread and a green salad to make a complete meal. It tastes even better the next day.

2 Tablespoons olive oil
½ cup chopped onions
¼ cup chopped celery
2 cloves garlic, minced
1 teaspoon red pepper flakes
1 teaspoon dried sage
2½ cups vegetable broth
1¼ cups chopped canned tomatoes (not drained)
1 cup cooked white beans (or canned Great Northern or white beans), drained
½ pound uncooked pasta

In a medium-size pot, heat oil and sauté onions and celery and cook until vegetables are soft. Add garlic, red pepper flakes, and sage and cook for 1 minute. Add broth, tomatoes, and beans. Bring to a boil over high heat. Add pasta and reduce heat to medium. Cook uncovered for 10 minutes or until pasta is just tender (al dente). If desired, continue to cook, but don't let the pasta absorb all the liquid.

Serve hot or refrigerate until ready to serve. Garnish with grated vegan cheese and chopped parsley.

Total Calories Per Serving: 306   Total Fat as % of Daily Value: 10%   Protein: 10 gm   Fat: 6 gm
Carbohydrates: 52 gm   Calcium: 59 mg   Iron: 3 mg   Sodium: 402 mg   Dietary Fiber: 5 gm

Cilantro, Bean, and Chili Soup

Serves 10

Vegetable oil spray
2 cups minced onions
2 cloves garlic, minced
4 chopped green onions (white section only)
2 fresh chilies, deseeded and chopped (about 3 Tablespoons, you choose the heat)
4 cups vegetable broth
3 cups cooked or canned, drained black beans
2 cups cooked or canned, drained, white or navy beans
3 Tablespoons minced fresh cilantro

Heat a large soup pot and spray with oil. Add onions and garlic and sauté until lightly golden, stirring about 4-5 minutes. Add green onions and allow them to wilt, about 2 minutes. Stir in chilies, broth, and beans. Allow soup to cook for 30 minutes or until vegetables are tender and flavors are married. Stir in cilantro. Continue to cook for 5 more minutes. Serve hot.

Note: For a thicker, creamier texture, purée about 2 cups of the soup in a blender, return to pot, and allow to heat.

Mediterranean Couscous Soup

Serves 10

Vegetable oil spray
2 cups minced onions
2 cloves garlic, minced
3 cups garbanzo beans
1 cup thinly sliced zucchini
2 cups thinly sliced green cabbage
¹/₂ cup cubed winter squash or pumpkin
1¹/₂ cups thinly sliced carrots
10 cups vegetable broth
2 teaspoons ground cumin
1 Tablespoon white pepper
1 cup Mediterranean uncooked couscous (also called "Israeli" or "Pearl" couscous,
**   not traditional or fine couscous)**
¹/₄ cup minced fresh parsley

Spray a large soup pot with oil and heat. Add onions and cook, stirring, until soft. Add garlic and cook, stirring for 1 minute. Add garbanzos, zucchini, cabbage, squash, carrots, broth, cumin, and white pepper. Bring to a fast boil; then lower to a simmer. Cover and allow to cook for 1 hour, or until all vegetables are tender.

Spray a large skillet with vegetable oil and heat. Stir in couscous and toast over high heat, stirring so all couscous is lightly coated. Skim 2 cups of broth from cooking soup and add to couscous. Lower heat, cover, and allow to simmer for 20 minutes or until all liquid is absorbed. Just before serving, add the couscous and parsley to the soup and stir. Allow soup to cook for 2 minutes and serve.

Total Calories Per Serving: 227   Total Fat as % of Daily Value: 3%   Protein: 10 gm   Fat: 2 gm
Carbohydrates: 42 gm   Calcium: 51 mg   Iron: 2 mg   Sodium: 820 mg   Dietary Fiber: 6 gm

Potage Crecy (Creamless Creamy Carrot Soup)

Serves 6

This vibrantly colored soup has everything going for it: bright orange color, smooth mouth feel, elegant appearance, lots of nutrients, and little fat.

1 Tablespoon oil or vegan margarine
1 cup chopped yellow onions
2 cloves garlic, minced
1 Tablespoon minced fresh ginger
2 pounds peeled and diced carrots
1 medium-size (about 6 ounces) peeled and diced baking potato
3 cups water or vegetable stock
¹/₂ teaspoon white pepper

1 teaspoon dried parsley

Heat oil or margarine in soup pot. Add onions, garlic, and ginger and sauté until onions are soft (about 8 minutes). Add carrots and potatoes, cover, and cook over low heat for 10 minutes. Add stock, pepper, and parsley. Cover and allow soup to cook until carrots are very tender (at least 30 minutes).

Place soup in a food processor or blender (or do it the old-fashioned way and push soup through a fine sieve by hand) and purée until smooth. Return to heat and cook soup until hot (about 5 minutes).

Serve on its own or garnished with chopped green onions and fresh parsley. To increase the illusion of creaminess, top with 1 teaspoon of vegan margarine or sour cream right before serving.

Total Calories Per Serving: 113   Total Fat as % of Daily Value: 3%   Protein: 2 gm   Fat: 2 gm
Carbohydrates: 22 gm   Calcium: 61 mg   Iron: 1 mg   Sodium: 127 mg   Dietary Fiber: 5 gm

Tuscan-Style Soup
Serves 10

1 Tablespoon olive oil
1 cup finely chopped onions
1 cup finely sliced fresh fennel
1 cup thinly sliced carrots
3 cups peeled, thinly sliced fresh eggplant (select eggplant with small diameters)
3 cloves garlic, minced
4 cups vegetable broth
1¹/₂ cups chopped canned tomatoes (not drained)
3 cups cooked or canned, drained navy or white beans
2 Tablespoons chopped fresh flat leaf (also called "Italian") parsley
2 cups finely shredded kale, collards, or escarole
2 teaspoons ground black pepper
2 teaspoons red pepper flakes

Heat olive oil in a large soup pot. Add onions, fennel, carrots, eggplant, and garlic. Sauté and stir for about 3 minutes or until carrots are just soft.

Add broth, tomatoes, and beans. Bring to a fast boil and immediately reduce to a simmer. Allow soup to simmer 20-30 minutes, covered, or until all vegetables are fork tender. Stir in greens, black pepper, and red pepper flakes. Cover and simmer 5-7 minutes or until greens are wilted. Serve hot.

Total Calories Per Serving: 138   Total Fat as % of Daily Value: 3%   Protein: 7 gm   Fat: 2 gm
Carbohydrates: 25 gm   Calcium: 74 mg   Iron: 2 mg   Sodium: 686 mg   Dietary Fiber: 7 gm

Creamy Red Pepper Soup
Serves 10

6 red peppers, destemmed, deseeded, and cut into quarters lengthwise (4 cups)
Olive oil
3 cups peeled and diced boiling potatoes
2 cups diced red onion
1 cup diced celery
2 Tablespoons olive oil
1 clove garlic, minced
1 Tablespoon chili powder
1 Tablespoon paprika
$^1/_2$ teaspoon white pepper
$^1/_4$ cup unbleached flour
4 cups vegetable stock, divided
$^1/_4$ cup dry sherry (optional)
1 cup soymilk or rice milk
$^1/_2$ cup shredded fresh basil

Place the red peppers, skin side up, on a cookie sheet. Using your fingers, coat the skins with a little olive oil. Place the peppers under the broiler and broil for several minutes or until the skin has charred and blackened. Remove the cookie sheet from the oven, place the peppers in a brown bag, and allow them to cool in the bag for 15 minutes.

Remove the peppers from the bag, remove and discard the blackened skins, place the peppers on a plate, and set aside.

In a large pot, sauté the potato, red onion, and celery in olive oil for 10 minutes or until lightly browned and soft. Add the garlic, chili powder, paprika, salt, and white pepper, and sauté an additional 2 minutes. Sprinkle the flour over the top of the vegetables, stir well, and cook an additional 1 minute. Remove the pot from the heat. Transfer the roasted red peppers and sautéed vegetables to a food processor. Add 1 cup vegetable stock and purée until smooth. Transfer the purée back to the large pot, add the remaining vegetable stock and sherry, and simmer over low heat until heated through. Stir in the soymilk, taste, and adjust the seasonings as needed. Garnish individual servings with shredded fresh basil.

Total Calories Per Serving: 126   Total Fat as % of Daily Value: 4%   Protein: 4 gm   Fat: 6 gm
Carbohydrates: 22 gm   Calcium: 37 mg   Iron: 1 mg   Sodium: 347 mg   Dietary Fiber: 4 gm

Curried Apple Soup

Serves 10

1 cup shallots, finely diced (onions will work, as well)
2 Tablespoons vegetable oil
1 Tablespoon curry powder
2 teaspoons minced ginger
¼ cup sherry (or 2 Tablespoons vinegar combined with 2 Tablespoons apple juice)
3 pounds green apples of choice, peeled, cored, and diced (about 8 cups)
4 cups vegetable stock
1 cup apple juice
1 cup soymilk
2 Tablespoons lemon juice
Salt and pepper to taste

In a large pot, sauté the shallots in oil for 5 minutes or until soft. Add the curry powder and ginger, and sauté an additional minute. Add the sherry and stir well. Add the diced apples, vegetable stock, and apple juice and bring the mixture to a boil. Cover, reduce the heat to low, and simmer 20-25 minutes or until the apples are tender. Remove from the heat and allow soup to cool for 10 minutes. In a food processor or blender, in batches, purée the soup until smooth and return the soup to the pot. Whisk in the soymilk, a little lemon juice, and season to taste with salt and pepper. If desired, add additional curry powder, apple juice, or lemon juice to the soup to adjust the sweetness or spicy flavor of the soup to your own taste. Serve hot or cold.

Total Calories Per Serving: 139   Total Fat as % of Daily Value: 6%   Protein: 2 gm   Fat: 4 gm
Carbohydrates: 27 gm   Calcium: 28 mg   Iron: 1 mg   Sodium: 329 mg   Dietary Fiber: 2 gm

Miso Soup with Mushrooms

Serves 5-6

1½ cups sliced fresh mushrooms
2 teaspoons vegetable oil
½ cup thinly sliced green onions
1 clove garlic, minced
1 Tablespoon minced fresh ginger
4 cups vegetable stock
2 cups stemmed, chopped Swiss chard leaves
2 Tablespoons red miso (or other miso of choice)
2 Tablespoons sesame seeds

In a large saucepan, sauté the mushrooms in the oil for 3 minutes or until soft. Add the green onion, garlic, and ginger, and sauté an additional 2 minutes. Add stock and Swiss chard and stir well to combine. Bring the mixture to a boil and boil for 3 minutes. In a small bowl, stir together the miso and a little of the cooking liquid from the saucepan. Add the miso mixture to the pot, stir well to combine, and remove the soup from the heat. Sprinkle sesame seeds over individual servings.

Total Calories Per Serving: 98   Total Fat as % of Daily Value: 7%   Protein: 4 gm   Fat: 5 gm
Carbohydrates: 13 gm   Calcium: 60 mg   Iron: 2 mg   Sodium: 1,088 mg   Dietary Fiber: 3 gm

Mushroom Barley Soup

Serves 6-8

1 cup chopped onions
½ cup chopped celery
1 cup minced carrots
2 cloves garlic, minced
1½ pounds sliced fresh mushrooms (about 5 cups)
3 Tablespoons soy sauce
1 cup uncooked barley
1 Tablespoon garlic powder
2 teaspoons dried dill
1 Tablespoon chopped fresh parsley
10 cups water (divided)

In a large pot, combine onions, celery, carrots, garlic, mushrooms, and 5 cups of water. Cover and allow soup to simmer until carrots are soft, about 10 minutes. Add soy sauce, barley, garlic powder, and the remaining 5 cups of water. Bring to a fast boil. Reduce heat, cover, and allow soup to simmer 5 minutes. Add dill and parsley and allow soup to simmer until barley is tender and soup has thickened.

Total Calories Per Serving: 176   Total Fat as % of Daily Value: 2%   Protein: 8 gm   Fat: 1 gm
Carbohydrates: 37 gm   Calcium: 47 mg   Iron: 2 mg   Sodium: 544 mg   Dietary Fiber: 8 gm

White Bean, Winter Squash, and Kale Soup

Serves 12

3 cups diced onion
2 cups diced celery (including the green tops)
2 Tablespoon olive oil
2 Tablespoons minced garlic
1 Tablespoon minced ginger
8 cups vegetable stock
6 cups winter squash, peeled, deseeded, and cut into 1-inch cubes
6 cups stemmed and roughly chopped fresh kale
2 teaspoons each dried basil and dried thyme
1 teaspoon ground cumin
Salt and pepper to taste
2 cups canned baby butter beans (baby limas) or cooked beans, drained and rinsed
2 cups Great Northern white beans or cooked beans, drained and rinsed

In a large pot, sauté the onion and celery in olive oil for 5 minutes to soften. Add the garlic and ginger and sauté for an additional 2 minutes. Add the vegetable stock, winter squash, kale, basil, thyme, cumin, salt, and pepper and bring to a boil. Cover the pot, reduce heat to low, and simmer 15-20 minutes or until the vegetables are tender. Add the beans and simmer an additional 5 minutes. Serve hot.

Total Calories Per Serving: 212   Total Fat as % of Daily Value: 5%   Protein: 8 gm   Fat: 3 gm
Carbohydrates: 42 gm   Calcium: 157 mg   Iron: 4 mg   Sodium: 871 mg   Dietary Fiber: 11 gm

Tomato Basil Soup
Serves 12

1¹⁄₂ cups diced onions
1 Tablespoon olive oil
1 Tablespoon minced garlic
4 cups vegetable stock
2¹⁄₂ cups chopped, canned tomatoes (not drained)
2 Tablespoons tomato paste
³⁄₄ cup frozen, thawed peas
¹⁄₃ cup orzo pasta (or star-shaped or other small shaped pasta)
1 Tablespoon sugar
1 teaspoon black pepper
2 cups washed, chopped fresh spinach
¹⁄₂ cup chopped fresh basil
3 Tablespoons chopped fresh Italian parsley (flat-leafed)
3 Tablespoons nutritional yeast flakes (as garnish)

Add oil to large pot and heat. Sauté onions in oil for 5 minutes to soften. Add the garlic and sauté an additional minute. Add vegetable stock, crushed tomatoes, and tomato paste. Stir well and bring the mixture to a fast boil. Reduce to medium heat. Add peas, orzo pasta, sugar, and pepper and cook 5-7 minutes or until the pasta is al dente. Add the spinach, basil, and parsley and simmer the soup an additional 2 minutes to allow the flavors to blend and the spinach to wilt. Garnish with nutritional yeast flakes, if desired.

Total Calories Per Serving: 62   Total Fat as % of Daily Value: 2%   Protein: 3 gm   Fat: 1 gm
Carbohydrates: 11 gm   Calcium: 24 mg   Iron: 1 mg   Sodium: 281 mg   Dietary Fiber: 2 gm

Fast Taco Soup
Serves 6

1 cup cooked or canned, drained kidney beans
1 cup cooked or canned, drained black beans (or two different types of beans of your choice)
3 cups canned diced tomatoes (with liquid)
¹⁄₂ cup chopped onions
2 Tablespoons taco seasoning (combination of chili powder, cumin, and black pepper)
1 cup canned, thawed, fresh or frozen, thawed cut corn
4 Tablespoons sliced black olives
2 cups vegetable broth
Baked tortilla chips and shredded vegan cheese or vegan sour cream (as garnish)

Combine all ingredients, except garnish, in a large pot. Stir to combine while heating. Bring to a fast boil, reduce heat, and allow to simmer 20-30 minutes, or until hot. Garnish, as desired, before serving.

Total Calories Per Serving (without garnish): 140   Total Fat as % of Daily Value: 3%   Protein: 7 gm   Fat: 2 gm
Carbohydrates: 26 gm   Calcium: 54 mg   Iron: 3 mg   Sodium: 322 mg   Dietary Fiber: 7 gm

Urkranian Borscht

Serves 8

8 cups vegetable broth
2 cups minced carrots
1 cup minced onion
1 cup minced green bell pepper
2 cups peeled, minced fresh beets
1 cup chopped fresh tomatoes
2 cups peeled and cubed boiling potatoes
1¹/₂ cups shredded green cabbage
1 clove garlic, minced
1 Tablespoon tomato purée
2 Tablespoons chopped fresh parsley
2 Tablespoons chopped fresh dill

In a large pot, heat broth. When warm add carrots, onions, pepper, and beets. Add tomatoes. Allow soup to cook for 5 minutes. Add potatoes, cabbage, and garlic. Allow soup to cook for 5 more minutes. Add purée, parsley, and dill. Allow soup to simmer 20-30 minutes, or until all vegetables are tender.

Total Calories Per Serving: 98   Total Fat as % of Daily Value: 1%   Protein: 1 gm   Fat: <1 gm
Carbohydrates: 23 gm   Calcium: 52 mg   Iron: 1 mg   Sodium: 846 mg   Dietary Fiber: 4 gm

Creamy Potato Soup

Serve 10

4 pounds golden (such as Yukon Gold) potatoes (about 10 cups)
¹/₂ cup chopped yellow onion
¹/₂ cup chopped celery
¹/₄ cup vegan margarine
1 teaspoon each black pepper and garlic powder
2 cups vegetable stock
5 cups plain soymilk
2 cups creamed corn
¹/₂ cup vegan bacon bits

Boil potatoes, cool, skin and dice in ¹/₂-inch cubes. In a large pot, sauté onion and celery with vegan margarine. Add pepper, garlic powder, stock, potatoes, soymilk, corn, and vegan bacon bits, stirring and simmering 20 minutes or until all vegetables are soft.

Total Calories Per Serving: 276   Total Fat as % of Daily Value: 11%   Protein: 9 gm   Fat: 7 gm
Carbohydrates: 45 gm   Calcium: 212 mg   Iron: 2 mg   Sodium: 337 mg   Dietary Fiber: 5 gm

Cold Avocado-Cilantro Soup

Serves 6-8

1 cup fresh cilantro leaves
2 fresh stemmed and seeded jalapeño chilies
2 cloves garlic
4 peeled, pitted, and cubed avocados (about 4 cups)
4 cups vegetable stock
1 cup orange juice
¹⁄₂ cup tequila (optional)
1 teaspoon ground cumin
¹⁄₄ chopped red bell pepper (as garnish)

In a food processor or blender, combine the cilantro, jalapeños, and garlic and process. Add half of all the remaining ingredients, except red bell pepper, and process with the cilantro mixture until smooth. Transfer the purée to a glass or plastic (not metal) bowl. Purée the remaining ingredients and stir the batches together. Cover and chill for at least 1 hour before serving. Garnish with red peppers before serving.

Total Calories Per Serving: 201   Total Fat as % of Daily Value: 23%   Protein: 3 gm   Fat: 15 gm
Carbohydrates: 18 gm   Calcium: 24 mg   Iron: 1 mg   Sodium: 815 mg   Dietary Fiber: 7 gm

Chilled Cantaloupe Soup

Serves 8

6 cups peeled and cubed cantaloupe
¹⁄₂ cup orange juice
3 Tablespoons lemon juice
1 cup plain soy yogurt
2 Tablespoons brown rice syrup

In a blender or food processor, combine the cantaloupe, orange juice, and lemon juice and blend well to form a smooth purée. Transfer the mixture to a glass or plastic bowl and whisk in the soy yogurt and brown rice syrup. Cover and chill for at least 2 hours before serving.

Total Calories Per Serving: 89   Total Fat as % of Daily Value: 1%   Protein: 2 gm   Fat: 1 gm
Carbohydrates: 19 gm   Calcium: 62 mg   Iron: 0 mg   Sodium: 28 mg   Dietary Fiber: 1 gm

Chilled Tomato Gazpacho

Serves 8

1 cup tomato paste
2 stemmed, seeded, and diced fresh chilies (you select the heat)
⅓ cup balsamic vinegar
2 Tablespoons lime juice
1 Tablespoon sugar
1 Tablespoon minced garlic
1 Tablespoon ground cumin
1 teaspoon Tabasco sauce or other hot sauce
1 teaspoon freshly ground black pepper
7 cups tomato juice
3 cups seeded and diced fresh tomatoes
2 cups peeled, seeded, and diced cucumbers
2 cups peeled and diced fresh jicama (if jicama is not available, use 2 cups cooked,
    peeled, diced potatoes)
1½ cups stemmed, seeded, and diced green bell peppers
1½ cups stemmed, seeded, and diced red bell peppers
1½ cups chopped green onion
1 cup each diced zucchini and diced summer squash
¼ cup freshly chopped parsley
¼ cup freshly chopped cilantro

In a blender or food processor, place the tomato paste, chilies, vinegar, lime juice, garlic, cumin, Tabasco sauce, pepper, and 3 cups of the tomato juice and process for 2 minutes or until smooth. Transfer the mixture to a large glass or plastic (not metal) bowl. Add the rest of the tomato juice and stir well to combine. Add the remaining ingredients and stir well to combine. Cover and chill for at least 2 hours before serving in chilled bowls.

Note: Will last well in the refrigerator for up to 3 days.

Total Calories Per Serving: 134   Total Fat as % of Daily Value: 1%   Protein: 6 gm   Fat: 1 gm
Carbohydrates: 31 gm   Calcium: 76 mg   Iron: 3 mg   Sodium: 1,074 mg   Dietary Fiber: 7 gm

Chapter 12: VEGETABLES AND GRAINS

Vegetables can add color and interest to party meals. There are so many types of vegetables and many cooking methods to use with them. Cooking affects vegetables in at least four ways, including altering texture, flavor, color, and nutritional content. The good news is that if you use cooking methods that preserve flavor and color, these methods also preserve nutritional content. Your guests will get a plate of goodness and think they're eating party food!

Vegetable Cooking Guidelines

- Lemon juice, vinegar, tomato products, citrus fruit juices, and sugar-containing ingredients, such as maple or rice syrup, make vegetable fiber firmer. If you want your grilled zucchini, which is very low in fiber, to maintain its shape, marinate in tomato juice prior to cooking. If you want your orange-glazed carrots, which are very high in fiber, to be very tender, do not add orange juice until the very end of cooking.

- Heat softens vegetable fiber. The longer you cook vegetables, they will be more tender; however, there will be more color and nutrient loss, so you'll need to balance texture and nutrient needs.

- Beans, peas, and lentils become soft by absorbing moisture. You can presoak beans, to ensure adequate moisture and to reduce cooking time, but you must always cook in enough water to allow maximum moisture absorption. Water needs vary from product to product.

- Attempt to use just enough cooking liquid to cook all vegetables (except beans, peas, and lentils). The less liquid, the more color, texture, and nutrients are saved.

- Cook vegetables for as short a time as possible and as close to serving time as possible. This makes for colorful vegetables with lots of "snap." If your schedule or cooking facilities don't allow you to cook vegetables close to serving time, think about serving cooked vegetables cold. For example, you could grill carrots, summer squash, zucchini, and red pepper, then chill them and serve as a cold side dish.

- Strong-flavored vegetables, such as Brussels sprouts, broccoli, rutabagas, or turnips, do not need their flavors developed. Attempt to cook them, uncovered, for as short a time as possible.

- White-colored vegetables, such as white potatoes, eggplant, zucchini, cauliflower, turnips, onions, and green cabbage, may benefit from a small amount of acid, such as lemon juice or vinegar, to keep the white from becoming pale or gray.

- Green-colored vegetables, such as kale, green beans, and spinach, will keep their color and texture well if cooked, uncovered, as quickly as possible. Try to avoid adding any acid, such as vinegar or orange juice, until just before serving, as acid can cause green vegetables to turn gray.

- Red or purple vegetables, such as beets or red cabbage, are loaded with antioxidants. You can preserve their bright color and the nutrients by cooking beets unpeeled, avoiding overcooking, and serving some of the cooking liquid as part of the sauce.

- The good news about yellow and orange vegetables, such as carrots, sweet potatoes, winter squash, and corn, is that their color and nutrients are very stable, holding up well to heat. Still, try to avoid overcooking, as the texture may become mushy.

- Clean vegetables with cold, running water. Try to avoid soaking vegetables, as the additional water may cause them to become mushy and may leach out some of the nutrients.

- Clean and peel vegetables as close to cooking as possible. Prewashing and peeling vegetables more than an hour or so before cooking can result in the growth of bacteria and the loss of some nutrients.

- When possible, cook vegetables with the peel on. This preserves some nutrients. If vegetables need to be peeled, peel them as thinly as possible after cooking, as many nutrients lie close to the surface.

- Root vegetables, such as potatoes, beets, carrots, parsnips, and turnips can be scrubbed with a clean, stiff vegetable brush rather than being peeled. Do this prior to cooking.

- Wash green leafy vegetables, such as spinach or mustard greens, several times in cold, running water, as quickly as possible. Drain well before cooking, so any sand or gravel is removed.

Most of the recipes in this chapter will work well with fresh or frozen vegetables, unless noted. If using canned vegetables, you may want to quickly rinse them to remove some of the salt.

When planning vegetable dishes, think seasonal. Seasonal vegetables may be more reasonable in price and should be at the height of their flavor and color. You can transform many vegetable dishes into entrées with the addition of cooked, seasoned beans, lentils, garbanzos, different types of nuts, or cubed, seasoned extra-firm tofu, seitan, or tempeh.

Flavor Your Fungus

Here are some marinating ideas for mushrooms. To a small amount of oil, add some of the herbs below. Allow mushrooms to marinate for at least 2 hours and then grill, sauté, barbecue, or bake them.

Turkish: caraway, dried mint, cumin, oregano, and red pepper flakes

Indian: cardamom, garam masala (a spice blend available in Indian markets), clove, cinnamon, fennel, and turmeric

Greek: cracked black pepper, oregano, cinnamon, and mint

Brazilian: bay leaf, black pepper, cloves, coriander, and nutmeg

Caribbean: jerk spice mixtures or allspice, nutmeg, ginger, clove, and chilies

Chinese: Chinese five-spice blend, star anise, dried orange peel, chili, and ginger

Mexican: fresh cilantro, chilies, cumin, and cinnamon

Moroccan: cinnamon, cumin, ginger, turmeric, saffron, and paprika

Thai: ginger, lemon grass, fresh mint, Thai basil, and chilies

Basic Bean Baking

To bake beans, you need cooked, drained beans and a sauce of liquid to bake them in. The sauce is used to moisten and flavor the beans. Decide on which role your baked beans will play, entrée, casserole, side dish, dessert, and then you can decide on the ingredients.

A rule of thumb for baking beans is to start with three-quarters of a cup of sauce for every cup and a quarter of cooked beans. The beans will absorb a lot of the liquid and will help to soften the fiber. If you would like your beans to taste strongly of a certain flavor, add it at the beginning of cooking. If you'd like just a hint of a flavor, add it during the last 10 minutes of cooking. For example, if you would like to have an oniony bean casserole, finely chop onions and mix them with the beans before putting them in the oven. If you'd like just a whisper of onions, sprinkle them lightly over the beans just several minutes before removing from the oven. Don't forget, bake beans benefit from slow baking. Try to bake them between 300-325 degrees over a long period of time, from 2-6 hours, depending on the amount. If you bake beans quickly, you may wind up with tough, dry beans.

Mix and Match

You can select one type of bean and vary the sauces, or vary both the beans and the sauces. We've given you some ideas below. If you use about 3 cups of cooked beans, you can add about $2^1/_4$ cups of sauce, and bake covered in an 8 x 8-inch glass casserole dish or a small glass loaf pan. It's always a good idea to bake beans in a non-reactive dish, so no off flavors develop.

If you like one type of sauce, then vary your beans for a different flavor. Tomato-based sauces work well with white, pinto, cranberry, black-eyed peas, and green and gray lentils. Garlic- and lemon-based sauces work well with kidney, appaloosa, garbanzo (chickpeas), red and lima beans, as well as split peas and yellow and orange lentils.

Baked Bean Sauces

Green Gratin: combine soymilk with fresh shredded spinach, kale, or collard greens (if using frozen greens, thaw them and squeeze out as much water as possible), dried thyme, dried sage, and fresh garlic. Add beans and bake. If desired, top with dried bread crumbs and place baked beans under a broiler for several minutes until browned.

Lemony Vegetable: combine vegetable broth with chopped onions, garlic, mint, and lemon juice. Toss with beans and bake.

Cacciatore Baked Beans: combine canned tomatoes (with juice), tomato purée, garlic, oregano, basil, black pepper, and white wine (optional). Toss with beans, top with a small amount of vegan Parmesan cheese or nutritional yeast and bake.

Curried: combine vegetable broth, chopped tomatoes, fresh ginger, curry powder, fresh cilantro or parsley, and ground cumin. Toss with beans and bake.

Traditional New England: combine chopped onions, prepared mustard, black pepper, vinegar, molasses, and maple syrup together. Toss with beans and bake.

Pizza Baked Beans: combine chopped tomatoes, prepared tomato sauce, sliced mushrooms, chopped bell pepper, chopped onions, basil, and black pepper. Toss with beans and bake.

Grains

All grains are low in fat and contain no cholesterol. They are low in sodium unless salt is added in cooking. They typically have between 5 and 10 grams of protein per cup. We rated grains in terms of their fiber, riboflavin, vitamin B-6, zinc, copper, and iron content. Vegetarians get significant amounts of these nutrients from grains. Our top choices are amaranth, quinoa, barley, triticale, and bulgur.

Think you can't do grains in a hurry? Get over the idea that it's just too much work to cook grains. While some grains do require a long time to cook, this cooking time can be reduced by soaking the grains overnight or by pressure-cooking them. Additionally, grains can be cooked in a crockpot for small amounts or commercial steamers. They do not require any attention while they are cooking. Quick-cooking grains, which require less than 30 minutes to prepare, include quick brown rice, couscous, quinoa, buckwheat groats (kasha), teff, and bulgur.

Tired of rice and pasta? Try cooking some quinoa or millet. Add herbs and spices, vegetables, tofu, seitan, tempeh, and a variety of sauces to make an unending selection of grain dishes.

The versatility of grains makes them the perfect ingredient for vegetarian dishes. For example, you can prepare basic, steamed, long grain white rice. Serve it as a bed for grilled vegetables, five-bean stew, a baked tofu "steak," or a brochette of mushrooms, sweet onions, and cherry tomatoes. Be sure to make enough to use as a thickening agent for soups. Make a vegetarian version of Avegolomono (Greek lemon and rice soup) with vegetarian stock and puréed rice. Add "creaminess" to vegetarian tomato, mushroom, and vegetable sauces with puréed rice. Toss cooked rice with pine nuts, basil, and olive oil and form into timbales (small drum shapes). Serve rice timbales as an accompaniment to stuffed sweet onions or marinated tempeh "steaks." Combine cooked rice with silken tofu, orange juice concentrate, and vanilla extract for an orange-rice pudding.

Cook up a pot of medium-texture kasha or whole wheat. Both these grains have a pleasant chewy texture and a slightly neutral, nutty flavor. Steamed with water, they make a good hot cereal. Serve them with heated maple syrup, chopped nuts, raisins, dried fruit, and fresh berries. Sauté cooked kasha or whole wheat with onions and a small amount of garlic and you have an accompaniment dish for vegetarian entrées, such as grilled portobello mushrooms or eggplant lasagna (use eggplant, cut lengthwise) to replace pasta. Add kasha or whole wheat pasta to vegetable soups to create a thick entrée stew. Reheat kasha or whole wheat with sliced mushrooms and minced carrots and celery for a pilaf. Combine cooked kasha with chopped vegetables and beans to make a stuffing for tomatoes, onion, and squash. Or mix cooked kasha with silken tofu, fresh chopped herbs, and dry bread crumbs and fry or bake as a savory grain pancake.

Grains You'll Want to Add to Your Menu

Barley: Barley has ancient origins and has been used as a food, a measuring standard, and even as money. Reach for whole barley, which is high in protein, fiber, potassium, calcium, niacin, and iron. Pearled barley has had its husks scoured off (along with nutrients) to reduce cooking time. Used most often as a thickener for soups and stews and as a partner in grain dishes, whole barley is also sprouted to produce barley malt syrup.

Millet: The closest many in this country get to millet is as birdseed. Yet with 6,000 varieties around the world, it is a staple for many cultures and has been for centuries. Millet is high in some B vitamins, copper, and iron. It is the easiest grain to digest and makes a great side to any meal. For a real taste treat, sauté millet with garlic and onions before steaming. When cooked and cooled, it has an ideal texture for making millet burgers.

Oats: Whole oats were long considered a weed before being cultivated. Now they are a tasty and healthy addition to everything from bread to cookies to hot breakfast cereals to granola. Oats are easily digestible, burning slowly in the body to provide extra energy. The bran and germ remain intact in each of the three most commonly sold forms of oats (steel cut, rolled, and whole [hulled] groats). Use oats as a cereal, thickener, and baking ingredient.

Quinoa: Quinoa has been called "the super grain" and is a relative of the baby green lamb's quarters. It grows quite tall and has a bushy head of seeds. Quinoa came originally from the Andes in South America, where it was cultivated by the Incas. The Incas referred to it as the "mother grain." After the Spanish conquests of the sixteenth century, it became a minor crop and was not commonly known until recently. Two Americans learned of quinoa in the 1980s and began to test-grow it in Colorado. It is now available in health-food stores and some supermarkets, where you may find it in pasta, snacks, and cereals as well as whole and as flour. Quinoa is very nutritious. It is high in protein and important vitamins and minerals as well as starch, sugar, and fat.

Quinoa has a smoky sesame-like taste. When ground into flour, it takes on a slightly bitter flavor. When quinoa is cooked, the grains, or seeds, become translucent. Quinoa can be used in place of rice. Complement quinoa with parsley, scallions, dill, citrus juices, flavored vinegars, or soy sauce.

Baked goods that are made with quinoa flour can be savory or sweet and lightly spiced. Whole quinoa nearly triples in volume when steamed. The exact proportion of water to grain and the length of the cooking time will differ depending on the size and weight of the pan, the intensity of the heat, and the desired degree of doneness.

RECIPES

Notes: All recipes can be easily doubled, tripled, or quadrupled. Instead of one or two entrées, select three or four of the following vegetable and grain recipes as centerpieces for your party meal.

Whole Grain Stuffing
Serves 15

Use this stuffing for bell peppers, small winter squash, tomatoes, small eggplants, and sweet onions. Fill vegetables with prepared stuffing and bake in a medium oven until the vegetables are tender.

Vegetable oil spray
1 quart vegetable stock or broth (about 4 cups)
2 cups whole kasha
¹/₂ cup brown rice
2 Tablespoons vegetable oil
³/₄ cup sliced, drained canned mushrooms
³/₄ cup cooked or canned, drained black beans
¹/₂ cup fresh chopped parsley
¹/₂ cup tomato purée
¹/₄ cup chopped fresh tomatoes
1 clove garlic, minced
2 teaspoons ground black pepper
15 small tomatoes, hollowed out

Preheat oven to 350 degrees. Place stock in a small pot. Heat until boiling. Reduce to simmer.

In a small bowl, combine kasha, rice, and oil. Heat a medium sauté pan. Sauté kasha until grains are separate and toasted. Slowly pour heated stock onto grains, stirring. Reduce heat to simmer. Cover and allow mixture to simmer until all liquid is absorbed, about 10-12 minutes. Stir in mushrooms, beans, parsley, tomato purée, chopped tomatoes, garlic, and black pepper. Allow stuffing to heat for 3 minutes. Your stuffing is now ready. Refrigerate until ready to use or stuff tomatoes and bake until tender.

Total Calories Per Serving: 71   Total Fat as % of Daily Value: 3%   Protein: 2 gm   Fat: 2 gm
Carbohydrates: 4 gm   Calcium: 10 mg   Iron: 1 mg   Sodium: 265 mg   Dietary Fiber: 2 gm

Maple-Glazed Carrots and Winter Squash with Pecans

Serves 10

¾ cup chopped pecans
1 Tablespoon each vegetable oil and maple syrup
2 pounds fresh peeled and diced butternut squash (about 4½ cups)
1 pound peeled and sliced carrots (about 2½ cups)
2 Tablespoons oil
½ cup apricot jam
2 teaspoons orange zest
4 Tablespoons maple syrup

Preheat oven to 400 degrees. Put pecans in a heavy skillet and toast over high heat, stirring constantly for about 3 minutes or until lightly toasted. Add oil and 1 Tablespoon maple syrup. Cook, stirring constantly for 1 more minute or until nuts are well coated. Remove from skillet and set aside. Turn off heat, but leave skillet on the stove.

In a large bowl, mix together squash, carrots, and 2 Tablespoons oil. Place squash mixture in the bottom of a heavy oven casserole (like a roasting pan) and roast in the oven, stirring occasionally for 30 minutes or until vegetables are tender.

In the skillet, mix jam, zest, and 4 Tablespoons syrup. Bring to a fast boil, stirring constantly, then lower heat. Allow to simmer until very thick, about 4 minutes.

Remove vegetables from oven. Stir in sauce and pecans. Place in a bowl and serve immediately.

Notes: If nuts are not desired, you can replace with roasted soybeans or shelled pumpkin seeds. Also, other hard winter squash may be used; frozen squash will not work in this recipe.

Total Calories Per Serving: 198   Total Fat as % of Daily Value: 16%   Protein: 2 gm   Fat: 10 gm
Carbohydrates: 26 gm   Calcium: 44 mg   Iron: 1 mg   Sodium: 39 mg   Dietary Fiber: 3 gm

Spinach Baked Mushrooms

Serves 8 entrées or 32 appetizers

2 teaspoons olive oil
½ cup diced onion
1 garlic clove, minced
⅛ teaspoon nutmeg
1 cup cooked rice (white or brown-begin with ⅓ cup uncooked)
1 cup frozen, thawed and squeezed dry chopped spinach
2 Tablespoons nutritional yeast
Vegetable oil spray
8 fresh large portobello mushroom caps, washed and patted dry

Preheat oven to 375 degrees. Pour oil into skillet and heat. Sauté onions and garlic for about 2 minutes, until soft. Place in a medium bowl. Add nutmeg, rice, spinach, and yeast to bowl and mix to combine.

Spray a baking sheet with oil. Place portobello caps, gill side up, on sheet. Divide spinach mixture into eight equal parts and fill each cap. Press filling down slightly. Bake for 15 minutes, or until mushrooms are soft and filling is hot.

Note: You can serve each person one whole cap as an entrée. For appetizers, cut each cap into 4 pieces.

Total Calories Per Serving: 77   Total Fat as % of Daily Value: 3%   Protein: 5 gm   Fat: 2 gm
Carbohydrates: 13 gm   Calcium: 44 mg   Iron: 1 mg   Sodium: 22 mg   Dietary Fiber: 3 gm

Asparagus with Lime and Onion Dressing

Serves 6-8

2 pounds fresh, trimmed asparagus (figure 10 thin stalks per pound)
½ cup vegan mayonnaise
2 Tablespoons water
1½ Tablespoons lime juice
1 clove garlic, minced
3 Tablespoons chopped green onion

Blanch asparagus quickly by filling a skillet that is as long as the asparagus with one or two inches of water (you need only cover the asparagus with about ½ inch of water). Half-fill a bowl or baking dish that is as long as the asparagus with a mixture of half ice water and half cold water. Bring water to a fast boil. Add asparagus and allow to cook for only 1-2 minutes, just until the asparagus turns bright green and gets the slightest bit tender (cooking time depends on the toughness of the asparagus). Remove the asparagus from the water and place immediately in ice water. Leave in ice water, turning, only until asparagus is cool to touch. Remove from ice water and place on a serving platter.

   To create sauce, place mayonnaise in a small bowl. Whisk in water and juice until combined, and then stir in garlic and onion. Allow sauce to chill for 10 minutes.

   To serve, drizzle sauce over asparagus, or allow guests to dip asparagus in sauce.

Note: If frozen asparagus spears are used, do not cook. Thaw quickly under cold running water, pat dry, and place on a serving plate.

Total Calories Per Serving: 42   Total Fat as % of Daily Value: 1%   Protein: 3 gm   Fat: 1 gm
Carbohydrates: 7 gm   Calcium: 39 mg   Iron: 3 mg   Sodium: 10 mg   Dietary Fiber: 3 gm

Kale with Two Peppers

Serves 5

1 cup chopped onion
Vegetable oil spray
2 pounds washed and cleaned kale (about 1 large bunch or about 8 cups)
2 teaspoons vinegar
1 teaspoon crushed red pepper flakes
1 teaspoon black pepper

Spray a large skillet with oil and cook onions, stirring, on low heat, until translucent. While onion is cooking, remove larger stems of kale leaves and chop roughly. Add kale to onions and cook, covered, stirring occasionally, until the leaves are wilted but still bright green. Quickly stir in vinegar and both peppers. Stir and serve immediately.

Total Calories Per Serving: 107   Total Fat as % of Daily Value: 2%   Protein: 6 gm   Fat: 1 gm
Carbohydrates: 22 gm   Calcium: 254 mg   Iron: 3 mg   Sodium: 79 mg   Dietary Fiber: 4 gm

Mashed Carrots

Serves 5

This can be a colorful side dish for creamy mushroom soup or potato chowder.

1 pound carrots, peeled, sliced, cooked, and drained (about 2¹/₂ cups)
1 Tablespoon vegan margarine
1 Tablespoon fresh dill
¹/₂ cup fresh seedless grapes, cut in halves

Place carrots in a blender or food processor and process them to mash them. Mix in margarine and dill. Add grapes and process for just 30 seconds, so grapes become slightly mashed.

Total Calories Per Serving: 63   Total Fat as % of Daily Value: 2%   Protein: 1 gm   Fat: 4 gm
Carbohydrates: 10 gm   Calcium: 31 mg   Iron: 0 mg   Sodium: 87 mg   Dietary Fiber: 3 gm

Corn and Asparagus Packets with Coconut Milk

Serves 6

¹/₂ cup chopped green bell pepper
¹/₄ cup chopped fresh cilantro
1 teaspoon hot sauce
1 cup drained, canned baby corn
1 cup frozen, thawed asparagus tips
¹/₂ cup chopped green onion (white part only)
1 cup long grain white rice
2 cups lowfat canned coconut milk
¹/₂ cup water
Oven-proof parchment paper or aluminum foil

Preheat oven to 400 degrees. Place bell pepper, cilantro, and hot sauce in a blender canister and process until thin and smooth. Set aside.

Cut corn and asparagus into 1-inch pieces. Mix corn, asparagus, and onions together with pepper sauce and set aside.

Assemble packets by cutting parchment or foil into large circles, about 10 inches across. Divide vegetable mixture into 6 equal amounts. Place mixture at one end of the circle. Twist the edges shut. If using parchment, you may use a sprinkle of water to help "glue" the edges. Place on a baking sheet and baked for 10 minutes.

While packets are baking, prepare rice by combining rice, coconut milk, and water in a small pot. Bring to a fast boil, reduce heat, and simmer, covered, until all liquid is absorbed, about 15 minutes. Turn off heat and allow rice to sit for 5 minutes.

To serve, place rice in the center of a serving platter and ring with vegetable packets. Guests can serve themselves rice, and then break open packets, on their plates, to enjoy the aroma.

Total Calories Per Serving: 127   Total Fat as % of Daily Value: 9%   Protein: 3 gm   Fat: 6 gm
Carbohydrates: 28 gm   Calcium: 64 mg   Iron: 2 mg   Sodium: 103 mg   Dietary Fiber: 2 gm

Roasted Eggplant Curry

Serves 5

2 pounds whole eggplant (about 2 medium)
1 cup chopped onions
2 cloves garlic, minced
1 teaspoon mustard seeds
1 teaspoon turmeric
¹/₂ teaspoon cayenne
1 teaspoon black pepper
1 teaspoon curry powder

Roast the eggplants, pricked in several places so they don't explode, on a barbeque or roast them in a 450-degree oven until charred on the outside and very soft on the inside. Cool and peel and set aside; you should have a large bowl of pulp.

Place onions in a large, non-stick pot and cook onions in just enough water to cover them until soft. Add garlic and mustard seeds. Cook until the onions begin to turn golden. Stir in the turmeric, cayenne, black pepper, and curry. Add the eggplant pulp, onion mixture, and tomato to a food processor and blend until the mixture looks thick. Return to pot and heat. Serve hot, over steamed rice.

Total Calories Per Serving: 66   Total Fat as % of Daily Value: 1%   Protein: 2 gm   Fat: 1 gm
Carbohydrates: 15 gm   Calcium: 33 mg   Iron: 1 mg   Sodium: 5 mg   Dietary Fiber: 7 gm

Creole Black-Eyed Peas

Serves 5

1 pound dried black-eyed peas (about 2¹/₂ cups)
¹/₂ teaspoon liquid smoke
¹/₂ cup chopped green bell pepper
¹/₂ cup chopped onion
¹/₂ cup chopped green onion
¹/₂ cup chopped celery
¹/₄ teaspoon garlic powder
1 teaspoon black pepper
1 teaspoon hot sauce
2 quarts water

Wash peas and soak overnight covered in cold water. Drain peas and discard water. Place all ingredients in a large pot and add 2 quarts water. Cook at least 2 hours or until peas are tender. If peas are not yet tender, but appear dry, add water, ¹/₂ cup at a time.

Total Calories Per Serving: 231   Total Fat as % of Daily Value: 2%   Protein: 15 gm   Fat: 1 gm
Carbohydrates: 42 gm   Calcium: 56 mg   Iron: 5 mg   Sodium: 43 mg   Dietary Fiber: 13 gm

Savory Barley and Eggplant

Serves 6

¹/₂ cup chopped onions
¹/₂ cup chopped mushrooms
¹/₄ cup chopped green bell peppers
1 Tablespoon minced garlic
1 Tablespoon water
1 cup peeled, cubed eggplant
2 Tablespoons water
2 cups canned chopped tomatoes (not drained)
1¹/₂ cups water
³/₄ cup quick-cooking or pearled barley
¹/₂ cup prepared chili sauce
¹/₄ cup chopped fresh parsley
1 teaspoon maple syrup
1 teaspoon nutritional yeast
¹/₂ teaspoon dried marjoram
1 teaspoon black pepper

Heat a large non-stick frying pan over medium heat. Add onions, mushrooms, peppers, and garlic and 1 Tablespoon of water and cook until vegetables soften, about 4 minutes. Add eggplant and 2 Tablespoons of water; cook and stir until softened, about 5 minutes. Add the tomatoes, 1¹/₂ cups water, barley, chili sauce, parsley, syrup, yeast, marjoram, and black pepper. Bring to a boil and simmer, covered, for 20 minutes or until barley is tender. Serve warm.

Total Calories Per Serving: 116   Total Fat as % of Daily Value: 1%   Protein: 5 gm   Fat: 1 gm
Carbohydrates: 24 gm   Calcium: 29 mg   Iron: 2 mg   Sodium: 14 mg   Dietary Fiber: 6 gm

Green Beans with Cranberry Sauce

Serves 12

1 pound cranberries, fresh or frozen, thawed (about 2¹/₂ cups)
1 cup peeled, seeded, chopped fresh orange
2 cups sugar
5 cups finely chopped canned or frozen, cooked and drained green beans
¹/₂ cup chopped walnuts (optional)

Combine cranberries and orange in canister of food processor or blender. Process until chunky, not puréed. Put mixture into a glass or plastic bowl; add sugar and stir well. Cover and refrigerate for 1 hour. Stir in green beans and walnuts. Return to refrigerator and allow dish to chill for 30 minutes. Can be served cold, or warmed slightly in a microwave.

Total Calories Per Serving (not nuts): 168   Total Fat as % of Daily Value: 0%   Protein: 1 gm   Fat: 0 gm
Carbohydrates: 43 gm   Calcium: 26 mg   Iron: 1 mg   Sodium: 4 mg   Dietary Fiber: 4 gm

Red Hot Potato Salad

Serves 10

5 pounds peeled and diced red skin potatoes (about 10¹/₂ cups)
2 cups diced red onion
1 cup diced sweet onions
2 Tablespoons vegetable oil
2 cloves garlic, minced
1 cup soymilk
¹/₃ cup fresh chopped parsley
¹/₂ teaspoon black pepper
¹/₄ cup vegan bacon bits (optional)

Place the diced potatoes in a large pot, cover them with water, and bring to a boil. Reduce heat to low and simmer for 20 minutes or until potatoes are tender. While potatoes are cooking, sauté the red onions and sweet onions in oil for 5 minutes or until lightly browned and very soft. Add the garlic to onions and cook an additional minute. Remove the pan from the heat and set aside. When the potatoes are tender, drain and return the cooked potatoes to the pot. Add the sautéed vegetables, soymilk, parsley, pepper, and vegan bacon bits to the potatoes. Using a potato masher, roughly mash all of the ingredients together, making the mixture as smooth or chunky as desired. Serve warm or cold.

Total Calories Per Serving: 261   Total Fat as % of Daily Value: 6%   Protein: 7 gm   Fat: 4 gm
Carbohydrates: 51 gm   Calcium: 44 mg   Iron: 2 mg   Sodium: 34 mg   Dietary Fiber: 5 gm

Scalloped Potatoes and Onions

Serves 10

1 Tablespoon olive oil
8 cups unpeeled, thinly sliced red skin potatoes
1 cup finely chopped red onion
¹/₄ cup nutritional yeast
2 teaspoons ground black pepper
2¹/₂ cups soy or rice milk
1 Tablespoon paprika
1 teaspoon mustard powder

Preheat oven to 375 degrees. Using a small amount of the oil, oil the bottom and sides of a 2-quart baking dish, and set aside.

   Layer approximately 2 cups of the sliced potatoes in the bottom of the prepared dish. Sprinkle ¹/₄ cup of the chopped onion, 1 Tablespoon of the nutritional yeast, and lightly season with a little pepper. Repeat the layering procedure with the remaining potatoes, onions, and nutritional yeast flakes. Drizzle the remaining oil over the top of the potatoes and then pour the milk over the top of the potatoes, allowing the milk to sink into the potatoes. Sprinkle top of potatoes with paprika and mustard. Cover and bake for 30 minutes or until potatoes are tender. Uncover and bake for 3-5 minutes to allow top to brown. Serve hot.

Total Calories Per Serving: 142   Total Fat as % of Daily Value: 2%   Protein: 7 gm   Fat: 2 gm
Carbohydrates: 26 gm   Calcium: 45 mg   Iron: 2 mg   Sodium: 43 mg   Dietary Fiber: 4 gm

Roasted Garlic Mashed Potatoes

Serves 8

12 unpeeled garlic cloves
4 pounds peeled, cubed boiling potatoes (such as Yukon golds or red rose)
1 cup soymilk or vegetable broth
2 teaspoons white pepper

Preheat oven to 450 degrees. Place the unpeeled garlic cloves in a pie pan and roast for 20 minutes or until cloves are soft enough to mash. Remove from oven and set aside to cool.

   While garlic is roasting, place cubed potatoes in a large pot and cover with water. Cover with lid and cook for 20 minutes or until tender. Drain the potatoes, saving the cooking liquid for use in the mashed potatoes. Place the drained potatoes in a large bowl and set aside for 5 minutes to dry. Squeeze garlic cloves from their skins (you can use your hands) and place in a small bowl. Mash garlic with a fork to form a paste. Add the mashed garlic, soymilk, and pepper to the potatoes and mash until smooth. If mixture is dry, add a small amount of reserved cooking liquid. Serve immediately or place in an oven-safe casserole and reheat at 350 degrees for 15 minutes when ready to serve.

Total Calories Per Serving: 183   Total Fat as % of Daily Value: 1%   Protein: 6 gm   Fat: 1 gm
Carbohydrates: 39 gm   Calcium: 42 mg   Iron: 2 mg   Sodium: 31 mg   Dietary Fiber: 6 gm

Oven-Roasted Mixed Potatoes

Serves 6

Vegetable oil spray
6 cups unpeeled, chunked sweet potatoes
2 cups unpeeled, chunked white potatoes
1 cup peeled, chunked onions
2 Tablespoons olive oil
2 teaspoons each dried rosemary and black pepper

Preheat oven to 375 degrees. Spray a 2-quart oven-proof casserole dish with oil. Add both types of potatoes and onions to casserole. Toss with olive oil. Cover and bake for 30 minutes, or until potatoes are tender. Uncover, mix with rosemary and pepper, and bake for an additional 5 minutes. Serve hot.

Total Calories Per Serving: 202   Total Fat as % of Daily Value: 7%   Protein: 3 gm   Fat: 5 gm
Carbohydrates: 37 gm   Calcium: 50 mg   Iron: 1 mg   Sodium: 77 mg   Dietary Fiber: 6 gm

Twice Baked Sweet Potatoes

Serves 6

6 large unpeeled sweet potatoes (about 4 pounds)
3 Tablespoons maple syrup
2 Tablespoons orange juice
2 teaspoons minced fresh ginger
1 teaspoon cinnamon
1 teaspoon orange zest

Preheat oven to 425 degrees. Using a fork, pierce the skins of the sweet potatoes in several places. Place sweet potatoes on a baking sheet and bake for 45 minutes or until soft enough to mash. Remove from oven and allow potatoes to cool enough to handle. Cut each potato in half lengthwise. Using a spoon, carefully scoop out the cooked flesh into a large bowl, leaving the skin intact to use as a shell. Set skins aside. Add maple syrup, orange juice, ginger, cinnamon, and zest to the bowl. Mash to form a paste. Place potato shells on a baking sheet. Fill each shell with potato mixture. Bake dish for 10 minutes or until mixture is thoroughly heated.

Total Calories Per Serving: 290   Total Fat as % of Daily Value: 0%   Protein: 5 gm   Fat: 0 gm
Carbohydrates: 69 gm   Calcium: 103 mg   Iron: 2 mg   Sodium: 167 mg   Dietary Fiber: 9 gm

Baked Sweet Potato Fries
Serves 6

Vegetable oil spray
2 pounds peeled sweet potatoes (about 4¹/₂ cups)
2 Tablespoon vegetable oil
2 teaspoons black pepper

Preheat oven to 375 degrees. Lightly spray oil on two non-stick baking sheets and set aside. Cut the peeled sweet potatoes into "French fries" or pieces ¹/₂-inch wide and 3-4 inches long. Transfer the cut sweet potato fries to the prepared baking sheets, dividing them evenly between the two sheets, and spread them to a single layer. Sprinkle potatoes with oil and pepper. Bake for 20 minutes. Stir at least once. Continue to bake until potatoes are tender on the inside and crispy on the outside. Place on a serving platter and serve hot.

Total Calories Per Serving: 179   Total Fat as % of Daily Value: 8%   Protein: 3 gm   Fat: 5 gm
Carbohydrates: 32 gm   Calcium: 61 mg   Iron: 1 mg   Sodium: 55 mg   Dietary Fiber: 5 gm

Brussels Sprouts Braised with Almonds
Serves 6

1 cup sliced almonds
2 Tablespoons vegetable oil
2 pounds washed and trimmed Brussels sprouts (about 4¹/₂ cups)
2 teaspoons minced fresh ginger
3 Tablespoons sugar
1 teaspoon soy sauce
¹/₄-¹/₂ cup water

Preheat a dry wok or large non-stick skillet and add almonds. Cook over high heat, stirring, to toast almonds. Remove almonds and set aside. In the same wok, heat oil and add ginger; cook for 30 seconds. Add the Brussels sprouts, toss well to coat, and stir-fry for 2 minutes. Add the sugar and soy sauce, stir well, and stir-fry an additional 2 minutes. Add a little of the water to the pan and stir-fry 1-2 minutes until the liquid cooks off. Repeat the procedure 1-2 more times or until the Brussels sprouts are tender. Add toasted almonds and stir well to combine. Place in a serving bowl and serve hot.

Total Calories Per Serving: 220   Total Fat as % of Daily Value: 20%   Protein: 8 gm   Fat: 13 gm
Carbohydrates: 23 gm   Calcium: 101 mg   Iron: 3 mg   Sodium: 95 mg   Dietary Fiber: 8 gm

Middle Eastern Vegetable and Garbanzo Stew
Serves 8

1 cup chopped onion
1 pound eggplant, peeled and cut into small cubes (about 2¹/₂ cups)
1 teaspoon black pepper
¹/₂ teaspoon cumin
2 cups diced fresh zucchini
1 cup tomato sauce
2 garlic cloves, minced
¹/₂ cup water
2 cups cooked or canned, drained garbanzos
¹/₃ cup chopped (flat-leaf) Italian parsley

Heat a large non-stick skillet over medium heat. Add onion and sauté for 5 minutes or until the onion starts to turn golden brown. If dry, add up to 2 Tablespoons of water. Add eggplant, pepper, and cumin. Reduce heat to simmer, cover and cook 5 minutes, stirring occasionally. Add zucchini, cover and cook an additional 3 minutes. Add tomato sauce, garlic, water, and garbanzos. Cover and simmer for 15 minutes or until eggplant is tender. When eggplant is tender, stir in parsley, cook for 1 additional minute and remove from heat. Serve warm.

Total Calories Per Serving: 187   Total Fat as % of Daily Value: 4%   Protein: 10 gm   Fat: 3 gm
Carbohydrates: 32 gm   Calcium: 50 mg   Iron: 3 mg   Sodium: 281 mg   Dietary Fiber: 8 gm

Mixed Greens with Red Peppers
Serves 10

2 cups diced onions
2 Tablespoons olive oil
3 cups seeded, chopped red bell peppers
2 Tablespoons minced garlic
2 cups vegetable broth
2 pounds washed, chopped collards or mustard greens
2 pounds washed, chopped spinach or kale
¹/₄ teaspoon each ground black pepper and crushed red pepper flakes
1 teaspoon hot sauce

In a large skillet, cook the onion in olive oil for 3-5 minutes or until soft. Add red peppers and garlic, and cook an additional minute. Add vegetable broth and bring to a fast boil. In batches, add the collard or mustard greens to the pan, covering the pan to help them wilt. When all of the collardor mustard greens have been added to the pan, cover, reduce the heat to medium, and cook for 2 minutes. Add the spinach or kale to the pan in batches, using the same procedure as with the collard greens, and cook for 3 minutes. Cover and cook an additional 3 minutes or until the greens are tender. Quickly stir in the black pepper, red pepper flakes, and hot sauce. This is a fast procedure; be certain not to overcook. Serve immediately.

Total Calories Per Serving: 83   Total Fat as % of Daily Value: 3%   Protein: 5 gm   Fat: 5 gm
Carbohydrates: 11 gm   Calcium: 167 mg   Iron: 3 mg   Sodium: 101 mg   Dietary Fiber: 5 gm

Basil Carrots with Maple

Serves 5

4 cups sliced carrots
¹/₃ cup olive oil
¹/₄ cup maple syrup
2 Tablespoons chopped fresh basil

In a large pot, steam carrots for 5 minutes or until tender-crisp. Remove form heat and set aside. In a large skillet, heat the oil, maple syrup, and basil until just hot. Add the carrots and toss until well coated. Serve warm.

Total Calories Per Serving: 216   Total Fat as % of Daily Value: 23%   Protein: 1 gm   Fat: 15 gm
Carbohydrates: 22 gm   Calcium: 83 mg   Iron: 1 mg   Sodium: 73 mg   Dietary Fiber: 4 gm

Sweet and Tangy Carrot Coins

Serves 6

1 cup sugar
²/₃ cup cider vinegar
¹/₄ cup vegetable oil
1 teaspoon mustard powder
¹/₄ teaspoon ground ginger
2 pounds peeled, thinly sliced carrots (about 4¹/₂ cups)
1 cup water
3 Tablespoon chopped fresh parsley

In a medium-size pot, combine sugar, vinegar, oil, dry mustard, and ginger, and bring to a fast boil. Reduce heat and continue to cook mixture for 5 minutes or until slightly thickened. Remove from heat and pour mixture into a glass bowl or large measuring cup; set aside. In the same saucepan, place the carrots and water, and bring to a boil. Cover, reduce heat to low, and simmer for 5-7 minutes or until the carrots are tender. Drain carrots and transfer the cooked carrots to a glass bowl. Pour the reserved mixture over the carrots, add the chopped parsley, and toss gently to combine. Serve hot, warm, or allow dish to cool.

Total Calories Per Serving: 282   Total Fat as % of Daily Value: 15%   Protein: 2 gm   Fat: 10 gm
Carbohydrates: 48 gm   Calcium: 58 mg   Iron: 1 mg   Sodium: 107 mg   Dietary Fiber: 4 gm

Roasted Beets with Garlic

Serves 8

Vegetable oil spray
2¹/₂ pounds beets, peeled, and cut into wedges (about 6 cups)
¹/₄ cup olive oil
2 teaspoons dried thyme
1 teaspoon black pepper
3 cloves garlic, minced

Preheat oven to 400 degrees. Lightly spray a 9 x 13-inch casserole dish. Place the beets in the bottom of the casserole dish and drizzle the olive oil over them. Sprinkle chopped thyme and pepper over the top and lightly toss the beets to evenly coat with oil and seasonings. Bake for 20 minutes, stir, then bake an additional 20 minutes. Add garlic to the pan, toss, and bake an additional 20-30 minutes or until the beets are tender and the garlic is soft. Remove from oven, toss, and serve hot.

Total Calories Per Serving: 112   Total Fat as % of Daily Value: 11%   Protein: 2 gm   Fat: 7 gm
Carbohydrates: 12 gm   Calcium: 28 mg   Iron: 1 mg   Sodium: 89 mg   Dietary Fiber: 3 gm

Corn and Quinoa Casserole

Serves 10

6 cups water
3 cups well-rinsed quinoa
¹/₂ cup pumpkin seeds
1 cup deseeded, diced red bell pepper
1 cup deseeded, diced yellow bell pepper
¹/₄ cup olive oil
2 cups cut corn
2 cloves garlic, minced
1 cup chopped green onions
¹/₂ cup minced black olives
¹/₄ cup chopped fresh parsley
¹/₄ cup lemon juice

In a saucepan, bring water to a boil. Add quinoa, cover, reduce heat and simmer for 10-15 minutes or until tender. Drain off excess water, transfer to a bowl, and fluff with a fork. While quinoa is cooking, heat a non-stick skillet and cook pumpkin seeds over medium heat for 3 minutes or until toasted. Transfer toasted pumpkin seeds to a bowl and set aside. In the same skillet, sauté the peppers in 1 Tablespoon olive oil for 2 minutes or until soft. Add corn and garlic, and cook for an additional 2 minutes. Add green onions and cook for 1 minute. Add cooked vegetables, pumpkin seeds, remaining oil, olives, parsley, and lemon juice to quinoa, and toss well to combine. Serve warm.

Total Calories Per Serving: 327   Total Fat as % of Daily Value: 20%   Protein: 10 gm   Fat: 13 gm
Carbohydrates: 47 gm   Calcium: 50 mg   Iron: 6 mg   Sodium: 79 mg   Dietary Fiber: 5 gm

Corn and Quinoa Casserole
Page 240

Savory Kebobs
Page 247

Green Beans Amandine

Serves 8

2 pounds fresh green beans, ends trimmed and strings removed
2 teaspoons white pepper
2 Tablespoons olive oil
2 Tablespoons lemon juice
1 cup sliced, toasted almonds
1½ Tablespoons chopped fresh parsley
2 teaspoons chopped fresh thyme

Place the green beans in a large steamer basket and steam for 3-5 minutes or until tender. Transfer the steamed green beans to a large bowl. Season the green beans with pepper, toss gently, and set aside. In a non-stick skillet combine lemon juice and almonds and cook over medium-high heat for 3-5 minutes or until the almonds are golden brown. Remove the skillet from the heat and stir in parsley and thyme and stir well to combine. Pour the hot almond mixture over the green beans and toss well to thoroughly coat. Serve warm.

Total Calories Per Serving: 117	Total Fat as % of Daily Value: 15%		Protein: 3 gm	Fat: 9 gm
Carbohydrates: 7 gm	Calcium: 61 mg	Iron: 2 mg	Sodium: 424 mg	Dietary Fiber: 3 gm

Apple Stuffed Acorn Squash

Serves 5

2 acorn squash
2 diced, peeled green apples
¼ cup brown sugar
1 teaspoon vegan margarine
½ teaspoon nutmeg

Preheat oven to 350 degrees. Slice squash in half; scrape and discard seeds. Place cut side down in a casserole dish and fill with 1 inch of water. Bake for 20 minutes or until just tender. While the squash is steaming in the oven, mix apples with brown sugar. Remove squash from oven, place face up, and fill the cavities with the apple mixture. Top each squash with a small amount of margarine and sprinkle with nutmeg. Cover with foil, and bake until the apples and the squash are very soft, about 20 minutes.

Total Calories Per Serving: 150	Total Fat as % of Daily Value: 2%		Protein: 2 gm	Fat: 1 gm
Carbohydrates: 37 gm	Calcium: 69 mg	Iron: 1 mg	Sodium: 17 mg	Dietary Fiber: 5 gm

Romanian Stuffed Cabbage

Makes 20-25 stuffed cabbage (depending on the number of leaves in each head of cabbage)

To eliminate the need to blanch the cabbage to separate the leaves, you can freeze the whole head of cabbage. When the cabbage is removed from the freezer, the leaves separate easily and are wilted enough to roll without cracking.

2 large heads of cabbage frozen, then defrosted
1 cup sliced onion

Filling mixture:
2 pounds vegan "ground round" or chopped Tofurky™ (about 4½ cups)
4 Tablespoons silken tofu
¼ cup brown sugar
3 Tablespoons lemon juice
½ cup cooked white rice (start with ¼ cup uncooked rice)

Sauce:
4 cups prepared tomato sauce
1 cup water
¼ cup raisins
½ cup dark brown sugar
3 Tablespoons of lemon juice

Topping:
½ cup reserved torn cabbage leaves (see recipe)
4 vegan ginger snap cookies or 1 Tablespoon crystallized ginger

Preheat oven to 350 degrees.

Peel leaves from the defrosted cabbage heads, careful not to tear them. Cut up smaller leaves and any torn leaves, place in bottom of deep baking pan (about 5-quart pan) with sliced onion, reserving about ½ cup torn cabbage leaves. Mix all the ingredients of the filling mixture together until well combined.

Put a small amount of filling mixture on the end of a cabbage leaf. Fold sides of leaves in and roll. Place finished rolls over cut-up cabbage and onion in pan.

Combine all sauce ingredients in a small saucepan and cook, stirring over medium heat for 3 minutes. Pour sauce over rolls. Top sauce with reserved cabbage leaves, spread in a thin layer and ginger snaps. Bake in oven, covered, for 2 hours. Check often, and baste with sauce. If cabbage leaves are not tender, continue to bake until they are. Remove from oven, remove torn cabbage leaves and ginger from top, and serve hot.

Total Calories Per Serving: 156   Total Fat as % of Daily Value: 2%   Protein: 13 gm   Fat: 1 gm
Carbohydrates: 26 gm   Calcium: 126 mg   Iron: 2 mg   Sodium: 570 mg   Dietary Fiber: 6 gm

Spanish-Influenced Stuffed Cabbage
Makes 10-12 rolls

A slight variation on traditional stuffed cabbage, with a little more "heat."

1 head cabbage

Filling:
1½ pounds vegan "ground round," chopped Tofurky™, or finely diced extra-firm tofu
½ cup dried bread crumbs
2 Tablespoons chopped onions
2 Tablespoons silken tofu
2 teaspoons black pepper

Sauce:
2 cups prepared tomato sauce
½ cup chopped canned tomatoes, not drained
2 Tablespoons lemon juice
2 Tablespoons sugar
2 teaspoons red pepper flakes
½ teaspoon ground cumin
½ cup sliced pimento-stuffed green olives

Preheat oven to 350 degrees. Clean cabbage and steam for 5 minutes or more until tender. Drain and set aside. In a large bowl, combine vegan ground round, bread crumbs, onion, tofu, and pepper; mix well. Place a small amount of filling mixture on each leaf. Fold ends of leaves in and roll. Place in a 2½ or 3 quart shallow baking dish. In a small pot, combine sauce ingredients and cook, stirring, for 3 minutes. Pour over rolls. Bake covered for 1 hour or until leaves are tender.

Variation: Kale or Swiss chard leaves would work well with this recipe.

Total Calories Per Serving: 173   Total Fat as % of Daily Value: 2%   Protein: 18 gm   Fat: 2 gm
Carbohydrates: 24 gm   Calcium: 191 mg   Iron: 4 mg   Sodium: 758 mg   Dietary Fiber: 7 gm

Almost Stuffed Cabbage

Serves 6

No time to roll? This recipe gives you the flavor of Polish stuffed cabbage without the extra rolling time. Prepare and mix the ingredients ahead of time, and allow it to slow-cook during the day.

2 cups shredded green cabbage
1 cup uncooked white rice
1/2 cup water
1/2 cup chopped onion
1/4 cup chopped bell pepper
2 cups chopped canned tomatoes, drained
1 pound (or 2 cups) chopped Tofurky™, seitan, or extra-firm tofu
1 cup tomato juice
1 teaspoon black pepper
1 teaspoon garlic powder
1/4 cup raisins

Combine all ingredients in a crockpot or slow cooker. Set on low. Allow to cook for 3-4 hours or until rice is cooked and cabbage is tender. Cooking time will vary depending on your equipment.

Total Calories Per Serving: 113   Total Fat as % of Daily Value: 1%   Protein: 3 gm   Fat: <1 gm
Carbohydrates: 26 gm   Calcium: 33 mg   Iron: 2 mg   Sodium: 39 mg   Dietary Fiber: 3 gm

Torta de Arroz (Three-Layer Rice Timbale)

Serves 10

1 garlic clove, minced
1/2 cup mined onion
4 Tablespoons minced chilies
2 Tablespoons oil
1 quart canned, diced tomatoes
1 1/2 cups white kernel corn (if canned, drained; if frozen, thawed)
5 cups cooked brown or white rice (start with 2 1/2 cups uncooked rice)
2 cups vegan sour cream
1/4 cup puréed silken tofu
1 1/2 cups mashed soft tofu
2 Tablespoons nutritional yeast

Preheat oven to 350 degrees. In a large saucepan, cook and stir garlic, onion, and chiles in hot oil until tender. Stir in tomatoes, corn, and rice. Simmer 5 minutes.

Place half of this mixture in a 2-quart oven-proof casserole dish. Combine sour cream and puréed silken tofu and spread half of this mixture over rice. Top with half of the mashed soft tofu. Sprinkle with nutritional yeast. Repeat the layers. Cover and bake for 30 minutes or until mixture is bubbling.

Total Calories Per Serving: 341   Total Fat as % of Daily Value: 22%   Protein: 10 gm   Fat: 14 gm
Carbohydrates: 46 gm   Calcium: 75 mg   Iron: 1 mg   Sodium: 272 mg   Dietary Fiber: 4 gm

Potato-Bread Stuffing

Serves 8

4 cups cubed bread
2 cups vegetable broth
2 cups mashed white or sweet potatoes
1 teaspoon poultry seasoning
2 Tablespoons chopped fresh parsley
1 Tablespoon chopped fresh thyme
¼ cup chopped onion
2 teaspoons black pepper

Preheat oven to 375 degrees. Soak bread in vegetable broth until just soft. Squeeze dry. In a large mixing bowl, mix all ingredients until well combined. Bake in a casserole dish or in individual muffin tins for 15 minutes or until browned on top.

Note: Can be frozen for later use, or can be used to stuff peppers, tomatoes, eggplant, or summer squash. Use instead of pasta or rice at meals.

Total Calories Per Serving: 115   Total Fat as % of Daily Value: 2%   Protein: 3 gm   Fat: 2 gm
Carbohydrates: 22 gm   Calcium: 61 mg   Iron: 2 mg   Sodium: 291 mg   Dietary Fiber: 1 gm

Wild Rice Stuffing

Serves 8

6 cups stale, cubed crusty bread
1 cup apple cider
3 cups cooked wild rice (start with 2 cups uncooked wild rice)
1 can sliced, canned, drained water chestnuts
½ cup dried cranberries
¼ cup dried, chopped apricots
¼ cup dried, chopped prunes
1 cup apple cider
1 teaspoon dried sage

Preheat oven to 350 degrees. In a large bowl, mix 1 cup cider with bread, let sit and soften for 5 minutes until bread is soft. Add all remaining ingredients and mix well to combine. Ladle into a 2-quart oven-proof casserole dish, cover, and bake for 30-40 minutes or until ingredients are tender and heated through.

Total Calories Per Serving: 572   Total Fat as % of Daily Value: 2%   Protein: 6 gm   Fat: 1 gm
Carbohydrates: 136 gm   Calcium: 505 mg   Iron: 2 mg   Sodium: 327 mg   Dietary Fiber: 3 gm

Chapter 13: FAST ENTRÉES

Introduction

You can offer one main hot or cold entrée with several side dishes or several entrées with fewer side dishes for your party menu, depending on time, space, occasion, and guest preference. It may be tricky to have only one entrée unless you are very familiar with your guests' taste in food. If you choose to offer one entrée, be sure to offer a variety of side dishes, so everyone can build a satisfying meal.

A chef's trick for meal preparation is to make a basic menu item that can be transformed into many different dishes. The initial preparation uses the most ingredients and most fuel for cooking. Subsequent cooking uses fewer ingredients and takes less time. You can see this if you look closely at most restaurant menus. At first glance, it seems that the restaurant is offering many different choices. On closer inspection, you'll see that many, many choices can be prepared from a minimum of ingredients. (Don't tell anyone I let you in on this secret!)

You can do the same thing at home. Try to buy or prepare ingredients or foods that can be used for many different purposes. For example, corn flakes are eaten, as is, at breakfast. They can be a coating for firm tofu or seitan, smashed into crumbs and used to thicken sauces or soups, added to muffin batter or cookie dough, and used as a dessert topping for frozen desserts, pudding, and fruit salad.

Plan your party meal by selecting the entrées first. Add side dishes, salads, breads, and beverages to fit the entrées. Many of the recipes included in this chapter can be prepared and frozen until needed.

The Layered Look

Lasagna is the entrée most closely identified as a classic Italian dish. At its most basic, lasagna is flat sheets of pasta alternated with layers of crumbled protein, sauce, and cheese. Lasagna is all about sharing. When you are preparing lasagna, think about families gathered at long tables under vine-covered canopies, sharing large bowls of steaming pasta and glasses of wine.

But before Italy, there was the ancient Greek enjoyment of lasagna. The Italian "lasagna" comes from the Greek "lasana," which means "chamberpot." This refers to the original shape of pottery-baked lasagna. The Romans upgraded the shape and the word into "lasanum," which means "cooking pot." As you can see, modern lasagna's shape has evolved beyond a pot with a rounded edge. Additionally, lasagna has evolved into an entrée embraced by many cultures. Lasagna ranges from Mexican-style to vegetarian to Asian. You name it, and it can be layered and sauced into lasagna.

Meat is not important for the success of lasagna. Traditional meatless lasagna has its origins in Calabria. Tomatoes are combined with minced garlic, chopped onion, olive oil, fresh basil, ricotta, mozzarella, and the whole dish is topped with chopped fresh parsley. You can add some heat with red pepper flakes and use vegan mozzarella cheese and crumbled soft tofu instead of ricotta.

Marinated, grilled, chopped portobellos can make up the "meat" layer, flavored with fresh fennel or fennel seed, basil, and oregano to create an elegant option to the usual meat and cheese lasagna. Spinach and arugula offer a mild-yet-snappy "meat" layer, as does zucchini combined with minced mushrooms and shallots (called a "duxelle" in classical terms), oregano, thyme, basil, shredded vegan mozzarella, and red wine. Swiss chard and roasted bell pepper lasagna is colorful on the plate and flavorful with olive oil, minced onions and garlic, shredded fresh basil, chopped tomatoes, and white pepper.

Use artichoke bottoms tossed with flour, soymilk, olive oil, fresh basil, vegan mozzarella, diced black olives, and garlic as the "meat" layer. Alternate the artichoke mixture with a thick cream sauce (made with puréed silken tofu) and top with grated vegan cheese. If you'd like a hint of heat, finely dice some peperocini (pickled Italian peppers) and add these to the sauce.

Pasta is not essential for excellent, nontraditional lasagna. Pasta ribbons can be replaced with thin slices of white or sweet potato, eggplant, summer squash, or zucchini. Try "seafood" lasagna, layering smoked tofu in a cream sauce with very thin slices of baguette, tomato, and vegan cheeses. If pasta ribbons are used, they can be flavored with spinach, carrots, tomatoes, basil, or cracked pepper.

Traditional sauces for lasagna include marinara, Bolognese, and cream. Marinara is a tomato and vegetable sauce, with no meat. Bolognese is also a tomato-based sauce, and it always contains meat. Most traditional sauce cooks would tell you that bolognese should have at least two kinds of meat. You can prepare a vegan bolognese by combining chopped vegan ground round or smoked tofu with chopped veggie sausage.

Traditional cheeses for lasagna are ricotta and parmigiana, a mixture of soft, creamy and mild, with tangy and al dente texture. You can use crumbled firm tofu for ricotta, nutritional yeast for the parmigiana, and shredded vegan mozzarella for texture.

Whether traditional, fusion, or new wave, lasagna is a crowd pleaser. It's also a make-ahead entrée that holds up well in the refrigerator or freezer. Once heated, lasagna makes a good banquet entrée, as it will stand up to the heat from chafing dishes or steam tables for longer amounts of time then nonlayered pastas.

Continental Lasagna

Let your imagination run wild when preparing your lasagna menu. Here are just a few ideas for replacing traditional meat, cheese, and pasta:

- Zorba the Lasagna: crumbled firm tofu, sliced black olives, and sliced red onions

- Lasagna Provencale: crumbled firm tofu, summer squash, herbes de provence seasoning, and bechamel or cream sauce

- Lasagna the Green: spinach noodles, vegan pesto sauce, bechamel sauce, and minced mild chilies

- Lasagna Southwest: chili beans, chili powder, cumin, any white vegan cheese, and tortilla strips (to replace pasta)

- Fiord Lasagna: finely minced smoked tofu or ground smoked seitan, sliced potatoes, and bechamel sauce

- Lasagna Jamaica: shredded seitan or tempeh tossed with jerk spice, spinach, and fiery hot tomato sauce

- Lasagna Mexico: wheat, carrot and spinach pasta layered with shredded vegan mozzarella cheese and a tomatillo sauce

- Lasagna Alfredo: creamy sauce, sliced crimini mushrooms, and vegan cheese

- Lasagna Primavera: Lasagna Alfredo with the addition of chopped fresh vegetables, such as carrots, sweet onions, and bell peppers

Kebobs

Kebobs, brochettes, or skewered food date way back in culinary history. Kebobs are a fast and convenient way to cook protein, vegetables, and fruit. Kebobs are the original "meal on a stick."

You can cook kebobs on a barbecue, stove-top or electric grill, a large skillet, or, if you are careful, in a broiler. If you want to both "kebob" fast and slow cook foods for one meal, place the fast-cookers on skewers separate from the slow-cookers. For example, cherry tomatoes, pineapples, fresh peaches or apricots, pearl onions or small onion chunks, extra-firm tofu, and button mushrooms all cook quickly, and can be placed on one skewer. Carrots, potatoes, apples, and winter squash cook slowly and should be placed together on another skewer.

If you are using wood or bamboo skewers, soak them in water for about 20 minutes prior to grilling, so they don't start to shred or catch on fire. You can purchase reusable metal skewers. If your fresh rosemary is growing long branches, you can cut and strip rosemary wood to use as a skewer, remembering to select ingredients that benefit from a rosemary flavor, such as mushrooms, tempeh, seitan, tofu, or potatoes. Spray skewers lightly with vegetable oil to prevent food from sticking to the skewers. If food seems to slip off skewers, double up and use two skewers together.

Basic savory kebob ingredients can include onions, tomatoes, white or golden potatoes, summer squash, bell peppers, carrots, elephant garlic, extra-firm tofu, seitan, and tempeh. Sweet kebobs can include fresh apples, pears, peaches, apricots, bananas, pineapple, and extra-firm tofu. Using different marinades, you can create many different flavored kebobs. Kebobs can be marinated ahead of time and stored in food bags or in plastic or glass containers. Avoid wood or metal containers, as they can interact with marinade ingredients.

Here are some kebob marinade ideas:
- Central American: Combine pineapple juice and a small amount of vegetable oil with ground smoked chili powder, oregano, cilantro, mango or tamarind, onion, and bell pepper.
- Middle Eastern: Use a small amount of olive oil combined with lemon juice, pomegranate juice, mint, garlic, sesame seeds, chopped dates, or a small amount of tahini paste.
- Mediterranean: Use a small amount of olive oil with vinegar and lemon juice, basil, oregano, garlic, dill, chopped olives, fresh fennel, and chopped parsley.
- Asian: Use a small amount of peanut or sesame oil combined with lime juice, soy sauce or miso, chili paste or wasabi, and minced fresh ginger and green onions. Instead of the oil, you can use coconut milk.
- Indian: Combine unflavored soy yogurt (or silken tofu mixed with lemon juice), chopped fresh mango, cilantro, cardamom, ginger, black pepper, and clove and mustard powder.

Round and Round They Go

"Neatballs" are the vegan answer to meatballs, and they make perfect party food. You can use "neatballs" to fill a pita or top a pizza. Just turn to some simple ingredients and you'll be dishing up pasta and topping the pizza in no time.

Neatballs require common ingredients and take very little kitchen expertise. Since they take some time to make (as opposed to a sandwich or a smoothie), we recommend that you make double batches of your neatballs and freeze one batch. If cooking from scratch is not an option, there are several speed-scratch alternatives. Thaw some "burger" (as in soy burger) crumbles, mix them well with chopped onions, bell pepper, garlic, and mashed firm tofu to make excellent neatballs that could be baked or fried. Falafel mix makes up great neatballs; after following the directions on the package, add cooked corn and chopped red peppers to make a Mediterranean neatball. Serve this with tabbouleh and couscous. Frozen veggie burgers can be thawed (in the refrigerator) and shaped into neatballs. Try topping a neatball sandwich with barbecue sauce, mushroom sauce, or salsa.

The key to neatballs is how you are going to get a wonderfully flavored mixture to stick together. Most moist ingredients, such as mashed potatoes, cooked brown rice or sticky (glutinous rice, found in Asian markets), or cooked cereal (such as cream of rice) and cooked whole wheat helped to hold together dry ingredients, such as cooked, chopped beans or chopped veggies. Dry ingredients, such as bread crumbs, whole-wheat flour, and ground nuts, help to hold together moist ingredients, such as tofu, cooked corn, and chopped mushrooms. Refrigerating uncooked neatballs helps to hold them together for cooking, as well.

If you find your neatball mixture needs thinning out, use liquid that will add flavor and/or color, such as tomato, carrot, celery, or vegetable cocktail juice, vegetable stock, mushroom broth, and puréed vegetables (such as carrots, celery, broccoli, and peas). If your mixture needs thickening, reach for seasoned bread crumbs, matzo meal (which can be seasoned with pepper and garlic and onion powder), ground nuts (such as walnuts or almonds), mashed potato mixes, and nut flours.

Neatballs can be as simple as rolled mashed potatoes, stiffened with bread crumbs or tofu thickened with wheat germ and matzo meal. You should try to add more interesting ingredients so your guests won't go to sleep in the mashed potatoes. For crunch, think chopped, toasted nuts (such as pecans or pine nuts), seeds (such as sesame or pumpkin), or soy bits (such as soy nuts or "bacon" bits). Flavor can be "hot" (think chili powder, Tabasco™, red pepper flakes, ginger, and chopped fresh or canned chilies), Asian (think soy sauce, tamari, miso, ginger, and lemon grass), Indian (think turmeric, curry powder mixes, garam masala, coriander, and fennel), Central American (think salsa, cilantro, chopped chilies, lemon or lime juice, and chopped tomatoes), Mediterranean (think sun-dried tomatoes, basil, oregano, balsamic vinegar, and parsley), or Southern French (think thyme, pepper, lavender, and sage).

Sauce for neatballs run the gamut. Take a can of your favorite soup (tomato or mushroom come to mind), add chopped veggies (such as tomatoes, carrots, and onions for tomato soup or celery and onions for the mushroom) and dilute with puréed tofu. This will make creamy gravy. Thicken vegetable or mushroom gravy with cornstarch for homestyle gravy. (You can sometimes cheat and use mashed potato mixes instead of cornstarch; it's faster and takes less concentration.) Tomato sauce is fine out of the can or "spiked" with chopped canned or fresh tomatoes, fresh or canned mushrooms, fresh or dried basil and oregano, and fresh or dried garlic. For a creamy tomato sauce, stir in some puréed tofu or soy yogurt (unflavored). Barbecue sauce is perfectly fine right out of the bottle or you can create your own with tomato purée, ketchup, mustard, and molasses.

Whether you serve your neatballs as an entrée, as sandwich stuffing, or stick toothpicks in them and offer them as an appetizer, the people around your table will enjoy neatballs.

RECIPES

Kebobs with Pineapple and Red Pepper
Serves 10

¹/₂ cup lite soy sauce
¹/₄ cup olive oil
¹/₂ cup dry white wine or ¹/₄ cup white vinegar combined with ¹/₄ cup cold water
¹/₂ cup minced onions
2 cloves garlic, minced
1 pound 1-inch chunks extra-firm tofu, seitan, or tempeh (about 3 cups)
2 cups 1-inch pieces red bell pepper
2 cups 1-inch chunks fresh pineapple

Combine soy sauce, oil, wine or vinegar and water, onions, and garlic in a large plastic or glass bowl. Add tofu, seitan, or tempeh and marinate in the refrigerator for 1 hour.

Remove tofu, seitan, or tempeh from marinade. Save marinade.

Preheat grill or broiler. On skewers, alternate tofu, seitan, or tempeh with red pepper and pineapple. Place kebobs in a shallow pan. Drizzle with marinade. If using a grill, place directly on grill. Grill or broil for 3-4 minutes, just until pepper begins to brown. Serve alone, on a bed of couscous or cooked bulgur wheat, or with a fresh spinach salad.

Potato Lasagna
Serves 8

Enjoy this change of pace from wheat noodles.

¼ cup oil
½ cup all-purpose flour
2 cups soymilk
2 cups vegetable or mushroom broth
¼ teaspoon nutmeg
3 cups vegan cheese (use different varieties if available)
1 teaspoon ground black pepper
Vegetable oil spray
5 large (about 2½ pounds) russet potatoes
1 cup thinly sliced red onion
¼ pound shredded vegan pepperoni
10 ounces frozen chopped spinach, thawed and drained
½ cup nutritional yeast

Preheat oven to 375 degrees. Combine oil and flour in pan and heat until bubbly. Remove from heat. Add soymilk, broth, and nutmeg. Return to heat and bring to a fast boil. Remove from heat and add grated cheeses slowly, stirring to combine. Continue to stir until smooth and add pepper.

Spray a 13 x 9-inch baking pan with oil. Peel potatoes, slice thinly, and place ¹/₃ of slices in the bottom of the pan. Cover with ¹/₂ the onion, ¹/₂ the vegan pepperoni, and ¹/₂ the spinach. Pour ¹/₃ of the cheese sauce over top. Repeat layers, ending with potatoes and cheese sauce. Bake, covered, for 30 minutes. Remove cover, sprinkle with nutritional yeast, and allow lasagna to bake for 30 more minutes. Remove from oven and allow lasagna to stand 10 minutes before serving.

Total Calories Per Serving: 440   Total Fat as % of Daily Value: 14%   Protein: 12 gm   Fat: 9 gm
Carbohydrates: 52 gm   Calcium: 457 mg   Iron: 5 mg   Sodium: 969 mg   Dietary Fiber: 7 gm

Chili Lasagna
Serves 6-8

Lasagna Goes Southwestern!

Vegetable oil spray
10 lasagna noodles
2 cups crumbled firm tofu
3 cups shredded vegan Cheddar cheese
3 green onions, diced
1 cup canned whole-kernel corn, drained
2 Tablespoons puréed silken tofu

¹/₂ **teaspoon salt**
¹/₂ **teaspoon black pepper**
3 cups prepared chili beans

Preheat oven to 350 degrees. Coat a 13 x 9-inch baking pan with oil spray.

Cook and drain lasagna noodles. Combine crumbled tofu, 2 cups vegan Cheddar cheese, half the green onions, corn, puréed tofu, and pepper; mix well.

Spread ³/₄ cup chili over the bottom of the baking dish. Place 3 lasagna noodles over the chili. Place half of the tofu mixture evenly over the noodles then top with half of the remaining chili. Place 3 noodles over the chili then top with the remaining tofu mixture. Place the 3 remaining noodles over the cheese mixture then top with the remaining chili. Cover tightly with aluminum foil and bake for 30 minutes. Remove foil and sprinkle lasagna with the remaining 1 cup Cheddar cheese. Bake 10 more minutes. Remove from oven, sprinkle with remaining scallions, and let sit for 5 minutes before serving.

Total Calories Per Serving: 565   Total Fat as % of Daily Value: 17%   Protein: 27 gm   Fat: 11 gm
Carbohydrates: 92 gm   Calcium: 298 mg   Iron: 6 mg   Sodium: 963 mg   Dietary Fiber: 13 gm

Zucchini Lasagna

Serves 10

Zucchini is a stand-in for lasagna noodles in this dish.

6 cups sliced fresh zucchini
¹/₄ **cup all purpose flour**
1 teaspoon black pepper
¹/₂ **cup oil for frying**
2 cups crumbled firm tofu
¹/₄ **cup puréed silken tofu**
1 teaspoon oregano
¹/₄ **cup nutritional yeast**
2 cups prepared spaghetti sauce
1 cup shredded vegan mozzarella

Preheat oven to 325 degrees. Slice zucchini lengthwise into ¹/₄-inch slices. Mix flour with pepper. Dip both sides of zucchini slices into mixture to coat.

Heat oil in a sauté pan and fry zucchini slices over medium heat until golden brown, turning them once. Remove zucchini to platter covered with a paper towel. In a bowl, combine both types of tofu, oregano, and 3 Tablespoons of nutritional yeast.

In bottom of a 13 x 9-inch baking pan, spread 1 cup of spaghetti sauce, top with half the zucchini slices, then half the tofu mixture, and half the mozzarella. Repeat the layers. Top the lasagna with remaining yeast. Bake lasagna in oven for 45 minutes or until lasagna is bubbly. Let stand 15 minutes before cutting and serving.

Total Calories Per Serving: 244   Total Fat as % of Daily Value: 27%   Protein: 12 gm   Fat: 17 gm
Carbohydrates: 14 gm   Calcium: 445 mg   Iron: 2 mg   Sodium: 352 mg   Dietary Fiber: 4 gm

Basic Tomato and Pasta Lasagna
Serves 12

The tomato sauce recipe makes enough to serve on the side or to freeze and enjoy later with pasta.

Tomato Sauce:
2 Tablespoons olive oil
1 cup chopped onion
3 cloves garlic, minced
One 6-ounce can tomato paste
Three 28-ounce cans peeled plum tomatoes, chopped (reserve juice)
$\frac{1}{2}$ cup each chopped fresh basil and fresh parsley
$1\frac{1}{2}$ teaspoons dried oregano
$\frac{1}{2}$ teaspoon crushed red pepper flakes (optional)
Salt and ground black pepper to taste

Lasagna:
1 Tablespoon salt
1 pound dry uncooked lasagna noodles
Two 16-ounce packages firm tofu, drained
2 cloves garlic, minced
$\frac{1}{4}$ cup chopped fresh basil
$\frac{1}{2}$ cup chopped fresh parsley
Salt and black pepper to taste

For the sauce, in a large heavy saucepan, heat oil over medium heat. Add onion and garlic and cook, stirring frequently, until onion is soft, about 5 minutes. Add tomato paste and cook, stirring, for 1 minute. Add tomatoes with juice, basil, parsley, oregano, and red pepper flakes. Cover and simmer over low heat about 1 hour. Season sauce with salt and pepper.

Preheat the oven to 375 degrees. Meanwhile, bring a large pot of water to boil. When the water boils, add salt and noodles. Cook until al dente, about 12 minutes, stirring occasionally. Drain, rinse with water, and drain again.

Crumble tofu into a medium-size bowl. Add garlic, basil, parsley, and salt and pepper. Stir until well blended. To assemble, spoon about 1 cup sauce over bottom of a 13 x 9-inch baking dish. Add a layer of noodles and top with one-third tofu mixture. Spoon over about $1\frac{1}{2}$ cups sauce and top with another layer of noodles. Cover with one-third tofu mixture and top with $1\frac{1}{2}$ cups of sauce and another layer of noodles. Top with remaining tofu mixture and 1 cup sauce. Cover and bake 30 minutes. Remove from oven and let stand about 15 minutes before cutting and serving.

Total Calories Per Serving: 329   Total Fat as % of Daily Value: 15%   Protein: 19 gm   Fat: 10 gm
Carbohydrates: 44 gm   Calcium: 558 mg   Iron: 5 mg   Sodium: 725 mg   Dietary Fiber: 7 gm

Flightless Tetrazini
Serves 12-14

Vegetable oil spray as needed
1 pound (2 cups) sliced mushrooms
¾ cup chopped onions
½ cup chopped bell pepper
1 pound (2 cups) cubed firm tofu
3 pounds cooked pasta (start with 1 pound, uncooked pasta)
1½ quarts (6 cups) prepared creamy white sauce (see note)
¾ cup cooked green peas
¾ cup cooked, diced carrots

In a large skillet, heat oil spray. Sauté mushrooms, onions, and peppers until soft. In a roasting pan or two 8 x 8-inch pans, combine mushrooms, onions, peppers, tofu, and pasta. Toss with sauce, then garnish with peas and carrots. Bake at 325 degrees for 30 minutes or until golden brown and bubbly. For extra garnish, use chopped red, green, and yellow bell peppers.

Note: A creamy sauce can be made by creating a roux with 6 Tablespoons of melted margarine and 3 ounces of flour, which are mixed together to form a thick paste. Heat 1½ quarts (6 cups) of soymilk. Slowly whisk into roux, and allow sauce to simmer, stirring occasionally, until slightly thickened.

Total Calories Per Serving: 368   Total Fat as % of Daily Value: 17%   Protein: 18 gm   Fat: 11 gm
Carbohydrates: 40 gm   Calcium: 140 mg   Iron: 3 mg   Sodium: 286 mg   Dietary Fiber: 5 gm

"Shrimp" Satay
Serves 6

2 pounds vegan shrimp or alternative (see variations below)
8 ounces fresh pineapple chunks
Vegetable oil
8 ounces ground roasted peanuts
¼ cup soy sauce
3 Tablespoons molasses
2 cloves garlic, minced
½ teaspoon red pepper flakes
Lemon slices for garnish

Alternate vegan shrimp and pineapple on wooden or metal skewers. Brush well with oil. In a small sauté pan, combine peanuts, soy sauce, molasses, garlic, and red pepper. Add enough water (about ¼ cup) to make a thin sauce. Simmer until slightly thickened, about 5 minutes.

Grill "shrimp" on a hot barbecue or charbroiler for 2 minutes on each side or until veagn shrimp are thoroughly cooked. Serve hot, with peanut dipping sauce.

Variations: This appetizer can also be made with Tofurky™, Field Roast™, or vegan scallops. If ground peanuts are not available, you can use smooth peanut butter as an alternative.

Total Calories Per Serving: 220   Total Fat as % of Daily Value: 5%   Protein: 2 gm   Fat: 3 gm
Carbohydrates: 47 gm   Calcium: 39 mg   Iron: 1 mg   Sodium: 592 mg   Dietary Fiber: 6 gm

Vegan Paella

Serves 10

Rice:
2 Tablespoons vegetable or olive oil
2¹/₂ cups long grain white rice (basmati or jasmine long grain will also work)
¹/₂ cup minced onion
2 cloves garlic, minced
1¹/₄ cups salsa
4¹/₂ cups hot vegetable broth

Heat oil in a large soup pot. Add rice and onion and cook, stirring, until onion is slightly browned, about 2-3 minutes. Add garlic and stir for 1 additional minute. Add salsa and cook, stirring, for 2-3 additional minutes or until mixture has little to no liquid remaining. Add hot broth and bring mixture to a fast boil. Reduce heat to a simmer, cover pot, and allow rice to cook for 20-25 minutes or until liquid is absorbed.

Topping:
Vegetable oil spray
2 cups chopped onions
1¹/₂ pounds vegan sausage, such as Soyrizo™, vegan knockwurst, or vegan kielbasa
1¹/₂ pounds extra-firm tofu or seitan
¹/₂ cup diced fresh carrots
¹/₂ cup diced fresh red bell pepper
¹/₄ cup diced fresh tomato
2 cloves garlic, minced
¹/₂ cup vegetable broth
1 Tablespoon cracked black pepper
1 pound smoked tofu, cubed
2 cups fresh or frozen (thawed) green peas
1 Tablespoon minced fresh cilantro or parsley

Spray a large frying pan with oil and allow to heat. Add onions and cook until soft, about 3 minutes. Next, slice the sausage and medium-chunk the tofu. Add to onions and quickly sauté, until sausage and tofu are hot. Lower heat, stir in carrots, bell pepper, tomato, and garlic. Spray in more oil if the mixture is dry. Stir and cook until all ingredients are well combined. Stir in broth, black pepper, and smoked tofu. Cover and simmer until vegetables are soft, about 15 minutes.

To serve, place rice on serving platter or in large serving bowl. Top with paella mixture. Garnish with peas and parsley. Serve warm.

Total Calories Per Serving: 464   Total Fat as % of Daily Value: 29%   Protein: 16 gm   Fat: 19 gm
Carbohydrates: 44 gm   Calcium: 259 mg   Iron: 6 mg   Sodium: 916 mg   Dietary Fiber: 9 gm

Pasta with Broccoli Florets, Garbanzo Beans, and Tomatoes
Serves 8

Vegetable oil spray
2¹/₂ cups canned, drained or cooked garbanzo beans
1 clove garlic, minced
2 teaspoons shredded fresh basil or parsley
1 teaspoon red pepper flakes
1 cup canned diced tomatoes (not drained)
3 cups cooked small pasta shells or other small pasta, such as rotini or elbows
**   (start with 1¹/₄ cups uncooked)**
1¹/₂ cups frozen, thawed broccoli florets or cut broccoli (see note)
2 Tablespoons nutritional yeast

Spray large skillet or electric frying pan with oil. Allow pan to heat, Add garbanzo beans, garlic, basil, and pepper flakes. Cook over low heat, stirring for 3 minutes. Stir in tomatoes and cover. Allow mixture to simmer 5 minutes. Add pasta and broccoli and stir. Allow to heat, uncovered, until hot, about 3 minutes. Spoon into serving bowl or individual bowls, top with yeast and serve.

Note: If fresh broccoli florets are used, first steam or microwave until just tender.

Total Calories Per Serving: 192   Total Fat as % of Daily Value: 2%   Protein: 10 gm   Fat: 1 gm
Carbohydrates: 36 gm   Calcium: 41 mg   Iron: 2 mg   Sodium: 233 mg   Dietary Fiber: 5 gm

Mediterranean White Bean and Eggplant Stew
Serves 10

Vegetable oil spray
2¹/₂ cups chopped onions
3 cloves garlic, minced
1 large eggplant, peeled and diced (about 3 cups)
3 cups diced fresh zucchini
One 28-ounce can chopped tomatoes
2 cups cooked or canned, drained small white beans
¹/₂ cup each chopped green bell pepper and red bell pepper
2 teaspoons dried basil
¹/₂ teaspoon black pepper
2 Tablespoons minced fresh parsley

Spray a large pot with non-stick spray and warm over medium-high heat for 1 minute. Add onions and garlic and sauté for 3 minutes. Add eggplant, zucchini, tomatoes, beans, sweet peppers, basil, and black pepper. Bring to a boil. Reduce heat to low. Cover and cook, stirring occasionally, until vegetables are tender, about 30 minutes. Stir in parsley before serving.

Total Calories Per Serving: 85   Total Fat as % of Daily Value: 1%   Protein: 4 gm   Fat: <1 gm
Carbohydrates: 18 gm   Calcium: 56 mg   Iron: 2 mg   Sodium: 12 mg   Dietary Fiber: 5 gm

Vegan "Chicken" Chili
Serves 8

Vegetable oil spray
3 pounds of chunked Chik'n™, Tofurky™, Wheatmeat™, or other vegan poultry-style
 meat that can be chunked
1 cup diced red bell pepper
1 cup diced green bell pepper
1 cup diced onion
1 deseeded and diced fresh chili (about 1 Tablespoon, you choose the heat!)
2 cups cooked or canned, drained kidney beans
2 cups canned, diced tomatoes (with liquid)
2 teaspoons cumin
1 Tablespoon chili powder
1 Tablespoon black pepper
1 Tablespoon hot sauce (or as desired)
2 Tablespoons shredded vegan cheese (optional)
2 Tablespoons vegan sour cream (optional)

Heat a large soup pot and spray with oil. Sauté vegan meat for 1 minute over high heat. Reduce heat to medium and add peppers, onion, and chilies. Continue to stir and sauté for 3 minutes or until onions are soft. Reduce heat to simmer. Add beans, tomatoes, cumin, chili powder, black pepper, and hot sauce. Cover and allow to simmer for 20 minutes or until flavors are blended. Place in a serving bowl. If desired, immediately before serving, garnish with vegan cheese and vegan sour cream.

Notes: For a buffet, purchase two or three round sourdough loaves. For a seated meal, purchase round, crusty rolls. Hollow out the center. Save the interior bread for fresh or dried bread crumbs. Serve chili in the sourdough "bowls" on the buffet or as individual servings.

Total Calories Per Serving: 409   Total Fat as % of Daily Value: 16%   Protein: 5 gm   Fat: 10 gm
Carbohydrates: 35 gm   Calcium: 96 mg   Iron: 6 mg   Sodium: 1,099 mg   Dietary Fiber: 14 gm

White, Green, and Red Gratin
Serves 8

Vegetable oil spray
2 cups frozen, thawed cauliflower florets
2 cups frozen, thawed Italian flat green beans or sugar snap peas
2 cups rinsed cherry tomatoes
1½ cups tomato juice
½ cup dry bread crumbs
4 Tablespoons nutritional yeast
½ cup shredded vegan cheese
1 Tablespoon olive oil
1 clove garlic, minced

Preheat oven to 400 degrees. Spray a large baking casserole (at least 8 x 8-inch) with oil. In a large medium-size bowl, toss cauliflower, green beans, tomatoes, and tomato juice. Evenly place vegetable mixture in pan. In a small bowl, combine bread crumbs, yeast, cheese, oil, and garlic. Spread evenly over vegetables.

Bake for about 12 minutes, or until vegetables are tender and topping is golden brown.

Note: If fresh cauliflower florets are used, steam or microwave until just tender. If desired, vegetable juice cocktail or mixtures of carrot and spinach juice may be used instead of tomato juice.

Total Calories Per Serving: 104   Total Fat as % of Daily Value: 5%   Protein: 5 gm   Fat: 3 gm
Carbohydrates: 15 gm   Calcium: 115 mg   Iron: 1 mg   Sodium: 141 mg   Dietary Fiber: 3 gm

"Seafood" Kebobs with Mushrooms
Serves 6

1 cup vegan fish fillets, thawed, cut into 6-8 pieces (see note)
2 cups vegan shrimp, thawed (see note)
12-16 small fresh button mushroom caps, washed
12-16 fresh cherry tomatoes
3 Tablespoon lite soy sauce
1 Tablespoon nutritional yeast
2 Tablespoons white vinegar
2 Tablespoons fresh lemon juice
1 teaspoon fresh lemon zest
2 Tablespoons minced fresh parsley
2 teaspoons white pepper
Olive oil (for brushing kebobs, about 2 Tablespoons)

Place cut vegan fish fillets, vegan shrimp, and mushrooms in a plastic or glass bowl. Set aside tomatoes. In a small bowl, combine soy sauce, yeast, vinegar, lemon juice, zest, parsely, and pepper and stir to combine. Pour marinade over "fish" and allow to marinate, refrigerated, for 30 minutes. Drain and save marinade.

Preheat grill or broiler. Thread vegan fish, veagn shrimp, mushrooms, and tomatoes on skewers. Place kebobs in a shallow pan and broil for 3-4 minutes, brushing with oil to prevent drying. If using a grill, place directly on grill. If desired, also brush with saved marinade. Remove from heat.

Serve alone, on a bed of couscous or cooked wheat, or with fresh spinach salad.

Notes: The number of kebobs depends on the length of the skewer. Vegan seafood products can be ordered online. Also, if vegan seafood products are not available, extra-firm tofu may be used instead.

Total Calories Per Serving: 111   Total Fat as % of Daily Value: 9%   Protein: 3 gm   Fat: 6 gm
Carbohydrates: 12 gm   Calcium: 11 mg   Iron: 1 mg   Sodium: 360 mg   Dietary Fiber: 3 gm

Oktoberfest Roulades (Sauerkraut and Tofu Balls in Mustard Sauce)

Makes approximately 20 balls

Sauce:
½ cup soymilk
3 Tablespoons prepared mustard
1 cup white wine or vegetable stock
1 teaspoon onion powder
1 teaspoon white pepper
1 Tablespoon white vinegar
1 pound silken tofu

Mix all ingredients, except tofu, in a medium bowl until combined. Gradually add tofu and mix until thoroughly blended. Refrigerate until ready to use.

Tofu Balls:
Vegetable oil spray
1½ pounds firm tofu, crumbled into very small pieces
1 cup diced onions
1⅓ cups canned or fresh sauerkraut, well drained
1 teaspoon mustard powder
¼ cup soymilk
¼ cup tomato paste
1 cup bread crumbs
1 Tablespoon paprika

Preheat oven to 375 degrees. Spray frying pan with vegetable oil spray and sauté tofu, onions, sauerkraut, and mustard until onions are soft (about 5 minutes).

Place sautéed mixture in blender canister and add soymilk and tomato paste. Blend for 1 minute or until just combined. Add bread crumbs and paprika and blend for 30 seconds or until just combined (if over-blended, mixture will not hold shape).

Roll mixture into about 20 balls. Spray baking sheet with oil; place balls in a single layer on the baking sheet and bake for 30 minutes or until browned. Remove from oven; then pour half of sauce in the bottom of a casserole dish. Place tofu balls on sauce and top with remaining sauce. Cover and bake for 20 minutes or until thoroughly heated.

Total Calories Per Tofu Ball In Sauce: 92   Total Fat as % of Daily Value: 5%   Protein: 6 gm   Fat: 3 gm
Carbohydrates: 8 gm   Calcium: 109 mg   Iron: 2 mg   Sodium: 163 mg   Dietary Fiber: 1 gm

Tofu and Bean Chili
Serves 8-10

2 teaspoons vegetable oil
1 cup each chopped green onions and diced red bell pepper
2 cloves garlic, minced
4 cups crumbled firm tofu
2 Tablespoons chili powder
2 teaspoons red pepper flakes
1 teaspoon ground cumin
14¹/₂-ounce can stewed tomatoes, not drained
2 Tablespoons red wine vinegar
4 cups drained, canned black beans or cooked black beans
1 Tablespoon minced cilantro

Pour oil in a 2-quart saucepan and allow to heat over medium heat. Add green onions, red peppers, and garlic, sautéing for 4-5 minutes or until soft, not browned.

Add tofu, and cook, stirring frequently for 5 minutes. Add the chili powder, red pepper flakes and cumin. Stir frequently for 2 minutes. Add the tomatoes and red wine vinegar. Bring to a boil. Reduce heat and simmer for 20 minutes. Stir in black beans and cilantro. Simmer for 5 minutes. Serve hot.

Note: This recipe can be prepared 1-2 days in advance, and kept refrigerated until ready to reheat.

Total Calories Per Serving: 278   Total Fat as % of Daily Value: 15%   Protein: 18 gm   Fat: 10 gm
Carbohydrates: 33 gm   Calcium: 330 mg   Iron: 5 mg   Sodium: 1,516 mg   Dietary Fiber: 12 gm

Pecan-Crusted "Roast"
Serves 8

One 3-pound Field Roast™ or other solid vegan meat, such as Tofurky™ (see note)
1 Tablespoon vegetable oil
2 cloves garlic, minced
¹/₂ cup chopped pecans
¹/₃ cup dry bread crumbs
1 teaspoon each dried sage and white pepper
¹/₂ cup canned cranberry sauce

Preheat oven to 400 degrees. Rub the roast with vegetable oil to coat. Place on a baking sheet and bake for 5 minutes. Remove roast from oven and cool.

In a small bowl, combine garlic, pecans, bread crumbs, sage, and pepper. Brush roast with cranberry sauce to coat. Press pecan mixture evenly over roast to make a coating. Return to oven and bake for 30 minutes, or until roast is thoroughly heated. Let stand 10 minutes before slicing.

Note: This will work for individual servings of extra-firm tofu, smoked tofu, seitan, or tempeh, if large vegan roasts are not available.

Total Calories Per Serving: 444   Total Fat as % of Daily Value: 26%   Protein: 2 gm   Fat: 17 gm
Carbohydrates: 33 gm   Calcium: 85 mg   Iron: 4 mg   Sodium: 1,036 mg   Dietary Fiber: 11 gm

Walnut Lemon Balls

Serves 8

These "neatballs" go well with a tomato or pesto sauce served over pasta, or used as a "neatball" sandwich in pita or on crusty French bread.

1¹/₂ cups walnuts
3 cups cooked brown rice
2 cups firm tofu, drained and mashed
1 cup dry bread crumbs or matzo meal
2 teaspoons basil
1 teaspoon thyme
1 Tablespoon cornstarch
¹/₈ cup lemon juice
1 Tablespoon miso

Preheat oven to 350 degrees. Place walnuts on an ungreased cookie sheet, place in the oven and toast for about 5 minutes. Allow walnuts to cool, place in a food processor, blender, or food mill and grind into a fine meal.

In a medium-size bowl, mix walnuts, rice, tofu, bread crumbs or matzo meal, basil, and thyme until combined.

In a small bowl, dissolve cornstarch in the lemon juice. Stir to dissolve and add miso.

Combine walnuts and cornstarch mixture. Using your hands is the best way to thoroughly moisten the dry ingredients; work with the mixture until it holds together. If the mixture is too dry or dense, add a small amount of water until the consistency is one that will hold together, but not too dry.

Roll mixture into small balls and place on a non-stick cookie sheet (or line with baking parchment or spray with vegetable oil spray). Bake for 15-20 minutes or until the balls are hot.

Note: This mixture can also be pressed into a loaf pan and baked as a "neatloaf." Allow loaf to cool (about 8-10 minutes) before slicing.

Total Calories Per Serving: 270   Total Fat as % of Daily Value: 16%   Protein: 15 gm   Fat: 10 gm
Carbohydrates: 32 gm   Calcium: 479 mg   Iron: 3 mg   Sodium: 193 mg   Dietary Fiber: 4 gm

Mushroom and Hazelnut Snacking Balls

Serves 6

The dough from this recipe can be shaped into balls and served as a cold appetizer on a bed of baby greens or cold couscous, pressed into a loaf pan and sliced (as a vegan paté), spread on veggies or crackers, or used as a sandwich spread.

Vegetable oil spray
¹/₂ medium onion, chopped
1 cup fresh button mushrooms, chopped
2 cloves garlic, minced
1 cup hazelnuts (also called filberts)
¹/₄ cup chopped fresh parsley

1 teaspoon soy sauce
¹/₂ teaspoon onion powder
2 teaspoons nutritional yeast
1 teaspoon black pepper

In a medium-size frying pan, spray vegetable oil and heat. Sauté onions, mushrooms, and garlic until soft, about 4 minutes. Add vegetables and all remaining ingredients into a blender or food processor and blend until smooth. Mixture will be very thick. Form into small balls or patties and refrigerate for at least 30 minutes before serving.

Total Calories Per Serving: 156   Total Fat as % of Daily Value: 21%   Protein: 5 gm   Fat: 14 gm
Carbohydrates: 7 gm   Calcium: 36 mg   Iron: 1 mg   Sodium: 60 mg   Dietary Fiber: 3 gm

Basic Veggie Balls
Serves 6

This is a great "pantry" recipe, as many of the ingredients should be on your shelf. This is also a great way to use leftover veggies. Serve with mashed potatoes and corn on the cob for a hearty meal.

One 16-ounce can (or 1¹/₂ cups) sliced carrots, drained (reserve liquid)
One 16-ounce can (or 1¹/₂ cups) cut green beans, drained
1¹/₂ cups cooked pinto or red beans
2¹/₂ cups bread crumbs
2 Tablespoons vegetable oil or melted vegan margarine
1 Tablespoon dried parsley
¹/₂ cup ketchup or chili sauce
2 Tablespoons silken tofu
¹/₂ teaspoon white pepper
¹/₂ teaspoon celery salt
1 teaspoon onion powder

Preheat oven to 325 degrees. Place carrots, green beans, and pinto beans in a blender or food processor canister and purée until almost smooth.

Place mixture in a large bowl. Stir in remaining ingredients until well combined. If mixture is too thick, add some of the reserved carrot liquid; if it is too thin, add additional bread crumbs.

Roll mixture into small balls and place on a non-stick cookie sheet (or spray with vegetable oil spray). Bake for 30-40 minutes or until thoroughly heated and lightly browned.

Note: This mixture can be pressed into a loaf pan and baked as a "neatloaf" or pressed into patties and fried or baked as "burgers."

Total Calories Per Serving: 326   Total Fat as % of Daily Value: 12%   Protein: 12 gm   Fat: 8 gm
Carbohydrates: 54 gm   Calcium: 141 mg   Iron: 4 mg   Sodium: 577 mg   Dietary Fiber: 8 gm

Tofu Balls

Serves 6-8

These are crunchy, toasty balls that would also make good burgers. Once again, you have the option of frying or baking. Make a double batch and freeze one batch; this makes a great quick dinner. Just microwave the tofu balls in tomato or mushroom sauce and serve with rice or pasta or in pita, tortillas, or rolls as a hot "neatball" sandwich.

2¹/₂ cups firm tofu, drained and crumbled
1 clove garlic, minced
¹/₄ cup onions, minced
¹/₂ cup wheat germ
³/₄ cup bread crumbs
1 Tablespoon soy sauce
¹/₄ cup chopped fresh parsley
¹/₂ cup celery, minced
¹/₄ cup chopped bell peppers
1 cup water or carrot juice
Oil for frying (about ¹/₈ cup)

In a large bowl, mash tofu until almost smooth. Add all ingredients except water and combine until well mixed. Slowly add water or juice until mixture is thick enough to form balls.

Form into small balls and refrigerate for 30 minutes. Fry in oil until browned or bake at 350 degrees for 20 minutes until heated and browned.

Total Calories Per Serving: 265   Total Fat as % of Daily Value: 17%   Protein: 22 gm   Fat: 11 gm
Carbohydrates: 23 gm   Calcium: 757 mg   Iron: 5 mg   Sodium: 295 mg   Dietary Fiber: 5 gm

Whole-Wheat "Neatballs"

Serves 8

This recipe requires some prep time, as the wheat needs to sit for at least 6 hours. You have a choice of cooking techniques; these "neatballs" can be fried in a small amount of oil or baked in the oven. Make an extra batch and freeze for later use. The "neatballs" go well with pasta as an entrée, can be crumbled and used as a pizza topping, or chopped and served with barbecue sauce as a sloppy Joe.

1 cup uncooked whole wheat or brown rice
¹/₂ cup diced, peeled potato (potato is uncooked)
¹/₂ cup sliced, peeled carrot (carrot is uncooked)
¹/₄ cup chopped onion
¹/₂ cup cooked corn
¹/₄ cup chopped radishes
1 teaspoon onion powder
1 clove garlic, minced
Oil for frying (about ¹/₄ cup)

Combine 1 cup whole wheat or brown rice with 2 cups of boiling water. Cover and let sit for at least 6 hours (overnight is better). You can make extra wheat and store it in the refrigerator to use as a side dish or as a cereal. You will use 2 cups of cooked whole wheat or brown rice for this recipe.

In a food processor, blender, or food mill, grind wheat, potatoes, carrots, onions, corn, and radishes until just smooth. Stir in onion powder and garlic. Form into small balls and refrigerate for 30 minutes.

Either heat oil in a frying pan and fry balls until heated and browned, or place neatballs on a greased cookie sheet and bake at 350 degrees for 20 minutes or until browned.

Variation: For a Southwestern flavor, add 2 Tablespoons chopped chilies to the wheat mixture and serve garnished with salsa. Serve with steamed tortillas and rice.

Total Calories Per Serving: 167   Total Fat as % of Daily Value: 12%   Protein: 3 gm   Fat: 8 gm
Carbohydrates: 23 gm   Calcium: 12 mg   Iron: 1 mg   Sodium: 11 mg   Dietary Fiber: 2 gm

Winter Pumpkin Stew with Apples
Serves 10

You'll need a good-looking pumpkin for this one! The completed stew can be served in the pumpkin shell, which has been hollowed out. Look for a sugar or pie pumpkin, not a jack-o-lantern, if you want to use the interior pulp in this stew. If you have a jack-o-lantern, you can scoop out the interior and discard (or use for good compost), save the seeds for roasting, and purchase winter squash to use in the stew.

3 Tablespoons whole wheat flour
2 teaspoons crushed fennel seeds
1 teaspoon cumin
1 teaspoon black pepper
2 pounds extra-firm tofu or seitan, cut into cubes
Vegetable oil spray
2 cups diced onions
2 cups vegetable broth
1 cup apple cider or unsweetened apple juice
¼ cup apple cider or red vinegar
2 pounds chunked fresh pumpkin or winter squash (peeled and seeded)
1 cup sliced, peeled carrots
1 cup sliced, peeled parsnips
1 cup peeled, cored, and chunked baking apples, such as Romes

In a medium-size bowl, combine flour, fennel, cumin, and black pepper. Add tofu or seitan chunks, tossing gently to coat. Remove coated tofu or seitan and set aside for 5 minutes.

Spray a large stew pot with vegetable oil and heat. Add onions and sauté only until soft, about 3 minutes. Add broth, cider, vinegar, pumpkin, carrots, and parsnips. Bring to a fast boil, reduce heat, and simmer until vegetables are tender, about 40 minutes.

While vegetables are stewing, spray a skillet with oil and allow to heat. Add tofu or seitan chunks and brown, tossing so that all sides are browned. Remove from skillet and set aside.

Add apples to stewing vegetables and allow to cook for 10 more minutes or until apples are tender. Add browned tofu or seitan and allow stew to heat for 5 minutes. Serve in a pumpkin shell, in individual bowls, or in a large serving bowl.

Note: You can also use large winter squash in place of the pumpkin shell and in the stew, instead of chunked pumpkin.

Total Calories Per Serving: 144   Total Fat as % of Daily Value: 6%   Protein: 9 gm   Fat: 4 gm
Carbohydrates: 21 gm   Calcium: 228 mg   Iron: 3 mg   Sodium: 24 mg   Dietary Fiber: 3 gm

Moo Shu Tempeh
Serves 8

Marinade:
4 Tablespoons low-sodium soy sauce
4 Tablespoons cold water
2 Tablespoons dark sesame oil
2 teaspoons orange juice concentrate
3 cloves garlic, minced

Combine all marinade ingredients in a large glass or plastic bowl. Set aside.

Tempeh:
2 Tablespoons dried mushrooms (shiitake are a good variety)
1 cup warm water
1¹/₂ pounds tempeh, cut into thin strips
Vegetable oil spray
4 cups finely shredded green cabbage
1 cup finely shredded carrots
1 cup diced green onions (white and green parts)
2 Tablespoons cornstarch
¹/₂ cup warm water
8 flour tortillas

Combine mushrooms and 1 cup warm water in a small bowl. Allow them to soak for 15 minutes or until soft. Discard water. Cut mushrooms into thin strips. Set aside.

Add tempeh to marinade, cover, and marinate for 30 minutes. Drain tempeh, reserve remaining marinade to use as sauce.

Spray a large skillet with oil and allow to heat. Add tempeh and allow to brown, about 3 minutes. Stir in mushrooms, cabbage, carrots, and green onions. Quickly mix cornstarch with ¹/₂ cup warm water and add to tempeh mixture. Stir and cook over high heat until cabbage is tender and mixture is hot. Remove from stove.

To serve, warm tortillas in the microwave or oven, rolled and wrapped in a towel. Place tortillas flat on a serving platter or on individual plates. Spoon a small amount, about 1 teaspoon of marinade in the center of each tortilla. Top marinade with ¹/₄ cup tempeh mixture. Fold bottom edge over tempeh mixture. Fold left and right sides of tortilla to the center to form a loose roll. Serve hot.

Total Calories Per Serving: 351   Total Fat as % of Daily Value: 19%   Protein: 13 gm   Fat: 12 gm
Carbohydrates: 49 gm   Calcium: 159 mg   Iron: 4 mg   Sodium: 767 mg   Dietary Fiber: 4 gm

Szechuan-Style Lo Mein

Serves 8

1¹⁄₂ pounds thin rice noodles, vermicelli, or thin spaghetti
2 Tablespoons sesame oil (divided)
1 Tablespoon fresh minced ginger
3 cloves garlic, minced
1 Tablespoon red pepper flakes
2 Tablespoons nutritional yeast
1 Tablespoon soy sauce
6 cups fresh bok choy or Napa cabbage, thinly sliced (about 2¹⁄₂ pounds)
1 cup thinly sliced red bell pepper
1¹⁄₂ cups vegetable broth
¹⁄₂ cup thinly sliced vegan Canadian bacon or breakfast strips
4 thinly sliced green onions
¹⁄₂ cup minced fresh cilantro
¹⁄₂ cup chopped cashews (optional)

Heat 4 quarts of water and bring to a boil. Break noodles in half and add to water. Reduce heat to medium and allow pasta to cook until just al dente (chewy). Drain and toss with 1 Tablespoon sesame oil. Set aside.

Heat 1 Tablespoon of sesame oil in a large skillet or wok. Add ginger, garlic, and pepper flakes and sauté for 1 minute. Quickly stir in yeast and soy sauce to combine and add bok choy and bell peppers. Stir and cook quickly until bok choy is wilted. Add broth, lower heat, and simmer 5 minutes uncovered. Stir in cooked noodles and vegan bacon and cook until thoroughly heated.

Place lo mein on a serving platter or in a serving bowl. Top with green onions and cilantro and cashews (if desired). Serve hot.

Total Calories Per Serving: 407   Total Fat as % of Daily Value: 8%   Protein: 7 gm   Fat: 5 gm
Carbohydrates: 83 gm   Calcium: 63 mg   Iron: 1 mg   Sodium: 526 mg   Dietary Fiber: 5 gm

Baked "Chicken" Fingers

Serves 10

2 pounds extra-firm tofu or smoked tofu, cut into thick strips
Vegetable oil spray
1 cup seasoned bread crumbs

Preheat oven to 375 degrees. Place tofu on a large plate and place bread crumbs in a large bowl. Spray a baking sheet with oil. Spray each piece of tofu lightly with oil and then dip and dredge into bread crumbs to coat. Brush or shake off excess bread crumbs. Place on baking sheet. Repeat until all tofu is coated.

Lightly spray the top of tofu with oil. Bake for 12-15 minutes or until thoroughly heated.

Note: If you like, you can use vegan meats that can be cut into thick strips, such as Chik'n™, Tofurky™, or Field Roast™. This also works with vegan fish fillets and shrimp. If products are frozen, do not thaw. This makes them difficult to cut, but improves the texture and keeps them moist.

Total Calories Per Serving: 106   Total Fat as % of Daily Value: 7%   Protein: 9 gm   Fat: 4 gm
Carbohydrates: 9 gm   Calcium: 202 mg   Iron: 2 mg   Sodium: 90 mg   Dietary Fiber: 1 gm

Thai Seitan Grill
Serves 6

Sauce:
¹⁄₄ cup vegan teriyaki sauce (prepared or see recipe on page 287)
3 Tablespoons water
¹⁄₄ cup creamy peanut (or soynut) butter
1 teaspoon red pepper flakes

Pour teriyaki sauce in a small bowl. Whisk water into teriyaki sauce until combined. Slowly add in peanut butter and whisk until smooth. Stir in red pepper flakes. If desired, sauce can be made in a food processor or blender by adding all ingredients to a canister and processing until smooth. Set sauce aside until ready to serve seitan.

Grill:
2 pounds seitan, cut into thin strips
1 cup very thinly sliced sweet onions
4 Tablespoons vegan teriyaki sauce (prepared or see recipe on page 287)

Preheat barbecue or indoor grill. If grills are not available, preheat oven to 425 degrees. Place seitan strips and onions on a hot grill and brush with teriyaki sauce. Grill and turn until heated through. Place on serving platter. Serve with prepared sauce on the side.

    If using an oven, place seitan on a non-stick baking sheet. Brush with teriyaki sauce and top with onions. Bake for 8-10 minutes or until hot.

Total Calories Per Serving: 898   Total Fat as % of Daily Value: 12%   Protein: 120 gm   Fat: 8 gm
Carbohydrates: 63 gm   Calcium: 1 mg   Iron: 11 mg   Sodium: 970 mg   Dietary Fiber: 11 gm

Olive and Tofu Stuffed Manicotti
Serves 6-8

16 jumbo shells or manicotti shells
Vegetable oil spray
2 cups sliced, fresh white or brown button mushrooms
¹⁄₂ cup pitted black olives
¹⁄₂ cup minced sweet onions, such as Vidalia or Maui
1 cup frozen, thawed, well-drained chopped spinach
2 cloves garlic, minced
2 Tablespoons minced fresh parsley
2 Tablespoons minced sun-dried tomatoes
1 pound extra-firm tofu, drained
4 cups spaghetti sauce

Boil 4 quarts of water in a large pot. Add pasta and cook only until just tender, about 3-4 minutes, depending on the size of the pot. Pasta should not be soft enough to eat. Drain, rinse, and set aside.

Preheat oven to 375 degrees. Heat large skillet and spray with oil. Add mushrooms and quickly sauté over high heat until fork tender. Remove from heat. Chop by hand or process in a food processor until finely minced. Place mushrooms in a large bowl. Chop olives and onions together by hand or in a food processor until almost a paste. Add to mushrooms and stir until combined. Chop spinach into a fine mince. Mix spinach with garlic, parsley, and dried tomatoes. Add spinach mixture to mushrooms and mix until well combined. Crumble tofu into mushroom mixture and mix until well combined. If mixture does not hold together, add a small amount of water or vegetable broth until mixture lightly holds together.

Pour sauce into a large baking dish to fill it 1 inch on the bottom. Fill each piece of pasta with approximately $1/4$ cup mushroom mixture. Place pasta, filled side up, into a baking dish. Cover pasta with 1 inch of sauce. Cover and bake for 15 minutes. Remove cover and baked for an additional 5 minutes or until sauce is bubbly and pasta is heated thoroughly.

Total Calories Per Serving: 392   Total Fat as % of Daily Value: 14%   Protein: 17 gm   Fat: 9 gm
Carbohydrates: 61 gm   Calcium: 217 mg   Iron: 5 mg   Sodium: 936 mg   Dietary Fiber: 9 gm

Stir-Fried Noodles

Serves 5

1½ pounds (about 3 cups) uncooked noodles, such as vermicelli or rice noodles
1 cup finely shredded green cabbage
1 cup fresh bean spouts
½ cup minced celery
¼ cup minced onions
½ cup drained, chopped canned bamboo shoots
1 cup fresh, thinly sliced button mushrooms
Vegetable oil spray
2 Tablespoons dark soy sauce
Vegetable broth (as needed, not more than 1 cup)

Put 3 quarts of water in a large pot and bring to a boil. Add noodles and cook until just soft (al dente), about 3-4 minutes. Drain.

Preheat wok or deep pot and spray with oil. Add vegetables and quickly stir-fry, stirring constantly over high heat until just soft, about 3-4 minutes.

Combine noodles with soy sauce and add to vegetables. Briskly stir-fry. If mixture is too dry for your taste, add vegetable broth by the Tablespoonful, allowing each addition to be absorbed before adding more. Serve immediately.

Total Calories Per Serving: 522   Total Fat as % of Daily Value: 1%   Protein: 6 gm   Fat: 1 gm
Carbohydrates: 119 gm   Calcium: 44 mg   Iron: 1 mg   Sodium: 827 mg   Dietary Fiber: 3 gm

Pasta Puttanesca
Serves 10

This is a spicy, colorful pasta entrée.

Vegetable oil spray
3 cloves garlic, minced
1 cup chopped sweet onions, such as Vidalia or Maui
¹/₂ cup each pitted black olives and pimento-stuffed green olives
4 each pepperoncini peppers (also known as Italian Pickled Peppers)
¹/₄ cup drained capers
2 Tablespoons seeded, chopped fresh chilies (you choose the heat!)
1 cup chopped fresh Italian parsley (also known as flat-leaf parsley)
4 cups chopped canned tomatoes, not drained
¹/₂ cup water
1 teaspoon ground oregano
¹/₂ teaspoon cayenne
2 pounds cooked pasta, such as spaghetti or angel hair (1 pound uncooked)

Spray a large pot liberally with oil and allow to heat. Add garlic and onions and cook, stirring, until onions are soft, but not brown, about 4 minutes. Add black olives and green olives, pepperoncini, capers, chilies, and parsley. Cover and simmer, about 5 minutes, stirring twice. Add tomatoes, water, oregano, and cayenne. Cover and allow dish to come to a boil. Lower to a simmer and allow to cook for 30 minutes or until flavors are married.

To serve, arrange pasta on serving platter or on individual plates. Top with hot sauce and serve.

Total Calories Per Serving: 177   Total Fat as % of Daily Value: 3%   Protein: 7 gm   Fat: 2 gm
Carbohydrates: 34 gm   Calcium: 38 mg   Iron: 1 mg   Sodium: 285 mg   Dietary Fiber: 4 gm

Fiery Black Bean Burritos
Serves 10

1¹/₂ cups hot cooked brown rice (start with ³/₄ cup uncooked rice)
1¹/₂ cups warm drained, canned black beans or cooked black beans
¹/₄ cup chopped onions
2 teaspoons cumin
¹/₂ cup minced fresh cilantro
2 Tablespoons seeded, chopped fresh chili (you choose the heat!)
Vegetable oil spray
Two 8-ounce packages extra-firm smoked tofu, cut into small cubes
10 whole wheat tortillas
2 cups shredded Romaine or fresh spinach
2 cups salsa

In a large bowl, combine rice, beans, onions, cumin, cilantro, and chili and set aside. Spray a large skillet with oil and heat. Add tofu and cook and stir for 2 minutes or until hot.

To assemble burritos, place a thin layer of rice and bean mixture on a tortilla. Top with tofu, greens, and salsa. Roll tightly. Serve warm or cold.

Total Calories Per Serving: 395   Total Fat as % of Daily Value: 12%   Protein: 13 gm   Fat: 8 gm
Carbohydrates: 67 gm   Calcium: 161 mg   Iron: 4mg   Sodium: 695 mg   Dietary Fiber: 6 gm

Polenta with Black Beans and Tomato-Basil Sauce
Serves 10

Polenta:
2 cups vegetable broth
1/2 cup or 4 ounces yellow corn meal
1 teaspoon cumin
2 teaspoons black pepper
2 teaspoons oregano

Bring 2 cups vegetable broth to a boil. Slowly whisk in cornmeal, whisking constantly to avoid lumps. Stir in cumin, pepper, and oregano. Reduce heat and simmer until polenta thickens, about 10 minutes. Set aside and keep warm.

Tomato-Basil Sauce:
1/2 cup sliced sundried tomatoes
1 clove garlic, minced
2 Tablespoons red vinegar
1 Tablespoon minced fresh basil or 2 teaspoons crumbled dried basil
2 Tablespoons chopped fresh parsley
2 Tablespoons capers, drained
1 cup chopped fresh tomatoes

Combine sundried tomatoes, garlic, vinegar, basil, parsley, capers, and fresh tomatoes in a large bowl and toss. Process in a food processor canister or blender until entire mixture is puréed. Pour into a bowl and set aside.

Black Beans:
2 cups cooked, drained black beans
1 clove garlic, minced
1 Tablespoon chopped canned jalapeño chili
1 teaspoon ground cumin
1 cup vegetable broth

Combine beans, garlic, jalapeño, and cumin in a large pot. Stir in broth and cook over medium flame until mixture is thoroughly heated.

To serve, layer polenta on a serving platter evenly. Top with sauce and then beans. Serve hot.

Total Calories Per Serving: 169   Total Fat as % of Daily Value: 1%   Protein: 6 gm   Fat: 1 gm
Carbohydrates: 34 gm   Calcium: 30 mg   Iron: 2 mg   Sodium: 441 mg   Dietary Fiber: 6 gm

Spiced Couscous with Tempeh

Serves 8

Spicy marinade:
2 cloves garlic, minced
2 teaspoons ground cumin
1 teaspoon cayenne
3 Tablespoons lemon juice
4 Tablespoons vegetable oil
¼ cup chopped fresh cilantro

Combine all marinade ingredients in a large bowl and whisk to combine.

1½ cups water
2 cups tempeh, cut into small pieces

Add water to marinade and stir. Add tempeh and mix so all the tempeh is coated. Cover and set aside.

Couscous:
Vegetable oil spray
½ cup minced onions
2 cloves garlic, minced
1 cup Israeli or Mediterranean or pearled couscous (not fine couscous)
2½ cups vegetable broth

Spray a large skillet liberally with oil and allow to heat. Add onions and garlic and cook and stir for 2 minutes. Add couscous, cook and stir until couscous is well coated. Add broth, reduce heat, and cover. Allow to simmer about 15 minutes or until all liquid is absorbed.

To assemble:
2 cups whole cherry tomatoes (about 2 pints)
¼ cup vegetable oil
1 teaspoon red pepper flakes
¼ cup chopped fresh parsley

Remove couscous from skillet and set aside, keeping warm. Add tomatoes and oil to the skillet and cook, stirring, until tomatoes begin to pop, about 2 minutes. Add red pepper flakes and parsley and stir to combine. Add tempeh and marinade. Cook, stirring, for 5 minutes or until most of the marinade is evaporated and tempeh is hot.

Place couscous on a serving platter or divide onto individual plates. Top with tempeh mixture and serve hot.

Total Calories Per Serving: 250   Total Fat as % of Daily Value: 29%   Protein: 9 gm   Fat: 19 gm
Carbohydrates: 14 gm   Calcium: 63 mg   Iron: 2 mg   Sodium: 254 mg   Dietary Fiber: 1 gm

Spaghetti with Sugo Crudo (Raw Tomato Sauce)

Serves 6-8

3 pounds very ripe tomatoes (about 8 cups)
2 Tablespoons cracked black pepper
2 cloves garlic, minced
½ cup olive oil
1½ pounds uncooked spaghetti

Bring a large pot of water to boil. Add whole tomatoes and simmer for 5 minutes; drain. Peel, core, and half the tomatoes. Chop tomatoes by hand or in a food processor and place in a large bowl. Toss with pepper. In a small cup, whisk garlic and olive oil. Cover and let sit for 30 minutes. Strain out garlic and discard. Add to tomatoes and toss to combine.

Bring a large pot with 3 quarts of water to boil. Add spaghetti and cook until al dente, slightly chewy. Drain, but do not rinse. Add pasta to tomato sauce, toss to coat, and serve immediately.

Total Calories Per Serving: 614   Total Fat as % of Daily Value: 31%   Protein: 16 gm   Fat: 20 gm
Carbohydrates: 92 gm   Calcium: 47mg   Iron: 5 mg   Sodium: 15 mg   Dietary Fiber: 6 gm

Peanut Pasta

Serves 6

1 pound uncooked fettuccini or flat spaghetti
2 cups carrots, cut into thin strips
1½ cups frozen green peas
½ cup red vinegar
1½ Tablespoons red pepper flakes
¼ teaspoon hot sauce
¼ cup peanut oil
1 Tablespoon soy sauce
2 Tablespoons creamy peanut butter
2 Tablespoons fresh chopped parsley (for garnish)
3 Tablespoons chopped peanuts (optional, for garnish)

Cook fettuccini in 1 gallon of boiling water until al dente (chewy). Drain and set aside, keeping warm. In a microwaveable bowl, combine carrots and peas. Microwave on HIGH for 3 minutes or until just tender. Drain and set aside. In a microwaveable bowl, combine vinegar, pepper flakes, hot sauce, peanut oil, and soy sauce. Microwave on HIGH for 1 minute. Whisk in peanut butter until well combined. Microwave on HIGH for 30 seconds. Place fettuccini in a serving bowl. Toss with carrots and peas and then peanut sauce until well coated. Serve immediately.

Note: You can use soynut butter and roasted soy nuts in place of the peanut products.

Total Calories Per Serving: 448   Total Fat as % of Daily Value: 20%   Protein: 14 gm   Fat: 13 gm
Carbohydrates: 68 gm   Calcium: 44 mg   Iron: 4 mg   Sodium: 232 mg   Dietary Fiber: 6 gm

Tofu and Mushrooms

Serves 6

Vegetable oil spray
2 pounds (about 4 cups) drained and cubed extra-firm tofu
1 cup soaked, dried shiitake mushrooms, sliced
6 green onions, chopped fine (white and green parts, about ¼ cup)
2 teaspoons dark soy sauce
2 teaspoons cornstarch mixed with 4 teaspoons water

Preheat wok or pot with deep sides. Spray with oil. Slowly add in a small amount of tofu, mushrooms, and onions at a time, stirring constantly over high heat, until onions are slightly soft, about 1 minute. Continue to add ingredients. When all the tofu, mushrooms, and onions are added, mix soy sauce and cornstarch together and quickly stir into wok to allow coating. Stir and cook for 1 minute and serve immediately.

Total Calories Per Serving: 185   Total Fat as % of Daily Value: 14%   Protein: 16 gm   Fat: 9 gm
Carbohydrates: 15 gm   Calcium: 281 mg   Iron: 3 mg   Sodium: 129 mg   Dietary Fiber: 2 gm

Tofu and Mushroom Stroganoff

Serves 10-12

Vegetable oil spray
½ cup minced onions
2 cloves garlic, minced
2 pounds extra-firm tofu, drained and cut into small cubes (about 4 cups)
1 pound sliced fresh button mushrooms
1 Tablespoon minced fresh basil
2 Tablespoons soy sauce
2 teaspoons cayenne
2 cups silken tofu
1 cup minced fresh parsley
2 pounds warm cooked pasta, such as bow ties (start with 1 pound uncooked pasta)

Spray large skillet with oil and heat. Add onions and cook until golden, about 2 minutes. Add garlic and cook for 1 minute. Add tofu and mushrooms to skillet, toss and cook until mushrooms are softened, about 4 minutes. Mix in basil, soy sauce, and cayenne and allow mixture to simmer. If necessary, purée silken tofu until smooth. Add to skillet and stir to combine. Taste. If desired, add additional soy sauce or cayenne. Cook until heated, about 5 minutes. Stir in parsley and remove from heat. Place pasta in a serving bowl or on individual plates. Top with stroganoff and serve.

Total Calories Per Serving: 243   Total Fat as % of Daily Value: 13%   Protein: 18 gm   Fat: 8 gm
Carbohydrates: 29 gm   Calcium: 232 mg   Iron: 4 mg   Sodium: 289 mg   Dietary Fiber: 1 gm

Chapter 14: DIPS AND SPREADS

Dips

Smooth dips and spreads create a pleasant contrast to crunchy vegetables. Dips with added ingredients, such as chopped vegetables or dried fruit, make a nice counterpart to soft breads or ripe fruit.

Most dips and spreads are more flavorful and smooth if prepared at least several hours before serving. They can be made ahead of time and require very little work at serving time. This makes them the perfect party food.

Pay attention to consistency when preparing dips. Dips should be thick enough to be easily scooped, but not so thick as to break chips or require a knife and fork! Don't panic if your dips thicken when they are refrigerated. Most dips tend to be thick when they are very chilled, and come to the correct consistency when served. If dips are too thick, try thinning them by simply mixing, adding a bit more of the main liquid, or even heating, depending on the dip. If a dip is too thin, try whisking in some softened vegan cream cheese, vegan sour cream, vegan yogurt, or puréed vegetables or fruit, depending on the dip's flavor.

Spreads are generally made to be thick enough so they don't slide off bread, crackers, or fruit or vegetable slices. Plan your spreads based on what it will be paired with. If you have mild bread or cucumber slices, you may want a savory spread, spiced with chopped chilies or a dash of hot sauce. If you are serving spicy crackers, plan on a mild spread.

Flavored vegan margarine and vegan cream cheese are easy spreads. Chop fresh parsley, cilantro, basil, chives, or tarragon or mince black or green olives, pimentos, radishes, or pickled vegetables. Choose two or three items and whip them into vegan margarine or vegan cream cheese. You can stir in dry or prepared mustard, curry powder, or capers to create colorful, flavorful spreads.

Traditional salsa (tomatoes, chilies, cilantro, and onions) is a great dip, marinade, and even a base for hot sauces and soups (add salsa to tomato or vegetable soup for flavor variety). But salsa does not have to be just tomato-based. You can make a citrus salsa with grapefruit and orange segments, chopped onion, cilantro, and chilies. Serve this on its own or add chopped pineapple, mango, or fresh peaches or apricots. You can roast vegetables, such as summer squash and red bell peppers, and add these to a tomato salsa. The variations are endless. Ditto for hummus. You can purchase different flavored hummus or make your own. To a basic hummus, add puréed red or yellow pepper, chilies, roasted corn, or tomatoes. Or use black beans or red beans to prepare the hummus, instead of garbanzos.

Bean dips are easy to make. Purée cooked beans and add garlic, onions, chilies, lemon juice, parsley, and other seasonings your guests might like. You can purchase vegan soy yogurt and sour cream and use them rather than dairy products. Puréed silken tofu, mixed with a small amount of lemon or lime juice can also be used as a base for savory dips, rather than dairy products.

Avocado is a great base for dips. Mash fresh ripe avocados or purchase frozen avocado pulp. Prepare a basic guacamole with mashed avocado, onion, cilantro, garlic, lemon juice, and chili. You can serve this as is or add seasonings.

Sauces are meant to add moisture, flavor, richness, or color to foods. Sauces should be thick enough to cling to food without being heavy or pasty. Take some time to create smooth, flavorful sauces. If you don't have the time or the inclination to stand and stir sauces, you can purchase prepared vegan sauces, such as vegan pesto or marinara. Flavorful sauces can be created by seasoning puréed cooked beans, rice, or vegetables. If sauces are too thick, thin them with a small amount of vegetable juice or broth. If sauces are too thin, thicken them with cornstarch, mashed potatoes, or vegan sour cream, depending on the sauce. Remember that a sauce enhances and accents the flavor of food.

Dip and Spread Recipes
The following recipes are all easily doubled, tripled, or quadrupled!

Vegan Cheeseball
Makes about 1½ cups serving 6 (1 large ball or 2 small balls)

Cheesballs displayed on a party buffet table seem to delight guests of all ages. Serve with crackers or vegetable chips.

1 package (usually 8 ounces, or one cup) vegan cream cheese, plain or French onion-flavored
2 Tablespoons diced green olives
1 Tablespoon diced black olives
2 Tablespoons minced green onions
1 Tablespoon nutritional yeast
3 Tablespoons minced almonds, minced fresh parsley, or minced vegan "bacon" bits (optional, for garnish)

Place cream cheese in a medium bowl and whip with a fork until softened. Slowly whip in olives, green onions, and yeast, mixing until well combined.

Here's the fun part: work mixture with your hands, forming one or two balls. If desired, roll in almonds, parsley, or "bacon" bits to coat exterior. Place on a serving plate and refrigerate for at least 1 hour before serving.

Total Calories Per Serving: 113   Total Fat as % of Daily Value: 14%   Protein: 2 gm   Fat: 9 gm
Carbohydrates: 5 gm   Calcium: 15 mg   Iron: 0 mg   Sodium: 190 mg   Dietary Fiber: 1 gm

Black and Green Olive Tapenade
Makes 1 quart (4 cups) serving 16

1 clove garlic, minced
1 cup chopped red onion
½ cup red vinegar
1½ cups each pitted black olives and pitted green olives
½ cup chopped roasted red peppers or canned, drained pimentos
¼ cup fresh basil leaves
1 Tablespoon dried oregano
1½ cups olive oil
1 Tablespoon red pepper flakes
1 Tablespoon black pepper

Place garlic, onion, and vinegar in a food processor canister or blender. Process until finely chopped. Add remaining ingredients. Purée until the texture of a dip is reached. Chill until ready to serve.

Total Calories Per Serving: 146   Total Fat as % of Daily Value: 10%   Protein: 1 gm   Fat: 10 gm
Carbohydrates: 15 gm   Calcium: 66 mg   Iron: 2 mg   Sodium: 223 mg   Dietary Fiber: 3 gm

Avocado Dip (Guacamole)

Makes about 2½ cups or five ½ cup servings

A twist on the traditional recipe!

2 cloves garlic, minced
¹/₂ cup chopped onions
1 teaspoon oil
2 avocados, pitted and peeled (about 1¹/₂ cups)
¹/₂ cup chopped red bell pepper
1 Tablespoon fresh cilantro, chopped (optional)
2 Tablespoons vegan mayonnaise
2 Tablespoons lime juice
¹/₄ cup vegan sour cream or unflavored soy yogurt
1 teaspoon red pepper flakes or Tabasco™ sauce

Mix garlic, onions, and oil in a small bowl and microwave on HIGH for 2 minutes or until tender.

In a large bowl, mash avocado. Add garlic mixture and remaining ingredients and mix and mash until well combined. Refrigerate in a plastic or glass container, covered. Chill for at least 1 hour before serving.

Note: If your avocado isn't soft enough to mash, you can microwave it on HIGH for 1 minute.

Total Calories Per Serving: 206   Total Fat as % of Daily Value: 27%   Protein: 2 gm   Fat: 17 gm
Carbohydrates: 13 gm   Calcium: 16 mg   Iron: 1 mg   Sodium: 129 mg   Dietary Fiber: 5 gm

Tzatziki (Greek Cucumber Dip)

Makes 1½ cups sauce or twelve 2 Tablespoons servings

2 cloves garlic, minced
2 Tablespoon minced fresh dill
1 cup peeled, deseeded and grated cucumber (see note)
1 teaspoon white pepper
¹/₂ cup vegan mayonnaise
¹/₂ cup vegan sour cream or unflavored soy yogurt

In a medium-size mixing bowl, combine garlic and dill. Squeeze any liquid from cucumber. Add cucumber, pepper, mayonnaise, and sour cream or yogurt to bowl and mix well. Chill for at least 1 hour before serving.

Note: To deseed cucumber, cut cucumber in half, lengthwise, and scoop out seeds.

Total Calories Per Serving: 92   Total Fat as % of Daily Value: 12%   Protein: 1 gm   Fat: 8 gm
Carbohydrates: 4 gm   Calcium: 12 mg   Iron: 0 mg   Sodium: 111 mg   Dietary Fiber: 0 gm

Capanata

Makes about 2¹/₂ cups or 6 servings

Use capanata as a dip for vegetables, breads, and crackers or as an ingredient in soups and casseroles.

1¹/₂ pounds eggplant (about 3¹/₂ cups)
2 cloves garlic, minced
³/₄ cup onions, chopped
¹/₄ cup celery, minced
3 Tablespoons olive oil (divided)
2 cups tomato sauce
3 Tablespoons tomato paste
2 Tablespoons vinegar
¹/₄ cup raisins
1 Tablespoon sugar
¹/₂ cup each green olives, sliced and black olives, sliced

Cut eggplant (do not peel) into small chunks. Cover with a paper towel and set aside. Place garlic, onions, celery, and 1 Tablespoon oil in a 2-cup bowl. Microwave on HIGH for 5 minutes or until onions are tender. Set aside. Combine eggplant and 2 Tablespoons olive oil and toss to coat eggplant. Place eggplant mixture in a medium-size bowl and microwave on HIGH for 6 minutes or until eggplant is tender. Drain eggplant and discard liquid. Add sauce, paste, vinegar, raisins, and sugar and mix. Microwave, covered, on HIGH for 10 minutes or until mixture is very tender. Let stand, covered, for 5 minutes to cool. Mix in olives. Serve hot or cold.

Total Calories Per Serving: 212   Total Fat as % of Daily Value: 16%   Protein: 4 gm   Fat: 10 gm
Carbohydrates: 29 gm   Calcium: 58 mg   Iron: 2 mg   Sodium: 571 mg   Dietary Fiber: 6 gm

Baba Ghanouj (Garlic-Eggplant Dip)

Makes about 2 cups or 4 servings

This Middle Eastern dish can be used as a spread for sandwiches, a dip for veggies or chips, or as a topping for rice, pasta, couscous, or roasted or steamed veggies.

1¹/₄ pounds eggplant (1 large eggplant)
3 cloves garlic, minced
¹/₄ cup minced onion
3 Tablespoons each vegan mayonnaise and lemon juice
2 Tablespoons chopped green onions
1 Tablespoon sliced black olives (for garnish)

Wash eggplant and dry it well. Pierce in several places with a fork. Place the eggplant on a microwave-safe rack. Microwave on HIGH, calculating 5 minutes per pound of eggplant. A 1¹/₄-pound eggplant should microwave in 7 minutes. Halfway through cooking, turn the eggplant over. Allow eggplant to cook until it is very tender when pieced with a fork. You want the eggplant to cook into a pulp. Remember that the eggplant will continue to cook as it stands, so you don't want it to become extremely soft in the microwave.

Remove eggplant from microwave and cool for 10 minutes. When eggplant is cool, cut it in half and scoop out the pulp.

In a food processor canister or blender, place the eggplant pulp and the remaining ingredients (except the black olive garnish). Process mixture until smooth. This can also be done by hand, in a mixing bowl. Spread baba ghanouj on a serving plate and garnish with black olives.

Total Calories Per Serving: 114   Total Fat as % of Daily Value: 11%   Protein: 2 gm   Fat: 7 gm
Carbohydrates: 10 gm   Calcium: 22 mg   Iron: 5 mg   Sodium: 86 mg   Dietary Fiber: 5 gm

Spinach and Parsley Dip
Makes about 2 cups or 4 servings

This dip is often served in a hollowed out round loaf of sourdough bread.

One 10-ounce package frozen chopped spinach (about 1¹/₂ cups)
¹/₄ cup chopped onion
¹/₂ cup chopped fresh parsley
1 cup vegan sour cream or unflavored soy yogurt
1 teaspoon black pepper

Cut spinach package in several places with a knife or scissors. Place on a microwave-safe plate. Microwave on HIGH for 4 minutes or until completely thawed. Remove from microwave, unwrap, and allow spinach to cool. Squeeze extremely dry and discard liquid.

Place spinach, parsley, sour cream or soy yogurt, and pepper in a medium-size bowl and mix until well combined. If a very smooth texture is desired, you can mix this in a blender or food processor.

Allow dip to chill for at least 2 hours before serving.

Variation: Use 1 cup of silken tofu blended with 2 teaspoons lemon juice instead of sour cream/yogurt.

Total Calories Per Serving: 195   Total Fat as % of Daily Value: 16%   Protein: 4 gm   Fat: 10 gm
Carbohydrates: 22 gm   Calcium: 85 mg   Iron: 3 mg   Sodium: 381 mg   Dietary Fiber: 2 gm

Raspberry Vinaigrette
Serves 8

¹/₂ cup olive oil
1 cup fresh or frozen, thawed raspberries
¹/₂ cup red wine or apple cider vinegar
2 teaspoons apple juice concentrate

Place all ingredients in a blender. Process dressing until smooth. Serve immediately or store in the refrigerator until ready to serve.

Total Calories Per Serving: 133   Total Fat as % of Daily Value: 21%   Protein: 0 gm   Fat: 14 gm
Carbohydrates: 3 gm   Calcium: 5 mg   Iron: 0 mg   Sodium: 2 mg   Dietary Fiber: 1 gm

Three-Colored Herbed Peppers

Makes 4 servings as a side dish or dip. If puréed, makes about 1¹/₂ cups sauce.

You can serve this dish as a side dish, sauce, dip, or condiment.

2 teaspoons olive oil
1 medium, seeded and cut into thin slices red bell pepper (about ³/₄ cup)
1 medium, seeded and cut into thin slices orange or yellow bell pepper (about ³/₄ cup)
1 medium, seeded and cut into thin slices green bell pepper (about ³/₄ cup)
1 clove garlic, minced
1 Tablespoon balsamic vinegar or red sherry
1 Tablespoon minced fresh basil
1 teaspoon each dried oregano and dried sage
1 teaspoon black pepper

In a 2-quart bowl or casserole, toss oil, peppers, and garlic. Microwave on HIGH for 2 minutes or until peppers are just tender. Add remaining ingredients, cover, and microwave on HIGH for 1 minute. Stir to combine flavors and serve.

Notes: If a smooth sauce is desired, microwave the cooked peppers for an additional 1 minute 30 seconds. Place in a food processor or blender and process until puréed. Serve over warm cooked vegetables or pasta, or as a sauce for baked tofu or a seitan "steak." Serve cold as a dipping sauce for veggies, chips, or breadsticks or use as a salad dressing.

Total Calories Per Serving: 48   Total Fat as % of Daily Value: 4%   Protein: 1 gm   Fat: 3 gm
Carbohydrates: 7 gm   Calcium: 27 mg   Iron: 1 mg   Sodium: 2 mg   Dietary Fiber: 2 gm

Dried Fig and Olive Tapenade

Makes about 4 cups or 8 servings

2 cups dried, quartered figs (about 14 ounces)
3 cups water
3 cups pitted, chopped black olives
¹/₄ cup lemon juice
3 Tablespoons prepared mustard
3 cloves garlic, minced
2 teaspoons cracked black pepper
1 teaspoon ground oregano
¹/₂ cup olive oil

Place figs in a large pot and add water. Cover and bring to a fast boil. Immediately reduce to simmer. Allow figs to cook until they are very tender, about 30-40 minutes. Remove from stove, drain, reserving ¹/₄ cup fig liquid, and cool.

   Place figs, olives, juice, mustard, garlic, black pepper, and oregano in the canister of a food processor or in a blender. Process until a thick paste is formed. Slowly drizzle in oil while processing on low, until all the oil is added and mixture is well combined. Place in a glass or plastic bowl, cover, and refrigerate for at least 3 hours before serving.

Total Calories Per Serving: 292   Total Fat as % of Daily Value: 31%   Protein: 3 gm   Fat: 20 gm
Carbohydrates: 30 gm   Calcium: 131 mg   Iron: 3 mg   Sodium: 446 mg   Dietary Fiber: 6 gm

Melon and Mint Salsa

Makes about 2 cups of salsa

This sweet-but-hot salsa is a good accompaniment to savory entrées, as a sandwich filler, or as a salad dressing.

1 cup diced cantaloupe
³/₄ cup diced honeydew or Persian melon
1 cup diced watermelon
1 teaspoon minced and seeded chili (you choose the heat!)
1 teaspoon chopped fresh mint
1 Tablespoon fresh lemon or lime juice
1 Tablespoon orange juice

In a non-reactive bowl, combine all ingredients. Allow salsa to chill at least 30 minutes before serving.

Total Calories Per Salsa: 157   Total Fat as % of Daily Value: 2%   Protein: 3 gm   Fat: 1 gm
Carbohydrates: 39 gm   Calcium: 38 mg   Iron: 1 mg   Sodium: 51 mg   Dietary Fiber: 3 gm

Artichoke and Corn Salsa

Serves 8

6 large diced cooked or canned, drained artichoke hearts (about 3 cups)
1 cup fresh, uncooked corn (1 cup after being cut from the cob)
¹/₂ cup freshly roasted, chopped red bell pepper or canned, drained pimentos
¹/₂ cup diced onions or shallots
¹/₂ cup diced jicama or water chestnuts
3 Tablespoons diced fresh chilies (you choose the heat!)
¹/₄ cup chopped fresh cilantro
4 Tablespoons fresh lime juice
2 teaspoons black pepper

In a large non-reactive bowl, combine artichokes, corn, red pepper, and onions. Add remaining ingredients and mix well to combine. Refrigerate, covered, for at least 1 hour before serving.

Total Calories Per Serving: 88   Total Fat as % of Daily Value: 1%   Protein: 5 gm   Fat: <1 gm
Carbohydrates: 20 gm   Calcium: 62 mg   Iron: 2 mg   Sodium: 119 mg   Dietary Fiber: 8 gm

Olive and Carrot Salsa
Makes about 2 cups or 4 servings

1½ cups grated carrots
8 large, pitted and chopped green olives
4 large, pitted and chopped black olives
2 teaspoons chopped bell pepper
¼ cup olive oil
1 teaspoon cayenne powder
1 Tablespoon fresh lemon juice

In a non-reactive bowl, combine all ingredients. Allow salsa to chill at least 30 minutes before serving.

Total Calories Per Serving: 159   Total Fat as % of Daily Value: 24%   Protein: 1 gm   Fat: 15 gm
Carbohydrates: 6 gm   Calcium: 39 mg   Iron: 1 mg   Sodium: 253 mg   Dietary Fiber: 2 gm

Savory Summer Peach and Avocado Salsa
Serves 10

2 cups diced fresh, ripe, pitted peaches (not peeled)
2 cups diced fresh, ripe, pitted, peeled apricots
2 Tablespoons minced fresh chilies (you choose the heat!)
½ cup diced, peeled, ripe avocado
¼ cup diced fresh red bell pepper
1 Tablespoon minced red onion
2 Tablespoons chopped fresh cilantro
2 Tablespoons peach nectar or orange juice

In a non-reactive bowl, combine ingredients. Allow salsa to chill for at least 30 minutes before serving.

Total Calories Per Serving: 45   Total Fat as % of Daily Value: 2%   Protein: 1 gm   Fat: 1 gm
Carbohydrates: 8 gm   Calcium: 8 mg   Iron: 0 mg   Sodium: 1 mg   Dietary Fiber: 2 gm

Strawberry Gazpacho
Serves 6

This elegant strawberry gazpacho can be served as a cold first course as a refreshing soup or else be used as a dip for breadsticks or chips. Please note that it does require advanced preparation.

Soup:
4 cups hulled and crushed fresh strawberries (see note)
½ cup thinly sliced white onions
½ cup thinly sliced red peppers
¾ cup peeled, thinly sliced English cucumber
1 clove garlic, minced
¼ cup each Balsamic vinegar and olive oil
2 teaspoons freshly ground black pepper

Place all soup ingredients in a glass or plastic bowl, cover, and allow to stand, refrigerated, for at least 8 hours. Place in a blender and purée. Chill.

Garnish:
¹/₂ cup diced strawberries
3 Tablespoons minced fresh chives
¹/₄ cup diced red peppers
¹/₄ cup peeled and diced English cucumbers

Mix strawberries, chives, peppers, and cucumber in a small bowl. Place a small mound of garnish in the center of each soup or serving dish. Pour soup around garnish. Serve immediately.

Note: To prepare the strawberries, first remove the leaves and stems (that's the "hulling"). Then place strawberries in a large bowl and working with a knife and a fork mash and crush the strawberries into small pieces.

Total Calories Per Serving: 148   Total Fat as % of Daily Value: 15%   Protein: 2 gm   Fat: 10 gm
Carbohydrates: 16 gm   Calcium: 39 mg   Iron: 1 mg   Sodium: 3 mg   Dietary Fiber: 4 gm

Roasted Red Bell Pepper Coulis

Serves 5

2 red bell peppers (about 1 pound or 2¹/₂ cups)
Vegetable oil spray
2 Tablespoons sweet onions, such as Vidalia or Maui
1 cup vegetable broth
1 teaspoon dry thyme
1 teaspoon black pepper

Roast bell pepper over a stove's gas burner or a barbecue. If these are not available, prick peppers in several places, place on a baking sheet and roast at 450 degrees for about 5-8 minutes or until skin has turned black.

Place roasted peppers in a bowl and cover for 2-3 minutes. Peel, seed, and coarsely chop pepper. Spray a large skillet with oil. Add onions and cook until very soft, about 2 minutes. Add pepper, stir, and cook for 2 minutes. Add broth, thyme, and black pepper, then stir and cook for 5 minutes. Pour sauce into a blender or food processor canister and process until smooth. Return to stove and allow sauce to simmer for 5 minutes. Serve warm.

Total Calories Per Serving: 31   Total Fat as % of Daily Value: 0%   Protein: 1 gm   Fat: 0 gm
Carbohydrates: 7 gm   Calcium: 14 mg   Iron: 1 mg   Sodium: 158 mg   Dietary Fiber: 2 gm

BBQ Sauce
Makes about 4 cups or 32 servings of 2 Tablespoons

1¹/₂ cups applesauce
¹/₂ cup canned tomato sauce or ketchup
1 cup sugar
¹/₄ cup maple syrup
¹/₄ cup lemon juice
1 teaspoon black pepper
¹/₂ teaspoon paprika
1 teaspoon garlic powder
¹/₈ teaspoon clove powder

Combine all ingredients in a medium-size pot or microwave-safe bowl. Stir to combine. Simmer on stove, stirring occasionally, for 10 minutes or until slightly thickened or microwave on HIGH, stirring once, for 5 minutes or until slightly thickened.

Total Calories Per Serving: 38   Total Fat as % of Daily Value: 0%   Protein: 0 gm   Fat: 0 gm
Carbohydrates: 10 gm   Calcium: 3 mg   Iron: 0 mg   Sodium: 21 mg   Dietary Fiber: 0 gm

Layered Spanish-Style Dip
Makes about 25 portions

Layered dips look attractive on a buffet table. They can be made 1-2 days ahead of time, actually acquiring more flavor. Assemble Mediterranean layered dips with tomatoes, pesto, vegan mozzarella cheese, and roasted peppers or Indian style with dahl (lentil dip), raita (plain soy yogurt flavored with cucumber and onion), cold curried garbanzos, and shredded carrots.

2 pounds (about 4 cups) canned bean dip or cold mashed and seasoned beans
1 pound (about 2 cups) guacamole or avocado pulp mixed with lemon juice and
**   chopped cilantro**
2¹/₂ cups vegan sour cream or plain soy yogurt
1 cup vegan mayonnaise
4 Tablespoons taco seasoning (or 1 Tablespoon each black pepper, cumin, chili
**   powder, and oregano)**
1¹/₂ pounds chopped fresh tomatoes (about 3 cups)
¹/₂ cup chopped green onions
1 pound sliced black olives (about 2 cups)
1 cup shredded vegan mozzarella cheese

Spread ¹/₃ of bean dip in the bottom of a round glass buffet dish able to hold at least 4 quarts. Layer ¹/₃ of guacamole over beans. Combine sour cream, mayonnaise, and taco mix and layer ¹/₃ over guacamole. Create a layer of tomatoes, onions, olives, and cheese over the sour cream. Repeat steps two more times. Chill for at least 2 hours before serving.

Total Calories Per Serving: 263   Total Fat as % of Daily Value: 19%   Protein: 9 gm   Fat: 12 gm
Carbohydrates: 29 gm   Calcium: 125 mg   Iron: 3 mg   Sodium: 370 mg   Dietary Fiber: 8 gm

Very Fast, Very Good Dipping Sauce

Serves 10-12

1¹/₂ cups tomato sauce
1 clove garlic, minced
2 teaspoons red pepper flakes

Combine all ingredients in a non-reactive (plastic or glass) container. Stir well to combine. Cover and refrigerate for 20 minutes before serving.

Total Calories Per Serving: 13   Total Fat as % of Daily Value: 0%   Protein: 1 gm   Fat: 0 gm
Carbohydrates: 3 gm   Calcium: 6 mg   Iron: 1 mg   Sodium: 193 mg   Dietary Fiber: 1 gm

Jalapeño and Garlic Salsa

Serves 10-12

3 cloves garlic, chopped
¹/₂ cup chopped onions
2 fresh or canned jalapeño chilies, deseeded and chopped
3¹/₂ cups canned chopped tomatoes, drained
1 Tablespoon fresh lime juice

Combine all ingredients in a non-reactive bowl. Stir well to combine. Chill for at least 30 minutes before serving.

Note: If jalapeños are too hot for your taste, instead use ¹/₄ cup chopped green bell peppers or other mild chilies.

Total Calories Per Serving: 20   Total Fat as % of Daily Value: 0%   Protein: 1 gm   Fat: 0 gm
Carbohydrates: 4 gm   Calcium: 11 mg   Iron: 0 mg   Sodium: 4 mg   Dietary Fiber: 1 gm

Fast Veggie Dip

Serves 4-6

12-ounces silken tofu (about 1¹/₂ cups)
2 Tablespoons dry onion soup or vegetable soup mix
2 teaspoons garlic powder
3 Tablespoons soymilk (optional)

Place all ingredients in a blender and process until smooth. If you would like a thicker dip, omit soymilk. If you would like a salad dressing or a thinner dip, add soymilk. Refrigerate for at least 1 hour before serving.

Total Calories Per Serving: 66   Total Fat as % of Daily Value: 5%   Protein: 6 gm   Fat: 3 gm
Carbohydrates: 5 gm   Calcium: 103 mg   Iron: 1 mg   Sodium: 316 mg   Dietary Fiber: 1 gm

Baked Pizza Dip
Serves 8-10

1 cup vegan cream cheese
1 Tablespoon dry Italian seasoning spice blend (or ½ teaspoon each: garlic powder, oregano, black pepper, and dry basil)
2 cups shredded vegan mozzarella cheese
3 cups tomato sauce (pizza sauce, if you've got it)

Preheat oven to 350 degrees. In a large bowl, whip vegan cream cheese and seasoning with a fork until blended cream cheese is soft. Spread half the cream cheese mixture on the bottom of an oven-proof pie plate or round, 8-inch oven-proof dish. Top with 1 cup vegan cheese. Then top with sauce and remaining cream cheese mixture. Repeat until all ingredients are used. Cover and bake for 15 minutes or until cheese is melted. Serve with fresh or baked veggie chips, breadsticks, or pieces of crusty bread.

Total Calories Per Serving: 127   Total Fat as % of Daily Value: 11%   Protein: 1 gm   Fat: 7 gm
Carbohydrates: 12 gm   Calcium: 163 mg   Iron: 1 mg   Sodium: 752 mg   Dietary Fiber: 1 gm

Fast and Lean Bean Dip
Makes about 3 cups or 6 servings

2 cups canned, drained beans (kidney or Great Northern work well)
1 cup salsa (you pick the heat!)
1 teaspoon garlic powder

Place beans in a bowl and mash with a fork. Stir in salsa and garlic powder. Mix until well combined. Serve immediately or chill until ready to serve.

Total Calories Per Serving: 77   Total Fat as % of Daily Value: 1%   Protein: 5 gm   Fat: 1 gm
Carbohydrates: 14 gm   Calcium: 32 mg   Iron: 1 mg   Sodium: 339 mg   Dietary Fiber: 4 gm

Lentil Dip
Serves 6

1½ cups cooked or canned, drained lentils (start with ½ cup dry lentils if cooking from scratch)
1 Tablespoon tomato purée
½ cup minced fresh onion
1 teaspoon hot sauce

Place all ingredients in a blender and process until just smooth. Pour into a glass or plastic bowl, cover, and allow dip to chill for at least 1 hour before serving.

Total Calories Per Serving: 64   Total Fat as % of Daily Value: 0%   Protein: 5 gm   Fat: 0 gm
Carbohydrates: 12 gm   Calcium: 13 mg   Iron: 2 mg   Sodium: 32 mg   Dietary Fiber: 4 gm

Black Bean Hummus

Serves 6-8

2 cups cooked, or canned, drained black beans
1 clove garlic, minced
2 Tablespoons tahini (sesame paste)
2 Tablespoons minced fresh parsley
2 teaspoons lemon juice

Place beans and garlic in a blender and process until just smooth. Add tahini and process until combined. Add remaining ingredients and process until just smooth. Place in a glass or plastic bowl and chill for at least 1 hour before serving.

Total Calories Per Serving: 110   Total Fat as % of Daily Value: 4%   Protein: 6 gm   Fat: 3 gm
Carbohydrates: 17 gm   Calcium: 58 mg   Iron: 2 mg   Sodium: 152 mg   Dietary Fiber: 4 gm

Sun-Dried Tomato Dip

Makes about 1 cup

½ cup sun-dried tomatoes
2 cloves garlic, minced
2 Tablespoons minced fresh basil
1 teaspoon hot sauce

Place tomatoes in a glass or plastic bowl, cover with cold water, and allow them to soak for at least 1 hour to soften and reconstitute. Place tomatoes in the canister of a food processor or in a blender. Process until smooth. Slowly add remaining ingredients and process until smooth. Serve immediately or chill until ready to use.

Total Calories Per Serving: 81   Total Fat as % of Daily Value: 1%   Protein: 4 gm   Fat: 1 gm
Carbohydrates: 17 gm   Calcium: 49 mg   Iron: 3 mg   Sodium: 691 mg   Dietary Fiber: 4 gm

Green Onion, Cashew, and Tofu Dip

Makes approximately 3 cups or 6 servings

2 cups silken tofu
¼ cup minced cashews
1 teaspoon each soymilk and soy sauce
1 Tablespoon nutritional yeast
¾ cup minced green onions

Place all ingredients, except green onions, in the canister of a food processor or blender. Process until smooth and combined. Add onions and process just until onions are combined (do not purée). Place in a glass or plastic bowl and refrigerate for at least 1 hour before serving.

Total Calories Per Serving: 98   Total Fat as % of Daily Value: 9%   Protein: 7 gm   Fat: 6 gm
Carbohydrates: 6 gm   Calcium: 101 mg   Iron: 1 mg   Sodium: 67 mg   Dietary Fiber: 1 gm

Black-Eyed Pea "Caviar"

Makes approximately 3¹/₂ cups or 7 servings

3 cups cooked, or canned, drained black-eyed peas
¹/₂ cup Italian salad dressing (oil and vinegar dressing with Italian spices)
3 cloves garlic, minced
2 Tablespoons canned, drained, minced jalapeños
2 Tablespoons canned, drained, minced pimentos
¹/₂ cup minced yellow or red bell pepper
¹/₄ cup minced green onion

Combine black-eyed peas and dressing in glass or plastic bowl. Add remaining ingredients and toss until well mixed. Cover and allow dish to chill for at least 1 hour before serving.

Total Calories Per Serving: 142	Total Fat as % of Daily Value: 8%	Protein: 6 gm	Fat: 5 gm
Carbohydrates: 19 gm	Calcium: 24 mg	Iron: 2 mg	Sodium: 495 mg	Dietary Fiber: 5 gm

Fast Garbanzo Spread

Makes approximately 2 cups or 4 servings

This makes a savory spread, but is a bit flaky.

1¹/₂ cups cooked or canned, drained garbanzo beans
1 clove garlic, minced
3 Tablespoons vegan mayonnaise (or just enough to moisten)
2 Tablespoons each minced onions and minced green bell peppers
1 Tablespoon minced red radish
1 Tablespoon minced carrots

Place garbanzo beans and garlic in a blender and blend until just smooth. Transfer into a glass or plastic bowl and mix in just enough mayonnaise to moisten. Add in vegetables and stir to combine. Cover and refrigerate for at least 1 hour before serving.

Total Calories Per Serving: 180	Total Fat as % of Daily Value: 8%	Protein: 5 gm	Fat: 12 gm
Carbohydrates: 22 gm	Calcium: 33 mg	Iron: 1 mg	Sodium: 335 mg	Dietary Fiber: 4 gm

Spicy Tempeh Spread

Serves 6

8 ounces tempeh (about 1 cup)
1 Tablespoon tomato purée
1 teaspoon chili powder
1 Tablespoon minced onions
2 teaspoons soy sauce
1 teaspoon each garlic powder and red pepper flakes
¹/₂ teaspoon ground cumin

Steam or microwave tempeh for 12 minutes or until soft. Allow to cool. Chop tempeh and place in the canister of a food processor. Add tomato purée and process until just smooth. Add remaining ingredients, process until ingredients combined. Transfer into a glass or plastic bowl, cover, and allow spread to chill for at least 30 minutes before serving.

Total Calories Per Serving: 79   Total Fat as % of Daily Value: 6%   Protein: 7 gm   Fat: 4 gm
Carbohydrates: 5 gm   Calcium: 46 mg   Iron: 1 mg   Sodium: 132 mg   Dietary Fiber: 0 gm

Teriyaki Sauce
Makes approximately 1 cup

May be used as a marinade for vegetables or veggie burgers, or as a basting liquid for grilling or roasting vegan "meats" or potatoes, or as an ingredient in salad dressings, soups, or sauces.

½ cup soy sauce
½ cup water
2 Tablespoons minced fresh ginger
2 cloves garlic, minced
¼ cup brown sugar

In a glass or plastic bowl whisk together all ingredients. Allow sauce to chill for at least 30 minutes before using.

Total Calories Per Sauce: 213   Total Fat as % of Daily Value: 0%   Protein: 4 gm   Fat: 0 gm
Carbohydrates: 51 gm   Calcium: 51 mg   Iron: 3 mg   Sodium: 8,209 mg   Dietary Fiber: 1 gm

Spinach and Basil Sauce
Makes approximately 1½ cups or 6 servings

3 cups washed, trimmed spinach leaves
1½ cups washed, fresh basil leaves
¾ cup washed, fresh Italian flat-leaf parsley
½ cup olive oil
2 Tablespoons water
1 Tablespoon nutritional yeast
1 clove garlic, minced

Place all ingredients in the canister of a food processor or blender and purée until smooth. If mixture is too thick, add additional water, by Tablespoonfuls. If mixture is too thin, allow it to chill for 30-40 minutes to "tighten."

Total Calories Per Serving: 174   Total Fat as % of Daily Value: 28%   Protein: 2 gm   Fat: 18 gm
Carbohydrates: 2 gm   Calcium: 43 mg   Iron: 1 mg   Sodium: 17 mg   Dietary Fiber: 1 gm

Creamy Hot "Cheese" Sauce

Makes approximately 1½ cups or 6 servings

½ cup nutritional yeast
3 Tablespoons unbleached flour
4 teaspoons cornstarch
½ teaspoon mustard powder
½ teaspoon garlic powder
1½ cups soymilk
1 Tablespoon vegetable oil

Place yeast, flour, cornstarch, mustard, and garlic powder in a small pot and stir together. Slowly add soymilk and oil, whisking over low heat until very smooth. You must whisk constantly to avoid lumps. Cook and whisk until sauce is desired consistency.

Total Calories Per Serving: 116   Total Fat as % of Daily Value: 6%   Protein: 9 gm   Fat: 4 gm
Carbohydrates: 13 gm   Calcium: 33 mg   Iron: 1 mg   Sodium: 37 mg   Dietary Fiber: 4 gm

Ketchup from Scratch

Makes approximately 2 cups or 16 servings of 2 Tablespoons

Vegetable oil spray
½ cup diced onion
1 Tablespoon minced garlic
1 Tablespoon olive oil
1½ pounds seeded, chopped fresh Roma (plum) tomatoes (about 3½ cups)
⅓ cup cider vinegar
¼ cup sugar
1 bay leaf
⅛ teaspoon cinnamon
¼ teaspoon cayenne

Spray a large skillet with oil, heat, and sauté the onion and garlic for 1 minute. Add olive oil and cook 1 more minute. Add the tomatoes and cook for an additional 5 minutes. Add remaining ingredients, reduce heat, cover, and simmer for 10 minutes, stirring occasionally. Remove and discard bay leaf.

Pour mixture into the canister of a food processor or blender and purée ketchup until smooth. If mixture is thinner than desired, return to skillet and allow ketchup to cook until desired thickness is obtained. Store in the refrigerator up to 1 week, covered in airtight glass or plastic containers.

Total Calories Per Serving: 32   Total Fat as % of Daily Value: 1%   Protein: 1 gm   Fat: 1 gm
Carbohydrates: 6 gm   Calcium: 6 mg   Iron: 0 mg   Sodium: 3 mg   Dietary Fiber: 1 gm

Corn Relish

Makes approximately 1 quart

2¹/₂ cups cut corn
²/₃ cup diced celery
²/₃ cup diced onion
²/₃ cup apple juice
²/₃ cup apple cider vinegar
2 Tablespoons diced, seeded fresh jalapeño
2 teaspoons mustard powder
2 teaspoons onion powder
¹/₂ teaspoon black pepper
²/₃ cup diced green bell pepper
²/₃ cup diced red bell pepper
²/₃ cup diced yellow or orange bell pepper

Combine all ingredients in a large pot and cook, simmering and stirring, for 15 minutes or until peppers are soft. Cool and store in airtight containers in the refrigerator.

Total Calories Per Serving: 623	Total Fat as % of Daily Value: 12%		Protein: 19 gm	Fat: 8 gm
Carbohydrates: 131 gm	Calcium: 165 mg	Iron: 6 mg	Sodium: 422 mg	Dietary Fiber: 21 gm

Aioli (Garlic Mayonnaise)

Makes ¹/₂ cup or four 2 Tablespoons servings

This is a very rich sauce/sandwich spread/dip; use it sparingly for a deep flavor. Also can be used as a coating for grilling vegetables, tofu, seitan, potatoes, or tempeh.

¹/₄ cup vegan mayonnaise
1 large clove garlic, chopped
1 teaspoon lemon juice
1 Tablespoon green onion
1 teaspoon white pepper
1 Tablespoon chopped fresh parsley

Place mayonnaise, garlic, lemon juice, and green onion in a blender and process until well blended. Transfer to small glass or plastic bowl and stir in pepper and parsley. Cover and refrigerate for at least 1 hour before serving.

Total Calories Per Serving: 95	Total Fat as % of Daily Value: 14%		Protein: 0 gm	Fat: 9 gm
Carbohydrates: 1 gm	Calcium: 5 mg	Iron: 0 mg	Sodium: 86 mg	Dietary Fiber: 0 gm

Chapter 15: SALADS AND DRESSINGS

The salad course of the meal, whether it is an entrée, accompaniment, appetizer, or a dessert can fit into an exciting vegan party menu. In season, green salads are great refreshers and look pretty on the plate. Out of season, they can be costly and may not be at the peak of attractiveness.

Frozen, canned, and dried products can be very forgiving. They are available in the same high quality year round and will retain their color, shape, and texture while being held and transported. Frozen vegetables can be crisped and hold their color well. Fruit frozen without sugar and unsweetened fruit juice concentrates, dried fruit, and fruit canned with juice or water would be appropriate and useful as vegan salad ingredients. Canned vegetables may be softer than fresh or frozen vegetables, adding more interest to the texture of the salad.

Salads from the pantry are a snap. We especially like green beans, wax beans, and beets as starter ingredients. How about lowfat sweet and sour green beans, wax beans, or beets made with a cornstarch, vinegar, orange juice concentrate, and soy sauce dressing? Prepare this dish hot and let it chill as a cold salad before serving.

Green beans tossed with a small amount of chopped vegan "ham" or smoked tofu and tossed with canned mushrooms and silken tofu or plain (unflavored) vegan yogurt is a soft, creamy, savory salad. Try the same salad with green beans, carrots, and chopped parsley and a vegan ranch dressing for a different color and flavor.

Vegan yogurt, vegan sour cream, or silken tofu can be tossed with sliced canned carrots or cooked, chilled frozen carrots and canned garbanzos or kidney beans, a little dill, some vinegar, and some chopped onions to create a salad. For a softer texture, finely chop the carrots and partially purée the garbanzo beans. You can completely purée this salad to make a cold dip for veggies and breadsticks. It will resemble Middle Eastern hummus.

Continuing in the pantry, how about a corn salad? This can be served as both a cold side dish or used as a cold condiment instead of high fat gravies or sauces. Combine canned (or frozen, cooked, and chilled) cut corn with canned sliced pimentos, chopped parsley, green onions, and bell peppers then toss with vinaigrette.

We love the idea of "Texas Caviar," also known as a cold black-eyed pea salad. Canned black-eyed peas are drained and rinsed and tossed with chopped onion and green bell pepper and barely dressed with oil and vinegar dressing. Prepare this with freshly cooked, frozen, thawed, or canned black-eyed peas.

Canned peas (or frozen, cooked, and chilled peas) can be tossed with soy vegan yogurt or vegan sour cream, garlic powder, and canned water chestnuts to make a smooth and crunchy salad. Use the yogurt or sour cream with a four or five bean salad instead of the traditional oil and vinegar. Choose from cut green beans, wax beans, green peas, lima beans, kidney beans, white beans, red beans, and garbanzo beans or black beans to create pantry bean salads. For a smoother texture, this type of salad can be partially puréed. Actually, you could totally purée this salad and use it as a lowfat dip for vege-tables or breadsticks.

Perfectly prepared pasta salad is easy. One pound (a 16-ounce package) of dried pasta requires a gallon (4 quarts) of boiling water. Cook pasta only until just tender. Drain, and rather than rinsing, spread pasta out on a serving platter or baking sheet to dry. One pound of dried pasta should yield about 3 pounds of cooked pasta. For every pound of uncooked pasta, plan on two pounds of salad fixings, such as chopped vegetables or fruit, nuts, crumbled tofu, cooked beans, sesame seeds, etc. Mix in fixings, add onions and herbs, as desired, toss in dressing, and you've got a picture-perfect pasta salad. Ideas for pasta salad fixings include: canned artichoke hearts, frozen or fresh asparagus spears, mushrooms, cucumbers, avocados, tomatoes, pea pods, green peas, wax or green beans, cooked kidney, black soy, black-eyed peas or white beans, zucchini, carrots, roasted eggplant or fennel, celery, caper, pickles, olives, almonds, walnuts, pecans, or pistachios.

Remember that avocados and fruit are your friends for salads. Mash avocado and season with onion and garlic powder (rather than chopped fresh onions and garlic) and a small amount of chopped canned tomatoes. If fresh avocado is too much of a hassle, purchase frozen avocado pulp. You can pack this into a loaf pan and make an avocado "pate," served sliced over fresh or steamed, chilled green spinach.

Canned peaches, pears, plums, and apricots can be finely chopped and tossed with vegan fruit-flavored yogurt, seasoned with cinnamon, ginger, or nutmeg for a sweet salad or light dessert. Spoon this over frozen melon balls and frozen berries.

Peeled and seeded cucumber can be finely chopped, tossed with yogurt, onion powder, lemon juice, and black pepper for a smooth salad. Mix with chopped canned tomatoes for extra color. Use vegetable juice cocktail combined with unflavored soy yogurt and freshly chopped herbs to make a creamy tomato dressing with lots of pizzazz.

Pasta, macaroni, and potato salads can be made vegan. Cook the pasta a bit past al dente and the potatoes until they are fork-tender. Toss pasta or potatoes with minced canned carrots and canned mild salsa for a fast and flavorful salad. Experiment with different shapes and types of pasta. Ditilini, small shells, penne, rotini, farfalle (bowties), and orzo are interesting, small shapes. Search for spinach-, carrot-, or tomato-flavored pasta. How about a sweet potato salad? Drain and rinse canned sweet potatoes and cut into uniform small pieces. Create a dressing by mincing canned pineapple and peaches and mixing with strawberry soy yogurt, vegan sour cream mixed with fruit preserves, or silken tofu blended with fruit juice.

Think about stuffing a salad. Use a scooped out tomato, onion, pepper, or small zucchini as a carrier for bean, pasta, rice, and potato salad. Instead of mayonnaise, try plain soy yogurt, vegan sour cream, or silken tofu blended with a small amount of lemon juice, chopped onions, and white pepper. Peach halves and pineapple rings can be stuffed with fruit-flavored soy yogurt, sweetened tofu, or firm tofu tossed with fruit juice and chopped frozen (thawed) strawberries or chopped canned peaches or apricots.

To maintain salad interest, offer unusual combinations, like a strawberry and spinach salad. Combine fresh baby spinach with sliced fresh or frozen unsweetened strawberries and toss with oil and vinegar flavored with ginger and lemon juice. Add teriyaki tofu or seitan pieces to a canned pear Waldorf salad. Replace the traditional apples and celery with canned pears and canned or frozen petite pois (baby peas). Toss frozen, cooked and chilled yellow squash and zucchini together with a soy yogurt, vegan sour cream, or silken tofu dressing flavored with chopped fresh parsley for a springtime, lightly flavored combination.

For dressings, use reserved liquid from drained fruit to thin mayonnaise-based dressings; this will cut down on the calories from fat, while replacing some of the flavor. Purchase vegan mayonnaise or prepare your own with silken tofu, lemon juice, dry mustard, and black pepper. Oil, vinegar, sugar, soy sauce, and prepared mustard all make good marinades for fresh or canned veggies.

Dress Up That Green Salad

Green salads are cool, crisp, and receptive to change! Build a basic salad with head and leaf lettuce, baby greens, endive, radicchio, and cabbage, and then go beyond.

As an Entrée, add:
- Cold black, white, kidney, lentil, and red beans
- Smoked, barbecued, baked, or grilled tofu
- Sliced vegan deli meats
- Grilled eggplant
- Bean and salsa combinations
- Hummus and olive combinations
- Grilled or marinated mushrooms
- Cold vegan ravioli, tortellini, and gnocchi
- Chopped walnuts, pistachios, pine nuts, and cashews
- Cold lentils tossed with mushrooms and tomatoes

As a Side Dish, add:
- Green and wax beans
- Cut corn
- Chopped onions, radishes, tomatoes, garlic, and olives
- Shredded carrots, beets, zucchini, and crookneck squash
- Chopped pickled vegetables
- Sliced marinated or fresh mushrooms
- Chopped nuts and seeds, such as walnuts, peanuts, cashews, and pumpkin or sesame seeds

Salad Artistry

A professional chef will tell you that every salad should be composed of four parts:

- underliner: Romaine lettuce, kale, or lettuce leaves, hollowed tomatoes, zucchini, or melons, tortilla shells, or shredded red cabbage are examples of salad underliners. Underliners add color to salads, as well as form an edible base.

- main ingredient: Chopped baby greens, marinated, diced tofu, cubed seasonal fresh fruit, diced, cooked potatoes, or shredded green cabbage are examples of a salad main ingredients. This is the first component of a salad on which you should decide, so you can plan a salad that has a pleasing texture, flavor, and color.

- dressing: Dressings can be tossed with salad ingredients, pooled on a serving plate under the salad, spooned on top, or served on the side. Hot or cold, dressings should complement all the salad components.

- garnish: The "cherry on top," adding color, complementing or adding to the flavor and texture, garnishes should be planned with seasonality and convenience in mind.

You may not be able to plan for every salad to have all four components. The salad moral here is offer your guests salads that are pleasing to the eye and interesting to the palate. Salads can be hot or cold, light or hearty, delicate or substantial, refreshing or filling. You make the call, depending on the menu for your event and availability of seasonal ingredients.

Vegetarian salads can start with cold rice, pasta, and grains (such as barley or kasha). Toss cold rice or pasta with chopped olives, celery, green onions, tomatoes, minced carrot, and garbanzo or black beans. Top with chopped nuts (think pine nuts, almonds, and pumpkin seeds), croutons, and shredded herbs (think basil, oregano, and rosemary) and then dress with oil and vinegar or a tomato and herb dressing. Firm tofu can be marinated overnight in Italian dressing, grilled, and served hot or cold. For a fat-free marinade try a combination of vinegar, lemon juice, ground oregano, cracked pepper, minced garlic, and chopped mushrooms.

Couscous can be served cold, tossed with basil, chopped mushrooms, and tomatoes or with chopped green, red, and yellow peppers, minced garlic, and onions. Try a sweet, cold couscous, tossing it with fresh blueberries, shredded fresh mint, and pine nuts. These combinations also work well with cold, cooked barley and with small pasta, such as orzo or pastina.

Utilize extra portions of cold spaghetti, pasta sauce, black olives, sliced mushrooms, oregano, and chopped canned tomatoes. Pair with a green salad and sliced baguette. Cold vegetarian tortellini or ravioli work well with this combination, too.

Depending on your menu plans, you may create a "composed" salad. That is a salad that has all the ingredients combined together. Or you may want to create a salad "buffet," lining up ingredients separately so guests can create their own salad. Create-your-own salads work especially well if any of your guests have food allergies, special preferences, or are watching their calorie, fat, or salt intake.

You may want to create salads from fresh, seasonal ingredients, a combination of fresh, frozen, canned, or dried ingredients, or convenience ingredients. Convenience salad ingredients can include bottled salad dressing or salad dressing mixes and precut fresh fruits and vegetables.

If you need to cut down the time you spend preparing salads, you may want to purchase precut green or fruit salad from grocery salad bars, adding some of your own ingredients for texture or crunch. Or you may want to try some of the "bagged" salads, which save you the trouble of purchasing and cutting many types of fresh vegetables or fruit.

When you plan your salads, think of mixing up textures, flavors, and colors. For example, you may want to add some pumpkin seeds (for crunch) and shredded red cabbage (for color) to a fresh mixed green salad. Fruit salad should include soft and crunchy ingredients, such as sliced, ripe bananas and crisp grapes.

Salad dressings should be used sparingly, just to moisten salads. Your salad ingredients should be the stars, not the dressing. Salad dressings add flavor, but they can also contribute extra fat and salt or cause the salad to lose its texture. You can prepare salad dressings a day or two ahead of time and store them in the refrigerator until needed. This allows the flavors to "marry" and saves you time the day of the event. Beyond salads, you may be able to use some of your salad dressings as marinades for grilled or roasted items, or as cold sauces for entrées.

Don't be afraid to mix fruits and vegetables in the same salad. Think tangerine or pink grapefruit sections in spinach salad, grapes or pineapple in coleslaw, or finely shredded Romaine in fresh fruit salad.

Some salads are meant to be served cool and crisp, such as green salads or coleslaw. Some salads can handle warm dressings, such as a cold spinach salad with a hot walnut dressing. And some salads can be served entirely warm, such as a German potato salad. To keep salads cold, fill a bowl bigger than your salad bowl about half way with crushed ice. Set the salad bowl into the ice bowl, checking occasionally to replenish ice if necessary.

Make your salad do double duty. Finely chopped savory salads can be used as part of a sandwich filling or as a bed for hot or cold entrées. Fresh fruit salads can serve as appetizers, side dishes for entrées, and as dessert.

SALAD DRESSING RECIPES

Mustard Basil Vinaigrette

Makes approximately 1 cup or eight 2 Tablespoons servings

⅓ cup minced onion
¼ cup cider vinegar
3 Tablespoons Dijon or spicy, prepared mustard
1 Tablespoon minced garlic
1 teaspoon freshly ground black pepper
½ cup olive oil
¼ cup vegetable broth
⅓ cup chopped fresh basil
2 Tablespoons chopped fresh parsley

In a small glass or plastic bowl, place the onion, vinegar, mustard, garlic, and pepper, and whisk well to combine. Slowly drizzle in the olive oil and broth, while whisking constantly, to form a smooth mixture. Add the basil and parsley and whisk well to combine. Store in an airtight container in the refrigerator.

Total Calories Per Serving: 138	Total Fat as % of Daily Value: 21%	Protein: 1 gm	Fat: 14 gm
Carbohydrates: 2 gm	Calcium: 26 mg	Iron: 1 mg	Sodium: 90 mg	Dietary Fiber: 1 gm

Citrus Walnut Vinaigrette

Makes approximately 1½ cups or twelve 2 Tablespoons servings

1 cup orange juice
2 teaspoons fresh orange zest
½ cup apple cider vinegar
⅓ cup minced onions
3 Tablespoons apple juice
1 Tablespoon minced fresh ginger
1 teaspoon black pepper
½ cup walnut oil (or ½ cup vegetable oil with 2 teaspoons minced walnuts)

Place orange juice, zest, and vinegar in the canister of a blender or food processor. Add the onions, juice, ginger, and pepper and process for 1 minute to combine. While the machine is running, slowly drizzle in the walnut oil and process for 1 minute. Store dressing in a glass or plastic airtight container in the refrigerator.

Total Calories Per Serving: 97	Total Fat as % of Daily Value: 14%	Protein: 0 gm	Fat: 9 gm
Carbohydrates: 3 gm	Calcium: 5 mg	Iron: 0 mg	Sodium: 1 mg	Dietary Fiber: 0 gm

Old-Fashioned Cooked Salad Dressing

Makes approximately 2 cups or sixteen 2 Tablespoons servings

This is a lowfat dressing!

1 cup vegetable stock
2 teaspoons cornstarch
¹/₂ cup sugar
¹/₃ cup minced onion
1 teaspoon mustard powder
¹/₄ cup vinegar
2 Tablespoons lemon juice
2 teaspoons celery seed

In a small pot, whisk together water and cornstarch and cook over low heat until thickened and clear. Remove from the heat and set aside to cool slightly.

In a blender or food processor canister, place the sugar, onion, and mustard powder and process for 10 seconds. Add the vinegar and lemon juice and process for 1 minute or until smooth. Add the water-cornstarch mixture and celery seed and process for a few seconds to incorporate. Transfer to an airtight container and store in the refrigerator for up to 2 weeks. If the dressing separates, stir before serving.

Total Calories Per Serving: 31   Total Fat as % of Daily Value: 0%   Protein: 0 gm   Fat: 0 gm
Carbohydrates: 8 gm   Calcium: 7 mg   Iron: 0 mg   Sodium: 50 mg   Dietary Fiber: 0 gm

Amino and Herb Salad Dressing

Makes approximately ³/₄ cup or six 2 Tablespoons servings

¹/₈ cup Bragg's Liquid Aminos™ or soy sauce
1 teaspoon Dijon or spicy prepared mustard
¹/₄ cup balsamic vinegar
3 cloves garlic, minced
1 teaspoon black pepper
1 Tablespoon minced fresh basil
1 Tablespoon minced fresh oregano
1 Tablespoon minced fresh parsley
¹/₂ cup olive oil

Place all ingredients in a bottle or covered bowl and shake or whisk to combine well. Cover and refrigerate for at least 30 minutes before serving. Stir or shake before serving.

Total Calories Per Serving: 168   Total Fat as % of Daily Value: 28%   Protein: 0 gm   Fat: 18 gm
Carbohydrates: 2 gm   Calcium: 22 mg   Iron: 1 mg   Sodium: 352 mg   Dietary Fiber: 1 gm

Ranch Dressing
Serves 10-12

2 cups vegan mayonnaise
1 Tablespoon minced garlic
2 teaspoons minced green onion
1 Tablespoon each chopped fresh flat-leaf parsley and chopped fresh basil
1 Tablespoon drained capers
½ cup plain soymilk
1½ teaspoons lemon juice
1 teaspoon ground black pepper

In a food processor or blender, place mayonnaise, garlic, green onion, parsley, basil, and capers. Process mixture until smooth. With the machine on slow, slowly pour in soymilk, lemon juice, and pepper. Store dressing in an airtight container in the refrigerator.

Total Calories Per Serving: 298   Total Fat as % of Daily Value: 45%   Protein: 1 gm   Fat: 29 gm
Carbohydrates: 2 gm   Calcium: 19 mg   Iron: 0 mg   Sodium: 305 mg   Dietary Fiber: 0 gm

Caesar Salad Dressing
Makes approximately 1 cup or eight 2 Tablespoons servings

½ cup lemon juice
2 cloves garlic, minced
1 Tablespoon nutritional yeast
1 teaspoon black pepper
½ cup olive oil

Place all ingredients in a blender or food processor canister. Process until well combined. Store dressing in an airtight container in the refrigerator. Stir before serving.

Total Calories Per Serving: 128   Total Fat as % of Daily Value: 21%   Protein: 1 gm   Fat: 14 gm
Carbohydrates: 2 gm   Calcium: 5 mg   Iron: 0 mg   Sodium: 4 mg   Dietary Fiber: 0 gm

Basic Tofu Salad Dressing
Makes approximately 2 cups or sixteen 2 Tablespoons servings

Use this as a "creamy" salad dressing.

1½ cups silken or soft tofu
3 Tablespoons minced onions
1 clove garlic, minced
1 Tablespoon chopped fresh parsley
1 Tablespoon lemon juice
1 teaspoon white pepper

Place all ingredients in a blender and process until smooth. Chill until ready to use.

Variations:
Tomato-basil: add 4 Tablespoons tomato purée and 1 Tablespoon chopped fresh basil
Mediterranean: add 2 Tablespoons chopped green olives, 2 teaspoons chopped bell pepper, 1 teaspoon oregano, and 2 teaspoons chopped tomatoes
Asian: add 2 Tablespoons soy sauce and 2 teaspoons fresh minced ginger
Thousand Island: add 2 Tablespoons tomato purée and 2 teaspoons pickle relish
Tangy Strawberry Orange: add 4 Tablespoons chopped fresh strawberries and 2 teaspoons orange juice concentrate

Total Calories Per Serving (not variations): 16   Total Fat as % of Daily Value: 1%   Protein: 2 gm   Fat: 1 gm
Carbohydrates: 1 gm   Calcium: 27 mg   Iron: 0 mg   Sodium: 2 mg   Dietary Fiber: 0 gm

SALAD RECIPES

Gazpacho Salad
Serves 6

Dressing:
1 cup tomato juice
2 teaspoons vegetable or olive oil
1 clove garlic, crushed
1 teaspoon chopped fresh cilantro or parsley
¼ teaspoon red pepper flakes
1 teaspoon black pepper

Salad:
1 cup peeled and cubed cucumber
½ cup shredded fresh zucchini or summer squash
½ cup chopped green bell pepper
½ cup chopped fresh tomato
¼ cup chopped green onions
2 cups bite-size salad greens

Combine all dressing ingredients and whisk until combined. Allow dressing to chill.

Place cucumber, squash, bell pepper, tomato, and onion in a medium-size salad bowl. Cover and chill for at least 30 minutes.

To serve, place salad greens on a serving platter. Cover with half the salad dressing. Top with the vegetable mixture. Serve with the remaining salad dressing.

Total Calories Per Serving: 37   Total Fat as % of Daily Value: 3%   Protein: 1 gm   Fat: 2 gm
Carbohydrates: 5 gm   Calcium: 22 mg   Iron: 1 mg   Sodium: 113 mg   Dietary Fiber: 1 gm

Lemon Cucumber Salad

Serves 6

3 cups peeled and sliced cucumbers (about 3 medium cucumbers)
1 cup plain soy yogurt or 1 cup silken tofu mixed with 1 Tablespoon lemon juice
$\frac{1}{4}$ cup chopped almonds
$\frac{1}{2}$ cup chopped dried apricots
$\frac{1}{4}$ cup chopped green onions
$\frac{1}{2}$ teaspoon chopped fresh mint
1 teaspoon black pepper

Toss all ingredients together in a glass or plastic bowl. Cover and allow salad to chill for at least 40 minutes prior to serving.

Total Calories Per Serving: 118   Total Fat as % of Daily Value: 6%   Protein: 3 gm   Fat: 4 gm
Carbohydrates: 20 gm   Calcium: 100 mg   Iron: 1 mg   Sodium: 9 mg   Dietary Fiber: 3 gm

Cabbage and Fruit Slaw

Serves 4

1 cup shredded green cabbage
$\frac{1}{2}$ cup chopped red apple (not peeled)
$\frac{1}{2}$ cup vegan mayonnaise or creamy salad dressing
$\frac{1}{2}$ cup sliced banana
2 Tablespoons raisins

In a large glass or plastic bowl, combine all ingredients and toss lightly. Cover and chill for at least 30 minutes before serving.

Total Calories Per Serving: 217   Total Fat as % of Daily Value: 28%   Protein: 1 gm   Fat: 18 gm
Carbohydrates: 9 gm   Calcium: 14 mg   Iron: 0 mg   Sodium: 175 mg   Dietary Fiber: 1 gm

Citrus and Greens Salad

Serves 10

Salad:
8 cups mixed green salad (make a colorful combination of fresh baby lettuces, spinach, romaine, etc.)
2$\frac{1}{2}$ cups diced pink grapefruit and/or tangerine sections
1 cup grated carrots
1 cup finely shredded red cabbage
$\frac{1}{2}$ cup raisins or dried cranberries

Dressing:
$\frac{1}{2}$ cup peeled and seeded fresh tangerine sections
1$\frac{1}{2}$ cups peeled and seeded fresh orange sections

½ cup peeled and sliced lemon
3 Tablespoons fresh lime juice
¼ cup minced sweet onion
½ cup olive oil
1 Tablespoon orange juice concentrate
1 Tablespoon black pepper

Combine all salad ingredients in a large glass or plastic bowl. Cover and refrigerate.

Place all dressing ingredients in a blender or food processor canister and process until just smooth. Place into a glass or plastic container, cover, and refrigerate for at least 30 minutes before serving.

Serve the chilled salad with the dressing on the side, or toss salad with dressing right before serving.

Note: If fresh tangerines are not available, more oranges can be used.

Total Calories Per Serving: 189   Total Fat as % of Daily Value: 17%   Protein: 2 gm   Fat: 11 gm
Carbohydrates: 24 gm   Calcium: 56 mg   Iron: 1 mg   Sodium: 16 mg   Dietary Fiber: 3 gm

Celery, Apples, and Walnuts

Serves 6

Salad:
2 cups cored, cubed apples
2 cups diced celery
2 cups hearts of palm
½ cup chopped walnuts
1 head red leaf lettuce

Dressing:
½ cup silken tofu or plain soy yogurt
¼ cup vinegar
1 Tablespoon prepared mustard
1 Tablespoon chopped onion
1 clove garlic, minced
1 Tablespoon diced fresh basil

In large bowl, toss all salad ingredients. Place in refrigerator.

In a medium-size bowl, whisk together tofu, vinegar, and mustard until well combined. Stir in onion, garlic, and basil until well combined. Place, covered, in the refrigerator.

Just before serving, toss salad with dressing. Serve immediately. Or place salad and dressing on the table and allow guests to select the amount of dressing they would like.

Total Calories Per Serving: 130   Total Fat as % of Daily Value: 12%   Protein: 5 gm   Fat: 8 gm
Carbohydrates: 13 gm   Calcium: 105 mg   Iron: 3 mg   Sodium: 278 mg   Dietary Fiber: 4 gm

Apple Cider-Tofu Entrée Salad

Serves 8

1½ pounds extra-firm tofu
1½ cups apple cider
1 cup sliced celery
½ cup chopped walnuts
1½ cups combined red and green seedless grapes, cut in half
1 cup vegan mayonnaise
1 red apple and 1 green apple, sliced (for garnish)

Cut tofu into bite-size pieces. Pour cider into a large pot. Bring to a boil, and then reduce to a simmer. Add tofu pieces. Allow tofu to poach (simmer, covered with liquid) for 1-2 minutes. Remove from stove, drain tofu, and allow tofu to cool.

    Put tofu and remaining ingredients in a large bowl. Toss gently until all ingredients are coated. Allow mixture to cool for at least 1 hour prior to serving. Immediately before service, garnish salad with apple slices.

Total Calories Per Serving: 600   Total Fat as % of Daily Value: 38%   Protein: 8 gm   Fat: 25 gm
Carbohydrates: 84 gm   Calcium: 379 mg   Iron: 1 mg   Sodium: 303 mg   Dietary Fiber: 2 gm

Peppery Potato Salad with Lemon

Serves 6

Dressing:
⅓ cup vegan sour cream
1 Tablespoon prepared mustard
1 Tablespoon lemon juice
2 teaspoons black pepper
¼ teaspoon fresh lemon zest

Salad:
8 boiling potatoes, cooked and cooled (about 1½ pounds)
1 Tablespoon lemon juice
½ cup drained and cubed extra-firm tofu
½ cup diced celery
¼ cup sliced black olives
¼ cup chopped green onions

To prepare dressing, combine all ingredients and mix well. Chill until ready to use.

    To prepare salad, first medium-slice potatoes (not thinly). You may leave the peel on if you like. Place potatoes on a serving platter or in a deep bowl. Sprinkle potatoes with lemon juice and then with tofu cubes. Cover tofu with olives and onions. Spoon dressing on top of salad. Cover and allow dish to chill for at least 30 minutes before serving.

Total Calories Per Serving: 154   Total Fat as % of Daily Value: 7%   Protein: 4 gm   Fat: 5 gm
Carbohydrates: 25 gm   Calcium: 73 mg   Iron: 2 mg   Sodium: 214 mg   Dietary Fiber: 4 gm

Peapod and Potato Salad

Serves 6

Use edible peapods (also called snow peas or Chinese peapods) or snap peas (edible peapods with small peas) for this salad.

2 pounds chunked, unpeeled boiling potatoes (about 4½ cups)
2 cups coarsely chopped peapods
½ cup chopped green onions (green and white parts)
¾ cup creamy vegan salad dressing

Place potatoes in a large pot, cover with water, and cook until fork tender. Drain and spread out on a serving platter to allow them to dry.

Place potatoes in a large bowl. Add remaining ingredients and toss to combine well. Cover and refrigerate for at least 1 hour before serving.

Total Calories Per Serving: 230   Total Fat as % of Daily Value: 13%   Protein: 5 gm   Fat: 9 gm
Carbohydrates: 35 gm   Calcium: 46 mg   Iron: 2 mg   Sodium: 146 mg   Dietary Fiber: 5 gm

Black Bean and Potato Salad

Serves 8

Dressing:
½ cup oil
3 Tablespoons fresh lime juice
2 teaspoons black pepper
1 teaspoon cayenne
2 Tablespoons minced fresh cilantro or parsley

Salad:
2 cups frozen, thawed, or canned, drained corn
2 cups cooked, or canned, drained black beans
¼ cup chopped green onions
1 cup chopped fresh tomatoes
2 pounds un-peeled boiling potatoes, chunked (about 4 cups)

Place dressing ingredients in a medium-size bowl and whisk until well combined. Cover and refrigerate until needed.

Add corn, beans, onions, and tomatoes to dressing, toss and return to refrigerator. Place potatoes in a large pot, cover with water, and cook until fork tender. Drain and spread out on a serving platter to allow them to dry.

Place potatoes in a large bowl, add black bean mixture, and toss to combine. Cover and refrigerate for at least 1 hour before serving.

Total Calories Per Serving: 299   Total Fat as % of Daily Value: 22%   Protein: 7 gm   Fat: 14 gm
Carbohydrates: 38 gm   Calcium: 35 mg   Iron: 2 mg   Sodium: 16 mg   Dietary Fiber: 8 gm

Deviled Potato Salad

Serves 6

2 pounds unpeeled boiling potatoes, chunked (about 4 cups)
¼ cup minced onion
3 Tablespoons prepared mustard
¾ cup vegan mayonnaise
2 teaspoons paprika
1 teaspoon hot sauce
2 teaspoons ground black pepper

Place potatoes in a large pot, cover with water, and cook until fork tender. Drain and spread out on a serving platter to allow them to dry.

In a large bowl, combine remaining ingredients. Add potatoes and toss to combine. Cover and refrigerate for at least 1 hour before serving.

Total Calories Per Serving: 227   Total Fat as % of Daily Value: 28%   Protein: 1 gm   Fat: 18 gm
Carbohydrates: 10 gm   Calcium: 16 mg   Iron: 1 mg   Sodium: 278 mg   Dietary Fiber: 2 gm

Broccoli-Avocado Salad

Serves 5

1½ pounds broccoli, chopped into small pieces (about 4 cups)
1 ripe avocado, peeled, pitted and cubed (about ¾ cup)
1 Tablespoon olive or vegetable oil
2 Tablespoons lemon juice
1 Tablespoon prepared mustard
1 teaspoon red pepper flakes

Broccoli can be used uncooked or lightly steamed. If you steam broccoli, allow it to cool before proceeding. Place broccoli in a medium-size salad bowl. Add avocado and toss very gently to combine. In a small bowl, whisk oil, juice, mustard, and pepper. Drizzle over vegetables. Serve warm or chill before serving.

Note: If you'd like to toss the salad to coat all the ingredients, dice the potatoes rather than slicing them. If you try to toss sliced potatoes, you'll wind up with crumbled potatoes.

Total Calories Per Serving: 133   Total Fat as % of Daily Value: 13%   Protein: 5 gm   Fat: 9 gm
Carbohydrates: 13 gm   Calcium: 72 mg   Iron: 1 mg   Sodium: 81 mg   Dietary Fiber: 6 gm

Marinated Mushroom Skewers

Serves 6

½ cup canned, drained whole mushrooms
¼ cup 1-inch bell pepper strips
1 teaspoon sugar

1 teaspoon mustard powder
⅓ cup water
⅓ cup red wine vinegar
6 skewers

Thread mushrooms and bell peppers onto skewers. In a large, shallow bowl or deep serving dish, combine remaining ingredients and mix well. Place skewers in marinade. Cover and place in refrigerator, turning skewers several times, for at least 3 hours. Serve cold or heat on indoor grill or barbecue or in microwave.

Total Calories Per Serving: 10   Total Fat as % of Daily Value: 0%   Protein: 0 gm   Fat: 0 gm
Carbohydrates: 1 gm   Calcium: 4 mg   Iron: 0 mg   Sodium:1 mg   Dietary Fiber: 0 gm

Salsa and Red Bean Salad

Serves 4

¼ cup chopped onions
1 cup chopped fresh tomato or canned, drained tomatoes
2 Tablespoons chopped fresh chili, seeded
1 Tablespoon chopped fresh cilantro or parsley
2 Tablespoons lime juice
1 teaspoon black pepper
2 cups canned, drained or cooked and cooled red beans (pinto beans)

Combine all ingredients in a large glass or plastic bowl. Cover and refrigerate for at least 30 minutes before serving.

Total Calories Per Serving: 122   Total Fat as % of Daily Value: 2%   Protein: 7 gm   Fat: 1 gm
Carbohydrates: 23 gm   Calcium: 68 mg   Iron: 2 mg   Sodium: 357 mg   Dietary Fiber: 6 gm

Minted Couscous with Blueberries

Serves 4

½ cup uncooked instant couscous
1½ cups fresh or frozen, thawed blueberries
2 Tablespoons shredded fresh mint
2 teaspoons olive oil
½ teaspoon cracked black pepper

Prepare couscous on the stove according to package directions, or microwave 1 cup of water on HIGH for 4 minutes or until boiling. Stir in couscous, cover, and let stand for 5 minutes or until all water is absorbed. Fluff prepared couscous with a fork and allow it to cool.

When couscous is thoroughly cool, stir in berries and mint. Toss to combine. Add oil and pepper, toss to combine, and serve.

Total Calories Per Serving: 135   Total Fat as % of Daily Value: 4%   Protein: 3 gm   Fat: 3 gm
Carbohydrates: 25 gm   Calcium: 22 mg   Iron: 1 mg   Sodium: 6 mg   Dietary Fiber: 3 gm

Spinach and Tomato Couscous Salad

Serves 4

Dressing:
2 Tablespoons white vinegar
1 Tablespoon vegetable oil or olive oil
2 teaspoons nutritional yeast
1 Tablespoon chopped fresh basil

Salad:
1 cup vegetable broth or water
³/₄ cup instant couscous
1 cup frozen, thawed chopped spinach, squeezed and drained of excess water
¹/₂ cup chopped fresh tomatoes
1 Tablespoon chopped fresh parsley

Place all dressing ingredients in a small bowl and whisk until well combined. Set aside.

Place the broth in a small pot and bring to a fast boil. Remove from heat and stir in couscous. Cover and let stand for 5 minutes or until all water is absorbed. Allow couscous to cool.

Place cooled couscous in a medium bowl. Toss with spinach, tomatoes, and parsley. Toss with dressing. Cover and serve warm or allow salad to chill for 30 minutes before serving.

Total Calories Per Serving: 162   Total Fat as % of Daily Value: 6%   Protein: 5 gm   Fat: 4 gm
Carbohydrates: 27 gm   Calcium: 48 mg   Iron: 1 mg   Sodium: 209 mg   Dietary Fiber: 3 gm

Udon Noodle Salad with Peanut Dressing

Serves 6

Dressing:
1 Tablespoon vegetable oil
2 Tablespoons minced garlic
2 Tablespoons minced ginger
¹/₂ cup peanut butter (or soynut or sunflower butter)
2 Tablespoons rice syrup
1 Tablespoon soy sauce
2 Tablespoons red wine or cider vinegar
¹/₂ cup cold water
2 Tablespoons fresh lime juice
2 teaspoons fresh deseeded and chopped chilies (you decide on the heat!)

Put oil in a medium-size sauce pot and heat gently. Add garlic and ginger. Cook and stir until garlic is soft, about 2 minutes. Add remaining ingredients. Bring to a simmer. Allow dressing to simmer for 2 minutes. Remove from heat. Pour into a blender or food processor canister and process until smooth. Pour into bowl and allow dressing to chill for at least 30 minutes.

Salad:
4 cups cooked udon noodles, chilled
½ cup minced fresh cilantro
1 cup fresh sugar snap peas
3 Tablespoons minced fresh Asian basil
4 Tablespoons roasted cashews (if desired)

Place noodles in large serving bowl. Add enough dressing to moisten noodles and toss to coat. You can toss the cilantro, sugar snaps, basil, and cashews with the noodles, or ring the salad with these ingredients, and allow guests to select.

Notes: If fresh cilantro is not available, you can use fresh parsley. If fresh Asian basil if not available, you can use 1 Tablespoon fresh basil.

Total Calories Per Serving: 356   Total Fat as % of Daily Value: 21%   Protein: 9 gm   Fat: 14 gm
Carbohydrates: 51 gm   Calcium: 70 mg   Iron: 3 mg   Sodium: 341 mg   Dietary Fiber: 4 gm

Couscous and Vegetable Salad

Serves 8

2 cups couscous
½ cup raisins
1½ cups boiling vegetable broth
1¼ cups chopped fresh zucchini
½ cup chopped green onion
2 Tablespoons minced onion
¼ cup olive oil
⅓ cup pine nuts (optional)
1 cup minced red bell peppers
5 Tablespoons lemon juice
1 teaspoon cumin
2 teaspoons nutritional yeast

Place couscous and raisins in large bowl. Pour boiling broth over couscous, stir quickly, cover, and allow couscous to stand for 5 minutes.

In a small bowl, combine zucchini and both onions. Add oil to a large skillet and heat. Add zucchini mixture and toss and cook for 2 minutes. Stir in pine nuts (optional) and stir and heat for 1 minute. Add bell peppers and stir and heat for 1 minute. Stir in couscous, lemon juice, cumin, and yeast and cook for 3 minutes. Remove from heat, place in a serving bowl, cover, and serve warm, or refrigerate and serve cold.

Total Calories Per Serving: 156   Total Fat as % of Daily Value: 11%   Protein: 3 gm   Fat: 7 gm
Carbohydrates: 22 gm   Calcium: 20 mg   Iron: 1 mg   Sodium: 155 mg   Dietary Fiber: 2 gm

Raspberry-Red Cabbage Salad
Serves 10

1½ pounds cored and thinly sliced red cabbage (about 2 small heads)
¾ cup oil
½ cup vinegar
½ cup mashed fresh or frozen, thawed raspberries
1 Tablespoon orange juice concentrate
2 teaspoons black pepper
1 cup grated, peeled fresh beets (not cooked)
1 cup peeled, seeded, chopped fresh pear
½ cup chopped walnuts (optional)

Place cabbage in a large bowl and set aside. In a small bowl, whisk oil, vinegar, raspberries, orange juice concentrate, and black pepper together until well combined. Set aside. Add beets and pears to cabbage and toss. Add dressing and walnuts (optional) and toss to coat. Cover and serve at room temperature, or refrigerate and serve cold.

Total Calories Per Serving: 189   Total Fat as % of Daily Value: 25%   Protein: 1 gm   Fat: 16 gm
Carbohydrates: 11 gm   Calcium: 39 mg   Iron: 1 mg   Sodium: 30 mg   Dietary Fiber: 3 gm

Asparagus in the Microwave Salad
Serves 8

30 stalks fresh asparagus (about 1½ pounds)
4 cups mixed salad greens (such as baby spinach, shredded kale, and arugula)
3 Tablespoons chopped walnuts or pecans (optional)

Dressing:
½ cup red wine or balsamic vinegar
2 Tablespoons oil
1 Tablespoon orange juice concentrate
2 teaspoons prepared mustard
1 teaspoon black pepper

Trim and wash asparagus. In batches, microwave asparagus by placing stalks, double layered and packed tightly, in a glass microwave-safe casserole. Cover and microwave on HIGH for 2-5 minutes, depending on your microwave and the asparagus. Remove asparagus from microwave and cool.

Place all dressing ingredients in a small bowl and whisk to combine. Pour over cooked asparagus, cover, and refrigerate for 1 hour.

Place greens on a serving platter or divide onto individual plates. Top with asparagus. Garnish with nuts, if desired.

Total Calories Per Serving: 65   Total Fat as % of Daily Value: 8%   Protein: 1 gm   Fat: 5 gm
Carbohydrates: 3 gm   Calcium: 20 mg   Iron: 1 mg   Sodium: 17 mg   Dietary Fiber: 1 gm

Savory Pomegranate, Spinach, and Orange Salad with Vinaigrette

Serves 9

Dressing:
¼ cup olive or vegetable oil
¼ cup cider vinegar
1 Tablespoon maple syrup
2 teaspoons orange juice concentrate

Salad:
1 cup pomegranate seeds (about 2 large pomegranates)
9 cups cleaned and torn fresh baby spinach leaves
3 navel oranges, peeled and thinly sliced (about 2 cups)
½ cup diced sweet onions, such as Maui or Vidalia
1 Tablespoon black pepper

In a small bowl or large cup, combine all dressing ingredients until well mixed. Set aside.

Combine pomegranate, spinach, and oranges in a large serving bowl. In a small bowl or cup, combine onions and black pepper. Add onions to spinach and toss to combine. Just before serving, whisk salad dressing and toss with salad. Serve immediately.

Total Calories Per Serving: 117   Total Fat as % of Daily Value: 10%   Protein: 2 gm   Fat: 6 gm
Carbohydrates: 15 gm   Calcium: 54 mg   Iron: 1 mg   Sodium: 26 mg   Dietary Fiber: 2 gm

Mustard-Crusted Tofu "Steak" Salad

Serves 8

3 pounds fresh, cleaned and washed baby spinach (about 8 cups)
1½ cups sliced fresh button mushrooms
4 Tablespoons Dijon or spicy mustard
1½ pounds tofu "steaks" or extra-firm tofu, cut into 1-inch slices
Vegetable oil spray
½ cup sliced white or red onions
2 cups halved cherry tomatoes
½ cup balsamic vinegar
¼ cup olive oil
2 Tablespoons nutritional yeast

Arrange spinach and mushrooms on a serving platter. Thinly coat each piece of tofu (both sides) with mustard. Spray large skillet with oil and allow to heat. Over high heat allow tofu to cook, turning until heated through, about 2 minutes. Arrange tofu on top of mushrooms. In a small cup or bowl mix vinegar, oil, and yeast until combined. Pour over tofu and serve immediately.

Total Calories Per Serving: 179   Total Fat as % of Daily Value: 15%   Protein: 13 gm   Fat: 10 gm
Carbohydrates: 16 gm   Calcium: 208 mg   Iron: 6 mg   Sodium: 279 mg   Dietary Fiber: 5 gm

Black Soybean and Pepper Salad

Serves 7

2 cups drained black soybeans
1¹/₂ cups drained canned corn
1 cup minced celery
¹/₂ cup chopped red bell pepper
1 cup chopped yellow or green bell pepper
2 Tablespoons minced onions
2 Tablespoons minced and deseeded fresh chili (you choose the heat!)
¹/₄ cup oil
¹/₄ cup balsamic vinegar
1 teaspoon white pepper

Combine soybeans, corn, celery, bell peppers, and onions in a large bowl. Add chili, oil, vinegar, and white pepper and toss to combine. Cover and refrigerate for at least 1 hour before serving.

Total Calories Per Serving: 198   Total Fat as % of Daily Value: 19%   Protein: 10 gm   Fat: 13 gm
Carbohydrates: 16 gm   Calcium: 63 mg   Iron: 3 mg   Sodium: 127 mg   Dietary Fiber: 5 gm

Cucumber and Red Onion Salad

Serves 6

3 cups thinly sliced, peeled seedless cucumber
1 cup peeled and finely diced red onion
¹/₄ cup chopped fresh dill
¹/₄ cup cider vinegar
1 Tablespoon black pepper
1 Tablespoon sugar

Place the cucumbers, onions, and dill in a large glass or plastic bowl and toss to combine. In a small bowl, combine vinegar, pepper, and sugar. Pour vinegar over cucumbers and toss to combine. Cover and chill for at least 1 hour before serving.

Total Calories Per Serving: 32   Total Fat as % of Daily Value: 0%   Protein: 1 gm   Fat: 0 gm
Carbohydrates: 7 gm   Calcium: 20 mg   Iron: 1 mg   Sodium: 3 mg   Dietary Fiber: 1 gm

Lemon-Tofu Cucumber Salad

Serves 8

Dressing:
1¹/₂ cups silken tofu
1 Tablespoon oil
2 Tablespoons lemon juice
1 clove garlic, minced
¹/₂ teaspoon each ground oregano and black pepper

2 teaspoons nutritional yeast
¹/₂ cup drained, crumbled extra-firm tofu

Salad:
3 cups peeled, sliced cucumbers
2¹/₂ cups coarsely chopped fresh tomatoes
2 cups chopped Romaine lettuce
3 cups washed baby spinach
¹/₂ cup chopped red onion
1 cup cooked, cooled, shelled edamame
¹/₂ cup pitted, chopped black olives

Place all dressing ingredients, except extra-firm tofu, in a blender or food processor canister. Process mixture until smooth. Pour into a medium-size bowl and stir in extra-firm tofu. Cover and refrigerate.

Place all salad ingredients in a large bowl and toss. Cover and chill for 30 minutes. Toss with dressing and serve immediately.

Total Calories Per Serving: 177   Total Fat as % of Daily Value: 15%   Protein: 14 gm   Fat: 9 gm
Carbohydrates: 13 gm   Calcium: 248 mg   Iron: 5 mg   Sodium: 95 mg   Dietary Fiber: 4 gm

Apple Slaw
Serves 10

4 cups peeled, cored, chopped Granny Smith apples
3 Tablespoons cider vinegar
¹/₂ cup silken tofu
1 cup soymilk
1 Tablespoon lemon juice
1 Tablespoon Dijon or spicy prepared mustard
1 Tablespoon sugar
¹/₂ teaspoon ginger powder
3 cups shredded green cabbage
3 cups shredded red cabbage
1 cup shredded carrot
¹/₂ cup thinly sliced green onion

Place apples in a large glass or plastic bowl and toss with 2 Tablespoons of vinegar. Set aside. In a blender or food processor canister, process the remaining 1 Tablespoon of vinegar and tofu, and blend for 30 seconds. Add soymilk, lemon juice, mustard, sugar, and ginger, and blend for 1 minute or until smooth and creamy. Pour the mixture over the apples and toss to combine. Cover apple mixture and chill for at least 30 minutes.

In a large bowl, place the remaining ingredients, pour the apple mixture over the top, and toss gently to combine. Allow slaw to chill for 20 minutes before serving.

Total Calories Per Serving: 66   Total Fat as % of Daily Value: 2%   Protein: 3 gm   Fat: 1 gm
Carbohydrates: 13 gm   Calcium: 81 mg   Iron: 1 mg   Sodium: 47 mg   Dietary Fiber: 2 gm

Bow Tie Pasta Salad
Serves 10

Salad:
12 ounces uncooked bow tie pasta (or other pasta of choice)
2 cups canned or cooked, drained garbanzo beans
1 cup diced carrots
1 cup diced red onion
1 cup diced green bell pepper
1 cup thinly sliced fresh zucchini
1 cup frozen, thawed or fresh, uncooked green peas
$^1/_2$ cup pitted and sliced black olives

Dressing:
$^1/_4$ cup olive oil
$^1/_4$ cup water
3 Tablespoons cider vinegar
3 Tablespoons freshly chopped parsley
2 Tablespoons nutritional yeast
1 Tablespoon Dijon or spicy prepared mustard
1 Tablespoon minced garlic
2 teaspoons minced fresh basil
1 teaspoon freshly ground black pepper

In a large pot, cook the bow tie pasta in boiling water until al dente (still chewy). Drain, rinse with cold water, and drain well again. Transfer the cooked pasta to a large bowl, add all of the vegetables, and toss well to combine.

In a small bowl, place all of the dressing ingredients, and whisk well to combine. Pour the dressing over the top of the pasta mixture and gently toss together. Cover and chill in the refrigerator for 1 hour or more to allow the flavors to blend. Toss gently again before serving.

Total Calories Per Serving: 184   Total Fat as % of Daily Value: 12%   Protein: 6 gm   Fat: 8 gm
Carbohydrates: 24 gm   Calcium: 51 mg   Iron: 2 mg   Sodium: 194 mg   Dietary Fiber: 4 gm

Section 3 ⁂ Entertaining a Crowd

Chapter 16: USING VEGAN INGREDIENTS

Many mainstream ingredients are used in vegan cooking. Fresh or frozen vegetables, fruit canned in juice or water, dried fruits and vegetables, fresh and dried herbs and spices, fresh, dried, or canned beans and lentils, unsweetened juices, vegetable oils… are readily available and easy to use. Many mainstream convenience items (including some salad dressings, canned soups, breads and crackers, and fruit preserves) are also available. Just do quick label reading to ensure that all the ingredients are vegan.

Depending on your cooking expertise, you may be very familiar with vegan ingredients or may have only a brief acquaintance with them. Using soy, rice, almond, or other vegan milks, tofu, vegan cheese, cream cheese and sour cream, and frozen vegan desserts may be second nature for you. If this is the case, you can share this chapter with a new-to-vegan-cooking friend!

"Vegan" ingredients are not specifically made for vegans. These ingredients are used by lots of people in many cuisines. Silken tofu, seitan, tempeh, other alternative meats, as well as vegan cheeses, are enjoyed by vegans and others. Depending on your geographical location, many of these ingredients are readily available in mainstream markets. If you search local supermarkets and specialty stores and still can't locate the vegan ingredients you need, you can turn to the internet or to mail order.

The remainder of this chapter contains information on locating and using vegan ingredients. If you are having a party and using a caterer, you may want to let your caterer take a look at this information.

Meatless Product Information

Boca Burger: www.bocaburger.com or (608) 285-3311
Burgers, chili, and ground burger (for tacos, "meat" sauce, "meat" balls, etc.).

Field Roast Grain Meat Company: www.fieldroast.com or (800) 311-9497
Field Roast™ is a wheat gluten product that can be used in place of roast beef. It is available in 3-pound roasts and in 3 flavors. Also stocked in 3-ounce patties. Recipes are available.

Garden Protein International: www.gardein.com or (604) 278-7300
Canadian company offering alternative meats including beefless strips and burgeres, breaded chick'n tenders, chick'n breasts, chick'n strips, chick'n cubes, breakfast patties, ground crumble, and stuffed turk'y roast

Lightlife Foods, Inc.: www.lightlife.com or (800) 769-3279
Vegan burgers and dogs; sliced vegan turkey, chicken, and beef style deli meats; vegan chili, and seitan.

Morningstar Farms: www.seeveggiesdifferently.com or (800) 243-1810
(division of Worthington Foods, a Kelloggs subsidiary) Burgers, crumbles (instead of ground beef), and chik'n and steak strips. Recipes available.

Spice of Life: www.spice-of-life.com or (800) 256-2253
Mock meats and TVP available in Mexican, Italian, and Teriyaki flavor.

Turtle Island Foods, Inc.: www.tofurky.com or (800) 508-8100
Tofurky™ "poultry" roast, tempeh, vegetarian sloppy joes (made with tempeh), soy and tempeh burgers, and soy hotdogs and sausages. Recipes available.

Yves Veggie Cuisine: www.yvesveggie.com or (800) 434-4246
This Canadian company offers vegan Canadian bacon and pepperoni, veggie ground round, deli slices, and more. Recipes available.

Meat alternatives can be made from any combination of soy, wheat, nuts, cooked grains, mushrooms, and beans. Tofu, soy "meats," seitan (wheat gluten), tempeh (fermented soy), and portobello mushrooms are good stand-in ingredients for beef, chicken, and pork. Meat alternatives are nothing new. A product called "Soy Bean Meat" was introduced to the U.S. market in 1922. "Protose," a combination of soy, nuts, and grains was marketed in the 1930's. In the 1950's, Loma Linda Foods developed meat alternatives for members of the largely vegetarian Seventh-day Adventist Church.

Some meat alternatives are mild or bland in flavor. This allows for culinary creativity. One day firm tofu can pass for poultry; another day marinated seitan can pass for roast beef. Other products are produced to taste like beef, pork, chicken, or fish. Stumped for no-fish tuna salad? Look for a vegan frozen mock "tuna" product, with a flavor and texture approximating tuna. Use this product to create fishless chowders, croquettes, burgers, and old-fashioned casseroles.

There are meat alternates for the creative and the sedate cook. As you know, tofu can be purchased in several textures. Extra-firm tofu can be cut and grilled, baked, or barbecued just like meat. The same goes for seitan and tempeh. All three need some assistance in the "sizzle" area, so experiment with seasonings and marinade. Fast and simple: marinate firm tofu, tempeh, or seitan in oil and vinegar dressing for 20 minutes. Broil for quick "steaks." Or place these foods in a baking pan, cover with savory marinara sauce, and bake until heated through.

If you're not into creativity this week, all three can be purchased already flavored, as in Southwestern, curry, and barbecue. It's easy to put together Southwestern "seitan steak" and "curried tofu steak" with these products. Flavored or not, remember to treat tofu, seitan, and tempeh as you would any meat product. Store and hold them at the correct temperature.

If you like one-stop meat alternate shopping, check out some of the sites we've listed. Turtle Island Foods offers Tofurky™ Roasts, made from tempeh that resemble turkey breast. This company also offers Tofurky™ deli slices that can be used on hot or cold sandwiches or in place of sliced turkey, and "giblet" gravy, to be served over vegan meats or used as part of a vegan casserole. Tofurky™ Jurky is a vegetarian jerky dried in a real smokehouse. Turtle Island also offers several styles of hot dogs and tempeh burgers. The Turtle Island Foods website offers recipes and serving ideas.

Portobello mushrooms have become a mainstay of non-meat entrées. Portobellos are chewy and tough (in a good way) and mimic meat. Marinate the caps (discard the stems, as they are tough, unless you are making a stock) in Italian dressing and grill or bake them or throw them, sliced, in stir-fries. Omnivores will think they are eating meat and vegans may become alarmed because it seems as if there's an animal product on their plate (clue them in!). If you don't have time to mess with fresh portobellos, several companies are selling pre-marinated mushrooms.

TVP or TSP, textured vegetable or soy protein, is the granddaddy of meat alternates. TVP is a dry product usually made with proteins isolated from soy flour. Over the years, it has been used as an ingredient in processed entrées and side dishes. TVP is an ingredient in many prepared vegetarian products, such as veggie dogs, chilies, and sausage.

You can purchase TVP fine or crumbled, flavored or plain. Use TVP where you would use ground beef. TVP needs to be rehydrated. A general rule of thumb is 1 cup of TVP to $^3/_4$ to 1 cup of boiling water, allowing 10 minutes for rehydration. Once TVP is rehydrated, use the fine texture in sauces, soups, casseroles, tacos, and chili. Use the crumble texture to replace beef in stews, stir-fries, soups, pot pies, and hot entrées. Dry TVP can stored in dry storage for up to 6 months. Rehydrated TVP needs to be refrigerated and used within 3 days.

Veggie Sloppy Joes

Serves 12

Use this recipe as a base for many entrées, soups, and stews. Add chopped or minced seasonal vegetables, a variety of tomatoes, peppers, and chilies or mushroom blends for variety. This dish can be made several days ahead and kept refrigerated until needed. Do not freeze, as the texture becomes soggy.

3 cups TVP
3 cups boiling water
1 cup minced onions
1 cup minced green bell pepper
3 cups canned diced tomatoes (with liquid)
1 cup tomato paste
2 cups prepared tomato sauce
2 Tablespoons granulated garlic
3 Tablespoons soy sauce
2 Tablespoons black pepper
2 teaspoons maple syrup

Place TVP in medium-size bowl. Add boiling water and stir. Allow TVP to soak for 5 minutes.

Place TVP in large pot. Add remaining ingredients and stir to combine. Simmer until vegetables are soft and mixture is hot, about 15 minutes.

Note: Serve over steamed rice, cornbread, or toasted buns or herbed rolls. Use as a hot sandwich filling in pita bread or wraps or to "stuff" a potato. Can also be used as an ingredient in hot appetizers, wrapped in phyllo or puff pastry dough, or as a stuffing ingredient for mushroom caps. Modify the seasonings and use as a vegetarian Bolognese sauce (Italian tomato sauce with "meat") for pasta.

Total Calories Per Serving: 148   Total Fat as % of Daily Value: 9%   Protein: 12 gm   Fat: 6 gm
Carbohydrates: 16 gm   Calcium: 156 mg   Iron: 3 mg   Sodium: 504 mg   Dietary Fiber: 4 gm

Understanding Soy

Soy hot dogs and veggie burgers have become familiar menu items. If you can't locate soy mayonnaise (Nayonaise is a nationally distributed brand; contact <www.vitasoy-usa.com> or try looking for Vegenaise; contact <www.followyourheart.com)> you can create your own by blending silken tofu with a small amount of lemon juice, mustard powder, and white pepper.

There are several brands of soy- and rice-based frozen vegan ice creams including frozen novelties, such as soy ice cream sandwiches and fudge bars.

Soy nuts are roasted soybeans that can used wherever you would use peanuts and are available in several flavors, as well as salted and unsalted. Soy butter is a bit blander than peanut butter. Use it on sandwiches, to thicken sauces or soups (think: Thai peanut sauce), or as a baking ingredient.

Soymilk is available in many forms and flavors. You can find soymilk in regular and lowfat forms, in pints and quarts, fresh or aseptically packaged, and plain or flavored with chocolate, mocha, strawberry, and vanilla. If you would like the same calcium, vitamin A, and vitamin D as cow's milk, you need to look for a brand of fortified soymilk. Once opened, soymilk needs to be refrigerated and used within 3-4 days. Chilled soymilk can be used as a beverage or used on cold or hot cereals. Use soymilk in pancake and waffle mixes, in quick breads, and in sauces.

Soymilk also can be used in sauces and soups, as long as you remember to stir. Soymilk tends to curdle if not stirred when added to hot liquids. Use soymilk to replace the cow's milk or water used to reconstitute condensed soups. Béchamel sauce is a combination of heated milk and roux (equal parts fat and flour). Make a soy béchamel with heated soymilk and vegan margarine. Soymilk tends to be blander than cow's milk, so increase the normal amount of seasonings you would use. Soymilk can also be used with instant puddings, dessert sauce mixes, and in baking mixes. If you have a recipe that calls for dairy buttermilk, you can use soymilk whisked vigorously with a small amount of vinegar. The proportions should be approximately 1 teaspoon of white vinegar (red vinegar will give an undesirable pinkish tinge) in 1 cup of soymilk. For extra tang, make your soy buttermilk two or three hours prior to use; keep refrigerated until ready to use.

The food industry uses soy, tofu, or isolated soy protein to make nondairy soy cheese, sour cream, and cream cheese. Vegetable gums, cornstarch, and tapioca starch are added to make a solid texture. Natural flavorings and colorings, rice, corn solids, and spices may also be used for coloring and flavor. Tofu is considered by some to simply be "soy cheese," as it is a solid curd formed from soymilk. But be advised that most vegan soy cheeses do not taste or melt like their dairy counterparts.

Want to use nondairy cheese, but don't know where to start? You can experiment with various brands. Go on the web and use the recipes companies have posted for their product.

Nondairy cheeses do not contain cholesterol, but they do contain fat, some of it saturated. About one ounce of dairy cheddar cheese has 114 calories with 9 grams of fat. Nondairy cheddar (Veganrella brand) has about 70 calories per serving, with 3 grams of fat. Both dairy and nondairy cheddar has about 180 milligrams of sodium.

Here are just some of the vegan cheeses we have sampled:
Cheezly comes in chunks (cheddar, edam, garlic and herb, gouda, nacho, and mozzarella) and as slices (cheddar and mozzarella)
Daiya comes in cheddar and mozzarella style shreds
Galaxy Foods chunks (cheddar and mozzarella), slices (American and mozzarella), and grated parmesan
Soymage vegan slices, cheddar and American
Teese comes in cheddar and mozzarella style, as well as nacho and cheddar sauce
Tofutti Better Than Cream Cheese Alternative (various flavors), vegan sour cream, as well as Tofutti slices (various flavors)
Vegan Gourmet Cheese Alternatives from Follow Your Heart (various flavors)

You really need to work with soy cheeses to find out their properties. Some have wonderful flavors when cold, but don't melt well. Some don't have a great taste when served cold, but melt well and taste good when hot. Some will incorporate into sauces with a creamy ease, and some prefer to stay in their original form. Some soy cheeses will hold up to browning (as in pizza or placed under a broiler) and some will simply spread. Be sure to try a variety of soy cheeses before making your decision. You may have to stock several different brands to meet your various needs.

Soy Foods

There are lots of prepared soy foods that require little or no special preparation. Here are a few:

<u>Turtle Island Foods</u> Tofurky <www.tofurky.com>
Tofurky is a frozen product that resembles cubed or sliced poultry. It can be used wherever you would use cooked turkey, such as a hot Tofurky sandwich (use a mushroom or vegetable gravy), Tofurky and stuffing, "chicken" vegetable soup, or no-turkey salad.

<u>Vitasoy USA</u> salad dressings, milk alternatives, tofu <www.vitasoy-usa.com>
Vitasoy has many soy products, including Nayonaise and prepared salad dressings. Nasoya Baked Tofu comes in Thai Peanut, Teriyaki, Mesquite Smoked Flavor, and Tex Mex flavors. This refrigerated product can be sliced and served as a cold sandwich or crumbled and used to top a salad. Served hot, it can be used as an entrée on its own or used as an ingredient in stir-fries, casseroles, and stews. The baked tofu is made from organic soybeans and has no preservatives. They also offer some tofu pudding mixes, so you can create your own puddings or pie filling.

<u>Eden Foods</u> soymilk and other beverages, tofu, dried and canned soybeans <www.edenfoods.com>
Eden Foods is one of the larger producers of soymilk and beverages in the United States. They offer enriched and non-enriched soymilk, lowfat and flavored soymilk and soymilk blends, such as soy and rice milk. They have a line of canned soybeans that can be used in soups, salads, and dips.

<u>Ener-G Foods</u> Soy nuts, Soyquik, gluten-free baking and cooking mixes, and powdered vegan Egg Replacer. <www.ener-g.com>
Soy nuts are crunchy and versatile. Use them in cold salads, hot soups and casseroles, in granola mixes, and as a garnish for sweet and savory items. Caters to individuals with special dietary needs.

<u>Galaxy Foods</u> soy cheeses, sour cream, spreads <www.galaxy.com>
Galaxy offers a variety of soy cheeses in various forms. Some are vegan.

Egg Substitutes

If you enjoy baking and have the time to experiment, you can find several vegan substitutes for eggs, including silken tofu, mixtures of oil and flour, and puréed fruit. If you bake "by the numbers," vegan egg replacer may be the ingredient for you. Powdered egg replacer can be substituted for whole eggs; egg replacer won't work if a recipe calls for egg yolks or egg whites. Approximately $1^1/_2$ teaspoons of egg replacer combined with 2 Tablespoons of warm (not hot!) water is equivalent to one large egg.

Most commercial egg substitutes are egg- and dairy-based. There are several products on the market that are plant-based, especially suitable for vegans and for people with an allergy to eggs or dairy. A dry product called Egg Replacer, produced by Ener-G Foods, (800) 331-5222 or <www.ener-g.com>, is the gold standard for plant-based egg substitutes. It comes packed in one pound boxes, which translates into the equivalent of approximately 80 large eggs. Egg Replacer's ingredients include potato starch, tapioca flour, carbohydrate gum (for body), citric acid, and calcium carbonate (for leavening). Once reconstituted, Egg Replacer must be handled with the same care as fresh eggs (that is, kept cold so as to avoid bacterial contamination). Another company producing vegan egg replacer in powdered form is Bob's Red Mill <www.bobsredmill.com>.

Other non-animal ingredients to replace eggs are soft tofu, mashed beans, mashed potatoes, and fruit purées. You will have to match the substitute with the menu item. For example, tofu can be scrambled with chopped vegetables and herbs to create a dish close to scrambled eggs or use as a filling for breakfast burritos. Fruit purées, such as banana and apple, can be used to replace some of the egg in baking recipes and puréed or mashed beans can be used as a thickener instead of eggs in soups and dips.

Soft and Silken Tofu

The soft consistency of tofu and its mild taste make it a perfect food for anyone. It is a good source of protein for people who prefer dishes that are easy to chew and digest. Soft tofu that has been puréed with fruits or vegetables is a good first protein food for infants.

Silken tofu, sometimes called Japanese tofu, is made from soymilk that is strained before a coagulant, such as a form of calcium, is added. The tofu is then made in a process similar to yogurt, where the protein is not hardened into curds and no whey is drained off. This process makes the texture generally smoother, creamier, and more custardlike than firmer tofu. Like traditional tofu, silken tofu comes in a range of firmnesses: soft, firm, and extra-firm. But even the extra-firm variety of silken tofu has a smoother consistency more similar to flan than other tofu. Silken tofu is best used for making dips, sauces, desserts, puddings, smoothies and "milk" shakes, or any recipe that requires blending. Silken tofu may be substituted for sour cream, cream cheese, salad dressing, mayonnaise, or yogurt. Silken tofu can be floated on top of soups or entrées, to be mixed in by your guest.

Silken tofu is an excellent combining ingredient. However, do not try to scramble, grill, or roast silken tofu. The texture is too soft and you will wind up with a sauce-like consistency, rather than a sandwich. Firm and extra-firm regular tofu is best when a firm, chewy texture is desired. If you do bake silken tofu, you can get a range of textures, from custard to cheesecake, depending on additional ingredients used.

You Say Potato

For those not accustomed to cooking with tofu, think of tofu as you would potatoes. Potatoes can be baked, boiled, broiled, grilled, mashed, puréed, or fried. Potatoes can be combined with hundreds of ingredients to form an unlimited number of dishes. Tofu is similar. Just as a plain, steamed potato is not so exciting to some people, so is unseasoned tofu. However, add a few ingredients and you have wonderful menu items.

Instead of Ricotta

Silken tofu has a soft creamy texture similar to soft, whipped cream cheese. Silken tofu is a good substitute for dairy products such as ricotta cheese and cream cheese. Substitute silken tofu for ricotta cheese in cheesecake recipes for a lower fat, no cholesterol, dairy-free alternative.

To create a dairy-free cream cheese, mix 12 ounces (about 1¼ cups) of silken tofu with 2 Tablespoons of lemon juice and a dash of salt. Allow mixture to chill for at least an hour, and you will have tofu cream cheese. For a lowfat, creamy dressing, combine 12 ounces of silken tofu with 2 Tablespoons of your favorite vinegar, 2 Tablespoons of olive oil or light vegetable oil, and a dash of ground white pepper. This forms a base for your creamy salad dressings. Add garlic and chopped parsley, or shredded chopped spinach and minced onion, or chopped chilies for a creamy bagel or toast spread, a vegetable dip, or a salad dressing.

Silken tofu is easy to use to create smoothies. To make one smoothie serving, blend 6 ounces (about ²/₃ cup) of silken tofu with 4 ounces of fresh or thawed frozen berries, and enough orange juice concentrate to sweeten. Leftovers can be refrigerated and re-blended or frozen for a fruit dessert. This combination could also be used to fill a prebaked pie shell, to create a "cream" pie.

Store Properly

Tofu is treated just like a dairy product in that it must be refrigerated and has a short shelf life. Fresh tofu generally has a refrigerated shelf life of 5-7 days. Silken tofu is often ultra-pasteurized and so has a very long shelf life. Check the packaging for expiration dates. No matter what type of tofu you use, it must be refrigerated once it is opened. Tofu can be frozen for up to 5 months. Defrosted silken tofu will be a little watery when thawed, but it is excellent for absorbing flavors and adding creaminess to menu items.

A Mighty Bean

All forms of tofu are rich in protein. Tofu is also a good source of B vitamins and iron. When the curdling agent used to make tofu is a calcium derivative (check the label), the tofu is an excellent source of calcium. While 50 percent of the calories in tofu come from fat, a 4-ounce serving of tofu contains just 6 grams of fat. It is low in saturated fat and contains no cholesterol. Generally, the softer the tofu the lower the fat content. Tofu is also very low in sodium, making it a perfect food for people on sodium-restricted diets. Tofu is now being marketed in low- and non-fat versions, as well.

Here are some additional ways to use silken tofu in your party menus:
1. Create an orange "frosty" by combining orange juice and silken tofu, allowing it to partially freeze before serving.
2. Instead of pudding, combine silken tofu with puréed fruit and use to create layered fruit parfaits.
3. Purée silken tofu with fruit and freeze to make a tofu-sherbet.
4. Combine silken tofu with prepared tomato sauce to make a creamy pasta sauce.
5. Instead of dairy sour cream, top baked potatoes with silken tofu, chopped green onions, sliced olives, and a scattering of cooked kidney beans.
6. Use silken tofu to replace some of the vegetable oil in quick-bread (such as carrot cake), pancake, and muffin recipes.
7. Whip silken tofu with vanilla extract to created a soy whipped topping.
8. Use silken tofu to create fast "cream" soups.
9. Use silken tofu to replace some of the mashed avocado in guacamole.
10. Mix silken tofu with dried onion soup mix to create a lowfat dip.
11. Blend silken tofu with melted chocolate chips and a sweetener to make a chocolate cream pie.

RECIPES

Silken Salad Dressing Base

Makes approximately 2 cups or sixteen 2 Tablespoons servings

1¹/₂ cups silken tofu
2 Tablespoons lemon juice or vinegar
2 Tablespoons olive oil
¹/₄ teaspoon salt

Place all ingredients in blender and process until smooth. Allow mixture to chill for at least 15 minutes before serving.

Note: Serve as is, or add chopped fresh or dried herbs and spices, vegetables, or prepared salsa to create your own blend.

Total Calories Per Serving: 30   Total Fat as % of Daily Value: 4%   Protein: 2 gm   Fat: 3 gm
Carbohydrates: 1 gm   Calcium: 26 mg   Iron: 0 mg   Sodium: 39 mg   Dietary Fiber: 0 gm

Tofu Chocolate Chip Cookies

Makes approximately four dozen 1-ounce cookies or 2 cookies per serving

2¹/₂ cups oatmeal
2 cups all-purpose flour
1 teaspoon baking powder
1 teaspoon baking soda
1 cup vegan margarine, softened
1 cup packed brown sugar
1 cup sugar
1 teaspoon vanilla extract
One 12.3-ounce package silken tofu (1¹/₄ cups)
1¹/₂ cups vegan chocolate chips

In a blender or food processor canister, process oatmeal until the consistency of coarse flour. Combine oatmeal, flour, baking powder, and baking soda. Set aside.

In a large bowl combine margarine, sugars, and vanilla until smooth. In a blender or food processor canister, process tofu until smooth. Stir into sugar mixture. Stir in flour mixture, 1 cup at a time, until combined. Stir in chocolate chips.

Drop by rounded teaspoons on ungreased baking sheet, 2 inches apart. Bake in a 375-degree oven 8-10 minutes or until golden around edges.

Total Calories Per Serving: 247   Total Fat as % of Daily Value: 16%   Protein: 3 gm   Fat: 10 gm
Carbohydrates: 36 gm   Calcium: 39 mg   Iron: 1 mg   Sodium: 158 mg   Dietary Fiber: 2 gm

Fruit Smoothie

Makes approximately five 1-cup servings

One 12.3-ounce package silken tofu (1¹/₄ cups)
1 medium banana
2 cups unsweetened orange-pineapple juice, chilled
One 8-ounce can unsweetened crushed pineapple, chilled (1 cup)

Combine all ingredients in blender; cover and process until smooth. Serve immediately.

Total Calories Per Serving: 125   Total Fat as % of Daily Value: 4%   Protein: 6 gm   Fat: 2 gm
Carbohydrates: 23 gm   Calcium: 77 mg   Iron: 1 mg   Sodium: 8 mg   Dietary Fiber: 1 gm

Tofu Alfredo

Serves 6

Alfredo creamy pasta sauce has long been a no-no on most peoples' lists of high-fat, high-cholesterol, and high-calorie food. But now you can have this sinful dish without the guilt! This creamy Alfredo pasta sauce is another excellent example of how tofu becomes "invisible" and is a great substitute for dairy cream.

One 12.3-ounce package silken tofu (1¼ cups)
2 cloves garlic, minced
1 teaspoon garlic powder
1 teaspoon onion powder
1 teaspoon pepper (or to taste)
1 teaspoon salt (or to taste)
1 cup plain soymilk
1 Tablespoon finely chopped fresh basil
1 Tablespoon finely chopped fresh tarragon
1-2 Tablespoons finely chopped fresh parsley
¼ cup grated vegan Parmesan
1 Tablespoon olive oil (optional)
1 package fettuccini noodles (or any pasta you prefer)

Place tofu in a blender or food processor canister. Add the garlic, garlic powder, onion powder, pepper, salt, and ¾ cup of the soymilk. If you want, at this time, add the fresh herbs. They will turn the sauce a beautiful light green when blended, so if you prefer the sauce to be white, wait to add the fresh herbs until after you've blended the ingredients. Blend everything until very smooth and creamy while scraping the sides occasionally. Add more soymilk a little at a time to make the sauce to your desired thickness.

Pour the sauce into a medium size saucepan and warm over low heat. Add the cheese and cook while constantly stirring, about 2-3 minutes. Do not boil or cook too long (the sauce will turn lumpy and separate). Add more soymilk if a thinner sauce is desired and add the fresh spices at this time if you prefer the sauce white. Quickly adjust seasonings after tasting by adding more salt or pepper as desired. You can add a little olive oil right before removing the pan from the heat to make the sauce richer in flavor. Remove from the stove but keep covered.

Cook the pasta as directed on the package and strain completely. Place the hot pasta in a large dish and pour the sauce over it. Sprinkle with fresh parsley and the other herbs and serve immediately.

Total Calories Per Serving: 281   Total Fat as % of Daily Value: 5%   Protein: 12 gm   Fat: 3 gm
Carbohydrates: 48 gm   Calcium: 139 mg   Iron: 2 mg   Sodium: 475 mg   Dietary Fiber: 2 gm

Vegan Luxury Sauces

It may be that you'd like to keep your party meal preparations to a minimum. No problem. Roasted tofu or grilled seitan or tempeh steaks can be made flavorful, moist, and luxurious with an excellent sauce.

Classic cuisine is based on four or five basic sauces. Ingredients are added to these basic sauces to create thousands of wonderful and varied sauces. So, prepare your protein, bake your potatoes, grill or steam your vegetables, and select a sauce or two from the following recipes to create easy and elegant sauces. The majority of sauce ingredients may already be found in your kitchen.

Note: If you don't care to use wine with your sauces, you can use 1 Tablespoon of white vinegar mixed with 1 Tablespoon of water for every 2 Tablespoons of wine listed in the recipe.

Veloute

Makes one quart (4 cups) or 4 servings

Veloute is a savory sauce, great for roasted or grilled protein, for baked potatoes, stuffed mushrooms, tomatoes or peppers, or served over noodles, steamed greens, or grilled vegetables.

Beat 8 Tablespoons of roux (4 Tablespoons of flour and 4 Tablespoons of fat, such as vegan margarine or vegetable oil worked into a paste) into 1 quart (4 cups) plus 1 cup of hot vegetable or mushroom stock. Simmer for at least 45 minutes, skimming if necessary. If the veloute is thinner than you'd like, allow it to cook awhile longer, or add more roux.

Variations on Veloute:
a. White Wine Sauce: reduce 8 Tablespoons of dry white wine by half, add one quart of veloute, and simmer for 10 minutes. Beat in 6 Tablespoons of soymilk (not fat-reduced) and 2 Tablespoons of lemon juice and beat until well combined.
b. Herb Sauce: add 1 teaspoon each chopped fresh parsley, chives, and tarragon to one quart of veloute or white wine sauce.
c. Hungarian Sauce: lightly cook 3 Tablespoons minced onions and 2 teaspoons of paprika in 2 Tablespoons of vegan margarine. Add 10 Tablespoons of white wine and reduce by half. Add one quart of veloute and allow sauce to simmer for 10 minutes.
d. Venetian: combine 2 Tablespoons chopped onions, 2 teaspoons chevril, 6 Tablespoons of white wine, and 4 Tablespoons of vinegar and reduce over low heat until only one-half of the original volume remains. Add 1-quart white wine sauce and simmer for 5 minutes.
e. Bercy Sauce: combine 10 Tablespoons white wine and 6 Tablespoons of chopped onions and reduce by one-third. Add one quart of veloute and reduce by one-fourth. Finish by swirling in 4 Tablespoon of vegan margarine, 1 Tablespoon of chopped parsley, and 2 teaspoons of lemon juice.

Total Calories Per Serving (not variations): 133   Total Fat as % of Daily Value: 17%   Protein: 1 gm   Fat: 11 gm
Carbohydrates: 7 gm   Calcium: 1 mg   Iron: 0 mg   Sodium: 315 mg   Dietary Fiber: 0 gm

Demiglaze

Makes 1 quart (4 cups) or 4 servings

Combine 1 quart of mushroom stock and 1 quart of mushroom sauce (mushroom stock flavored with carrots, onions and celery, tomato purée, bay leaf, and thyme), and thicken with roux (4 Tablespoons of flour and 4 Tablespoons of vegan margarine). Allow to simmer until it is reduced by half. Don't be impatient with demiglaze. The thickness comes from allowing it to reduce down on the stove. Demiglaze is best made the day before the event, and reheated as needed.

Variations on Demiglaze:
a. Diable Sauce: combine 10 Tablespoons of white wine, 4 Tablespoons of chopped onions, and 1 teaspoon of cracked black pepper and allow to reduce by half. Add 1 quart demiglaze and simmer for 15 minutes. Finish with cayenne to taste.
b. Madeira Sauce: combine 12 Tablespoons of Madeira wine with 1 quart of demiglaze and allow sauce to reduce by one fourth.
c. Red Wine Sauce: combine $^3/_4$ cup chopped carrots, $^1/_2$ cup chopped celery, $^1/_2$ cup minced onions, 2 cloves chopped garlic with $1^1/_2$ quarts red wine. Reduce by one-half. Add 1 quart demiglaze and reduce again by one-half.

d. <u>Mushroom Sauce</u>: brown $^1/_2$ cup of sliced mushrooms and 2 Tablespoons of minced onions in 2 Tablespoons of vegan margarine. Add 1 quart demiglaze and simmer for 10 minutes. Finish with 12 Tablespoons of sherry and 2 Tablespoons of lemon juice.

Total Calories Per Serving (not variations): 216   Total Fat as % of Daily Value: 20%   Protein: 4 gm   Fat: 13 gm
Carbohydrates: 20 gm   Calcium: 3 mg   Iron: 1 mg   Sodium: 1,560 mg   Dietary Fiber: 1 gm

Bechamel
Makes 1 quart (4 cups) or 8 servings

Beat 8 Tablespoons of roux (4 Tablespoons of flour and 4 Tablespoons of fat, such as vegan margarine or vegetable oil, worked into a paste) into 1 quart (4 cups) of slightly warmed soymilk. You'll need to whisk briskly and control the heat, so the soymilk does not curdle. When the roux is blended into the milk, add 2 whole cloves and 1 bay leaf. Allow mixture to simmer, stirring occasionally, for 10 minutes. Remove cloves and bay leaf before serving.

Bechamel is a creamy sauce. You can alter the thickness by adding more or less roux, or by carefully allowing it to reduce while simmering.

Variations of Bechamel:
a. <u>Herb Sauce</u>: add 1 teaspoon each chopped fresh parsley, chives, and tarragon to 1 quart of bechamel; stir to incorporate and simmer.
b. <u>Hungarian Sauce</u>: lightly cook 3 Tablespoons minced onions and 2 teaspoons of paprika in 2 Tablespoons of vegan margarine. Add to 2 quarts of bechamel and simmer for 10 minutes.
c. <u>Mushroom Sauce</u>: brown $^1/_2$ cup of sliced mushrooms and 2 Tablespoons of minced onions in 2 Tablespoons of vegan margarine. Add 1 quart of bechamel and simmer for 10 minutes
d. <u>Mustard Sauce</u>: stir $^1/_4$ cup prepared mustard into 1 quart of bechamel. Allow to simmer, stirring occasionally, for 10 minutes.
e. <u>Dessert Sauce</u>: omit bay leaf when preparing bechamel and add 2 teaspoons of vanilla extract. Stir 2 Tablespoons of maple syrup and 1 Tablespoon of orange juice concentrate into 1 quart of warm bechamel. Allow sauce to simmer until flavors are combined. This sauce can be served warm or cold.

Total Calories Per Serving (not variations): 328   Total Fat as % of Daily Value: 12%   Protein: 10 gm   Fat: 8 gm
Carbohydrates: 52 gm   Calcium: 195 mg   Iron: 4 mg   Sodium: 109 mg   Dietary Fiber: 2 gm

Chapter 17: BASIC PARTY PLANNING

Planning a party calls for lots of organization so you can enjoy the event as well. Here are some suggestions followed by professional party planners:

1. Things to think about when planning a party or gathering:

- Who is the party for? (business, family, friends, etc.)
- What is the reason for the party? (theme, birthday, special occasion)
- When is the party? (day of the week, time of day)
- Where is the party going to be? (home, office, etc.)
- How many people are you inviting?
- What type of party is it? (brunch, lunch, dinner, hors d'oeuvres, dessert, buffet, sit-down meal)

2. After thinking about these questions, you can start planning your party. Here is a checklist to help:

- Make a list of people to invite.
- Mark the date on your calendar.
- Send invitations (by mail, e-mail, or phone).
- Plan menu, including the beverages.
- Make shopping list (food, paper goods, decorations, etc.).
- Plan cooking schedule: Determine what will be purchased, what can be prepared ahead and frozen the day before and that day, and what items you may get delivered (such as ice or a wedding cake!).
- Make a list of equipment needed (rental chairs and tables, outdoor heaters, microphone, etc.).
- Plan the layout of the room(s). (Make sure all the food tables are not right on top of each other to ensure smooth flow and room for people to mingle.)
- Plan music, if appropriate.
- Plan lighting.
- Buy or make centerpieces or other decorations.
- Buy cleaning supplies for before and after the party.
- Make a checklist of what you are preparing with appropriate cooking equipment needed for each recipe.
- Make sure you have all the platters and serving pieces you will need.
- If people will be helping you, communicate with them and let them know what you expect from them (time of arrival, serving guests, staying after guests have left, etc.), so they have a clear idea of what they will be doing.

3. During the Party Here are some considerations to think about for your guests:
- Coat rack (hangers or a separate room to put coats)
- A place to put boots or umbrellas
- Ice, ice bucket, ice tongs or scoop
- Cocktail napkins (have enough for 2 per person)
- Toothpicks

- Candles
- Paper towels
- Extra toilet paper (for powder room)
- Pretty guest soaps (for powder room)
- Paper hand towels (for powder room)
- Plates (appetizer, salad, dinner, dessert)
- Glasses (water, wine, mixed drink, beer, soda, coffee); some beverages can use the same type of glass
- Silverware (remember all of the courses, a fresh spoon or stirrer is necessary for coffee)
- If grilling, check the tank, charcoal, lighter fuel
- Coffee and assortment of tea bags
- Vegan milk and sugar for beverages, lemon slices for tea
- Salt and pepper
- Chilled beverages
- Brewed hot beverages
- Bottle openers
- Film, memory cards for the camera
- Garbage bags
- Dishwashing soap
- Club soda (for any thing that may spill, a great spot remover)
- Space to chill beverages. It only takes beer, wine, juice, and soda 20 minutes to chill on ice. A large tub or cooler can be used in a back room.

4. Keep a Journal

After any party, it is a good idea to record in a journal how much was left over and what people liked and didn't enjoy. This information will be a big help when you plan your next party. Think of your party journal as a time saver for your next party. If possible, record recipes, quantities purchased, stores that were good resources for ingredients, etc.

The Art of the Buffet

The space you have will help you to determine what type of service you will have at your party. If you don't have a lot of space, buffets are the easiest way to serve a large group of people and will give your guests time to eat, drink, and mingle. Buffets can help to keep the cook out of the kitchen and let the host enjoy the party as much as the guests.

As with any type of entertaining, the trick to hosting a successful party buffet meal is to plan ahead. Here are some ideas to help you structure your buffet planning.

1. First, pick your theme. This is a very important part of your planning process, since everything else from the food to the decorations may be involved. Cocktail party, appetizing hors d'oeuvre buffet, dessert buffet, barbecue, full-course dinner buffet . . . the choices are endless. After you've picked a theme, set a date and send out the invitations. The sooner you do this the better.

2. Create the Menu. Keep it simple. Allow at least two weeks to plan your menu and assess your supplies. Get as much done ahead of time as possible so on the day of your party you only have to prepare

the food and get yourself ready. Straighten the house, or visit the site where you will be serving, such as a local park, classroom, social hall, etc., and prepare any dishes that can be made ahead of time.

Plan your menu so there are plenty of options for your guests. While some people may pile their plates high, others will just nibble. A good mix would include a tray of cubed vegan cheese and crackers or vegetables and dip in addition to the main entrée. This way you'll still be able to serve some adventurous dishes, confident that there'll be something everyone will like.

To make sure you have enough food, prepare one extra portion of each dish for every six guests. Depending on your menu and the time allowed for people to eat, plan on replenishing certain platters of food, or removing platters when they are empty.

3. Think the entire event through before setup. Consider things like strategic locations of tables at your buffet. A buffet table near the entrance may cause a bottleneck. Don't forget these details: How long it will take for your guests to move through the buffet line? How many tables will you need? One table with two lines or several tables with different courses? Your buffet table may be set against a wall or in the center of the room. For only six or eight guests, it's often placed with the long side against a wall; more guests may require both sides to prevent traffic jams. In that case, set up a double-sided buffet that people can get to from both sides. If you don't have the space, ask half of the people to go through at a time.

Setting the Table

When setting up the buffet, think functional. Where are the plates? Where are the utensils? If your guests have to hold a plate in their lap, you can't serve something that requires a knife and fork.

Set the buffet table to make it as easy as possible for your guests to serve themselves. Arrange the buffet in order of how people eat their meal (salad, appetizer, sides, then entrée). Place a stack of dinner plates at the point where guests start and a basket of silverware and napkins at the end of the buffet. Make enough so guests may go back for seconds and have fresh flatware. Stack extra plates, too. Also, it's a good idea to set an additional table away from the main buffet for coffee, juice, other drinks, and desserts. Don't forget, this is a party. Make it festive! Vary textures, colors, shapes, heights, and placement of food. Be creative with decorations.

Serving Made Easy

The one thing all buffet food must have in common is that it must be easy to get from table to plate to mouth and not require much in the way of cutting. It is customary to serve bite-size foods that can be eaten with a fork. Carefully consider the utensils you're using to serve each dish. Use tongs if necessary to prevent spillage and avoid putting food trays two-deep on a table to prevent spilling into other dishes. It is also recommended that covered dishes be used, where possible, for hot dishes. Remember, food safety is an important part of planning holiday parties and buffets as well.

Once the date arrives and the doorbell rings, relax, gather around the table and enjoy the company of friends. The preparation should pay off and everyone should have a wonderful time.

More Party Basics

You've just invited 50 of your closest friends over for a party meal and you have no idea what you're going to do. Here are some more tips to help you prepare for a party with a minimum of frazzle.

Selecting a Theme

Creating a theme for your party is an easy way to create atmosphere. It will get your guests into a celebratory mood. If you're planning a celebration for a holiday, use the traditional elements of that holiday to add color to your event. For example, for an Independence Day party, make the event special by incorporating ready-made ideas into your theme: flags; red, white, and blue paper plates and napkins; selected "patriotic" music, and sparklers as party favors.

Christmas, Halloween, Chanukah, and Valentine's Day are examples of holidays with built-in theme elements; how about some lesser-known holidays:

- Earth Day is April 22. Opt for an environmental theme, and play up this international holiday that celebrates environmentalism. Prepare a vegan meal with locally grown, seasonal ingredients, and decorate with environmentally friendly décor (green plants, globes, and recycled-paper products). You might even make a tree- or garden-planting ceremony part of the party.

- September is National Sewing Month. Consider throwing a craft brunch to celebrate. You can decorate with sewing notions, prepare simple fare, and invite your friends over to work on a beginner-level sewing project. Use this "holiday" to inspire a monthly craft party!

Because holidays recur every year, you have ample opportunity to stock up long before your next party-and save a ton of money. Shop after-holiday sales at gift, party, and houseware stores, and pick up themed paper plates, napkins and linens, decorations, favors, and other odd items that might come in handy during next year's events.

Combining Party Themes

Birthdays, anniversaries, and other milestone occasions are perfect for theme parties. However, why not get really creative and go beyond traditional milestone themes? "Happy Birthday" balloons are fun for kids, but adults have more sophisticated sensibilities. They appreciate eclectic ideas and funky themes. For example:

- Instead of throwing a traditional birthday party for a friend turning 40 or 50, consider throwing a '40s Party with a swing theme or a '50s Party with a rock'n roll theme. Prepare food and beverages appropriate to the era, hire a swing or oldies band or stock up on CDs, and ask your guests to come in costume.

- Incorporate traditional "bon voyage" theme elements into a retirement party or celebration for a co-worker who received a promotion or landed a great new job. Get "island" with the planning, including palm trees, beach-themed décor, tropical drinks and food, and Hawaiian and beach music.

Meal parties, perhaps the most frequently thrown type of party, focus on the food and drink: breakfast, brunch, lunch, high tea, cocktails, dinner, or dessert. Although the food is central to the party, you can still incorporate a theme to your meal party, providing both good food and conversation flow.

- Instead of having a casual party, why not have a disco party? Send out '70s-style invitations, rent a disco ball, and throw some '70s tunes in the CD player. Play up the menu with food and drink popular in the 1970s: lots of appetizers, fast food-style munchies (they can be done healthy), and cold frozen beverages, such as slushes. Costumes are optional, but would add a lot of fun.

- Have a high tea or brunch to celebrate spring, inviting guests to a garden party with elegant décor, fresh-cut flowers, an assortment of tea sandwiches (with the crusts cut off!), and a very dignified lemonade punch or champagne, if appropriate. Ask guests to wear their best fancy hats. Suggest thrift-store shopping or incorporate hat decorating as a party activity, using items purchased at a craft store, such as huge flowers, leaves, wide ribbons, and sparkles.

- If hosting a simple dinner party, you could transform it into Game Night without adding much extra planning; you just need decks of cards or assorted board games and some extra tables and chairs.

Theme-Based Party

Some parties are planned around themes: costume parties, decade parties, movie nights, or girls' night out parties. Why not try the following?

- An entertainment-based party, such as a karaoke, film, or Super Bowl party, in which the theme event is central to the party's concept.
- A crafting group, in which the guests work on a specific yarn, sewing, or other craft project, perhaps for a community agency.
- A game night, dice party, or scavenger hunt, at which guests participate in an activity or game.

Whether it be music, activities, or professional entertainment, your guests will have a great time if the entertainment is fun or enjoyable.

- Create a soundtrack for your party.
- Plan a "solve a mystery" party.
- Research how to find quality, professional entertainment.

As you're planning a theme party, you'll need to determine any specific tools you or your guests will need to supply, directions you need to print up, or special equipment you'll need to buy, rent, or borrow. Theme parties don't need to cost a lot of money. Shop in ethnic markets, dollar stores, or big-box stores for theme-based party supplies. Most likely, you'll spend a lot less money than at a party-supply store.

Choosing Party Décor

By just adding a few details, you can turn your party into a real event. Instead of focusing on traditional elements, try a little creativity:

- Having a barbecue? Make it a "western barbecue" by covering your tables with red-and-white checkerboard tablecloths, second-hand store condiment squeeze bottles, vintage cowboy-printed fabric squares as napkins, and a centerpiece made of chili peppers and Tabasco sauce.
- Planning a dessert and beverage reception? Fluff things up with a "swing" theme: vintage bar glasses, mood lighting in low pinks and yellows (use inexpensive colored light bulbs), and drink-recipe cocktail napkins.
- Turn an ordinary luncheon into high tea by investing in a three-tiered serving platter; linen napkins; clean, polished silver and crystal; and a lovely bouquet of tulips.

Remember to keep safety in mind when you're planning your party décor. Although items sold at deep discounts might be good for your budget, they might not be safe for your guests, especially if you are inviting children. Use common sense: Don't place highly flammable decorative items near an open flame, don't use plastic bags or anything with accessible string if you're hosting a party with children in attendance, and don't encourage guests (especially if they have been drinking alcohol) to toast their own kebobs or veggie dogs with short, wooden skewers.

Simple (and Inexpensive) Ambience: Candles and Other Forms of Lighting

Even if you can't afford a single decorative item for your adult party, you can still create an abundance of ambience just by placing candles around your home. Try a few bright ideas.

- Set floating candles in clear glass bowls filled halfway with water and place in several areas: the living room, the dining room, and, of course, the bathroom.

- Purchase tiki torches and plant them around your front walkway and backyard or patio.

- Dim overhead lighting and cover lamps with sheer, colored scarves. Check your local thrift store for pieces that you might not be caught dead in, but that would look great draped over your too-bright living-room light. Keep safety in mind, ensuring anything draped doesn't touch the light bulb or feel hot to the touch.

- Combine radiance with aroma by lighting assorted scented candles in each room. Keep the flavors the same in each room so your guests don't get overwhelmed by different odors.

Understanding Party Food Basics

Food will probably be the largest, most important variable at any party you host. You should know a few basics about what kinds of food go with what kinds of parties.

- Standing parties (cocktail, casual gatherings) call for nibblets and finger foods, and at least six different kinds of appetizers, including dips and sweets.

- At buffet parties, plan for one or two main courses and up to six side dishes, including vegetables, grains, salads, breads, and desserts.

- At seated parties, one main course and related side dishes are all that is required, but you will want to serve an appetizer and/or salad before the entrée, and follow it with dessert. Don't forget to have a few pre-dinner noshes available for guests: chunked vegan cheese and crackers, chips and dips, and an additional appetizer or two.

Try to keep your menu varied, but don't make it overly challenging. For example, you might make an exotic main course, but you should pair it with a relatively mild side dish, allowing guests to take a break from spicy flavors. Likewise, spend your time (and money) preparing one or two elegant appetizers, and then round out the menu with dips and breads.

Don't go overboard with food! You might think a sagging table will impress your guests, but if you overdo it, you'll only have leftovers that ultimately might get discarded.

Planning Beverages and Drinks for Your Party

Although the beverage selection should vary from party to party, a few basic rules hold true:

- Stock up on bottled water and assorted soft drinks and juices for guests that don't drink alcohol.

- Make sure you have plenty of ice! A few hours ahead of time, fill a large bucket with ice and chill a selection of drinks.

- If you are serving alcohol, take into account your guests' varying preferences. Include red and white wine and assorted cocktails.

- Regardless of the event, always have regular and decaffeinated coffee ready to brew toward the end of the night, as well as soy or rice milk, sweeteners, and a few interesting coffee condiments, such as cinnamon or vanilla syrup.

Don't forget two critical planning elements with respect to beverages: space and chill time. Make sure you have enough space in your freezer for the amount of ice you'll need, or plan to hit the store just before the party so the ice doesn't melt before your guests arrive. Remember to chill your cold drinks at least 24 hours before the party so that your drinks are cold when the guests arrive. You might think you only need a few hours of chilling; however, your refrigerator will cool down 80 cans of warm soda more slowly than you might think. You'll need to make room in your refrigerator for all those cans and bottles, too, so keep your cold food requirements in mind.

Although water, juice, and soft drinks are fine, you might also add a few different options, such as freshly brewed iced tea, flavored sparkling water, or sparkling juice. Although you can't be expected to stock every type of beverage your guests could possibly demand, a good host will have enough of a variety on hand to suit most requests.

Basic Tools for Dining and Drinking

No matter what kind of party you're planning, if food and drink are involved, your guests will need something from which to drink and eat.

- Paper, disposable, or glass cups from which guests can drink cold beverages; guests will grab a clean glass at least once, so plan accordingly
- Insulated cups or mugs for hot beverages
- Large plates for eating the main meal
- Small plates for desserts and appetizers
- Enough knives, forks, and spoons-plastic or metal-so that each guest has a complete set, plus a few extra, just in case
- Twice as many paper napkins as you think you will need (linen napkins are great for the table, but guests will need cocktail napkins for drinks and appetizers)
- An adequate supply of serving bowls, pitchers, and platters in assorted sizes, shapes, and colors
- Any serving utensils you will need to actually serve the food and drinks: large spoons, serving forks, a ladle, a corkscrew, a bottle opener, and a carving knife

How much alcohol/beverages do you need?

If you're serving alcohol at your party, how much will you need? Here is a bit of basic beverage math:

- Plan for two drinks per person for the first two hours of the party, and then one drink per person for every hour thereafter.
- One 750-milliliter bottle of alcohol (wine, champagne, or liquor) will yield about six 4-ounce glasses.
- Plan two cans or bottles of soda per person; change that quantity to three if you are hosting a party without alcohol.
- If you're hosting a party heavy on drinks that require ice, such as iced soft drinks or blended or shaken cocktails, you'll need a half pound of ice per person.

Based on these facts, we can calculate that for a 4-hour party of 20 expected guests, you would plan to serve a total of 120 drinks.

Thrifty Ways to Stock Up for a Party

Consider starting a "party closet." A party closet is a storage container large enough to safely store your party tools: dishes, cutlery, glassware, linens, candles, and leftover favors that might be put to some future use. Because these items are stored in one place, and only pulled out for parties, you'll always have a good supply on hand.

Scour local second-hand stores for dishes, glassware, and flatware. Keep one element the same, color, style, or pattern, and your guests will be impressed with your decorating style. Whether you're using matched china or thrift-store finds, make sure your party tools are clean, polished, and in good repair.

If you are thrift-store shopping for your party tools, avoid any plates or glasses made with lead. Generally, old china, glazed terra cotta or clay dishes, or dishes with highly decorated, multicolored interior surfaces can contain lead. If you are in doubt, err on the side of caution. Lead poisoning can lead to serious health consequences.

Take a hint from restaurants and make "rollups" several days before your party. Place a complete set of cutlery-knife, fork, and spoon-in one napkin, and roll it up. Secure the roll with clear tape (if you're using paper napkins) or some other festive touch, such as theme-related napkin holders, or tuck the end of the napkin into the roll.

Napkin Folding

Cloth napkins don't have to be expensive! Most houseware stores sell white cloth napkins in bulk for under $20. Invest in a couple of packages and you'll be covered for a long time. Also look for plain, matching napkins at discount and closeout stores. Starched napkins fold and retain their shape better than limp napkins, so bust out that can of spray starch and heat up the iron. Some basic skill with napkin folding will add an elegant touch to your table.

- Triangle-Fold napkin in half diagonally. Fold corners up to meet the top point. Turn napkin over and fold in half diagonally. Pick up at center and stand on base of triangle.

- Glass Fan-Fold napkin in half lengthwise. Accordion pleat napkin from top to bottom. Fold bottom third of napkin back under. Place bottom in wine glass and spread out top pleats of napkin so that it resembles a fan.

- Standing Fan-Fold napkin in half lengthwise. Fold into $1/2$-inch accordion pleats, beginning at the bottom of the napkin and only pleating half the napkin. Fold the whole napkin in half, so that pleat meets pleat, with the accordion fold on the outside. Fold upper-right corner of unpleated sides diagonally down to folded base of pleats, and turn under edge, adjusting the fan until it feels stable. Place on table and spread pleats to form fan.

- Tower-Fold napkin in half diagonally. Fold corners to meet at top point. Turn napkin over and fold bottom two thirds way up. Turn napkin around and bring corners together, tucking one corner into the other. Turn napkin around and stand on base.

- Simple (the kids can help)-Fold napkin in half diagonally. Holding the top point of the triangle, pull it through a round napkin holder. Attractively arrange bottom portion of napkin.

Putting Your Party to Music

Music sets the atmosphere; consider carefully the soundtrack for your party. If you can, coordinate your music with your party's theme: country/western for barbecues, disco for disco parties, and swing for martini parties. Also think about the types of activities you'll feature, and coordinate your soundtrack to reflect the mood you'll want to set.

- For a seated dinner, plan a few lively CDs for pre-dinner festivities. When the guests move to the dining table, switch to mellow music-classical, vocals, or ambient house music, so you can hear conversation without shouting. Also remember to adjust the volume accordingly.

- A casual mixer will fare well with classic or contemporary rock, country, bluegrass, or R&B-just make sure to keep the volume loud enough to hear, but quiet enough to encourage chatter.

- If you're having a cocktail party, opt for smooth jazz, swingy '60s vocals (Peggy Lee or Frank Sinatra) or low-key house music. Again, watch the volume.

Whatever your soundtrack, select your CDs ahead of time. You don't want to waste valuable party time fumbling with CD cases or rifling through your collection. Stack up about 10 CDs next to the player in the order you would like to play them.

You'll want to experiment with different sounds and styles before the party. Try to achieve a mix of the standard and the unexpected. For interesting ideas, visit your local independent music store and chat with the clerks. After you select your party soundtrack, check each CD to ensure there aren't any scratches. Also, make sure you keep the remote in your pocket at all times, just to make certain the volume fluctuates with the party. If you're on a budget and your CD collection reflects it, visit used CD stores, where you can find great albums at rock-bottom prices. Also considering visiting your local public library, where you may find many great CDs you can borrow!

Incorporating Activities

When presented with the proper attitude, games and activities can add an element of fun to many gatherings. You might be surprised by how many guests will enjoy participating in games and activities at your party. Although you'll do best wandering through a game store or consulting a party activities book, keep in mind a few options that have stood the test of time:

- Adult party games: Allowing guests to showcase their particular talents, knowledge, and skills, adult party games can bring disparate guests together into a cohesive group. Although you probably don't want to pull out the Trivial Pursuit game for a party of 40 people, smaller gatherings are perfectly suited for an hour or two of challenging mind games.

- Scavenger hunts: This childhood favorite can become a favorite with adults when given a mature spin. At the beginning of a destination party, hand the guests a list of items they should be able to locate throughout the evening. You also can host a video or musical scavenger hunt, or plan an entire party around a city-wide scavenger hunt.

- Shower games: Although some guests will claim to abhor the silly little games played at wedding and baby showers, I adore them. Keep it simple, no more than two or three games per party, and offer fun prizes. If you adopt a festive spirit, your guests will, too.

Although some gatherings, such as a Games Night, demand certain activities, games should never be forced on anyone. Don't forget to offer prizes for winners! Although selecting and wrapping these small gifts might seem like one extra chore, prizes make the games even more fun, giving guests something to vie for. The prizes don't have to be expensive-scented candles, a CD or DVD, or a funky coffee mug, but they should reflect some thought. Don't forget to remove the price tags! Also, before your party, make sure all your boxed games contain all the pieces and that any tools you'll need are on hand.

If you don't want to spend a lot of money on games, hit the kids' section of your local store and select a few low-priced options, such as Uno, Yahtzee, or Operation. Find games allowing many players.

Party Games

If you and your guests love charades, go for it. And you might want to check out one of these other games, all suitable for adults and many for children.

- Pictionary: Whether you make your own set or buy the game, Pictionary is a great group game just about anyone can play.

- Twister: Yes, it's retro, but isn't that the point?

- Taboo: This cheeky game is a great ice-breaker for adults who think they know one another. Don't take the game too seriously, and you'll have a great time.

- Hide-and-seek: Best played outdoors, in a park or while camping, hide-and-seek when played with adults can be just as fun as it was when you were a kid.

- Trivial Pursuit: It's a classic, with good reason. Playing in teams allows to you match skills and knowledge, and players can have a great time arguing about their final answers.

- Cranium: Another game marketed for adults, but teenagers do very well with it. Cranium contains a little bit for everyone: trivia, acting skills, drawing, and modeling with clay. Best suited for smaller gatherings, Cranium is one of the more fun games to emerge in recent years.

Hiring Entertainment

Consider hiring professional entertainment for your party. Although not every gathering is suited to this type of activity, a little creativity and effort on your part can make your evening's entertainment spectacular. Here are some ideas:

- Music: Quality performers are always welcome at any party, especially when they function more as ambience, rather than the central focus. Consider a string quartet, jazz trio, or even a harpist, all of whom can add wonderful atmosphere to your gathering without overpowering it.

- If you're working with a limited budget, but are dying for professional musicians at your party, contact a local university or music school, where you can often find talented students who are more than happy to play for the exposure and a small fee.

- Live entertainment: A hypnotist, comedian, or balloon artist can add a lively, silly element to the right party, such as a barbecue, retirement or reunion party, children's party, or picnic. Before you dismiss this idea as childish, think about it: What could be more entertaining than a group of adults laughing their heads off at a professional clown?

Always keep your guests' happiness in mind. Not everyone will appreciate a comedian who tells off-color jokes. If your guests are on the conservative side, plan accordingly.

If you have the budget for a professional entertainer or service provider, don't skimp on quality. Ask for references, attend an event at which the person will be performing, and make sure you are getting your money's worth. Give yourself plenty of time to research, evaluate, and select your entertainment. Because this is one task you can definitely perform far ahead of your party date, don't leave it to the last minute, or else you might find yourself settling for second-rate talent.

Offering Party Favors

Although not absolutely essential to the success of a party, small favors are a nice way of thanking your guests for attending your party. Because many people will bring wine, food, or hostess gifts, it's a gracious touch to offer something in return. Party favors should be inexpensive and specific to your party's theme or occasion. Although almost any small, interesting memento will suffice, here are a few suggestions for favors that work:

- Digital pictures taken and printed at the event, and then slipped into preprinted cards; guests pick up the cards on their way out the door.

- For "Girls Night Out," little makeup bags filled with hair accessories, cosmetics, or nail polish.

- Small boxes of incense, tied with an inexpensive burner.

- For an outdoor or garden party, individual seed packets or flower bulbs wrapped in cheesecloth, with instructions for growing attached.

Favors also serve as a memento of your party, reminding guests what a fabulous time they had at your event and possibly prompting them to plan something of their own.

Elegant Party Menu Ideas

<u>Summertime Dinner</u>:
Appetizer: Chilled artichokes with curried rice
Entrée: Onion tart with mango salsa
Sides: Chilled greens (spinach, swiss chard, etc.) with lemon dill vinaigrette, roasted corn with pimento vegan margarine
Intermezzo: Sliced melon with cucumber dressing
Dessert: Chilled cherry-vanilla soup or strawberry-balsamic pie with white and black pepper crust

<u>Winter Dinner</u>:
Appetizer: Potato-pumpkin ragout or Potato-leek soup
Entrée: Curried vegetables in a polenta crust
Sides: Barley with ginger and shiitake mushrooms, lemon-tarragon vegetable salad
Intermezzo: Apple-calvados sorbet (calvados is an apple liqueur)
Dessert: Rum cake with seasonal fruit compote

<u>Dinner With A Mediterranean Flair</u>:
Appetizer: Roasted eggplant and pepper dip served with focaccia and artisan breads
Entrée: Asparagus and mushroom risotto
Side: Wilted greens with roasted garlic, white beans with sun-dried tomatoes
Intermezzo: Sliced citrus scented with orange-blossom water
Dessert: Assorted biscotti and tea cookies

Holiday Theme Party Menu Ideas

<u>Thanksgiving</u>:
Assorted crudites and dips
Herbed lentil loaf with mushroom gravy
Baked, candied sweet potatoes with cranberry-walnut gravy
Broccoli and cauliflower medley
Tofu pumpkin pie
Assorted cookies and fresh fruit
Or
Butternut squash soup with herbed vegan margarine
Seasonal vegetable pie with mushroom sauce
Baked sweet potatoes with praline topping
Garlic mashed potatoes
Glazed lemon carrots
Apple-cinnamon pie

<u>Winter Holiday Meal</u>:
Tomato-lentil soup with herbed croutons
Assorted vegan ravioli with three-pepper coulis (peeled, puréed bell peppers used as a sauce)
Torta rustica (a layered vegetable pie)
Sautéed greens
Mashed turnip and rutabagas
Assorted breads and rolls
Lemon-tofu cheesecake

New Year Menu:
Holiday hors d'oeurve platter (assorted olives, radishes, marinated veggies such as asparagus, cauliflower, artichokes, whole green onions, cherry tomatoes, cucumber, and carrot sticks, assorted breadsticks, and salsas and dips)
Black-eyed peas and tofu (black-eyes peas are considered to bring good luck for the New Year)
Mushroom risotto
Mashed sweet potatoes (seasoned with orange zest and lemon zest, nutmeg, and vanilla)
Braised greens (braise greens of choice with white wine, minced garlic, and pepper)
Assorted sorbets and cookies

Fourth of July Grill-Out:
Assorted veggie burgers (purchase commercially or make your own; see page 162)
Veggie hotdogs
Grilled lemon-herb tofu steaks
Corn on the cob and baked white and sweet potatoes (cooked right in the coals)
Potato and pasta salad
Confetti broccoli slaw (can purchase shredded broccoli or can do it yourself)
Watermelon wedges and seasonal fresh fruit (served iced)

Passover:
Crunchy vegetable tray with a variety of dressings
Matzo balls in carrot-vegetable broth
Mushroom-matzo-nutloaf with vegetable gravy
Fruit compote (stewed dried fruit with orange juice concentrate, flavored with ginger and cinnamon)
Baked sweet potatoes
Braised greens
Plum tart (made with matzo meal crust)
Baked apples with raisins

Halloween:
Purée of carrot soup served in a pumpkin shell (scoop out pumpkin, toast seeds and use as garnish)
"Monster" sandwich: 6-foot submarine bread filled with grilled veggies, sliced tomatoes, onions, etc.
Cole slaw and potato salad (if available, try purple potatoes)
Assorted veggie chips (bake thinly sliced potatoes, carrots, beets, etc.) with flavored hummus
"Dirt and worms" dessert: frozen sorbet or rice or soy frozen desserts, mixed with cookie and cake crumbs, chopped raisins, along with canned fruit cut into strips

Easter:
Fresh spinach salad with mandarin orange segments, sliced almonds, and vinaigrette dressing
Stuffed tomatoes
Brown rice pilaf with dates, raisins, and pineapple
Baby carrots tossed with dill and vegan margarine
Broccoli and cauliflower florets tossed with garlic and lemon
Peach upside down cake

<u>Rosh Hashanah:</u>
Mock chopped liver with assorted crackers
Mushroom barley soup
Vegetarian kishke
Stuffed baked potatoes
"Creamed" spinach (use puréed tofu and soymilk to create a "cream" sauce)
Sliced carrots tossed with apple juice and parsley
Sliced citrus (slices of oranges, pink grapefruit, tangerines, etc.)
Assorted fruit breads (carrot, zucchini, pumpkin, etc.)

Special Occasion Menu Ideas

<u>Light Reception</u> (for early afternoon dining, such as a late morning wedding or communion):
Sliced and wedged seasonal fruit with soy yogurt dressing, crudities (crunchy vegetables) with garlic vinaigrette and Thai peanut dressing, mock "pate," assortment of breadsticks with dipping sauces, assorted canapés (cold, marinated tofu on French bread rounds, tofu "egg" salad on Melba toast, chopped marinated vegetables on focaccia, etc.), dolmas (grape leaves stuffed with herbed rice), hot tempura veggies (carrots, cauliflower, sweet potatoes, green beans) with tamari dipping sauce, assorted pastries and beverages.

<u>Hot and Cold Reception</u> To the "Light Reception" above add:
Hot hors d'oeurves, such as stuffed mushrooms (and stuffed cherry tomatoes if you have the time and the concentration), vegan egg rolls, and spring rolls
Light entrées, such as vegetable stir-fries and pastas (you can have these pre-set in chafing dishes or set up stations, where your guests can watch the items being prepared).
Specialty items, such as tamales (savory made with chilies or sweet made with raisins and pineapple), enchiladas, Asian steam buns, mini-stuffed cabbage, stuffed zucchini blossoms, filled pastas (such as gnocchi, ravioli, or tortellini), pierogi (pasta stuffed with potato and sauerkraut or with prune filling), knishes (pastry stuffed with potato or kasha), or blintzes (crepes with fruit filling).

<u>Dessert Reception:</u>
Fruit: Sliced melons (honeydew, cantaloupe, Persian, watermelon, muskmelon, casaba, etc), grape clusters, fruit brochettes (short skewers of strawberries, pineapple wedges, grapes, etc.)
Baked Goods: assorted cookies (if purchasing, watch out for non-vegan ingredients, such as eggs and honey), vegan gingerbread squares, assorted fruit tarts (purchase individual puff pastry or tart shells and fill with pie filling), cake rounds, sliced fruit breads (cranberry, carrot, zucchini, blueberry, persimmon, etc.) served with fruit preserves
If you have the facilities, offer assorted fruit sorbets or soy or rice ice cream, either garnished with fresh fruit or prepared as mini-sundaes (sundaes can be made ahead of time and frozen until ready to use).

In addition to the receptions mentioned above, some of the following dishes can be included on menus, depending on the occasion.

<u>Jewish Celebration:</u>
Matzo ball soup
Stuffed cabbage with sweet and sour sauce
Potato pancakes with applesauce
Glazed carrots/Green beans amandine

Assorted breadbasket, including rye and pumpernickel rolls
Baked apples with cinnamon and ginger
Plum tart

Wedding (Sit-down):
Champagne reception with trays of fresh strawberries and grapes
Ratatouille (eggplant stew with tomatoes, garlic, zucchini, and black olives)
Crepes with savory filling (e.g., marinated, sautéed mushrooms)
Duchesse potatoes/minted green peas (duchesse potatoes are finely mashed potatoes mixed with vegan milk, nutmeg and white pepper, piped through a pastry bag to resemble large rosettes and baked until golden)
Assorted fruit trays
Assorted crudite trays with dips
Assorted bread baskets
Raspberry and lemon sorbet
Wedding cake

Communion:
Wine reception with fruit kebobs, tofu-cheesecake squares, and assorted vegan cookies
Finger sandwiches
Fresh veggie tray with dips
Antipasto (marinated veggies, olives, pickles, pepperocini, etc.)

Putting Together Party Themes and Menus
1. Wine Tasting at Home
The Wines: select four vegan wines from several different regions, such as Napa Valley, California, Willamette Valley, Oregon, Central Coast, California, and Upstate New York. Figure on one bottle of wine serving four people. Select wines that are the same quality, using price as a guide.

The Room(s) Set Up: plan on this as a buffet. Set up five "stations" or tables. One table will contain a bottle of each wine. The remaining tables will have a different wine and a matching food dish. Plan on an appetizer on one table, a salad on another, an entrée on another, and dessert on the last table. For example, with a fragrant pinot noir pairing, offer a creamy potato soup as the appetizer, a pear, fennel and walnut salad, roasted seitan and dill "steaks" as the entrée, and a vegan chocolate, cheese and berry selection as dessert.

The Game Plan: guests will taste all wines twice. At the first table, guests will have an opportunity to taste all the wines against each other. At each food table, they will taste the wines with their paired foods. If you like, prepare ranking cards, so everyone can compare when coffee is served.

2. Camping in the Backyard
The "Campground": this should be planned for the late afternoon or early evening. In a spacious back-yard, pitch a small tent, create a fire pit, being sure to take safety precautions, and plan on flashlights for the kids to "explore." Have comfy cushions, blankets, and outdoor chairs for guests. Citronella candles add ambience and keep the bugs at bay.

The Menu: lots of easy dips, such as hummus and black bean dip (you can create a third dip by combining the hummus and the black bean dip), veggie hotdogs and buns, vegetable kebobs, and roasted potatoes and corn. Beverages can include bottled water, juice boxes, and pitchers of lemonade. Dessert can include fresh fruit, popcorn balls, trail mix, and s'mores (see page 340).

The Game Plan: this is meant to be an easy-going get together. The children can "explore" and identify insects and plants, while still being in eyesight of the adults. Adults can grill, lounge, and enjoy visiting.

3. Girls Night Out
The Game Plan: "save" up all the birthday and special occasion gifts you "owe" and arrange to have a manicurist, masseuse, or yoga instructor be the main event at your get-together.

The Room(s): you'll want to have three areas including a lounge area, an eating area, and a "spa" area. Stock the spa area with towels, new cushy socks or flip flops for your guests, and arrange appropriate lighting, temperature and music (if necessary).

The Menu: lots of finger foods and foods that can hold up for several hours without heat. Plan on one or two green and fruit salads, such as a baby greens with roasted pears and figs or an endive, spinach and grape salad, lots of cut fresh seasonal fruit and dips, hot and cold herbal teas, cold fresh juice, freshly baked breads, and an assortment of muffins and cookies.

Szechuan-Style Lo Mein
Page 265

Chapter 18: ENTERTAINING CHILDREN

Kid's Party for 12-25 Children

More and more parents are asking for vegetarian or vegan food for their children, in schools, child care centers, and recreational programs. It's often not feasible to prepare a variety of snacks, as preparation space is limited and time is short. The solution is to offer one snack menu that appeals to both veggie and non-veggie children.

Kids are kids and they all enjoy crunchy, colorful, smooth, and tasty snacks. The more kids participate, the more they will enjoy snack time. Let them build "pebbles on a log" by stuffing celery with peanut butter or vegan cream cheese and sprinkling raisins, chopped dates, or dried cranberries on top. Dipping is always fun. Dips can include peanut, soy, or almond butter, vegan cream cheese or sour cream, blended tofu (especially the flavored variety), mashed avocado, and various flavors of hummus. Sweet dips can be made by puréeing bananas with fresh or frozen fruit, or by using soy yogurt or vegan cream cheese. Good "dip sticks" can include cut-up carrots, celery, peppers, mushrooms, cucumbers, pita wedges, breadsticks, pretzels, crackers, and apple or pear sections.

Decorating cupcakes is always fun. See Chapter 2 for some ideas. You can bake muffins or cupcakes from scratch, from a mix, or purchase vegan products, frosted or unfrosted. Toppings can include cake crumbs, mashed cold cereals, chopped nuts, shredded coconut, diced dried apricots, figs, apples, raisins, cranberries or peaches, or other seasonal ingredients.

Have a portable pudding party. Pack assorted vegan pudding flavors in individual cups, with a spoon taped to each cup. Place each cup in a small bag. Using waxed paper, make up multiple packets, containing about a teaspoon each, with chopped dried fruit, shredded coconut, cookie crumbs, and crushed cold cereal or granola. Place all the packets in a large bag. Have the guest of honor distribute the toppings, allowing the guests to pick and choose their pudding toppings. When they are finished, they can use the small bag for their trash, or they can have a decorating party, making fancy bags or small paper bag puppets.

If you're looking for a warm snack, try macaroni tossed with tomato sauce, small pieces of baked white potato or sweet potato, or small portions of veggie hot dogs or burgers on whole wheat buns. If the kids are old enough, cook up some fresh or frozen corn on the cob for a quick snack.

Make up a "house blend" of crunchy snacks by mixing several types of cold cereals (look for whole grain, no sugar varieties), pretzel pieces, and smashed vegan cookies with dried fruit. For a sweet snack, keep sorbet on hand. You can serve it in cones or topped with chopped fruit. Fruit salad made with a combination of fresh, frozen, and canned fruits are fast to make.

Bring on the crispy, crunchy finger foods and the cool desserts. Depending on the setting, you may be able to get children involved with the preparation, from mixing dips to filling snack bags to creating desserts. (One particularly popular preschool treat was the creation of a "beagle pear." On a bed of shredded lettuce, invert a pear half; use prune or plum halves for ears, raisins for eyes, and a grape for the nose. We couldn't decide if the kids had more fun making them or eating them.)

A favorite snack is a dessert "club." You'll need cookies with a flat surface, softened vegan ice cream or sorbet, and peanut or soynut butter that has been combined with granola (the stickier the better). Assemble the club by placing the first cookie on a dessert plate, top with ice cream, add a layer of peanut butter, and put on a second layer of ice cream and top with a second cookie. These can be made ahead of time and frozen (be sure to wrap them, as they will absorb freezer flavors). Kids can help assemble these (and they'll have fun doing it). For an "ice cream" cake, bake larger cookies and go higher on the layers.

Menu Ideas for Teenagers

Teenagers may still have the same tastes as younger children, may have moved to more adult selections, or may be on a weird planet all their own. We won't even attempt to solve adolescent angst, but we can give some ideas for feeding them at a gathering.

1. The All-American Fifties' Theme

Snacks: Pretzels, potato and veggie chips (buy them or slice potatoes and carrots thinly, bake off in the oven; use seasonings, like chili or onion powder, if you think your troops will like them), fresh veggie sticks (carrots, celery, zucchini, jicama, cherry tomatoes, radishes, cucumbers) and dips, popcorn

Beverages: Root beer floats (use vanilla or chocolate soy or rice ice cream), fruit punch (color it in weird colors, like blue or purple), assorted sparkling waters, lemonade.

Entrées: Veggie pizza (pile on the tomatoes, mushrooms, peppers, onions), veggie burgers and veggie dogs (remember the condiments: include relish, ketchup, veggie mayonnaise, onions, etc.), foot-long (or longer) subs with a base of vegan deli slices and vegan cheese and heaped with sliced cucumbers, tomatoes and green peppers, and shredded lettuce, carrots, and onions

Sides: Baked French-fries, tossed salad, coleslaw, macaroni salad

Desserts: Frozen soy/rice ice cream or sorbet sundaes (have chopped fruit, nuts, and vegan whipped topping available), watermelon wedges, cookies

2. Mama Mia, 'atsa Gooda Party Food

Snacks: Veggie chips, assorted olives, pickles, mini-bagel or muffin pizzas

Beverages: Assorted sparkling waters, lemonade, sparkling apple or grape juice

Entrées: Veggie lasagna, rotini with marinara sauce, assorted vegan ravioli

Sides: Garlic breadsticks, tossed salad

Desserts: Neapolitan soy or rice ice cream (vanilla, chocolate and strawberry ice cream combo) with chocolate sauce and chopped pistachios, melon balls

3. Make Mine Spicy

Snacks: Tortillas and veggie chips with salsa and guacamole

Beverages: Iced fruit drinks, horchatas (rice and fruit drinks which can be made by combining rice milk, raspberry or strawberry syrup, and a sprinkle of cinnamon), virgin margaritas (fruit slushes with margarita mix, hold the tequila)

Entrées: Veggie tacos and/or burritos with black bean and red chili sauce, four-bean chili (include chopped onions, chopped chilies, chopped bell peppers, chopped fresh cilantro, and shredded vegan soy cheese on the side)

Sides: Steamed and Spanish rice, mini corn cobs (cut corn cobs into 3-inch lengths or purchase, frozen, already cut) dusted with chili powder and garlic, steamed tortillas, green salad (to cool off some heat)

Desserts: Fruit smoothies, fresh berries, peanut butter cookies

Of course, if you don't have time to cook and assemble, you could order a three-foot long veggie sub from a local sandwich shop. Depending on the children's age, you should plan on ordering from three inches of sandwich (for preschoolers through first grade) all the way to twelve inches (for middle schoolers) of sandwich per child. You can ask a local bagel shop to assemble a bagel sandwich basket. Ask for an assortment of bagel flavors, avoiding the strong flavors, such as garlic and onion, and an assortment of spreads, including vegan margarine and peanut butter. If you have the time, you may want to supply the spreads, such as vegan cream cheese, soynut or sunflower butter, and hummus, if the bagel shop does not have them. Finally, pizza is always a hit, and what a surprise to have veggie pizzas delivered right to the party.

Beyond the Food

Parties are not just about the food. Have pre-made decorations, or have children create their own "ambience." Here are some ideas:

- Paint miniature pumpkins or gourds for Halloween.
- Make spiders using black pipe cleaners at Halloween.
- Fashion ghosts out of vegan lollipops or small apples with a popsicle-like stick inserted as a "stem" covered with squares of white fabric tied on the stick and decorated.
- Create snowmen out of recycled styrofoam balls, pom-poms, and buttons for winter parties.
- Make gingerbread houses at a winter party. Give each child a small, empty, clean juice carton. Let them cover the carton with vegan graham crackers using a flour and water mixture as glue.
- Make hearts with pipe cleaners and beads for Valentine's Day.
- Decorate large cut-out hearts at Valentine's Day.
- Paint and plant small flower pots for a springtime party.
- Create tissue paper flowers for a springtime party.
- Create marble art by placing a sheet of paper in a shallow box, dipping marbles into different color paints, and roll around in box for a colorful design.

Kids-Can-Cook

Kids can help "prepare" party food, if you have the space for them to set up various work stations and you have enough adults to help supervise. Here is a general idea of age-related tasks kids should be able to successfully accomplish:

Age 3: wash fruits and vegetables, tear lettuce and greens, toss salad, stir cold beverages and sauces

Age 4-5: open packages, mash bananas or beans with a fork, line up bread slices or crackers

Age 6-7: help to garnish food ("put three grapes on top of each bowl of pudding"), measure cold and liquid ingredients, assemble sandwiches

Ages 8-9: roll cookies, place muffin papers in tins and fill muffin tins with batter, use a whisk or fork to beat ingredients, assemble parfaits

Ages 10-12: help to design meal, microwave ingredients, stir soups and sauces, help to arrange food on platters

Ages 13-15: prepare food by following recipes, shred ingredients with a box grater, use a blender (with supervision) and an electric mixer, remove baked goods and light pans from the oven, arrange items on platters, and help to serve guests

Ages 16-18: prepare food by following recipes with more complicated instructions such as creating edible fruit basket centerpieces by pushing a flower shape cookie cutter through sliced pineapple and using a melon baller to create flower centers, then arranging the fruit flowers on skewers in a basket

Kids-Can-Cook Sample Recipes
See previous chapters for additional ideas

Peanut Butter Pinwheels
Serves 3-4

This easy-to-pack snack is perfect for a road trip, a day at the beach, a classroom party, or an after-school snack.

1 apple, cored and thinly sliced (about 1 cup)
1 Tablespoon orange juice
4 Tablespoon peanut butter, sunflower butter, or soynut butter
2 large flour tortillas
¼ cup raisins

Toss the apple in the orange juice until completely covered. Spread the peanut butter onto the tortillas. Evenly distribute the raisins and apples on the tortillas. Roll the tortillas tightly and slice into 1-inch sections. Push a toothpick through each pinwheel to keep them from falling apart.

Total Calories Per Serving: 444   Total Fat as % of Daily Value: 26%   Protein: 12 gm   Fat: 17 gm
Carbohydrates: 64 gm   Calcium: 119 mg   Iron: 3 mg   Sodium: 584 mg   Dietary Fiber: 6 gm

Indoor S'mores
Makes 10

¼ cup canned diced pears, drained
10 vegan graham cracker boards
½ cup vegan chocolate or carob chips
¼ cup shredded coconut

Preheat broiler. Pat pears dry. Break each graham cracker into 2 pieces. Place 10 pieces on a cookie sheet. Sprinkle pears, chips, and coconut over graham crackers. Broil, until chips are just melting, about 20-30 seconds. Remove from broiler, top with second cracker and serve.

Total Calories Per Serving: 72   Total Fat as % of Daily Value: 5%   Protein: 1 gm   Fat: 3 gm
Carbohydrates: 11 gm   Calcium: 2 mg   Iron: 0 mg   Sodium: 49 mg   Dietary Fiber: 1 gm

Some More Party Menu Ideas for Kids
<u>Pita Pockets:</u> Purchase mini-pitas or cut regular-sized pitas in quarters and fill with:
Nut butter (peanut, hazelnut, soy, sunflower) mixed with raisins or dried cranberries
Nut butter and shredded carrots
Vegan cream cheese with chopped carrots and zucchini
Vegan cream cheese with chopped dried apricots or fresh or canned pineapple
Hummus with chopped red bell pepper
Shredded Romaine and spinach tossed with salad dressing

Note: These sandwich fillings work well with whole wheat tortillas, vegetable wraps, or mini-bagels.

Lettuce Roll-Ups

Separate Romaine leaves. Wash and remove some of the center core so you can roll the leaves. Place a thin layer of any or the following:

Sliced vegan cheese

Sliced or minced fresh tomatoes

Shredded carrots

Hummus

"Egg" salad made with finely chopped extra-firm tofu tossed with vegan mayonnaise

Sliced vegan deli meats

Tightly roll and refrigerate until ready to serve.

Classroom Bento or Lunch Kits

Your own personal lunch box is always fun! Look for disposable individually sized compartmented boxes or inexpensive bento boxes. We have found them in some office supply stores, party supply stores, and in Asian markets. Fill a lunch box for each child, or allow them to make their own choices, depending on time, space, and age. Here are some ideas for menu items:

Pretzel nuggets or baked tortilla chips	Whole wheat or matzo crackers
Dry cold cereal mixture	Baked croutons
Popcorn	Cherry tomatoes
Baby carrots	Cucumber, zucchini, or carrot slices
Broccoli florets	Raisins, dried cranberries, or dried apple slices
Fresh strawberries or seedless grapes	Orange wedges or tangerines slices
Cubed vegan cheese	Flavored, cubed seitan or extra-firm tofu

Tips for Parents

Parties can be fun and healthy. Below are some tips to help plan a healthy party, as suggested by the American Dietetic Association, the Michigan Dietetic Association, and the Child Studies Center at California State University, Long Beach.

Safety Tips:

Remember to follow these 4 steps for serving safe food:

- Clean (wash hands and food-contact surfaces)
- Chill (refrigerate promptly)
- Cook (cook foods to proper temperatures)
- Separate (be aware of and avoid potentials for cross-contamination)

Be familiar with potential choking hazards:

If you are planning a party for young children, items such as whole grapes, sliced hot dogs, hard candies, or other items small enough to lodge in a child's throat should not be served.

Be familiar with the most common food allergens:

- Eight foods account for 90% of food-allergic reactions: milk, eggs, peanuts, tree nuts (walnuts, cashews, etc.), fish, shellfish, soy, and wheat.
- The most common food allergens for children are eggs, milk, and peanuts.

Healthy Tips:

- Incorporate physical activity through active games or dancing.
- Limit the quantity of food provided or consider a celebration without food.
- Plan a menu full of healthy choices.
- Try to limit the amount of sweets and high-fat snacks to 25% or less of the food being served.

Quick and Easy Snack Ideas:

- Air-popped popcorn
- Pretzels
- Crackers and peanut butter
- Baked chips and salsa
- Fresh fruit (with soy yogurt dip or peanut butter)
- Veggie sticks (with lowfat dip)
- 100% juice or sparkling water
- Vegan ginger snaps or graham crackers

Classroom Party Coordination

If you keep your event simple and stay in touch with the teacher, a classroom party will be a great success. Start the planning as early as possible so that you'll have enough time to gather ideas, supplies, and parents to help you.

Talk to the Teacher

Before you do anything, communicate with your child's teacher. Many parents feel pressured to turn a class party into a county fair, but it's more likely the teacher would prefer the event to be as simple as cookies and punch. You might want to have two conversations, the first to settle on the general details and then a second conversation to run a few of your ideas by him or her. But whether you have one chat or more, be sure to ask these questions before the event:

- What is the party date and duration, and how many kids are in the class?
- Are there any particular kinds of food or refreshments expected? Does any child in the class have a food allergy or dietary restriction you should be aware of?
- Is there a small kitchen, an area with a counter and a sink or do you need to provide your own work table and handwashing facilities, and finally do you need to bring all food ready to serve?
- Is there a particular theme? If not, is there something the class is studying that would be appropriate? Perhaps a favorite book character or science subject would be fun as well as excite the kids.
- Will the party be inside the classroom? On the playground? In the gym or cafeteria?
- How much time will you have to prep the party area? Time to clean up?

Plan the Party

Whether you're planning a classroom birthday party or the class holiday festival, keep it simple. Traditional food, games, and crafts are popular because they have timeless appeal to kids. Plus, you don't run into problems explaining game rules or placating picky eaters. Get creative by adapting traditional games, food, and activities to match your theme.

- Choose a theme. Try to tailor your choice to a subject the class has been studying (such as the environment or a favorite book) or to the time of year. Keep the focus on cultural (rather than religious) celebrations when planning a holiday party.

- If you're short on time, choose a craft or activity over competitive games. It keeps everyone calm, engaged, and wards off potential tantrums. Also, you don't have to worry about prizes. Making a craft also gives each child a favor to bring home.

- If you do plan competitive games, try to choose challenges that reward different kinds of skills, like memory, word, number, and physical achievement. Keep prizes conservative and come prepared with a few extras in case of ties or judging disputes.

- Think about inexpensive and quick ways to create ambiance, such as bringing in a boom box or iPod for party music. (Be aware of neighboring classes before you blast the volume.)

- Consider buying any supplies (such as napkins, cups, etc.) in bulk. It will save you time and money when you plan the next event. This is especially true in the younger grades, where there are parties almost every month!

- Even if you've discussed the students' dietary issues with the teacher, it's probably best to stay away from foods like peanuts and peanut butter, which can cause a severe allergic reaction in some kids.

- Try to send each child home with a party souvenir. These can be as simple as the craft made or a sheet of stickers.

The Day of the Event

The key to success here is arriving prepared and staying calm. You may be lucky enough to get set-up time while the students are in the library or at recess, but if not, try to be as unobtrusive as possible while you're getting ready. Here are a few suggestions for a satisfying and smooth event:

- Arrive with any supplies portioned individually so that you don't have to waste time getting organized. For example, if the kids are making hats, try to provide each student with his own bag filled with the basic materials. For the supplies students will share, offer enough choices so kids don't need to wait too long for their turn with a favorite marker.

- If you can't set up beforehand, have a quick craft activity that can keep kids busy at their desks while setting up. Another option is passing out refreshments at their desks while you finish getting ready.

- Be flexible. If students aren't responding to a game or activity, move on to the next idea.

- Particularly for younger students, alternate active events with quiet ones so that you don't send their energy levels out of control. Sharing a story or picture book is a great way to restore calm.

- Remember that you are the party planner, not the behavior warden. Let the teacher handle discipline problems.

Chapter 19: COOKING FOR A CROWD

If you're cooking for a crowd, careful planning can take the worry out of the event. With careful menu planning, advanced preparation, and easy-to-make and easy-to-serve dishes, you can present a meal that everyone, including the cook, can enjoy.

Stress-Reducing Tips for Entertaining a Crowd

- Start with smart shopping by stocking up on pantry items a week in advance and for perishables 1-2 days in advance.
- Select menu items that can be made a day or two in advance so you don't run out of space or energy the day of the event.
- Select foods that can be served cold or at room temperature and that can be served family style on large platters for quick serving.
- Incorporate healthy foods into your menu by adding fresh, frozen, or dried fruits and vegetables and grains to your menu. Don't be afraid to add color because the more colorful the food, the higher the nutrient content.
- Buffets usually mean that people eat more. If you want to serve buffet-style, remember your guests will have a tendency to eat one-third more food because it all looks so good. Think about lower calorie options for those that are concerned about their intake.
- Stay with the types of dishes you're comfortable preparing. Go for familiar foods with a twist and easy but beautiful presentations. If you don't have the time or space to prepare all your meal items, be certain to sample prepared items from local stores. Check out ordering and/or delivery information so you have all the details prior to the event.
- Set the table the night before if you're planning seating arrangements. Set up serving tables and map out where each platter (with serving utensils) will be if you are hosting a buffet. If you are decorating, plan on doing this the night before as well.
- If you are using a facility other than your home, check out all the details at least one week before the event. Information that will help your event go smoothly includes:

    - How soon can we get into our room to set up?
    - Can we store food in your refrigerators overnight or several hours before the event?
    - Is the kitchen stocked with pots, pan, cooking utensils, serving dishes, silverware, china, coffee urns or glasses; is there a cost to use them?
    - How long do we have the room?
    - Do you provide clean-up materials, including mops, brooms, trash bags, and soap?
    - Can we rearrange the furniture?
    - What are parking arrangements?

No Time and the Whole Family's Coming in Two Days!

Don't panic, but do set a schedule. Before you get started, first take stock of your time and skills, then map out a plan. Allow more time for the things you do well yourself. For example, if you are great cook, but not so great on decorating, we suggest that you cook, and your roommates/family members take care of the ambiance. Here are some more guidelines:

- Speed Dust. Focus on the obvious clutter, not if the shelves need new paper! Expect guests to use all the rooms. Carefully clean counters and other visible areas.

- Food is important. Cook ahead and serve from the freezer, if possible. Find out which local markets have frozen vegan hors d'oeurves, which bakeries have great vegan carrot cakes or cupcakes, and which market has the greatest variety of vegan frozen desserts. If you think you will need more than two or three containers of a particular item, you may want to speak to the manager to ensure the amount you need will be in stock when it is needed.

- Plan a realistic menu. This means preparing dishes that you really have the time to shop for and to cook and to purchase those dishes that take more time or equipment than you have.

- Include lots of healthy options, such as hummus and veggies, seasonal fruit plates, roasted vegetable or fruit salsas, rice pilafs, tropical fruit sorbets, etc. You get the idea. Remember to include colorful garnishes. Hummus isn't very pretty on its own, but becomes glamorous in a colorful bow, garnished with ribbons of green, yellow, and red bell pepper.

- Depending on how extensively you want to plan, you can go to cooking software, such as Master Cook. Master Cook is not exclusively vegetarian, but if you are planning a party for 10 (or 5 or 50) Master Cook suggests menus for all tastes, prepares shopping lists and will modify for vegetarian, diabetic, low-sodium, or lowfat guests.

- Think about the table setting, since this is the stage for your food performance. Centerpieces can be very simple (several candles framed by seasonal flowers) or ornate. Our favorite type is edible center pieces, such as bouquets of herbs and edible flowers, arrangements of seasonal fruit and vegetables, or, if you have the patience and the talent, carved vegetables and flowers. If you are familiar with salt dough (the type of dough used in bread sculptures) you may want to fashion centerpieces out of it. Inquire of your local bakeries, as they may do bread sculptures for special occasions. These bread sculptures last for several months if kept in a cool dry place between uses.

Serving, Simmering, and Sitting

In addition to food, you'll need to think about serving platters and serving utensils, various sizes of plates, cups and glasses, eating utensils, napkins, salt and pepper shakers, and anything else that will be needed on the table. The best way to plan for this is to "map" out your menu and match it with the serving platters you have. For example, "the hummus is to go into the orange bowl, served with the black-handled large spoon." With a map, you'll know you have all the necessary equipment and people can help you dish up and serve the various menu items. Decide whether you want to fill platters just once, or if you will be able to refill as needed. This will help you to decide how many and what size serving dishes you need.

Buffets, rather than seated meals, offer guests a variety of choices. They can select exactly the menu items they want in the quantity they want. They can acquire a taste for new food items and enjoy old favorites. You'll need to coordinate your serving possibilities when you plan your buffet. Depending on your space and the number people helping you, a self-service buffet may be the way to go.

Think about your everyday menus and see what can be "gussied up" for an entertaining meal. For example, your lentil loaf can be encased in puff pastry (buy it frozen) or pie crust and turned into a lentil "wellington" served with mushroom gravy, garlic mashed potatoes (simply add 2 Tablespoons of sautéed, minced garlic for every pound of potatoes), and curried greens. Or try baked tomatoes filled with cornbread stuffing (add kernel corn, sautéed onions, carrots and celery, and toasted pine nuts), sweet potato fritters, and braised kale (braised in vegetable stock and seasoned with garlic and white pepper). We were served a marinated and sautéed portobello "steak" on a bed of a trio of grains (brown rice flavored with onion, couscous flavored with cilantro, and barley flavored with dill) and a charred pepper sauce (bell peppers roasted over a flame, peeled, seeded, puréed and heated with minced garlic) at a holiday party and have recreated this menu many times, with great guest satisfaction.

Many food items are versatile. For example, ravioli can be steamed, sauced, and served as a hot or cold appetizer or entrée. Or you can steam ravioli, drain, and pat dry. Then dip ravioli in soymilk, dip in seasoned bread crumbs, and oven fry. Serve as a crispy appetizer or as part of a pasta platter. Cooked and chilled ravioli served with a variety of dipping sauces (think of marinara, pesto, and lemon vinaigrette) makes a festive and fast appetizer. The same goes for veggies. Serve sliced bell peppers (get them in their rainbow of colors), baby carrots, whole green onions, cherry tomatoes or tomato wedges, sliced zucchini and summer squash, and fresh green and wax beans in their natural state (raw, that is) with dipping sauces as a cold crudite (translation: crunchy stuff) platter, or go one step further and use the same veggies for hot tempura (you can purchase tempura batter mixes or you can create your own with rice flour and soymilk).

Desserts can be simple, yet elegant for a large gathering, especially if everyone is feeling a little stuffed after a big meal. Here are some fast, yet fancy dessert ideas:

1. Drizzle fresh berries or orange slices with orange liqueur and shredded fresh mint.
2. Serve a small, peeled tangerine with three or four halved dates and some toasted macadamia or hazelnuts.
3. Toss grapefruit sections with pomegranate seeds or sliced fresh grapes, orange juice, and (optional) some rose water.
4. Serve a ripe pear with almond or chocolate biscotti.
5. Serve lemon sorbet topped with fresh or frozen berries and a splash of blackberry liqueur.
6. Serve vanilla soy or rice ice cream drizzled with amaretto and topped with a chocolate cookie wafer.
7. Serve melon slices tossed with fresh shredded mint and chilled champagne.

Secrets of Cooking Large Amounts of Food

So what is the secret to cooking in large quantities? Like cooking any size meal, the secret is in the planning. You will need extra and larger everything. Take your recipes and list all the ingredients you need to buy. Plan your menu and inventory your serving dishes, pots and pans, plates, forks, knives, spoons, and drinking glasses at least a week in advance. Buy everything you need ahead of time, right down to spreads for bread and ice for drinks.

Once you have your menu and inventory planned, figure out a time schedule. Have the house cleaned and seating arrangements completed the day before so you can focus on the meal, otherwise you'll be pulling your hair out trying to get everything done on time. The easiest thing to cook is a one-dish meal with few side dishes.

Sample Planning Sketch

Prepared Dishes:

Main dish: Vegetable Lasagna (Prepare one week prior to party, triple recipe)
Day of Event: 2:00 pm take prepared lasagna out of freezer, cook in roaster for 2 hours in oven; serve on platter with red-handled spatula
Side vegetable: Steamed Broccoli
Day of event: 3:00 pm place in 3-quart steamer, plan on 20 minutes stove top time; serve in blue bowl
Bread, buy brown-and-serve rolls (or make from scratch ahead of time) and put in oven for 15 minutes; last thing to cook, serve in basket, buy new towel

Equipment and Ingredients Needed:
Lasagna pan
10-inch skillet
3 boxes lasagna noodles
2 cans (28 ounces) chopped tomatoes
1 large or 2 mediuim onions, sliced
6 carrots (or more as needed)
6 potatoes (or more as needed)
1 can vegan onion soup
1 can vegan mushroom soup
3 Tablespoons Braggs Liquid Aminos or soy sauce
1-2 cups mushrooms (optional)
1-2 packages onion soup mix, per directions

It can't be emphasized enough that you should read through the directions before starting a recipe, so you can assemble all the necessary equipment, preheat ovens, allow for cooking or cooling time, etc. If possible, do a dry run with a recipe before using it in an important situation. (Thanksgiving morning is not the time to find out that the pineapple-sweet potato pie needs a longer baking time in your oven.) Make notes if you find the recipe needs to be "tweaked." For example, a cornbread recipe may need more soymilk or water than originally called for; note it for future reference.

Speaking of adjusting recipes, let's walk through how to convert a recipe (if you need more or less than the amount on the recipe). It takes a few minutes to do the calculations, but you'll benefit in the long run since you'll wind up with the right amount of food (saving time, face, and costs).

Yields

Say you have a soup recipe with a yield of $1^1/_2$ gallons and you need to make 10 gallons. You could "eyeball" the recipe and triple it plus a little more. It might work, as soup recipes may not be that sensitive. If the soup comes out too thin, you can thicken it. If it comes out too thick, you can thin it. Of course, you'll then have to adjust the seasonings and some of the ingredients. You might wind up with too much or too little.

"Eyeballing" recipes or guestimating how much to change recipes rarely works well. Sensitive recipes, such as baking recipes or recipes that require a balance of spices, don't translate well when you add an additional pinch here or an extra can of tomato purée there. The following is a conversion formula that will allow you to increase or decrease recipe yields without the guesswork.

To Convert Total Yields

1. Divide the yield you want (the new yield) by the yield you have on the recipe (the original yield). It makes no difference if you are increasing or decreasing the new amount. You use the same procedure.

2. The number you have just gotten is called the "conversion factor." Simply multiply every ingredient by the conversion factor to get the new amount of each ingredient.

For example, if the original recipe has 10 portions, but you need 15, just divide 15 by 10 (original into new) to get the conversion factor, which is 1.5. So, if the original recipe called for 3 pounds of tomatoes, the new amount would be 4 lbs 8 oz (3 lbs tomatoes x 1.5 = 72 ounces or 4 lbs 8 oz).

Portions

What if only portion numbers are listed on a recipe you would like to change? You need to do two steps to find the yield of the recipe and then can proceed as explained above.

You find the yield (so you can get the conversion factor) by multiplying original portions times the portion size (twenty-five 4-oz portions becomes 100 oz or a 6 lbs 4 oz yield). Do the same for the new amount you desire (e.g., thirty 5-oz portions becomes 150 oz or 9 lbs 6 oz for the new yield). Then proceed as above. This might sound like a lot of numbers, but after you've done this several times, it will seem easy.

Once you have your recipes converted, you will need to do a bit of guestimation to decide how much of each recipe to prepare. If you are doing a buffet or creating platters, here are some guidelines:

1. Entrées: estimate by pieces (for individual items, such as enchiladas, cabbage rolls, or corn cakes) or portions (for casserole-type dishes). Assume 2 pieces for adults and one piece for children or 8 ounces per adult (for casserole-type dishes) and 3 ounces for children. Multiply the number of portions needed and you will have the amount to prepare, as in 45 tamales or 10 pounds of lentil loaf. Some caterers like to prepare ten per cent over the anticipated number of guests, for insurance. That's up to you.

2. Side dishes: estimate 4 ounces for adults and 2 ounces for children for most hot side dishes.

3. Salads: for green or tossed salads, estimate 8 ounces (or the amount of salad that will fill a measuring cup) for adults and 3 ounces for children along with 3 ounces of salad dressing for adults and 1 ounce for children. For solid salads (fruit, potato, pasta, etc.), estimate 5 ounces for adults and 2 ounces for children.

4. Sauces/gravies: depending on your entrées and side dishes, estimate 2 ounces for adults and 1 ounce for children.

5. Fruit or vegetable trays: estimate 6-8 pieces (cherry tomatoes, radishes, carrot sticks) for adults and 2-3 pieces per child or 6-7 ounces per adult and 2 ounces per child.

6. Desserts: this is a little harder to standardize; estimate by the slice (rule of thumb is 96 two-inch slices for a whole cake sheet), by the piece (cupcakes, cookies, etc.), or by the ounce (about 5 ounces of sorbet or ice cream is a standard portion).

Measurement Refresher

A. Liquid
1 cup = 8 ounces
1 pint = 2 cups or 16 ounces
1 quart = 4 cups or 32 ounces or 2 pints
$\frac{1}{2}$ gallon = 8 cups or 64 ounces or 2 quarts or 4 pints
1 gallon = 128 ounces or 16 cups or 4 quarts or 8 pints
1 Tablespoon = 3 teaspoons
2 Tablespoons = 1 ounce

B. Solid
1 pound = 16 ounces

Sample Recipe Conversion: GOING UP!

Let's say you have your Aunt Mary's wonderful marinara sauce recipe, which has a yield of 1 quart (32 ounces). You would like to make 5 gallons (128 ounces x 5, or 640 ounces) for a big spaghetti party. To get the conversion factor, divide 640 ounces by 32 ounces. The answer is 20. This is your conversion factor and you will multiply every ingredient by 20 to get the new amount.

Original Recipe Amount (1 quart total)	x Conversion Factor	= New Recipe Amount (5 gallons total)
8 ounces tomato purée	x 20	160 oz (or 1 gal 1 qt)
4 ounces tomato paste	x 20	80 oz (or $1/2$ gal 1 pint)
10 ounces vegetable stock	x 20	200 oz (or $1^1/2$ gal 1 cup)
4 ounces minced onions	x 20	80 oz (or 5 lbs)

Sample Recipe Conversion: GOING DOWN!

Your Uncle Ernie has a wonderful hash brown potato recipe he learned in the Army. His recipe makes about 75 pounds. You only need 10 pounds. So, divide 75 into 10. The answer is 0.13 (rounding the answer). This is your conversion factor for all the ingredients.

Original Recipe Amount (75 lbs)	x Conversion Factor	= New Recipe Amount (10 lbs)
60 pounds peeled potatoes	x 0.13	7.8 lbs (or 7 lbs 14 oz)
3 pounds minced onions	x 0.13	0.40 lbs (or 7 oz)
1 pound flour	x 0.13	0.13 lbs (or $1^1/2$ oz)
1 quart vegetable oil (32 oz)	x 0.13	$3^1/2$ oz

A note of caution about using conversions with baking recipes: The converted amounts don't always work. You'll have to do the mathematical conversion and then work with the recipe to make it an exact fit. Remember that baking recipes are akin to chemical formulas and rely on fairly exact interactions between ingredients. If you convert a baking formula, do a test run before putting it on the menu.

How Much to Prepare

Deciding how much to make is not an exact science. However, we can give you some basic guidelines.

1. Coffee: just work backwards. If you have 6-ounce coffee cups and you think you will serve about 75 cups, then you'll need 450 ounces of prepared coffee or about $2^1/2$ gallons (450 divided by 128 ounces/gallon). One pound of coffee makes approximately 3 gallons of brewed coffee. The rest will depend on your coffee maker (do you make 16 ounce pots? 1 gallon urns? etc.).

2. Juice can be figured out in the same way. Decide which glasses you'll be serving in, figure total need, and then decide on type of juice. Will you be diluting concentrates, purchasing canned and ready to use, purchasing individual juices, etc.

3. Hot cereals and grains: most cereal and grains expand $2^1/2$ times from raw to cooked, so 16 ounces of raw oats should cook up to about 48 ounces of prepared oatmeal. If you want to serve twenty-five 4-ounce portions of oatmeal, then you'll need 100 ounces; divided by 2.5 to figure out the raw amount to cook (you should have gotten about 40 ounces or 2 pounds 8 ounces of raw oats).

4. Fruit: you'll need to take into account the percentage of waste depending on the type of fruit chosen. For example, berries and grapes don't need to be peeled, so if you buy 20 pounds of them, you can serve 20 pounds. Peeled melons, apples and oranges will loss some weight during processing, so be sure to buy more than you actually need.

Sample amounts for 25:

- Coffee (8-ounce cups): approximately 2 gallons (or $1\frac{1}{2}$ pounds of coffee)
- Soymilk (4 ounces, for coffee and cereal): approximately 3 quarts
- Fresh mixed fruit salad ($\frac{1}{3}$-cup portion): 4 pounds, 11 ounces prepared
- Toast (1 slice): $1\frac{1}{4}$ loaves (most store-bought loaves have 20 slices of bread, with ends discarded)

Pass the Party Food

Your event may not lend itself to sit-down service or even to a buffet. Here are some tips for easy entertaining using party trays and platters that can be easily passed around to your guests.

- Chips and crackers are great for dipping. Mix it up with celery and carrot sticks, fresh strawberries, raw green beans, summer squash slices, and broccoli florets.
- Offer guests an assortment. For eight or more people, serve 4 different kinds of vegan rolled deli slices and chunked vegan cheeses.

Here are some amounts to help make sure there's plenty of food to go around.

- For platters or sandwiches:

# of Guests	Vegan Deli Slices	Vegan Sliced Cheese	Rolls	Bread	Salad	Chips	Vegan Cookies
4	1 lb	$\frac{1}{2}$ lb	8	12 slices	1 lb	4 ozs	8
8	2 lbs	1 lb	16	24 slices	2 lbs	8 ozs	16
12	3 lbs	$1\frac{1}{2}$ lbs	24	36 slices	3 lbs	12 ozs	24
16	4 lbs	2 lbs	32	48 slices	4 lbs	16 ozs	32
24	6 lbs	3 lbs	48	72 slices	6 lbs	24 ozs	48
32	8 lbs	4 lbs	64	96 slices	8 lbs	32 ozs	64
40	10 lbs	5 lbs	80	120 slices	10 lbs	40 ozs	80

- Beverages

Coffee: Use 1 pound of coffee for fifty 8-ounce servings.
Tea: Use 1 cup of loose tea for fifty 8-ounce servings.
Vegan Milk for Coffee: Use 1 pint (2 cups) for 25 servings.
Vegan Milk to Drink: Use $1\frac{1}{2}$ gallons (10 quarts) for twenty-four 8-ounce servings.

- Salads

Fruit Salad: 2 quarts (about 8 cups) for 24 people
Potato Salad: 3 quarts (about 12 cups) for 24 people
Vegetable Salad: 5 quarts (about 20 cups) for 25 people

- Vegetables

Lettuce: 4 heads of Romaine or iceberg for 24 people
Carrot Strips: 1 pound carrots for 25 people

Celery: 1 pound celery for 25 people
Olives: 1 quart olives for 25 people (3-4 olives per person)
Pickles: 1 quart pickles for 25 people
Mashed Potatoes: 7 pounds of raw potatoes for 25 people
Baked Potatoes: 25 small potatoes for 25 people (approximately 10 pounds)

- Miscellaneous

Vegan Margarine: $1/2$ pound margarine for 32 people (about 1 teaspoon each)
Juice: Two 46-ounce cans for twenty-three 4-ounce servings
French Bread: Two 18-inch loaves for 24 servings
Extra-Firm Tofu: 4 pounds for 24 people (this is served chunked, in a casserole)

- Desserts

Cake: A $15^1/_2$ x $10^1/_2$ x 1-inch sheet cake will feed 24 people
This is usually what is considered a half sheet.
Vegan Ice Cream: 3 quarts of ice cream for 24 people.
Fruit Pie: Five 9-inch pies will serve 30 people.
Canned Fruit: Eight 28-ounce cans for 24 people

- Rice and Pasta

Long Grain Rice: $10^1/_2$ cups uncooked rice for 24 people
Spaghetti or Noodles: 10 to $12^1/_2$ pounds uncooked pasta for 25 people

Sample Large Scale Recipe

Salad Bowl for 20

Serves 20

**2 heads chicory
2 pounds endives
24 tomatoes, sliced
6 cucumbers, sliced and peeled
2 heads lettuce
24 radishes, sliced
6 green peppers, chopped
Vegan French dressing as needed, approximately 2 pints (4 cups)
2 bunches watercress**

Line a large salad bowl with chicory and endive. Next, alternate layers of tomatoes and cucumbers. In a separate bowl, mix the lettuce, radishes, and green peppers with the French dressing. Put in the center of the large salad bowl and garnish the top with watercress. Chill before serving.

Total Calories Per Serving: 285   Total Fat as % of Daily Value: 38%   Protein: 3 gm   Fat: 25 gm
Carbohydrates: 16 gm   Calcium: 57 mg   Iron: 1 mg   Sodium: 405 mg   Dietary Fiber: 4 gm

Some More Tips for Cooking for a Crowd

Some menu items are better suited for cooking for a crowd than others. Here are a few ideas:

-Items cooked in a pan, frozen, and reheated as needed, such as lasagna, shepherd's pie, quiche, pot pies, stuffed pasta shells, or cabbage rolls.

-Items cooked in a big pot on the stove or a crockpot, such as chilies, vegetable and potato stews, curries, gumbo, lentil stew, and Southwestern bean and hominy stew.

-Grilled items get the cook out of the kitchen and allow guests to get involved if they want to. Beyond veggie burgers and veggie dogs, premake seitan, tempeh, or veggie kebobs, marinated seitan or portobello mushroom "steaks," baked potatoes, roasted fruit (such as pineapple and mango slices) or roasted vegetables (such as summer squash, tomatoes, mini-corn on the cob, and sliced sweet onions).

Depending on the party, you may be able to get your guests involved in meal preparation.

- Pasta party: premake pasta dough or purchase vegan wonton or eggroll wrappers (wonton and eggroll wrappers can do double-duty as ravioli pasta) and premake filling; have a short "how to stuff pasta" lesson. Allow guests to fill and finish their own stuffed pasta. This is a lot easier than making ravioli by yourself! Have pots of boiling water ready to cook the prepared pasta and sauces warming on the stove for serving the pasta.

- Assemble your own: think about setting out all the fixings for stuffing your own taco or rolling your own burrito, stuffing your own baked potato, or assembling your own bowl of chili.

- The world's longest sandwich: many submarine sandwich shops will sell you just the bread. Order as many three-foot long sliced rolls as you think you'll need (figure about 6 inches of sandwich per adult, 3 inches per child). Put out the sandwich fixings and let your guests prepare a communal sandwich.

Keep it Simple

Sometimes a get-together is all about the food, and sometimes the food is just one of the elements. If the food is in the background of your large event, you can keep the preparation and service easy, while serving enjoyable food.

- Bread: if you are not a bread baker, seek out the best vegan bread baker in your area. Purchase a variety of freshly baked bread, rolls, bagels, bialies, etc., that can be simply sliced and served with a variety of homemade or purchased dips and spreads.

- Fresh fruit: rather than elaborate desserts, if the situation is appropriate, purchase low-labor seasonal fruit, such as oranges, blueberries, strawberries, raspberries, grapes, and other fruit that require little cutting and peeling. Serve on chilled platters, with or without dips.

- Fresh vegetables: minimize your labor by purchasing baby carrots, radishes, cherry or grape tomatoes, mushrooms, fresh green or wax beans, sugar snap peas, and other vegetables that require little to no peeling or chopping.

- Jarred, marinated or pickled vegetables: olives, cucumbers, jalapeños, artichoke hearts, roasted red peppers, and pickled or marinated vegetable mixes add color and flavor to fresh vegetable platters.

- Prebaked pizza crusts: you can make your own crusts or purchase them. Heat them just prior to serving and pile high with chopped olives, sundried tomatoes, shredded vegan cheese, canned pineapple tidbits, chopped fresh herbs, artichoke hearts, sliced mushrooms, or diced vegan meats.

- Rolled breads, such as large tortillas or lavash: rather than trying to create a thousand small sandwiches, stuff, roll, and slice filled breads. They'll look like elegant pinwheels and take very little time to create. Ingredients can be as simple as vegan cream cheese with sliced olives or as complex as baby spinach, shredded vegan cheese, shredded roasted red peppers, and a homemade dressing.

Chapter 20: WORKING WITH A CATERER

Finding a Caterer

Just as it is with any cuisine, caterers have varying abilities to work with vegetarian menus. You may be able to locate a vegetarian caterer in your area or a caterer who offers vegetarian menus along with other cuisines. If you can't get recommendations from friends, you may want to contact vegetarian restaurants or markets that offer prepared vegetarian cuisine. Other catering-locator resources may be the food editor of your local paper or institutions that offer vegetarian cuisine, such as Jain or Seventh-day Adventist groups.

When selecting a caterer, be certain to sample the food they offer. If a vegetarian restaurant or market offers catering services, taste menu items they have prepared before making your selection. If you will be using a caterer, ask for a menu tasting. Be reasonable when you do your tasting. If you are having a small buffet event, with less than 25 people, you should expect only very small samples. If you are having a larger, served event, more than 100 people, you may expect to see and taste an entire plate, so you can get an idea of how the menu items will appear and if the flavors are well matched.

Lots of Catering Concerns

We will leave the finances to you. Needless to say, have a firm idea of your budget before you start "auditioning" caterers. Many caterers charge by the "head," or number of people attending the event. In addition to the menu chosen, prices will differ for served versus buffet meals. Per-head charges may include some or all of the following:

> appetizers
> entrée and side dishes
> bread and condiments
> standard dessert (not specialty cakes)
> hot beverages (coffee and tea)
> service style (e.g., buffet vs served)
> standard linen (table clothes and napkins)
> room rental
> standard centerpieces
> taxes and gratuity

Catering charges differ greatly, as events and locations differ greatly. The following items are usually not included in per-head charges:

> alcoholic beverages
> nonstandard cold beverages (such as sparkling cider)
> nonstandard desserts (such as wedding cakes)
> nonstandard-colored linen
> entertainment (such as live music)
> audiovisual equipment (such as microphones, projectors, etc.)
> parking
> specialty centerpieces (such as ice or vegetable carvings, seasonal decorations, etc.)
> flowers or room decorations
> meals for nonguests (such as parking valets, musicians, hostesses, etc.)
> specialty rentals (such as outdoor tents, podiums, champagne fountains, etc.)

The above mentioned items are in no way absolutes. Every caterer has a different way of handling costs.

You need to be aware of what can be charged for and don't be afraid to ask questions. Negotiations are always a possibility. For example, if a caterer quotes you $25 per head for a seated wedding meal, you need to find out what this includes. Most caterers will have referrals for items they don't handle, such as flowers or music. Be certain to audition the non-food people the same way you auditioned the caterer.

The caterer will want a guarantee for the number of meals to be served. Remember that the final guarantee you give, usually three to four days before the event, is the number for which you will pay. Also remember that the caterer is only responsible for preparing meals for the number given in the final guarantee.

Do not assume that the caterer will "have it" or "do it." For example, if flowers are not discussed, there probably won't be flowers on the table. If centerpieces are not discussed, the caterer will probably place their standard centerpiece on each table, if they have one. If you do not ask for a microphone, the caterer cannot magically produce one.

This is your party. The more details you communicate, the more the event will please you. If you select a buffet, coordinate with the caterer how people will proceed to the buffet tables. If the meal is to be served, specify the order of service. For example, you may want the head table or the guest of honor to be served first. If you are having presentations or speeches between courses, tell the caterer. This way they can keep the salad cold and the entrée hot. Let the caterer know if it is all right for the servers to serve food and beverages or pick up used plates while speeches are being made.

If you have guests with special dietary needs supply the caterer with the information and ask how this will be handled. If you would like a small reception table set up at the room entrance, or an extra table for gifts or awards, you must tell the caterer, so they can order sufficient amounts of tables, chairs, and linen. You get the idea. The caterer can make certain the food is tasty, served at the correct temperature, and looks good. Beyond that, the caterer needs you to help with the "choreography" of the event.

Vegetarian Concerns

In addition to the linen, flowers, and music, the caterer may need direction in selecting and preparing menus that meet your specifications. Since there are so many nuances to vegetarian cuisine, even the most experienced vegetarian caterer should be offered a "short course" in the types of ingredients you do and do not prefer to have included in your meals.

Caterers are busy people and may not have the time or level of understanding to read a lot of information. The remainder of this chapter is designed to help you communicate your food preferences to caterers. Read them yourself so you are familiar with the contents. Make copies and highlight the areas that are important for the caterer. Rather than just handing the caterer a "reading assignment," be certain to review the information, so everyone is on the same page.

Basic Vegetarianism

If you see that it is necessary, use the following information to purvey pertinent vegetarian information to your caterer. You can make copies of this article, or visit www.vrg.org and download "Vegetarianism in a Nutshell."

Before giving this to your caterer, review it and see if you need to make any additions or deletions, depending on your food preferences.

Vegetarianism in a Nutshell

What is a Vegetarian?

Vegetarians do not eat meat, fish, and poultry. Vegans are vegetarians who abstain from eating or using all animal products, including milk, cheese, other dairy items, eggs, wool, silk, and leather. Among the many reasons for being a vegetarian are health, ecological, and religious concerns, dislike of meat, compassion for animals, belief in non-violence, and economics. The American Dietetic Association has affirmed that a vegetarian diet can meet all known nutrient needs. The key to a healthy vegetarian diet, as with any other diet, is to eat a wide variety of foods, including fruits, vegetables, plenty of leafy greens, whole grain products, nuts, seeds, and legumes. Limit your intake of sweets and fatty foods.

Making the change to a Vegetarian Diet

Many people become vegetarian instantly. They totally give up meat, fish, and poultry overnight. Others make the change gradually. Do what works best for you. Being a vegetarian is as hard or as easy as you choose to make it. Some people enjoy planning and preparing elaborate meals, while others opt for quick and easy vegetarian dishes.

Vegetarian Nutrition

Protein

Vegetarians easily meet their protein needs by eating a varied diet, as long as they consume enough calories to maintain their weight.

It is not necessary to plan combinations of foods. A mixture of proteins throughout the day will provide enough "essential amino acids." (See "Position of the American Dietetic Association: Vegetarian Diets," JADA, July 2009; Simply Vegan; and nutrition information on www.vrg.org)

Good protein sources are: beans, lentils, tofu, nuts, seeds, tempeh, chickpeas, peas... Many common foods, such as whole grain bread, greens, potatoes, and corn, quickly add to protein intake.

Iron

Good iron sources are: dried beans, tofu, tempeh, spinach, chard, baked potatoes, cashews, dried fruits, bulgur, and iron-fortified foods (such as cereals, instant oatmeal, and veggie "meats"). To increase the amount of iron absorbed at a meal, eat a food containing vitamin C, such as citrus fruit or juices, tomatoes, or broccoli. Using iron cookware also adds to iron intake.

Calcium

Good calcium sources include: broccoli, collard greens, kale, mustard greens, tofu prepared with calcium, fortified soymilk, and fortified orange juice.

Vitamin B12

The adult recommended intake for vitamin B12 is very low. Vitamin B12 comes primarily from animal-derived foods. A diet containing dairy products or eggs provides adequate vitamin B12. Fortified foods, such as some brands of cereal, nutritional yeast, soymilk, or veggie "meats," are good non-animal sources. Check labels to discover other products that are fortified with vitamin B12. Tempeh and sea vegetables are not a reliable source of vitamin B12. To be on the safe side, if you are vegan and do not consume fortified foods regularly, you should take a non-animal derived supplement.

Children and Vegetarianism

According to The American Dietetic Association, vegetarian and vegan diets can meet all nitrogen needs and amino acid requirements for growth. Diets for children should contain enough calories to support growth and have reliable sources of key nutrients, such as iron, zinc, vitamin D, and vitamin B12.

Vegetarian Catering: Helpful Hints

Vegan menu items are easy to prepare and offer. Here are some suggestions.

Entrées

Three-Bean Tamale Pie: alternate 3 types of cooked beans with salsa, top with prepared cornbread mix, bake

Chili Sauté: add chopped bell peppers, onions, and garlic to vegetarian chili and sauté quickly; serve over steamed brown or white rice or cornbread

Veggie Shepherd's Pie: top vegetable stew (try a mixture of carrots, celery, onions, and mushrooms) with prepared mashed potatoes, bake

Pasta Bake: toss cooked pasta with marinara sauce, chopped tomatoes, and diced mushrooms, season with fresh basil and oregano, bake

Lentil Stew: combine cooked lentils with cooked quartered new potatoes, sliced carrots, diced celery, and chopped tomatoes, season with pepper and dill, allow to simmer, serve

Side Dishes

Garlic Mashed Potatoes: from scratch, roast whole garlic heads, peel and mash with potatoes; for speed scratch, add granulated garlic to mashed potato mixture

Herbed Potatoes: coat new potatoes with olive oil (use a spray to save time and cost), toss with dried herbs, and bake until crisp

Refried Beans: mash cooked pinto beans with sautéed onions, and bell peppers, sauté to heat

O'Brien Potatoes: add diced peppers, chopped onions, and cut corn with hash browns, bake or sauté

Rice Pilaf: sauté rice in a small amount of vegetable oil, then steam in vegetable stock, garnish with cooked peas, carrots, mushrooms, and slivered almonds

Grab-and-Go

Very Veggie Pita Pizza: coat the inside of a pita with marinara sauce, stuff with sliced mushrooms, chopped tomatoes, onions and bell peppers, minced garlic, and diced olives, heat in oven or microwave, serve hot

Veggie Size: serve veggie burger of your choice with vegetarian chili and chopped veggies, serve on whole-grain bun or in a pita

Burrito Wrap: fill a large tortilla or wrap with vegetarian refried beans, sliced chilies, chopped tomatoes or salsa, sliced onions and avocado slices, heat in oven or microwave, serve hot

Grilled Vegetable Brochette: skewer cherry tomatoes, whole mushrooms, chunks of bell pepper, zucchini, eggplant, and tomatoes, marinate in teriyaki or soy sauce for several hours. Grill until veggies are lightly brown, serve hot or cold

Desserts

Couscous with Berries: toss cooked couscous with thawed, frozen berries and chopped fresh mint, serve alone or with sorbet

Peach Cobbler: top frozen or canned pie filling with strips of piecrust, chopped nuts and raisins, bake

Baked Apple: stuff cored apples with chopped dried fruit, cinnamon, ginger and orange zest, sweeten with orange juice concentrate, bake

Apple Bread Pudding: combine shredded bread with apple pie filling (use applesauce for additional moisture), bake

Fruit Compote: stew dried fruit (raisins, apricots, prunes, apples work well) with peeled, sliced apples and pears, season with cinnamon, mace, and lemon zest. Serve hot or chilled, alone or over sorbet.

Vegetarian cuisine is becoming more and more popular. Making your kitchen and menu veggie-friendly includes creativity and a veggie mindset. No new equipment or expensive ingredients are required.

- Who Wants What: Before adding menu items, ascertain what you guests' needs are. After assessing your needs, educate your staff. Include both staff and guests in mini-taste panels, product samplings, and cooking demos.

- Secrets of the Storeroom: Review your inventory and identify vegan ingredients. Here are some suggestions of items to have on hand (you'll be surprised at how veggie-friendly you already are).

- Freezer: frozen vegetables and fruit, frozen potatoes, frozen pie crust (made with vegetable shortening), fruit juice concentrates (to be used as a cooking sweetener in place of sugar)

- Refrigerator: fresh produce, fresh herbs, fresh garlic and ginger, fresh potatoes, tortillas (made with vegetable oil), assorted breads, vegan margarine, prepared salsas, chutneys, oil-based salad dressings (made without dairy or eggs), juices

- Nonperishable storage: canned tomato products, canned and dried beans (lentils, pinto, kidney, navy, garbanzos, black-eyed peas, split peas, white, lima, etc.), pasta, rice, potato mixes (made without dairy), grains (couscous, kasha, oats, bulgur, etc.), peanut butter and other nut butters, fruit preserves, vinegars, mustard, oils, dried herbs and spices, flavoring extracts, and zests

  Inspect the labels if you are using processed products, such as bakery mixes, frozen entrées, prepared salad dressings, etc. Some animal-derived ingredients are obvious (powdered egg, dried milk, bacon bits) and some are less obvious (casein, rennet, or enzymes used)

- Speed or Scratch: Preparation of vegetarian menu items can be made from scratch or speed-scratch. If your kitchen and staff have the time and capacity, beans, veggie burgers, and pasta dishes can be made from scratch (these items stand up well to cook-chill). If time and skill are lacking, utilize speed-scratch ingredients, such as canned beans, frozen or chilled veggie burgers, and frozen pasta entrées. Add your own touches to create signature dishes.

  Vegetarian ingredients are versatile, easily adaptable to different dishes. Canned or "scratch" lentils can be mashed with stewed eggplant, fresh tomatoes, onions, and garlic and used as a dip for vegetables, a spread for garlic bread, or as a sandwich condiment. Tomato salsa can be a salad dressing, chip or vegetable dip, flavoring for soup, and an ingredient in casseroles. Orange or apple juice concentrate can flavor a salad dressing or marinade, replace sugar in baking recipes, or add "zip" to a sweet and sour sauce (served over grilled vegetables). Cooked black bean beans can be tossed in salads, simmered in soups, baked into breads, smashed into spreads or can stand on their own, garnished with sliced red onion and avocado.

- Think efficiency: Develop timesaving production techniques for times when your are preparing both vegan and non-vegetarian menu items. For example, preparing steamed vegetables with vegan margarine or olive oil, rather than butter, or using vegetable stock or base, rather than meat stock, means making only one batch for everyone. Purchase canned vegetarian refried beans (the price is the same), canned fruit packed in juice or water, and frozen fruit, processed without sugar.

Soy Speak

Soy products have been around for the last two thousand years or so. Incorporate them into your menus for health and interest. The following information will provide your caterer with an introduction to soy-based vegan ingredients.

Tofu: Tofu is probably the most familiar soy product. Nothing more than "firm" soymilk (think: cheese making), tofu is available in different firmness and flavors. Silken tofu is custard-like and can be the "cream" in pies, soups, puddings, and sauces. Soft tofu blends well and can be used instead of dairy in smoothies, salad dressings, and dips. Firm and extra-firm tofu can be marinated, chopped, diced, sautéed, baked, etc.

Tofu has a neutral flavor so it will take on whatever personality you give it. Marinate tofu in fresh or dried herbs, salad dressings, vinegars, barbecue sauce, chili sauce, etc. If you need really firm tofu, such as for grilling or roasting, you can drain blocks of extra-firm tofu. Place tofu between weights, such as several china dinner plates, and drain for several hours. This will condense and compress the tofu and works well for tofu "steaks," fajita strips, and barbecued tofu sandwiches.

There are commercially available flavored tofus, both sweet and savory. Try almond-flavored tofu for dessert items, and barbecue, Southwestern, Mediterranean, and Asian flavored for entrées.

Freezing is okay for tofu and makes it chewier in texture. Drain tofu and slice before freezing. To use frozen tofu, let it thaw in the refrigerator, squeeze out excess fluid, and marinate or cook the tofu.

Soymilk: Soymilk is available in several flavors and fat levels. Soymilk is naturally high in protein but low in calcium, vitamins A, D, and B12. If nutrition is a concern, look for fortified brands. We have seen vanilla, almond, mocha, and chocolate soymilk available in individual and food service packs.

Tempeh: Tempeh is a firm cake of pressed, fermented soybeans, sometimes mixed with grains, such as rice or wheat. Tempeh's mild smoky flavor and chewy texture works well in chili, casseroles, stir-fries, and hot sandwiches. Tempeh is sold in blocks and is usually available in various flavors.

Soynuts: Soynuts are roasted soybeans and have a nutty, peanut flavor. Use them in Thai dishes, as salad toppings, and as an ingredient in baking and trail mixes.

Soy Cheese and Yogurt: Soy cheese and yogurt can be used just like their dairy cousins. Soy cheese is available in various types, such as mozzarella and cheddar. Look for vegan soy cheese that does not contain casein (an animal product). Soy yogurt is generally available as a sweetened, fruit-flavored product. Use it as is in sauces or freeze it for a fast dessert. Frozen soymilk and rice milk are the vegan equivalents of ice cream and are available in many flavors and forms (sandwiches, cones, etc.).

Soy Protein: Meat analogs, such as tofu hot dogs, burgers, crumbles, breakfast strips, and "fake" sandwich meats are generally made from soy protein and are designed to mimic their animal counterparts. Experiment with different brands to find the type that have the flavor and texture acceptable for your guests. For example, several brands of soy burgers should be fried, which may defeat the purpose of your healthy offerings.

Food Safety

Food safety procedures are important for all vegan protein products. Except for aseptically packaged products (tofu and soymilk are available in this packaging), all soy and protein products must be kept refrigerated until used and have use-by dates to which you must adhere. Once opened, all soy and protein products must be handled just like meat or eggs. Avoid time-temperature abuse, cross-contamination, multiple reheating of leftovers, etc.

Although not a soy product, seitan is a popular vegetarian meat substitute. Seitan is compressed gluten (wheat protein). It is available in blocks, strips, and crumbles and can be frozen until ready to use. Seitan has a very firm texture and will hold up to poaching, roasting, grilling, and baking. Serve it as a "steak" (marinated in lemon or lime juice, garlic, and onions) or add it where you would use beef or chicken strips. There are commercially available meat analogs made with seitan, some in the shape of roasts, which can be flavored and served just like roast beef.

Tofu, tempeh, soymilk, and seitan (wheat gluten that can be used in place of meat) can be frozen. They must be thawed in the refrigerator. The frozen tofu, tempeh, and seitan will be tougher when thawed and the soymilk will be watery. Plan on using thawed products as ingredients rather than as stand-alone items.

All soy products are available in organic or standard forms and may be fortified or not. The products used to process them may differ. For example, some tofu is process with calcium, some with nigari (a sea vegetable). Save the labels, as some of your customers may request this information.

Soy Instead

Instead of:	Soy Substitute:
8 ounces ricotta cheese	8 ounces mashed firm tofu or 5 ounces okara (soy pulp remaining after soymilk production)
8 ounces milk	8 ounces soymilk
8 ounces yogurt	8 ounces blended silken tofu or soy yogurt
1 large egg	2 Tablespoons blended firm tofu
1 ounce baking chocolate (may contain dairy)	3 ounces unsweetened cocoa powder and 1 Tablespoon soy oil
1 pound ground beef (for burritos, meat sauce, etc.)	1 pound diced firm tofu, 12 ounces crumbled seitan or tempeh (marinate for extra flavor before cooking)

Soy Suggestions

Tempeh: marinate in Italian dressing or barbecue sauce and grill; dice and mix into soups or chilies; or slice and grill and serve as a "tempeh" dip sandwich

Soymilk: use in place of cow's milk in puddings, custards, and sauces; make hot chocolate or coffee beverages; or use in soups

Soy Crumbles: sauté, bake, or grill with fresh or dry herbs and use as pizza toppings, in chili, in "beef" and mac casseroles or "meat" sauces, and in tacos; or with tofu as a "morning scramble"

Soft Tofu: use instead of ricotta cheese in stuffed shells and lasagna, make fruit smoothies, use in salad dressings; or scramble instead of eggs (remember to season with pepper, hot sauce, sautéed veggies, etc.)

Silken Tofu: use instead of mayonnaise or sour cream in recipes, use to make pudding, pie fillings or custard; smooth out sauces (tofu Alfredo or primavera) or soups; and make a frosting by blending a small amount of tofu with an instant vegan pudding mix

<u>Firm Tofu</u>: add to brochettes instead of meat; use in stir-frys; cut in cubes to make an egg-less or chicken-less salad (toss with celery, onions, pickles, vegan mayonnaise); or grill, roast (use the same seasonings as you do for meat), or bake with bread stuffing

Soy Product Manufacturers

Eden Foods, Inc.
701 Tecumseh Road
Clinton, MI 49236
www.edenfoods.com
producers of soymilk and soy sauce

Follow Your Heart/Earth Island
PO Box 9400
Chatsworth, CA 91309
www.followyourheart.com
produces vegan soy cheese, mayonnaise, and chicken-free chicken

House Foods America Corporation
7351 Orangewood Avenue
Garden Grove, CA 92841
www.house-foods.com
producers of Japanese-style tofu

Lightlife Foods
PO Box 870
Greenfield, MA 10302
www.lightlife.com
producers of soy hot dogs, sausage, and deli slices

Morinaga Nutritional Foods
2441 W. 205th St.
Torrance, CA 90501
www.morinu.com
producers of Mori-Nu aseptic packaged tofu

Toffuti Brands, Inc.
50 Jackson Drive
Cranford, NJ 07016
www.toffuti.com
producers of soy-based frozen desserts, vegan soy cheese, and soy cream cheese

Turtle Island Foods, Inc.
PO Box 176
601 Industrial Ave.
Hood River, OR 97031
www.tofurky.com
producers tempeh, veggie "meats", and pizza

Vitasoy USA, Inc.
1 New England Way
Ayer, MA 01432
www.vitasoy-usa.com
producer of soymilk

White Wave, Inc.   producers of soy yogurt, tempeh,
1990 N. 57th Street   tofu, and soy beverages including creamer
Boulder, CO 80301
www.whitewave.com

WholeSoy and Company   produces soy yogurt, soy smoothies, and frozen desserts
353 Sacramento St.
San Francisco, CA 94111
www.wholesoyco.com

Suggestions for Vegan Replacements

Instead of:	Use:
Hot roast beef in a sandwich	Hot Field Roast™ with mushroom sauce
Sausage and egg burrito	Soyrizo™ and scrambled tofu or vegan breakfast crumbles and tofu
Roast beef, lamb, or pork in a French dip sandwich	Sliced veggie meats with onion sauce
Steak in a steak dinner	Grilled whole portobello caps, seitan, or tempeh
Meat loaf	Combination of soy ground round and TVP with chopped vegetables, formed and baked into a loaf
Pork loin for a pork roast dinner	Sliced Tofurky™ with an onion-garlic gravy
Ground beef for tamale or shepherd's pie	Crumbled Field Roast™ or soy ground round
Filling for lasagna	Thinly sliced eggplant, zucchini, summer squash, mushrooms, tomatoes, vegan cheeses, olives, and smoked tofu
Filling for enchiladas	Chopped tomatoes, bell peppers, chilies, mushrooms, shredded vegan cheeses, mashed or whole beans, brown rice, cut corn
Turkey in hot turkey sandwich	Sliced Tofurky™ or extra-firm tofu marinated, poultry seasoning, served with vegetable gravy and cranberry sauce
Burger with the "works"	Veggie or mushroom burger with sliced tomato, shredded carrots, shredded beets, sliced cucumbers, diced bell peppers, sliced chopped onions, and shredded red and green cabbage

Additional Explanations

If you need to get more in-depth with your caterer, the following goes into label-reading and acceptable vegan ingredients.

Wine: The Fruit of the Vine May Have More Than Fruit

How can wine (and vinegar) not be vegetarian, you ask? It's true that wine usually contains only grapes or other fruit, yeast, and perhaps a small amount of sulfites, which are added and created during fermentation. Wine and vinegar ingredients are vegetarian and vegan. It's the processing of wine and vinegar that may introduce small amounts of animal products. Don't be surprised if vegan customers inquire about the brand of wine or vinegar you use.

Most people prefer their wine and vinegar to be clear. A clarifying or fining agent makes wine clear by removing proteins from the wine. The agents eventually settle out of the wine. Different proteins serve as clarifying agents depending upon both the type of wine and the desired flavor. Lab trials determine both the clarifying agent and quantities used. The fining agents have an opposite polarity to that of the wine. Therefore, the agents solidify with the protein and they remain in the wine, although they can be removed.

Some finers are animal-based products and some are earth-based. Animal-based agents include egg whites, milk, casein, gelatin, and isinglass. Animal-based finers are generally less expensive. Isinglass is prepared from the bladder of the sturgeon fish. Bentonite, a clay earth product that is vegetarian, serves as a popular fining agent.

Egg whites from chicken eggs are used for red wine clarification and are removed before the wine is bottled. The egg whites are not specially processed or separately distributed for the wine industry. They are regular, store-bought eggs or farm eggs. Two or three egg whites can clarify a 55-gallon wine barrel.

Winemakers in areas of France generally utilize egg whites in their production because they can use the whites of the eggs after the yolks have already been added to food products. Large producers of wine in the United States do not usually use egg whites as a fining agent. They may select potassium caseinate as a substitute for eggs. Whole milk and casein are two other possible fining agents in some red wines.

Gelatin can clarify either white or red wine. Gelatin pulls suspended material out of wine, and less expensive wines may use this material. One ounce of gelatin can clarify 1,000 gallons of wine.

Fining agents coagulate on the bottom of the wine tank or barrel. They are then removed through either a settling process or a cellulose fiber filter. The ingredient list of a wine will not state the clarifier as an ingredient because it is removed from the final product. Calling or writing to a particular wine company may be the best way to discover which fining agent they use. Also, keep in mind that some vegans choose not to consume alcohol for religious reasons.

The animal-fining issue includes vinegars that are produced from wines. Search for vegan sources of wine or vinegar online.

Vegan Sugar

Refined sugar is avoided by some vegetarians because its processing may involve a bone char filter. An activated carbon filter, sometimes made of bone char, whitens sugar through an absorption process. While the bone char filter is used by some major sugar companies, it is not used to produce all refined sugar.

The two major ingredients in refined sugar produced in the United States are beet sugar and cane sugar. Cane sugar is mainly grown in Florida, California, Louisiana, Hawaii, and Texas. Beet sugar is grown in states located in the middle part of the United States. Much sugar cane is actually imported.

According to beet sugar producers, beet and cane sugar are nutritionally equivalent and one cannot usually taste any difference between them. They are both composed of sucrose.

Beet sugar refineries never use a bone char filter in processing because this type of sugar does not require an extensive whitening procedure. Beet sugar can be refined with a pressure lead filter and an ion exchange system.

Bones from cows are used to make bone char. Bone is heated to an extremely high temperature, which results in a physical change in the bones composition. The bone becomes pure carbon before it is used in a refinery. Refined sugar does not contain any bone particles. The bone char removes impurities from the sugar, but does not become a part of the sugar. Individual pieces of bone char, like granular carbon, can be used for several years. They must be continuously washed to remove the sugar deposits.

Some labels on sugar packages seem to indicate that the product is raw sugar, but all commercial sugar has undergone some refining. Genuine raw sugar cannot be bought and sold to the general consumer in the USA according to FDA regulations, as it is considered unfit for human consumption.

Turbinado sugar is a product that is made by separating raw cane sugar crystals in a centrifuge and washing them with steam. Turbinado sugar does not pass through a bone char filter because its brown color is desirable. You may also find date palm sugar and other "fruit" sugars that have not been filtered. They have a slightly different taste, texture, and absorbing ability. You'll want to try out a small-batch recipe before using these sugars in large batches. The good news is that organic sugars are usually free of bone char. (See page 20.)

Even the Maple Syrup?

The process of making maple syrup requires an agent to reduce the foam on the syrup by adding a small amount of fat to the liquid. The traditional process of reducing the foam in maple syrup has included the use of lard. Previously, local producers would hang pork fat over a tub of maple syrup and let drops of fat drip into the syrup. Others used milk, cream, or butter. If animal products are used in the form of lard or milk, the amount is minute. For example, eight to ten gallons of syrup will involve a quarter of a teaspoon of cream or a pea-sized drop of butter.

Vegetable oil is a common defoaming agent. It can be applied to the end of a wooden stick and dipped into the foaming part of the maple syrup. Most manufacturers of maple syrup now use vegetable oil or synthetic defoamers instead of lard.

The List Goes On

Red food coloring, frozen French fries, and ready-to-use pie crust may contain animal products, as may many other items perceived as vegetarian. Read the label and select the products which best meet everyone's needs.

The Ins and Outs of Vegetarian Label Reading

The following can help as you attempt to decipher if particular processed foods are veggie or not:

1. Natural flavors: "natural" does not necessarily equal "vegetarian." Natural only means that ingredients are derived from unprocessed products, such as herbs, spices, eggs, dairy, meat, or fish.

2. Are all French fries vegetarian? Not necessarily; most commercial French fries are blanched prior to freezing. Blanching may be done in animal fat. Also, fries are sometimes seasoned with beef or chicken flavor. Check the label or with the manufacturer.

3. What is cochineal (carmine)? Some red food coloring is made from the shell of the cochineal beetle. This can be labeled as cochineal, carmine, or carminic acid. Cochineal is not considered vegetarian.

4. What about whey? Whey is the liquid that remains after most of the protein and fat has been removed from milk during the cheese-making process. It is also the liquid that rises to the top of yogurt. Whey is vegetarian but not vegan.

5. How about when I see "enyzmes" listed on the label? Enzymes are proteins added to foods to enhance flavor or improve texture. They can be animal, vegetable, bacterial, or plant-based. Those used in cheese-making may be animal-derived, so even a vegetarian who eats cheese may not eat brands of cheese made with animal-based enzymes. Examples of enzymes are: lactase (bacterial), lipase (animal or plant), papain (vegetable), pectinase (fruit), protease (animal, vegetable, bacterial, or plant), rennet (animal), and trypsin (animal).

6. Are mono- and diglycerides okay? Monoglycerides and diglycerides are common food additives used as emulsifiiers and/or preservatives. The commercial source may be either animal (cow- or pork-derived) or vegetable, or they may be synthesized in a food laboratory. They are often found in bakery products, beverages, ice cream, chewing gum, shortening, whipped toppings, margarine, and confections. Once again, you need to check with the manufacturer to find out the source.

7. Stearic acid comes from steers, right? Stearic is used as a binder or flavor agent in foods. Its source may be either animal or vegetable. It is found in vegetable and animal oils, animal fats, cascarilla bark extract, and in synthetic form. It is used in butter flavoring, vanilla flavoring, chewing gum and candy, fruit waxes, and may not be vegetarian.

8. Calcium lactate sounds as if it comes from milk (as in "lactose"). Believe it or not, calcium lactate is typically vegan. It is generally fermented from cornstarch or beets.

9. What are agar-agar and guar gum? Both are very traditional, vegan thickening agents. Agar (also known as agar-agar) is a vegetable gum obtained from seaweeds used to thicken foods. Guar gum is also a vegetable gum.

10. Where does casein come from? Casein is a milk derivative. It is sometimes used to improve texture in soy and rice cheeses, yogurt, and sour cream. This means that some soy and rice products may be vegetarian, but not vegan.

11. I see "lecithin" on a lot of labels. Is it vegetarian? Lecithin is naturally found in egg yolks, dairy products, and meat, as well as some vegetables such as soybeans, peanuts, and corn. Lecithin is commonly used in foods that require emulsification or blending. Nowadays, most manufacturers use soy or corn as a basis for lecithin product.

12. Is "gluten" a protein from meat? Gluten is a mixture of proteins from wheat flour and is generally a vegan product. It may also be called wheat gluten or seitan.

13. Is kosher gelatin vegetarian? Kosher gelatin can be made with fish or beef bones. This means that it is not always vegetarian. Some Kosher jells are vegan.

Putting it all Together

The proceeding information should give your caterer a solid base for vegan menu planning. You may want to share menu-planning ideas or recipes from previous chapters in this book, to make your party meal as close to perfection as possible.

If you are looking for some "upscale" ideas for your caterer, you might want to share the following two menus. These multi-course, elegant menus were designed and prepared for many upscale events by Executive Chef Michael Valvik in the Indianopolis area.

Upscale Menu # 1
Tofu and Vegetable Sushi Rolls with Mizuno Salad Mix laced with soy-ginger emulsion accompanied by Lotus Chips, Enoki Mushrooms, Pickled Ginger, and Wasabi,

Marinated Portobello and Roast Vegetable Napoleon topped with fried Leeks laced with Port Wine Reduction accompanied by Six Grain Rice, Herb, and Pecan Medley, Rapini, and Petite Carrots

Strudel Purse filled with Fresh Fruit and Hazelnuts bound with Lavender Rice Syrup, Baked Golden Brown, and Dusted with Powder Sugar and Chocolate Sauce

Upscale Menu # 2
Potage of Tomato and Basil Purée, garnished with Roasted Corn, Asparagus Tips, and Polenta Croutons

Marinated Grilled Eggplant Roulades filled with White Bean Ragout, Roasted Peppers, and Broccoli Flowerets on a bed of Rice Noodles tossed with Fresh Spinach and Mushrooms, and Drizzled with Balsamic Reduction

Vanilla and Pear Sorbet topped with Berries, Candied Pecans, and Fresh Mint

Chapter 21: PARTY PLANNING FOR PEOPLE WITH DIABETES

Fast Overview

Just as a fast review, there are two basic types of diabetes. People with Type I diabetes are reliant on injectable insulin. In the past, Type I diabetes was called juvenile diabetes. Individuals with Type II diabetes many times can be treated without insulin, with diet and exercise being important parts of treatment. In the past, Type II diabetes was called adult-onset diabetes. Neither type of diabetes limits itself to a particular age group, and so the more appropriate Type I and Type II terms are used today.

Everybody's cells get their energy from a sugar called glucose. Glucose is obtained from many different types of foods, such as potatoes, fruit, breads, pasta, etc. Glucose is stored in the liver. Your liver releases glucose into the blood when your body needs energy. The organs that needed the energy capture the glucose and use it. Insulin, a substance released by the pancreas helps glucose get inside cells. If you are a Type II diabetic, your pancreas might not be able to release all the insulin it makes. Without insulin, the body doesn't know how to use glucose. When the glucose can't get inside the cells, it accumulates in the blood. Too much glucose in the blood can lead to many medical problems. If necessary, you can help your body use the glucose it needs by taking diabetic medication properly, exercising, and eating properly. It has been found that just a ten-pound weight loss (in people who need to lose weight) helps insulin to work better and that regular exercise also helps your body use insulin.

What to Eat?

In the 1920's, after it was understood that injected insulin alone was not enough to control diabetes and that the way one ate affected one's diabetes, researchers set out to find exactly what type of diet should be recommended to people with diabetes. One theory, in the 1930's, was that people with diabetes knew intuitively what to eat. In other words, researchers thought that your body would tell you what it needed. That didn't work. Eliminating all sugar from the diet didn't either. After much trial and error, it was found that people with diabetes did best when they ate a balanced diet that kept them at their ideal body weight.

Based on the balanced diet theory, the American Dietetic Association began to formulate diabetic diets. From observation it was found that the avoidance of certain foods did little to control diabetes, where a diet balanced in protein, fat, and carbohydrates seemed to help the condition. But how do you design balanced menus for all people with diabetes all the time? It couldn't be expected that every diabetic would visit their dietitian regularly to pick up menus. It was also not realistic to expect that people with diabetes could or would adhere strictly to menus for which they gave no input. This is when a great solution was devised — the exchange lists for meal planning.

Back to the Future

The exchange lists for meal planning, with variations on a theme, are what dietitians and healthcare workers have used to calculate diabetic diets for the past four decades. The exchanges are arranged into three groups. The carbohydrate group includes starch, fruit, milk, and vegetable exchanges; the meat group includes very lean, lean, medium-fat, and fat meats, seafood, poultry, and meat substitute exchanges; and the fat group includes saturated and unsaturated fat exchanges. Each exchange is assigned a calorie level; for example, one fat exchange is 45 calories. Each food within the exchange is assigned a portion amount. For example, one slice of bacon, one-eighth of an avocado, and one tea-spoon of margarine are all one fat exchange and all worth 45 calories. People who have worked with the exchanges for a while find they can analyze a recipe or a menu in a matter of minutes.

The exchanges give patients and menu planners freedom of choice. Instead of being told that they must have grapefruit juice at breakfast time, a patient is told that they are entitled to one fruit exchange in the morning. This can be translated into the correct portion size of juice, fresh fruit, dried fruit, or canned or frozen unsweetened fruit.

People with diabetes are counseled as to the correct calorie level for maintenance of good health. The exchange lists allow them to select types and amounts of food while maintaining a healthy calorie level. For example, if told they could have 1 fruit exchange, 2 lean meat exchanges, 2 starch exchanges, and 1 fat exchange for breakfast, one person might select cantaloupe wedges, steamed tofu, and 2 slices of toast and margarine, while another individual might select tomato juice, hummus (as the meat exchange), and a toasted bagel. Both meals comply with the exchanges.

Let's Party

Holidays and special meal events can be frustrating times for people with diabetes and the people providing meals for them. While current theory has it that no foods need be excluded from diabetic diets (except for severe cases), daily intake must be balanced and within the person's calorie level. And although an occasional piece of cake might be allowed, holiday meals often have very few options for people with diabetes.

When designing festive menus, consider that everyone, including people with diabetes, can benefit from menu items that are tasty and fun yet lower in fat and concentrated sweets. Rather than having to create separate dishes for people with diabetes, offer lots of dishes that everyone can enjoy, with perhaps a portion variation for some of the more controlled people with diabetes.

Many of your favorite festive menu items already fit the bill, especially entrées (serve the sauces on the side). Instead of cranberry sauce, offer stewed apples with almonds, raisins, and cinnamon. Instead of chocolate sauce, offer fruit coulis made with frozen fruit, flavoring extracts, and fruit juice concentrate. Tofu makes a creamy base for savory or sweet sauces, requiring little sugar for sweetness (make a creamy dessert sauce with silken tofu, puréed strawberries, and orange zest). Poached or stewed fruit or salsas make low-sugar, lowfat accompaniments to roasted tempeh or seitan or other savory entrées. Once you get into this, you will be surprised at how easy it is to convert your party menus into diabetic-friendly meals.

Here's a traditional festive meal (and our thoughts on making it diabetic-friendly):
- Crudités platter with sour-cream based dip (replace dip with a bean or lowfat soy yogurt-based dip) Assorted dinner rolls (no problem)
- Roasted seitan with rosemary and mushroom gravy (seitan is fine; serve gravy on the side or offer a fresh berry relish)
- Cranberry sauce (offer stewed fruit compote or hot seasoned applesauce)
- Mashed potatoes made with soymilk and vegan margarine (no problem; for a lower fat version, try using lowfat soymilk or lowfat vegetable broth)
- Canned sweet potatoes with pineapple (Have you ever tasted baked fresh sweet potatoes? They put canned to shame. Simply bake, cube, and serve with a bit of vegan margarine, or mash them with a small amount of vegan margarine, nutmeg, and ginger. Canned, unsweetened pineapple is fine.)
- Green beans with almonds (no problem)
- Bread stuffing (no problem; a little high in fat, but it's a party!)
- Traditional pumpkin pie (several choices here: for example, make a lower sugar, lower fat pumpkin custard with canned pumpkin, silken tofu, and apple juice concentrate)

Partys for Everybody

With an eye to individual people with diabetic needs, here are some suggestions for festive foods that can fit into a diabetic pattern.

Company Breakfast:

- Fresh fruit slices with citrus-maple syrup dip (dip made with 2 cups lowfat soy yogurt, 1 Tablespoon orange or lime juice, and 2 Tablespoons maple syrup to serve 12 people)

- Baked apples seasoned with cinnamon, nutmeg, ginger, and apple juice

- Peaches with raspberry sauce (frozen or juice-packed peaches; sauce made with soy yogurt, frozen unsweetened raspberries, and orange juice concentrate)

- Silken tofu omelets with fresh chopped herbs and veggies

- Cornbread and zucchini muffins (made with juice concentrate rather than sugar) with raisins and nuts and served with hot fruit compote (stewed apples, pears, peaches, and dried fruit)

- Baked oatmeal (made with layers of prepared oatmeal, unsweetened canned or frozen fruit, dried fruit, and fruit-flavored soy yogurt)

Buffet:

- Grilled vegetable platter (zucchini, onions, tomatoes, bell peppers sliced, brushed with olive oil, sprinkled with chopped oregano and basil then grilled); served with fresh salsa

- Twice-baked potatoes (stuffed with potatoes mashed with silken tofu and unflavored soy yogurt, chopped fresh parsley, and onion and garlic powder)

- Mock "Shrimp" and "crab" stuffed mini-pitas (vegan shrimp and crab products chopped with fresh vegetables) or vegan "shrimp" wrapped with snow peas

- Stuffed mushrooms (bread stuffing made with water chestnuts, chopped onions, and minced garlic)

- Spinach dip (thawed frozen chopped spinach mixed with soy yogurt, fresh bread crumbs, chopped fresh parsley, and chopped green onions)

- Crudités with creamy dill dip (dip made with dill weed, soy yogurt or sour cream, chopped bell peppers, and black pepper); crudités can be any crunchy veggie, such as jicama, carrots, broccoli, cauliflower, cherry tomatoes, radishes, canned asparagus, canned baby corn, snow peas, or mushrooms.

Desserts:

- Banana cake (see recipe later in this chapter) served with a fresh or frozen fruit sauce (purée strawberries with a small amount of orange juice concentrate and vanilla extract)

- Chocolate banana cake (banana cake made with the addition of 2 Tablespoons of cocoa powder) served with fresh or frozen berries

- Poached pears (poach pears in apple juice flavored with cinnamon and ginger)

- Fruit smoothies (made with fresh or frozen fruit, soy yogurt or silken tofu, and juice concentrate)

- Pudding parfaits (made from vegan pudding mix and lowfat soymilk, layered with unsweetened granola and chopped dried fruit)

- Fruit tarts (purchase prepared tart shells or arrange vanilla wafers or ginger snaps in individual dishes; fill with low-calorie vegan pudding and top with fruit)

- Mini sundaes (made with sorbet or frozen vegan desserts, topped with chopped nuts, chopped fruit, and fruit sauce)

- Ice cream club sandwiches (made with vegan graham crackers, sorbet or frozen vegan dessert, chopped fruit, and chopped nuts)

Beverages:
- Flavored coffees
- Hot herbed tea with citrus slices and mint sprigs
- Fruit punch (made with unsweetened juices, sparkling water, and sherbet)
- Fruit smoothies (made with unflavored soy yogurt or tofu, fresh or frozen fruit, spices)

The following recipes are written in amounts for caterers, or for prepping ahead and freezing or storing for later use.

Oatmeal Apricot Bars
Makes fifty 2 x 3-inch bars

1 pound vegan margarine
1 pound brown sugar or sugar
$\frac{1}{2}$ pound unsweetened applesauce (1 cup)
3 ounces unsweetened apple juice concentrate ($\frac{1}{3}$ cup)
$1\frac{1}{2}$ pounds all purpose flour (or half and half unbleached and whole wheat flour)
1 pound 12 ounces uncooked quick oats ($4\frac{3}{4}$ cups)
3 Tablespoons baking soda
2 pounds chopped dried apricots ($3\frac{1}{2}$ cups)
1 pound chopped golden raisins (2 cups)

Preheat oven to 325 degrees. In a mixer bowl, combine margarine and sugar and beat until well mixed. Add applesauce and concentrate and beat until smooth.

Combine flour, oats, and soda. Add to margarine and mix until just combined. Mixture should be crumbly.

Spread half of mixture evenly on 4-5 ungreased baking sheets. Cover mixture with chopped fruit. Top evenly with remaining mixture. Bake for 35 minutes or until golden brown. Depending upon oven space, you may have to do this in batches.

Cut into bars and serve warm or allow bars to cool. Serve with stewed fruit or yogurt with chopped dried fruit

Note: Make this recipe ahead of time and either store in airtight containers in the freezer, or in a cool, dark area.

One bar = 245 calories, 46 grams carbohydrate, 8 grams fat, and 3 grams of protein. Approx. $2\frac{1}{2}$ starch exchanges and $1\frac{1}{2}$ fat exchanges.

Banana Cake

Makes three 9-inch cakes or 25 portions

$^1/_2$ pound vegan margarine (about 1 cup)
$^1/_2$ pound sugar (about 1 cup)
1 pound applesauce (about 4 cups)
2 Tablespoons vanilla extract
1 cup silken tofu
$2^1/_2$ pounds mashed bananas (about $5^1/_2$ cups)
2 pounds cake flour (about 4 cups)
3 Tablespoons baking powder
2 teaspoons baking soda
8 ounces unflavored or vanilla soy yogurt (about 1 cup)

Preheat oven to 350 degrees. In a mixer bowl, combine margarine, sugar, applesauce, and vanilla and mix until well combined and fluffy. Add tofu and mix until well combined. Add bananas and mix at medium speed for 2 minutes.

Combine flour, powder, and soda. With the mixer at low speed, alternate adding dry ingredients and yogurt. Mix until well combined.

Place batter into 3 greased and floured 9-inch cake pans (if loaf pans are used instead, baking time will have to be increased). Bake at 350 degrees for 25 minutes or until a toothpick inserted in the center of the pan comes out clean.

Cool and then remove from pans. Serve as breakfast bread with fresh fruit or as a dessert, served with sorbet.

One portion = 250 calories, 40 grams carbohydrates, 11 grams fat, and 3 grams protein, or approx. $3^1/_2$ bread exchanges, 2 fat exchanges.

Roasted Two-Pepper Soup

Serves 10 (4-ounce or $^1/_2$ cup portions)

1 pound green bell peppers (about 2 cups)
$1^1/_2$ pounds red bell peppers (about 3 cups)
1 ounce olive oil (about 2 Tablespoons)
1 clove garlic, minced
$^1/_2$ cup finely diced onions
$^1/_2$ cup finely diced fresh tomatoes
2 Tablespoons ground oregano
$1^1/_2$ pints vegetable stock (about 3 cups)
1 teaspoon white pepper

Pierce whole peppers and rub with oil. Place on ungreased baking sheet and roast in 375 degree oven until skins are blistered. Remove from oven, place in a plastic bag, and allow to cool (this makes removing the skin easier). Peel, seed, and chop peppers. Set aside.

Lightly sauté garlic and onions in a medium stockpot (use oil or vegetable spray). Add tomatoes and oregano. Sauté until soft. Add stock, white pepper, and chopped peppers and bring to a boil, stirring occasionally. Reduce heat and allow to simmer for 15 minutes.

If desired, purée for a creamy texture. Pair with crudities and crunchy bread for a light supper.

One portion= 96 calories, 15 grams carbohydrate, 3 grams fat, 3 grams protein, or approx. 1 bread exchange, $^1/_2$ fat exchange

Fruit Cobbler with Biscuit Topping
Makes ten 3 x 2-inch portions

Use a combination of unsweetened peaches, apples, pears, cherries, and berries in this cobbler.

3 pounds mixed frozen fruit (peaches, apples, pears, cherries, and berries), drained (about 6 cups)
3 cups juice (juice drained from fruit plus unsweetened apple juice to make total amount)
1 cup sugar
6 Tablespoons cornstarch
1 Tablespoon fresh orange zest
2 teaspoons fresh lemon zest
2 teaspoons ground cinnamon
2 teaspoons ground ginger
1 cup cold water
2 cups vegan biscuit mix
³/₄ cup water

Reserve fruit in large mixing bowl. Preheat oven to 425 degrees.

In a small stockpot, heat juice to boiling. Lower heat. Mix sugar, cornstarch, zests, cinnamon, and ginger together and add to juice. Stir to combine. Add water and whisk until thickened.

Place fruit in a 9 x 12-inch casserole or baking dish. Pour thickened juice over fruit.

In a separate bowl, combine biscuit mix and water. Mix until soft dough is formed. Roll biscuit dough on a floured board to a 2-inch thickness. Place rolled dough on top of fruit. Bake at 425 degrees for 25 minutes or until browned.

Serve warm and use for breakfast, or allow to cool and serve as a holiday dessert with flavored whipped topping.

One portion = 195 calories, 30 grams carbohydrate, 8 grams fat, and 1 gram protein or approx. $2^1/_2$ starch exchanges, 2 fat exchanges

Red Onion and Basil Salad Dressing

Makes 1 pint or 2 cups

3 Tablespoons diced red onions
1 Tablespoon diced white onion
1 Tablespoon dried basil
2 Tablespoons olive oil
½ cup cold vegetable broth
2 Tablespoons vegan mayonnaise (or 3 Tablespoons soft tofu)
1 teaspoon black pepper

Combine all ingredients in a non-reactive bowl until well mixed. Cover and refrigerate until ready to use.

One portion (1 ounce) = 20 calories, 3 grams carbohydrate, 1 gram fat, and no protein, or approx. $^1/_3$ bread exchange, $^1/_8$ fat exchange

BOOKS FROM
THE VEGETARIAN RESOURCE GROUP

If you are interested in purchasing any of the following VRG titles, please send a check or money order made out to The Vegetarian Resource Group (Maryland residents must add 6% sales tax) and mail it along with your order to The Vegetarian Resource Group, P.O. Box 1463, Baltimore, MD 21203. Make sure you include your shipping address. You can fax your order to (410) 366-8804 or call (410) 366-8343 Monday through Friday 9 am to 6 pm EST to order with a Visa or MasterCard credit card. Price given includes postage in the United States. Outside the USA please contact us first to find out the correct cost for postage and shipping. You can also order these books online at www.vrg.org

SIMPLY VEGAN

Quick Vegetarian Meals
By Debra Wasserman & Reed Mangels, Ph.D., R.D.

Simply Vegan is an easy-to-use vegetarian guide that contains over 160 kitchen-tested vegan recipes (no meat, fish, fowl, dairy, or eggs). Each recipe is accompanied by a nutritional analysis.

Reed Mangels, Ph.D., R.D., has included an extensive vegan nutrition section on topics such as Protein, Fat, Calcium, Iron, Vitamin B12, Pregnancy and the Vegan Diet, Feeding Vegan Children, and Calories, Weight Gain, and Weight Loss. A Nutrition Glossary is provided, along with sample menus, meal plans, and a list of the top recipes for Iron, Calcium, and Vitamin C.

Also featured are food definitions and origins, and a comprehensive list of mail-order companies that specialize in selling vegan food, natural clothing, cruelty-free cosmetics, and ecologically-based household products. TRADE PAPERBACK $15

VEGAN HANDBOOK

Edited by Debra Wasserman & Reed Mangels, Ph.D., R.D.

Over 200 vegan recipes including the basics, international cuisine, and gourmet dishes can be found in this book. Also includes sports nutrition, a seniors' guide to good nutrition, one week of menus for diabetics, poll information, feeding vegan kids, vegetarian history, and much more. The book is 256 pages. TRADE PAPERBACK, $20

MEATLESS MEALS FOR WORKING PEOPLE

Quick and Easy Vegetarian Recipes
By Debra Wasserman & Charles Stahler

Vegetarian cooking can be simple or complicated. The Vegetarian Resource Group recommends using whole grains and fresh vegetables whenever possible. For the busy working person, this isn't always possible. Meatless Meals For Working People contains over 100 delicious fast and easy recipes, plus ideas which teach you how to be a vegetarian within your hectic schedule using common convenient vegetarian foods. This 192-page handy guide also contains a spice chart, party ideas, information on quick service restaurant chains, and much more. TRADE PAPERBACK, $12

CONVENIENTLY VEGAN

By Debra Wasserman

Prepare meals with all the natural foods products found in stores today, including soymilk, tempeh, tofu, veggie hot dogs, etc. You'll find 150 recipes using convenience foods (including canned beans) along with grains, fresh fruits, and vegetables. Menu ideas, product sources, and food definitions are included. TRADE PAPERBACK $15

VEGAN MEALS FOR ONE OR TWO

By Nancy Berkoff, RD, EdD, CCE

Whether you live alone, are a couple, or are the only one in your household who is vegetarian, this 216-page book is for you. Each recipe is written to serve one or two people and is designed so that you can realistically use ingredients the way they come packaged from the store. Information on meal planning and shopping is included, as well as breakfast ideas, one-pot wonders, recipes that can be frozen for later use, grab-and-go suggestions, everyday and special occasion main dishes, plus desserts and snacks. A glossay is also provided. TRADE PAPERBACK $15

VEGAN MENU FOR PEOPLE WITH DIABETES

By Nancy Berkoff, RD, EdD, CCE

This 96-page book gives people with (or at risk for) diabetes a four-week meal plan, exchange listings for meat substitutes and soy products, and recipes for enjoyable dishes such as Creamy Carrot Soup, Tangy Tofu Salad, Baked Bean Quesadillas, and French Toast. TRADE PAPERBACK $10

VEGAN MICROWAVE COOKBOOK

By Nancy Berkoff, RD, EdD, CCE

This 288-page cookbook contains 165 recipes, some of which take less than 10 minutes to cook. It also includes information for converting traditional recipes to the microwave, microwave baking and desserts, making breakfasts in a snap, and suggestions and recipes for holidays and parties. TRADE PAPERBACK $16.95

VEGAN IN VOLUME

By Nancy Berkoff, RD, EdD, CCE

This 272-page quantity cookbook is loaded with terrific recipes serving 25. Suitable for catered events, school and college food services, restaurants, parties in your own home, weddings, and much more. TRADE PAPERBACK $20

THE LOWFAT JEWISH VEGETARIAN COOKBOOK
By Debra Wasserman

The Lowfat Jewish Vegetarian Cookbook contains over 150 lowfat, vegan international recipes. Savor potato knishes, Polish plum and rhubarb soup, Indian curry and rice, Greek pastries, and spinach pies. Feast on Romanian apricot dumplings, North African barley pudding, pumpernickel and Russian flat bread, sweet fruit kugel, Czechoslovakian noodles with poppy seeds, and Russian blini. Celebrate with eggless challah, hamentashen for Purim, Chanukah latkes, mock "chopped liver," Russian charoset, eggless matzo balls, and Syrian wheat pudding.

Breakfast, lunch, and dinner menus are provided, as well as 33 unique Passover dishes and Seder ideas, and Rosh Hashanah Dinner suggestions. Each recipe is accompanied by a nutritional analysis. TRADE PAPERBACK $15

NO CHOLESTEROL PASSOVER RECIPES
By Debra Wasserman

For many, low-calorie Passover recipes are quite a challenge. Here is a wonderful collection of Passover dishes that are non-dairy, no-cholesterol, eggless, and vegetarian. It includes recipes for eggless blintzes, dairyless carrot cream soup, festive macaroons, apple latkes, sweet and sour cabbage, knishes, broccoli with almond sauce, mock "chopped liver," no oil lemon dressing, eggless matzo meal pancakes, and much more. TRADE PAPERBACK $9

VEGAN SEAFOOD
By Nancy Berkoff, RD, EdD, CCE

Chef Nancy Berkoff has created these unique and good-tasting vegan fish and seafood recipes. After using this book, you'll agree with millions of vegetarians who say: Sea animals - Don't Eat Them! Inside these 96 pages you will find sections about cooking with vegan 'fish,' 'seafood' stocks and sauces, websites offering 'seafood' products, and information about omega 3 fatty acids for vegans. Avoid fish but still enjoy the taste of the sea with 'Fish' Sticks, Ethiopian-Style 'Shrimp' and Sweet Potato Stew, 'Crab' Rangoon, 'Tuna' Salad, Gefilte 'Fish,' Spicy 'Fish' Cakes, and much more! TRADE PAPERBACK $12

VEGETARIAN QUANTITY RECIPES
From The Vegetarian Resource Group

Here is a helpful kit for people who must cook for large groups and institutional settings. It contains 28 vegan recipes including main dishes, burgers, sandwich spreads, side dishes, soups, salads, desserts, and breakfast. Each recipe provides a serving for 25 and 50 people, and a nutritional analysis. The kit also contains a listing of over 100 companies offering vegetarian food items in institutional sizes and "Tips for Introducing Vegetarian Food into Institutions." PACKET $15

To order additional copies of
VEGANS KNOW HOW TO PARTY
send $25 (postage included) per book to
The Vegetarian Resource Group, PO Box 1463, Baltimore, MD 21203.
(Outside the USA, please contact us first to find out
the exact cost for shipping and handling.)

WHAT IS THE VEGETARIAN RESOURCE GROUP?

Our health professionals, activists, and educators work with businesses and individuals to bring about healthy changes in your school, workplace, and community. Registered dietitians and physicians aid in the development of practical nutrition related publications and answer member or media questions about the vegetarian lifestyle.

Vegetarian Journal is one of the benefits members enjoy. Readers receive practical tips for vegan meal planning, articles on vegetarian nutrition, recipes, natural food product reviews, and an opportunity to share ideas with others. All nutrition articles are reviewed by a registered dietitian or medical doctor.

To Join The Vegetarian Resource Group
and Receive the Quarterly Vegetarian Journal for One Year

Send $20.00 to The Vegetarian Resource Group
PO Box 1463, Baltimore, MD 21203.
(Mexico/Canada send $32 and other foreign countries
send $42 in US funds only.)
Orders can be charged over the phone by calling (410) 366-8343
or faxed by calling (410) 366-8804. Our e-mail address is vrg@vrg.org
Also, visit our web site at: www.vrg.org

INDEX